DISCARD

ESSENTIAL WORKS OF SOCIALISM

ESSENTIAL WORKS
OF SOCIALISM

edited by Irving Howe

New Haven and London, Yale University Press

1976

Printed in the United States of America by
The Colonial Press, Inc., Clinton, Massachusetts.

Published in Great Britain, Europe, and Africa by
Yale University Press, Ltd., London.
Distributed in Latin America by Kaiman & Polon,
Inc., New York City; in Australasia by Book & Film
Services, Atarmon, N.S.W., Australia; in Japan by
John Weatherhill, Inc., Tokyo.

ACKNOWLEDGMENTS

"Letters on the Historical Method," by Friedrich Engels; translated by Sidney Hook for his **Toward the Understanding of Karl Marx.** Copyright 1933 by John Day Publishing Company, Inc. Reprinted by permission of Sidney Hook.

"Dual Power," by Leon Trotsky from **The History of the Russian Revolution,** Vol. I. Reprinted by permission of the University of Michigan Press.

"Three Concepts of the Russian Revolution," by Leon Trotsky. Copyright © 1941 by Harper & Brothers. Copyright renewed 1969 by Stein & Day, Inc. From the book **Stalin.** Reprinted with permission of Stein and Day Publishers, MacGibbon & Kee, and Granada Publishing Limited.

"Soul of Man Under Socialism," by George Orwell from **The Collected Essays, Journalism and Letters of George Orwell,** Volume IV, edited by Sonia Orwell and Ian Angus, copyright © 1968 by Sonia Brownell Orwell. Reprinted by permission of Harcourt Brace Jovanovich, Inc. and Secker & Warburg.

Section 79 of **The Intelligent Woman's Guide to Socialism,** by George Bernard Shaw. Reprinted by permission of The Society of Authors on behalf of the Bernard Shaw Estate.

"Science and Art Under Socialism," by Bertrand Russell from **Roads to Freedom.** Reprinted by permission of George Allen & Unwin, Ltd. and Barnes & Noble, Inc.

"Why Fascism Won," from **School for Dictators** by Ignazio Silone, published by Atheneum Publishers. Copyright 1938 by Harper & Brothers. Copyright under the title **La Scuola Dei Dittatori,** copyright © 1962 by Arnoldo Mondadori Editore. Reprinted by permission of Atheneum Publishers and Victor Gollancz, Ltd.

Excerpt from **Marxism and Democracy** by Lucien Laurat. Reprinted by permission of Victor Gollancz, Ltd.

Chapter VI from **The Unperfect Society** by Milovan Djilas, translated by Dorian Cooke, © 1969 by Harcourt Brace Jovanovich, Inc. and reprinted with their permission and that of Associated Book Publishers, Ltd. First published in Great Britain in 1969 by Methuen & Co., Ltd.

"With the Head Through the Wall," by Ivan Svitak in **Studies in Comparative Communism,** July–October, 1968. Reprinted by permission of the author.

To the memory of
Norman Thomas

A Debt of Friendship

It is a pleasure to acknowledge the help, in making the selections for this book, of Emanuel Geltman, a life-long friend and colleague, with whom I have shared some of the experiences of American socialism.   **I.H.**

Contents

III The Bolshevik Tradition

Preface

As this book enters, happily, its second incarnation, I find that there is little for me to add except to underscore once again the statement in the Introduction: "This book has been edited out of a conviction that no compromise is possible between democratic socialists and the various defenders of authoritarian and totalitarian despotism who have appropriated and blemished the name of socialism."

After its first appearance in 1970, the book met with an occasional criticism from certain kinds of academics who complained that it did not present an "ecumenical" range of left-wing thought. But no such presentation is possible —and if one tried it, the result could only be a disaster, unsatisfactory to all opinions. The range of views in this book is wide, from right-wing to left-wing socialists, and with significant extensions beyond either. But it is a collection dedicated to the view that democracy is the very essence of socialism, that without democracy socialism becomes a cruel travesty, and that the liberation of humanity, which has been the traditional socialist goal, is possible only through political freedom and its extension into the other realms of existence.

About these matters there can be no intellectual or moral compromise. Almost everywhere in the world today, bitter political struggles are being enacted between contending parties and groups which hold basically different values yet speak in the name of socialism. As these lines are being written, for example, there is continuing in Portugal a conflict, not yet resolved, between the Socialists, committed to political freedom as the setting for social change, and the Communists, Maoists, and various freelance left-authoritarians who seek to establish a dictatorship. So powerful does the hold of the tradition and vocabulary of socialism remain that both sides speak in its name. Yet intellectual candor and moral hygiene require that the lines be drawn clearly, sharply, beyond doubt.

Once that has been done, there remains, of course, the widest possibility, indeed, the greatest need for lively reflection and polemic as to the meaning, value, perspective, and desirability of the socialist idea—both among socialists themselves and their critics. The reader will find in these pages many differences of opinion. This is not a collection meant to further any narrow ideology or party line. But it starts out, as it ends, with an unambiguous premise as to what socialism signifies in relation to democracy—once that is agreed upon, the debate can proceed.

December 1975   I. H.

Introduction

I

Compiling this anthology has proved to be a far more difficult task than I had at first supposed it would be, far more difficult than merely bringing together authoritative texts of socialism and then appending other writings which, if less authoritative than controversial, would yield a contemporary socialist perspective. For both as movement and idea, socialism now finds itself, like all other serious movements and ideas, in a state of deep and chronic crisis. Crisis means a breakdown of certainties and boundaries, a blurring of self-definition, a loss of assertiveness. There remain, to be sure, socialists who content themselves with repeating old phrases and doctrines—some of these good people are intellectually asleep, others were never awake—but the serious socialists of our time are those who choose to start over again, from the very beginning, as if to say: We will cling to the original hope and value that inspired some of the best men of the last century and brought millions out of historical muteness into the dignity of consciousness; other than that, we can take nothing for granted, neither heritage nor dogma.

The difficulties in choosing texts for this anthology that would be valuable both as political reflection and historical evidence were enormous. Given the subject and the editor, there could be no pretense to objectivity. This collection represents a certain response to the tradition, which must also include the problems and failures, of socialist thought. While far from agreeing with everything in this book, the editor would claim that for both an understanding of the socialist past and the creation of a socialist future, the writings gathered here matter in

1

significant ways, sometimes as guides to opinion and action, sometimes as inducements to argument and disagreement.

Here, then, are the guiding premises by which selections were made for this book:

■ This is an anthology of socialist thought and not of Marxism. Whole areas of Marxist writing—philosophy, anthropology, literary criticism, historical narrative—are consequently not present or present only in a minor way. Yet Marxism, of course, has been the single most influential strand of thought in the development of modern socialism, and it would be impossible to present the socialist critique of capitalist society, or the socialist discussions concerning the path toward a good society, or the socialist analyses of the welfare state as a modified form of capitalism, without including a large sampling of the writings of Marx and Engels, as well as their major followers, both orthodox and revisionist. Representatives of non-Marxist socialism do appear in this book, but not as a dominant tendency, a fact reflecting both the course of history in the past century and a judgment as to the relative intellectual weights of Marxist and non-Marxist socialism.

■ The writings of major socialist figures have often been extremely polemical, a condition that may be unavoidable in oppositional movements and especially those claiming an overall or total view of society. Yet nothing can seem more faded or boring than yesterday's apparently brilliant polemic. I have tried, though not with complete success, to keep the more esoteric and "internal" kinds of radical polemics out of this volume; from the vantage point of time many of these come to seem mere outbursts of vanity, or exercises in dogmatism, or occasions for releasing upon comrades the frustrations that follow from political powerlessness. But to have omitted polemics entirely would have been a grave error intellectually and a distortion historically. What "outsiders" or hostile critics may regard as scholastic disputation often contains debates of an important kind—debates concerning topics which liberal and conservative thinkers, using *their* parochial jargon, are also trying to cope with. No anthology of socialist thought could, for example, dis-

pense with the classical controversy between the orthodox revolutionary views of Rosa Luxemburg and the heterodox revisionist views of Eduard Bernstein, or with the
prescient critiques offered by Luxemburg and Julian
Martov of early Bolshevism, or with the brilliant assault
Trotsky launched against Stalinism. In one or two instances I have thought it valuable to include a still more
recondite polemic, such as the previously untranslated
essay by George Plekhanov in which he glancingly anticipates a possible social development, revolution as the
road to a new Asiatic despotism, that the later course of
Russian history seems to have confirmed. Nevertheless, it
can be said that by and large the selections in this volume are self-contained and require no special knowledge
in the internal history of socialist debate and schism.

▪ Many wings of the socialist movement are represented
in these pages. Right-wing socialists are here, left-wing
socialists are here, and so too are many who do not fit
either label. There are even a few writers who discuss the
problems of socialism cogently but may not quite be socialists themselves. Yet, at a time when the term *socialism*
has been used in confusing, contradictory, and even scandalous ways, it is a requirement of intellectual hygiene
that some lines be drawn—and drawn as unambiguously
as possible. This book has been edited out of a conviction
that no compromise is possible between democratic socialists and the various defenders of authoritarian and
totalitarian despotism who have appropriated and blemished the name of socialism. Despite popular and sometimes scholarly assumptions to the contrary, there is a line
of belief, a line of value, a line of blood between socialism and the modern apologists for both Stalinism and
such post-Stalinist authoritarians as the Maoists and Cas-
troites. The latter political tendencies, which, in any case,
hardly lack opportunities to express themselves, do not appear in this book. They are obviously important, and
their ideas merit study, but not, in my judgment, in an
anthology of *socialist* thought.

There remains the more complicated and ambiguous
problem of such Bolshevik theorists as Lenin, Trotsky,
Bukharin, and Rakovsky, about whom it might be said, as
many of their opponents have, that at least some of their

ideas helped prepare the foundation for Stalinist and post-Stalinist dictatorships. Without pretending that the matter can be discussed adequately in a few sentences, I will simply state my own views, so that the reader will grasp the premises on which this book has been edited: there are indeed important elements in the thought of men such as Lenin and Trotsky and even more in their political practice that either encourage or lead to authoritarianism. A good portion of the criticism launched against the theory and practice of Bolshevism by Luxemburg and Martov seems to me still valid. Nevertheless, I have included selections from Lenin, Trotsky, Bukharin, and Rakovsky, first because of their intrinsic political value, second because on one side of their work these men are close to the views of such revolutionary socialists as Luxemburg, and third because there are also democratic components in their thought, some of which are brought into strong relief in these pages.

▪ This anthology does not attempt to offer either a history of socialism or a history of socialist thought. Limitations of space have forced me to exclude all but a very few examples of historical writing from a socialist point of view. What I have tried to present are crucial texts propounding socialists' views on political, economic, and social topics, as well as some that serve to illustrate the internal evolution of socialist thought. The selections are arranged in a rough historical order, but again, there are omissions: the pre-Marxist or "utopian socialists" are omitted simply because choices had to be made.

II

It may now be helpful to say a few words about the historical setting and special contribution of the groups into which the contributors have been divided.

About the intellectual preeminence and historical centrality of Marx there can be no doubt. A brilliant agitator and polemicist, a profound economist, a great sociologist, an incomparable historian, Marx was the first thinker to bring together the various strands of socialist thought into both a coherent world view and an impassioned doctrine of struggle. He drew upon German philosophy, French political thought, and English economics—that is the standard formula employed by his disciples. More important, he was the first major spokesman for socialism to remove the earlier utopian fantasies and eccentricities, the first to present the socialist ideal not as a mere pleasing dream but as an historically realizable goal, indeed as a goal that history had brought to the very threshold of possibility. Marx found the sources of revolt within the self-expanding and self-destroying rhythms of capitalist economy; he argued that capitalism itself was a transitory social order, ardent and progressive in its youth insofar as it helped break down particularistic and feudal barriers to economic development and led to a quickening of social energies, but sluggish and reactionary in its late stages, when it would serve as a brake upon the means of production and corrupt the culture of mankind. Marx located the working class as the motor of revolutionary action, the force that would, or at least could, alone bring to an end the historical sequence of class society and oppression. In this sense, Marx's theoretical system is profoundly democratic: it envisages the self-activity of the masses of human beings, the vast majority of the population, as the central impetus to historical transformation.

It was the power of Marx's vision that it was also a system; the power of his system that it was also a vision. His writings fuse, or combine, a sophisticated sociology, a strategy for political change, and at times, elements of a secular religion. He spoke of a necessary sequence or pattern in history, a determined progression of social transformation; he spoke in behalf of heroic action, the collective will of the exploited to break their chains; but above all he tried to show that history—that is, the development of economy under capitalism—had reached the point where objective prerequisites and subjective energies for socialism could, so to say, meet. Previously men had dreamed of a good society, but without possessing the material resources for creating one; now the development of industry and technique, together with the historical position of the proletariat as a revolutionary class, made possible the leap from necessity to freedom.

That the course of modern history has not quite conformed to Marx's schema of prediction; that the revolutions made in his name have occurred only in backward and preindustrial societies where the proletariat was weak and democracy barely known; that the working class, at least in the developed capitalist nations, has not, or not yet, fulfilled the "mission" assigned to it; that the breakdown of the economy, together with the expected immiseration of the masses, is at the very least a moot point—all this may well be true. Yet only in part does it detract from the power of Marx's work. His theory of historical materialism, with its stress "in the last analysis" on the primacy of the economic mode of production as the major causal factor in human affairs, may be open to serious challenge or may require complex modification once an effort is made to scrutinize closely exactly what it purports to be saying; but it has had an overwhelming impact on modern historical investigation, shaping and coloring the work even of those who reject Marx. The theory of class struggle may be coarse in some of its applications and inadequate with respect to those problems of social psychology that must necessarily arise for anyone who wishes to apply, as distinct from merely repeating, what Marx said; but it has proven to be a powerful tool in the study of both capitalist and precapitalist societies, as also, we have recently come to see, in the study of postcapitalist societies. Marx's ethical views, in their balder versions, may seem inadequate through their dismissal of the power of ethical idealism as an independent causative factor in history; but his own towering idealism and devotion to the cause for which he lived and worked has itself proven to be a major historical fact, inspiring both segments of the European working class and many intellectuals.

There is obviously far more to Marx's thought than can be glimpsed in these pages: I have chosen selections which stress his work as social analyst, political spokesman, and economist. But there is enough here, I think, to substantiate Marx's own claim in a letter written in 1852:

   . . . as for myself, no credit is due me for discovering the existence of classes in modern society nor yet the struggle between them. Long before me bourgeois historians had described the historical development of this class struggle and bourgeois economists the economic anatomy of the classes. What I did that was new was to prove: 1) that the *existence of classes* is only bound up with *particular, historic phases in the development of production*; 2) that the class struggle necessarily leads to *the dictatorship of the proletariat*; 3) that this dictatorship itself only constitutes the transition to the *abolition of all classes and to a classless society*.

By now, almost all socialists have abandoned the treacherous phrase "dictatorship of the proletariat," both because it is open to obvious misconstruction and because it has acquired, in the Stalinist and post-Stalinist dictatorships, abhorrent connotations. Marx himself had written that he differentiated himself from "those communists who were out to destroy personal liberty and who wished to turn the world into one large barracks or into a gigantic warehouse." A useful gloss on this matter is provided by Sidney Hook:

The phrase "dictatorship of the proletariat" which was later to prove such a fateful bone of contention among those who called themselves Marxists was not used in any major published work of Marx and only twice in his correspondence. According to Marx, even under a political democracy, so long as the instruments of production are owned by a few, in effect, a social dictatorship exists. For those who own and control these instruments, by their power to give work or withdraw it, exercise an arbitrary power over the lives of those who must live by the use of these instruments. The state, functioning as an instrument of the dominant economic class, enforces that power. When the workers establish their own state, the situation is reversed. By socializing production, the workers expropriate the former owners. No matter how democratic the political forms and processes by which this is done, it is in effect a social dictatorship by the workers over the former owners.

As Marx conceived it, the political expression of the social "dictatorship of the proletariat" takes the form of a workers' democracy. Engels and Marx both regarded the Paris Commune, in which many parties participated and in which the followers of Marx were a tiny minority, as a "dictatorship of the proletariat." The political processes of democracy as they exist under capitalism are broadened so that the people by referendum and recall have a greater direct influence upon the agencies of the state. As Marxism as a movement developed, the phrase "dictatorship of the proletariat" fell into almost total disuse in every politically democratic country until it was revived by the followers of Lenin and Trotsky.

The problems and contradictions which such concepts as "dictatorship of the proletariat" raised for the burgeoning socialist movement in the last third of the nineteenth century were by no means unique; they reflect a whole series of difficulties which must always arise when a mass movement is created with the aid of an ideology but which must confront conditions for which no ideology can prepare it. With time the unfortunate phrase "dictatorship of the proletariat" was abandoned, as was the whole side of Marxist thought and activity reflecting the Jacobin or insurrectionary tradition of early nineteenth-century European radicalism.

Between approximately 1870 and the First World War there grew up in Europe an increasingly strong group of Social Democratic parties, proclaiming their orthodox devotion to Marxist principles but contenting themselves in practice with a struggle for political and economic reforms. Engels, shortly before his death, could write: "We, the 'revolutionaries,' the 'overthrowers'—we are thriving far better on legal methods than on illegal methods and overthrow," while at the same time, as if still to recall his earlier views, adding that if the ruling class tried to nullify through force of arms a socialist parliamentary victory, the socialists would reserve the right to take up arms. The language of revolution lingered on, often used sincerely by both leaders and working-class followers; but meanwhile concrete victories were being scored through parliamentary and trade-union action, and these victories, far from whetting the appetites of the workers for revolution, tended in some respects to integrate them into the society of democratic capitalism and persuade them that their aims could best be realized through a politics of gradualism.

After Engels' death, the mantle of intellectual leadership in the European Social Democracy fell to Karl Kautsky, a man of scholarly inclinations but slight intellectual originality. Enormously influential among all European socialists—at least until 1914 he was admired even by Lenin—Kautsky guided the socialist parties along the ambiguous, yet at least partially fruitful, road of continuing to speak in behalf of revolution while defining the forthcoming revolution not as a complete political rupture or an insurrectionary apocalypse but as a process of historical and social transformation that might well occur through democratic means. Trying to maintain this "centrist" course, Kautsky found himself challenged from two directions: on the left by Rosa Luxemburg and the right by Eduard Bernstein, both of them figures of greater intellectual brilliance than himself.

Though completely devoted to the idea of democracy and contemptuous of all elitist and putschist notions, Luxemburg spoke within the Social Democracy for an independent kind of Marxist orthodoxy. She sharply attacked reformism in all its versions, focusing mainly on the outspoken Bernstein, but also casting a glance at the increasingly circumspect Kautsky; she attacked the idea, once anathema to socialists but soon to be all-too-easily accepted, of socialists participating in coalition governments with bourgeois parties; she championed the spontaneous activity and initiative of the working class, especially the general strike as the highest form of mass action. When the First World War broke out, Luxemburg attacked the "social patriotism" to which almost all the Social Democratic parties succumbed, that is, their policy of supporting "their" governments in the war despite their earlier proclamations of internationalism and threats of a general strike in case the imperialist powers did go to war.

At the opposite pole from, yet a worthy intellectual antagonist of the formidable Rosa, was Eduard Bernstein, the spokesman for "revisionism." What Kautsky was more and more inclined quietly to accept, Bernstein developed as a theory with candor and courage. Bernstein argued that the activity of the working class in general, and the socialist movement in particular, had begun to transform the character of capitalism, modulating and humanizing it. The labor movement and its middle-class allies, he argued, had a stake in the preservation of democracy; the theory of immanent—and imminent—economic breakdown was becoming open to challenge, in part precisely because of the social changes effected through the working-class movement; and while class struggle would continue, it need not take a violent form. For Bernstein what mattered most was the continuous political and economic activity of the socialist movement within and in behalf of the democratic structure, and it might well be that the ideal of the classless society could not be reached but would have to be regarded as a limit forever to be approached. Bernstein rejected a "final conflict," a messianic mission, a total apocalypse, and chose instead a continued striving for reform. "What is generally called the goal of socialism is nothing to me, the movement is everything," he wrote, meaning that not an "end of days" nor an end of history, a secular equivalent to eschatological yearning, was the true purpose of socialism, but rather a continuous pragmatic activity. The argument advanced against this position—apart from such considerations, more technical in nature, as to whether capitalism would indeed eventuate in a disastrous crack-up—was that without a clear goal in view there could be no intelligent choice of means, and that, unless the ideal of a classless society were significantly alive in the experience of the socialist movement, it would decline into a mere bargaining agency within the inherently unjust system of capitalism. Another problem raised by Bernstein's views has been well expressed by Peter Gay in his study of the revisionist wing of German Social Democracy:

A democratic Socialist movement that attempts to transform a capitalist into a Socialist order is necessarily faced with the choice between two incompatibles—principles and power. Socialist parties that are dedicated to democracy proceed on the fundamental assumption that their enemies are human, too, an assumption that limits the range of their weapons. Discussion, vote-getting, parliamentarism—rather than terrorism, violence, revolution—constitute the arsenal of the democratic Socialist. Again, the Socialist who is also a democrat will eschew dictatorship to maintain himself in power and rely, instead, on persuasion.

But a democratic Socialist movement that remains faithful to its principles may never achieve power. Or, if an accident should put control into its hands, it may soon lose it to less scrupulous adversaries. Is democratic Socialism, then, impossible? Or can it be achieved only if the party is willing to abandon the democratic method temporarily to attain power by violence in the hope that it may return to parliamentarism as soon as control is secure? Surely this second alternative contains tragic possibilities: a democratic movement that resorts to authoritarian methods to gain its objective may not remain a democratic movement for long. Still, the first alternative—to cling to democratic procedures under all circumstances—may doom the party to continual political impotence.

For a time Bernstein was steadily excoriated within the Social Democratic movement, most forcefully by Luxemburg but also by Kautsky; yet it became clear, even to many of his former critics, that he had indeed described the actual character and operative goals of the Social Democratic parties. The decisive challenge to Social Democratic reformism would come, however, only with the Bolshevik Revolution in Russia, which led to the creation of Communism as a worldwide revolutionary movement. Under the leadership of Lenin and Trotsky, men of brilliant political gifts and enormous personal will, the Bolsheviks expounded a politics that not only restored to Marxism the revolutionary élan of its early years but also imposed upon it a rigid organizational discipline that had never been present in any previous Marxist movement and that seems peculiarly derived from the conditions of Russian autocracy under which the Bolsheviks had been forced to work.

The Leninist outlook does not deny either the need for a continual struggle in behalf of reforms under capitalism or for active participation in electoral work; it merely insists that these not become ends in themselves or ends so overwhelmingly immediate as to blot out the need for a total social transformation. To Leninism, the reformist politics of Social Democracy signifies a capitulation to bourgeois society, often as a consequence of the economic advantages enjoyed by skilled workers said to constitute "an aristocracy of labor" and thereby to have lost the values of class solidarity. At the center of their politics the Bolsheviks put the goal of revolution, a seizure of power requiring violence all but inevitably, for, they argued, no ruling class can be expected to yield its power without offering armed resistance. The "dictatorship of the proletariat," that uncomfortable legacy from Marx, was declared by the Leninists to be the necessary transitional period from capitalism to socialism. But perhaps

the most distinctive political contribution of the Leninist
movement was its theory of "the vanguard party," that is,
the view that the working class cannot by itself move
beyond limited economic struggles within the confines of
capitalism and that it must therefore be educated, prod-
ded, and led to its revolutionary tasks by an elite party
composed of highly disciplined and full-time Marxists.
Where the model of Social Democracy—the German
party—grew into a great mass movement resting upon
the organized working class, participating in democratic
or semidemocratic institutions, and priding itself on a
free and loose internal life, the Leninist organizational
model was the Bolshevik underground of the pre-World
War I years, composed of a narrow and often declassed
stratum of revolutionary intellectuals and workers, highly
centralized in structure, and demanding of its members
complete loyalty and participation, far more so than ordinary parties, even Social Democratic parties.

The Bolshevik outlook was crucially shaped by the
Russian experience, and to that experience it had a distinct relevance. In Tsarist Russia there was little possibility for a normal democratic politics, little opportunity for
reaching the masses of people through legal newspapers,
meetings, and appeals. As a result, the conspiratorial
mode of organization employed by the Bolsheviks seems,
if not attractive, then at least authentic under the circumstances. Furthermore, in Russia there was a strong pre-
Marxist tradition of revolutionary conspiratorial organization that unquestionably left a strong imprint on the
mind of Lenin, despite his frequent attacks during the
prerevolutionary years on both the populist and terrorist
wings of Russian radicalism and despite the fact that he
considered himself an orthodox Marxist. Differences in
national experience resulted in differences of political
outlook, which became a tragedy for the socialist movement, however, when the followers of Lenin exalted the
Russian experience into a universally applicable model.

There were inherent dangers in Leninist thought. The
insistence upon the central role of the revolutionary party
could easily lead—as in fact it did lead—to a fatal identification between party and class, vanguard and history, so

that whatever the party considered necessary or desirable or even expedient could easily be declared to be in the interest of the entire working class or a measure ordained by the inexorable logic of history itself. The idea of the vanguard party, an elite of the self-chosen, led to authoritarian haughtiness, manipulation of followers, contempt for the masses, and finally to a two-caste system, with the upper caste the ordained revolutionists to whom all was permissible and the lower caste the herd of miscellaneous followers. It is true that Lenin and his colleagues in the years before and even after the revolution would have denied that such was the ultimate or necessary character of their thought; and certainly in the fierce inner discussions within the Bolshevik movement—for a short while, even after the revolution—there was a readiness to abide internally by democratic norms. But once they had seized power and come to confront the difficulties of ruling as a regime that could count on the support of only a minority of the people, the Bolsheviks more and more succumbed to the identification of the "dictatorship of the proletariat" with the dictatorship of their own party. And then, all but unavoidably, their rule became a dictatorship over the proletariat. Anti-Stalinist defenders of early Bolshevism have noted, with some cogency, that nothing in original Leninist doctrine specifically endorsed the kind of one-party dictatorship that emerged shortly after the revolution; indeed, that this dictatorship could at least in part be explained by the breakdown of Russian society during and after the war, as well as by the pressures to which the new Bolshevik state was subjected by the external bourgeois world. Perhaps so; almost certainly so. But what also seems clear is the extent to which the original Leninist doctrine, together with its utopian egalitarianism, contained a strongly elitist authoritarianism enabling the Bolsheviks to accept the idea of maintaining a dictatorship in which all civil liberties were destroyed and rule in the name of workers power became a rule of power over the workers.

All of these problems are reflected in the passages that have been selected for this anthology from the writings of the Bolshevik leaders, as are also the efforts some of them made in the mid-1920s to stop the degeneration of Bolshevik rule from a revolutionary dictatorship to a totalitarian state.

No contrast could be sharper than that between the ideological totalism of Bolshevik thought, with its claims to certainty, coherence, and completeness, and the liberal empiricism one finds in such non-Marxian socialists as Shaw, Wilde, and Morris. By comparison with the Marxists, these English writers seem impressionistic and even amateurish, offering little in the way of economic or sociological analysis and nothing about the problems of political action. With the exception of Shaw in his Fabian phase, they are not party or organizational men at all. Yet their writing retains the freshness and value of imaginative projections of socialism as a mode of freedom. In their work, the vision of socialism remains alive and attractive, full of the pleasure and diversity that is possible to free men, and perhaps more significant for socialist reconstruction than the militaristic utopianism of the Bolsheviks or the drab utilitarianism of the Social Democrats.

III

The concluding section of this anthology is concerned with the politics of the last half-century, and the essays that appear in it are necessarily—anything else would be intolerable—more tentative and problematic than those in the previous sections. By and large, the contributors speak for themselves and what they say can be judged by the reader himself; but it may be helpful to some readers if I briefly sketch one or two of the main problems that have preoccupied reflective socialists in the twentieth century and that keep recurring in the essays in Section V.

The Problem of Stalinism   A crucial, perhaps *the* crucial, experience of our century has been the appearance of totalitarian systems yoking terror and ideology and claiming to dominate and shape the entirety of existence:

what Richard Lowenthal has called "the permanent revolution from above," that is, the relentless assault by the party-state upon a defenseless population in the name of a vision of total utopia. Fascism and Stalinism were by no means identical, but they were, as Trotsky remarked, symmetrical: they employed similar political methods for different social ends and in both societies the enormity of the methods was far more important than the declared ends. The rise of fascism in the twenties and thirties destroyed major socialist movements and took the lives of many individual socialists; it caused despair as to the possibility of creating a decent human society, not, of course, among socialists alone. But only seldom did it threaten the fundamental commitment of socialists. Fascism might be analyzed as "the last stage of capitalism," or it might be seen as a new kind of society superseding capitalism; but no matter what designation one employed, fascism still seemed a cancerous growth, a horrible affliction, that had arisen out of a detested society. In some tragic sense it thereby reinforced the socialist conviction that major changes were needed if humanity was not to destroy itself.

Intellectually, however, Stalinism was far more disturbing. It seemed a cruel parody, perhaps a self-parody, of the socialist dream, and it forced thoughtful socialists to reconsider the terms of their conviction. In Russia a Marxist party had seized power; it had destroyed private property in the means of production; it had elicited overwhelming sacrifice and idealism; yet the result was a brutal and oppressive society, ruled by terror, intent upon erasing the slightest trace of free expression, allowing the working class none of the rights it possessed even under capitalism, and in its essential quality as alien to the socialist vision as anything could be.

Within this society there sprang up a new social stratum: the party-state bureaucracy which found its roots in the bureaucratic intelligentsia, the factory managers, the military officials, and above all the Communist functionaries. This new social stratum looked upon the workers as material to be shaped, upon intellectuals as propagandists to be employed, upon the international Communist movement as an auxiliary to be exploited, and upon Marxist thought as a crude process for rationalizing its power and ambitions.

What was the nature of the new society that had arisen in Russia during the twenties and thirties? A few socialists continued to believe that Stalinism, because it had abolished private property, retained some "socialist elements." (It should be clear that when speaking of Stalinism here, we refer not merely to the rule of one person but to a social system that could persist, and has persisted, beyond his lifetime; in popular usage, *Communism* signifies the same system.) Some held with Trotsky that Stalinist Russia should be designated a "degenerated workers state" because it preserved the nationalized property forms that were a "conquest" of the Russian Revolution. In Trotsky's view, the party-state dictatorship had no independent historical perspective and would soon have to give way either to a capitalist restoration or a workers democracy.

A growing number of socialists, such as Hilferding, Shachtman, and Djilas, insisted, however, that the loss of political power by the Russian working class meant that it no longer ruled in any social sense, for, as a propertyless class, it could exercise power only through direct political means and not in those indirect ways that the bourgeoisie had sometimes employed in its youthful phase. Stalinism, they continued, showed no signs of producing from within itself a bourgeois restoration or of gliding into democracy. The bureaucracy had become a new ruling class, with interests of its own fundamentally opposed to both capitalism and socialism.

This view of Communist society—which Djilas has popularized through the phrase, The New Class—held that what is decisive is not the forms of property ownership (i.e., nationalized economy) but the realities of property relations (i.e., who controls the state that owns the property). Can the workers, in whose name power is held, organize themselves into trade unions to strike against "their state"? Can they form parties freely and openly challenge the domination of "their party"? As Djilas has remarked: "An unfree people can have no scope in the economic organism."

From such theoretic analyses and speculations (developed in detail in several of the selections in Section V) enormous consequences followed for socialist thought:

- There is no necessary or inevitable sequence from capitalism to socialism, as many Marxists had believed, nor is there any inherently "progressive" movement within history. New, unforeseen, and retrogressive societies can appear or intervene in the sequence of change.

- The mere abolition of capitalism is not, in and of itself, necessarily a step toward either freedom in general or socialism in particular; it can lead—indeed, in some instances it has led—to societies more repressive than capitalism at its worst.

- Neither working-class rule nor socialism can be defined merely as a society in which private property has been abolished or the means of production nationalized; what is decisive is the nature of the political regime exercised over postcapitalist or nationalized property.

- In the long run the Communist movement may come to seem, not the vanguard of proletarian revolution that it has declared itself to be, but a movement that could achieve success only in underdeveloped countries, where there was neither a self-confident bourgeoisie nor an advanced working class, and that had as its "historic function" the provision of ideological rationales for a draconian socioeconomic modernization of backward societies.

- The idea of a total transformation of humanity under the guidance of the "vanguard party" is a corrupt fantasy which soon leads to an alternation of terror and apathy. A Czech socialist, Erazim Kohak, has written some memorable words on this matter:

According to Utopian rhetoric from Lenin on, new institutions, social relations, and new men, free, unalienated, should have sprung from socialist praxis. . . . But nothing of the sort happened. The new institutions expressed nothing but the new masters' conception of Utopia. Creatures of theory, they remained theoretical—alien, lifeless, apathetic. The people proved apathetic rather than zealous, preferring their lost freedom, even their folly, to perfection. . . .

It was at this point that the hidden logic of all social messianism came to the fore. The rhetorical Utopians convinced them-

selves that they had found the recipe for perfection. When their
fellow men failed to share their enthusiasm, they embarked on a
crusade to eliminate whatever was blinding them to their superior
insights—Jews, capitalists, sinners. But when their crusade succeeded and men still failed to conform to their true faith, they
found themselves forced to resort to coercion. Like all Utopians
they were convinced they were coercing men for their own good,
and that in time the coercion would become unnecessary. . . .
Coercion produces not enthusiasm and agreement, but alienation
and apathy, which in turn can be dislodged only by greater coercion, leading to still greater apathy.

■ Socialism must then be redefined—or better, thought
through once again—as a society in which the means of
production, to an extent that need not be determined
rigidly in advance, are collectively owned and in which
they are democratically controlled; a society requiring as
its absolute prerequisite the preservation and extension of
democracy. Without socialism, democracy tends to
wither, to be limited in social scope, to apply its benefits
unequally, and to suffer from co-existence with unjust
arrangements of social power; but without democracy,
socialism is impossible.

The Problem of the Welfare State At least in the
democratic and industrialized Western nations, capitalism has undergone significant internal changes during the
last half century: it has become a welfare or semiwelfare
state, more frequently, a welfare-garrison state. The welfare state—to employ an abstract model—preserves the
essential character of capitalist economy, in that the interplay of private or corporate owners in the free market
remains dominant; but it modifies the workings of that
economy, in that the powers of free disposal by property
owners are regulated and controlled through political organs. A more detailed description of the welfare state as
a static model is provided by Henry Pachter:

The welfare state is a capitalistic economy which largely depends on the free market but in which the countervailing powers
have been politicized and are consciously employed to balance
the economy, to develop the national resources or to pursue fixed
goals of social policy. . . . The fully developed welfare state has
at its disposal a wide range of economic instruments, classical as

well as Keynesian and statist. . . . The welfare state may achieve
techniques of industry-wide planning, price-fixing and over-all control of development, but though it will nationalize the coal industry in France and England, erect a TVA in the United States
and build a government steel mill for India, it stops short of expropriation. On the contrary, its proclaimed aim is to preserve the
structure of property and to protect the formation of a free market. Whatever expropriating is to be done must come through the
free play of the market, as is being done, e.g., in our farm
economy despite price supports. The basic relationships of buyer
and seller, employer and employee, owner and nonowner are no
different from those prevailing under pure capitalism, but they are
supplemented by state interference in two important areas: where
classical capitalism is indifferent to the distribution of income, the
welfare state at least tries to make income differential less steep; also,
whereas under pure capitalism the development of resources is but
an accidental by-product of the profit incentive, the welfare state
sets itself definite goals of developing public and private facilities. . . .
. . . we should not be misled by its efforts to plan, regulate and
control production, to redistribute income and to curb the uninhibited use of private property. At the hub of its mechanics, it is
different from socialism. Though some prices and wages are determined politically, on the whole they are still determined by
the market, and that is true even of the public enterprises; the
regime of property prevails throughout, with the dead weight of
past investments burdening the calculation of profit and the decisions on future investments, with at least a theoretical obligation to balance all budgets, and with remuneration still tightly
ruled by a man's contribution to the value of the product. Public
projects still need to be justified in terms of national policy rather
than human needs, and expenditure for defense and similar competitive purposes still exceeds the welfare expenditure.

What this excellent description does not claim to provide is any sense of the way in which the welfare state
tends to be open-ended at both sides, the way, within
limits that need not be rigidly fixed in advance, the welfare state is an algebraic container that can be filled with
the arithmetic of varying sociopolitical contents. Nor does
it provide a sense of the welfare state as the outcome, not
necessarily a "final" one, of prolonged social struggle to
modulate and humanize capitalist society. It would be
hard, perhaps impossible, to say to what extent the welfare state is the result of a deliberate intent to stabilize
capitalist society from above, so that it will avoid breakdown and revolutionary crises, and to what extent it is

the partially realized triumph in the struggle of masses of men to satisfy their desires. As against those who see the welfare state merely as the outcome of autonomous economic processes or as a device for maintaining, through diversions and concessions, the traditional forms of economic power, it needs to be stressed that welfarism represents, both in achievement and potential, a conquest that has been *wrested* through struggle by the labor, socialist, and liberal movements.

There have been many debates among socialists as to the appropriate social analysis and political attitudes in regard to the welfare state. Some have felt, and most European Social Democratic parties have behaved, as if the welfare state were, in all but name, a sufficient political goal, so that all that remained on the foreseeable agenda was a series of reforms which did not, in effect, challenge the prevailing relationships of power. Others have seen the welfare state as characteristic of all forms of advanced industrial society, offering bread and television, palliatives and opiates, to disarm opposition and thereby perpetuate, more subtly but more insidiously than in the past, class domination.

Both of these views tend to underestimate the value of the welfare state as a society which, its numerous and grave injustices notwithstanding, embodies achievements won by the working class and its allies over the past century. Still more important, they neglect the importance of the welfare state as an arena permitting further social advance.

Meanwhile, as a result of the appearance of the welfare state, a wide range of serious problems has arisen for socialists, though not, of course, for them alone:

▪ The classical Marxist theory of the inevitability of periodic economic crisis in capitalist society has, at the least, come under serious challenge. Is the relative stability of the welfare state due to the fact that in many Western nations it depends heavily on armament production—war economy—as a major crutch? What then of those societies, such as the Swedish, that are among the most advanced welfare states yet have only a modest armament budget? Would the decline of the war economy in the Western capitalist nations lead to a traditional kind of economic crisis or could the new and sophisticated methods associated with the welfare state—government regulation of and intervention in the economy, fiscal measures, public works programs—provide, so to say, social equivalents to war expenditure? Would the difficulties in such a situation arise from the intrinsic failures of the economic system or would they be the result of political failures, that is, an unwillingness on the part of those in power to take the necessary measures?

■ The development of the welfare state raises fundamental questions about the role and importance of the working class in modern society and thereby, of course, about key points in socialist theory. Does the increasing trend toward automation and computerization signify a gradual decline in both the numerical size and social strength of the working class? Has the welfare state succeeded in politically disarming the working class and thereby removing from the scene the one force which socialists have regarded as the basis of insurgent politics? Has the traditional Marxist expectation of proletarian revolution been invalidated by the seeming integration of the working class into modern industrial society? And if so, does this mean that we must now expect and yield to a future of social stasis? These are obviously complex questions, which those contributors to this volume who discuss the welfare state, G. D. H. Cole, Henry Pachter, and Michael Walzer, answer in different ways. But all would probably agree with the view of the English socialist writer Alisdair MacIntyre concerning the welfare state:

It was only gradually that people in Britain became conscious of themselves as living in a society where a right to minimal standards of welfare was presupposed. . . . Even a modern affluent working class, even a working class with a socialist tradition . . . has to learn that the welfare state is *essentially a realm of conflict* in which the real benefits of welfare are always in danger of being undermined by defense spending, by the encroachments of private interests, or simply by inflation, and thus a realm in which it needs a good deal of running even to keep standing in the same place. So a working-class political self-consciousness about welfare as a point at which elementary rights have continually to be reclaimed seems to be one of the preconditions of the maintenance of welfare in an advanced capitalist society.

The problem of a politics that goes further than this is partly the problem of a working class that sixty years ago had to set itself the goals of welfare and now has to find for itself new political goals. . . .

The Problem of Socialism   Does a great historical movement ever get a second chance? Suppose Saul of Tarsus and the rest of the original "cadre" had been destroyed or had committed some incredible blunder, could Christianity have regained its momentum after an interval of isolation and despair? For socialism, it is clear, the great historical opportunity came in the first quarter of this century, and for a variety of reasons—the Social Democrats and Leninists were keen enough in their criticism of each other—the chance was not taken.

Historical energy and idealism cannot be whipped up at demand; once a generation becomes exhausted or an idea contaminated, it takes a long time before new efforts can be made, if they can be made at all. Meanwhile history does not stand still. Socialism having failed to transform Western society in the first quarter of the century, part of what it had supposed to be its "historical mission" was appropriated by the existing society. Where that did not happen, as in the backward countries, there arose a corrupt mockery of socialism, a total state (I quote Proudhon's uncanny anticipation)

having the appearance of being founded on the dictatorship of the masses, but in which the masses have no more power than is necessary to ensure a general serfdom in accordance with the precepts and principles borrowed from the old absolutism; indivisibility of public power, all-consuming centralization, systematic destruction of all individual, corporative and regional thought, and inquisitorial police.

Whether socialism as a movement—I leave aside the European Social Democracy, which by now has at most a formal relation to the idea of socialism—can be revived, or whether it will have served historically as a bridge toward some new radical humanism, it is too soon to say.

Socialists remain. They are people devoted to a problem, or a memory that gives rise to a problem. The socialist idea signifies, first, a commitment to the values of fraternity, libertarianism, egalitarianism, and freedom. It means, secondly, commitment to an envisioned society in which a decisive proportion of the means of production shall be commonly and democratically controlled. What, however, is the relation between these two commitments?

One great failing of the socialist movement in the past was that it did not recognize, or recognize sufficiently, the inherent tension between the values it claimed to embody and the social scheme it proposed to enact. Traditionally, it was assumed that a particular change in property forms and relations would be adequate to, or at least largely prepare for, the desired change in the quality of life. Now we know from sad experience that the transformation of economy from private to public forms of ownership is not necessarily "progressive" and that such transformations seem, in any case, to be part of a general worldwide drift.

The dominant stress of the Marxist movements has been upon political means (strategy, tactics, propaganda) concerning which it often had sophisticated theories; but in regard to the society it envisaged, the content of its hope, it had surprisingly little to say, sometimes no more than the threadbare claim that once "we" take power, "we" will work things out. Martin Buber is right in saying:

To the questions of the elements of social restructure, Marx and Engels never gave a positive answer, because they had no inner relation to this idea. . . . The political act remained the one thing worth striving for. . . .

By now the more reflective socialists feel differently, but as often happens in human affairs, a growth in awareness does not necessarily facilitate confidence in action. If today we are asked what we mean or envision by socialism, our first instinctive response, even if it never reaches our lips, is likely to be in negative terms: "We don't mean such and such, we don't mean simply nationalization of industry. . . ." Our first response, that is, rests upon a deviation from a previously held norm and thereby constitutes a kind of self-criticism. (That listeners may not even know the tradition from which we are deviating, is one of the perils of the passage of time and American ahistoricism.)

We now try to describe our vision of the good society in terms of qualities, sentiments of freedom and fraternity, norms of conduct and value, priorities of social allocation; whereas, by and large, the tradition of socialism has been to speak in terms of changing institutions and power relationships. Yet in undertaking this shift of emphasis we cannot but admit the cogency of a certain kind of criticism: "A society, even one envisaged in the future, cannot be described simply by specifying desired qualities. You may hope to infuse a future society with those qualities; you may expect that a new social structure will promote or encourage those qualities. But a society must also, perhaps even primarily, be described or foreseen in structural terms."

For most of the European Social Democratic parties, this problem barely exists, since they have decided, usually in practice and sometime in program, to abandon the idea of socialization of the economy. In doing so, they become little more than liberal welfarist parties. Arguing against Anthony Crosland's theoretical defense of such a course, George Lichtheim properly remarks:

. . . the Conservative party could in principle accept all his reform demands and still retain control of the country. What would really undermine its hold—a major shift in the ownership of property—is precisely the thing he regards as unnecessary. The residual demand for it is, he thinks, a vestige of Marxism. In that case, the Tories must be regarded as full-blooded Marxists, for the one thing they seem determined to prevent is a drastic change in the social balance which would transfer the power of decision-making from private firms to public authorities.

If, then, we do retain the perspective of a long-range socialization of economy, the problem becomes how to reconcile the traditional socialist emphasis upon property forms, an emphasis necessary but not sufficient, with a more sophisticated understanding of the relationship between social structure and humane values. In any case, we neither can nor should wish to recapture the innocence of traditional socialism. We may try to develop schemes for autonomous and pluralistic social institutions within a collectivist economy. We may wish to place a decisive stress upon the idea of democratic participation. We may argue that the trend toward economic collectivism is historically unavoidable and the only choice facing men is whether it should be allowed to drift into bureaucratic authoritarianism or brought under the sponsorship of a democratic polity. But in the end we know that "history" guarantees us nothing: everything is now a question of human will.

Another way of saying all this is to insist that the socialist vision remains a genuine option—a profound need. Perhaps the accumulation of defeats can yet provide a premise for new beginnings.

I
The Founding Fathers

Karl Marx and Friedrich Engels

The Communist Manifesto, Part I

Issued in 1848 as the joint work of the young revolutionists Karl Marx (1818–1883) and Friedrich Engels (1820–1895), The Communist Manifesto is the first complete and popular statement of the Marxist view of society and proposal for social transformation. "It was published," wrote Engels in his 1888 preface to a reprint of the Manifesto, "as the platform of the Communist League, a workingmen's association, first exclusively German, later on international. . . ." Brilliantly composed, it is surely the most influential socialist pamphlet ever to appear. We print here the first section of the Manifesto, in which the critique of capitalism is presented with great force.

It should be remarked that when Marx and Engels chose to use the term Communist, it did not, of course, have the totalitarian associations which it has acquired in the mid-twentieth century. They had in mind setting themselves in opposition to the early nineteenth-century "utopian socialists," those who did not try to anchor their analysis of society in a concrete historical examination of the relationship of classes but instead dreamed of states of perfection achieved through reason, universal harmony, or a benevolent despot. In the last third of the nineteenth century, the movement inspired by Marx and Engels usually described itself as socialist or social democratic.

A specter is haunting Europe—the specter of communism. All the powers of old Europe have entered into a holy alliance to exorcise this specter: Pope and Czar,

Metternich and Guizot, French radicals and German police spies.

Where is the party in opposition that has not been decried as communistic by its opponents in power? Where the opposition that has not hurled back the branding reproach of communism against the more advanced opposition parties, as well as against its reactionary adversaries?

Two things result from this fact:

1. Communism is already acknowledged by all European powers to be itself a power.

2. It is high time that communists should openly, in the face of the whole world, publish their views, their aims, their tendencies, and meet this nursery tale of the specter of communism with a Manifesto of the party itself.

To this end, communists of various nationalities have assembled in London and sketched the following Manifesto, to be published in the English, French, German, Italian, Flemish, and Danish languages.

1 Bourgeois and Proletarians*

The history of all hitherto existing society† is the history of class struggles.

Free man and slave, patrician and plebeian, lord and

---

* By "bourgeoisie" is meant the class of modern capitalists, owners of the means of social production and employers of wage labor. By proletariat, the class of modern wage laborers who, having no means of production of their own, are reduced to selling their labor in order to live. [Note by Engels to the English edition of 1888.]

† That is, all *written* history. In 1857 the prehistory of society, the social organization existing previous to recorded history, was all but unknown. Since then Haxthausen discovered common ownership of land in Russia, Maurer proved it to be the social foundation from which all Teutonic races started in history, and by and by village communities were found to be, or have been, the primitive form of society everywhere from India to Ireland. The inner organization of this primitive communistic society was laid bare, in its typical form, by Morgan's crowning discovery of the true nature of the *gens* and its relation to the *tribe*. With the dissolution of these primeval communities, society begins to be differentiated into separate and finally antagonistic classes. I have attempted to retrace this process of dissolution in *Der Ursprung der Familie, des Privateigenthums und des Staats* [*The Origin of the Family Private Property and the State*], second edition, Stuttgart, 1886. [Note by Engels to the English edition of 1888.]

serf, guild master* and journeyman, in a word, oppressor and oppressed, stood in constant opposition to one another, carried on an uninterrupted, now hidden, now open fight, a fight that each time ended either in a revolutionary reconstitution of society at large or in the common ruin of the contending classes.

In the earlier epochs of history we find almost everywhere a complicated arrangement of society into various orders, a manifold gradation of social rank. In ancient Rome we have patricians, knights, plebeians, slaves; in the Middle Ages, feudal lords, vassals, guild masters, journeymen, apprentices, serfs; in almost all of these classes, again, subordinate gradations.

The modern bourgeois society that has sprouted from the ruins of feudal society has not done away with class antagonisms. It has but established new classes, new conditions of oppression, new forms of struggle in place of the old ones.

Our epoch, the epoch of the bourgeoisie, possesses, however, this distinctive feature: it has simplified the class antagonisms. Society as a whole is more and more splitting up into two great hostile camps, into two great classes directly facing each other: bourgeoisie and proletariat.

From the serfs of the Middle Ages sprang the chartered burghers of the earliest towns. From these burgesses the first elements of the bourgeoisie were developed.

The discovery of America, the rounding of the Cape opened up fresh ground for the rising bourgeoisie. The East Indian and Chinese markets, the colonization of America, trade with the colonies, the increase in the means of exchange and in commodities generally, gave to commerce, to navigation, to industry an impulse never before known, and thereby, to the revolutionary element in the tottering feudal society, a rapid development.

The feudal system of industry, under which industrial production was monopolized by closed guilds, now no longer sufficed for the growing wants of the new markets. The manufacturing system took its place. The guild masters were pushed to one side by the manufacturing mid-

* Guild master, that is, a full member of a guild, a master within, not a head of a guild. [Note by Engels to the English edition of 1888.]

dle class; division of labor between the different corporate guilds vanished in the face of division of labor in each single workshop.

Meantime the markets kept ever growing, the demand ever rising. Even manufacture no longer sufficed. Thereupon steam and machinery revolutionized industrial production. The place of manufacture was taken by the giant, modern industry, the place of the industrial middle class by industrial millionaires, the leaders of whole industrial armies, the modern bourgeois.

Modern industry has established the world market, for which the discovery of America paved the way. This market has given an immense development to commerce, to navigation, to communication by land. This development has, in its turn, reacted on the extension of industry; and in proportion as industry, commerce, navigation, railways extended, in the same proportion the bourgeoisie developed, increased its capital, and pushed into the background every class handed down from the Middle Ages.

We see, therefore, how the modern bourgeoisie is itself the product of a long course of development, of a series of revolutions in the modes of production and of exchange.

Each step in the development of the bourgeoisie was accompanied by a corresponding political advance of that class. An oppressed class under the sway of the feudal nobility, it became an armed and self-governing association in the medieval commune*; here independent urban republic (as in Italy and Germany), there taxable "third estate" of the monarchy (as in France), afterwards, in the period of manufacture proper, serving either the semifeudal or the absolute monarchy as a counterpoise against the nobility, and, in fact, cornerstone of the great monarchies in general, the bourgeoisie has at last, since the establishment of modern industry and of the world mar-

---

* "Commune" was the name taken in France by the nascent towns even before they had conquered from their feudal lords and masters local self-government and political rights known as the "third estate." Generally speaking, for the economic development of the bourgeoisie, England is here taken as the typical country; for its political development, France. [Note by Engels to the English edition of 1888.]

ket, conquered for itself, in the modern representative state, exclusive political sway. The executive of the modern state is but a committee for managing the common affairs of the whole bourgeoisie.

The bourgeoisie, historically, has played a most revolutionary part:

■ The bourgeoisie, wherever it has got the upper hand, has put an end to all feudal, patriarchal, idyllic relations. It has pitilessly torn asunder the motley feudal ties that bound man to his "natural superiors," and has left remaining no other nexus between man and man than naked self-interest, than callous "cash payment." It has drowned the most heavenly ecstasies of religious fervor, of chivalrous enthusiasm, of Philistine sentimentalism in the icy water of egotistical calculation. It has resolved personal worth into exchange value and, in place of the numberless indefeasible chartered freedoms, has set up that single, unconscionable freedom—free trade. In one word, for exploitation, veiled by religious and political illusions, it has substituted naked, shameless, direct, brutal exploitation.

■ The bourgeoisie has stripped of its halo every occupation hitherto honored and looked up to with reverent awe. It has converted the physician, the lawyer, the priest, the poet, the man of science into its paid wage laborers.

■ The bourgeoisie has torn away from the family its sentimental veil, and has reduced the family relation to a mere money relation.

■ The bourgeoisie has disclosed how it came to pass that the brutal display of vigor in the Middle Ages, which reactionists so much admire, found its fitting complement in the most slothful indolence. It has been the first to show what man's activity can bring about. It has accomplished wonders far surpassing Egyptian pyramids, Roman aqueducts, and Gothic cathedrals; it has conducted expeditions that put in the shade all former exoduses of nations and crusades.

■ The bourgeoisie cannot exist without constantly revolutionizing the instruments of production, and thereby the relations of production and with them the whole relations of society. Conservation of the old modes of production in unaltered form was, on the contrary, the first condition

of existence for all earlier industrial classes. Constant revolutionizing of production, uninterrupted disturbance of
all social conditions, everlasting uncertainty and agitation
distinguish the bourgeois epoch from all earlier ones. All
fixed, fast-frozen relations, with their train of ancient and
venerable prejudices and opinions, are swept away, all
new-formed ones become antiquated before they can ossify. All that is solid melts into air, all that is holy is
profaned, and man is at last compelled to face with sober
senses his real conditions of life and his relations with his
kind.

The need of a constantly expanding market for its
products chases the bourgeoisie over the whole surface of
the globe. It must nestle everywhere, settle everywhere,
establish connections everywhere.

▪ The bourgeoisie has through its exploitation of the
world market given a cosmopolitan character to production and consumption in every country. To the great cha-
grin of reactionists, it has drawn from under the feet of
industry the national ground on which it stood. All old-
established national industries have been destroyed or are
daily being destroyed. They are dislodged by new industries, whose introduction becomes a life and death question for all civilized nations, by industries that no longer
work up indigenous raw material, but raw material
drawn from the remotest zones; industries whose products are consumed not only at home, but in every quarter
of the globe. In place of the old wants, satisfied by the
productions of the country, we find new wants, requiring
for their satisfaction the products of distant lands and
climes. In place of the old local and national seclusion
and self-sufficiency we have intercourse in every direction, universal interdependence of nations. And as in material, so also in intellectual production. The intellectual
creations of individual nations become common property.
National one-sidedness and narrowmindedness become
more and more impossible, and from the numerous national and local literatures there arises a world literature.

▪ The bourgeoisie, by the rapid improvement of all instruments of production, by the immensely facilitated
means of communication, draws all, even the most barbarian, nations into civilization. The cheap prices of its

commodities are the heavy artillery with which it batters down all Chinese walls, with which it forces the barbarians' intensely obstinate hatred of foreigners to capitulate. It compels all nations, on pain of extinction, to adopt the bourgeois mode of production; it compels them to introduce what it calls civilization into their midst, i.e., to become bourgeois themselves. In one word, it creates a world after its own image.

▪ The bourgeoisie has subjected the country to the rule of the towns. It has created enormous cities, has greatly increased the urban population as compared with the rural and has thus rescued a considerable part of the population from the idiocy of rural life. Just as it has made the country dependent on the towns, so it has made barbarian and semibarbarian countries dependent on the civilized ones, nations of peasants on nations of bourgeois, the East on the West.

▪ The bourgeoisie keeps more and more doing away with the scattered state of the population, of the means of production, and of property. It has agglomerated population, centralized means of production, and has concentrated property in a few hands. The necessary consequence of this was political centralization. Independent, or but loosely connected provinces, with separate interests, laws, governments, and systems of taxation, became lumped together into one nation, with one government, one code of laws, one national class interest, one frontier, and one customs tariff.

▪ The bourgeoisie, during its rule of scarce one hundred years, has created more massive and more colossal productive forces than have all preceding generations together. Subjection of nature's forces to man, machinery, application of chemistry to industry and agriculture, steam navigation, railways, electric telegraphs, clearing of whole continents for cultivation, canalization of rivers, whole populations conjured out of the ground—what earlier century had even a presentiment that such productive forces slumbered in the lap of social labor?

We see then that the means of production and of exchange, on whose foundation the bourgeoisie built itself up, were generated in feudal society. At a certain stage in the development of these means of production and of exchange, the conditions under which feudal society produced and exchanged, the feudal organization of agriculture and manufacturing industry, in one word, the feudal relations of property, became no longer compatible with the already developed productive forces; they became so many fetters. They had to be burst asunder; they were burst asunder.

Into their place stepped free competition, accompanied by a social and political constitution adapted to it, and by the economic and political sway of the bourgeois class.

A similar movement is going on before our own eyes. Modern bourgeois society with its relations of production, of exchange, and of property, a society that has conjured up such gigantic means of production and of exchange, is like the sorcerer who is no longer able to control the powers of the nether world whom he has called up by his spells. For many a decade past, the history of industry and commerce is but the history of the revolt of modern productive forces against modern conditions of production, against the property relations that are the conditions for the existence of the bourgeoisie and of its rule. It is enough to mention the commercial crises that by their periodic return put on trial, each time more threateningly, the existence of the entire bourgeois society. In these crises a great part not only of the existing products but also of the previously created productive forces are periodically destroyed. In these crises there breaks out an epidemic that in all earlier epochs would have seemed an absurdity—the epidemic of overproduction. Society suddenly finds itself put back into a state of momentary barbarism; it appears as if a famine, a universal war of devastation had cut off the supply of every means of subsistence; industry and commerce seem to be destroyed; and why? Because there is too much civilization, too much means of subsistence, too much industry, too much commerce. The productive forces at the disposal of society no longer tend to further the development of the conditions of bourgeois property; on the contrary, they have become too powerful for these conditions, by which they are fettered, and as soon as they overcome these fetters they bring disorder into the whole of bourgeois society, endanger the existence of bourgeois property.

The conditions of bourgeois society are too narrow to comprise the wealth created by them. And how does the bourgeoisie get over these crises? On the one hand, by enforced destruction of a mass of productive forces; on the other, by the conquest of new markets, and by the more thorough exploitation of the old ones. That is to say, by paving the way for more extensive and more destructive crises, and by diminishing the means whereby crises are prevented.

The weapons with which the bourgeoisie felled feudalism to the ground are now turned against the bourgeoisie itself.

But not only has the bourgeoisie forged the weapons that bring death to itself; it has also called into existence the men who are to wield those weapons—the modern working class—the proletarians.

In proportion as the bourgeoisie, i.e., capital, is developed, in the same proportion is the proletariat, the modern working class, developed—a class of laborers, who live only so long as they find work, and who find work so long as their labor increases capital. These laborers, who must sell themselves piecemeal, are a commodity, like every other article of commerce, and are consequently exposed to all the vicissitudes of competition, to all the fluctuations of the market.

Owing to the extensive use of machinery and to division of labor, the work of the proletarians has lost all individual character and, consequently, all charm for the workman. He becomes an appendage of the machine, and it is only the simplest, most monotonous, and most easily acquired knack that is required of him. Hence the cost of production of a workman is restricted, almost entirely, to the means of subsistence that he requires for his maintenance and for the propagation of his race. But the price of a commodity, and therefore also of labor, is equal to its cost of production. In proportion, therefore, as the repulsiveness of the work increases, the wage decreases. Nay, more, in proportion as the use of machinery and division of labor increases, in the same proportion the burden of toil also increases, whether by prolongation of the working hours, by increase of the work exacted in a given time, or by increased speed of the machinery, etc.

Modern industry has converted the little workshop of the patriarchal master into the great factory of the industrial capitalist. Masses of laborers, crowded into the factory, are organized like soldiers. As privates of the industrial army they are placed under the command of a perfect hierarchy of officers and sergeants. Not only are they slaves of the bourgeois class, and of the bourgeois state; they are daily and hourly enslaved by the machine, by the overlooker, and, above all, by the individual bourgeois manufacturer himself. The more openly this despotism proclaims gain to be its end and aim, the more petty, the more hateful, and the more embittering it is.

The less the skill and exertion of strength implied in manual labor, in other words, the more modern industry becomes developed, the more is the labor of men superseded by that of women. Differences of age and sex have no longer any distinctive social validity for the working class. All are instruments of labor, more or less expensive to use, according to their age and sex.

No sooner is the exploitation of the laborer by the manufacturer over, to the extent that he receives his wages in cash, than he is set upon by the other portions of the bourgeoisie, the landlord, the shopkeeper, the pawnbroker, etc.

The lower strata of the middle class—the small tradespeople, shopkeepers, and retired tradesmen generally, the handicraftsmen and peasants—all these sink gradually into the proletariat, partly because their diminutive capital does not suffice for the scale on which modern industry is carried on, and is swamped in the competition with the large capitalists, partly because their specialized skill is rendered worthless by new methods of production. Thus the proletariat is recruited from all classes of the population.

The proletariat goes through various stages of development. With its birth begins its struggle with the bourgeoisie. At first the contest is carried on by individual laborers, then by the workspeople of a factory, then by the operatives of one trade, in one locality, against the individual bourgeois who directly exploits them. They direct their attacks not against the bourgeois conditions of production, but against the instruments of production themselves; they destroy imported wares that compete with their labor, they smash to pieces machinery, they set factories ablaze, they seek to restore by force the vanished status of the workman of the Middle Ages.

At this stage the laborers still form an incoherent mass scattered over the whole country and broken up by their mutual competition. If anywhere they unite to form more compact bodies, this is not yet the consequence of their own active union, but of the union of the bourgeoisie, which class, in order to attain its own political ends, is compelled to set the whole proletariat in motion and is moreover yet, for a time, able to do so. At this stage, therefore, the proletarians do not fight their enemies, but the enemies of their enemies, the remnants of absolute monarchy, the landowners, the nonindustrial bourgeois, the petty bourgeoisie. Thus the whole historical movement is concentrated in the hands of the bourgeoisie; every victory so obtained is a victory for the bourgeoisie.

But with the development of industry the proletariat not only increases in number; it becomes concentrated in greater masses, its strength grows, and it feels that strength more. The various interests and conditions of life within the ranks of the proletariat are more and more equalized, in proportion as machinery obliterates all distinctions of labor and nearly everywhere reduces wages to the same low level. The growing competition among the bourgeois and the resulting commercial crises make the wages of the workers ever more fluctuating. The unceasing improvement of machinery, ever more rapidly developing, makes their livelihood more and more precarious; the collisions between individual workmen and individual bourgeois take more and more the character of collisions between two classes. Thereupon the workers begin to form combinations (trade unions) against the bourgeois; they club together in order to keep up the rate of wages; they found permanent associations in order to make provision beforehand for these occasional revolts. Here and there the contest breaks out into riots.

Now and then the workers are victorious, but only for a time. The real fruit of their battles lies not in the immediate result, but in the ever expanding union of the workers. This union is helped on by the improved means of

communication that are created by modern industry and
that place the workers of different localities in contact
with one another. It was just this contact that was needed
to centralize the numerous local struggles, all of the same
character, into one national struggle between classes. But
every class struggle is a political struggle. And that union,
to attain which the burghers of the Middle Ages, with
their miserable highways, required centuries, the modern
proletarians, thanks to railways, achieve in a few years.

This organization of the proletarians into a class, and
consequently into a political party, is continually being
upset again by the competition between the workers
themselves. But it ever rises up again, stronger, firmer,
mightier. It compels legislative recognition of particular
interests of the workers by taking advantage of the divisions among the bourgeoisie itself. Thus the ten-hour bill
in England was carried.

Altogether collisions between the classes of the old society further, in many ways, the course of development of
the proletariat. The bourgeoisie finds itself involved in a
constant battle, at first with the aristocracy; later on, with
those portions of the bourgeoisie itself whose interests
have become antagonistic to the progress of industry; at
all times, with the bourgeoisie of foreign countries. In all
these battles it sees itself compelled to appeal to the
proletariat, to ask for its help, and thus to drag it into the
political arena. The bourgeoisie itself, therefore, supplies
the proletariat with its own elements of political and
general education: in other words, it furnishes the proletariat with weapons for fighting the bourgeoisie.

Further, as we have already seen, entire sections of the
ruling classes are, by the advance of industry, precipi-
tated into the proletariat, or are at least threatened in
their conditions of existence. These also supply the proletariat with fresh elements of enlightenment and progress.

Finally, in times when the class struggle nears the decisive hour, the process of dissolution going on within the
ruling class, in fact, within the whole range of old society,
assumes such a violent, glaring character that a small
section of the ruling class cuts itself adrift and joins the
revolutionary class, the class that holds the future in its
hands. Just as, therefore, at an earlier period, a section

of the nobility went over to the bourgeoisie, so now a portion of the bourgeoisie goes over to the proletariat, and in particular a portion of the bourgeois ideologists, who have raised themselves to the level of comprehending theoretically the historical movement as a whole.

Of all the classes that stand face to face with the bourgeoisie today, the proletariat alone is a really revolutionary class. The other classes decay and finally disappear in the face of modern industry; the proletariat is its special and essential product.

The lower-middle class, the small manufacturer, the shopkeeper, the artisan, the peasant, all these fight against the bourgeoisie, to save from extinction their existence as fractions of the middle class. They are therefore not revolutionary, but conservative. Nay, more, they are reactionary, for they try to roll back the wheel of history. If by chance they are revolutionary they are so only in view of their impending transfer into the proletariat; they thus defend not their present but their future interests, they desert their own standpoint to place themselves at that of the proletariat.

The "dangerous class," the social scum, that passively rotting mass thrown off by the lowest layers of old society, may, here and there, be swept into the movement by a proletarian revolution; its conditions of life, however, prepare it far more for the part of a bribed tool of reactionary intrigue.

In the conditions of the proletariat those of old society at large are already virtually swamped. The proletarian is without property; his relation to his wife and children has no longer anything in common with the bourgeois family relations; modern industrial labor, modern subjection to capital, the same in England as in France, in America as in Germany, has stripped him of every trace of national character. Law, morality, religion are to him so many bourgeois prejudices, behind which lurk in ambush just as many bourgeois interests.

All the preceding classes that got the upper hand sought to fortify their already acquired status by subjecting society at large to their conditions of appropriation. The proletarians cannot become masters of the productive forces of society, except by abolishing their own previous mode of appropriation, and thereby also every other previous mode of appropriation. They have nothing of their own to secure and to fortify; their mission is to destroy all previous securities for, and insurances of, individual property.

All previous historical movements were movements of minorities, or in the interest of minorities. The proletarian movement is the self-conscious, independent movement of the immense majority, in the interest of the immense majority. The proletariat, the lowest stratum of our present society, cannot stir, cannot raise itself up, without the whole superincumbent strata of official society being sprung into the air.

Though not in substance, yet in form, the struggle of the proletariat with the bourgeoisie is at first a national struggle. The proletariat of each country must, of course, first of all settle matters with its own bourgeoisie.

In depicting the most general phases of the development of the proletariat, we traced the more or less veiled civil war, raging within existing society, up to the point where that war breaks out into open revolution and where the violent overthrow of the bourgeoisie lays the foundation for the sway of the proletariat.

Hitherto every form of society has been based, as we have already seen, on the antagonism of oppressing and oppressed classes. But in order to oppress a class certain conditions must be assured to it under which it can, at least, continue its slavish existence. The serf, in the period of serfdom, raised himself to membership in the commune, just as the petty bourgeois, under the yoke of feudal absolutism, managed to develop into a bourgeois. The modern laborer, on the contrary, instead of rising with the progress of industry, sinks deeper and deeper below the conditions of existence of his own class. He becomes a pauper, and pauperism develops more rapidly than population and wealth. And here it becomes evident that the bourgeoisie is unfit any longer to be the ruling class in society, and to impose its conditions of existence upon society as an overriding law. It is unfit to rule because it is incompetent to assure an existence to its slave within his slavery, because it cannot help letting him sink into such a state that it has to feed him instead of being fed by him. Society can no longer live under this bourgeoisie: in other words, its existence is no longer compatible with society.

The essential condition for the existence, and for the sway of the bourgeois class, is the formation and augmentation of capital; the condition for capital is wage labor. Wage labor rests exclusively on competition between the laborers. The advance of industry, whose involuntary promoter is the bourgeoisie, replaces the isolation of the laborers, due to competition, by their revolutionary combination, due to association. The development of modern industry, therefore, cuts from under its feet the very foundation on which the bourgeoisie produces and appropriates products. What the bourgeoisie, therefore, produces, above all, is its own gravediggers. Its fall and the victory of the proletariat are equally inevitable.

Karl Marx and Friedrich Engels

Ideology and History*

The following selection is taken from an early work by Marx and Engels called German Ideology, *composed in 1845–46 and unpublished for the most part until after Marx's death. The passage is a clear if not yet fully developed statement of the materialist conception of history that has played a central role in the thought of Marxist socialism.*

The premises from which we start are not arbitrary, they are not dogmas; they are real premises, from which abstraction can be made only in imagination. They are real individuals, their action and their material conditions of life, both those which they find in existence and those produced through their own action. These premises can therefore be verified in a purely empirical way.

The first premise of all human history is, of course, the existence of living human individuals. The first fact to be established is therefore the physical organization of these individuals and their consequent relation to the rest of nature. We cannot here, of course, go into either the physical characteristics of men, themselves, or the natural conditions found by men—the geological, orohydrographical, climatic, and other conditions. All historical work must start on the basis of these natural conditions and their modification in the course of history through the action of men.

Men may be distinguished from animals by consciousness, religion, or anything else. They begin to differentiate themselves from animals as soon as they begin to

* Title supplied by editor.

44

produce their means of subsistence, a step which is conditioned by their physical organization. By producing their means of existence men indirectly produce their material life itself.

The mode in which men produce their means of existence depends in the first place on the nature of the means of existence themselves—those which they find at their disposal and have to reproduce.

This mode of production must not be considered merely from the aspect that it is the reproduction of the physical existence of individuals. It is rather, in fact, a definite form of activity of these individuals, a definite form of expressing their life, their definite *mode of life*. As individuals express their life, so they are. What they are therefore coincides with their production—*what* they produce as well as *how* they produce. What individuals are therefore depends on the material conditions of their production.

This production first makes its appearance with the *increase of population*. It in turn itself presupposes *intercourse* of the individuals among themselves. The form of this intercourse is again determined by production. . . .

The fact is therefore that definite individuals, who are productively active in a definite way, enter into these definite social and political relations. In every single instance, empirical observation must show the connection of the social and political structure with production—empirically and without any mystification and speculation. The social structure and the state always arise from the life-process of definite individuals, but of these individuals, not as they may appear in their own or other people's ideas, but as they *really* are, that is, as they act, produce in a material way, therefore as they produce under definite limitations, presuppositions, and conditions which are material and independent of their will.

The production of ideas, concepts, of consciousness is at first directly interwoven with the material activity and the material intercourse of men, the language of actual life. Conception, thought, the mental intercourse of men then still appear as the direct efflux of their material relations. The same is true of mental production, as expressed in the language of the politics, laws, morality,

religion and metaphysics of a people. Men are the products of their concepts, ideas, etc.—but real, producing
men, as they are conditioned by a definite development
of their productive forces and the intercourse, up to its
most far-reaching forms, which correspond with these.
Consciousness can never be anything else than conscious
existence, and the existence of men is their actual life-
process. If in all ideology men and their relations appear
upside down, as in a camera obscura, this phenomenon
arises just as much from their historical life-process as the
reversal of objects on the retina does from their directly
physical life-process.

In direct contrast to German philosophy, which de-
scends from heaven to earth, here the ascent is made
from earth to heaven. That is to say, we do not start from
what men say, imagine, conceive, nor from men as described, thought of, imagined, and conceived, in order
thence and thereby to reach corporeal men; we start from
real, active men, and from their life-process also show the
development of the ideological reflexes and echoes of this
life-process. Even the phantasmagoria in men's brains are
necessary supplements of their material life-process, empirically demonstrable and bound up with material premises. Morals, religion, metaphysics, and all other ideology
and the corresponding forms of consciousness thus no
longer maintain the appearance of independence. They
have no history, they have no development; but men,
developing their material production and their material
intercourse, change, along with this their real existence,
also their thinking and the products of their thought. It is
not consciousness that determines life, but life that determines consciousness. In the first mode of observation, the
starting point is consciousness taken as the living individual; in the second, in conformity with actual life, it is the
real living individual himself, and consciousness is considered only as *his* consciousness.

The mode of observation is not without a basis. It sets
out from real premises and never for a moment leaves
them. Its premises are men not in any imaginary isolation
and state of fixation, but in their actual empirically observable process of development in definite conditions.
From the moment this active life-process is shown, his-

tory ceases to be a collection of dead facts, as it is with the empiricists, themselves still abstract, or an imaginary activity of imaginary persons, as it is with the idealists.

There, where speculation ends, with real life, real positive science therefore begins, the representation of practical activity, of the practical process of the development of men. The empty phrases of consciousness break off; real knowledge must take their place. With the representation of reality, independent philosophy loses the medium for its existence. Its place can at best be taken by a collection of the most general results which can be extracted from observation of men's historical development. The abstractions in themselves, separated from actual history, have absolutely no value. They can only serve to facilitate the arrangement of the historical material, to indicate the sequence of its separate strata. But they do not, like philosophy, in any way provide a recipe or formula by which the historical epochs can be neatly trimmed. On the contrary, the difficulty begins precisely when a start is made with the examination and arrangement, the actual presentation, of the material, whether of a past epoch or of the present. The overcoming of these difficulties is conditioned by premises which cannot be given at this stage but can only result from the study of the real life-process and the action of individuals of every epoch.

Karl Marx

Address to the Communist League

In 1850, Marx delivered an Address to the Communist League, the group on behalf of which he had two years earlier composed The Communist Manifesto. *The Address is notable not only for its analysis of class and political relations, foreshadowing Marx's brilliant writings on French politics and society; it is also the first major statement of his view that even in the course of a bourgeois revolution, the working class must play an independent political role, pressing for reforms which the dominant bourgeois forces are likely to resist and thereby driving the bourgeois revolution to a point further than the bourgeoisie itself might desire. The Address is a major document in the long line of strategic analyses concerning relations between socialist and nonsocialist liberal parties; it was also a major source for the ideas of Lenin and Trotsky concerning the problems of working-class movements in countries where the bourgeois revolution had not yet been completed.*

. . . Brethren, we have told you as far back as in 1848, that German liberalism would soon come to power and would at once use it against the working class. You have seen how this has been fulfilled. It was the bourgeoisie, who, after the victorious movement of March, 1848, took the reins of government, and the first use they made of their power was to force back the workingmen, their allies in the fight against absolutism, to their former oppressed condition. They could not achieve their purpose without the assistance of the defeated aristocracy, to whom they even transferred governmental power, securing, however, for themselves the ultimate control of the government through the budget. . . .

The part which the Liberals played in 1848, this treacherous role will at the next revolution be played by the democratic petty bourgeoisie, who, among the parties opposing the government, are now occupying the same position which the liberals occupied prior to the March revolution. This democratic party, which is more dangerous to the workingmen than the Liberal Party was, consists of the following three elements:

1. The more progressive members of the upper bourgeoisie, whose object it is to sweep away all remnants of feudalism and absolutism;
2. The democratic-constitutional petty bourgeosie, whose main object it is to establish a democratic federation of the Germanic states;
3. The republican petty bourgeoisie, whose ideal it is to turn Germany into a sort of Swiss republic. These republicans are calling themselves "reds" and "social democrats" because they have the pious wish to remove the pressure of large capital upon the smaller one and of the big bourgeoisie upon the petty bourgeoisie.

All these parties, after the defeat they have suffered, are calling themselves republicans or reds, just as in France the republican petty bourgeoisie are calling themselves socialists. Where, however, they have the opportunity of pursuing their aims by constitutional methods, they are using their old phraseology and are showing by deed that they have not changed at all. It is a matter of course that the changed name of that party does not alter their attitude towards the working class; it merely proves that in their struggle against the united forces of absolutism and large capitalists they require the support of the proletariat.

The petty bourgeois Democratic Party in Germany is very powerful. It embraces not only the great majority of the town population, the small traders and craftsmen, but also the peasantry and the agricultural laborers, insofar as the latter have not yet come into contact with the proletariat of the towns. The revoluionary working class acts in agreement with that party as long as it is a question of fighting and overthrowing the aristocratic-liberal coalition; in all other things the revolutionary working class must act independently. The democratic petty bourgeoisie, far from desiring to revolutionize the whole society, are aiming only at such changes of the social conditions as would make their life in existing society more comfortable and profitable. They desire above all a reduction of national expenditure through a decrease of bureaucracy, and the imposition of the main burden of taxation on the landowners and capitalists. They demand, likewise, the establishment of state banks and laws against usury, so as to ease the pressure of the big capitalist upon the small traders and to get from the state cheap credit. They demand also the full mobilization of the land, so as to do away with all remnants of manorial rights. For these purposes they need a democratic constitution which would give them the majority in Parliament, municipality, and parish.

With a view to checking the power and the growth of big capital, the Democratic Party demands a reform of the laws of inheritance and legacies, likewise the transfer of the public services and as many industrial undertakings as possible to the state and municipal authorities. As to the workingmen—well, they should remain wage workers: for whom, however, the Democratic Party would procure higher wages, better labor conditions, and a secure existence. The Democrats hope to achieve that partly through state and municipal management and through welfare institutions. In short, they hope to bribe the working class into quiescence and thus to weaken their revolutionary spirit by momentary concessions and comforts.

The democratic demands can never satisfy the party of the proletariat. While the democratic petty bourgeoisie would like to bring the revolution to a close as soon as their demands are more or less complied with, it is our interest and our task to make the revolution permanent, to keep it going until all the ruling and possessing classes are deprived of power, the governmental machinery occupied by the proletariat, and the organization of the working classes of all lands is so far advanced that all rivalry and competition among themselves has ceased; until the more important forces of production are concentrated in the hands of the proletarians. With us it is not a

matter of reforming private property, but of abolishing it;
not of hushing up the class antagonism, but of abolishing
the classes; not of ameliorating the existing society, but of
establishing a new one. There is no doubt that, with the
further development of the revolution, the petty bourgeois democracy may for a time become the most influential party in Germany. The question is, therefore, what
should be the attitude of the proletariat, and particularly
of the League, towards it:

1. During the continuation of the present conditions in which
the petty bourgeois democracy is also oppressed?
2. In the ensuing revolutionary struggles which would give them
momentary ascendancy
3. After those struggles, during the time of their ascendancy
over the defeated classes and the proletariat?

1 At the present moment when the democratic petty
bourgeoisie are everywhere oppressed, they lecture the
proletariat, exhorting it to effect a unification and conciliation; they would like to join hands and form one great
opposition party, embracing within its folds all shades of
democracy. That is, they would like to entangle the proletariat in a party organization in which the general social
democratic phrases predominate, behind which their particular interests are concealed, and in which the particular proletarian demands should not, for the sake of peace
and concord, be brought forward. Such a unification
would be to the exclusive benefit of the petty bourgeois
democracy and to the injury of the proletariat. The organized working class would lose its hard-won independence and would become again a mere appendage of the
official bourgeois democracy. Such a unification must be
resolutely opposed.

Instead of allowing themselves to form the chorus of
the bourgeois democracy, the workingmen, and particularly the League, must strive to establish next to the
official democracy an independent, a secret as well as a
legal organization of the working-class party, and to
make each community the center and nucleus of working-class societies in which the attitude and the interests
of the proletariat should be discussed independently of
bourgeois influences. How little the bourgeois democrats

care for an alliance in which the proletarians should be regarded as co-partners with equal rights and equal standing is shown by the attitude of the Breslau democrats, who in their organ the *Oder-Zeitung* are attacking those workingmen who are independently organized and whom they nickname socialists, subjecting them to severe persecutions. The gist of the matter is this: In case of an attack on a common adversary no special union is necessary; in the fight with such an enemy the interests of both parties, the middle-class democrats and the working-class party, coincide for the moment, and both parties will carry it on by a temporary understanding. This was so in the past, and will be so in the future. It is a matter of course that in the future sanguinary conflicts, as in all previous ones, the workingmen by their courage, resolution, and self-sacrifice, will form the main force in the attainment of victory. As hitherto, so in the coming struggle, the petty bourgeoisie as a whole will maintain an attitude of delay, irresolution, and inactivity as long as possible, in order that, as soon as victory is assured, they may arrogate it to themselves and call upon the workers to remain quiet, return to work, avoid so-called excesses, and thus to shut off the workers from the fruits of victory. It is not in the power of the workers to prevent the petty bourgeois democrats from doing that; but it is within their power to render their ascendancy over the armed proletariat difficult and to dictate to them such terms as shall make the rule of the bourgeois democracy carry within itself from the beginning the germ of dissolution, and its ultimate substitution by the rule of the proletariat considerably facilitated.

The workers, above all during the conflict and immediately afterwards, must try as much as ever possible to counteract all bourgeois attempts at appeasement and compel the democrats to carry out their present terrorist phases. They must act in such a manner that the revolutionary excitement does not subside immediately after the victory. On the contrary, they must endeavour to maintain it as long as possible. Far from opposing so-called excesses and making examples of hated individuals or public buildings to which hateful memories are attached by sacrificing them to popular revenge, such deeds must not only be tolerated, but their direction must be taken in hand. During the fight and afterwards the workers must seize every opportunity to present their own demands beside those of the bourgeois democrats. They must demand guarantees for the workers as soon as the democrats propose to take over the reins of government. If necessary, they must exact these guarantees, and generally see to it that the new rulers should bind themselves to every possible concession and promise, which is the surest way to compromise them. The workers must not be swept off their feet by the general elation and enthusiasm for the new order of things which usually follow upon street battles; they must quench all ardour by a cool and dispassionate conception of the new conditions, and must manifest open distrust of the new government. Beside the official government, they must set up a revolutionary workers' government, either in the form of local executives and communal councils, or workers' clubs or workers' committees, so that the bourgeois democratic governments not only immediately lose all backing among the workers, but from the commencement find themselves under the supervision and threats of authorities, behind whom stands the entire mass of the working class. In short, from the first moment of victory we must no longer direct our distrust against the beaten reactionary enemy, but against our former allies, against the parties who are now about to exploit the common victory for their own ends only.

2   In order that this party, whose betrayal of the workers will begin with the first hour of victory, should be frustrated in its nefarious work, it is necessary to organize and arm the proletariat. The arming of the whole proletariat with rifles, guns, and ammunition must be carried out at once; we must prevent the revival of the old bourgeois militia, which has always been directed against the workers. Where the latter measure cannot be carried out, the workers must try to organize themselves into an independent guard, with their own chiefs and general staff, to put themselves under the order, not of the government, but of the revolutionary authorities set up by the workers. Where workers are employed in state service, they must arm and organize in special corps, with chiefs chosen by

themselves, or form part of the proletarian guard. Under
no pretext must they give up their arms and equipment,
and any attempt at disarmament must be forcibly resisted. Destruction of the influence of bourgeois democracy over the workers, immediate independent and armed
organization of the workers, and the exaction of the most
irksome and compromising terms from the bourgeois democracy, whose triumph is for the moment unavoidable
—these are the main points which the proletariat, and
therefore also the League, has to keep in eye during and
after the coming upheaval.

3 As soon as the new government is established, they
will commence to fight the workers. In order to be able
effectively to oppose the petty bourgeois democracy, it is
in the first place necessary that the workers should be
independently organized in clubs, which should soon be
centralized. The central authority, after the overthrow of
the existing governments, will at the earliest opportunity
transfer its headquarters to Germany, immediately call
together a congress, and make the necessary proposals for
the centralization of the workers' clubs under an Executive Committee, who will have their headquarters in the
center of the movement. The rapid organization, or at
least the establishment of a provincial union of the workers' clubs, is one of the most important points in our
considerations for invigorating and developing the Workers' Party. The next result of the overthrow of the existing
government will be the election of a national representation. The proletariat must see to it first that no worker
shall be deprived of his suffrage by the trickery of the
local authorities for government commissioner; secondly,
that beside the bourgeois democratic candidates there
shall be put up everywhere working-class candidates,
who, as far as possible, shall be members of the League,
and for whose success all must work with every possible
means. Even in constituencies where there is no prospect
of our candidate being elected, the workers must nevertheless put up candidates in order to maintain their independence, to steel their forces, and to bring their revolutionary attitude and party views before the public. They
must not allow themselves to be diverted from this work
by the stock argument that to split the vote of the demo-

crats means assisting the reactionary parties. All such talk is but calculated to cheat the proletariat. The advance which the Proletarian Party will make through its independent political attitude is infinitely more important than the disadvantage of having a few more reactionaries in the national representation. The victorious democrats could, if they liked, even prevent the reactionary party having any success at all, if they only used their newly won power with sufficient energy.

The first point which will bring the democrats into conflict with the proletariat is the abolition of all feudal rights. The petty bourgeois democrats, following the example of the first French Revolution, will hand over the lands as private property to the peasants; that is, they will leave the agricultural laborers as they are, and will but create a petty bourgeois peasantry, who will pass through the same cycle of material and spiritual misery in which the French peasant now finds himself.

The workers, in the interest of the agricultural proletariat as well as in their own, must oppose all such plans. They must demand that the confiscated feudal lands shall be nationalized and converted into settlements for the associated groups of the landed proletariat; all the advantages of large-scale agriculture shall be put at their disposal; these agricultural colonies, worked on the cooperative principle, shall be put in the midst of the crumbling bourgeois property institutions. Just as the democrats have combined with the small peasantry, so we must fight shoulder to shoulder with the agricultural proletariat. Further, the democrats will either work directly for a federal republic, or at least, if they cannot avoid the republic one and indivisible, will seek to paralyze the centralization of government by granting the greatest possible independence to the municipalities and provinces. The workers must set their face against this plan, not only to secure the one and indivisible German republic, but to concentrate as much power as possible in the hands of the central Government. They need not be misled by democratic platitudes about freedom of the communes, self-determination, and the like. In a country like Germany, where there are so many medieval remnants to be swept away and so much local and provincial obstinacy to be overcome, under no circumstances must parishes, towns, and provinces be allowed to be made into obstacles in the way of revolutionary activity which must emanate from the center. That the Germans should have to fight and bleed, as they have done hitherto, for every advance over and over again in every town and in every province separately cannot be tolerated. As in France in 1793, so it is today the task of the revolutionary party in Germany to centralize the nation.

We have seen that the democrats will come to power in the next phase of the movement and that they will be obliged to propose measures of a more or less socialistic nature. It will be asked what contrary measures should be proposed by the workers. Of course they cannot in the beginning propose actual communist measures, but they can (1) compel the democrats to attack the old social order from as many sides as possible, disturb their regular procedure and compromise themselves, and concentrate in the hands of the state as much as possible of the productive forces, means of transport, factories, railways, etc.; (2) The measures of the democrats, which in any case are not revolutionary but merely reformist, must be pressed to the point of turning them into direct attacks on private property; thus, for instance, if the petty bourgeoisie propose to purchase the railways and factories, the workers must demand that such railways and factories, being the property of the reactionaries, shall simply be confiscated by the state without compensation. If the democrats propose proportional taxation, the workers must demand progressive taxation; if the democrats themselves declare for a moderate progressive tax, the workers must insist on a tax so steeply graduated as to cause the collapse of large capital; if the democrats propose the regulation of the national debt, the workers must demand state bankruptcy. The demands of the workers will depend on the proposals and measures of the democrats.

If the German workers will only come to power and to the enforcement of their class interests after a prolonged revolutionary development, they will at least gain the certainty that the first act of this revolutionary drama will coincide with the victory of their class in France, and this will surely accelerate the movement of their own emancipation. But they themselves must accomplish the greater part of the work; they must be conscious of their class interests and take up the position of an independent party. They must not be diverted from their course of proletarian independence by the hypocrisy of the democratic petty bourgeoisie. Their battle cry must be: "The revolution in permanence."

Friedrich Engels

Manchester in 1844

The Condition of the Working Class in England in 1844 first appeared in a German edition in 1845. It is a work in which acute sociological observation concerning the effects of the Industrial Revolution on the factory workers of England is combined with blazing indignation against the social wretchedness Engels observed. In the following selections, Engels writes first about a proletarian slum in Manchester and then about the beginnings of working-class politics.

I will now give a description of the working-class districts of Manchester. The first of them is the Old Town, which lies between the northern limit of the commercial quarter and the River Irk. Here even the better streets, such as Todd Street, Long Millgate, Withy Grove, and Shudehill are narrow and tortuous. The houses are dirty, old, and tumble-down. The side streets have been built in a disgraceful fashion. If one enters the district near the Old Church and goes down Long Millgate, one sees immediately on the right-hand side a row of antiquated houses where not a single front wall is standing upright. This is a remnant of the old Manchester of the days before the town became industrialized. The original inhabitants and their children have left for better houses in other districts, while the houses in Long Millgate, which no longer satisfied them, were left to a tribe of workers containing a strong Irish element. Here one is really and truly in a district which is quite obviously given over entirely to the working classes, because even the shopkeepers and the publicans of Long Millgate make no effort to give their establishments a semblance of cleanliness. The condition of this street may be deplorable, but it is by no means as bad as the alleys and courts which lie behind it, and which can be approached only by covered passages so narrow that two people cannot pass. Anyone who has never visited these courts and alleys can have no idea of the fantastic way in which the houses have been packed together in disorderly confusion in impudent defiance of all reasonable principles of town planning. And the fault lies not merely in the survival of old property from earlier periods in Manchester's history. Only in quite modern times has the policy of cramming as many houses as possible on to such space as was not utilized in earlier periods reached its climax. The result is that today not an inch of space remains between the houses and any further building is now physically impossible. It is by no means the worst slum in Manchester, and it does not cover one-tenth of the area of Manchester.

This sketch will be sufficient to illustrate the crazy layout of the whole district lying near the River Irk. There is a very sharp drop of some 15 to 30 feet down to the south bank of the Irk at this point. As many as three rows of houses have generally been squeezed on to this precipitous slope. The lowest row of houses stands directly on the bank of the river while the front walls of the highest row stand on the crest of the ridge in Long Millgate. Moreover, factory buildings are also to be found on the banks of the river. In short, the layout of the upper part of Long Millgate at the top of the rise is just as disorderly and congested as the lower part of the street. To the right and left a number of covered passages from Long Millgate give access to several courts. On reaching them, one meets with a degree of dirt and revolting filth, the like of which is not to be found elsewhere. The worst courts are those leading down to the Irk, which contain unquestionably the most dreadful dwellings I have ever seen. In one of these courts, just at the entrance where the covered passage ends, there is a privy without a door. This privy is so dirty that the inhabitants of the court can only enter or leave the court if they are prepared to wade through puddles of stale urine and excrement. Anyone

who wishes to confirm this description should go to the
first court on the bank of the Irk above Ducie Bridge.
Several tanneries are situated on the bank of the river,
and they fill the neighborhood with the stench of animal
putrefaction. The only way of getting to the courts below
Ducie Bridge is by going down flights of narrow dirty
steps, and one can only reach the houses by treading over
heaps of dirt and filth. The first court below Ducie Bridge
is called Allen's Court. At the time of the cholera (1832)
this court was in such a disgraceful state that the sanitary
inspectors (of the local Board of Health) evacuated the
inhabitants. The court was then swept and fumigated
with chlorine. In his pamphlet, Dr. Kay gives a horrifying
description of conditions in this court at that time. Since
Kay wrote this pamphlet, this court appears to have been
at any rate partly demolished and rebuilt. If one looks
down the river from Ducie Bridge, one does at least see
several ruined walls and high piles of rubble, side by side
with some recently built houses. The view from this
bridge, which is mercifully concealed by a high parapet
from all but the tallest mortals, is quite characteristic of
the whole district. At the bottom the Irk flows, or rather,
stagnates. It is a narrow, coal-black, stinking river full of
filth and rubbish which it deposits on the more low-lying
right bank. In dry weather this bank presents the spectacle of a series of the most revolting blackish-green puddles of slime from the depths of which bubbles of mias-
matic gases constantly rise and create a stench which is
unbearable even to those standing on the bridge forty or
fifty feet above the level of the water. Moreover, the flow
of the river is continually interrupted by numerous high
weirs, behind whcih large quantities of slime and refuse
collect and putrefy. Above Ducie Bridge there are some
tall tannery buildings, and further up there are dye
works, bone mills, and gasworks. All the filth, both liquid
and solid, discharged by these works finds its way into
the River Irk, which also receives the contents of the
adjacent sewers and privies. The nature of the filth de-
posited by this river may well be imagined. If one looks
at the heaps of garbage below Ducie Bridge one can
gauge the extent to which accumulated dirt, filth and
decay permeates the courts on the steep left bank of the

river. The houses are packed very closely together and since the bank of the river is very steep it is possible to see a part of every house. All of them have been blackened by soot, all of them are crumbling with age and all have broken window panes and window frames. In the background there are old factory buildings which look like barracks. On the opposite, low-lying, bank of the river, one sees a long row of houses and factories. The second house is a roofless ruin, filled with refuse, and the third is built in such a low situation that the ground floor is uninhabitable and has neither doors nor windows. In the background one sees the paupers' cemetery, and the stations of the railways to Liverpool and Leeds. Behind these buildings is situated the workhouse, Manchester's "Poor Law Bastille." The workhouse is built on a hill and from behind its high walls and battlements seems to threaten the whole adjacent working-class quarter like a fortress.

Above Ducie Bridge the left bank of the Irk becomes flatter and the right bank of the Irk becomes steeper and so the condition of the houses on both sides of the river becomes worse rather than better. Turning left from the main street which is still Long Millgate, the visitor can easily lose his way. He wanders aimlessly from one court to another. He turns one corner after another through innumerable narrow dirty alleyways and passages, and in only a few minutes he has lost all sense of direction and does not know which way to turn. The area is full of ruined or half-ruined buildings. Some of them are actually uninhabited and that means a great deal in this quarter of the town. In the houses one seldom sees a wooden or a stone floor, while the doors and windows are nearly always broken and badly fitting. And as for the dirt! Everywhere one sees heaps of refuse, garbage and filth. There are stagnant pools instead of gutters and the stench alone is so overpowering that no human being, even partially civilized, would find it bearable to live in such a district. The recently constructed extension of the Leeds railway which crosses the Irk at this point has swept away some of these courts and alleys, but it has thrown open to public gaze some of the others. So it comes about that there is to be found immediately under the railway bridge a court which is even filthier and more revolting than all the others. This is simply because it was formerly so hidden and secluded that it could only be reached with considerable difficulty (but is now exposed to the human eye). I thought I knew this district well, but even I would never have found it had not the railway viaduct made a breach in the slums at this point. One walks along a very rough path on the river bank, in between clothesposts and washing lines to reach a chaotic group of little, one-storyed, one-roomed cabins. Most of them have earth floors, and working, living and sleeping all take place in the one room. In such a hole, barely six feet long and five feet wide, I saw two beds—and what beds and bedding!—which filled the room, except for the fireplace and the doorstep. Several of these huts, as far as I could see, were completely empty, although the door was open and the inhabitants were leaning against the door posts. In front of the doors filth and garbage abounded. I could not see the pavement, but from time to time, I felt it was there because my feet scraped it. This whole collection of cattle sheds for human beings was surrounded on two sides by houses and a factory and on a third side by the river. (It was possible to get to this slum by only two routes.) One was the narrow path along the river bank, while the other was a narrow gateway which led to another human rabbit warren which was nearly as badly built and was nearly in such a bad condition as the one I have just described.

Enough of this! All along the Irk slums of this type abound. There is an unplanned and chaotic conglomeration of houses, most of which are more or less uninhabitable. The dirtiness of the interiors of these premises is fully in keeping with the filth that surrounds them. How can people dwelling in such places keep clean! There are not even adequate facilities for satisfying the most natural daily needs. There are so few privies that they are either filled up every day or are too far away for those who need to use them. How can these people wash when all that is available is the dirty water of the Irk? Pumps and piped water are to be found only in the better-class districts of the town. Indeed no one can blame these helots of modern civilization if their homes are no cleaner than the occasional pigsties which are a feature of these slums. There are actually some property owners who are not ashamed to let dwellings such as those which are to be found below Scotland Bridge. Here on the quayside a mere six feet from the water's edge is to be found a row of six or seven cellars, the bottoms of which are at least two feet beneath the low-water level of the Irk. What can one say of the owner of the corner house—situated on the opposite bank of the river above Scotland Bridge—who actually lets the upper floor although the premises downstairs are quite uninhabitable, and no attempt has been made to board up the gaps left by the disappearance of doors and windows? This sort of thing is by no means uncommon in this part of Manchester, where, owing to the lack of conveniences, such deserted ground floors are often used by the whole neighborhood as privies.

Working-Class Movements in England 1844

Even if I had not given so many examples as I have done to illustrate the condition of the working classes in England, it would still be self-evident that the proletariat can hardly feel happy at the present situation. It will surely be granted that the state of affairs I have described is not one in which either an individual or a social class can think, feel, and live in a civilized manner. The workers must strive to escape from this position, which degrades them to the level of animals. They must try to achieve for themselves a better and more human status. They can do this only by attacking the interests of the middle classes who live by exploiting the workers. But the bourgeoisie defends its interests in the most vigorous fashion. It has at its disposal not only the power of property, but also the resources of the authority of the state. Every attempt the worker makes to free himself from his present bondage meets with the open hostility of the bourgeoisie.

Moreover, the worker is made perpetually aware of the fact that the middle classes treat him as if he were an inanimate object and a piece of property rather than a human being, and for this reason alone he is the declared enemy of the bourgeoisie. I have already given a hundred examples, and I could have given another hundred, to

illustrate the fact that under present circumstances the
worker can only retain his self-respect by rising in anger
against the middle classes. There can be no doubt that
the worker is well able to protest with all the fury at his
command against the tyranny of the capitalist, if only
because of the way in which he has been brought up—or
rather his lack of proper upbringing. In addition, the fact
that there is now a large hot-blooded Irish element in the
English proletariat also stimulates the workers' animosity
against their oppressors. The English worker today is no
longer an Englishman (of the old school). He no longer
resembles his capitalist neighbor in being a mere machine
for making money. His capacity for feeling has developed. He has thrown off his native Nordic reserve. He
has cast aside his inhibitions. Given a free rein, his passions have therefore been able to develop so that they
now readily stimulate him to action. Among the middle
classes the emphasis laid on the cultivation of the reasoning faculty has greatly increased the tendency towards
selfishness and, indeed, has promoted greed to the position of a guiding principle in the conduct of affairs. For
the bourgeoisie, love of money has become the ruling
passion of life. All this is lacking in the worker, who is
therefore able to give full play to passions as strong and
unbridled as those of the foreigner. All feelings of patriotism have been crushed in the heart of the worker.

We have seen the only way in which the worker can
retain his self-respect is by fighting against the way of life
imposed upon him. It is natural, therefore, that it is when
he is taking action against his oppressors that the English
worker is seen at his best. It is then that he appears to the
fullest advantage—manly, noble and attractive. We shall
see that all the vigor and activity of the worker is concentrated upon this struggle. We shall see that even his
efforts to cultivate his mind have a direct connection with
his fight against the bourgeoisie. It is true that we shall
have to report isolated cases of violence and even brutality. It must be remembered, however, that in England the
social war has been openly declared. There are occasions
on which it is in the interest of the middle classes to wage
this war with the weapons of hypocrisy and to try and
cover up their deeds under the disguise of peace and

even of philanthropy. When this happens, the worker can reply only by tearing off his mask of hypocrisy, so as to reveal the true state of affairs. Acts of violence committed by the working classes against the bourgeoisie and their henchmen are merely frank and undisguised retaliation for the thefts and treacheries perpetrated by the middle classes against the workers.

Since its beginning in the early days of the Industrial Revolution the revolt of the workers against the middle classes has passed through several phases. I do not propose to examine here the historical significance of these phases in the history of the English people. This must be reserved for a later study. For the time being, I propose to confine myself to a brief survey of the principal facts concerning the hostility of the workers to the middle classes in order to show what effect this has had upon the development of the English proletariat.

Criminal activities were the first, the crudest, and the least successful manifestation of this hostility. The worker lived in poverty and want and saw that other people were better off than he was. The worker was not sufficiently intelligent to appreciate why he, of all people, should be the one to suffer—for after all he contributed more to society than the idle rich, and sheer necessity drove him to steal in spite of his traditional respect for private property. We have already pointed out how crime has increased as industry has expanded. It has been shown that there has been a constant relationship between the number of arrests and the annual consumption of bales of cotton.

The workers, however, soon realized that crime did not forward their cause. The criminals, by their thefts, could protest against the existing social order only as individuals. All the mighty forces of society were hurled against the individual lawbreaker and crushed him with their overwhelming power. In addition theft was the blindest and most stupid form of protest and consequently this never became the universal expression of the workers' reaction to industrialization, although many workers doubtless sympathized privately with those who broke the law. The first organized resistance of the workers, as a class, to the bourgeoisie, was the violence associated with the movements against the introduction of machinery. This occurred in the earliest stage of the Industrial Revolution. Even the earlier inventors of new machines, such as Arkwright, were attacked in this way and their machines destroyed. Subsequently there were many instances of machine breaking. These generally followed the same course as the printers' riots in Bohemia in 1844, when both workshops and machines were destroyed.

This type of protest was also far from universal. It was limited to certain localities and was confined to resistance to one aspect of industrial change. If the immediate object of the machine breaker was attained, then the defenseless law breakers had to face the full fury of the established order. The criminals were severely punished and the introduction of the new machinery went on unchecked. It was clearly necessary for the workers to find a new method of expressing their discontent. . . .

In 1818 a union of coal miners was strong enough to bring about a general stoppage of work throughout Scotland. These unions bound their members by an oath of fidelity and secrecy, and kept accurate membership lists, possessed funds and rendered regular financial accounts. Local branches were established, but the secrecy in which affairs of these unions had to be conducted crippled their development. As soon as the workers were granted the right of free association in 1824 trade unions sprang up all over England and they became powerful. Unions were set up by workers in all branches of industry, their declared object being to protect the individual artisan against the tyranny and indifference of the middle classes. They aimed at fixing wages by collective bargaining with their employers. They wished to regulate wages according to the profits of the employers. They desired to raise wages whenever a favorable opportunity presented itself. Their policy was to maintain uniform rates of wages in different occupations throughout the country. Consequently the trade unions negotiated with the capitalists to secure the establishment of wage scales which would be universally applied, and they threatened to strike against any individual employer who refused to pay wages at this level. Trade unionists tried to restrict the number of apprentices in each trade. By setting limits on the expansion of the labor force in this way they hoped to maintain competition between employers for the available skilled workers, and so to keep wages high.

Unionists also strenuously opposed attempts to reduce wages by such underhand methods as the introduction of new machinery and tools. Finally unemployed workers received financial assistance from their unions. This was done either by a direct grant from the union funds or by supplying the unemployed worker with a card, which certified that he was a union member, and therefore entitled to receive subsistence and information about vacant jobs, from other branches when he was seeking work in other parts of the country. These arrangements are called "the tramping system," and those who use them to find work are called "tramps." In order to carry out their policy, the trade unions appoint two salaried officials known as the president and the secretary. It is necessary to pay these officials, because no employers can be expected to give them work. The affairs of the trade union are controlled by a committee which is responsible for collecting the weekly subscriptions of the members and for seeing that the funds are used for carrying out the objects of the association. Should some real advantage appear to be gained from doing so, the skilled workers in one district try, if possible, to combine with similar unions in other districts to form a federation which holds regular meetings of delegates. There have been isolated attempts to hold national conferences representing unionists in particular trades. On several occasions, the first being in 1830, efforts have been made to establish a universal trade union for the whole country, delegates from all types of trade unions being summoned. Attempts to form nationwide associations, however, have generally proved abortive, and even when initially successful, have never lasted for very long. Only if circumstances brought about a quite exceptional wave of enthusiasm would a union of this kind be both possible and successful. . . . The history of trade unionism is the story of many defeats of the workers and of only a few isolated victories. It is obvious that all these efforts on the part of trade unionists cannot change the economic law by which wages are fixed according to supply and demand in the labor mar-

ket. Consequently the trade unions are helpless in the
face of the major factors influencing the economy. Thus if
there is a trade depression, the unions themselves have to
acquiesce in a reduction of wages or go out of existence.
Similarly if there is a striking increase in the demand for
labor the trade unions are not in a position to secure for
their members higher wages than those which they would
in any case obtain as a result of free competition between
the capitalists for skilled men. On the other hand, the
trade unions are in a position to exercise considerable
influence over minor and less important factors in the
economy. If the manufacturers did not have to face mass
organized opposition from the workers they would always increase their own profits by continually reducing
wages. Competition between the manufacturers themselves would force the individual capitalist to depress the
wages of his workers to the minimum. Unless exceptional
circumstances prevail, it is true to say that the united
opposition of the workers can limit the evil consequences
of unrestrained competition between manufacturers. It is
one thing for a manufacturer to reduce wages when all
other manufacturers are doing the same thing because
the general state of the economy makes this necessary. It
is another matter for one employer to attempt to cut
wages on his own account at a time when there is no
economic justification for doing so. The manufacturer
who does this knows that he will have to meet a strike,
which will injure him because his capital will lie idle and
his machinery will go rusty. He knows that he cannot be
sure of imposing a reduction in wages, while he can be
certain that, if successful, his example will be followed by
his rivals. This will lead to a fall in the price of the goods
he is making and will soon deprive him of any advantage
gained by the original reduction in wages.

Again the trade unions are often able to bring about a
more rapid increase in wages after a trade crisis than
would occur if the workers were entirely unorganized. It
is not in the interest of the individual manufacturer to
raise wages until he is forced to do so by the competition
of rival manufacturers. In fact, the workers themselves
demand more wages as soon as business improves, and
they are often able to force the manufacturer to pay

higher wages by threatening a strike. If the manufacturer is short of workers, he is not able to resist such a demand. But as we have pointed out, the trade unions are unable to make any headway against the more important factors influencing the state of the labor market. In such circumstances hunger gradually forces the operatives to go back to work on whatever terms the employer dictates. Even if only a few of the strikers return to work, the power of the union is broken, since the labor of the blacklegs and the fact that there are still supplies of goods in the market enable the middle classes to overcome the worst consequences of the disturbance caused to business by the stoppage. Union funds are soon exhausted if large sums have to be disbursed in strike-pay. Small shopkeepers are prepared to sell goods on credit, at a high rate of interest, but only for a short time. Consequently necessity forces the worker back under the yoke of the middle classes. The workers have discovered that most strikes are unsuccessful. In their own interests the manufacturers do not wish to cut wages unless a reduction is unavoidable. Indeed it is the organized opposition of the workers that has forced the employers to adopt this policy.

If a reduction in wages has to take place because the state of business makes this imperative the workers' standard of life naturally falls. It may well be asked why the workers go on strike when it is clear that the stoppage cannot prevent a reduction in wages, which cannot be avoided owing to slack trade. The answer is, simply, that the workers must protest both against a reduction in wages and also against the circumstances which make that reduction necessary. They must assert that since they are human beings they do not propose to submit to the pressure of inexorable economic forces. On the contrary they demand that economic forces should be adapted to suit *their* convenience. If trade unionists failed to register their protest by striking, their silence would be regarded as an admission that they acquiesced in the preeminence of economic forces over human welfare. Such acquiescence would be a recognition of the right of the middle classes to exploit the workers when business was flourishing and to let the workers go hungry when business was slack. The workers must protest against this state of affairs so long as they have not lost all human feeling. Their protest takes the form of strikes because Englishmen are practical people, who believe in the efficacy of deeds rather than words. They are not German theorists, who cheerfully go to sleep as soon as their protest has been officially received and left to slumber in a pigeonhole for ever. The practical manner in which Englishmen protest has helped to set certain limits to the greed of the middle classes. It has kept alive the opposition of the workers to the overweening political and social power of the capitalist class.

But the workers are also learning from practical experience that trade unions and strikes are not of themselves sufficient to break the might of the middle classes. The real importance, however, of trade unions and strikes is that they constitute the first attempt of the workers to put an end to competition amongst themselves. They are based on a recognition of the fact that the power of the middle classes over the workers is due entirely to the existence of competition between workers themselves—that is to say, their lack of solidarity and their internecine rivalries. Trade unions have proved to be so dangerous to the existing social order simply because they have—if only to a limited degree—firmly opposed that competition of workers among themselves, which is the very cornerstone of modern society. The workers could not have chosen a more vulnerable chink in the armour of the middle classes and of the present social structure than by organizing trade unions and strikes. The sovereign power of property must come to an end if competition among workers is impaired and if all the operatives are determined not to allow themselves to be exploited by the middle classes.

Wages have come to depend upon the law of supply and demand and upon the state of the labor market at any particular moment, simply because the workers have hitherto allowed themselves to be treated as chattels which can be bought and sold. The whole modern system of political economy, with its law of wages, will collapse as soon as the workers make up their minds that they are not going to allow themselves to be passively bought and sold any longer. Its doom is sealed as soon as they act like human beings who can think as well as toil and show their determination to secure a just share of the fruits of their labour. It is true that the law of wages would eventually come into force again if the workers went no further than to secure the removal of competition amongst themselves. But such a limitation of their aims would bring the present trade union movement to an end and would actually cause a revival of competition among the workers. Such a policy is out of the question. Necessity will force the trade unions to bring to an end not merely *one* aspect of competition, but all competition. And this result will be achieved. Every day it becomes clearer to workers how they are affected by competition. They appreciate even more clearly than the middle classes that it is competition among the capitalists that leads to those commercial crises which cause such dire suffering among the workers. Trade unionists realize that commercial crises must be abolished, and they will soon discover *how* to do it.

Karl Marx

The Eighteenth Brumaire of Louis Bonaparte

Nothing Marx ever wrote compares in brilliance of historical analysis to his The Eighteenth Brumaire of Louis Bonaparte. *He composed this book in 1852, as an account of the revolutionary and counterrevolutionary events in France between 1848 and 1852, beginning with the democratic revolution and ending with the coup of Louis Bonaparte. This work is a classical portrait of the bourgeois revolution and of the parts played in it by the whole ensemble of modern classes. The first section of* The Eighteenth Brumaire *follows.*

Hegel remarks somewhere that all facts and personages of great importance in world history occur, as it were, twice. He forgot to add: the first time as tragedy, the second as farce. Caussidière for Danton, Louis Blanc for Robespierre, the *Montagne* of 1848 to 1851 for the *Montagne* of 1793 to 1795, the nephew for the uncle. And the same caricature occurs in the circumstances attending the second edition of the eighteenth Brumaire!

Men make their own history, but they do not make it just as they please; they do not make it under circumstances chosen by themselves, but under circumstances directly encountered, given, and transmitted from the past. The tradition of all the dead generations weighs like a nightmare on the brain of the living. And just when they seem engaged in revolutionizing themselves and things, in creating something that has never yet existed, precisely in such periods of revolutionary crisis they anxiously conjure up the spirits of the past to their service and borrow from them names, battle cries, and costumes in order to present the new scene of world history in this time-honored disguise and this borrowed language. Thus Luther donned the mask of the apostle Paul, the Revolution of 1789 to 1814 draped itself alternately as the Roman Republic and the Roman Empire, and the Revolution of 1848 knew nothing better to do than to parody, now 1789, now the revolutionary tradition of 1793 to 1795. In like manner a beginner who has learned a new language always translates it back into his mother tongue, but he has assimilated the spirit of the new language and can freely express himself in it only when he finds his way in it without recalling the old and forgets his native tongue in the use of the new.

Consideration of this conjuring up of the dead of world history reveals at once a salient difference. Camille Desmoulins, Danton, Robespierre, St. Just, Napoleon, the heroes, as well as the parties and the masses of the old French Revolution performed the task of their time in Roman costume and with Roman phrases, the task of unchaining and setting up modern *bourgeois* society. The first ones knocked the feudal basis to pieces and mowed off the feudal heads which had grown on it. The other created inside France the conditions under which alone free competition could be developed, parceled landed property exploited, and the unchained industrial productive power of the nation employed; and beyond the French borders he everywhere swept the feudal institutions away, so far as was necessary to furnish bourgeois society in France with a suitable up-to-date environment on the European continent. The new social formation once established, the antediluvian colossi disappeared and with them resurrected Romanity—the Brutuses, Gracchi, Publicolas, the tribunes, the senators, and Caesar himself. Bourgeois society in its sober reality had begotten its true interpreters and mouthpieces in the Says, Cousins, Royer-Collards, Benjamin Constants, and Guizots; its real military leaders sat behind the office desks, and the hogsheaded Louis XVIII was its political chief. Wholly absorbed in the production of wealth and in peaceful competitive struggle, it no longer comprehended that ghosts from the days of Rome had watched over its cradle. But unheroic as bourgeois society is, it nevertheless took heroism, sacrifice, terror, civil war, and battles of peoples to bring it into being. And in the classically austere traditions of the Roman Republic its gladiators found the ideals and the art forms, the self-deceptions that they needed in order to conceal from themselves the bourgeois limitations of the content of their struggles and to keep their enthusiasm on the high plane of the great historical tragedy. Similarly, at another stage of development, a century earlier, Cromwell and the English people had borrowed speech, passions, and illusions from the Old Testament for their bourgeois revolution. When the real aim had been achieved, when the bourgeois transformation of English society had been accomplished, Locke supplanted Habakkuk.

Thus the awakening of the dead in those revolutions served the purpose of glorifying the new struggles, not of parodying the old; of magnifying the given task in imagination, not of fleeing from its solution in reality; of finding once more the spirit of revolution, not of making its ghost walk about again.

From 1848 to 1851 only the ghost of the old revolution walked about, from Marrast, the *républician en gants jaunes*, who disguised himself as the old Bailly, down to the adventurer who hides his commonplace repulsive features under the iron death mask of Napoleon. An entire people, which had imagined that by means of a revolution it had imparted to itself an accelerated power of motion, suddenly finds itself set back into a defunct epoch and, in order that no doubt as to the relapse may be possible, the old dates arise again, the old chronology, the old names, the old edicts, which had long become a subject of antiquarian erudition, and the old minions of the law, who had seemed long decayed. The nation feels like that mad Englishman in Bedlam who fancies that he lives in the times of the ancient Pharaohs and daily bemoans the hard labor that he must perform in the Ethiopian mines as a gold digger, immured in this subterranean prison, a dimly burning lamp fastened to his head, the overseer of the slaves behind him with a long whip, and at the exits a confused welter of barbarian mercenaries, who understand neither the forced laborers in the mines nor one another, since they speak no common language. "And all this is expected of me," sighs the mad Englishman, "of me, a free-born Briton, in order to make gold for the old Pharaohs." "In order to pay the debts of the Bonaparte family," sighs the French nation. The Englishman, so long as he was in his right mind, could not get rid of the fixed idea of making gold. The French, so long as they were engaged in revolution, could not get rid of the memory of Napoleon, as the election of December 10 proved. They hankered to return from the perils of revolution to the fleshpots of Egypt, and December 2, 1851, was the answer. They have not only a caricature of the old Napoleon, they have the old Napoleon himself, caricatured as he must appear in the middle of the nineteenth century.

The social revolution of the nineteenth century cannot draw its poetry from the past, but only from the future. It cannot begin with itself before it has stripped off all superstition in regard to the past. Earlier revolutions required recollections of past world history in order to drug themselves concerning their own content. In order to arrive at its own content, the revolution of the nineteenth century must let the dead bury their dead. There the phrase went beyond the content; here the content goes beyond the phrase.

The February revolution was a surprise attack, a *taking* of the old society *unawares*, and the people proclaimed this unexpected *stroke* as a deed of world importance, ushering a new epoch. On December 2, the February revolution is conjured away by a cardsharper's trick, and what seems overthrown is no longer the monarchy but the liberal concessions that were wrung from it by centuries of struggle. Instead of *society* having conquered a new content for itself, it seems that the *state* only returned to its oldest form, to the shamelessly simple domination of the saber and the cowl. This is the answer to the *coup de main* of February, 1848, given by the *coup d'état* of December, 1851. Easy come, easy go. Meanwhile the interval of time has not passed by unused. During the years 1848 to 1851 French society has made up, and that by an abbreviated because revolutionary method, for the studies and experiences which, in a regular, so to speak, textbook course of development would have had to precede the February revolution, if it was to be more than a ruffling of the surface. Society now seems to have fallen back behind its point of departure; it has in truth first to create for itself the revolutionary point of departure, the situation, the relations, the conditions under which alone modern revolution becomes serious.

Bourgeois revolutions, like those of the eighteenth century, storm swiftly from success to success; their dramatic effects outdo each other; men and things seem set in sparkling brilliants; ecstasy is the everyday spirit; but they are short-lived; soon they have attained their zenith, and a long crapulent depression lays hold of society before it learns soberly to assimilate the results of its storm-and-stress period. On the other hand, proletarian revolutions, like those of the nineteenth century, criticize themselves constantly, interrupt themselves continually in their own course, come back to the apparently accomplished in order to begin it afresh, deride with unmerciful thoroughness the inadequacies, weaknesses, and paltrinesses of their first attempts, seem to throw down their adversary only in order that he may draw new strength from the earth and rise again, more gigantic, before them, recoil ever and anon from the indefinite prodigiousness of their own aims, until a situation has been created which makes all turning back impossible, and the conditions themselves cry out:

> *Hic Rhodus, hic salta**
> Here is the rose, here dance!

For the rest, every fairly competent observer, even if he had not followed the course of French developments step by step, must have had a presentiment that an unheard-of fiasco was in store for the revolution. It was enough to hear the self-complacent howl of victory with which Messieurs the democrats congratulated each other on the expected gracious consequences of the second Sunday in May, 1852. In their minds, the second Sunday

---

* "Here is Rhodes, jump here!" from the Latin version of a fable by Aesop.

in May, 1852 had become a fixed idea, a dogma, like the day on which Christ should reappear and the millennium begin, in the minds of the Chiliasts. As ever, weakness had taken refuge in a belief in miracles, fancied the enemy overcome when he was only conjured away in imagination, and it lost all understanding of the present in a passive glorification of the future that was in store for it and of the deeds it had *in petto* but which it merely did not want to carry out as yet. Those heroes who seek to disprove their demonstrated incapacity by mutually offering each other their sympathy and getting together in a crowd had tied up their bundles, collected their laurel wreaths in advance, and were just then engaged in discounting on the exchange market the republics *in partibus* for which they had already providently organized the government personnel with all the calm of their unassuming disposition. December 2 struck them like a thunderbolt from a clear sky, and the peoples that in periods of pusillanimous depression gladly let their inward apprehension be drowned out by the loudest bawlers will perchance have convinced themselves that the times are past when the cackle of geese could save the Capitol.

The Constitution, the National Assembly, the dynastic parties, the blue and the red republicans, the heroes of Africa, the thunder from the platform, the sheet lightning of the daily press, the entire literature, the political names and the intellectual reputations, the civil law and the penal code, the *liberté, égalité, fraternité,* and the second Sunday in May, 1852—all has vanished like a phantasmagoria before the spell of a man whom even his enemies do not make out to be a magician. Universal suffrage seems to have survived only for a moment, in order that with its own hand, it may make its last will and testament before the eyes of all the world and declare in the name of the people iself: All that exists deserves to perish.

It is not enough to say, as the French do, that their nation was taken unawares. A nation and a woman are not forgiven the unguarded hour in which the first adventurer that came along could violate them. The riddle is not solved by such turns of speech, but merely formulated differently. It remains to be explained how a nation of thirty-six million can be surprised and delivered unresisting into captivity by three swindlers.

Let us recapitulate in general outline the phases that the French revolution went through from February 24, 1848, to December, 1851.

Three main periods are unmistakable: *the February period*; May 4, 1848, to May 28, 1849: *the period of the constitution of the republic*, or *of the Constituent National Assembly*; May 28, 1849, to December 2, 1851: *the period of the constitutional republic or of the Legislative National Assembly*.

The *first period*, from February 24, or the overthrow of Louis Philippe, to May 4, 1848, the meeting of the Constituent Assembly, the *February period* proper, may be described as the *prologue* to the revolution. Its character was officially expressed in the fact that the government improvised by it itself declared that it was *provisional* and, like the government, everything that was mooted, attempted, or enunciated during this period proclaimed itself to be only *provisional*. Nothing and nobody ventured to lay claim to the right of existence and of real action. All the elements that had prepared or determined the revolution, the dynastic opposition, the republican bourgeoisie, the democratic-republican petty bourgeoisie, and the social-democratic workers, provisionally found their place in the February *government*.

It could not be otherwise. The February days originally intended an electoral reform by which the circle of the politically privileged among the possessing class itself was to be widened and the exclusive domination of the aristocracy of finance overthrown. When it came to the actual conflict, however, when the people mounted the barricades, the National Guard maintained a passive attitude, the army offered no serious resistance, and the monarchy ran away, the republic appeared to be a matter of course. Every party construed it in its own way. Having secured it arms in hand, the proletariat impressed its stamp upon it and proclaimed it to be a *social republic*. There was thus indicated the general content of the modern revolution, a content which was in most singular contradiction to everything that, with the material available, with the degree of education attained by the masses, under the given circumstances and relations, could be immediately realized in practice. On the other hand, the claims of all the remaining elements that had collaborated in the February revolution were recognized by the lion's share that they obtained in the government. In no period do we, therefore, find a more confused mixture of high-flown phrases and actual uncertainty and clumsiness, of more enthusiastic striving for innovation and more deeply rooted domination of the old routine, of more apparent harmony of the whole of society and more profound estrangement of its elements. While the Paris proletariat still reveled in the vision of the wide prospects that had opened before it and indulged in seriously meant discussions on social problems, the old powers of society grouped themselves, assembled, reflected, and found unexpected support in the nation, the peasants and petty bourgeois, who all at once stormed onto the political stage, after the barriers of the July monarchy had fallen.

The *second period*, from May 4, 1848, to the end of May 1849, is the period of the *constitution, the foundation, of the bourgeois republic*. Directly after the February days not only had the dynastic opposition been surprised by the republicans and the republicans by the socialists, but all France by Paris. The National Assembly, which met on May 4, 1848, had emerged from the national elections and represented the nation. It was a living protest against the pretensions of the February days and was to reduce the results of the revolution to the bourgeois scale. In vain the Paris proletariat, which immediately grasped the character of this National Assembly, attempted on May 15, a few days after it met, forcibly to negate its existence, to dissolve it, to disintegrate again into its constituent parts the organic form in which the proletariat was threatened by the reacting spirit of the nation. As is known, May 15 had no other result save that of removing Blanqui and his comrades, that is, the real leaders of the proletarian party, from the public stage for the entire duration of the cycle we are considering.

The *bourgeois monarchy* of Louis Philippe can be followed only by a *bourgeois republic*; that is to say, whereas a limited section of the bourgeoisie ruled in the name of the king, the whole of the bourgeoisie will now rule on behalf of the people. The demands of the Paris proletariat are utopian nonsense, to which an end must be put. To this declaration of the Constituent National Assembly the Paris proletariat replied with the *June insurrection*, the most colossal event in the history of European civil wars. The bourgeois republic triumphed. On its side stood the aristocracy of finance, the industrial bourgeoisie, the middle class, the petty bourgeois, the army, the *lumpenproletariat* organized as the Mobile Guard, the intellectual lights, the clergy, and the rural population. On the side of the Paris proletariat stood none but itself. More than three thousand insurgents were butchered after the victory and fifteen thousand were transported without trial. With this defeat the proletariat passes into the *background* of the revolutionary stage. It attempts to press forward again on every occasion, as soon as the movement appears to make a fresh start, but with ever decreased expenditure of strength and always slighter results. As soon as one of the social strata situated above it gets into revolutionary ferment, the proletariat enters into an alliance with it and so shares all the defeats that the different parties suffer, one after another. But these subsequent blows become the weaker, the greater the surface of society over which they are distributed. The more important leaders of the proletariat in the Assembly and in the press successively fall victims to the courts, and ever more equivocal figures come to head it. In part it throws itself into *doctrinaire experiments, exchange banks, and workers' associations, hence into a movement in which it renounces the revolutionizing of the old world by means of the latter's own great, combined resources and seeks, rather, to achieve its salvation behind society's back, in private fashion, within its limited conditions of existence, and hence necessarily suffers—shipwreck*. It seems to be unable either to rediscover revolutionary greatness in itself or to win new energy from the connections newly entered into, until *all classes* with which it contended in June themselves lie prostrate beside it. But at least it succumbs with the honors of the great, world-historic struggle; not only France, but all Europe trembles at the June earthquake while the ensuing defeats of the upper classes are so cheaply bought that they require barefaced exaggeration by the victorious party to be able to pass for events at all and become the more ignominious the further the defeated party is removed from the proletarian party.

The defeat of the June insurgents, to be sure, had now prepared, had leveled the ground on which the bourgeois republic could be founded and built up, but it had shown at the same time that in Europe the questions at issue are other than that of "republic or monarchy." It had revealed that here *bourgeois republic* signifies the unlimited despotism of one class over other classes. It had proved that in countries with an old civilization, with a developed formation of classes, with modern conditions of production, and with an intellectual consciousness in which all traditional ideas have been dissolved by the work of centuries, *the republic signifies in general only the political form of the revolution of bourgeois society and not its conservative form of life*, as, for example, in the United States of North America, where, though classes already exist they have not yet become fixed, but continually change and interchange their elements in constant flux, where the modern means of production, instead of coinciding with a stagnant surplus population, rather compensate for the relative deficiency of heads and hands, and where, finally, the feverish, youthful movement of material production, which has to make a new world its own, has left neither time nor opportunity for abolishing the old spirit world.

During the June days, all classes and parties had united in the *party of order* against the proletarian class as the *party of anarchy*, of socialism, of communism. They had "saved" society from "*the enemies of society*." They had given out the watchwords of the old society, "*property, family, religion, order*," to their army as passwords and had proclaimed to the counterrevolutionary crusaders: "In this sign thou shalt conquer!" From that moment, as soon as one of the numerous parties which had gathered under this sign against the June insurgents has sought to hold the revolutionary battlefield in its own class interest, it has gone down before the cry: "Property, family, religion, order." Society is saved just as often as the circle of its rulers contracts, as a more exclusive interest is maintained against a wider one. Every demand of the simplest bourgeois financial reform, of the most ordinary liberalism, of the most formal republicanism, of the most shallow democracy is simultaneously castigated as an "attempt on society" and stigatized as "socialism." And, finally, the high priests of "the religion of order" themselves are driven with kicks from their Pythian tripods, hauled out of the beds in the darkness of night, put in prison vans, thrown into dungeons, or sent into exile; their temple is razed to the ground, their mouths are sealed, their pens broken, their law torn to pieces in the name of religion, of property, of the family, of order. Bourgeois fanatics for order are shot down on their balconies by mobs of drunken soldiers, their domestic sanctuaries profaned, their houses bombarded for amusement —in the name of property, of the family, of religion, and of order. Finally, the scum of bourgeois society forms the *holy phalanx of order* and the hero Crapulinski installs himself in the Tuileries as the *"savior of society."*

Friedrich Engels

The Rise of Capitalism and the Working Class*

> Socialism: Scientific and Utopian, *from which the following selection is taken, is itself part of a larger work, commonly known as* Anti-Dühring, *which Engels wrote in 1887 as a polemic against Eugan Dühring, a German professor who had undergone a conversion to socialism and had challenged many Marxist views. Three years later, writes Engels, "at the request of my friend, Paul Lafargue . . . I arranged three chapters of this book as a pamphlet, which he translated and published in 1890, under the title: Socialisme utopique et socialisme scientifique." The selection below is an example of Marxist sociology as it deals with the conflict of social orders and classes.*

The materialist conception of history starts from the proposition that the production of the means to support human life and, next to production, the exchange of things produced, is the basis of all social structure; that in every society that has appeared in history, the manner in which wealth is distributed and society divided into classes or orders is dependent upon what is produced, how it is produced, and how the products are exchanged. From this point of view the final causes of all social changes and political revolutions are to be sought, not in men's brains, not in men's better insight into eternal truth and justice, but in changes in the modes of production and exchange. They are to be sought not in the *philosophy*, but in the *economics* of each particular epoch. The growing perception that existing social institutions are

---

* Title supplied by editor.

unreasonable and unjust, that reason has become unreason and right wrong, is only proof that in the modes of production and exchange changes have silently taken place with which the social order, adapted to earlier economic conditions, is no longer in keeping. From this it also follows that the means of getting rid of the incongruities that have been brought to light must also be present, in a more or less developed condition, within the changed modes of production themselves. These means are not to be invented by deduction from fundamental principles, but are to be discovered in the stubborn facts of the existing system of production.

What is, then, the position of modern socialism in this connection?

The present structure of society—this is now pretty generally conceded—is the creation of the ruling class of today, of the bourgeoisie. The mode of production peculiar to the bourgeoisie, known, since Marx, as the capitalist mode of production, was incompatible with the feudal system, with the privileges it conferred upon individuals, entire social ranks, and local corporations, as well as with the hereditary ties of subordination which constituted the framework of its social organization. The bourgeoisie broke up the feudal system and built upon its ruins the capitalist order of society, the kingdom of free competition, of personal liberty, of the equality, before the law, of all commodity owners, of all the rest of the capitalist blessings. Thenceforward the capitalist mode of production could develop in freedom. Since steam, machinery, and the making of machines by machinery transformed the older manufacture into modern industry, the productive forces evolved under the guidance of the bourgeoisie developed with a rapidity and in a degree unheard of before. But just as the older manufacture, in its time, and handicraft, becoming more developed under its influence, had come into collision with the feudal trammels of the guilds, so now modern industry, in its more complete development, comes into collision with the bounds within which the capitalistic mode of production holds it confined. The new productive forces have already outgrown the capitalistic mode of using them. And this conflict between productive forces and modes of production is not a conflict engendered in the mind of man, like that between original sin and divine justice. It exists, in fact, objectively, outside us, independently of the will and actions even of the men that have brought it on. Modern socialism is nothing but the reflex, in thought, of this conflict in fact; its ideal reflection in the minds, first, of the class directly suffering under it, the working class.

Now, in what does this conflict consist?

Before capitalistic production, i.e., in the Middle Ages, the system of petty industry obtained generally, based upon the private property of the labourers in their means of production; in the country, the agriculture of the small peasant, freeman, or serf; in the towns, the handicrafts organised in guilds. The instruments of labour—land, agricultural implements, the workshop, the tool—were the instruments of labour of single individuals, adapted for the use of one worker, and, therefore, of necessity, small, dwarfish, circumscribed. But, for this very reason they belonged, as a rule, to the producer himself. To concentrate these scattered, limited means of production, to enlarge them, to turn them into the powerful levers of production of the present day—this was precisely the historic role of capitalist production and of its upholder, the bourgeoisie. In the fourth section of *Capital*, Marx has explained in detail, how since the fifteenth century this has been historically worked out through the three phases of simple cooperation, manufacture, and modern industry. But the bourgeoisie, as is also shown there, could not transform these puny means of production into mighty productive forces without transforming them, at the same time, from means of production of the individual into *social* means of production, only workable by a collectivity of men. The spinning wheel, the hand loom, the blacksmith's hammer, were replaced by the spinning machine, the power loom, the steam hammer; the individual workshop, by the factory implying the cooperation of hundreds and thousands of workmen. In like manner, production itself changed from a series of individual into a series of social acts, and the products from individual to social products. The yarn, the cloth, the metal articles that now came out of the factory, were the joint product of many workers, through whose hands they had successively to pass before they were ready. No one person could say of them: "I made that; this is *my* product."

But where, in a given society, the fundamental form of production is that spontaneous division of labour which creeps in gradually and not upon any preconceived plan, there the products take on the form of *commodities*, whose mutual exchange, buying and selling, enable the individual producers to satisfy their manifold wants. And this was the case in the Middle Ages. The peasant, for instance, sold to the artisan agricultural products and bought from him the products of handicraft. Into this society of individual producers, of commodity producers, the new mode of production thrust itself. In the midst of the old division of labour, grown up spontaneously, and upon *no definite plan,* which had governed the whole of society, now arose division of labour upon a *definite plan,* as organised in the factory; side by side with *individual* production appeared *social* production. The products of both were sold in the same market, and, therefore, at prices at least approximately equal. But organisation upon a definite plan was stronger than spontaneous division of labour. The factories working with the combined social forces of a collectivity of individuals produced their commodities far more cheaply than the individual small producers. Individual production succumbed in one department after another. Socialised production revolutionised all the old methods of production. But its revolutionary character was, at the same time, so little recognised that it was, on the contrary, introduced as a means of increasing and developing the production of commodities. When it arose, it found ready made, and made liberal use of, certain machinery for the production and exchange of commodities: merchants' capital, handicraft, wage labour. Socialised production thus introducing itself as a new form of the production of commodities, it was a matter of course that under it the old forms of appropriation remained in full swing, and were applied to its products as well.

In the medieval stage of evolution of the production of commodities, the question as to the owner of the product of labour could not arise. The individual producer, as a rule, had, from raw material belonging to himself, and generally his own handiwork, produced it with his own tools, by the labour of his own hands or of his family. There was no need for him to appropriate the new product. It belonged wholly to him, as a matter of course. His property in the product was, therefore, based *upon his own labour*. Even where external help was used, this was, as a rule, of little importance, and very generally was compensated by something other than wages. The apprentices and journeymen of the guilds worked less for board and wages than for education, in order that they might become master craftsmen themselves.

Then came the concentration of the means of production and of the producers in large workshops and manufactories, their transformation into actual socialised means of production and socialised producers. But the socialised producers and means of production and their products were still treated, after this change, just as they had been before, i.e., as the means of production and the products of individuals. Hitherto, the owner of the instruments of labour had himself appropriated the product, because, as a rule, it was his own product and the assistance of others was the exception. Now the owner of the instruments of labour always appropriated to himself the product, although it was no longer *his* product but exclusively the product of the *labour of others*. Thus, the products now produced socially were not appropriated by those who had actually set in motion the means of production and actually produced the commodities, but by the *capitalists*. The means of production, and production itself, had become in essence socialised. But they were subjected to a form of appropriation which presupposes the private production of individuals, under which therefore, everyone owns his own product and brings it to market. The mode of production is subjected to this form of appropriation, although it abolishes the conditions upon which the latter rests.*

---

* It is hardly necessary in this connection to point out that, even if the *form* of appropriation remains the same, the *character* of the appropriation is just as much revolutionised as production is by the changes described above. It is, of course, a very different matter whether I appropriate to myself my own product or that of another. Note in passing that wage labour, which contains the whole capitalistic mode of

This contradiction, which gives to the new mode of production its capitalistic character, *contains the germ of the whole of the social antagonisms of today.* The greater the mastery obtained by the new mode of production over all important fields of production and in all manufacturing countries, the more it reduced individual production to an insignificant residuum, *the more clearly was brought out the incompatibility of socialised production with capitalistic appropriation.*

The first capitalists found, as we have said, alongside of other forms of labour, wage labour ready-made for them on the market. But it was exceptional, conplementary, accessory, transitory wage labour. The agricultural labourer, though, upon occasion, he hired himself out by the day, had a few acres of his own land on which he could at all events live at a pinch. The guilds were so organized that the journeyman of today became the master of tomorrow. But all this changed, as soon as the means of production became socialised and concentrated in the hands of capitalists. The means of production, as well as the product, of the individual producer became more and more worthless; there was nothing left for him but to turn wage worker under the capitalist. Wage labour, aforetime the exception and accessory, now became the rule and basis of all production; aforetime complementary, it now became the sole remaining function of the worker. The wage worker for a time became a wage worker for life. The number of these permanent wage workers was further enormously increased by the breaking up of the feudal system that occurred at the same time, by the disbanding of the retainers of the feudal lords, the eviction of the peasants from their homesteads, etc. The separation was made complete between the means of production concentrated in the hands of the capitalists, on the one side, and the producers, possessing nothing but their labour power, on the other. *The contradiction between socialised production and capitalistic ap-*

---

production in embryo, is very ancient; in a sporadic, scattered form it existed for centuries alongside of slave labour. But the embryo could duly develop into the capitalistic mode of production only when the necessary historical preconditions had been furnished. [Note by Engels.]

*propriation manifested itself as the antagonism of prole-
tariat and bourgeoisie.*

We have seen that the capitalistic mode of production
thrust its way into a society of commodity producers, of
individual producers, whose social bond was the exchange of their products. But every society based upon
the production of commodities has this peculiarity: that
the producers have lost control over their own social interrelations. Each man produces for himself with such
means of production as he may happen to have and for
such exchange as he may require to satisfy his remaining
wants. No one knows how much of his particular article
is coming on the market, nor how much of it will be
wanted. No one knows whether his individual product
will meet an actual demand, whether he will be able to
make good his costs of production or even to sell his
commodity at all. Anarchy reigns in socialised production.

But the production of commodities, like every other
form of production, has its peculiar, inherent laws inseparable from it; and these laws work, despite anarchy, in
and through anarchy. They reveal themselves in the only
persistent form of social interrelations, i.e., in exchange,
and here they affect the individual producers as compulsory laws of competition. They are, at first, unknown to
these producers themselves and have to be discovered by
them gradually and as the result of experience. They
work themselves out, therefore, independently of the
producers, and in antagonism to them, as inexorable natural laws of their particular form of production. The
product governs the producers.

In medieval society, especially in the earlier centuries,
production was essentially directed towards satisfying the
wants of the individual. It satisfied, in the main, only the
wants of the producer and his family. Where relations of
personal dependence existed, as in the country, it also
helped to satisfy the wants of the feudal lord. In all this
there was, therefore, no exchange; the products, consequently, did not assume the character of commodities.
The family of the peasant produced almost everything
they wanted: clothes and furniture, as well as means of
subsistence. Only when it began to produce more than

was sufficient to supply its own wants and the payments in kind to the feudal lord, only then did it also produce commodities. This surplus, thrown into socialised exchange and offered for sale, became commodities.

The artisans of the towns, it is true, had from the first to produce for exchange. But they, also, themselves supplied the greatest part of their own individual wants. They had gardens and plots of land. They turned their cattle out into the communal forest, which, also, yielded them timber and firing. The women spun flax, wool, and so forth. Production for the purpose of exchange, production of commodities, was only in its infancy. Hence, exchange was restricted, the market narrow, the methods of production stable; there was local exclusiveness without, local unity within; the mark in the country; in the town, the guild.

But with the extension of the production of commodities, and especially with the introduction of the capitalist mode of production, the laws of commodity production, hitherto latent, came into action more openly and with greater force. The old bonds were loosened, the old exclusive limits broken through, the producers were more and more turned into independent, isolated producers of commodities. It became apparent that the production of society at large was ruled by absence of plan, by accident, by anarchy; and this anarchy grew to greater and greater height. But the chief means by aid of which the capitalist mode of production intensified this anarchy of socialised production was the exact opposite of anarchy. It was the increasing organisation of production, upon a social basis, in every individual productive establishment. By this, the old, peaceful, stable condition of things was ended. Wherever this organisation of production was introduced into a branch of industry, it brooked no other method of production by its side. The field of labour became a battleground. The great geographical discoveries, and the colonisation following upon them, multiplied markets and quickened the transformation of handicraft into manufacture. The war did not simply break out between the individual producers of particular localities. The local struggles begot in their turn national conflicts, the commercial wars of the seventeenth and the eighteenth centuries.

Finally, modern industry and the opening of the world market made the struggle universal, and at the same time gave it an unheard of virulence. Advantages in natural or artificial conditions of production now decide the existence or nonexistence of individual capitalists, as well as of whole industries and countries. He that falls is remorselessly cast aside. It is the Darwinian struggle of the individual for existence transferred from nature to society with intensified violence. The conditions of existence natural to the animal appear as the final term of human development. The contradiction between socialised production and capitalistic appropriation now presents itself as *an antagonism between the organisation of production in the individual workshop and the anarchy of production in society generally.*

The capitalistic mode of production moves in these two forms of the antagonism immanent to it from its very origin. It is never able to get out of that "vicious circle" which Fourier had already discovered. What Fourier could not, indeed, see in his time is that this circle is gradually narrowing; that the movement becomes more and more a spiral, and must come to an end, like the movement of the planets, by collision with the centre. It is the compelling force of anarchy in the production of society at large that more and more completely turns the great majority of men into proletarians; and it is the masses of the proletariat again who will finally put an end to anarchy in production. It is the compelling force of anarchy in social production that turns the limitless perfectibility of machinery under modern industry into a compulsory law by which every individual industrial capitalist must perfect his machinery more and more, under penalty of ruin.

But the perfecting of machinery is making human labour superfluous. If the introduction and increase of machinery means the displacement of millions of manual by a few machine workers, improvement in machinery means the displacement of more and more of the machine workers themselves. It means, in the last instance, the production of a number of available wage workers in excess of the average needs of capital, the formation of a complete industrial reserve army, as I called it in 1845,* available at the times when industry is working at high pressure, to be cast upon the street when the inevitable crash comes, a constant dead weight upon the limbs of the working class in its struggle for existence with capital, a regulator for the keeping of wages down to the low level that suits the interests of capital. Thus it comes about, to quote Marx, that machinery becomes the most powerful weapon in the war of capital against the working class; that the instruments of labour constantly tear the means of subsistence out of the hands of the labourer; that the very product of the worker is turned into an instrument for his subjugation. Thus it comes about that the economising of the instruments of labour becomes at the same time, from the outset, the most reckless waste of labour power, and robbery based upon the normal conditions under which labour functions; that machinery, "the most powerful instrument for shortening labour time, becomes the most unfailing means for placing every moment of the labourer's time and that of his family at the disposal of the capitalist for the purpose of expanding the value of his capital." (Marx, *Capital.*) Thus it comes about that the overwork of some becomes the preliminary condition for the idleness of others, and that modern industry, which hunts after new consumers over the whole world, forces the consumption of the masses at home down to a starvation minimum, and in doing thus destroys its own home market. "The law that always equilibrates the relative surplus population, or industrial reserve army, to the extent and energy of accumulation, this law rivets the labourer to capital more firmly than the wedges of Vulcan did Prometheus to the rock. It establishes an accumulation of misery, corresponding with accumulation of capital. Accumulation of wealth at one pole is, therefore, at the same time, accumulation of misery, agony of toil slavery, ignorance, brutality, mental degradation, at the opposite pole, i.e., on the side of the class that produces *its own product in the form of capi-*

---

* *The condition of the Working Class in England.*

tal." (Marx, *Capital*.) And to expect any other division of the products from the capitalistic mode of production is the same as expecting the electrodes of a battery not to decompose acidulated water, not to liberate oxygen at the positive, hydrogen at the negative pole, so long as they are connected with the battery.

We have seen that the ever increasing perfectibility of modern machinery is, by the anarchy of social production, turned into a compulsory law that forces the individual industrial capitalist always to improve his machinery, always to increase its productive force. The bare possibility of extending the field of production is transformed for him into a similar compulsory law. The enormous expansive force of modern industry, compared with which that of gases is mere child's play, appears to us now as a *necessity* for expansion, both qualitative and quantitative, that laughs at all resistance. Such resistance is offered by consumption, by sales, by the markets for the products of modern industry. But the capacity for extension, extensive and intensive, of the markets is primarily governed by quite different laws that work much less energetically. The extension of the markets cannot keep pace with the extension of production. The collision becomes inevitable, and as this cannot produce any real solution so long as it does not break in pieces the capitalist mode of production, the collisions become periodic. Capitalist production has begotten another "vicious circle."

As a matter of fact, since 1825, when the first general crisis broke out, the whole industrial and commercial world, production and exchange among all civilised peoples and their more or less barbaric hangers-on, are thrown out of joint about once every ten years. Commerce is at a standstill, the markets are glutted, products accumulate, as multitudinous as they are unsaleable, hard cash disappears, credit vanishes, factories are closed, the mass of the workers are in want of the means of subsistence, because they have produced too much of the means of subsistence; bankruptcy follows upon bankruptcy, execution upon execution. The stagnation lasts for years; productive forces and products are wasted and destroyed wholesale, until the accumulated mass of commodities finally filters off, more or less depreciated in value, until production and exchange gradually begin to move again. Little by little the pace quickens. It becomes a trot. The industrial trot breaks into a canter, the canter in turn grows into the headlong gallop of a perfect steeplechase of industry, commercial credit, and speculation which finally, after breakneck leaps, ends where it began—in the ditch of a crisis: And so over and over again. We have now, since the year 1825, gone through this five times, and at the present moment we are going through it for the sixth time. And the character of these crises is so clearly defined that Fourier hit all of them off when he described the first as *"crise pléthorique,"* a crisis from plethora.

In these crises, the contradiction between socialised production and capitalist appropriation ends in a violent explosion. The circulation of commodities is, for the time being, stopped. Money, the means of circulation, becomes a hindrance to circulation. All the laws of production and circulation of commodities are turned upside down. The economic collision has reached its apogee. *The mode of production is in rebellion against the mode of exchange.*

The fact that the socialised organisation of production within the factory has developed so far that it has become incompatible with the anarchy of production in society, which exists side by side with and dominates it, is brought home to the capitalists themselves by the violent concentration of capital that occurs during crises, through the ruin of many large, and a still greater number of small, capitalists. The whole mechanism of the capitalist mode of production breaks down under the pressure of the productive forces, its own creations. It is no longer able to turn all this mass of means of production into capital. They lie fallow, and for that very reason the industrial reserve army must also lie fallow. Means of production, means of subsistence, available labourers, all the elements of production and of general wealth, are present in abundance. But "abundance becomes the source of distress and want" (Fourier), because it is the very thing that prevents the transformation of the means of production and subsistence into capital. For in capitalistic society the means of production can only function when they have undergone a preliminary transformation into capital, into the means of exploiting human labour power. The necessity of this transformation into capital of the means of production and subsistence stands like a ghost between these and the workers. It alone prevents the coming together of the material and personal levers of production; it alone forbids the means of production to function, the workers to work and live. On the one hand, therefore, the capitalistic mode of production stands convicted of its own incapacity to further direct these productive forces. On the other, these productive forces themselves, with increasing energy, press forward to the removal of the existing contradiction, to the abolition of their quality as capital, to the *practical recognition of their character as social productive forces.*

The rebellion of the productive forces, as they grow more and more powerful, against their quality as capital, this stronger and stronger command that their social character shall be recognised, forces the capitalist class itself to treat them more and more as social productive forces, so far as this is possible under capitalist conditions. The period of industrial high pressure, with its unbounded inflation of credit, not less than the crash itself, by the collapse of great capitalist establishments, tends to bring about that form of the socialisation of great masses of means of production which we meet with in the different kinds of joint-stock companies. Many of these means of production and of distribution are, from the outset, so colossal that, like the railways, they exclude all other forms of capitalistic exploitation. At a further stage of evolution this form also becomes insufficient. The producers on a large scale in a particular branch of industry in a particular country unite in a trust, a union for the purpose of regulating production. They determine the total amount to be produced, parcel it out among themselves, and thus enforce the selling price fixed beforehand. But trusts of this kind, as soon as business becomes bad, are generally liable to break up, and on this very account compel a yet greater concentration of association. The whole of the particular industry is turned into one gigantic joint-stock company; internal competition gives place to the internal monopoly of this one company. This has happened in 1890 with the English alkali production, which is now, after the fusion of 48 large works, in the hands of one company, conducted upon a single plan, and with a capital of £6,000,000.

In the trusts, freedom of competition changes into its very opposite—into monopoly; and the production without any definite plan of capitalistic society capitulates to the production upon a definite plan of the invading socialist society. Certainly this is so far still to the benefit and advantage of the capitalists. But in this case the exploitation is so palpable that it must break down. No nation will put up with production conducted by trusts, with so barefaced an exploitation of the community by a small band of dividend mongers.

In any case, with trusts or without the official representative of capitalist society—the state—will ultimately have to undertake the direction of production.* This necessity for conversion into state property is felt first in the great institutions for intercourse and communication—the post office, the telegraphs, the railways.

If the crises demonstrate the incapacity of the bourgeoi-

---

* I say "have to." For only when the means of production and distribution have *actually* outgrown the form of management by joint-stock companies, and when, therefore, the taking them over by the state has become *economically* inevitable, only then—even if it is the state of today that effects this—there is an economic advance, the attainment of another step preliminary to the taking over of all productive forces by society itself. But of late, since Bismarck went in for state ownership of industrial establishments, a kind of spurious socialism has arisen, degenerating, now and again, into something of flunkeyism, that without more ado delcares *all* state ownership, even of the Bismarckian sort, to be socialistic. Certainly, if the taking over by the state of the tobacco industry is socialistic, then Napoleon and Metternich must be numbered among the founders of socialism. If the Belgian state, for quite ordinary political and financial reasons, itself constructed its chief railway lines; if Bismarck, not under any economic compulsion, took over for the state the chief Prussian lines, simply to be the better able to have them in hand in case of war, to bring up the railway employees as voting cattle for the government, and especially to create for himself a new source of income independent of parliamentary votes—this was, in no sense, a socialistic measure, directly or indirectly, consciously or unconsciously. Otherwise, the Royal Maritime Company, the Royal porcelain manufacture, and even the regimental tailor shops of the Army would also be socialistic institutions, or even, as was seriously proposed by a sly dog in Frederick William III's reign, the taking over by the state of the brothels. [Note by Engels.]

sie for managing any longer modern productive forces, the transformation of the great establishments for production and distribution into joint-stock companies, trusts, and state property shows how unnecessary the bourgeoisie are for that purpose. All the social functions of the capitalist are now performed by salaried employees. The capitalist has no further social function than that of pocketing dividends, tearing off coupons, and gambling on the Stock Exchange, where the different capitalists despoil one another of their capital. At first the capitalistic mode of production forces out the workers. Now it forces out the capitalists and reduces them, just as it reduced the workers, to the ranks of the surplus population, although not immediately into those of the industrial reserve army.

But the transformation, either into joint-stock companies and trusts or into state ownership, does not do away with the capitalistic nature of the productive forces. In the joint-stock companies and trusts this is obvious. And the modern state, again, is only the organisation that bourgeois society takes on in order to support the external conditions of the capitalist mode of production against the encroachments as well of the workers as of individual capitalists. The modern state, no matter what its form, is essentially a capitalist machine, the state of the capitalists, the ideal personification of the total national capital. The more it proceeds to the taking over of productive forces, the more does it actually become the national capitalist, the more citizens does it exploit. The workers remain wage workers—proletarians. The capitalist relation is not done away with. It is rather brought to a head. But, brought to a head, it topples over. State ownership of the productive forces is not the solution of the conflict, but concealed within it are the technical conditions that form the elements of that solution.

This solution can only consist in the practical recognition of the social nature of the modern forces of production, and therefore in the harmonising of the modes of production, appropriation, and exchange with the socialised character of the means of production. And this can only come about by society openly and directly taking possession of the productive forces which have outgrown all control except that of society as a whole. The social character of the means of production and of the products today reacts against the producers, periodically disrupts all production and exchange, acts only like a law of nature working blindly, forcibly, destructively. But with the taking over by society of the productive forces, the social character of the means of production and of the products will be utilised by the producers with a perfect understanding of its nature, and instead of being a source of disturbance and periodical collapse, will become the most powerful lever of production itself.

Active social forces work exactly like natural forces: blindly, forcibly, destructively, so long as we do not understand, and reckon with, them. But when once we understand them, when once we grasp their action, their direction, their effects, it depends only upon ourselves to subject them more and more to our own will, and by means of them to reach our own ends. And this holds quite especially of the mighty productive forces of today. As long as we obstinately refuse to understand the nature and the character of these social means of action—and this understanding goes against the grain of the capitalist mode of production and its defenders—so long these forces are at work in spite of us, in opposition to us, so long they master us, as we have shown above in detail.

But when once their nature is understood, they can, in the hands of the producers working together, be transformed from master demons into willing servants. The difference is as that between the destructive force of electricity in the lightning of the storm, and electricity under command in the telegraph and the voltaic arc; the difference between a conflagration, and fire working in the service of man. With this recognition, at last, of the real nature of the productive forces of today, the social anarchy of production gives place to a social regulation of production upon a definite plan, according to the needs of the community and of each individual. Then the capitalist mode of appropriation, in which the product enslaves first the producer and then the appropriator, is replaced by the mode of appropriation of the products that is based upon the nature of the modern means of production: upon the one hand, direct social appropriation, as means to the maintenance and extension of production; on the other, direct individual appropriation, as means of subsistence and of enjoyment.

Whilst the capitalist mode of production more and more completely transforms the great majority of the population into proletarians, it creates the power which, under penalty of its own destruction, is forced to accomplish this revolution. Whilst it forces on more and more the transformation of the vast means of production, already socialised, into state property, it shows itself the way to accomplishing this revolution. *The proletariat seizes political power and turns the means of production into state property.*

But, in doing this, it abolishes itself as proletariat, abolishes all class distinctions and class antagonisms, abolishes also the state as state. Society thus far, based upon class antagonisms, had need of the state. That is, of an organisation of the particular class which was *pro tempore* the exploiting class, an organisation for the purpose of preventing any interference from without with the existing conditions of production, and, therefore, especially, for the purpose of forcibly keeping the exploited classes in the condition of oppression corresponding with the given mode of production (slavery, serfdom, wage labour). The state was the official representative of society as a whole; the gathering of it together into a visible embodiment. But it was this only in so far as it was the state of that class which itself represented, for the time being, society as a whole: in ancient times, the state of slaveowning citizens; in the Middle Ages, the feudal lords; in our own time, the bourgeoisie. When at last it becomes the real representative of the whole of society, it renders itself unnecessary. As soon as there is no longer any social class to be held in subjection; as soon as class rule, and the individual struggle for existence based upon our present anarchy in production, with the collisions and excesses arising from these, are removed, nothing more remains to be repressed, and a special repressive force, a state, is no longer necessary. The first act by virtue of which the state really constitutes itself the representative of the whole of society—the taking possession of the means of production in the name of society—this is, at the same time, its last independent act as a state. State interference in social relations becomes, in one domain after another, superfluous, and then dies out of itself; the government of persons is replaced by the administration of things and by the conduct of processes of production. The state is not "abolished." *It dies out.* This gives the measure of the value of the phrase "*a free state,*" both as to its justifiable use at times by agitators and as to its ultimate scientific insufficiency; and also of the demands of the so-called anarchists for the abolition of the state out of hand.

Since the historical appearance of the capitalist mode of production, the appropriation by society of all the means of production has often been dreamed of, more or less vaguely, by individuals, as well as by sects, as the ideal of the future. But it could become possible, could become a historical necessity, only when the actual conditions for its realisation were there. Like every other social advance, it becomes practicable, not by men understanding that the existence of classes is in contradiction to justice, equality, etc., not by the mere willingness to abolish these classes, but by virtue of certain new economic conditions. The separation of society into an exploiting and an exploited class, a ruling and an oppressed class, was the necessary consequence of the deficient and restricted development of production in former times. So long as the total social labour only yields a produce which but slightly exceeds that barely necessary for the existence of all; so long, therefore, as labour engages all or almost all the time of the great majority of the members of society—so long, of necessity, this society is divided into classes. Side by side with the great majority, exclusively bond slaves to labour, arises a class freed from directly productive labour, which looks after the general affairs of society: the direction of labour, state business, law, science, art, etc. It is, therefore, the law of division of labour that lies at the basis of the division into classes. But this does not prevent this division into classes from being carried out by means of violence and robbery, trickery and fraud. It does not prevent the ruling class, once having the upper hand, from consolidating its power at the expense of the working class, from turning its social leadership into an intensified exploitation of the masses.

But if, upon this showing, division into classes has a certain historical justification, it has this only for a given period, only under given social conditions. It was based upon the insufficiency of production. It will be swept away by the complete development of modern productive forces. And, in fact, the abolition of classes in society presupposes a degree of historical evolution at which the existence, not simply of this or that particular ruling class, but of any ruling class at all, and, therefore, the existence of class distinction itself has become an obsolete anachronism. It presupposes, therefore, the development of production carried out to a degree at which appropriation of the means of production and of the products, and, with this, of political domination, of the monopoly of culture, and of intellectual leadership by a particular class of society, has become not only superfluous but economically, politically, intellectually, a hindrance to development. . . .

Friedrich Engels

The Road to Power*

> When Engels wrote this essay in 1895, he could look
> upon the transformation of the European Marxist
> movement from a tiny sect into a major political
> movement. Taking the occasion of a reprint of several
> articles dealing with political struggles in France that
> Marx had written in 1850, Engels sharply attacked
> the more adventurist and romantic notions concern-
> ing insurrection that had earlier prevailed among Eu-
> ropean radicals. In this late work, Engels stresses the
> need to build a mass movement based on the entire
> working class and to use to the full the resources of
> parliamentary democracy. Understandably, Engels'
> essay has been a favorite text among reformist social-
> ists.
>
> The essay has itself had a fascinating history. When
> first printed in Vorwärts, the organ of the German
> social democracy, several passages were cut by the
> editors for reasons of political caution; these pas-
> sages (which Lenin strongly emphasized in his State
> and Revolution) indicate that Engels, while repudiat-
> ing conspiratorial insurrection, did not rule out the
> possibility of armed struggles as a necessary prelimi-
> nary to achieving power. The present text restores the
> cut passages.

. . . In judging the events and series of events of day-to-
day history, it will never be possible for anyone to go
right back to the final economic causes. Even today,
when the specialised technical press provides such rich
materials, in England itself it still remains impossible to

---

* Title supplied by editor.

follow day by day the movement of industry and trade in the world market and the changes which take place in the methods of production, in such a way as to be able to draw the general conclusion, at any point of time, from these very complicated and ever changing factors: of these factors, the most important, into the bargain, generally operate a long time in secret before they suddenly and violently make themselves felt on the surface. A clear survey of the economic history of a given period is never contemporaneous; it can only be gained subsequently, after collecting and sifting of the material has taken place. Statistics are a necessary help here, and they always lag behind. For this reason, it is only too often necessary, in the current history of the time, to treat the most decisive factor as constant, to treat the economic situation existing at the beginning of the period concerned as given and unalterable for the whole period, or else to take notice only of such changes in this situation as themselves arise out of events clearly before us, and as, therefore, can likewise be clearly seen. Hence, the materialist method has here often to limit itself to tracing political conflicts back to the struggles between the interests of the social classes and fractions of classes encountered as the result of economic development, and to show the particular political parties as the more or less adequate expression of these same classes and fractions of classes.

It is self-evident that this unavoidable neglect of contemporaneous changes in the economic situation, of the very basis of all the proceedings subject to examination, must be a source of error. But all the conditions of a comprehensive presentation of the history of the day unavoidably imply sources of error—which, however, keeps nobody from writing contemporary history.

When Marx undertook this work,* the sources of error mentioned were, to a still greater degree, impossible to avoid. It was quite impossible during the period of the Revolution of 1848/49 to follow the economic transformations which were being consummated at the same time, or even to keep a general view of them. It was just the

---

* Essays for the *Neue Rheinische Zeitung* (1850), reprinted as *Class Struggles in France*.

same during the first months of exile in London, in the autumn and winter of 1849/50. But that was just the time when Marx began this work. And, in spite of these unfavorable circumstances, his exact knowledge both of the economic situation in France and of the political history of that country since the February Revolution made it possible for him to give a picture of events which laid bare their inner connections in a way never attained since, and which later brilliantly withstood the double test instituted by Marx himself. . . .

The thing which still gives this work of ours a quite special significance is that, for the first time, it expresses the formula in which, by common agreement, the workers' parties of all countries in the world briefly summarise their demand for economic reconstruction: the appropriation by society of the means of production. In the second chapter, in connection with the "right to work," which is characterised as "the first clumsy formula wherein the revolutionary aspirations of the proletariat are summarised," it is said: "But behind the right to work stands the power over capital; behind the power over capital, the appropriation of the means of production, their subjection to the associated working class and, therefore, the abolition of wage labour as well as of capital and of their mutual relationships." Thus, here, for the first time, the proposition is formulated by which modern working-class socialism is equally sharply differentiated both from all the different shades of feudal, bourgeois, petty bourgeois, etc., socialism and also from the confused community of goods of utopian and spontaneous worker communism. If, later, Marx extended the formula to appropriation of the means of exchange also, this extension, which, in any case, was self-evident after *The Communist Manifesto*, only expressed a corollary to the main proposition. . . . After the defeats of 1849, we in no way shared the illusions of the vulgar democracy grouped around the would-be provisional governments *in partibus*. This vulgar democracy reckoned on a speedy and finally decisive victory of the "people" over the "usurpers"; we looked to a long struggle, after the removal of the "usurpers," between the antagonistic elements concealed within this "people" itself. Vulgar democracy expected a renewed outbreak from day to day; we declared as early as autumn 1850 that at least the first chapter of the revolutionary period was closed and that nothing further was to be expected until the outbreak of a new world crisis. For this reason we were excommunicated, as traitors to the revolution, by the very people who later, almost without exception, have made their peace with Bismarck—so far as Bismarck found them worth the trouble.

But we, too, have been shown to have been wrong by history, which has revealed our point of view of that time to have been an illusion. It has done even more; it has not merely destroyed our error of that time; it has also completely transformed the conditions under which the proletariat has to fight. The mode of struggle of 1848 is today obsolete from every point of view, and this is a point which deserves closer examination on the present occasion.

All revolutions up to the present day have resulted in the displacement of one definite class rule by another; all ruling classes up till now have been only minorities as against the ruled mass of the people. A ruling minority was thus overthrown; another minority seized the helm of state and remodeled the state apparatus in accordance with its own interests. Thus was on every occasion the minority group able and called to rule by the degree of economic development, and just for that reason, and only for that reason, it happened that the ruled majority either participated in the revolution on the side of the former or else passively acquiesced in it. But if we disregard the concrete content of each occasion, the common form of all these revolutions was that they were minority revolutions. Even where the majority took part, it did so—whether wittingly or not—only in the service of a minority; but because of this, or simply because of the passive, unresisting attitude of the majority, this minority acquired the appearance of being the representative of the whole people.

As a rule, after the first great success, the victorious minority became divided; one half was pleased with what had been gained, the other wanted to go still further, and put forward new demands, which, to a certain extent at least, were also in the real or apparent interests of the great mass of the people. In individual cases these more radical demands were realised, but often only for the moment; the more moderate party again gained the upper hand, and what had eventually been won was wholly or partly lost again; the vanquished shrieked of treachery, or ascribed their defeat to accident. But in truth the position was mainly this: the achievements of the first victory were only safeguarded by the second victory of the more radical party; this having been attained, and, with it, what was necessary for the moment, the radicals and their achievements vanished once more from the stage.

All revolutions of modern times, beginning with the great English revolution of the seventeenth century, showed these features, which appeared inseparable from every revolutionary struggle. They appeared applicable, also, to the struggles of the proletariat for its emancipation; all the more applicable, since in 1848 there were few people who had any idea at all of the direction in which this emancipation was to be sought. The proletarian masses themselves, even in Paris, after the victory, were still absolutely in the dark as to the path to be taken. And yet the movement was there, instinctive, spontaneous, irrepressible. Was not this just the situation in which a revolution had to succeed, led certainly by a minority, but this time not in the interests of the minority, but in the real interests of the majority? If, in all the longer revolutionary periods, it was so easy to win the great masses of the people by the merely plausible and delusive views of the minorities thrusting themselves forward, how could they be less susceptible to ideas which were the truest reflex of their economic position, which were nothing but the clear, comprehensible expression of their needs, of needs not yet understood by themselves, but only vaguely felt? To be sure, this revolutionary mood of the masses had almost always, and usually very speedily, given way to lassitude or even to a revulsion to its opposite, so soon as illusion evaporated and disappointment set in. But here it was not a question of delusive views, but of giving effect to the very special interests of the great majority itself, interests which at that time were certainly by no means clear to this great majority, but which must soon enough become clear in the course of giving practical effect to them, by their convincing obviousness. And if now, as Marx showed in the third article, in the spring of 1850, the development of the bourgeois republic that had arisen out of the "social" revolution of 1848 had concentrated the real power in the hands of the big bourgeoisie —monarchistically inclined as it was—and, on the other hand, had grouped all the other social classes, peasants as well as petty bourgeoisie, round the proletariat, so that, during and after the common victory, not they, but the proletariat grown wise by experience, must become the decisive factor—was there not every prospect here of turning the revolution of the minority into the revolution of the majority?

History has proved us, and all who thought like us, wrong. It has made it clear that the state of economic development on the Continent at that time was not, by a long way, ripe for the removal of capitalist production; it has proved this by the economic revolution which, since 1848, has seized the whole of the Continent, has really caused big industry for the first time to take root in France, Austria, Hungary, Poland, and, recently, in Russia, while it has made Germany positively an industrial country of the first rank—all on a capitalist basis, which in the year 1848, therefore, still had great capacity for expansion. But it is just this industrial revolution which has everywhere for the first time produced clarity in the class relationships, which has removed a number of transition forms handed down from the manufacturing period and in Eastern Europe even from guild handicraft, and has created a genuine bourgeoisie and a genuine large-scale industrial proletariat and pushed them into the foreground of social development. But, owing to this, the struggle of these two great classes, which, apart from England, existed in 1848 only in Paris and, at the most, a few big industrial centres, has been spread over the whole of Europe and has reached an intensity such as was unthinkable in 1848. At that time the many obscure evangels of the sects, with their panaceas; today the one generally recognised, transparently clear theory of Marx, sharply formulating the final aims of the struggle. At that time the masses, sundered and differing according to locality and nationality, linked only by the feeling of common suffering, undeveloped, tossed to and fro in their perplexity from enthusiasm to despair; today a great international army of socialists, marching irresistibly on and growing daily in number, organisation, discipline, insight, and assurance of victory. If even this mighty army of the proletariat has still not reached its goal, if, a long way from winning victory with one mighty stroke, it has slowly to press forward from position to position in a hard, tenacious struggle, this only proves, once and for all, how impossible it was in 1848 to win social reconstruction by a simple surprise attack. . . .

It was believed that the militant proletariat had been finally buried with the Paris Commune. But, completely to the contrary, it dates its most powerful advance from the Commune and the Franco-German war. The recruitment of the whole of the population able to bear arms into armies that could be counted in millions and the introduction of firearms, projectiles, and explosives of hitherto undreamt of efficacy created a complete revolution in all warfare. This, on the one hand, put a sudden end to the Bonapartist war period and insured peaceful industrial development, since any war other than a world war of unheard of cruelty and absolutely incalculable outcome had become an impossibility. On the other hand, it caused military expenditure to rise in geometrical progression, and thereby forced up taxes to exorbitant levels, and so drove the poorer classes of people into the arms of socialism. The annexation of Alsace-Lorraine, the most immediate cause of the mad competition in armaments, might set the French and German bourgeoisie chauvinistically at each other's throats; for the workers of the two countries, it became a new bond of unity. And the anniversary of the Paris Commune became the first universal commemoration day of the whole proletariat.

The war of 1870/71 and the defeat of the Commune had transferred the centre of gravity of the European workers' movement for the time being from France to Germany, as Marx foretold. In France it naturally took years to recover from the bloodletting of May, 1871. In Germany, on the other hand, where industry was, in addition, furthered (in positively hot-house fashion) by the blessing of the French milliards and developed more and more quickly, Social Democracy experienced a much more rapid and enduring growth. Thanks to the understanding with which the German workers made use of the universal suffrage introduced in 1866, the astonishing growth of the party is made plain to all the world by incontestable figures: 1871, 102,000; 1874, 352,000; 1877, 493,000 Social Democratic votes. Then came recognition of this advance by high authority in the shape of the Anti-Socialist Law: the party was temporarily disrupted; the number of votes sank to 312,000 in 1881. But that was quickly overcome, and then, though oppressed by the Exceptional Law, without press, without external organisation, and without the right of combination or meeting, the rapid expansion really began: 1884, 550,000; 1887, 763,000; 1890, 1,427,000 votes. Then the hand of the state was paralysed. The Anti-Socialist Law disappeared; socialist votes rose to 1,787,000, over a quarter of all the votes cast. The government and the ruling classes had exhausted all their expedients—uselessly, to no purpose, and without success. The tangible proofs of their impotence, which the authorities, from night watchman to the imperial chancellor, had had to accept—and that from the despised workers—these proofs were counted in millions. The state was at the end of its Latin, the workers only at the beginning of theirs.

But the German workers did a second great service to their cause in addition to the first, which they rendered by their mere existence as the strongest, best disciplined, and most rapidly growing socialist party. They supplied their comrades of all countries with a new weapon, and one of the sharpest, when they showed them how to use universal suffrage.

There had long been universal suffrage in France, but it had fallen into disrepute through the misuse to which the Bonapartist government had put it. After the Commune there was no workers' party to make use of it. Also in Spain it had existed since the republic, but in Spain boycott of the elections was ever the rule of all serious opposition parties. The Swiss experiences of universal suffrage, also, were anything but encouraging for a workers' party. The revolutionary workers of the Latin countries had been wont to regard the suffrage as a snare, as an instrument of government trickery. It was otherwise in Germany. *The Communist Manifesto* had already proclaimed the winning of universal suffrage, of democracy, as one of the first and most important tasks of the militant proletariat, and Lassalle had again taken up this point. When Bismarck found himself compelled to introduce the franchise as the only means of interesting the mass of the people in his plans, our workers immediately took it in earnest and sent August Bebel to the first constituent Reichstag. And from that day on they have used the franchise in a way which has paid them a thousandfold and has served as a model to the workers of all countries. The franchise has been, in the words of the French Marxist programme, *"transformé, de moyen de duperie qu'il a été jusqu'ici, en instrument d'émancipation"*—they have transformed it from a means of deception, which it was heretofore, into an instrument of emancipation. And if universal suffrage had offered no other advantage than that it allowed us to count our numbers every three years; that by the regularly established, unexpectedly rapid rise in the number of votes it increased in equal measure the workers' certainty of victory and the dismay of their opponents, and so became our best means of propaganda; that it accurately informed us concerning our own strength and that of all hostile parties, and thereby provided us with a measure of proportion for our actions second to none, safeguarding us from untimely timidity as much as from untimely foolhardiness—if this had been the only advantage we gained from the suffrage, then it would still have been more than enough. But it has done much more than this. In election agitation it provided us with a means, second to none, of getting in touch with the mass of the people, where they still stand aloof from us; of forcing all parties to defend their views and actions against our attacks before all the people; and further, it opened to our representatives in the Reichstag a platform from which they could speak to their opponents in Parliament and to the masses without, with quite other authority and freedom than in the Press or at meetings. Of what avail to the government and the bourgeoisie was their

Anti-Socialist Law when election agitation and socialist speeches in the Reichstag continually broke through it?

With this successful utilisation of universal suffrage, an entirely new mode of proletarian struggle came into force, and this quickly developed further. It was found that the state institutions, in which the rule of the bourgeoisie is organised, offer still further opportunities for the working class to fight these very state institutions. They took part in elections to individual diets, to municipal councils and to industrial courts; they contested every post against the bourgeoisie in the occupation of which a sufficient part of the proletariat had its say. And so it happened that the bourgeoisie and the government came to be much more afraid of the legal than of the illegal action of the workers' party, of the results of elections than of those of rebellion.

For here, too, the conditions of the struggle had essentially changed. Rebellion in the old style, the street fight with barricades, which up to 1848 gave everywhere the final decision, was to a considerable extent obsolete.

Let us have no illusions about it: a real victory of an insurrection over the military in street fighting, a victory as between two armies, is one of the rarest exceptions. But the insurgents, also, counted on it just as rarely. For them it was solely a question of making the troops yield to moral influences, which, in a fight between the armies of two warring countries do not come into play at all, or do so to a much less degree. If they succeed in this, then the troops fail to act, or the commanding officers lose their heads, and the insurrection wins. If they do not succeed in this, then, even where the military are in the minority, the superiority of better equipment and training, of unified leadership, of the planned employment of the military forces and of discipline makes itself felt. The most that the insurrection can achieve in actual tactical practice is the correct construction and defence of a single barricade. Mutual support; the disposition and employment of reserves; in short, the cooperation and harmonious working of the individual detachments, indispensable even for the defence of one quarter of the town, not to speak of the whole of a large town, are at best

defective, and mostly not attainable at all; concentration
of the military forces at a decisive point is, of course,
impossible. Hence the passive defence is the prevailing
form of fight: the attack will rise here and there, but only
by way of exception, to occasional advances and flank
assaults; as a rule, however, it will be limited to occupation of the positions abandoned by the retreating troops.
In addition, the military have, on their side, the disposal
of artillery and fully equipped corps of skilled engineers,
resources of war which, in nearly every case, the insurgents entirely lack. No wonder, then, that even the barricade struggles conducted with the greatest heroism—
Paris, June, 1848; Vienna, October, 1848; Dresden, May,
1849—ended with the defeat of the insurrection, so soon
as the leaders of the attack, unhampered by political
considerations, acted from the purely military standpoint,
and their soldiers remained reliable.

The numerous successes of the insurgents up to 1848
were due to a great variety of causes. In Paris in July,
1830 and February, 1848, as in most of the Spanish street
fights, there stood between the insurgents and the military a civic militia, which either directly took the side of
the insurrection, or else by its lukewarm, indecisive attitude caused the troops likewise to vacillate and supplied
the insurrection with arms into the bargain. Where this
citizens' guard opposed the insurrection from the outset,
as in June, 1848, in Paris, the insurrection was vanquished. In Berlin in 1848, the people were victorious
partly through a considerable accession of new fighting
forces during the night and the morning of the 19th,
partly as a result of the exhaustion and bad victualing of
the troops, and, finally, partly as a result of the paralysed
command. But in all cases the fight was won because the
troops failed to obey, because the officers lost their power
of decision or because their hands were tied.

Even in the classic time of street fighting, therefore, the
barricade produced more of a moral than a material effect. It was a means of shaking the steadfastness of the
military. If it held out until this was attained, then victory was won; if not, there was defeat. This is the main
point, which must be kept in view, likewise when the
chances of contingent future street fights are examined.

The chances, however, were in 1849 already pretty poor. Everywhere the bourgeoisie had thrown in its lot with the governments, "culture and property" had hailed and feasted the military moving against the insurrections. The spell of the barricade was broken; the soldier no longer saw behind it "the people," but rebels, agitators, plunderers, levellers, the scum of society; the officer had in the course of time become versed in the tactical forms of street fighting, he no longer marched straight ahead and without cover against the improvised breastwork, but went round it through gardens, yards, and houses. And this was now successful, with a little skill, in nine cases out of ten.

But since then there have been very many more changes, and all in favour of the military. If the big towns have become considerably bigger, the armies have become bigger still. Paris and Berlin have, since 1848, grown less than fourfold, but their garrisons have grown more than that. By means of the railways, the garrisons can, in twenty-four hours, be more than doubled, and in forty-eight hours they can be increased to huge armies. The arming of this enormously increased number of troops has become incomparably more effective. In 1848, the smooth-bore, percussion muzzle-loader, today, the small-calibre, magazine, breech-loading rifle, which shoots four times as far, ten times as accurately, and ten times as fast as the former. At that time the relatively ineffective round shot and grapeshot of the artillery; today the percussion shells, of which one is sufficient to demolish the best barricade. At that time the pickaxe of the sapper for breaking through walls; today the dynamite cartridge.

On the other hand, all the conditions on the insurgents' side have grown worse. An insurrection with which all sections of the people sympathise will hardly recur; in the class struggle all the middle sections will never group themselves round the proletariat so exclusively that the reactionary parties gathered round the bourgeoisie well-nigh disappear. The "people," therefore, will always appear divided, and with this a powerful lever, so extraordinarily effective in 1848, is lacking. Even if more soldiers who have seen service were to come over to the insurrectionists, the arming of them becomes so much the more difficult. The hunting and luxury guns of the gunshops— even if not previously made unusable by removal of part of the lock by the police—are far from being a match for the magazine rifle of the soldier, even in close fighting. Up to 1848, it was possible to make the necessary ammunition oneself out of powder and lead; today the cartridges differ for each rifle, and are everywhere alike only in one point, that they are a special product of big industry, and therefore not to be prepared *extempore*, with the result that most rifles are useless as long as one does not possess the ammunition specially suited to them. And, finally, since 1848 the newly built quarters of the big towns have been laid out in long, straight, broad streets, as though made to give full effect to the new cannons and rifles. The revolutionary would have to be mad, who himself chose the working class districts in the North and East of Berlin for a barricade fight. Does that mean that in the future the street fight will play no further role? Certainly not. It only means that the conditions since 1848 have become far more unfavourable for civil fights, far more favourable for the military. A future street fight can therefore only be victorious when this unfavourable situation is compensated by other factors. Accordingly, it will occur more seldom in the beginning of a great revolution than in its further progress and will have to be undertaken with greater forces. These, however, may then well prefer, as in the whole Great French Revolution on September 4 and October 31, 1870, in Paris, the open attack to the passive barricade tactics.

Does the reader now understand why the ruling classes decidedly want to bring us to where the guns shoot and the sabres slash? Why they accuse us today of cowardice, because we do not betake ourselves without more ado into the street, where we are certain of defeat in advance? Why they so earnestly implore us to play for once the part of cannon fodder?

The gentlemen pour out their prayers and their challenges for nothing, for nothing at all. We are not so stupid. They might just as well demand from their enemy in the next war that he should take up his position in the line formation of old Fritz, or in the columns of whole divisions *à la* Wagram and Waterloo, and with the flint-lock in his hands at that. If the conditions have changed in the case of war between nations, this is no less true in the case of the class struggle. The time of surprise attacks, of revolutions carried through by small conscious minorities at the head of unconscious masses, is past. Where it is a question of complete transformation of the social organisation, the masses themselves must also be in it, must themselves already have grasped what is at stake, what they are going in for with body and soul. The history of the last fifty years has taught us that. But in order that the masses may understand what is to be done, long, persistent work is required, and it is just this work which we are now pursuing, and with a success which drives the enemy to despair.

In the Latin countries, also, it is being more and more recognised that the old tactics must be revised. Everywhere the unprepared onslaught has gone into the background, everywhere the German example of utilising the suffrage, of winning all posts accessible to us, has been imitated. In France, where for more than a hundred years the ground has been undermined by revolution after revolution, where there is no single party which has not done its share in conspiracies, insurrections, and all other revolutionary actions; in France, where, as a result, the government is by no means sure of the army and where, in general, the conditions for an insurrectionary *coup de main* are far more favourable than in Germany—even in France the Socialists are realising more and more that no lasting victory is possible for them, unless they first win the great mass of the people, i.e., in this case, the peasants. Slow propaganda work and parliamentary activity are being recognised here, too, as the most immediate tasks of the party. Successes were not lacking. Not only have a whole series of municipal councils been won; fifty Socialists have seats in the Chambers, and they have already overthrown three ministries and a President of the Republic. In Belgium last year, the workers enforced the franchise, and have been victorious in a quarter of the constituencies. In Switzerland, in Italy, in Denmark, yes, even in Bulgaria and Rumania the Socialists are represented in the Parliaments. In Austria, all parties agree that our admission to the Reichsrat can no longer be withheld. We will get in, that is certain; the only question still in dispute is: by which door? And even in Russia, when the famous *Zemsky Sobor* meets, that National Assembly to which young Nicholas offers such vain resistance, even there we can reckon with certainty on also being represented in it.

Of course, our foreign comrades do not renounce their right to revolution. The right to revolution is, after all, the only real "historical right," the only right on which all modern states without exception rest, Mecklenburg included, whose aristocratic revolution was ended in 1755 by the "hereditary settlement," the glorious charter of feudalism still valid today. The right to revolution is so incontestably recognised in the general consciousness that even General von Boguslawski derives the right to a *coup d'état*, which he vindicates for his Kaiser, solely from this popular right.

But whatever may happen in other countries, German Social Democracy has a special situation and therewith, at least in the first instance, a special task. The two million voters, whom it sends to the ballot box, together with the young men and women, who stand behind them as nonvoters, form the most numerous, most compact mass, the decisive *"shock force"* of the international proletarian army. This mass already supplies over a fourth of the recorded votes; and as the by-elections to the Reichstag, the diet elections in individual states, the municipal council and industrial court elections demonstrate, it increases uninterruptedly. Its growth proceeds as spontaneously, as steadily, as irresistibly, and at the same time as tranquilly as a natural process. All government interventions have proved powerless against it. We can count even today on two and a half million voters. If it continues in this fashion, by the end of the century we shall conquer the greater part of the middle section of society, petty bourgeois and small peasants, and grow into the decisive power in the land, before which all other powers will have to bow, whether they like it or not. To keep this growth going without interruption until of itself it gets beyond the control of the ruling governmental system, not to fritter away this daily increasing shock force in advance guard fighting, but to keep it intact until the day of the decision, that is our main task. And there is only one means by which the steady rise of the socialist fighting forces in Germany could be momentarily halted, and even thrown back for some time: a clash on a big scale with the military, a bloodbath like that of 1871 in Paris. In the long run that would also be overcome. To shoot out of the world a party which numbers millions—all the magazine rifles of Europe and America are not enough for this. But the normal development would be impeded, the shock force would, perhaps, not be available at the critical moment, the decisive struggle would be delayed, protracted, and attended by heavy sacrifices.

The irony of world history turns everything upside down. We, the "revolutionaries," the "rebels"—we are thriving far better on legal methods than on illegal methods and revolt. The parties of order, as they call themselves, are perishing under the legal conditions created by themselves. They cry despairingly with Odilon Barrot: *la légalité nous tue*, legality is the death of us; whereas we, under this legality, get firm muscles and rosy cheeks and look like eternal life. And if we are not so crazy as to let ourselves be driven into street fighting in order to please them, then nothing else is finally left for them but themselves to break through this legality so fatal to them. . . .

It is now, almost to the year, sixteen hundred years since a dangerous party of revolt made a great commotion in the Roman Empire. It undermined religion and all the foundations of the state; it flatly denied that Cæsar's will was the supreme law; it was without a fatherland, international; it spread over all countries of the Empire from Gaul to Asia, and beyond the frontiers of the Empire. It had long carried on an underground agitation in secret; for a considerable time, however, it had felt itself strong enough to come out into the open. This party of revolt, who were known by the name of Christians, was also strongly represented in the army; whole legions were Christian. When they were ordered to attend the sacrificial ceremonies of the pagan-established church, in order to do the honours there, the soldier rebels had the audacity to stick peculiar emblems—crosses—on their helmets in protest. Even the wonted barrack cruelties of their superior officers were fruitless. The Emperor Diocletian could no longer quietly look on while order, obedience, and discipline in his army were being undermined. He intervened energetically, while there was still time. He passed an anti-socialist, I should say, anti-Christian, law. The meetings of the rebels were forbidden, their meeting halls were closed or even pulled down, the Christian badges, crosses, etc., were, like the red handkerchiefs in Saxony, prohibited. Christians were declared incapable of holding offices in the state, they were not to be allowed even to become corporals. Since there were not available at that time judges so well trained in "respect of persons" as Herr von Köller's antirevolt bill assumes, the Christians were forbidden out of hand to seek justice before a court. This exceptional law was also without effect. The Christians tore it down from the walls with scorn; they are even supposed to have burnt the Emperor's palace in Nicomedia over his head. The latter revenged himself by the great persecution of Christians in the year 303, according to our chronology. It was the last of its kind. And it was so effective that seventeen years later the army consisted overwhelmingly of Christians, and the succeeding autocrat of the whole Roman Empire, Constantine, called the Great by the priests, proclaimed Christianity as the state religion.

Karl Marx

Commodities

It would be foolish to suppose that any excerpts, or even summary, could yield an adequate picture of the complexities, richness, and difficulties of Marx's Capital. *The sections provided below should, however, give the reader an introductory glimpse into Marxian economics. They deal with the commodity as the basic economic unit, with the working day as an example of capitalist social organization, and with "the fetishism of commodities," perhaps the most brilliant instance of Marx's socioeconomic analysis. Volume I of* Capital *was published in 1867; the remaining volumes not until after Marx's death. Because of space limitations, Marx's footnotes, often very rich in historical material, have been omitted.*

The wealth of those societies in which the capitalist mode of production prevails, presents itself as "an immense accumulation of commodities,"* its unit being a single commodity. Our investigation must therefore begin with the analysis of a commodity.

A commodity is, in the first place, an object outside us, a thing that by its properties satisfies human wants of some sort or another. The nature of such wants, whether, for instance, they spring from the stomach or from fancy, makes no difference. Neither are we here concerned to know how the object satisfies these wants, whether directly as means of subsistence or indirectly as means of production.

---

* Karl Marx, "A Contribution to the Critique of Political Economy," London, 1859, p. 19.

Every useful thing, as iron, paper, etc., may be looked at from the two points of view of quality and quantity. It is an assemblage of many properties and may therefore be of use in various ways. To discover the various use of things is the work of history. So also is the establishment of socially recognised standards of measure for the quantities of these useful objects. The diversity of these measures has its origin partly in the diverse nature of the objects to be measured, partly in convention.

The utility of a thing makes it a use-value. But this utility is not a thing of air. Being limited by the physical properties of the commodity, it has no existence apart from that commodity. A commodity, such as iron, corn, or a diamond is, therefore, so far as it is a material thing, a use-value, something useful. This property of a commodity is independent of the amount of labour required to appropriate its useful qualities. When treating of use-value, we always assume to be dealing with definite quantities, such as dozens of watches, yards of linen, or tons of iron. The use-values of commodities furnish the material for a special study, that of the commercial knowledge of commodities. Use-values become a reality only by use or consumption: they also constitute the substance of all wealth, whatever may be the social form of that wealth. In the form of society we are about to consider, they are, in addition, the material depositories of exchange value.

Exchange value, at first sight, presents itself as a quantitative relation, as the proportion in which values in use of one sort are exchanged for those of another sort, a relation constantly changing with time and place. Hence exchange value appears to be something accidental and purely relative, and consequently an intrinsic value, i.e., an exchange value that is inseparably connected with, inherent in commodities, seems a contradiction in terms. Let us consider the matter a little more closely.

A given commodity, e.g., a quarter of wheat, is exchanged for x blacking, y silk, or z gold, in short, for other commodities in the most different proportions. Instead of one exchange value, the wheat has, therefore, a great many. But since x blacking, y silk, or z gold each represents the exchange value of one quarter of wheat, x blacking, y silk, z gold, must as exchange values be replaceable by each other, or equal to each other. Therefore, first: the valid exchange values of a given commodity express something equal; secondly, exchange value, generally, is only the mode of expression, the phenomenal form, of something contained in it, yet distinguishable from it.

Let us take two commodities, e.g., corn and iron. The proportions in which they are exchangeable, whatever those proportions may be, can always be represented by an equation in which a given quantity of corn is equated to some quantity of iron: e.g., 1 quarter corn = x cwt. iron. What does this equation tell us? It tells us that in two different things—in 1 quarter of corn and x cwt. of iron, there exists in equal quantities something common to both. The two things must therefore be equal to a third, which in itself is neither the one nor the other. Each of them, so far as it is exchange value, must therefore be reducible to this third.

A simple geometrical illustration will make this clear. In order to calculate and compare the areas of rectilinear figures, we decompose them into triangles. But the area of the triangle itself is expressed by something totally different from its visible figure, namely, by half the product of the base into the altitude. In the same way the exchange values of commodities must be capable of being expressed in terms of something common to all, of which thing they represent a greater or lesser quantity.

This common "something" cannot be either a geometrical, a chemical, or any other natural property of commodities. Such properties claim our attention only in so far as they affect the utility of those commodities, make them use-values. But the exchange of commodities is evidently an act characterised by a total abstraction from use-value. Then one use-value is just as good as another, provided only it be present in sufficient quantity. Or, as old Barbon says, "one sort of wares are as good as another, if the values be equal. There is no difference or distinction in things of equal value. . . . An hundred pounds' worth of lead or iron, is of as great value as one hundred pounds' worth of silver or gold." As use-values, commodities are, above all, of different qualities, but as exchange values they are merely different quantities, and consequently do not contain an atom of use-value.

If then we leave out of consideration the use-value of commodities, they have only one common property left, that of being products of labour. But even the product of labour itself has undergone a change in our hands. If we make abstraction from its use-value, we make abstraction at the same time from the material elements and shapes that make the product a use-value; we see in it no longer a table, a house, yarn, or any other useful thing. Its existence as a material thing is put out of sight. Neither can it any longer be regarded as the product of the labour of the joiner, the mason, the spinner, or of any other definite kind of productive labour. Along with the useful qualities of the products themselves, we put out of sight both the useful character of the various kinds of labour embodied in them, and the concrete forms of that labour; there is nothing left but what is common to them all; all are reduced to one and the same sort of labour, human labour in the abstract.

Let us now consider the residue of each of these products; it consists of the same unsubstantial reality in each, a mere congelation of homogeneous human labour, of labour power expended without regard to the mode of its expenditure. All that these things now tell us is, that human labour power has been expended in their production, that human labour is embodied in them. When looked at as crystals of this social substance, common to them all, they are—Values.

We have seen that when commodities are exchanged, their exchange value manifests itself as something totally independent of their use-value. But if we abstract from their use-value, there remains their Value as defined above. Therefore, the common substance that manifests itself in the exchange value of commodities, whenever they are exchanged, is their value. The progress of our investigation will show that exchange value is the only form in which the value of commodities can manifest itself or be expressed. For the present, however, we have to consider the nature of value independently of this, its form.

A use-value, or useful article, therefore, has value only

because human labour in the abstract has been embodied or materialised in it. How, then, is the magnitude of this value to be measured? Plainly, by the quantity of the value-creating substance, the labour, contained in the article. The quantity of labour, however, is measured by its duration, and labour-time in its turn finds its standard in weeks, days, and hours.

Some people might think that if the value of a commodity is determined by the quantity of labour spent on it, the more idle and unskilful the labourer, the more valuable would his commodity be, because more time would be required in its production. The labour, however, that forms the substance of value, is homogeneous human labour, expenditure of one uniform labour power. The total labour power of society, which is embodied in the sum total of the values of all commodities produced by that society, counts here as one homogeneous mass of human labour power, composed though it be of innumerable individual units. Each of these units is the same as any other, so far as it has the character of the average labour power of society and takes effect as such; that is, so far as it requires for producing a commodity, no more time than is needed on an average, no more than is socially necessary. The labour time socially necessary is that required to produce an article under the normal conditions of production and with the average degree of skill and intensity prevalent at the time. The introduction of power looms into England probably reduced by one half the labour required to weave a given quantity of yarn into cloth. The hand loom weavers, as a matter of fact, continued to require the same time as before; but for all that, the product of one hour of their labour represented after the change only half an hour's social labour, and consequently fell to one-half its former value.

We see then that that which determines the magnitude of the value of any article is the amount of labour socially necessary, or the labour time socially necessary for its production. Each individual commodity, in this connexion, is to be considered as an average sample of its class. Commodities, therefore, in which equal quantities of labour are embodied, or which can be produced in the same time, have the same value. The value of one commodity is to the value of any other, as the labour time necessary for the production of the one is to that necessary for the production of the other. "As values, all commodities are only definite masses of congealed labour time."

The value of a commodity would therefore remain constant, if the labour time required for its production also remained constant. But the latter changes with every variation in the productiveness of labour. This productiveness is determined by various circumstances, amongst others, by the average amount of skill of the workmen, the state of science, and the degree of its practical application, the social organisation of production, the extent and capabilities of the means of production, and by physical conditions. For example, the same amount of labour in favourable seasons is embodied in 8 bushels of corn, and in unfavourable, only in four. The same labour extracts from rich mines more metal than from poor mines. Diamonds are of very rare occurrence on the earth's surface, and hence their discovery costs, on an average, a great deal of labour time. Consequently much labour is represented in a small compass. Jacob doubts whether gold has even been paid for at its full value. This applies still more to diamonds. According to Eschwege, the total produce of the Brazilian diamond mines for the eighty years, ending in 1823, had not realised the price of one-and-a-half years' average produce of the sugar and coffee plantations of the same country, although the diamonds cost much more labour, and therefore represented more value. With richer mines, the same quantity of labour would embody itself in more diamonds and their value would fall. If we could succeed at a small expenditure of labour, in converting carbon into diamonds, their value might fall below that of bricks. In general, the greater the productiveness of labour, the less is the labour time required for the production of an article, the less is the amount of labour crystallised in that article, and the less is its value; and *vice versa*, the less the productiveness of labour, the greater is the labour time required for the production of an article, and the greater is its value. The value of a commodity, therefore, varies directly as the quantity, and inversely as the productiveness, of the labour incorporated in it.

A thing can be a use-value, without having value. This is the case whenever its utility to man is not due to labour. Such are air, virgin soil, meadows, and the like. A thing can be useful, and the product of human labour, without being a commodity. Whoever directly satisfies his wants with the produce of his own labour, creates, indeed, use-values, but not commodities. In order to produce the latter, he must not only produce use-values, but use-values for others, social use-values. Lastly, nothing can have value, without being an object of utility. If the thing is useless, so is the labour contained in it; the labour does not count as labour, and therefore creates no value.

The Working Day

Capital has not invented surplus labour. Wherever a part of society possesses the monopoly of the means of production, the labourer free or not free must add to the working time necessary for his own maintenance an extra working time in order to produce the means of subsistence for the owners of the means of production, whether this proprietor be the Athenian *kalos kagatnos*, Etruscan theocrat, civis Romanus, Norman baron, American slave owner, Wallachian Boyard, modern landlord or capitalist. It is, however, clear that in any given economic formation of society, where not the exchange value but the use-value of the product predominates, surplus labour will be limited by a given set of wants which may be greater or less, and that here no boundless thirst for surplus labour arises from the nature of the production itself. Hence in antiquity, overwork becomes horrible only when the object is to obtain exchange value in its specific independent money form, in the production of gold and silver. Compulsory working to death is here the recognized form of overwork. Only read Diodorus Siculus. Still these are exceptions in antiquity. But as soon as people, whose production still moves within the lower forms of slave labour, corvée labour, and the like, are drawn into the whirlpool of an international market dominated by the capitalistic mode of production, the sale of their products for export becoming their principal interest, the civilised horrors of overwork are grafted on the barbaric horrors of slavery and serfdom. Hence the Negro labour in the Southern States of the American Union preserved something of a patriarchal character so long as production was chiefly directed to immediate local consumption. But in proportion, as the export of cotton became of vital interest to these states, the overworking of the Negro and became a factor in a calculated and calculating system. It was no longer a question of obtaining from him a certain quantity of useful products. It was now a question of production of surplus labour itself. So was it also with the corvée, e.g., in the Danubian Principalities (now Roumania).

The comparison of the greed for surplus labour in the Danubian Principalities with the same greed in English factories has special interest, because surplus labour in the corvée has an independent and palpable form.

Suppose the working day consists of 6 hours of necessary labour and 6 hours of surplus labour. Then the free labourer gives the capitalist every week 6 × 6 or 36 hours of surplus labour. It is the same as if he worked 3 days in the week for himself, and 3 days in the week gratis for the capitalist. But this is not evident on the surface. Surplus labour and necessary labour glide one into the other. I can, therefore, express the same relationship by saying, e.g., that the labourer in every minute works 30 seconds for himself and 30 for the capitalist, and so on. It is otherwise with the corvée. The necessary labour which the Wallachian peasant does for his own maintenance is distinctly marked off from his surplus labour on behalf of the Boyard. The one he does on his own field, the other on the seignorial estate. Both parts of the labour time exist, therefore, independently, side by side one with the other. In the corvée, the surplus labour is accurately marked off from the necessary labour. This, however, can make no difference with regard to the quantitative relation of surplus labour to necessary labour. Three days' surplus labour in the week remain three days that yield no equivalent to the labourer himself, whether it be called corvée or wage labour. But in the capitalist, the greed for surplus labour appears in the straining after an unlimited extension of the working day, in the Boyard more simply in a direct hunting after days of corvée.

In the Danubian Principalities, the corvée was mixed up with rents in kind and other appurtenances of bondage, but it formed the most important tribute paid to the ruling class. Where this was the case, the corvée sometimes the using up of his life in 7 years' of labour

rarely arose from serfdom; serfdom much more frequently on the other hand took origin from the corvée.
This is what took place in the Roumanian Provinces.
Their original mode of production was based on community of the soil, but not in the Slavonic or Indian form.
Part of the land was cultivated in severalty as freehold by
the members of the community, another part, *ager publi-
cus*, was cultivated by them in common. The products of
this common labour served partly as a reserve fund
against bad harvests and other accidents, partly as a public store for providing the costs of war, religion, and other
common expenses. In course of time military and clerical
dignitaries usurped, along with the common land, the
labour spent upon it. The labour of the free peasants on
their common land was transformed into corvée for the
thieves of the common land. This corvée soon developed
into a servile relationship existing in point of fact, not in
point of law, until Russia, the liberator of the world,
made it legal under pretence of abolishing serfdom. The
code of the corvée, which the Russian General Kisseleff
proclaimed in 1831, was of course dictated by the Bo-
yards themselves. Thus Russia conquered with one blow
the magnates of the Danubian provinces and the applause of liberal crétins throughout Europe.

According to the *Règlement organique*, as this code of
the corvée is called, every Wallachian peasant owes to
the so-called landlord, besides a mass of detailed payments in kind: 1) 12 days of general labour; 2) 1 day of
field (labour; 3) 1 day of wood carrying. In all, 14 days
in the year. With deep insight into political economy, however, the working day is not taken in its ordinary sense, but
as the working day necessary to the production of an average daily product; and that average daily product is determined in so crafty a way that no Cyclops would be
done with it in 24 hours. In dry words, the *Règlement*
itself declares with true Russian irony that by 12 working
days one must understand the product of the manual
labour of 36 days, by 1 day of field labour 3 days, and by
1 day of wood carrying in like manner three times as
much. In all, 42 corvée days. To this had to be added the
so-called *jobagie*, service due to the lord for extraordinary
occasions. In proportion to the size of its population,

every village has to furnish annually a definite contingent to the *jobagie*. This additional corvée is estimated at 14 days for each Wallachian peasant. Thus the prescribed corvée amounts to 56 working days yearly. But the agricultural year in Wallachia numbers in consequence of the severe climate only 210 days, of which 40 for Sundays and holidays, 30 on an average for bad weather, together 70 days, do not count. One hundred and forty working days remain. The ratio of the corvée to the necessary labour $^{55}\!/_{84}$ or 66⅔ percent gives a much smaller rate of surplus value than that which regulates the labour of the English agricultural or factory labourer. This is, however, only the legally prescribed corvée. And in a spirit yet more "liberal" than the English Factory Acts, the *Règlement organique* has known how to facilitate its own evasion. After it has made 56 days out of 12, the nominal day's work of each of the 56 corvée days is again so arranged that a portion of it must fall on the ensuing day. In one day, e.g., must be weeded an extent of land, which, for this work, especially in maize plantations, needs twice as much time. The legal day's work for some kinds of agricultural labour is interpretable in such a way that the day begins in May and ends in October. In Moldavia conditions are still harder. "The corvée days of the *Règlement organique*," cried a Boyard, drunk with victory, "amount to 365 days in the year."

If the *Règlement organique* of the Danubian provinces was a positive expression of the greed for surplus labour which every paragraph legalised, the English Factory Acts are the negative expression of the same greed. These acts curb the passion of capital for a limitless draining of labour power, by forcibly limiting the working day by state regulations, made by a state that is ruled by capitalist and landlord. Apart from the working-class movement that daily grew more threatening, the limiting of factory labour was dictated by the same necessity which spread guano over the English fields. The same blind eagerness for plunder that in the one case exhausted the soil, had, in the other, torn up by the roots the living force of the nation. Periodical epidemics speak on this point as clearly as the diminishing military standard in Germany and France.

The Factory Act of 1850 now in force (1867) allows for the average working day 10 hours, i.e., for the first 5 days 12 hours from 6 a.m. to 6 p.m., including ½ an hour for breakfast, and an hour for dinner, and thus leaving 10½ working hours, and 8 hours for Saturday, from 6 a.m. to 2 p.m., of which ½ an hour is subtracted for breakfast. Sixty working hours are left, 10½ for each of the first 5 days, 7½ for the last. Certain guardians of these laws are appointed, Factory Inspectors, directly under the Home Secretary, whose reports are published half-yearly by order of Parliament. They give regular and official statistics of the capitalistic greed for surplus labour.

Let us listen, for a moment, to the Factory Inspectors.

The fraudulent millowner begins work at a quarter of an hour (sometimes more, sometimes less) before 6 a.m. and leaves off a quarter of an hour (sometimes more, sometimes less) after 6 p.m. He takes 5 minutes from the beginning and from the end of the half hour nominally allowed for breakfast, and 10 minutes at the beginning and end of the hour nominally allowed for dinner. He works for a quarter of an hour (sometimes more, sometimes less) after 2 p.m. on Saturday. Thus, his gain is

	MINUTES
Before 6 A.M.	15
After 6 P.M.	15
At breakfast time	10
At dinner time	20
	60
Five days—300 minutes	
On Saturday before 6 A.M.	15
At breakfast time	10
After 2 P.M.	15
	40
Total weekly	340

Or 5 hours and 40 minutes weekly, which multiplied by 50 working weeks in the year (allowing two for holidays and occasional stoppages) is equal to 27 working days.

Five minutes a day's increased work, multiplied by 50 weeks, are equal to two and a half days of produce in the year.

An additional hour a day gained by small installments before 6 a.m., after 6 p.m., and at the beginning and end of the times nominally fixed for meals, is nearly equivalent to working 13 months in the year.

Crises during which production is interrupted and the factories work "short time," i.e., for only a part of the week, naturally do not affect the tendency to extend the working day. The less business there is, the more profit has to be made on the business done. The less time spent in work, the more of that time has to be turned into surplus labour time.

Thus the Factory Inspector's report on the period of the crisis from 1857 to 1858:

It may seem inconsistent that there should be any overworking at a time when trade is so bad; but that very badness leads to the transgression by unscrupulous men, they get the extra profit of it. . . . In the last half year, says Leonard Horner, 122 mills in my district have been given up; 143 were found standing. [yet, overwork is continued beyond the legal hours].

For a great part of the time, [says Mr. Howell] owing to the depression of trade, many factories were altogether closed, and a still greater number were working short time. I continue, however, to receive about the usual number of complaints that half, or three-quarters of an hour in the day, are snatched from the workers by encroaching upon the times professedly allowed for rest and refreshment.

The same phenomenon was reproduced on a smaller scale during the frightful cotton crisis from 1861 to 1865:

It is sometimes advanced by way of excuse, when persons are found at work in a factory, either at a meal hour, or at some illegal time, that they will not leave the mill at the appointed hour, and that compulsion is necessary to force them to cease work [cleaning their machinery, etc.], especially on Saturday afternoons. But, if the hands remain in a factory after the machinery has ceased to revolve . . . they would not have been so employed if sufficient time had been set apart specially for cleaning, etc., either before 6 a.m. [*sic!*] or before 2 p.m. on Saturday afternoons.

The profit to be gained by it (overworking in violation of the Act) appears to be, to many, a greater temptation than they can resist; they calculate upon the chance of not being found out; and when they see the small amount of penalty and costs, which those who have been convicted have had to pay, they find that if they should be detected there will still be a considerable balance of gain. . . . In cases where the additional time is gained by a multiplication of small thefts in the course of the day, there are insuperable difficulties to the inspectors making out a case.

These "small thefts" of capital from the labourer's meal and recreation time, the factory inspectors also designate as "petty pilfering of minutes," "snatching a few minutes," or, as the labourers technically called them, "nibbling and cribbling at meal times."

It is evident that in this atmosphere the formation of surplus value by surplus labour, is not secret. "If you allow me," said a highly respectable master to me, "to work only ten minutes in the day overtime, you put one-thousand a year in my pocket." "Moments are the elements of profit."

Nothing is from this point of view more characteristic than the designation of the workers who work full time as "full-timers," and the children under thirteen who are only allowed to work 6 hours as "half-timers." The worker is here nothing more than personified labour time. All individual distinctions are merged in those of "full-timers" and "half-timers."

The Fetishism of Commodities

A commodity appears, at first sight, a very trivial thing, and easily understood. Its analysis shows that it is, in reality, a very queer thing, abounding in metaphysical subtleties and theological niceties. So far as it is a value in use, there is nothing mysterious about it, whether we consider it from the point of view that by its properties it is capable of satisfying human wants or from the point that those properties are the product of human labour. It is as clear as noon day, that man, by his industry, changes the forms of the materials furnished by nature in such a way as to make them useful to him. The form of wood, for instance, is altered, by making a table out of it. Yet, for all that, the table continues to be that common, everyday thing, wood. But, so soon as it steps forth as a commodity, it is changed into something transcendent. It not only stands with its feet on the ground, but, in relation to all other commodities, it stands on its head, and evolves out of its wooden brain grotesque ideas, far more wonderful than "table-turning" ever was.

The mystical character of commodities does not originate, therefore, in their use-value. Just as little does it proceed from the nature of the determining factors of value. For, in the first place, however varied the useful kinds of labour, or productive activities, may be, it is a physiological fact, that they are functions of the human organism and that each such function, whatever may be its nature or form, is essentially the expenditure of human brain, nerves, muscles, and so on. Secondly, with regard to that which forms the groundwork for the quantitative determination of value, namely, the duration of that expenditure, or the quantity of labour, it is quite clear that there is a palpable difference between its quantity and quality. In all states of society, the labour time that it

133

costs to produce the means of subsistence must necessarily be an object of interest to mankind, though not of equal interest in different stages of development. And lastly, from the moment that men in any way work for one another, their labour assumes a social form.

Whence, then, arises the enigmatical character of the product of labour, so soon as it assumes the form of commodities? Clearly from this form itself. The equality of all sorts of human labour is expressed objectively by their products all being equal values; the measure of the expenditure of labour power by the duration of that expenditure, takes the form of the quantity of value of the products of labour; and finally, the mutual relations of the producers, within which the social character of their labour affirms itself, take the form of a social relation between the products.

A commodity is therefore a mysterious thing, simply because in it the social character of men's labour appears to them as an objective character stamped upon the product of that labour; because the relation of the producers to the sum total of their own labour is presented to them as a social relation, existing not between themselves, but between the products of their labour. This is the reason why the products of labour become commodities, social things whose qualities are at the same time perceptible and imperceptible by the senses. In the same way the light from an object is perceived by us not as the subjective excitation of our optic nerve, but as the objective form of something outside the eye itself. But, in the act of seeing, there is at all events, an actual passage of light from one thing to another, from the external object to the eye. There is a physical relation between physical things. But it is different with commodities. There, the existence of the things *qua* commodities, and the value relation between the products of labour which stamps them as commodities, have absolutely no connection with their physical properties and with the material relations arising therefrom. There it is a definite social relation between men, that assumes, in their eyes, the fantastic form of a relation between things. In order, therefore, to find an analogy, we must have recourse to the mist-enveloped regions of the religious world. In that world the productions of the human brain appear as independent beings endowed with life and entering into relation both with one another and the human race. So it is in the world of commodities with the products of men's hands. This I call the *fetishism* which attaches itself to the products of labour, so soon as they are produced as commodities, and which is therefore inseparable from the production of commodities.

This fetishism of commodities has its origin, as the foregoing analysis has already shown, in the peculiar social character of the labour that produces them.

As a general rule, articles of utility become commodities only because they are products of the labour of private individuals or groups of individuals who carry on their work independently of each other. The sum total of the labour of all these private individuals forms the aggregate labour of society. Since the producers do not come into social contact with each other until they exchange their products, the specific social character of each producer's labour does not show itself except in the act of exchange. In other words, the labour of the individual asserts itself as a part of the labour of society, only by means of the relations which the act of exchange establishes directly between the products, and indirectly, through them, between the producers. To the latter, therefore, the relations connecting the labour of one individual with that of the rest appear, not as direct social relations between individuals at work, but as what they really are, material relations between persons and social relations between things. It is only by being exchanged that the products of labour acquire, as values, one uniform social status, distinct from their varied forms of existence as objects of utility. This division of a product into a useful thing and a value becomes practically important only when exchange has acquired such an extension that useful articles are produced for the purpose of being exchanged, and their character as values has therefore to be taken into account, beforehand, during production.

From this moment the labour of the individual producer acquires socially a twofold character. On the one hand, it must, as a definite useful kind of labour, satisfy a definite social want, and thus hold its place as part and parcel of the collective labour of all, as a branch of a social division of labour that has sprung up spontaneously. On the other hand, it can satisfy the manifold wants of the individual producer himself only in so far as the mutual exchangeability of all kinds of useful private labour is an established social fact, and therefore the private useful labour of each producer ranks on an equality with that of all others. The equalization of the most different kinds of labour can be the result only of an abstraction from their inequalities, or of reducing them to their common denominator, viz., expenditure of human labour power or human labour in the abstract. The twofold social character of the labour of the individual appears to him, when reflected in his brain, only under those forms which are impressed upon that labour in everyday practice by the exchange of products. In this way, the character that his own labour possesses of being socially useful takes the form of the condition that the product must be not only useful, but useful for others, and the social character that his particular labour has of being the equal of all other particular kinds of labour takes the form that all the physically different articles that are the products of labour have one common quality, viz., that of having value.

Hence, when we bring the products of our labour into relation with each other as values, it is not because we see in these articles the material receptacles of homogeneous human labour. Quite the contrary; whenever, by an exchange, we equate as values our different products, by that very act we also equate, as human labour, the different kinds of labour expended upon them. We are not aware of this, nevertheless we do it. Value, therefore, does not stalk about with a label describing what it is. It is value, rather, that converts every product into a social hieroglyphic. Later on, we try to decipher the hieroglyphic, to get behind the secret of our own social products; for to stamp an object of utility as a value is just as much a social product as language. The recent scientific discovery that the products of labour, so far as they are values, are but material expressions of the human labour spent in their production, marks, indeed, an epoch in the history of the development of the human race, but, by no means, dissipates the mist through which the social character of labour appears to us to be an objective character of the products themselves. The fact that in the particular form of production with which we are dealing, viz., the production of commodities, the specific social character of private labour carried on independently consists in the equality of every kind of that labor by virtue of its being human labour, which character, therefore, assumes in the product the form of value—this fact appears to the producers, notwithstanding the discovery above referred to, to be just as real and final as the fact that, after the discovery by science of the component gases of air, the atmosphere itself remained unaltered.

What, first of all, practically concerns producers when they make an exchange is the question, how much of some other product they get for their own? in what proportions the products are exchangeable? When these proprotions have, by custom, attained a certain stability, they appear to result from the nature of the products, so that, for instance, one ton of iron and two ounces of gold appear as naturally to be of equal value as a pound of gold and a pound of iron in spite of their different physical and chemical qualities appear to be of equal weight. The character of having value, when once impressed upon products, obtains fixity only by reason of their acting and reacting upon each other as quantities of value. These quantities vary continually, independently of the will, foresight, and action of the producers. To them, their own social action takes the form of the action of objects which rule the producers instead of being ruled by them. It requires a fully developed production of commodities before, from accumulated experience alone, the scientific conviction springs up that all the different kinds of private labour, which are carried on independently of each other and yet as spontaneously developed branches of the social division of labour, are continually being reduced to the quantitive proportions in which society requires them. And why? Because, in the midst of all the accidental and ever fluctuating exchange-relations between the products, the labour time socially necessary for their production forcibly asserts itself like an overriding law of nature. The law of gravity thus asserts itself when a house falls about our ears. The determination of the magnitude of value by labour time is therefore a secret, hidden under the apparent fluctuations in the relative values of commodities. Its discovery, while removing all appearance of mere accident from the determination of the magnitude of the values of products, yet in no way alters the mode in which that determination takes place.

Man's reflections on the forms of social life and consequently also, his scientific analysis of those forms take a course directly opposite to that of their actual historical development. He begins, *post-factum,* with the results of the process of development ready to hand before him. The characters that stamp products as commodities, and whose establishment is a necessary preliminary to the circulation of commodities, have already acquired the stability of natural, self-understood forms of social life before man seeks to decipher, not their historical character, for in his eyes they are immutable, but their meaning. Consequently it was the analysis of the prices of commodities that alone led to the determination of the magnitude of value, and it was the common expression of all commodities in money that alone led to the establishment of their characters as values. It is, however, just this ultimate money form of the world of commodities that actually conceals, instead of disclosing, the social character or private labour and the social relations between the individual producer. When I state that coats or boots stand in a relation to linen, because it is the universal incarnation of abstract human labour, the absurdity of the statement is self-evident. Nevertheless, when the producers of coats and boots compare those articles with linen or, what is the same thing, with gold or silver, as the universal equivalent, they express the relation between their own private labour and the collective labour of society in the same absurd form.

The categories of bourgeois economy consist of such like forms. They are forms of thought expressing with social validity the conditions and relations of a definite, historically determined mode of production, viz., the production of commodities. The whole mystery of commodities, all the magic and necromancy that surrounds the products of labour as long as they take the form of commodities, vanishes therefore so soon as we come to other forms of production.

Since Robinson Crusoe's experiences are a favorite theme with political economists, let us take a look at him on his island. Moderate though he be, yet some few wants he has to satisfy and must therefore do a little useful work of various sorts, such as making tools and furniture, taming goats, fishing, and hunting. Of his prayers and the like we take no account, since they are a source of pleasure to him, and he looks upon them as so much recreation. In spite of the variety of his work, he knows that his labour, whatever its form, is but the activity of one and the same Robinson and, consequently, that it consists of nothing but different modes of human labour. Necessity itself compels him to apportion his time accurately between his different kinds of work. Whether one kind occupies a greater space in his general activity than another depends on the difficulties, greater or less as the case may be, to be overcome in attaining the useful effect aimed at. This our friend Robinson soon learns by experience, and having rescued a watch, ledger, and pen and ink from the wreck, commences, like a true-born Briton, to keep a set of books. His stock-book contains a list of the objects of utility that belong to him, of the operations necessary for their production; and lastly, of the labour time that definite quantities of those objects have, on an average, cost him. All the relations between Robinson and the objects that form this wealth of his own creation, are here so simple and clear as to be intelligible without exertion, even to Mr. Sedley Taylor. And yet those relations contain all that is essential to the determination of value.

Let us now transport ourselves from Robinson's island bathed in light to the European Middle Ages shrouded in darkness. Here, instead of the independent man, we find everyone dependent, serfs and lords, vassals and suzerains, laymen and clergy. Personal dependence here characterises the social relations of production just as much as it does the other spheres of life organized on the basis of that production. But for the very reason that personal dependence forms the groundwork of society, there is no necessity for labour and its products to assume a fantastic form different from their reality. They take the shape, in the transactions of society, of services in kind and payments in kind. Here the particular and natural form of labour, and not, as in a society based on production of commodities, its general abstract form, is the immediate social form of labour. Compulsory labour is just as properly measured by time, as commodity-producing labour; but every serf knows that what he expends in the service of his lord is a definite quantity of his own personal labour power. The tithe to be rendered to the priest is more matter of fact than his blessing. No matter, then, what we may think of the parts played by the different classes of people themselves in this society, the social relations between individuals in the performance of their labour appear at all events as their own mutual personal relations and are not disguised under the shape of social relations between the products of labour.

For an example of labour in common or directly associated labour we have no occasion to go back to that spontaneously developed form which we find on the threshold of the history of all civilised races. We have one close at hand in the patriarchal industries of a peasant family, that produces corn, cattle, yarn, linen, and clothing for home use. These different articles are, as regards the family, so many products of its labour, but as between themselves, they are not commodities. The different kinds of labour, such as tillage, cattle tending, spinning, weaving, and making clothes, which result in the various products, are in themselves, and such as they are, direct social functions, because functions of the family, which just as much as a society based on the production of commodities, possesses a spontaneously developed system of division of labour. The distribution of the work within the family, and the regulation of the labour time of the several members, depend as well upon differences of age and sex as upon natural conditions varying with the seasons. The labour power of each individual, by its very nature, operates in this case merely as a definite portion of the whole labour power of the family, and therefore, the measure of the expenditure of individual labour power by its duration appears here by its very nature as a social character of their labour.

Let us now picture to ourselves, by way of change, a community of free individuals, carrying on their work with the means of production in common, in which the labour power of all the different individuals is consciously applied as the combined labour power of the community. All the characteristics of Robinson's labour are here repeated, but with this difference, that they are social, instead of individual. Everything produced by him was exclusively the result of his own personal labour, and therefore simply an object of use for himself. The total product of our community is a social product. One portion serves as fresh means of production and remains social. But another portion is consumed by the members as means of subsistence. A distribution of this portion amongst them is consequently necessary. The mode of this distribution will vary with the productive organization of the community and the degree of historical development attained by the producers. We will assume, but merely for the sake of a parallel with the production of commodities, that the share of each individual producer in the means of subsistence is determined by his labour time. Labour time would, in that case, play a double part. Its apportionment in accordance with a definite social plan maintains the proper proportion between the different kinds of work to be done and the various wants of the community. On the other hand, it also serves as a measure of the portion of the common labour borne by each individual and of his share in the part of the total product destined for individual consumption. The social relations of the individual producers, with regard both to their labour and to its products, are in this case perfectly simple and intelligible, and that with regard not only to production but also to distribution.

The religious world is but the reflex of the real world. And for a society based upon the production of commodities, in which the producers in general enter into social relations with one another by treating their products as commodities and values, whereby they reduce their individual private labour to the standard of homogeneous human labour—for such a society, Christianity with its *cultus* of abstract man, more especially in its bourgeois developments, Protestantism, Deism, and so on, is the most fitting form of religion. In the ancient Asiatic and other ancient modes of production, we find that the conversion of products into commodities, and therefore the conversion of men into producers of commodities, holds a subordinate place, which, however, increases in importance as the primitive communities approach nearer and nearer to their dissolution. Trading nations, properly so called, exist in the ancient world only in its interstices, like the gods of Epicurus in the Intermundia or the Jews in the pores of Polish society. Those ancient social organisms of production are, as compared with bourgeois society, extremely simple and transparent. But they are founded either on the immature development of man individually, who has not yet severed the umbilical cord that unites him with his fellow men in a primitive tribal community, or upon direct relations of subjection. They can arise and exist only when the development of the productive power of labour has not risen beyond a low state and when, therefore, the social relations within the sphere of material life, between man and man and between man and nature, are correspondingly narrow. This narrowness is reflected in the ancient worship of Nature and in the other elements of the popular religions. The religious reflex of the real world can, in any case, only then finally vanish, when the practical relations of everyday life offer to man none but perfectly intelligible and reasonable relations with regard to his fellowmen and to nature.

The life-process of society, which is based on the process of material production, does not strip off its mystical veil until it is treated as production by freely associated men and is consciously regulated by them in accordance with a settled plan. This, however, demands for society a certain material groundwork or set of conditions of existence which in their turn are the spontaneous product of a long and painful process of development.

Political economy has indeed analysed, however incompletely, value and its magnitude and has discovered what lies beneath these forms. But it has never once asked the question why labour is represented by the value of its product and labour time by the magnitude of that value. These formulae, which bear stamped upon them in unmistakable letters that they belong to a state of society in which the process of production has the mastery over man, instead of being controlled by him, such formulae appear to the bourgeois intellect to be as much a self-evident necessity imposed by nature as productive labour itself. Hence forms of social production that preceded the bourgeois form are treated by the bourgeoisie in much the same way as the Fathers of the Church treated pre-Christian religions.

To what extent some economists are misled by the fetishism inherent in commodities, or by the objective appearance of the social characteristics of labour, is shown, amongst other ways, by the dull and tedious quarrel over the part played by nature in the formation of exchange value. Since exchange value is a definite social manner of expressing the amount of labour bestowed upon an object, nature has no more to do with it than it has in fixing the course of exchange.

The mode of production in which the product takes the form of a commodity, or is produced directly for exchange, is the most general and most embryonic form of bourgeois production. It therefore makes its appearance at an early date in history, though not in the same predominating and characteristic manner as nowadays. Hence its fetish character is comparatively easy to be seen through. But when we come to more concrete forms, even this appearance of simplicity vanishes. Whence arose the illusions of the monetary system? To it gold and silver, when serving as money, did not represent a social relation between producers but were natural objects with strange social properties. And modern economy, which looks down with such disdain on the monetary system, does not its superstition come out as clear as noonday, whenever it treats of capital? How long is it since economy discarded the physiocratic illusion that rents grow out of the soil and not out of society?

But not to anticipate, we will content ourselves with yet another example relating to the commodity form. Could commodities themselves speak, they would say:

Our use-value may be a thing that interests men. It is no part of us as objects. What, however, does belong to us as objects, is our value. Our natural intercourse as commodities proves it. In the eyes of each other we are nothing but exchange values. Now listen how those commodities speak through the mouth of the economist. "Value (i.e., exchange value) is a property of things, riches (i.e., use-value) of man. Value, in this sense, necessarily implies exchanges, riches do not." "Riches (use-value) are the attribute of men, value is the attribute of commodities. A man or a community is rich, a pearl or a diamond is valuable. . . . A pearl or a diamond is valuable" as a pearl or diamond. So far no chemist has ever discovered exchange value either in a pearl or a diamond. The economical discoverers of this chemical element, who by-the-bye lay special claim to critical acumen, find however that the use-value of objects belongs to them independently of their material properties, while their value, on the other hand, forms a part of them as objects. What confirms them in this view is the peculiar circumstances that the use-value of objects is realised without exchange, by means of a direct relation between the objects and man, while, on the other hand, their value is realised only by exchange, that is, by means of a social process. Who fails here to call to mind our good friend Dogberry, who informs neighbour Seacoal that, "To be a well-favoured man is the gift of fortune; but reading and writing comes by nature."

The Secret of Primitive Accumulation

We have seen how money is changed into capital; how through capital surplus value is made, and from surplus value more capital. But the accumulation of capital presupposes surplus value; surplus value presupposes capitalistic production; capitalistic production presupposes the pre-existence of considerable masses of capital and of labour power in the hands of producers of commodities. The whole movement, therefore, seems to turn in a vicious circle, out of which we can only get by supposing a primitive accumulation (previous accumulation of Adam Smith) preceding capitalistic accumulation, an accumulation not the result of the capitalist mode of production, but its starting point.

This primitive accumulation plays in political economy about the same part as original sin in theology. Adam bit the apple, and thereupon sin fell on the human race. Its origin is supposed to be explained when it is told as an anecdote of the past. In times long gone by there were two sorts of people; one, the diligent, intelligent, and above all, frugal élite; the other, lazy rascals, spending their substance and more, in riotous living. The legend of theological original sin tells us certainly how man came to be condemned to eat his bread in the sweat of his brow; but the history of economic original sin reveals to us that there are people to whom this is by no means essential. Never mind! Thus it came to pass that the former sort accumulated wealth, and the latter sort had at last nothing to sell except their own skins. And from this original sin dates the poverty of the great majority that, despite all its labour, has up to now nothing to sell but itself, and the wealth of the few that increases constantly although they have long ceased to work. Such insipid childishness is every day preached to us in the defence of property. M. Thiers, e.g., had the assurance to repeat it with the solemnity of a statesman, to the French people, once so *spirituel*. But as soon as the question of property crops up, it becomes a sacred duty to proclaim the intellectual food of the infant as the one thing fit for all ages and for all stages of development. In actual history it is notorious that conquest, enslavement, robbery, murder, briefly force, play the great part. In the tender annals of political economy, the idyllic reigns from time immemorial. Right and "labour" were from all time the sole means of enrichment, the present year of course always excepted. As a matter of fact, the methods of primitive accumulation are anything but idyllic.

In themselves, money and commodities are no more capital than are the means of production and of subsistence. They want transforming into capital. But this transformation itself can only take place under certain circumstances that centre in this, viz., that two very different kinds of commodity possessors must come face to face and into contact; on the one hand, the owners of money, means of production, means of subsistence, who are eager to increase the sum of values they possess, by buying other people's labour power; on the other hand, free labourers, the sellers of their own labour power, and therefore the sellers of labour. Free labourers, in the double sense that neither they themselves form part and parcel of the means of production, as in the case of slaves, bondsmen, and the like, nor do the means of production belong to them, as in the case of peasant proprietors; they are, therefore, free from, unencumbered by, any means of production of their own. With this polarisation of the market for commodities, the fundamental conditions of capitalist production are given. The capitalist system presupposes the complete separation of the labourers from all property in the means by which they can realise their labour. As soon as capitalist production is once on its own legs, it not only maintains this separation, but reproduces it on a continually extending scale. The process, therefore, that clears the way for the capitalist system can be none other than the process which takes away from the labourer the possession of his means of production; a process that transforms, on the one hand, the social means of subsistence and of production into capital, on the other, the immediate producers into wage labourers. The so-called primitive accumulation, therefore, is nothing else than the historical process of divorcing the producer from the means of production. It appears as primitive, because it forms the prehistoric stage of capital and of the mode of production corresponding with it.

The economic structure of capitalistic society has grown out of the economic structure of feudal society. The dissolution of the latter set free the elements of the former.

The immediate producer, the labourer, could only dispose of his own person after he had ceased to be attached to the soil and ceased to be the slave, serf, or bondman of another. To become a free seller of labour power, who carries his commodity wherever he finds a market, he must further have escaped from the regime of the guilds, their rules for apprentices and journeymen, and the impediments of their labour regulations. Hence, the historical movement which changes the producers into wage workers, appears, on the one hand, as their emancipation from serfdom and from the fetters of the guilds, and this side alone exists for our bourgeois historians. But, on the other hand, these new freedmen became sellers of themselves only after they had been robbed of all their own means of production and of all the guarantees of existence afforded by the old feudal arrangements. And the history of this, their expropriation, is written in the annals of mankind in letters of blood and fire.

The industrial capitalists, these new potentates, had on their part not only to displace the guild masters of handicrafts but also the feudal lords, the possessors of the sources of wealth. In this respect their conquest of social power appears as the fruit of a victorious struggle both against feudal lordship and its revolting prerogatives and against the guilds and the fetters they laid on the free development of production and the free exploitation of man by man. The *chevaliers d'industrie*, however, only succeed in supplanting the *chevaliers* of the sword by making use of events of which they themselves were wholly innocent. They have risen by means as vile as those by which the Roman freedman once on a time made himself the master of his *patronus.*

The starting point of the development that gave rise to the wage labourer as well as to the capitalist was the servitude of the labourer. The advance consisted in a change of form of this servitude, in the transformation of feudal exploitation into capitalist exploitation. To understand its march, we need not go back very far. Although we come across the first beginnings of capitalist production as early as the fourteenth or fifteenth century, sporadically, in certain towns of the Mediterranean, the capitalistic era dates from the sixteenth century. Wherever it appears, the abolition of serfdom has been long effected, and the highest development of the Middle Ages, the existence of sovereign towns, has been long on the wane.

In the history of primitive accumulation, all revolutions are epoch-making that act as levers for the capitalist class in the course of formation; but, above all, those moments when great masses of men are suddenly and forcibly torn from their means of subsistence, and hurled as free and "unattached" proletarians on the labour market. The expropriation of the agricultural producer, of the peasant, from the soil, is the basis of the whole process. The history of this expropriation of the agricultural producer, of the peasant, from the soil, is the basis of the whole process. The history of this expropriation, in different countries, assumes different aspects, and runs through its various phases in different orders of succession, and at different periods. In England alone, which we take as our example, has it the classic form.

Friedrich Engels

Letters on Historical Method*

The four letters that follow were written by Engels toward the end of his life. They are notable for his awareness of the many difficulties in the Marxist approach to history and for his effort to restate some of the major premises of the materialistic historical approach in more subtle and complex ways than had usually been done either by Marx and Engels in their early writings or by many of their socialist followers in the decades following.

1 *To Conrad Schmidt*

London, Oct. 27, '90

Dear Schmidt:

. . . Society gives rise to certain public functions which it cannot dispense with. The people who are delegated to perform them constitute a new branch of the division of labor *within society*. They acquire therewith special interest in opposition to those who have elected them, make themselves relatively independent of them, and the *state* is already here. The same thing takes place, as we observed, in commercial exchange and later in money exchange. The new independent power must, of course, submit to the movement of production as a whole. But it also *reacts*, by virtue of the strength of its immanent, i.e., its once borrowed but gradually developed relative independence, upon the conditions and course of production. There is a *reciprocity* between two *unequal* forces, on the one side the economic movement, on the other the new political power which strives for the greatest possible

---

* Title supplied by editor.

independence and which having once arisen is endowed with its *own movement*. The economic movement, upon the whole, asserts itself but it is affected by the reaction of the relatively independent political movement which it itself had set up. This political movement is on the one hand the state power, on the other, the opposition which comes to life at the same time with it. Just as the money market reflects as a whole, with the qualifications indicated, the movement of the industrial market, but naturally in an *inverted* fashion, so there is reflected in the struggle between government and opposition, the struggle between already existing and opposing classes but again in an inverted form, no longer direct but indirect, not as open class struggle but as a struggle between *political principles*. So inverted is this reflection that it required thousands of years to discover what was behind it.

The reaction of the state power upon economic development can take a threefold form. It can run in the same direction, and then the tempo of development becomes accelerated; it can buck up against that development in which case today among every large people the state power is sure to go to smash before long; or it can block economic development along some directions and lay down its path along others. This last case is ultimately reducible to one of either of the foregoing two. It is clear that in the second and third cases the political power can do great damage to the course of economic development and result in a great waste of energy and materials.

We must add to the above the cases of conquest and brutal destruction of economic resources in which under certain circumstances it was possible in the past for a local or national economic development to be completely destroyed. Today situations of this kind produce opposite effects, at least among the large nations. Often it is the conquered who in the long run wins more economically, politically, and morally than the conqueror.

The same is true for law. Just as soon as the new division of labor makes necessary the creation of *professional jurists*, another new independent domain is opened which for all its dependence upon production and trade in general, still possesses a special capacity to react upon these fields. In a modern state, law must not only correspond to the general economic situation and be its expression; it must also be a *coherently unified expression* and free from glaring internal inconsistencies. In order to achieve this, the fidelity with which the law directly reflects economic conditions becomes less and less. This is all the truer, in those rare cases, when the legal code expresses the harsh, unrelieved and naked fact of class rule. For that contradicts the very *principle of justice* and law. The pure and consistent jural concept of the revolutionary bourgeoisie of 1792–96 already appears falsified in many respects in the Code Napoleon. And in so far as it is carried out, it is subject to daily modification because of the growing power of the proletariat. That doesn't prevent the Napoleonic code from serving as a legal model for new codifications of law in all parts of the world. The course of legal development is to be explained in large part first by this attempt to erect an harmonious system of law by eliminating the contradictions between jural propositions which are themselves the direct translation of economic relations; and then by the influence and compulsion exerted by the further economic development which keeps on upsetting the system and plunging it into new contradictions. (I speak here for the time being only of civil law.)

The reflection of economic relations as principles of law is necessarily an inverted one. The process takes place without the participants becoming conscious of it. The jurist imagines that he is operating with *a priori* propositions while the latter are only reflections of the economic process. And so everything remains standing on its head. This inverted reflex so long as it is not recognized for what it is constitutes what we call *ideological conceptions*. That it is able to set up a counteraction on the economic basis and within certain limits to modify it seems to me to be self-evident. The foundations of the law of inheritance, corresponding stages in the development of the family being presupposed, are economic. Nonetheless it would be very hard to prove that, e.g., the absolute freedom of testamentary disposition in England, and the strongly restricted right in France, in all particu-

lars have only economic causes. Yet both methods react
in a very significant way upon the economic system in
that they influence the distribution of wealth.

And now as concerns those ideological realms which
tower still higher in the clouds—*religion, philosophy,* etc.
—they all possess from prehistorical days an already discovered and traditionally accepted fund of—what we
would today call bunk. All of these various mistaken
ideas of nature, of the creation of man, of spirits and
magical forces have as their basis, in the main, negative
economic grounds. False ideas of nature are supplemen-
tary to the primitive economic development of the prehistorical period; but in places they are often conditioned
and even caused by economic development. However,
even if economic need has been the chief driving force in
the advance of natural knowledge, and has become even
more so, it would be altogether pedantic to seek economic causes for all this primitive original superstition.
The history of science is the history of the gradual elimination of this superstition, i.e., its replacement by new,
but always less absurd, superstitions. The people who
supply it belong again to a special sphere in the division
of labor and imagine that they are working in an independent domain. And in so far as they constitute an independent group within the social division of labor, their
production, inclusive of their errors, exerts a *counteracting influence* upon the entire social development, even
upon the economic. Nonetheless they still remain under
the *dominant influence of economic development.* For
example, in philosophy this is easiest to demonstrate for
the bourgeois period. Hobbes was the first modern materialist (in the sense of the eighteenth century) but an
absolutist at a time when in the whole of Europe absolute monarchy was enjoying the height of its power and
in England had taken up the struggle against the people.
Locke was, in religion as in politics, a son of the class
compromise of 1668. The English Deists, and their more
consistent followers, the French materialists, were the
genuine philosophers of the bourgeoisie—the French,
even of the bourgeois revolution. In German philosophy
from Kant to Hegel, the German philistine makes his way
—now positively, now negatively. But as a definite do-

main within the division of labor the philosophy of every age has as its presuppositions a certain intellectural material which it inherits from its predecessors and which is its own point of departure. That is why philosophy can play first violin in economically backward countries; e.g., France in the eighteenth century as opposed to England upon whose philosophy her own was based, and later Germany as opposed to both. But in France as in Germany, philosophy and the general outburst of literary activity of that time were a result of an economic upswing. The final supremacy of economic development even in these realms is established, but it takes place within the conditions which are set down by the particular realm; in philosophy, e.g., through the effect of economic influences (which again exert influence through disguised political, etc., forms) upon the existing philosophical material which our philosophical predecessors have handed down. Of itself economics produces no effects here directly; but it determines the *kind of change* and development the already existing intellectual material receives, and even that, for the most part, indirectly, since it is the political, jural, and moral reflexes which exercise the greatest direct influence upon philosophy. . . .

2 *To J. Bloch*

London, Sept. 21, 1890

Dear Sir:

. . . To Point II.* I qualify your first major proposition as follows: According to the materialistic conception of history, the production and reproduction of real life constitutes in the *last instance* the determining factor of history. Neither Marx nor I ever maintained more. Now when someone comes along and distorts this to mean that the economic factor is the *sole* determining factor he is converting the former proposition into a meaningless, ab-

---

* Bloch had asked how the fundamental principle of the materialistic conception of history was understood by Marx and Engels themselves; whether the production and reproduction of life constituted the *sole* determining factor or was only the foundation upon which all other relations developed a further activity of their *own*.

stract, and absurd phrase. The economic situation is the basis but the various factors of the superstructure, the political forms of the class struggles and their results—constitutions, etc., established by victorious classes after hard-won battles, legal forms, and even the reflexes of all these real struggles in the brain of the participants, political, jural, philosophical theories, religious conceptions which have been developed into systematic dogmas—all these exercise an influence upon the course of historical struggles and in many cases determine for the most part their form. There is a reciprocity between all these factors in which, finally, through the endless array of contingencies (i.e., of things and events whose inner connection with one another is so remote, or so incapable of proof, that we may neglect it, regarding it as nonexistent) the economic movement asserts itself as necessary. Were this not the case, the application of the theory to any given historical period would be easier than the solution of a simple equation of the first degree.

We ourselves make our own history, but, first of all, under very definite presuppositions and conditions. Among these are the economic, which are finally decisive. But there are also the political, etc. Yes, even the ghostly traditions which haunt the minds of men play a role albeit not a decisive one. The Prussian state arose and developed through historical, in the last instance, economic causes. One could hardly, however, assert without pedantry that among the many petty principalities of North Germany, just Brandenburg was determined by economic necessity and not by other factors also (before all, its involvement in virtue of its Prussian possessions, with Poland and therewith international political relations—which were also decisive factors in the creation of the domestic power of Austro-Hungary) to become the great power in which was to be embodied the economic, linguistic, and, since the Reformation, also the religious differences of North and South. It would be very hard to attempt to explain by economic causes without making ourselves ridiculous the existence of every petty German state of the past or present, or the origin of modern German syntax, which reinforced the differences that existed already in virtue of the geographical separating wall formed by the mountains from Sudeten to Taunus.

Secondly, history is so made that the end result always arises out of the conflict of many individual wills in which every will is itself the product of a host of special conditions of life. Consequently there exist innumerable intersecting forces, an infinite group of parallelograms of forces which give rise to one resultant product—the historical event. This again may itself be viewed as the product of a force acting as a Whole without consciousness or volition. For what every individual wills separately is frustrated by what every one else wills, and the general upshot is something which no one willed. And so the course of history has run along like a natural process; it also is subject essentially to the same laws of motion. But from the fact that the wills of individuals—who desire what the constitution of their body as well as external circumstances, in the last instance economic (either personal or social), determine them to desire—do not get what they wish but are sunk into an average or common result, from all that one has no right to conclude that they equal zero. On the contrary, every will contributes to the result and is in so far forth included within it.

I should further like to beg of you to study the theory from its original sources and not at second hand. It is really much easier. Marx hardly wrote a thing in which this theory does not play a part. *The Eighteenth Brumaire of Louis Napoleon* is an especially remarkable example of its application. There are many relevant passages also in *Capital*. In addition, permit me to call your attention to my own writings, *Herrn E. Dühring's Unwälzung der Wissenschaft* and *L. Feuerbach und der Ausgang der klassischen deutschen Philosophie* where I give the most comprehensive exposition of historical materialism which to my knowledge exists anywhere.

Marx and I are partly responsible for the fact that at times our disciples have laid more weight upon the economic factor than belongs to it. We were compelled to emphasize its central character in opposition to our opponents who denied it, and there wasn't always time, place, and occasion to do justice to the other factors in the reciprocal interactions of the historical process. But just as soon as it was a matter of the presentation of an historical chapter, that is to say, of practical application, things became quite different; there, no error was possible. Unfortunately it is only too frequent that a person believes he has completely understood a new theory and is capable of applying it when he has taken over its fundamental ideas—and even then in an incorrect form. And from this reproach I cannot spare many of the recent "Marxists." They have certainly turned out a rare kind of tommyrot. . . .

Yours, etc.

3   *To Hans Starkenburg*

London, January 25, 1894

Dear Sir:

Here are the answers to your questions: *

1   By economic relations, which we regard as the determining basis of the history of society, we understand the way in which human beings in a definite society produce their necessities of life and exchange the product among themselves (in so far as division of labor exists). Consequently the *whole technique* of production and transportation is therein included. According to our conception, this technique determines the character and method of exchange, further, the distribution of the products and therewith, after the dissolution of gentile society, the relationships of ruler to ruled, and thence, the state, politics, law, etc. Under economic relations are included further, the geographical foundations upon which they develop and the actually inherited remains of earlier economic stages of development which have persisted, often through traditon only or *vis inertiae*, and also, naturally, the external surrounding milieu of society.

If the technique, as you properly say, its to a large extent dependent upon the state of science, how much

---

* To what extent are economic relations *causally* effective, i.e., are they sufficient causes or necessary conditions or occasions, etc., of social development? What roles do the factors of *race* and historical *personality* play in Marx-Engels' conception of history?

more is science dependent upon the *state* and *needs* of technique. If society has a technical need, it serves as a greater spur to the progress of science than do ten universities. The whole of hydrostatics (Torricelli, etc.) was produced by the needs of controlling the mountain streams in Italy in the sixteenth and seventeenth centuries. We only acquired some intelligible knowledge about electricity when its technical applications were discovered. Unfortunately, in Germany, people have been accustomed to write the history of the sciences as if the sciences had fallen from the sky.

2 We regard the economic conditions as determining, in the last instance, historical development. But there are two points here which must not be overlooked.

(*a*) The political, legal, philosophical, religious, literary, artistic, etc., development rest upon the economic. But they all react upon one another and upon the economic base. It is not the case that the economic situation is the *sole active cause* and every thing else only a passive effect. But there is a reciprocal interaction within a fundamental economic necessity which *in the last instance* always asserts itself. The state, e.g., exerts its influence through tariffs, free trade good or bad taxation. Even that deadly supineness and impotence of the German philistine which arose out of the miserable economic situation of Germany from 1648 to 1830 and which expressed itself first in pietism, then in sentimentalism and crawling servility before prince and noble, were not without their economic effects. They constituted one of the greatest hindrances to a progressive movement and were only cleared out of the way by the revolutionary and Napoleonic wars which made the chronic misery acute. It is not true, as some people here and there conveniently imagine, that economic conditions work themselves out automatically. Men make their own history but in a given, conditioning milieu, upon the basis of actual relations already extant, among which, the economic relations, no matter how much they are influenced by relations of a political and ideological order, are ultimately decisive, constituting a red thread which runs through all the other relations and enabling us to understand them.

(b) Men make their own history but until now not with collective will according to a collective plan. Not even in a definitely limited given society. Their strivings are at cross-purposes with each other, and in all such societies therefore reigns a *necessity* which asserts itself under the form of contingency. The *necessity* which here expresses itself through all those contigencies is ultimately, again, economic. Here we must treat of the so-called great man. That a certain particular man and no other emerges as a definite time in a given country is naturally pure chance. But even if we eliminate him, there is always a need for a substitute, and the substitute is found *tant bien que mal;* in the long run he is sure to be found. That Napoleon—this particular Corsican—should have been the military dictator made necessary by the exhausting wars of the French Republic—that was a matter of chance. But that in default of a Napoleon, another would have filled his place, that is established by the fact that whenever a man was necessary he has always been found: Caesar, Augustus, Cromwell, etc. Marx, to be sure, discovered the materialistic conception of history, but the examples of Thierry, Mignet, Guizot, the whole school of English historians up to 1850 show they were working towards it; and its rediscovery by Morgan serves as proof that the time was ripe for it and that it *had* to be discovered.

So with all other accidents and apparent accidents in history. The wider the field we investigate, the further removed from the economic, the closer to the domain of pure, abstract ideology, the more we find that it reveals accidents in its development, the more does the course of its curve run in zigzag fashion. But fit a trend to the curve; and you will find that the longer the period taken, the more inclusive the field treated, the more closely will this trend run parallel to the trend of economic development. . . .

4 *To F. Mehring*

July 14, 1893

. . . Only one point is lacking which Marx and I did not sufficiently stress and in relation to which we are equally to blame. We both placed and *had to place* the chief weight upon the *derivation* of political, legal, and other ideological notions, as well as the actions which they led up to, from fundamental economic facts. In consequence, we neglected the formal side, i.e., the way in which these ideas arose, for the sake of the content. That gave our opponents a welcome occasion for misunderstanding. Paul Barth is a striking example.

Ideology is a process which of course is carried on with the consciousness of so-called thinkers but with a false consciousness. The real driving force which moves it remains unconscious otherwise it would not be an ideological process. It imaginatively creates for itself false or apparent driving forces. Because it is a thought process, it derives both its content and form from pure thought, either its own or that of its predecessors. It works with pure conceptual material which it unwittingly takes over as the product of thought and therefore does not investigate its relations to a process further removed from and independent of thought. Indeed it seems to be self-evident that since all activity is mediated by thought, it is ultimately *grounded* in thought. The historical ideologist (and historical means here political, jural, philosophical, theological, in short, all domains which belong to society and not merely to nature)—the historical ideologist is confronted in every scientific field by material which has been built up independently out of the thought of earlier generations and which through the minds of these successive generations has undergone an independent development peculiar to itself. External facts from this or other fields may have contributed to determine this development, but these facts, according to the tacit presuppositions made, are themselves mere fruits of a thought process. And so we still remain in the realm of pure thought which has succeeded so well in digesting the hardest facts.

It is this appearance of an independent history of state

constitutions, systems of law, of ideologies in every special field, which, above all, has blinded so many people. When Luther and Calvin "transcend" the official Catholic religion; when Hegel "transcends" Fichte and Kant; and Rousseau, indirectly with his social contract, the constitutionalist, Montesquieu, it is a process which remains within theology, philosophy, and political science. It merely reveals a stage in the history of these intellectual domains and never emerges from the field of pure thought at all. Ever since the illusion of the eternity and ultimacy of the system of capitalist production arose, the refutation of the Mercantilists through the physiocrats and A. Smith has been regarded, not as the intellectual reflection to different economic facts, but only as a victory of thought, as a correct insight, won at last, into actual conditions existing always and everywhere. If only Richard the Lion-hearted and Philip Augustus had introduced free trade, instead of involving themselves in crusades, five hundred years of misery and stupidity would have been spared us.

This side of affairs, which I can here only indicate, we have all neglected, more than is necessary. It's the old story. In the beginning the form is always neglected for the content. As already said, I myself have made that error, and it has always been thrown up to me. I am far from reproaching you with it. As an older sinner in this respect, I have hardly the right. But I wish to call your attention to this point for the future.

This is bound up with the stupid conception of the ideologists. Because we denied that the different ideological spheres, which play a part in history, have an independent historical development, we were supposed therewith to have denied that they have any *historical efficacy*. At the basis of this is the ordinary undialectical notion of cause and effect as fixed, mutually opposed, polar relations and a complete disregard of reciprocity. These gentlemen forget, almost intentionally, that an historical factor, once it has been brought into the world by another, ultimately economic fact is able to react upon its surroundings and even affect its own causes. . . .

TRANSLATED BY SIDNEY HOOK

II

The
Social Democratic
Tradition

Karl Kautsky

The Commonwealth of the Future

During the years before the First World War, when the Social Democratic movement became a major force in European political life, its outstanding intellectual spokesman was Karl Kautsky (1854–1938). Executor of Marx's writings and editor of the distinguished German socialist journal, Neue Zeit, Kautsky became the spokesman for the dominant trend in European social democracy: opposed in theory to the "revisionist" or reformist wing of the movement, yet increasingly committed, in practice, to its pragmatic and reformist politics. Even as he continued to engage in a strict interpretation and defense of the Marxist texts, Kautsky rarely showed a spark of the revolutionary passion that had animated Marx and Engels. Under his guidance, the German Social Democratic movement became a party rooted in the daily life of the working class and in parliamentary and electoral work.

The following selection is taken from Kautsky's book Das Erfurter Programm, written in 1892 and translated into English as The Class Struggle. It offers a statement on the problems of the transition from capitalism to socialism, as well as reflecting on occasion some of the political and intellectual ambiguities of his position.

The abolition of the present system of production means substituting production for use for production for sale.

Production for use may be of two forms:

First, individual production for the satisfaction of individual wants; and,

Second, social or cooperative production for the satisfaction of the wants of a commonwealth.

The first form of production has never been a general form of production. Man has always been a social being, as far back as we can trace him. The individual has always been thrown upon cooperation with others in order to satisfy some of his principal wants; others had to work for him and he, in turn, had to work for others. Individual production for self-consumption has always played a subordinate part; today it hardly deserves mention.

Until the present system of production (production for sale) was developed, cooperative production for common use was the leading form; it is as old as production itself. If any one system of production could be considered better adapted than any other to the nature of man, then cooperative production must be pronounced the natural one. In all probability for every thousand years of production for sale, cooperative production for use numbers tens of thousands. The character, extent, and power of cooperative societies have changed along with the instruments and methods of production which they adopted. Nevertheless, whether such a commonwealth was a horde or a tribe or any other form of community, they all had certain essential features in common. Each satisfied its own wants, at least the most vital ones, with the product of its own labor; the instruments of production were the property of the community; its members worked together as free and equal individuals according to some plan inherited or devised, and administered by some power elected by themselves. The product of such cooperative labor was the property of the community and was applied either to the satisfaction of common wants, whether these were occasioned by production or consumption, or were distributed among the individuals or groups which composed the community.

The well-being of such self-supporting communities or societies depended upon natural and personal conditions. The more fertile the territory they occupied, the more diligent, inventive, and vigorous their members, the greater was the general well-being. Droughts, freshets, invasions by more powerful enemies, might afflict, or even destroy, them, but there was one visitation they were free from, the fluctuations of the market. With this they were either wholly unacquainted, or they knew it only in connection with articles of luxury.

Such cooperative production for use is nothing less than communistic or, as it is called today, socialist production. Production for sale can be overcome only by such a system. Socialist production is the only system of production possible when production for sale has become impossible.

This fact does not, however, imply that it is necessary to revive the dead past or to restore the old forms of community property or communal production. These forms were adapted to certain means of production; they were, and continue to be, inapplicable to more highly developed instruments of production. It was for that reason that they disappeared almost everywhere in the course of economic development at the approach of the system of production for sale, and wherever they did resist the latter, their effect was to interfere with the development of productive powers. As reactionary and hopeless as were the efforts to resist the system of production for sale, would be today any endeavor to overthrow the present by a revival of the old communal system.

The system of socialist production which has become necessary, owing to the impending bankruptcy of our present system of production for sale, will and must have certain features in common with the older systems of communal production, in so far, namely, as both are systems of cooperative production for use. In the same way, the capitalist system of production bears some resemblance to the system of small and individual production, which forms the transition between it and communal production; both produce for sale. Just as the capitalist system of production, as a higher development of commodity production, is different from small production, so will the form of social production, that has now become necessary be different from the former systems of production for use.

The coming system of socialist production will not be the sequel to ancient communism; it will be the sequel to the capitalist system of production, which itself develops the elements that are requisite for the organization of its successor. It brings forth the new people whom the new system of production needs. But it also brings forth the social organization which, as soon as the new people have mastered it, will become the foundation stone of the new system of production. . . . .

The Economic Significance of the State

All communities have had economic functions to fulfill. This must, self-evidently, have been the case with the original communist societies which we encounter at the threshold of history. In proportion as individual small production, private ownership in the means of production, and production for sale underwent their successive development, a number of social functions came into existence, the fulfillment of which either exceeded the power of the individual industries or were from the start recognized as too important to be handed over to the arbitrary conduct of individuals. Along with the care for the poor, the young, the old, the infirm (schools, hospitals, poorhouses), the community reserved the functions of promoting and regulating commerce, i.e., building highways, coining money, superintending highways, and the management of certain general and important matters pertaining to production. In medieval society these several functions developed upon the towns and sometimes upon religious corporations. The medieval state was little concerned with such functions. All this changed as the state took on its modern form, that is, became the state of office holders and soldiers, the tool of the capitalist class. Like all previous states, the modern state is the tool of class rule. It could not, however, fulfill its mission and satisfy the needs of the capitalist class without either dissolving, or depriving of their independence, those economic institutions which lay at the foundation of the pre-capitalist social system, and taking upon itself their functions. Even in places where the modern state tolerated the continuance of medieval organizations, these fell into decay and became less and less able to fulfill their functions. These functions became, however, broader and broader with the development of the capitalist system; they grew with such rapidity that the state was gradually compelled to assume even those functions which it cares least to trouble itself about. For instance, the necessity of taking over the whole system of charitable and educational institutions has become so pressing upon the state that it has in most cases surrendered to this necessity. From the start it assumed the function of coining money; since then, forestry, care of the water supply, building of roads, come constantly more under its jurisdiction.

There was a time when the capitalist class, in its self-confidence, imagined it could free itself from the economic activities of the state; the state should only watch over their safety at home and abroad, keep the proletarians and foreign competitors in check, but keep its hands off the whole economic life. The capitalist class had good reasons for desiring this. However great the power of the capitalists, the power of the state had not always shown itself as subservient as they wished. Even where the capitalist class had virtually no competitor with whom to dispute the overlordship, and where, accordingly, the power of the state showed itself friendly, the office holders often became disagreeable friends to deal with.

The hostility of the capitalist class to the interference of the state in the economic life of a country came to the surface first in England, where it received the name of the Manchester School. The doctrines of that school were the first weapons with which the capitalist class took the field against the socialist-labor movement. It is therefore no wonder that the opinion took hold of many a socialist workingman that a supporter of the Manchester School and a capitalist were one and the same thing and that, on the other hand, socialism and the interference of the state in the economic affairs of a country were identical. No wonder that such workingmen believed that to overthrow the Manchester School was to overthrow capitalism itself. Nothing less true. The Manchester teaching was never anything more than a teaching which the capitalist class played against the workingman or the government whenever it suited its purposes, but from the logical practice of which it has carefully guarded itself. Today the Manchester School no longer influences the capitalist class. The

reason of its decline was the increasing force with which
the economic and political development urged the necessity of the extension of the functions of the state.

These functions grew from day to day. Not only do
those which the state assumed from the start become ever
larger, but new ones are born of the capitalist system
itself, of which the former generations had no conception
and which affect ultimately the whole economic system.
Formerly, statesmen were essentially diplomats and jurists; today they must, or should, be economists. Treaties
and privileges, ancient researches and matters of precedent are of little use in the solution of modern political
problems; economic principles have become the leading
arguments. What are today the chief matters with which
statesmen concern themselves? Are they not finance, colonial affairs, tariff, protection and insurance of workingmen?

Nor is this all. The economic development forces the
state, partly in self-defense, partly for the sake of better
fulfilling its functions, partly also for the purpose of increasing its revenues, to take into its own hands more and
more functions or industries.

During the Middle Ages the rulers derived their main
income from their property in land; later, during the sixteenth, seventeenth, and eighteenth centuries, their trea-
suries derived large accessions from the plundering of
church and other estates. On the other hand, the need of
money frequently compelled the rulers to sell their land
to the capitalists. In most European countries even now,
however, very considerable survivals of the former state
ownership of land can be found in the domains of the
crown and the state mines. Furthermore, the development of the military system added arsenals and wharves;
the development of commerce added postoffices, railroads, and telegraphs; finally, the increasing demand for
money on the part of the state has given birth, in European countries, to all manner of state monopolies.

While the economic functions and the economic power
of the state are thus steadily increased, the whole economic mechanism becomes more and more complicated,
more and more sentitive, and the separate capitalist undertakings become, as we have seen, proportionately

more interdependent upon one another. Along with all this grows the dependence of the capitalist class upon the greatest of all their establishments, the state or government. This increased dependence and interrelation increases also the disturbances and disorders which afflict the economic mechanism, for relief from all of which, the largest of existing economic powers, the state or government, is, with increasing frequency, appealed to by the capitalist class. Accordingly, in modern society the state is called more and more to step in and take a hand in the regulation and management of the economic mechanism, and ever stronger are the means placed at its disposal and employed by it in the fulfillment of this function. The economic omnipotence of the state, which appeared to the Manchester School as a socialist utopia, has developed under the very eyes of that school into an inevitable result of the capitalist system of production itself.

State Socialism and the Social Democracy

The economic activity of the modern state is the natural starting point of the development that leads to the cooperative commonwealth. It does not, however, follow that every nationalization of an economic function or of an industry is a step towards the cooperative commonwealth and that the latter could be the result of a general nationalization of all industries without any change in the character of the state. . . .

If the modern state nationalizes certain industries, it does not do so for the purpose of restricting capitalist exploitation, but for the purpose of protecting the capitalist system and establishing it upon a firmer basis, or for the purpose of itself taking a hand in the exploitation of labor, increasing its own revenues, and thereby reducing the contributions for its own support which it would otherwise have to impose upon the capitalist class. As an exploiter of labor, the state is superior to any private capitalist. Besides the economic power of the capitalists, it can also bring to bear upon the exploited classes the political power which it already wields.

The state has never carried on the nationalizing of industries further than the interests of the ruling classes demanded, nor will it ever go further than that. So long as the property-holding classes are the ruling ones, the nationalization of industries and capitalist functions will never be carried so far as to injure the capitalists and landlords or to restrict their opportunities for exploiting the proletariat.

The state will not cease to be a capitalist institution until the proletariat, the working class, has become the ruling class; not until then will it become possible to turn it into a cooperative commonwealth.

From the recognition of this fact is born the aim which the Socialist Party has set before it: to call the working class to conquer the political power to the end that, with its aid, they may change the state into a self-sufficing cooperative commonwealth. . . .

The Structure of the Future State

It is not our purpose to meet all the objections, misconceptions and misstatements with which the capitalist class strives to combat socialism. . . .

There is, however, one objection that should be met. It is important enough to merit thorough treatment, and its removal will make clearer the point of view and purpose of socialism.

Our opponents declare that the cooperative commonwealth cannot be considered practicable and cannot be the object of the endeavors of intelligent people until the plan is presented to the world in a perfected form and has been tested and found feasible. They claim that no sensible man would start to build a house before he had perfected his plan and before experts had approved of it; that least of all would he pull down his only dwelling before he knew what else to put in its place. Socialists are, accordingly, told that they must come out with their plan of a future state; if they refuse, it is a sign that they themselves have not much confidence in it. . . .

The construction of a plan upon which the future social order is to be built has become, not only purposeless, but wholly irreconcilable with the point of view of modern science. In the course of the nineteenth century a great revolution took place, not only in the economic world, but also in men's minds. Insight into the causes of social development has increased tremendously. As far back as the forties Marx and Engels showed—and from that time on every step in social science has proved it— that, in the last analysis, the history of mankind is determined, not by ideas, but by an economic development which progresses irresistibly, obedient to certain underlying laws and not to anyone's wishes or whims. In the foregoing chapters we have seen how it goes on; how it brings about new forms of production which require new forms of society; how it starts new wants among men which compel them to reflect upon their social condition and to devise means whereby to adjust society to the new system in accordance with which production is carried on. For, we must always remember, this process of adjustment does not proceed of itself; it needs the aid of the human brain. Without thought, without ideas, there is no progress. But ideas are the means to social development; the first impulse does not proceed from them, as was formerly believed, and as many still think; the first impulse comes from economic conditions.

Accordingly it is not the thinkers, the philosophers, who determine the trend of social progress. What the thinkers can do is to discover, to recognize, the trend; and this they can do in proportion to the clearness of their understanding of the conditions which preceded, but they can never themselves determine the course of social evolution.

And even the recognition of the trend of social progress has its limits. The organization of social life is most complex; even the clearest intellect finds it impossible to probe it from all sides and to measure all the forces at work in it with sufficient accuracy to enable him to foretell accurately what social forms will result from the joint action of all these forces.

A new social form does not come into existence through the activity of certain especially gifted men. No man or group of men can conceive of a plan, convince people by degrees of its utility, and, when they have acquired the requisite power, undertake the construction of a social edifice according to their plan.

All social forms have been the result of long and fluctuating struggles. The exploited have fought against the exploiting classes; the sinking reactionary classes against the progressive, revolutionary ones. In the course of these struggles the various classes have merged in all manner of combination to battle with their opponents. The camp of the exploited at times contains both revolutionary and reactionary elements; the camp of the revolutionists may contain at times both exploiters and exploited. Within a single class different factions are frequently formed according to the intellect, the temperament, or the station of individuals or whole sections. And, finally, the power wielded by any single class has never been permanent; each has risen or fallen as its understanding of the surrounding conditions, the compactness and size of its organization, and its importance in the mechanism of production increased or diminished.

In the course of the fluctuating struggles of these classes the older social forms, which had become untenable, were pushed aside for new ones. The social order which took the place of the old was not always immediately the best possible. In order to have made it so the revolutionary class of each epoch would have had to be in possession of the sole political power and the most perfect understanding of their social conditions. As long as this was not the case, mistakes were inevitable. Not infrequently a new social order proved itself partially, if not wholly, as untenable as the one overthrown. Nevertheless, the stronger the pressure of economic development, the clearer became its demands and the greater the ability of the revolutionary classes to do what was required of them. The institutions of the revolutionary class which were in opposition to the demands of economic development fell into decay and were soon forgotten. But those which had become necessary quickly struck root and could not be exterminated by the upholders of the former system.

It is in this way that all new social orders have arisen. Revolutionary periods differ from other periods of social development only by virtue of the fact that during them the phenomena of development proceed at an unusually rapid pace.

The genesis of a social institution is, it thus appears,

very different from that of a building. Previously perfected plans are not applicable to the construction of the former. In view of this fact, sketching plans for the future social state is about as rational as writing in advance the history of the next war.

The course of events is, however, by no means independent of the individual. Everyone who is active in society affects it to a greater or less extent. A few individuals, especially prominent through their capacity or social position, may exercise great influence upon the whole nation. Some may promote the development of society by enlightening the people, organizing the revolutionary forces, and causing them to act with vigor and precision; others may retard social development for many years by turning their powers in the opposite direction. The former tend, by the promotion of the social evolution, to diminish the sufferings and sacrifices that it demands; the latter, on the contrary, tend to increase these sufferings and sacrifices. But no one, whether he be the mightiest monarch or the wisest and most benevolent philosopher, can determine at will the direction that the social evolution shall take or prophesy accurately the new forms that it will adopt.

Few things are, therefore, more childish than to demand of the socialist that he draw a picture of the commonwealth which he strives for.

Confiscation of Property

Our opponents declare that socialism can never come into power except through a wholesale confiscation of property, confiscation without compensation not only of house and farm but of superfluous furniture and savings bank deposits. Next to the charge of intending to forcibly dissolve all family ties, this is the trump card played against us.

The program of the Socialist Party has nothing to say about confiscation. It does not mention it, not from fear of giving offense, but because it is a subject upon which nothing can be said with certainty. The only thing that can be declared with certainly is that the tendency of economic development renders imperative the social ownership and operation of the means of large production. In what way this transfer from private and individual into collective ownership will be effected, whether this inevitable transfer will take the form of confiscation, whether it will be a peaceable or a forcible one—these are questions no man can answer. Past experience throws little light on this matter. The transition may be effected, as was that from feudalism to capitalism, in as many different ways as there are different countries. The manner of the transition depends wholly upon the general circumstances under which it is effected, the power and enlightenment of the classes concerned, for instance, all of them circumstances that cannot be calculated for the future. In historical development, the unexpected plays the most prominent role.

It goes without saying that the Socialist Party wishes this unavoidable expropriation of large industry to be effected with as little friction as possible, in a peaceful way, and with the consent of the whole people. But the historical development will take its course regardless of the wishes of either socialists or their adversaries.

In no case can it be said that the carrying out of the socialist program demands under all circumstances that the property whose expropriation has become necessary will be confiscated.

Nevertheless, it may be said with certainty that economic development can render necessary the confiscation of only a part of existing property. The economic development demands social ownership of the implements of labor only; it does not concern itself with the part of property that is devoted to personal and private uses. This is applicable not only to food, furniture, etc. We recall what was said in a previous chapter about savings banks. They are the means whereby the private property of the noncapitalist classes is rendered accessible to capitalists. The deposits of every single depositor, taken separately, are too insignificant to be applied to capitalist industry; not until many deposits have been gathered together are they in a condition to fulfill the function of capital. In the measure in which capitalist undertakings pass from private into social concerns, the opportunities will be lessened for patrons of savings banks to draw interest upon their deposits; these will cease to be capital and will become merely noninterest-bearing funds. But this is a very different thing from the confiscation of savings bank deposits.

The confiscation of such property is, moreover, not only economically unnecessary but politically improbable. These small deposits come mainly from the pockets of the exploited classes, from those classes to whose efforts the introduction of socialism will be due. Only those who consider these classes to be utterly unreliable can believe that they would begin by robbing themselves of their hard-earned savings in order to regain possession of the means of production.

But not only does the introduction of socialist production not require the expropriation of nonproductive wealth, it does not even require the expropriation of all property in the means of production.

That which renders the socialist society necessary is large production. Cooperative production requires also cooperative ownership in the means of production. But just as private property in the means of production is irreconcilable with cooperative work in large industry, so cooperative or social ownership in the means of production is irreconcilable with small production. This requires, as we have seen, private ownership in the means of production. The aim of socialism is to place the worker in possession of the necessary means of production. The expropriation of the means of production in small industry would mean merely the senseless proceeding of taking them from their present owner and returning them again to him.

Accordingly, the transition to the socialist society does not at all require the expropriation of the small artisan and the small farmer. This transition not only will deprive them of nothing, but it will bring them many advantages. Since the tendency of socialist society is to substitute production for use for production for sale, it must be its endeavor to transform all social dues (taxes, interest upon mortgages on property that has been nationalized, etc., so far as these may have been not wholly abolished) from money payments into payments in products. But this means the raising of a tremendous burden from the farmer. In many ways that is what he is striving for today, but it is impossible under the supremacy of production for sale. Only the socialist society can bring it, and with it remove the main cause of the ruin of the farming industry.

It is the capitalists who expropriate the farmers and artisans. Socialist society puts an end to this expropriation.

Certainly, socialism will not put an end to economic development. On the contrary, it is the only means to ensure its progress beyond a certain point. In socialist society, as in society today, large industry will develop more and more and increasingly absorb small industry. But here, too, the same conclusion holds good as in the case of the family and marriage. The direction of the evolution remains the same, but socialism removes all the painful and shocking manifestations that under the present system are the accompaniments of the social evolution.

Today the transformation of the small farmer and the small producer from workers in the field of small production to workers in the field of large production means their transformation from property holders into proletarians. In a socialist society, a farmer or artisan who becomes a worker in a large socialized industry will become a sharer in all the advantages of large industry; his condition is plainly bettered. His transition from large to small industry is no more to be compared with the change from a property holder to a proletarian, but rather to the transformation of a small property holder into a large property holder.

Small production is doomed to disappear. Only the socialist system can make it possible for farmers and handicraftmen to become participants in the advantages of large production without sinking into the proletariat. Only under the socialist system can the inevitable downfall of the small producer, industrial and agricultural, result in an improvement of their condition.

The mainspring of economic development will no longer be the competition which grinds down and expropriates those who fall behind, it will be the power of attraction which the more highly developed forms of production exercise upon the less developed ones.

A development of this sort is not only painless, it proceeds much more rapidly than that brought out by the spur of competition. Today, when the introduction of new and higher forms of production is impossible without ruining and expropriating the owners of industries carried on under inferior forms, and without inflicting suffering and privation upon the large masses of workers who have become through this means superfluous, every economic progress is doggedly resisted. We see on all sides instances of the tenacity with which producers cling to antiquated forms of production and of their desperate efforts to preserve them. Never yet was any system of production known as revolutionary as the present one; never did any revolutionize so completely within the space of a hundred years all human activities. And yet how many ancient ruins of antiquated, outlived forms of production still exist!

Just as soon as the fear disappears of being thrown into the proletariat if an independent industry is abandoned; just as soon as the present prejudices against large production disappear because of the advantages which the social ownership of large production will bestow upon all; just as soon as it is possible for everyone to share these advantages, only fools will strive to preserve antiquated forms of production.

What capitalist large production has not accomplished within a hundred years, socialist large production will bring about within a short time—the absorption of outgrown small production. It will accomplish this without expropriation, through the attractive power of improved industrial methods. In places where agricultural production is still not production for sale, but prevailingly production for use, small farming will perhaps continue for some time under the socialist society. In the end, the advantages of cooperative large production will be discerned in these districts also. The change from small to large production in agriculture will be hastened and made easy by the steadily progressing disappearance of the contrast between city and country and by the tendency to locate industries in rural districts.

Division of Products in the Future State

There is still a point, the most important of all, that should be touched upon. The first question which is put to a socialist is usually: How will you go about the division of wealth? Shall each have an equal share?

"Dividing up!" That sticks in the crop of the Philistine. Their whole conception of socialism begins and ends with that word. Indeed, even among the cultured the idea prevails that the object of socialism is to divide the whole wealth of the nation among the people.

That this view still prevails, despite all protests and proofs on the part of socialists, is to be ascribed not only to the malice of our opponents, but also, and perhaps to a greater extent, to their inability to understand the social conditions that have been created by the development of large production. Their horizon is still, to a great extent, bounded by the conceptions that belong only to small production. From the standpoint of small production, "dividing up" is the only possible form of socialism. The notion of dividing has long been familiar to the small businessman and farmer. From the beginning of production for sale in antiquity, it has happened innumerable times that as soon as a few families had heaped up great wealth and reduced farmers and artisans to a state of dependence, these latter rose in rebellion and attempted to improve their condition through the expulsion of the rich and the division of their property. They succeeded in this for the first time during the French Revolution, which laid such stress on the rights of private property. Peasants, artisans, and the class that was about to develop into capitalists, divided among themselves the church estates. "Dividing up" is the socialism of small production, the socialism of the conservative ranks of society, not the socialism of the proletariat engaged in large industry.

Socialists do not propose to divide: on the contrary, their object is to concentrate in the hands of society the instruments of production that are now scattered in the hands of various owners.

But this does not dispose of the question of "dividing up." If the means of production belong to society, to it must belong also, as a matter of course, the function of disposing of the products that are brought forth by the use of these means. In what way will society distribute these among its members? Shall it be according to the principle of equality or according to the labor performed by each? And in the latter case, is every kind of labor to receive the same reward, whether it be pleasant or unpleasant, hard or easy, skilled or unskilled?

The answer to this question seems to be the central point of socialism. Not only does it greatly preoccupy the opponents of socialism, but even the early socialists devoted a great deal of attention to it. From Fourier to Weitling and from Weitling to Bellamy, there runs a steady stream of the most diversified answers, many of which reveal a wonderful cleverness. There is no lack of positive propositions, many of which are as simple as they are practicable. Nevertheless, the question has not the importance generally ascribed to it.

There was a time when the distribution of products was looked upon as wholly independent of production. Since the contradictions and ills of the capitalist system manifest themselves first in its peculiar method of distributing its products, it was quite natural that the exploited classes and their friends should have found the root of all evil in the "unjust" distribution of products. Of course, they proceeded, in accordance with the ideas prevalent at the beginning of the nineteenth century, upon the supposition that the existing system of distribution was the result of the ideas of the day, especially of the legal system in force. In order to remove this unjust distribution, all that was needed was to invent a juster one and to convince the world of its advantages. The just system could be no other than the reverse of the existing one. "Today the grossest inequality rules; the principle upon which distribution should be based must be one of equality." Today the idler rolls in wealth while the laborer starves, so others said: "To each according to his deeds" (or in newer form, "To each the product of his labor"). But doubts arose as to both these formulas, and so arose a third: "To each according to his needs."

Since then socialists have come to realize that the distribution of products in a community is determined, not by the prevailing legal system, but by the prevailing system of production. The share of the landlord, the capitalist, and the wage-earner in the total product of society is determined by the part which land, capital, and labor power play in the present system of production. Certainly in a socialist society the distribution of products will not be left to the working of blind laws concerning the operation of which those concerned are unconscious. As today in a large industrial establishment, production and the payment of wages are carefully regulated, so in a socialist society, which is nothing more than a single gigantic industrial concern, the same principle must prevail. The rules according to which the distribution of products is to be carried out will be established by those concerned. Nevertheless, it will not depend upon their pleasure what these rules shall be; they will not be adopted arbitrarily according to this or that "principle," they will be determined by the actual conditions of society and, above all, by the conditions of production.

For instance, the degree of productivity of labor, at any given time, exercises a great influence upon the manner in which distribution is effected. We can conceive a time when science shall have raised industry to such a high level of productivity that everything wanted by man will be produced in great abundance. In such a case, the formula, "To each according to his needs," would be applied as a matter of course and without difficulty. On the other hand, not even the profoundest conviction of the justice of this formula would be able to put it into practice if the productivity of labor remained so low that the proceeds of the most excessive toil could produce only the bare necessities. Again, the formula, "To each according to his deeds," will always be found inapplicable. If it has any meaning at all, it presupposes a distribution of the total product of the commonwealth among its members. This notion, like that of a general division with which the socialist regime is to be ushered in, springs from the modes of thought that are peculiar to the modern system of private property. To distribute all products at stated intervals would be equivalent to the gradual reintroduction of private property in the means of production.

The very principle of socialist production limits the possible distribution to only a portion of the products. All those products which are requisite to the enlargement of production cannot, as a matter of course, be the subject of distribution; and the same holds good with regard to all such products as are intended for common use, *i.e.*, for the establishment, preservation, or enlargement of public institutions.

Already in modern society the number and size of such institutions increases steadily. It is in this domain especially that large production crowds down small production. It goes without saying that so far from being checked, this development will be greatly stimulated in a socialist society.

The quantity of products that can be absorbed by private consumption and, accordingly, be turned into private property, must inevitably be a much smaller portion of the total product in a socialist, than in modern society, where almost all the products are merchandise and private property. In socialist society, it is not the bulk of the products, but only the residue that is distributed.

But even this residue socialist society will not be able to dispose of at will; there, too, the requirements of production will determine the course to be pursued. Such production is undergoing steady changes; the forms and methods of distribution will be subject to manifold changes in a socialist society.

It is entirely utopian to imagine that a special system of distribution is to be manufactured and that it will stand for all time. In this matter, as little as any other, is socialist society likely to move by leaps and bounds or start all over anew; it will go on from the point at which capitalist society ceases. The distribution of goods in a socialist society might possibly continue for some time under forms that are essentially developments of the existing system of wage payment. At any rate, this is the point from which it is bound to start. Just as the forms of wage labor differ today, not only from time to time, but also in various branches of industry, and in various sections of the country, so also may it happen that in a socialist society the distribution of products may be carried on under a variety of forms corresponding to the various needs of the population and the historical antecedents of the industry. We must not think of the socialist society as something rigid and uniform, but rather as an organism, constantly developing, rich in possibilities of change, an organism that is to develop naturally from increasing division of labor, commercial exchange, and the dominance of society by science and art.

Next to the thought of "dividing up," that of "equal shares" troubles the foes of socialism most. "Socialism," they declare, "proposes that everyone shall have an equal share of the total product; the industrious is to have no more than the lazy; hard and disagreeable labor is to receive no higher reward than that which is light and agreeable; the hod carrier who has nothing to do but carry the material is to be on a par with the architect himself. Under such circumstances everyone will work as little as possible; no one will perform the hard and disagreeable tasks; knowledge, having ceased to be appreciated, will cease to be cultivated; and the final result will be the relapse of society into barbarism. Consequently, socialism is impracticable."

The fallacy of this reasoning is too glaring to need exposure. This much may be said: Should socialist society ever decide to decree equality of incomes, and should the effect of such a measure threaten to be the dire one prophesied, the natural result would be, not that socialist production, but that the principle of equality of incomes, would be thrown overboard.

The foes of socialism would be justified in concluding from the equality of incomes that socialism is impracticable if they could prove:

1. That this equality would be under all circumstances irreconcilable with the progress of production. This they never have, and never can, prove, because the activity of the individual in production does not depend solely upon his remuneration, but upon a great variety of circumstances—his sense of duty, his ambition, his dignity, his pride, etc.—none of which can be the subject of positive prophecy but only of conjecture, a conjecture which makes against and not for, the opinion expressed by the opponents of socialism.

2. That the equality of incomes is so essential to a

socialist society that the latter cannot be conceived without the former. The opponents of socialism will find it equally impossible to prove this. A glance over the various forms of communist production from the primitive communism down to the latest communist societies will reveal how manifold are the forms of distribution that are applicable to a community of property in the instruments of production. All forms of modern wage-payment—fixed salaries, piece wages, time wages, bonuses—all of them are reconcilable with the spirit of a socialist society; and there is not one of them that may not play a role in socialist society, as the wants and customs of its members, together with the requirements of production, may demand.

It does not, however, follow from this that the principle of equality of incomes—not necessarily identical with their uniformity—will play no part in socialist society. What is certain is that it will do so not as the aim of a movement for leveling things generally, forcibly, artificially, but as the result of a natural development, a social tendency.

In the capitalist sytem of production, there exist two tendencies, one to increase and the other to decrease the differences in incomes; one to increase, one to diminish inequality. By dissolving the middle classes of society and swelling constantly the size of individual fortunes, the capitalist system broadens and deepens the chasm that exists between the masses of the population and those who are at its head; the latter tower higher and higher above the former. Together with this tendency is noticed another, which, operating within the circle of the masses themselves, steadily equalizes their incomes. It flings the small producers, farmers, and manufacturers, into the class of the proletariat, or at least, pushes their incomes down to the proletarian level and wipes out existing differences among the proletarians themselves. The machine tends steadily to remove all differences which originally appeared in the proletariat. Today the differences in wages among the various strata of labor fluctuate incessantly and come nearer and nearer to a point of uniformity. At the same time, the incomes of the educated proletariat are irresistibly tending downward. The equalization of incomes among the masses—that which the opponents of socialism, with the greatest moral indignation, brand as the purpose of socialism—is going on before their eyes in the society of today.

Under the socialist system, as a matter of course, all those tendencies that sharpen inequalities and that proceed from private ownership in the means of production would come to an end. On the other hand, the tendency to wipe out inequalities of incomes would find stronger expression. But here, again, the observations made upon the dissolution of existing family forms and the downfall of small production hold good. The tendency of economic development remains in socialist, as in capitalist, society, but it finds a very different expression. Today the equalization of incomes among the mass of the population proceeds by the depression of the higher incomes to the level of the lower ones. In a socialist society it must inevitably proceed by the raising of the lower to the standard of the higher.

The opponents of socialism seek to frighten the small producers and the workingmen with the claim that equalization of incomes can mean for them nothing else than a lowering of their condition, because, they say, the incomes of the wealthy classes are not sufficient, if divided among the poor, to preserve the present average income of the working and middle classes; consequently, if there is to be an equality of incomes, the upper classes of workers and the small producers will have to give up part of their incomes and will thus be the losers under socialism.

Whatever truth there may be in this claim lies in the fact that the wretchedly poor, especially the slum proletariat, are today so numerous and their need so great that to divide among them the immense incomes of the rich would scarcely be enough to make possible for them the existence of a worker of the better-paid class. Whether this is a sufficient reason for preserving our glorious social system may very well be doubted. We are of the opinion, however, that a diminution of the misery, which would be accomplished through such a division, would mean a step forward.

There is, however, no question of "dividing up"; the

only question is concerning a change in the method of production. The transformation of the capitalist system of production into the socialist system of production must inevitably result in a rapid increase of the quantity of wealth produced. It must never be lost sight of that the capitalist system of production for sale hinders today the progress of economic development, hinders the full expansion of the productive forces that lie latent in society. Not only is it unable to absorb the small industries as rapidly as the technical development makes possible and desirable, but it has even become impossible for it to employ all the labor forces that are available. The capitalist system of production squanders these forces; it steadily drives increasing numbers of workers into the ranks of the unemployed, the slum proletariat, the parasites, and the unproductive middlemen.

Such a state of things would be impossible in a socialist society. It could not fail to find productive labor for all its available labor forces. It would increase, it might even double, the number of productive workers; in the measure in which it did this it would multiply the total wealth produced yearly. This increase in production would be enough in itself to raise the incomes of all workers, not only of the poorest.

Furthermore, since socialist production would promote the absorption of small production by large production and thus increase the productivity of labor, it would be possible, not only to raise the incomes of the workers, but also to shorten the hours of labor.

In view of this, it is foolish to claim that socialism means the equality of pauperism. This is not the equality of socialism; it is the equality of the modern system of production. Socialist production must inevitably improve the condition of all the working classes, including the small industrialist and the small farmer. According to the economic conditions under which the change from capitalism to socialism is effected this improvement will be greater or less, but in any case it will be marked. And every economic advance beyond that will produce an increase and not, as today, a decrease in the general well-being.

This change in the tendency of incomes is, in the eyes

of socialists, of much more importance than the absolute increase of incomes. The thoughtful man lives more in the future than in the present; what the future threatens or promises preoccupies him more than the enjoyment of the present. Not what is, but what will be, not existing conditions, but tendencies, determine the happiness both of individuals and of whole states.

Thus we become acquainted with another element of superiority in socialist over capitalist society. It affords, not only a greater well-being but also certainty of livelihood—a security that today the greatest fortune cannot guarantee. If greater well-being affects only those who have hitherto been exploited, security of livelihood is a boon to the present exploiters, whose well-being demands no improvement or is capable of none. Uncertainty hovers over both rich and poor, and it is, perhaps, more trying than want itself. In imagination it forces those to taste the bitterness of want who are not yet subject to it; it is a specter that haunts the palaces of the wealthiest.

George Plekhanov

Terrorism and Populism*

George Plekhanov (1856–1918) was the first major
intellectual spokesman for Russian Marxism. In the
early 1870's and 1880's the Russian radicals had
been mainly populists. They believed that the motor
force for social change in Russia would be the peasants and the basis for a new society would be the
peasant commune, thereby enabling Russia to escape
the destructive consequences of Western capitalism.
In the late 1870's, the populists broke into two
groups, one devoted to the policy of "going to the
people," that is, trying to educate groups of peasants,
and the other turning to revolutionary terrorism
against Czarist officials.

Plekhanov was the first socialist theoretician in
Russia who, in the name of Marxism, attacked both
wings of populism. He argued against the idealization of the peasantry; he denied that the peasant
commune could provide an adequate basis for socialism, since, among other reasons, socialism could be
built only on an advanced economy and a modern
democratic society; and he urged the creation of a
broad socialist party, based largely on the nascent
Russian working class, which would collaborate with
progressive bourgeois elements to overthrow the
Czarist monarchy and establish a democratic republic.

In 1883, he published Socialism and Political
Struggle, a fierce attack on both populists and terrorists, from which the following passages are taken.
Like other dusty polemics in the literature of socialism, Plekhanov's arguments against the populists,

---

* Title supplied by editor.

*terrorists, and anarchists—though all but unknown
to English-language readers—take on a new cogency
in the light of political developments at the present
moment.*

. . . From the anarchist point of view, the political question is the touchstone of any working-class program. The anarchists not only deny any deal with the modern state, they go so far as to exclude from their notions of "future society" anything that recalls the idea of the state in one way or another. "Autonomy of the individual in an autonomous community"—such has been the motto of all consistent supporters of this trend. We know that its founder, Proudhon, set himself the not quite modest task "to do, as regards the government" (which he confused with the state) "what Kant did as regards religion" and carried his antistate zeal so far as to declare that Aristotle himself was "a skeptic in matters of state."* The accomplishment of the task he had set himself was very simple and followed, if you like, quite logically from the economic doctrines of the French Kant. Proudhon was never able to imagine the economic system of the future otherwise than in the form of commodity production, corrected and supplemented by a new, "just" form of exchange on the basis of "constituted value." For all its "justice," this new form of exchange does not, of course, preclude the purchase, sale, or promissory notes which go with commodity production and circulation. All these transactions naturally presuppose various contracts, and it is these that determine the mutual relations between the transacting sides. But in modern society, "contracts" are based on common legal standards compulsory for all citizens and safeguarded by the state. In the "future society" everything would supposedly proceed somewhat differently. Revolution, according to Proudhon, was to abolish "laws," leav-

---

* To what extent Aristotle was "a skeptic in matters of state" is obvious from the first chapter of the first volume of his *Politics*, in which he says that "the state is the most accomplished form of community," that its purpose is "the supreme good," and that it is therefore a phenomenon "natural in the highest sense of the word, and man is an animal predestined by his very nature to the state form of community." [Note by Plekhanov to the 1905 edition.]

ing only "contracts." "There is no need for laws voted by a majority or unanimously," he says in his *Idée générale de la Révolution au XIX siècle*, "every citizen, every commune and corporation will establish their own particular laws." With such a view of the matter, the political program of the proletariat was simplified to the extreme. The state, which recognizes only general laws compulsory for all citizens, could not even be a means for attaining socialist ideals. Making use of it for their aims, the socialists only consolidate the evil by the rooting out of which "social liquidation" should begin. The state must "decline," thus affording "every citizen, every commune and corporation" full freedom to decree "their own particular laws" and to conclude the "contracts" which they require. . . .

The task of the Russian anarchists was simplified still more. "The destruction of the state" (which little by little replaced in the anarchist program its "decline" recommended by Proudhon) was to clear the way for the development of the "ideals" of the Russian people. And as community land tenure and organization of crafts into cartels occupy a very prominent place in these "ideals," it was presumed that the "autonomous" Russians of democratic origin would conclude their "contracts," not in the spirit of Proudhon's reciprocity, but rather of agrarian communism. As "born socialists," the Russian people would not be long in understanding that mere community land tenure does not guarantee the desired "equality" and would be forced to set about organizing "autonomous communities" on completely communist foundations.

The Russian anarchists, however—at least those of the so-called "rebel" shade—bothered little about the economic consequences of the popular revolution they preached. They considered it their duty to remove those social conditions which, in their opinion, hindered the normal development of national life; but they did not ask themselves which road that development would take once it was freed from external hindrances. That this peculiar refashioning of the famous motto of the Manchester School, *laissez faire, laissez passer*, to make it look revolutionary, precluded all possibility of seriously ap-

praising the contemporary condition of our social and
economic life and did away with every criterion for determining even the concept of the "normal" course of its
development—this did not occur either to "rebels" or to
the "Narodniks" (Populists) who appeared later. At the
same time it would be utterly hopeless to attempt such an
appraisal as long as Proudhon's teachings remained the
point of departure of our revolutionaries' considerations.
The weakest point of those teachings, the point in which
they offend logic, is the concept of commodity and of
exchange value, i.e., those very premises on which alone
the correct conclusions about the mutual relations of the
products in the future economic organization can be
based. From the standpoint of Proudhon's theories, no
special importance attaches to the circumstance that contemporary Russian village community land tenure by no
means precludes commodity production. The Proudhonist
has no inkling of the "inner, inevitable dialectics" which
transform commodity production at a definite stage of its
development into . . . capitalist production. And that is
why it did not occur to his Russian cousin to ask himself
whether the divided efforts of "autonomous" persons,
communes, and corporations would suffice for the struggle against this tendency of commodity production which
threatens one fine day to supply a certain proportion of
the "born" Communists with "honorably acquired" capi-
tals and to turn them into exploiters of the remaining
masses of the population. . . .

We cannot enter here into a detailed analysis of anarchism in general or of Bakuninism in particular. We
wish merely to point out that both Proudhon and the
Russian anarchists were completely right from their point
of view when they raised "political noninterference" to
the position of main dogma in their practical program.
The social and political composition of Russian life in
particular, it seemed, justified the negation of "politics"
which is compulsory for all anarchists. Before entering
the field of political agitation, the *inhabitant of Russia
has to become a citizen,* i.e., to win for himself at least
some political rights, and first of all, of course, the right
to think as he pleases and to say what he thinks. Such a

task amounts in practice to a political revolution, and the experience of Western Europe has clearly "shown" all anarchists that such revolutions have not brought, do not and cannot bring any benefit to the people. As for the consideration that the people must be educated politically by taking part in their country's public life, that could not be put into practice, if only for the reason that the anarchists consider, as we have already seen, that such participation is not education, but perversion of the popular masses: it develops in the "belief in the state" and therefore the tendency to statehood, or, as the late M. A. Bakunin would have said, "infects them with its official and social venom, and, in any case, distracts them at least for a short time from what is now the only useful and salutary matter—from revolt." And at the same time, according to the philosophy of history of our "rebels," it appeared that the Russian people had shown its antistate tendency by a whole series of large and small movements and could therefore be considered mature enough politically. So down with all "dabbling in politics!" Let us help the people in its antistate struggle. Let us unite its dispersed efforts in one revolutionary stream—and then the awkward edifice of the state will crash, opening by its fall a new era of social freedom and economic equality. These few words expressed the whole program of our "rebels."

In this sketchy review of the programs of the different groups of Russian revolutionaries we must not forget that the views according to which "all constitutions" were only more or less unprofitable contracts with the devil, as old F. H. Jacobi put it—such views, we say, were typical not only of the Narodniks and anarchists. If the reader knows about Frederick Engels' polemic with P. Tkachov, he will probably remember that the editor of *Nabat* (a Narodnik journal), who disagreed with the Bakuninists on the question of practical struggle, was in perfect agreement with them on their basic views about the social and political condition of our country. He looked at it through the same prism of Russian exceptionalism and the "inborn communist tendencies of the Russian people." Like a genuine Blanquist, he did not deny "politics," of course, but he understood it exclusively as a plot whose purpose is to seize state power. This purpose, it seems, occupied the whole field of vision of our Blanquists of that time and led them to many contradictions. To remain consistent, they had to admit that their activity could be useful to the cause of progress only in the exceptional case that the blow they dealt would not deviate a hair's breadth from its target. If their plot is discovered or the revolutionary government is overthrown by the Liberal Party, the Russian people, far from winning anything, will risk losing much. The last of the supposed cases is particularly disastrous. The liberals will establish a strong government which will be far more difficult to fight than the modern "absolutely absurd" and "absurdly absolute" monarchy while "the fire of economic progress" will destroy the radical bases of the people's life. Under its influence, exchange will develop, capitalism will consolidate itself, the very principle of the village community will be destroyed—in a word, the river of time will wash away the stone from which the communist heaven is within hand's reach. In cases of failure, the Russian Blanquists would be bound to inflict terrible damage on the cause of popular emancipation and thus fall into the tragic position of William Tell, who had to risk the life of his own son. . . .

Such a narrow and hopeless philosophy of Russian history was bound to lead logically to the amazing conclusion that Russia's economic backwardness was a most reliable ally of the revolution and that stagnation was to be blazoned as the first and only paragraph of our "minimum program." Every day brings us new enemies, creates new social factors hostile to us, we read in the first, November issue of *Nabat* for 1875. "Fire is creeping up to our state forms, too. Now these are dead, lifeless. Economic progress will stir life in them, will breathe into them a new spirit, will give them the strength and the fortitude which they have so far lacked," and so forth. But if Joshua succeeded, as the Bible relates, in stopping the sun "for ten degrees," the time of miracles has passed and there is not a single party which could shout: "Stop, productive forces! Do not move, capitalism!" History pays as little attention to the fears of revolutionaries as to the jeremiads of reaction. "Economic progress" does its work without waiting for the anarchists or the Blanquists to put their intentions into practice. Every factory founded in Petersburg, every new wageworker employed by a Yaroslavl handicraftsman strengthens the "flame of progress," which is supposed to be fatal to the revolution, and consequently decreases the probability of popular victory. Can such a view of the mutual relations of the various social forces in Russia be called revolutionary? We do not think so. In order to make themselves revolutionary in substance and not in name alone, the Russian anarchists, Narodniks, and Blanquists should first of all have revolutionized their own heads, and to do so they should have learned to understand the course of historical development. . . .

Can our revolutionaries really seize power and retain it, if only for a short time, or is all talk of this nothing else than cutting the skin of a bear that has not been killed and which, by force of circumstances, is not even going to be killed? That is a question which has recently become an urgent one for revolutionary Russia. . . .

Let us hasten to make a reservation. We do not belong to the opponents in principle of such an act as the seizure of power by a revolutionary party. In our opinion that is the last, and what is more, the absolutely inevitable conclusion to be drawn from the political struggle which every class striving for emancipation must undertake at a definite stage in social development. Having gained political domination, a revolutionary class will retain that domination and be relatively secure against the blows of reaction only when it uses against reaction the mighty weapon of state power.

But there is no more difference between heaven and earth than between the dictatorship of a class and that of a revolutionary clique. This applies in particular to the dictatorship of the working class, whose present task is not only to overthrow the political domination of the unproductive classes in society, but also to do way with the anarchy now existing in production and consciously to organize all functions of social and economic life. The

mere *understanding* of this task calls for an advanced
working class with political experience and education, a
working class free from bourgeois prejudices and able to
discuss its situation by itself. In addition to this, its *solution* presupposes that socialist ideas are spread among the
proletariat and that the proletariat is conscious of its own
strength and confident in victory. But *such* a proletariat
will not allow even the sincerest of its well-wishers to
seize power. It will not allow it for the simple reason that
it has been to the school of political education with the
firm intention of finishing it at some time and coming
forward as an independent figure in the arena of historical life, not to pass eternally from one guardianship to
another; it will not allow it because such a guardianship
would be unnecessary, as the proletariat could then solve
the problem of the socialist revolution itself; and finally it
will not allow it because such a guardianship would be
harmful, for the conscious participation of the producers
in organizing production cannot be replaced by any conspiratorial skill, any daring or self-sacrifice on the part of
the conspirators. The mere thought that the social problem can be solved in practice by anybody but the workers themselves shows complete misunderstanding of this
problem, irrespective of whether the idea is held by an
"Iron Chancellor" or a revolutionary organization. Once
the proletariat has understood the conditions of its emancipation and is mature to emancipate itself, it will take
state power in its own hands in order to finish off its
enemies and build up social life, not, of course, on the
basis of *an*-archy, which would bring new disasters, but
of *pan*-archy, which will give all adult members of society the possibility to take part in the discussion and
settlement of social matters. And until the working class
is sufficiently developed to be able to fulfill its great
historical task, the duty of its supporters is to accelerate
the process of its development, to remove the obstacles
preventing its strength and its consciousness from growing and not to invent social experiments and vivisection,
the outcome of which is always more than doubtful.

That is how we understand the seizure of power in the
socialist revolution. Applying this point of view to Rus-

sian reality we must admit that we by no means believe in the early possibility of a socialist government in Russia. . . .

Considering all that has been said we think that only one aim of the Russian socialists would not be fantastic now: to achieve free political institutions, on the one hand, and to create elements for the setting up of the future *workers' socialist party* of Russia, on the other. They must put forward the demand for a democratic constitution which shall guarantee the workers the "rights of citizen" as well as the "rights of man" and give them, by universal suffrage, the possibility to take an active part in the political life of the country. Without trying to scare anybody with the yet remote "red specter," such a political program would arouse sympathy for our revolutionary party among all those who are not systematic enemies of democracy; it could be subscribed to by very many representatives of our liberalism as well as by the socialists. And whereas the seizure of power by some secret revolutionary organization will always be the work only of that organization and of those who are initiated in its plans, agitation for the program mentioned would be a matter for the whole of Russian society, in which it would intensify the conscious striving for political emancipation. Then the interests of the liberals would indeed "force" them to "act jointly with the socialists against the government," because they would cease to meet in revolutionary publications the assurance that the overthrow of absolutism would be the signal for a social revolution in Russia. At the same time another less timid and more sober section of liberal society would no longer see revolutionaries as unpractical youths who set themselves unrealizable and fantastic plans. This view, which is disadvantageous for revolutionaries would give place to the respect of society not only for their heroism but also for their political maturity. This sympathy would gradually grow into active support, or more probably into an independent social movement, and then the hour of absolutism's fall would strike at last. The socialist party would play an extremely honorable and beneficial role in this emancipation movement. Its glorious past, its selflessness and

energy would give weight to its demands, and it would
at least stand chances of thus winning *for the people*
the possibility of political development and education and
for itself the right to address its propaganda openly to the
people and to organize them openly into a separate
party.

George Plekhanov

Anarchist Tactics and Morality

The following item is a slightly condensed chapter from Anarchism and Socialism, *originally published in 1895.*

The anarchists are utopians. Their point of view has nothing in common with that of modern socialism. But there are Utopias and Utopias. The great utopians of the first half of the 19th century were men of genius; they helped forward social science, which in their time was still entirely utopian. The utopians of today, the anarchists, are the abstracters of quintessence, who can only fully draw forth some poor conclusions from certain mummified principles. . . . Their "profound thinkers," their "lofty theorists," do not even succeed in making the two ends of their reasoning meet. They are the *decadent* utopians, stricken with incurable intellectual anaemia. The great utopians did much for the development of the working-class movement. The utopians of our days do nothing but retard its progress. And it is especially their so-called tactics that are harmful to the proletariat.

We already know that Bakunin interpreted the Rules of the first International in the sense that the working class must give up all political action and concentrate its efforts upon the domain of the "immediately economic" struggle for higher wages, a reduction of the hours of labour, and so forth. Bakunin himself felt that such tactics were not very revolutionary. He tried to complete them through the action of his Alliance; he preached riots.* But the more the class consciousness of the proletariat develops, the more it inclines towards political action and give up the "riots," so common during its infancy. It is more difficult to induce the working men of Western Europe, who have attained to a certain degree of political development, to riot, than, for example, the credulous and ignorant Russian peasants. As the proletariat has shown no taste for the tactics of "riot," the Companions have been forced to replace it by "individual anarchist action." It was especially after the attempted insurrection at Benevento in Italy in 1877 that the Bakuninists began to glorify the "propaganda of deed." But if we glance back at the period that separates us from the attempt of Benevento, we shall see that this propaganda too assumed a special form: very few "riots," and these quite insignificant, a great many personal attempts against public edifices, against individuals, and even against property—"individually hereditary," of course. It could not be otherwise.

"We have already seen numerous revolts by people who wished to obtain urgent reforms," says Louise Michel, in an interview with a correspondent of the *Matin*. . . . "What was the result? The people were shot down. Well, we think the people have been sufficiently bled; it is better large-hearted people should sacrifice themselves, and, at their own risk, commit acts of violence whose object is to terrorise the Government and the bourgeois."

This is exactly what we have said—only in slightly different words. Louise Michel has forgotten to say that revolts, causing the bloodshed of the people, figured at the head of the anarchists' program until the anarchists became convinced, not that these partial risings in no way serve the cause of the workers, but that the workers, for the most part, will not have anything to do with these risings.

---

* In their dreams of riots and even of the revolution, the anarchists burn with real passion and delight all title deeds of property and all governmental documents. It is Kropotkin especially who attributed immense importance to these *autos-da-fé*. Really, one would think him a rebellious civil servant.

Error has its logic as well as truth. Once you reject the political action of the working class, you are fatally driven—provided you do not wish to serve the bourgeois politicians, to accept the tactics of the Vaillants and the Henrys. The so-called "independent" members of the German Socialist Party have proved this in their own persons. They began by attacking "parliamentarism," and to the "reformist" tactics of the "old" members they opposed—on paper, of course—the "revolutionary struggle," the purely "economic" struggle. But this shruggle, developing naturally, must inevitably bring about the entry of the proletariat into the arena of political struggles. Not wishing to come back to the very starting-point of their negation, the Independents, for a time, preached what they called "political demonstrations," a new kind of old Bakuninist riots. As riots, by whatever name they are called, always come too late for the fiery "revolutionists," there was only left to the Independents to "march forward," to become converts to anarchy, and to propagate —in words—the propaganda of deed. . . .

Kropotkin turns the materialist conception of history against the Social Democrats. "To each new economical phase of life corresponds a new political phase," he assures us. "Absolute monarchy—that is court rule—corresponded to the system of serfdom. Representative government corresponds to capital rule. Both, however, are class rule. But in a society where the distinction between capitalist and labourer has disappeared, there is no need of such a government; it would be an anachronism, a nuisance." If Social Democrats were to tell him they know this at least as well as he does, Kropotkin would reply that possibly they do, but that then they will not draw a logical conclusion from these premises. He, Kropotkin, is your real logician. Since the political constitution of every country is determined by its economic condition, he argues, the political action of socialists is absolute nonsense. "To seek to attain socialism or even (!) an agrarian revolution by means of a political revolution, is the merest Utopia, because the whole of history shows us that political changes flow from the great economic revolutions, and not *vice versa*. . . ." Basing his argument upon this impregnable foundation, Kropotkin advises the Russian revolutionists to give up their political struggle against Tzarism. They must follow an "immediately economic end." "The emancipation of the Russian peasants from the yoke of serfdom that has until now weighed upon them, is therefore the first task of the Russian revolutionist. In working along these lines he directly and immediately works for the good of the people. . . . and he moreover prepares for the weakening of the centralised power of the state and for its limitation."

Thus the emancipation of the peasants will have prepared the way for the weakening of Russian Tzarism. But how to emancipate the peasants before overthrowing Tzarism? Absolute mystery! . . .

However this may be, the whole political action of the working class must be summed up in these few words: "No politics! Long live the purely economic struggle!" This is Bakuninism, but perfected Bakuninism. Bakunin himself urged the workers to fight for a reduction of the hours of labour and higher wages. The anarchists of our day seek to "make the workers understand that they have nothing to gain from such child's play as this, and that society can only be transformed by destroying the institutions which govern it." The raising of wages is also useless. "North America and South America, are they not there to prove to us that whenever the worker has succeeded in getting higher wages, the prices of articles of consumption have increased proportionately, and that where he has succeeded in getting 20 francs a day for his wages, he needs 25 to be able to live according to the standard of the better class workman, so that he is always below the average?" The reduction of the hours of labour is at any rate superfluous since capital will always make it up by a "systematic intensification of labour by means of improved machinery. Marx himself has demonstrated this as clearly as possible" (J. Grave).

We know, thanks to Kropotkin, that the anarchist ideal has a double origin. And all the anarchist "demonstrations" also have a double origin. On the one hand, they are drawn from the vulgar hand books of political economy, written by the most vulgar bourgeois economists, e.g., Grave's dissertation upon wages, which Bastiat would have applauded enthusiastically. On the other hand, the "Companions," remembering the somewhat Communist origin of their ideal, turn to Marx and quote, without understanding, him. Even Bakunin has been "sophisticated" by Marxism. The latter-day anarchists, with Kropotkin at their head, have been even more sophisticated. . . .

All this would be very ridiculous, if it were not too sad, as the Russian poet Lermontoff says. And it is sad indeed. Whenever the proletariat makes an attempt to somewhat ameliorate its economic position, "large-hearted people," vowing they love the proletariat most tenderly, rush in from all points of the compass, and depending on their halting syllogisms, put spokes into the wheel of the movement, do their utmost to prove that the movement is useless. We have had an example of this with regard to the eight-hour day, which the anarchists combatted, whenever they could, with a zeal worthy of a better cause. When the proletariat takes no notice of this and pursues its "immediately economic" aims undisturbed—as it has the fortunate habit of doing—the same "large-hearted people" reappear upon the scene armed with bombs and provide the government with the desired and sought-for pretext for attacking the proletariat. We have seen this in Paris on May 1, 1890; we have seen it often during strikes. Fine fellows these "large-hearted men"!

An anarchist will have nothing to do with "parliamentarism," since it only lulls the proletariat to sleep. He will have none of "reforms," since reforms are but so many compromises with the possessing classes. He wants the revolution, a "full, complete, immediate, and immediately economic" revolution. To attain this end, he arms himself with a saucepan full of explosive materials and throws it amongst the public in a theatre or a café. He declares this is the "revolution." For our own part it seems to us nothing but "immediate" madness.

It goes without saying that the bourgeois governments, whilst inveighing against the authors of these attempts, cannot but congratulate themselves upon these tactics. "Society is in danger!" *Caveant consules!* And the police "consuls" become active, and public opinion applauds all the reactionary measures resorted to by ministers in order to "save society." . . .

Kropotkin would have us believe that anarchist morality, a morality free from all obligations or sanctions, opposed to all utilitarian calculations, is the same as the natural morality of the people, "the morality from the habit of well doing." The morality of the anarchists is that of persons who look upon all human action from the abstract point of view of the unlimited rights of the individual, and who, in the name of these rights, pass a verdict of "not guilty" on the most atrocious deeds, the most revoltingly arbitrary acts. "What matter the victims," exclaimed the anarchist poet Laurent Tailhade, at the banquet of the "Plume" Society, "provided the gesture is beautiful?"

Tailhade is a decadent, who, because he is blasé has the courage of his anarchist opinions. In fact the anarchists combat democracy because democracy, according to them, is nothing but the tyranny of the majority as against the minority. The majority has no right to impose its wishes upon the minority. But if this is so, in the name of what moral principle do the anarchists revolt against the bourgeoisie? Because the bourgeoisie are not a minority? Or because they do not do what they "will" to do?

"Do as thou would'st," proclaim the anarchists. The bourgeoisie "want" to exploit the proletariat, and do it remarkably well. They thus follow the anarchist precept, and the "Companions" are very wrong to complain of their conduct. They become altogether ridiculous when they combat the bourgeoisie in the name of their victims. "What matters the death of vague human beings," continues the Anarchist logician Tailhade, "if thereby the individual affirms himself?" Here we have the true morality of the anarchists; it is also that of the crowned heads.

Thus in the name of the revolution, the anarchists serve —the cause of reaction; in the name of morality they approve the most immoral acts; in the name of individual liberty they trample under foot all the rights of their fellows.

And this is why the whole anarchist doctrine founders

upon its own logic. If any maniac may, because he "wants" to, kill as many men as he likes, society, composed of an immense number of individuals, may certainly bring him to his senses, not because it is its caprice, but because it is its duty, because such is the *conditio sine qua non* of its existence.

George Plekhanov

Absolutism in Russia*

The following essay, here translated into English for the first time, has a special importance in the history of socialist thought. Though, on the surface, it is merely a dispute of one Russian socialist with another over the "agrarian question," the work actually anticipates some of the most crucial problems of twentieth-century politics.

Plekhanov was arguing against those Russian socialists who proposed to nationalize the land in the coming revolution. He, instead, favored the distribution of the land among the peasants, even though he recognized that such a policy would be "bourgeois" in character. He argued that in a country like Russia the division of the land among independent peasants, despite its many disadvantages, would "deal a deathblow to our old order, in which both the land and the men who tilled it were the property of the state, and which is nothing but the Muscovite version of the economic order on which all the great Oriental despotisms are founded" (emphasis added).

There was already, said Plekhanov, too much of "the Chinese system" in Russian society, too much of that state despotism that served, in his later formulation, as "the economic foundation of Caesarism." A further concentration of land ownership in the hands of the state, even a "progressive" state, would contribute toward a new despotism in a traditional Russian style. How suggestive and even prescient Plekhanov was, the history of totalitarianism in Russia indicates.

---

* Title supplied by editor.

In the translation that follows, most of Plekhanov's
rather heavy-handed polemical thrusts have been cut,
but the line of his argument remains unobstructed.
The original version, entitled "On the Agrarian Ques-
tion in Russia," appeared in Drevnik Sotsialdemok-
rata, February, 1906.

In the November, 1905, edition of Pravda Comrade Maslov discusses the agrarian question. . . .

He says that the transfer of the landlords' land into the
hands of the peasants "may have enormous progressive or
reactionary significance, according to the hands into
which these lands fall. In France, the transfer of the lands
confiscated by the Revolution to the petty bourgeoisie, as
its private property, made that bourgeoisie produce vast
numbers of adherents to Bonapartism and believers in
bourgeois 'order.' The division or sale of these lands only
turns tens of thousands of landlords into hundreds of
thousands of new landlords, which, obviously, could only
play into the hands of reaction."

First, a word about France. It is true that the petty
bourgeoisie, which obtained a part of the lands confiscated by the Revolution—not all of it, as Maslov seems to
think—*subsequently* often played a reactionary part. But
since we are talking about the petty bourgeoisie, Maslov
should explain the role it played *during* the Revolution.
This is important in our particular case. And he would
also do well to explain to us the precise historical significance of the confiscation of lands carried out by the
French Revolution.

Should it be considered reactionary? If so, then we
should have to change our entire concept of the economic
meaning of the great French storm. We would have to
regret the confiscation itself, which dealt such a heavy
blow to the economic foundation of the old order, we
should have to regret that petty-bourgeois property replaced the big feudal estates. We would even have to
regret that the Revolution took place at all, because
undoubtedly it "could only play into the hands of reaction."

But perhaps we should regret something else altogether? Namely, the fact that the Great French Revolution was a *bourgeois* revolution? . . . But this would mean "to play into the hands of" a utopian conception of history.

The great upheaval that took place in France at the end of the eighteenth century had an enormous progressive significance in both cities and countryside. In both places, it abolished obsolete relationshps of production, characteristic of the "old order," and replaced them with bourgeois relationships. This gave a great impetus to the economic development of France and, through the economic, to the political. . . . If any country should find itself today in a situation like that of France at the end of the eighteenth century, and history put to it the dilemma of choosing between the relationships of production characteristic of the "old order" and the transfer of land from the landlords to the petty bourgeoisie, then not a single socialist could hesitate about his choice—nor would he have the right to wash his hands like Pontius Pilate. He would have the duty to promote, by all means at his disposal, the downfall of the semifeudal relationships of production and their replacement by bourgeois relationships.

And what if Russia should be in exactly that situation? It may be objected that Russia today, unlike France in the eighteenth century, has a proletarian party. I do not forget this. But I am assuming that in the "committee" or in the authority that decides on the agrarian question, the proposal of the proletarian party will have fallen through, so that a choice has now to be made among the proposals of other, nonproletarian parties. . . . The question will now be: nationalization of the land or transfer of the confiscated lands to peasants as their property?

After all, Maslov himself recognizes that the landlords' right to their lands expresses itself only in their exploitation of their tenants. But if things are so, then the expropriation of the landlords can only raise the living standards of the peasants who lease their lands. And this, in turn, will not hurt the economic position of the country but, on the contrary, improve it.

If, then, we have to choose between nationalization and division of lands, we must choose division. To be sure, it would have many disadvantages from our point of view. But, compared to nationalization, it has the very great advantage, *that it would deal a deathblow to our old order, in which both the land and the men who tilled it were the property of the state, and which is nothing but the Muscovite version of the economic order on which all the great Oriental despotisms are founded.* Nationalization of land would mean an attempt to restore that order, which had already received some serious blows in the eighteenth century and which was severely shaken by the course of economic development in the second half of the nineteenth.

If our present-day peasant movement represents a danger to the further economic development of Russia, it is only to the extent that it could lead to the restoration of the above-mentioned order, and we are entitled to fear its consequences to that extent. Fortunately, this tendency, though it undoubtedly exists, has few chances of victory.

This needs explaining.

You may have read, in the seventh volume of the geography of Elisee Reclus, the pages on China. If you did, you will surely remember the curious story of how, after many peripeties which produced revolutions and changes of dynasty, the Chinese "socialists" abandoned the idea of common property in land ("as it had existed before") and "attempted to introduce a new system." In 1069 A.D. Wang An-Shih, friend and counselor of the then Chinese Emperor Cheu-Tsung, issued a decree abolishing private property. By this decree the state became the sole proprietor and undertook the distribution of all products whose production was managed by government officials. This measure provoked a strong opposition of the mandarins and the former big landlords, but Wang An-Shih—according to Reclus—maintained his system of state communism for fifteen years. "But a change of ruler was sufficient to abolish the new regime, which corresponded as little to the desires of the people as to the aspirations of highly placed persons, and which produced a whole class of inquisitors who became real landlords."

Reclus says that this communist attempt of the Chinese imperial court was the greatest of all government attempts to transform the social system. This remark was

not made without reflection. The anarchist Reclus is aiming at the Social Democrats whose aspirations assume, in
the minds of the anarchists, the form of Chinese "communism." The story of Wang An-Shih's policy is, obviously, told as a new argument against the alleged state
socialism of international Social Democracy. It is a pity
that this argument cannot survive serious criticism.

I will ignore the fact that the methods by which Social
Democrats realize thier aspirations have nothing in common with decrees issued by more or less people-loving
imperial courts. But the whole attempt to draw an analogy between the internal history of China and the history
of a nineteenth century Western European society is a
sign of great naiveté. Reclus was a pretty good geogra-
pher but a bad sociologist. He uncritically took over the
story of the "communist" revolution in the eleventh century, and yet there is, even in his own account, enough
material to reduce the truth contained in that story to its
proper proportions.

It is clear from his own account that the history of
China, for over 1,000 years, "coincided with the history of
land ownership and that its most original feature was,
therefore, the struggle for the land between the people
and the feudal landlords." It is also clear from it that
already in the ninth century A.D. a law was passed by
which land was proclaimed the property of the government. This was as much a "communist" revolution as the
attempt of Wang An-Shih. True, the latter also applied,
according to Reclus, to movable property. But that this is
so is more than doubtful. It is much more likely that the
information about the revolution carried out by Wang
An-Shih refers to undertakings something like the government farms which the authorities started among us, to the
great dissatisfaction of the peasants, in portions of medieval Russia. However, these Russian undertakings were
clearly on a much larger scale and were preceded by a
distribution of land throughout the country, which seriously affected the interests of the landlords who farmed
their lands by feudal law. In any case, given the economic condition of China, this revolution could only have
been agrarian and should be viewed only as an episode in
the history of the public economy of China. And it is

clear from our rejection of the nationalization of land how unattractive this episode is to Social Democrats in their analogous attempts. . . .

For our part, we expect nothing except bad things from the undertaking of the Russian Wang An-Shihs, but will concentrate our efforts upon making them politically and economically impossible.

We must, however, admit, to our sorrow, that there has been quite a lot of "Chineseness" in the agrarian history of Muscovite Russia. Under the influence of many unfavorable historical conditions—among the most important, economic backwardness and the Tartar yoke—property in land gradually passed from the landlords to the Grand Duke (later the Tsar), who used the land as a kind of reserve fund to provide for the needs of the state. The St. Petersburg period of Russian history perfected and systematized what the Moscow period had started. As far as the interests of the peasants were concerned, the well-known "window to Europe" (i.e., St. Petersburg, in Pushkin's famous phase) brought no substantial change in the government's agrarian policy.

As regards the landlords' interests, there has been, on the contrary, a substantial change, which undoubtedly influenced the psychology of the peasantry. But before we deal with the change, and in order to understand its influence, we must recall that, for a considerable period of time, there were two parallel processes: the peasants were turned into serfs of the state; and the old patrimonial landlords had their rights curtailed and were gradually equalized with the new type of landlord who owed service to the state. (Ivan the Terrible is known to have been largely responsible for this change.) The result was that the population of Russia was divided into government orphans (peasants and other taxable people), government bondmen (people liable to state service), and government prayermen (the clergy). "Given the political and economic situation at the time, the ownership of land was the necessary condition for properly performing military service as it then existed," writes the historian, Klyuchevsky. This is true not only of military service, but also of any kind of service. . . .

And so the Russian state gradually became the Leviathan of which Hobbes had dreamed, the Leviathan who gives each person a piece of land, with due regard to his occupation and position. It is hardly necessary to point out that our notorious common ownership of land in the village, with its periodic redistributions, was a substantial consequence of the enslavement of both land and peasant by the state. The old prejudice about this system is by now destroyed in Russian and Western European science. But it is still necessary to deal with the following important circumstance.

If the possession of land is a necessity for the "taxable people," so that they may fulfill their duty to the state, the "government orphans" also need—in their own orphanly way, to be sure—a new distribution of land whenever a "land squeeze" occurs. It is also natural that the new government tries, as much as it can, to fill this need by giving the peasants new, empty lands, sending them to "new places," or remedying inequalities of landholding through redistributions. We all know the importance of "revisions" in the lives of government peasants. . . .

But that is not all. If land ownership was an essential condition of service for the "government bondmen," then it was logical to take away the land of any "bondman" who did not serve. This was the situation of the entire "serving nobility" when "freedom" relieved them of their obligation to serve.

And so a thought dawned in the heads of the "orphans": why should the "gentlemen" still own their estates? As their need for land increased, the "orphans" tended to answer that these estates were a crying injustice which would soon be remedied. They hoped for the "black division" [of land]. When these hopes were disappointed, the "orphans" helped themselves to the gentlemen's land, just as they had helped themselves to their common lands, without waiting for a new revision.

We are told that our present agrarian unrest is due to the influence of revolutionary propaganda. To begin with, this influence is not big enough to explain all cases of agrarian "disorder." And, then, the question arises: why could the revolutionaries influence the peasants in that particular direction? What made it possible for the revolutionaries?

This is my answer: the peasant psychology has been historically formed by the nationalization of land. That psychology existed long before the peasants were subjected to revolutionary propaganda. It was produced not by revolutionaries but by the "history of the Russian state." This psychology showed itself even in last year's famous "peasant congresses." If the majority of the delegates so easily agreed that the landlords should be given no compensation for their lands, it is because the peasants were convinced that the landlords had originally received their lands from the state. As the delegate from Smolensk put it: "You received it as a gift; you should return it as a gift." . . .

When the peasant who is not affected by revolutionary propaganda—and very few of them are—talks about the necessity of taking land from the landlords, it does not enter his head that he is shaking any foundations. Quite the contrary! He views himself as the preserver of the economic foundation, hallowed by the course of centuries, because the Russian state rested on it for centuries. He quite sincerely views the landlords who resist the distribution of land as rebels. And in a certain sense—in the sense of his conscious striving—he is indeed a preserver. What is more, if he should successfully reestablish that economic foundation of our old government order, the wheel of Russian history would make a strong backward turn.

That is why, when we support the peasant demands, we must not for one monent forget the reactionary side of the peasant movement. It is obvious that we must "resist" that part, even though we are not officials of the Ministry of Internal Affairs. We must come out for the distribution of land because it is required of us by the interests of the working class and of the whole social and political development of Russia. The Smolensk delegate to one of the peasant congresses said: "The Tsars took the land from the people and gave it to their retainers." What should be done then? Take the land from the "retainers." Apart from that, the congresses said nothing. After that, their resolutions enter an area in which Utopia prevails: everybody "receives" as much land as he needs, etc. But, after all, the Chinese social upheavals took land from the "retainers" and returned to the Leviathan state, after which history repeated itself by spawning new "retainers," who caused new upheavals and revived the old "Chineseness."

We do not need "Chineseness." This is why we support the peasant movement only to the extent that it destroys the old and does not attempt to create something that would make the old, by comparison, a new and progressive phenomenon.

It is easy now to establish the general leading principles of our "economic policy." We try to remove the bourgeois relationships of production where we can replace them by others, our own; but we prepare the way for them, where the choice is between them and obsolete, prebourgeois relationships.

TRANSLATED BY I. A. LANGNAS

Jean Jaurès

From the Rights of Man to Socialism

Jean Jaurès (1859–1914) was the leader of French socialism during the early years of this century. He was assassinated by a chauvinist gunman, and his death marked the end of all the hopes that European socialism, presumably inspired by international sentiments, might keep the great powers from launching a ghastly world war.

It has been customary in radical circles to praise Jaurès as a brilliant personality, a scintillating orator, a fine leader, but meanwhile to condescend a little toward his intellectual powers, often because he was far from Marxist orthodoxy. But time is a cruel teacher. Many of the clogged Marxist tracts of theoreticians allegedly more profound than Jaurès are now all but unreadable, while his writings, for all their oratorical quality, retain a clear vision of the indissoluble link between democracy and socialism. "From the Rights of Man to Socialism," here translated into English for the first time, is taken from Volume II of his Oeuvres, 1901.

Only socialism will give the Declaration of the Rights of Man its entire meaning. Revolutionary bourgeois law has, indeed, freed the human personality from any shackles. But it forces new generations to pay a duty on the capital accumulated by their predecessors, and, by granting to a minority the right to collect that duty, it imposes upon human personality as a whole a kind of mortgage in favor of the past and to the advantage of a single class.

We, on the contrary, claim that all the means of production and wealth accumulated by humanity must be

213

put at the disposal of all human activities and help to make them free. We hold that every man has, from now onward, a right to all the means of development created by humanity. Man does not come into the world weak and naked, exposed to all kinds of oppressions and exploitations. He comes into it as a person vested with a right, who can claim for his entire development the free use of the work tools accumulated by the effort of humanity. Every individual has a right to demand of humanity everything that will aid his effort: he has the right to work, to produce, to create, and no category of men may draw usury from this work or put it under its yoke. And, since the community can assure the right of the individual only by putting the means of production at his disposal, the community must be vested with the sovereign right of property over these means. . . .

The Declaration of the Rights of Man was also an affirmation of life, an appeal to life. The French Revolution proclaimed in it the rights of living man. It did not grant to past humanity the right to bind present humanity. It did not grant to the past services of kings and nobles the right to weigh upon present and living humanity and check its growth. On the contrary, living humanity seized all the live forces bequeathed by the past and put them to its use. French unity, created by the kings, became the decisive weapon against the kings. Similarly, the big forces of production accumulated by the bourgeoisie will become the decisive weapon of human liberation against capitalist privilege.

Life does not abolish the past; it subdues it. The Revolution is not a break; it is a conquest. And when the proletariat achieves that conquest, when socialism is established, all the human effort accumulated through the centuries will be like a rich and benevolent nature receiving all persons from their birth and assuring them a full development.

This is why there is a root of socialism even in bourgeois revolutionary law, in the Declaration of the Rights of Man. But this internal logic of the idea of right and humanity would have remained dormant and ineffective without the vigorous external action of the proletariat. It intervened in the Revolution from its first days. It does

not listen to the absurd *class* advice of those who like
Marat tell it: "What are you doing? And why do you
march to take the Bastille, which never locked up proletarians?" The proletariat marched; it attacked; it decided
the success of the great days; it went to the frontiers; it
saved the Revolution at home and abroad; it became a
necessary force and picked up, on the way, the prize of
its unceasing action. In three years, from 1789 to 1792, it
turned a semibourgeois, semidemocratic regime into a
pure democracy, in which proletarian action is sometimes
dominant. By deploying its force, the proletariat becomes
self-confident; it ended by saying, with Baboeuf, that,
having created a common power, that of the nation, it
must use it to achieve the common welfare.

Thus socialism ceased to be a vague philosophical
speculation and became a living force. Socialism arose
from the French Revolution by the combined action of
two forces: the force of the idea of right, and the force of
the nascent proletarian action. So it is not an abstract
utopia. It surges from the most boiling and effervescent
hot springs of modern life.

After many trials, partial victories, and failures, the
new bourgeois order developed through a variety of political regimes. Under the Empire, during the Restoration,
the economic system of the bourgeoisie, founded upon
unlimited competition, began to produce its effects: an
undoubted increase of wealth, but also immorality, cunning, perpetual struggle, disorder, and oppression. The
genius of Fourier consisted in realizing that it was possible to remedy the disorder and to cleanse and order the
social system, not only without lowering the production
of wealth, but actually increasing it. It was not an ascetic
ideal, but rather a free scope for all talents, for all instincts. The same association that will abolish crises will
multiply wealth by coordinating and combining efforts.
The touch of asceticism, with which the Revolution dark-
ened socialism, was now mingled with the great current
of modern production and affluence. Through Fourier,
through Saint-Simon, socialism appeared as a force able
not only to repel capitalism, but to overtake it.

In the new order glimpsed by these men of genius,
justice will not be bought at the price of the joys of life.

On the contrary, the just organization of human forces
will increase their productive power. The splendor of
wealth will make manifest the victory of right, and joy
will be the radiance of justice. Baboeuf's idea had not
been the negation of the Revolution, but rather its bold-
est throb. In the same way, Fourierism and Saint-Simonism are not the negation or restriction of modern life, but
rather its passionate enlargement. Always and everywhere, socialism is a living force, moving with the ardent
current of life.

To these great dreams of harmony and wealth for all,
to these grand constructive designs of Fourier and Saint-
Simon, the bourgeoisie of Louis-Philippe replied with an
increased class exploitation, with an intensive and exhausting utilization of the strength of the workers, and
with an orgy of government concessions, monopolies, dividends, and premiums. It would have been naive, to say
the least, to fight this daring exploitation for any length
of time with idyllic dreams. Proudhon replied with a
bitter criticism of property, rent, and profit; here, too,
what had to be said was said from the bitter inspiration
and at the actual dictation of life.

But how can this work of criticism be completed by a
work of organization? How can all the social elements
menaced or oppressed by the powers of banks, monopolies, and capitalism group themselves into a vast fighting
unit? Proudhon quickly saw that the army of social democracy was heterogeneous, composed of a factory proletariat still insufficient in numbers and strength, a merchant and industrial petty bourgeoisie, and craftsmen
doomed but not yet abolished by capitalist concentration
and absorption. Hence the hesitations and contradictions
of the positive part of Proudhon's work; hence a strange
mixture of reaction and revolution as he tries to save by
factitious combinations the credit of the petty bourgeoisie
while he foresees the coming of the working class as the
revolutionary force. Proudhon would have liked to sus-
pend the course of history, to adjourn the revolutionary
crisis of 1848 to give economic revolution time to clarify
its outline and give human minds a better orientation.
These hesitations, these scruples, these contradictory ef-

forts could come only from the contact of sincere socialist thought with a complex and still uncertain reality.

In 1848, the grand, decisive, and substantial force manifested and organized itself. The growth of big industry stimulated the rise of a proletariat, ever more numerous, more coherent, more conscious. Those who, with Marx, hailed the coming of this decisive power, those who understood that it will transform the world, could exaggerate the speed of economic process. Less prudent than Proudhon, less aware than he of the powers of resistance and change of small industry, they could simplify the problem unduly and magnify the absorptive strength of concentrated capital.

But, with all the reservations and restrictions produced by the study of an ever-complex and multiplied reality, it remains true that the purely proletarian class is growing in numbers, that it represents an ever growing proportion of human societies, that it is grouped in ever vaster centers of production. And it remains true that this proletarian clan is prepared to conceive, through large-scale production, a large-scale property, whose *limit* is social property.

With Baboeuf, socialism had been the most ardent shiver of the democratic Revolution; with Fourier and Saint-Simon, the most magnificent enlargement of the promises of wealth and power that daring capitalism lavished upon the world; with Proudhon, the sharpest warning to the societies devoured by the bourgeoisie. Now socialism is, with and in the proletariat, the strongest of social powers. . . .

Socialism is not an arbitrary and utopian conception; it moves and develops in full reality; it is a great force of life, blended into the whole of life, and soon capable of directing life. To the imcomplete application of justice and human rights by the bourgeois and democratic Revolution, it has opposed the full and decisive interpretation of the Rights of Man. To the incomplete, narrow, and chaotic organization of wealth attempted by capitalism, it has opposed a magnificent conception of harmonious wealth, where the effort of each individual is strengthened by the mutual effort of all. To the aridity of bourgeois arrogance and egotism, shrunken by monopolist and elitist exploitation, it has opposed a revolutionary bitterness, an avenging and provoking irony, a deadly analysis that dissolves lies. Finally, to the social primacy of capital, it has opposed organization on ever-stronger class lines of a growing proletariat. . . .

While the real, substantial forces of socialism grow, the technical means of putting it into practice appear ever more definite. The nation is becoming more united and more sovereign; it is forced to take over more and more economic functions—a rough prelude to social property. In the great urban and industrial communities, democracy is becoming more and more involved in problems of property and administration of collective domains through questions of public hygiene, housing, lighting, education, and food supply. Cooperatives of all kinds, of consumers and of producers, are multiplying. Labor and professional organizations are growing and becoming more subtle and diversified. . . .

It is henceforth certain that capitalist privilege will not be replaced by the ponderous monopoly of a central bureaucracy. Rather, the nation, sovereign of property and guardian of the social right, will have innumerable organs —communes, cooperatives, unions—which will give social property the freest and subtlest of movements and harmonize with the infinite mobility and variety of individual forces. There exists a technical as well as a social and intellectual preparation for socialism. Those who, excited by the work already accomplished, believe that a socialist world can be created at once by decree, by a proletarian *fiat lux* (let there be light), are like children. But those who cannot see that an irresistible force of evolution spells the doom of the class system and of the reign of the bourgeoisie are mad.

TRANSLATED BY I. A. LANGNAS

Paul Lafargue

The Right to Be Lazy

> A French Socialist and the son-in-law of Marx, Paul
> Lafargue (1842–1911) wrote The Right to Be Lazy
> in 1883, partly as a jeu d'esprit but also partly as
> an effort to rid socialist thought of a residual puritan-
> ism concerning the virtues of work. Unlike many a
> weightier document, Lafargue's essay holds up ex-
> tremely well, anticipating many discussions of work
> and leisure that would occupy us in the second half
> of the twentieth century.

A strange delusion possesses the working classes of the
nations where capitalist civilization holds its sway. This
delusion drags in its train the individual and social woes
which for two centuries have tortured sad humanity. This
delusion is the love of work, the furious passion for work,
pushed even to the exhaustion of the vital force of the
individual and his progeny. Instead of opposing this mental aberration, the priests, the economists, and the moralists have cast a sacred halo over work. Blind and finite
men, they have wished to be wiser than their God; weak
and contemptible men, they have presumed to rehabili-
tate what their God had cursed. I, who do not profess to
be a Christian, an economist, or a moralist, I appeal from
their judgement to that of their God; from the preachings
of their religious, economic, or free-thought ethics to the
frightful consequences of work in capitalist society.

In capitalist society, work is the cause of all intellectual
degeneracy, of all organic deformity. Compare the thor-
ough-bred in Rothschild's stables, served by a retinue of

bipeds, with the heavy brute of the Norman farms that plows the earth, carts the manure, hauls the crops. Look at the noble savage whom the missionaries of trade and the traders of religion have not yet corrupted with Christianity, syphilis, and the dogma of work, and then look, at our miserable slaves of machines.

When, in our civilized Europe, we would find a trace of the native beauty of man, we must go seek it in the nations where economic prejudices have not yet uprooted the hatred of work. Spain, which, alas, is degenerating, may still boast of possessing fewer factories than we have of prisons and barracks; but the artist rejoices in his admiration of the hardy Andalusian, brown as his native chestnuts, straight and flexible as a steel rod; and the heart leaps at hearing the beggar, superbly draped in his ragged *capa*, parleying on terms of equality with the Duke of Ossuna. For the Spaniard, in whom the primitive animal has not been atrophied, work is the worst sort of slavery. The Greeks in their era of greatness had only contempt for work: their slaves alone were permitted to labor: the free man knew only exercises for the body and mind. And so it was in this era that men like Aristotle, Phidias, Aristophanes moved and breathed among the people; it was the time when a handful of heroes at Marathon crushed the hordes of Asia, soon to be subdued by Alexander. The philosophers of antiquity taught contempt for work, that degradation of the free man, the poets sang of idleness, that gift from the Gods.

Jesus, in his sermon on the Mount, preached idleness: "Consider the lilies of the field, how they grow: they toil not, neither do they spin: and yet I say unto you that even Solomon in all his glory was not arrayed like one of these." Jehovah the bearded and angry god, gave his worshipers the supreme example of ideal laziness; after six days of work, he rests for all eternity.

On the other hand, what are the races for which work is an organic necessity? The Auvergnians; the Scotch, those Auvergnians of the British Isles; the Galicians, those Auvergnians of Spain; the Pomeranians, those Auvergnians of Germany; the Chinese, those Auvergnians of

Asia. In our society, which are the classes that love work for work's sake? The peasant proprietors, the little shopkeepers; the former bent double over their fields, the latter crouched in their shops, burrow like the mole in his subterranean passage and never stand up to look at nature leisurely.

And meanwhile the proletariat, the great class embracing all the producers of civilized nations, the class which in freeing itself will free humanity from servile toil and will make of the human animal a free being,—the proletariat, betraying its instincts, despising its historic mission, has let itself be perverted by the dogma of work. Rude and terrible has been its punishment. All its individual and social woes are born of its passion for work.

We have seen that by diminishing the hours of labor new mechanical forces will be conquered for social production. Furthermore, by obliging the laborers to consume their products the army of workers will be immensely increased. The capitalist class once relieved from its function of universal consumer will hasten to dismiss its train of soldiers, magistrates, journalists, procurers, which it has withdrawn from useful labor to help it in consuming and wasting. Then the labor market will overflow. Then will be required an iron law to put a limit on work. It will be impossible to find employment for that swarm of former unproductives, more numerous than insect parasites, and after them must be considered all those who provide for their needs and their vain and expensive tastes. When there are no more lackeys and generals to decorate, no more free and married prostitutes to be covered with laces, no more cannons to bore, no more palaces to build, there will be need of severe laws to compel the working women and workingmen who have been employed on embroidered laces, iron workings, buildings, to take the hygienic and calisthenic exercises requisite to reestablish their health and improve their race. When once we begin to consume European products at home instead of sending them to the devil, it will be necessary that the sailors, dock handlers, and the draymen sit down and learn to twirl their thumbs. The happy Polynesians may then love as they like without fearing the civilized Venus and the sermons of European moralists.

And that is not all: In order to find work for all the nonproducers of our present society, in order to leave room for the industrial equipment to go on developing indefinitely, the working class will be compelled, like the capitalist class, to do violence to its taste for abstinence and to develop indefinitely its consuming capacities. Instead of eating an ounce or two of gristly meat once a day, when it eats any, it will eat juicy beefsteaks of a pound or two: instead of drinking moderately of bad wine, it will become more orthodox than the pope and will drink broad and deep bumpers of Bordeaux and Burgundy without commercial baptism and will leave water to the beasts.

The proletarians have taken into their heads to inflict upon the capitalists ten hours of forge and factory: that is their great mistake, because of social antagonisms and civil wars. Work ought to be forbidden and not imposed. The Rothschilds and other capitalists should be allowed to bring testimony to the fact that throughout their whole lives they have been perfect vagabonds, and if they swear they wish to continue to live as perfect vagabonds in spite of the general mania for work, they should be pensioned and should receive every morning at the city hall a five-dollar gold piece for their pocket money. Social discords will vanish. Bond holders and capitalists will be first to rally to the popular party, once convinced that far from wishing them harm, its purpose is rather to relieve them of the labor of over-consumption and waste, with which they have been overwhelmed since their birth. As for the capitalists who are incapable of proving their title to the name of vagabond, they will be allowed to follow their instincts. There are plenty of disgusting occupations in which to place them. . . .

But vengeance, harsh and prolonged, will be heaped upon the moralists who have perverted nature, the bigots, the canters, the hypocrites, and other such sects of men who disguise themselves like maskers to deceive the world. . . . On the days of great popular rejoicing, when instead of swallowing dust as on the 15th of August and 14th of July under capitalism, the communists and collectivists will eat, drink and dance to their hearts' content, the members of the Academy, of moral and political sciences, the priests with long robes and short, of the economic, Catholic, Protestant, Jewish, positivist and freethought church; the propagandists of Malthusianism, and of Christian, altruistic, independent, or dependent ethics, clothed in yellow, shall be compelled to hold a candle until it burns their fingers, shall starve in sight of tables loaded with meats, fruits and flowers and shall agonize with thirst in sight of flowing hogsheads. Four times a year with the changing seasons they shall be shut up like the knife grinders' dogs in great wheels and condemned to grind wind for ten hours.

The lawyers and legislators shall suffer the same punishment. Under the regime of idleness, to kill the time, which kills us second by second, there will be shows and theatrical performances always and always. And here we have the very work for our bourgeois legislators. We shall organize them into traveling companies to go to the fairs and villages, giving legislative exhibitions. The generals in riding boots, their breasts brilliantly decorated with medals and crosses, shall go through the streets and courts levying recruits among the good people. . . . If, uprooting from its heart the vice which dominates it and degrades its nature, the working class were to arise in its terrible strength, not to demand the Rights of Man, which are but the rights of capitalist exploitation, not to demand the Right to Work which is but the right to misery, but to forge a brazen law forbidding any man to work more than three hours a day, the earth, the old earth, trembling with joy would feel a new universe leaping within her. But how should we ask a proletariat corrupted by capitalist ethics, to take a manly resolution. . . .

Like Christ, the doleful personification of ancient slavery, the men, the women, and the children of the proletariat have been climbing painfully for a century up the hard Calvary of pain; for a century compulsory toil has broken their bones, bruised their flesh, tortured their nerves; for a century hunger has torn their entrails and their brains. O Laziness, have pity on our long misery! O Laziness, mother of the arts and noble virtues, be thou the balm of human anguish!

Eduard Bernstein

Crisis and Adjustment in Modern Economy

Eduard Bernstein (1850–1932) began his political career as an intellectual spokesman for the German Social Democratic party, soon to become the strongest section of the Socialist (Second) International. During the time of the German "anti-socialist laws" in the 1880's, Bernstein left Germany to spend two decades abroad, in Switzerland and England. He came under the strong influence of English parliamentary institutions and was greatly impressed by both the English unions and the Fabian (gradualist) socialists. In 1896, Bernstein began to publish a series of studies that would become the classic work of evolutionary or reformist socialism, Die Voraussetzungen des Sozialismus and die Aufgaben der Sozialdemokratie. An English translation appeared in 1900 under the title of Evolutionary Socialism. Bernstein argued that economic crises under capitalism could be averted or at least modulated by state action; that the traditional Marxist expectations of proletarian impoverishment and middle-class disintegration were turning out to be false; that parliamentary action, not proletarian dictatorship, was the road to socialist change. Though his views were officially condemned by the German party, most of the Social Democratic movements in Europe gradually took them over bit by bit. The two selections below from Evolutionary Socialism show Berstein engaged first in economic and then political analysis.

The contradictions inherent in the movement of capitalist society impress themselves upon the practical bourgeoisie most strikingly in the changes of the periodic cycle through which modern industry runs and whose crowning point is the universal crisis.—Marx, Preface to the second edition of *Capital*.

In socialist circles the most popular explanation of economic crises is their derivation from underconsumption. Friedrich Engels, however, has on several occasions combated this idea sharply—most sharply, probably, in the third part of the third chapter of the polemical treatise against Dühring, where Engels says that underconsumption by the masses may well be "also a condition of crises," but that it explains their presence today just as little as their former absence. Engels illustrates this by the conditions of the English cotton industry in the year 1877 and declares it to be a strong measure in the face of those conditions "to explain the present total stagnation in the sale of cotton yarns and textile fabrics by the underconsumption of the English masses and not by the over-production of the English cotton manufacturers."*

But Marx himself has also occasionally pronounced very sharply against the derivation of crises from underconsumption. "It is pure tautology," he writes in the second volume of *Capital*, "to say that crises rise from a want of consumers able to pay." If one wished to give this tautology an appearance of greater reality by saying that the working classes receive too small a portion of what they produce, and that the grievance would therefore be redressed if they had a larger share, it can only be observed that "the crises are each time preceded by a period in which the workers' wages rise and the working classes actually receive a relatively greater share than usual of the yearly produce destined for consumption." It thus would appear that capitalist production "includes conditions independent of good or evil intentions—conditions which only permit temporarily relative prosperity for the working classes and then always as a stormy bird

---

* Third edition, pp. 308, 309. [In a footnote to this Engels remarks: "The explanation of crises by underconsumption originated with Sismondi and had with him a certain justification." "Rodbertus," he says, "borrowed it from Sismondi and Dühring copied it from him." In the preface to the *Poverty of Philosophy*, Engels also argues in similar fashion against the theory of crises put forth by Rodbertus.]

of a crisis."* To which Engels adds in a footnote: "*Ad notam* for the adherents of Rodbertus' theory of crises."

A passage in the second part of the third volume of *Capital* stands in apparent contradiction to all these statements. There Marx says about crises: "The last reason for all social crises always is the poverty and limitation of consumption of the masses as opposed to the impulse of capitalist production to develop the productive forces, as though only the absolute capacity for consumption of the community formed their limit."† That is not very different from Rodbertus' theory of crises, for with him also crises are not occasioned simply by underconsumption by the masses, but, just as explained here, by it in conjunction with the increasing productivity of labour. In the passage quoted by Marx, underconsumption of the masses is emphasised even in contradistinction to the anarchy of production—disparity of production in the various branches and changes of prices which produce temporarily general depressions—as the last reason of all true crises.

As for any real difference of conception appearing here from that expressed in the quotation given above from the second volume, an explanation must be sought in the very different times in which the two sentences were written. There is an interval of between thirteen to fourteen years between them, and the passage from the third volume of *Capital* is the earlier one. It was written by 1864 or 1865, while the one out of the second volume must have been written about 1878.‡ In another passage of this second volume, which had been written by 1870, the periodic character of crises—which is approximately a ten-year cycle of production—is brought into conjunction with the length of the turnover of fixed capital (laid out in machinery, etc.). The development of capitalistic production has a tendency on the one hand to extend the bulk of value and the length of life of fixed capital, and

---

* *Ibid.*
† *Ibid.*
‡ Compare for this the statement of Engels in the preface to the second volume of *Capital*. Generally speaking the second volume contains the latest and ripest results of Marx's work of research.

on the other to diminish this life by a constant revolution of the means of production, hence the "moral wearing out" of this portion of fixed capital before it is "physically spent." Through this cycle of connected turnovers comprehending a series of years in which capital is confined through its fixed portion, arises a material cause for periodic crises in which the business passes through periods following one another of exhaustion, medium activity, precipitancy, crisis.*

The periods for which capital is invested are certainly very diverse and do not coincide, but the crisis always forms the starting point of a great fresh investment and therewith—from the standpoint of the whole community —a more or less new material foundation for the next cycle.† This thought is taken up again in the same volume in the chapters on the reproduction of capital, and it is there shown how even with reproduction on the same scale and with unchanged productivity of labour, differences in the length of life of the fixed capital which appear temporarily (if, for example, in one year more constituent portions of fixed capital decay than in the previous year) must have as a consequence crises of production. Foreign trade can indeed help out, but so far as it does not remove these differences it only transfers "the conflicts to a wider sphere and opens to them a greater scope." A communistic society could prevent such disturbance by continued relative overproduction which in its case would be "only the control of the community over its own means of production"; but in a capitalistic society this overproduction is an anarchical element.

This example of disturbances merely through the differences of length of life of fixed capital is striking. Want of proportion in the production of fixed and circulating capital is one of the favourite arguments of the economists for explaining crises. It is something quite new to them to hear that such a want of proportion can and must arise from the simple maintenance of fixed capital; that it can and must arise with the assumption of an ideal nor-

---

* Vol. II., p. 164.
† P. 165.

mal production and the simple reproduction of the social capital already in use.* In the chapter on "Accumulation and Reproduction on a Larger Scale," overproduction and crises are only mentioned cursorily as self-evident results of possibilities of combination which follow from the process depicted. Yet here again the idea of "overproduction" is very vigorously maintained. "If," we find on page 499, "Fullarton, for example, will know nothing of overproduction in the ordinary meaning of the term, but only of the overproduction of capital—that is, pecuniary capital—that only shows again how very little even the best bourgeois economists understand the mechanism of their system." And on page 524 it is shown that if, as can occasionally happen even with capitalistic accumulation, the constant part of the portion of capital destined for the production of the means of consumption is greater than wages capital plus the surplus value derived from the portion of capital destined for the creation of the means of production, this would be overproduction in the former sphere and "would only be adjusted by a great commercial crash."

The thought above developed, that the opening out of markets would extend the conflicts of capitalistic economy to wider spheres and therefore increase them, is in the third volume applied by Engels on different occasions to the newer phenomena. The notes on page 97 in the first part of this volume, and on page 17 in the second part, are much the most worthy of notice. In the latter note, which recapitulates and completes what is written in the former, he mentions the enormous extension, since the time when Marx wrote, of the means of traffic, which has really made the whole world a market, particularly the entry of every fresh industrial country into competition with England, and the unlimited extension of the region for the investment of surplus European capital. All these are, according to him, factors which have set aside or greatly weakened "most of the old incubators of crises and opportunities for the formation of crises." But after characterising the cartels and trusts as a means for limit-

---

* *Ibid.*

ing competition in the inner market, and the protective duties with which the non-English world surrounds itself as "armour for the final, universal industrial campaign which is to decide the government of the world market," he ends: "Thus each of the elements which strives against a repetition of the old crises conceals in itself the seed of a more powerful future crisis." Engels raises the question whether the industrial cycle which in the infancy of worldwide commerce (1815–1847) used to last about five years, and from 1847 to 1867 ten years, has not undergone a new extension, and whether we do not "find ourselves in the preparatory period of a new world-crash of unheard-of violence," but he also leaves this alternative open, that the acute form of the periodic process with its hitherto ten-year cycle may have yielded to a "more chronic rotation allotted to different lands at different times of relatively shorter, feebler improvement of trade, with a relatively long, indecisive depression."

The time that has elapsed since this was written has left the question unanswered. Signs of an economic worldwide crash of unheard-of violence have not been established, nor can one describe the improvement of trade in the intervals between the crises as particularly short-lived. Much more does a third question arise which after all is partly contained already in the second, namely: (1) whether the enormous extension of the world market, in conjunction with the extraordinary shortening of time necessary for the transmission of news and for the transport trade, has so increased the possibilities of adjustment of disturbances; and (2) whether the enormously increased wealth of the European states, in conjunction with the elasticity of the modern credit system and the rise of industrial cartels, has so limited the reacting force of local or individual disturbances that, at least for some time, general commercial crises similar to the earlier ones are to be regarded as improbable.

This question, raised by me in an essay on the "Socialist Theory of a Catastrophic Development of Society," has experienced all kinds of opposition. Among others, it has caused Rosa Luxemburg to lecture me in a series of articles published in the *Leipzig Volkszeitung* of September, 1898, on the nature of credit and the possibilities of capitalism in regard to adaptation. As these articles, which have also passed into other socialist papers, are true examples of false dialectics, but handled at the same time with great skill, it appears to me to be opportune to examine them here.

Rosa Luxemburg maintains that the credit system, far from working against crises, is the means of pushing them to an extremity. It first made possible the unmeasured extension of capitalistic production, the acceleration of the exchange of goods and of the cyclic course of the process of production, and in this way it is the means of bringing into active conflict as often as possible the differences between production and consumption. It puts into the hand of the capitalist the disposal of the capital of others, and with it the means of foolhardy speculation, and if depression sets in it intensifies the crisis. Its function is to banish the residue of stability from all capitalist conditions, to make all capitalist forces in the highest degree elastic, relative, and sensitive.

Now all that is not exactly new to anyone who knows a little of the literature of socialism in general and of Marxist socialism in particular. The only question is whether it rightly represents the real facts of the case today, or whether the picture has not another side. According to the laws of dialectic evolution to which Rosa Luxemburg so much likes to give play, it ought certainly to be the case; but even without falling back upon these, one should realise that a thing like credit, capable of so many forms, must under different conditions work in different ways. Marx treats credit by no means from the point of view that it is only a destructive agent in the capitalist system. He assigns to it, amongst other things,* the function of "creating the form of transition to a new modus of production," and with regard to it he expressly brings into prominence "the double-sided characteristics of the credit system." Frau Luxemburg knows the passage referred to very well; she even reprints the sentence from it where Marx speaks of the mixed character, "half swindler,

* Vol. III., i., p. 429.

half prophet," of the chief promulgators of credit (John Law, Isaac Pereire, and others). But she refers exclusively to the destructive side of the credit system and mentions not a word of its capacity for establishing and creating, which Marx expressly includes. Why this amputation, why this noteworthy silence with respect to the "double-sided characteristics"? The brilliant dialectical fireworks by means of which the power of the credit system is represented as a means of adaptation in the light of a "one-day fly," end in smoke and mist as soon as one looks more closely at this other side which Frau Luxemburg passes by so shyly.

That the credit system makes speculation easier is an experience centuries old; and very old, too, is the experience that speculation does not stop production when industrial circumstances are far enough developed to suit it. Meanwhile, speculation is conditioned by the relation of the knowable to the unknown circumstances. The more the latter predominate the more will speculation flourish; the more it is restrained by the former, the more the ground is cut from under its feet. Therefore the maddest outburst of commercial speculation comes to pass at the dawn of the capitalistic era, and speculation celebrates its wildest orgies usually in the countries where the capitalistic development is youngest. In the domain of industry, speculation flourished most luxuriantly in new branches of production. The older a branch of production is under modern forms—with the exception of the manufacture of mere articles of fashion—the more does the speculative momentum cease to play a decisive part in it. The conditions and movements of the market are then more exactly foreseen and are taken into consideration with greater certainty.

Nevertheless, this certainty is only relative, because competition and technical development exclude an absolute control of the market. Overproduction is to a certain extent unavoidable. But overproduction in single industries does not mean general crises. If it leads to such a one, either the industries concerned must be of such importance as consumers of the manufactures of other industries, as that their stagnation also stops these indus-

tries, or indeed they must take from them, through the
medium of the money market—that is, through the paralysis of general credit—the means of carrying on production. But it is evident that there is always a lessening
probability of this latter result. The richer a country is,
the more developed its credit organisation—which is not
be be confused with a more widely spread habit to produce with borrowed capital. For here the possibilities of
adjustment multiply in an increasing measure. In some
passage, which I cannot find at the moment, Marx said
once—and the correctness of the sentence can be proved
by the most abundant evidence—that the contractions in
the centre of the money market are much more quickly
overcome than in the different points of the circumfer-
ence. But the change of the means of communication
brought about in the meantime has more than neutralised
the consequences of great distances in this respect.*

If the crises of the money market are not quite banished from the world yet, as far as concerns us here, the
tightenings of that market by vast commercial undertakings controlled with difficulty are very much reduced.

The relations of financial crises to trade and business
crises are not yet so fully explained that one can say with
any certainty when both happen together that it was the
trade crises, i.e., overproduction, which directly caused
the money crises. In most cases it was quite clear that it
was not actual overproduction, but overspeculation,
which paralysed the money market and by this depressed
the whole business. That is proved from the isolated facts
which Marx mentions in the third volume of *Capital*,
taken from the official inquiries into the crises of 1847
and 1857, as well as from the facts which Professor Herk-

---

* Engels calculates that America and India have been brought nearer
to the industrial countries of Europe by means of the Suez Canal,
steamer transport, etc., by 70 to 90 percent. and adds "that owing
to this the two great incubators of crises from 1825 to 1857 lost a
great part of their destructive power" (*Capital*, Vol. III., Part I., p.
45). On p. 395 of the same volume, Engels maintains that certain
speculative business formed on risky schemes of credit, which Marx
pictures as factors of crises in the money market, have been brought
to an end through the oceanic cable. The correcting parenthesis of
Engels on p. 56 of the second part of Vol. III. is also worthy of
notice for its criticism on the development of the credit system.

ner adduces on these and other crises in his sketch of
the history of trade crises in his *Handworterbuch der
Staatswissenschaften.* Frau Luxemburg deduces on the
basis of the facts adduced by Herkner that the crises
hitherto have not at all been the right crises, but that
they were only infantile illnesses of the capitalistic economy, the accompanying phenomena not of narrowing but
of widening the domain of the capitalistic economy—that
we "have not yet entered upon that phase of perfect
capitalistic maturity which is presumed in the Marxist
scheme of the periodicity of crises." According to her, we
find ourselves "in a phase where crises no longer accom-
pany the rise of capital nor yet its decline." This time will
only come when the world market is fully developed and
can be enlarged by no sudden extensions. Then the struggle between the productive powers and the limits of exchange will become continually sharper and more stormy.

To that one must observe that the formula of the crises
in and for Marx was no picture of the future, but a
picture of the present day which it was expected would
recur in the future in always sharper forms and in greater
acuteness. As soon as Frau Luxemburg denies to it the
significance which Marx imputed to it for the whole
epoch lying behind us and sets it up as a deduction
which did not yet correspond with reality, but was only a
logical forecast based on the existence of certain elements
in an embryonic state, she immediately questions the
whole Marxist prediction of the coming social evolution,
so far as this is based on the theory of crises. For if this
was not based on experience at the time when it was set
up and has not become manifest in the interval between
then and now, in what more distant future can one place
its formula as coming true? Its relegation to the time
when the world market has been fully developed is a
flight into the next world.

No one knows when the world market will be fully
developed. Frau Luxemburg is not ignorant of the fact
that there is an intensive as well as an extensive broadening of the world market and that the former is today of
much greater importance than the latter.

In the trade statistics of the great industrial countries,

exports play by far the greatest part in regard to the countries longest occupied. England exports to the whole of Australasia (all the Australian colonies, New Zealand, etc.) values less in amount than to a single country, France; to the whole of British North America (Canada, British Columbia, etc.) not so much as to Russia only; to both colonial territories together, which are indeed of a respectable age, not so much as to Germany. Its trade with all its colonies, including the whole of the immense Indian Empire, is not a third of its trade with the rest of the world; and as regards the colonial acquisitions of the last twenty years, the exports thither have been ridiculously small. The extensive widenings of the world market are accomplished much too slowly to allow sufficient outlet for the actual increase of production if the countries already drawn into it did not offer it an increasing market. A limit to this increasing and intensive amplifying of the world market, along with the extension of its area, cannot be set up *a priori*. If the universal crisis is the inherent law of capitalistic production, it must prove its reality now or in the near future. Otherwise the proof of its inevitableness hovers in the air of abstract speculation.

We have seen that the credit system today undergoes less, not more, contractions leading to the general paralysis of production and so far, therefore, takes a minor place as a factor in forming crises. But so far as it is a means of a hothouse forcing of overproduction, the associations of manufacturers meet this inflation of production in separate countries, and even internationally here and there, ever more frequently, by trying to regulate production as a cartel, a syndicate, or a trust. Without embarking in prophecies as to its final power of life and work, I have recognised its capacity to influence the relation of productive activity to the condition of the market so far as to diminish the danger of crises. Frau Luxemburg refutes this also.

First she denies that the association of manufacturers can be general. She says the final aim and effect of such associations are, by excluding competition within a branch, to increase their share of the total amount of profit gained in the market of commodities. But, she adds, one branch of industry could only attain this at the cost of another, and the organisation could not possibly, therefore, be general. "Extended into all branches of production it would itself put an end to its effect."

This proof does not differ by a hair's breadth from the proof, long ago abandoned, of the uselessness of trades unions. Its support is even immeasurably more fragile than the wages fund theory of blessed memory. It is the presumption unproven, unprovable, or, rather, proved to be false, that in the commodity market only a fixed amount of profit is to be divided. It presumes, amongst other things, a fixing of prices independently of the movements in the cost of production. But even given a fixed price, and, moreover, a fixed technological basis of production, the amount of profit in a branch of industry can be raised without thereby lessening the profits of another, namely, by the lessening of unproductive expenses, the ceasing of cutting competition, better organisation of production, and the like. That the association of manufacturers is an effective means towards this is self-evident. The problem of the division of profits is the last obstacle of all which stands in the way of a general union of associations of employers.

It stands somewhat better with the last objection of Frau Luxemburg. According to it, the cartels are unsuitable for preventing the anarchy of production because the cartels of manufacturers as a rule obtain their higher profit rate on the home market, because they use the portion of capital that cannot be applied to this for manufacturing products for foreign countries at a much less profit rate. The consequence is, increased anarchy on the world market, the opposite to the object aimed at.

"As a rule" this maneuver can only be upheld where a protective duty affords the cartel protection, so as to make it impossible for the foreign country to repay it in like coin. Meanwhile we are concerned here neither with denying the harmful effects of the present simple and high protectionist system nor with an apology for the syndicates of manufacturers. It has not occurred to me to maintain that cartels and the like are the last word of economic development and are suited to remove forever the contradictions of modern industrial life. I am, on the contrary, convinced that where in modern industrial countries cartels and trusts are supported and strengthened by protective duties, they must, in fact, become factors of the crises in the industry concerned—also, if not at first, in any case finally, for the "protected" land itself. The question only arises how long the people concerned will be content with this arrangement. Protective tariffs are in themselves no product of economy but an encroachment on economy by the political power seeking to secure economic results. It is otherwise with the industrial cartel. It has, although favoured by protective tariffs, grown out of the economic soil and is a national means of adapting production to the movements of the market. That it is, or can be, at the same time the means of monopolist exploitation is another matter. But it is just as much beside the question that in the former capacity it means an increase of all earlier remedial measures for overproduction. With much less risk than the individual undertaking, it can, in times of a glut on the market, temporarily limit production. Better than this, it is also in a position to meet foreign cutting competition abroad. To deny this is to deny the superiority of organisation over anarchic competition. But we do so, if we deny on principle that cartels can work as a modifying influence on the nature and frequency of crises. How *far* they can do so is for the present a matter for conjecture, for we have not sufficient experience to allow of a conclusive judgment in this respect. But still fewer conclusive facts can be given under these circumstances for anticipating future general crises as they hovered before Marx and Engels, repetitions on a larger scale of the crises of 1825, 1836, 1847, 1857, 1873. The mere fact that whilst for a long time socialists generally believed in an increasing contraction of the industrial cycle as the natural consequence of the increasing concentration of capital, a development in the form of a spiral, Friedrich Engels in 1894 found himself driven to question whether a new enlarging of the cycle was not in front of us, and thus to suggest the exact contrary of the former assumption, and he warned us against the abstract deduction that these crises must repeat themselves in the old form.*

The history of individual industries shows that their crises by no means always coincide with the so-called general crises. Marx, as we have seen, believed he could establish on the need of an accelerated renewal of fixed capital (implements of production, etc.) a material foundation for periodic crises,† and it is undoubtedly true that an important reason for crises is to be found here. But it is not accurate, or not more accurate, that these periods of renewal coincide as to time in the various industries. And therewith a further factor of the great general crisis is done away with.

There remains then only so much, that the capacity for production in modern society is much greater than the actual demand for products determined by the buying capacity; that millions live insufficiently housed, insufficiently clad, and insufficiently nourished, in spite of abundant means at hand for sufficient housing, nourishment, and clothing; that out of this incongruity, overproduction appears again and again in different branches of production, so that either actually certain articles are produced in greater amounts than can be used—for example, more yarn than the present weaving mills can work—or that certain articles are produced, not indeed in a greater quantity than can be used, but in a greater quantity than can be bought; that in consequence of this, great irregularity occurs in the employment of the workers, which makes their situation extremely insecure, weighs them down in unworthy dependence, brings forth overwork here and want of work there; and that of the means

---

* We are, of course, only speaking here of the purely economic foundation of crises. Crises as results of political events (wars and serious threatenings of war) or of very widespread failures of crops—local failures no longer exercise any effect in this respect—are of course always possible.

† The use of the word *material* in the passage mentioned (Vol. II., p. 164) is not without interest in judging how Marx understood this word. According to the present usual definition of the word, the explanation of crises from underconsumption would be quite as materialistic as founding it on changes in the process of production or in implements.

employed today to counteract the most visible part of this evil, the cartels, represent monopolist unions—on the one side against the workers, and on the other against the great public—which have a tendency to carry on warfare over the heads of these and at their cost with the same kind of monopolist unions in other industries or other lands, or, by international or interindustrial agreements, arbitrarily to adapt production and prices to their need of profit. The capitalistic means of defence against crises virtually bear within themselves the possibilities of a new and more hopeless serfdom for the working classes, as well as of privileges of production which revive in acute form the old guild privileges. It appears to me to be much more important at present, from the standpoint of the workers, to keep before our eyes the possibilities of cartels and trusts than to prophesy their "impotence." It is for the working class a subordinate question whether these combinations will be able, in the course of time, to attain their first-mentioned object, the warding off of crises. But it becomes a question full of importance as soon as expectations of any kind as regards the movement for the emancipation of the working classes are made dependent upon the question of the general crisis. For then the belief that cartels are of no effect against crises may be the cause of very disastrous neglect.

The short sketch which we gave in the introduction to this chapter of the Marx-Engels explanations of economic crises will suffice, in conjunction with the corresponding facts adduced, to show that the problem of crises cannot be solved by a few well-preserved catchwords. We can only investigate what elements of modern economy work in favour of crises and what work against them. It is impossible to prejudge *a priori* the ultimate relation of these forces to one another, or their development. Unless unforeseen external events bring about a general crisis, and as we have said that can happen any day, there is no urgent reason for concluding that such a crisis will come to pass for purely economic reasons. Local and partial depressions are unavoidable; general stagnation is not unavoidable with the present organisation and extension of the world market, and particularly with the great extension of the production of articles of food. The latter phenomenon is of peculiar importance for our problem. Perhaps nothing has contributed so much to the mitigation of commercial crises or to the stopping of their increase as the fall of rent and of the price of food.

Evolutionary Socialism

. . . I set myself against the notion that we have to expect shortly a collapse of the bourgeois economy and that social democracy should be induced by the prospect of such an imminent, great, social catastrophe to adapt its tactics to that assumption. That I maintain most emphatically.

The adherents of this theory of a catastrophe base it especially on the conclusions of *The Communist Manifesto*. This is a mistake in every respect.

The theory which *The Communist Manifesto* sets forth of the evolution of modern society was correct as far as it characterized the general tendencies of that evolution. But it was mistaken in several special deductions, above all in the estimate of the *time* the evolution would take. The last has been unreservedly acknowledged by Friedrich Engels, the joint author with Marx of the *Manifesto*, in his preface to *The Class War in France*. But it is evident that if social evolution takes a much greater period of time than was assumed, it must also take upon itself *forms* and lead to forms that were not foreseen and could not be foreseen then.

Social conditions have not developed to such an acute opposition of things and classes as is depicted in the *Manifesto*. It is not only useless, it is the greatest folly to attempt to conceal this from ourselves. The number of members of the possessing classes is today not smaller but larger. The enormous increase of social wealth is not accompanied by a decreasing number of large capitalists but by an increasing number of capitalists of all degrees. The middle classes change their character, but they do not disappear from the social scale.

The concentration in productive industry is not being accomplished even today in all its departments with equal thoroughness and at an equal rate. In a great many branches of production, it certainly justifies the forecasts of the socialist critic of society; but in other branches it lags even today behind them. The process of concentration in agriculture proceeds still more slowly. Trade statistics show an extraordinarily elaborated graduation of enterprises in regard to size. No rung of the ladder is disappearing from it. The significant changes in the inner structure of these enterprises and their interrelationship cannot do away with this fact.

In all advanced countries, we see the privileges of the capitalist bourgeoisie yielding step by step to democratic organizations. Under the influence of this, and driven by the movement of the working classes which is daily becoming stronger, a social reaction has set in against the exploiting tendencies of capital, a counteraction which, although it still proceeds timidly and feebly, yet does exist and is always drawing more departments of economic life under its influence. Factory legislation, the democratization of local government, and the extension of its area of work, the freeing of trade unions and systems of cooperative trade from legal restrictions, the consideration of standard conditions of labour in the work undertaken by public authorities—all these characterize this phase of the evolution.

But the more the political organizations of the modern nations are democratized the more the needs and opportunities of great political catastrophes are diminished. He who holds firmly to the catastrophic theory of evolution must, with all his power, withstand and hinder the evolution described above, which, indeed, the logical defender of that theory formerly did. But is the conquest of political power by the proletariat simply to be by a political catastrophe? Is it to be the appropriation and utilization of the power of the state by the proletariat exclusively against the whole nonproletarian world?

He who replies in the affirmative must be reminded of two things. In 1872, Marx and Engels announced in the preface to the new edition of *The Communist Manifesto* that the Paris Commune had exhibited a proof that "the working classes cannot simply take possession of the ready-made state machine and set it in motion for their own aims." And in 1895 Friedrich Engels stated in detail in the preface to *Class Struggles in France* that the time of political surprises, of the "revolutions of small conscious minorities at the head of unconscious masses" was today at an end, that a collision on a large scale with the military would be the means of checking the steady growth of social democracy and of even throwing it back for a time—in short, that social democracy would flourish far better by lawful than by unlawful means and by violent revolution. And he points out in conformity with this opinion that the next task of the party should be "to work for an uninterrupted increase of its vote" or to carry on a slow *propaganda of parliamentary activity*.

Thus Engels, who, nevertheless, as his numerical examples show still somewhat overestimated the rate of process of the evolution! Shall we be told that he abandoned the conquest of political power by the working classes, because he wished to avoid the steady growth of social democracy secured by lawful means being interrupted by a political revolution?

If not, and if one subscribes to his conclusions, one cannot reasonably take any offense it it is declared that for a long time yet the task of social democracy is, instead of speculating on a great economic crash, "to organize the working classes politically and develop them as a democracy and to fight for all reforms in the state which are adapted to raise the working classes and transform the state in the direction of democracy."

That is what I have said in my impugned article and what I still maintain in its full import. As far as concerns the question propounded above it is equivalent to Engels' dictum, for democracy is, at any given time, as much government by the working classes as these are capable of practising according to their intellectual ripeness and the degree of social development they have attained. Engels, indeed, refers at the place just mentioned to the fact that *The Communist Manifesto* has "proclaimed the conquest of the democracy as one of the first and important tasks of the fighting proletariat."

In short, Engels is so thoroughly convinced that the tactics based on the presumption of a catastrophe have had their day, that he even considers a revision of them necessary in the Latin countries where tradition is much more favourable to them than in Germany. "If the conditions of war between nations have altered," he writes, "no less have those for the war between classes." Has this already been forgotten?

No one has questioned the necessity for the working classes to gain the control of government. The point at issue is between the theory of social cataclysm and the question whether with the given social development in Germany, and the present advanced state of its working classes in the towns and the country, a sudden catastrophe would be desirable in the interest of the social democracy. I have denied it and deny it again, because in my judgment a greater security for lasting success lies in a steady advance than in the possibilities offered by a catastrophic crash.

And, as I am firmly convinced that important periods in the development of nations cannot be leapt over, I lay the greatest value on the next tasks of social democracy, on the struggle for the political rights of the working man, on the political activity of working men in town and country for the interests of their class, as well as on the work of the industrial organization of the workers.

In this sense I wrote the sentence that the movement means everything for me and that what is *usually* called "the final aim of socialism" is nothing: and in this sense I write it down again today. Even if the word "usually" had not shown that the proposition was only to be understood conditionally, it was obvious that it *could* not express indifference concerning the final carrying out of socialist principles, but only indifference—or, as it would be better expressed, carelessness—as to the form of the final arrangement of things. I have at no time had an excessive interest in the future, beyond general principles; I have not been able to read to the end of any picture of the future. My thought and efforts are concerned with the duties of the present and the nearest future, and I only busy myself with the perspectives beyond so far as they give me a line of conduct for suitable action now.

The conquest of political power by the working classes, the expropriation of capitalists, are no ends in themselves but only means for the accomplishment of certain aims and endeavours. As such they are demands in the program of social democracy and are not attacked by me. Nothing can be said beforehand as to the circumstances of their accomplishments; we can only fight for their realization. But the conquest of political power necessitates the possession of political *rights*; and the most important problem of tactics which German social democracy has at the present time to solve, appears to me to be to devise the best ways for the extension of the political and economic rights of the German working classes. . . .

Rosa Luxemburg

The Conquest of Political Power

One of the towering and most attractive figures in European radicalism, Rosa Luxemburg (1870–1919), was at first active in the Polish and then in the German socialist movement. She quickly rose to prominence as publicist and theoretician, standing at the far left of the Social Democrats but steadily distinguishing herself from the Bolsheviks. Rosa Luxemburg became known as an exponent of "revolutionary spontaneity," the idea that the masses would rise in revolt without the educative or manipulative guidance of a "vanguard party." The selections that follow show her in two characteristic political stances. In the excerpt from her Reform or Revolution (1899), entitled "The Conquest of Political Power," she argues vigorously against the "revisionism" of Bernstein and his cothinkers. In the chapter from The Russian Revolution (1919), entitled "The Problem of Dictatorship," she is, even while declaring herself a supporter of the October Revolution, arguing strongly against the Bolshevik denial of political freedom to their political opponents. For those left socialists who have refused both Social Democratic reformism and Bolshevik authoritarianism, Rosa Luxemburg has been an inspiring ancestor.

The fate of democracy is bound up, we have seen, with the fate of the labor movement. But does the development of democracy render superfluous or impossible a proletarian revolution, that is, the conquest of the political power by the workers?

Bernstein settles the question by weighing minutely the good and bad sides of social reform and social revolution He does it almost in the same manner in which cinnamon or pepper is weighed out in a consumers' cooperative store. He sees the legislative course of historic development as the action of "intelligence," while the revolutionary course of historic development is for him the action of "feeling." Reformist activity, he recognizes as a slow method of historic progress, revolution as a rapid method of progress. In legislation he sees a methodic force; in revolution, a spontaneous force.

We have known for a long time that the petty-bourgeois reformer finds "good" and "bad" sides in everything. He nibbles a bit at all grasses. But the real course of events is little affected by such combinations. The carefully gathered little pile of the "good sides" of all things possible collapses at the first fillip of history. Historically, legislative reform and the revolutionary method function in accordance with influences that are much more profound than the consideration of the advantages or inconveniences of one method or another.

In the history of bourgeois society, legislative reform served to strengthen progressively the rising class, the latter was sufficiently strong to seize political power, to suppress the existing juridical system, and to construct itself a new one. Bernstein, thundering against the conquest of political power as a theory of Blanquist violence, has the misfortune of labeling as a Blanquist error that which has always been the pivot and the motive force of human history. From the first appearance of class societies having the class struggle as the essential content of their history, the conquest of political power has been the aim of all rising classes. Here is the starting point and end of every historic period. This can be seen in the long struggle of the Latin peasantry against the financiers and nobility of ancient Rome, in the struggle of the medieval nobility against the bishops and in the struggle of the artisans against the nobles, in the cities of the Middle Ages. In more modern times, we see it in the struggle of the bourgeoisie against feudalism.

Legislative reform and revolution are not different methods of historic development that can be picked out at pleasure from the counter of history, just as one chooses hot or cold sausages. Legislative reform and revolution are different *factors* in the development of class society. They condition and complement each other, and are at the same time reciprocally exclusive, as are the north and south poles, the bourgeoisie and the proletariat.

Every legal constitution is the *product* of a revolution. In the history of classes, revolution is the act of political creation, while legislation is the political expression of the life of a society that has already come into being. Work for reform does not contain its own force, independent from revolution. During every historic period, work for reforms is carried on only in the direction given to it by the impetus of the last revolution and continues as long as the impulsion of the last revolution continues to make itself felt. Or, to put it more concretely, in each historic period work for reforms is carried on only in the framework of the social form created by the last revolution. Here is the kernel of the problem.

It is contrary to history to represent work for reforms as a long-drawn-out revolution and reduction as a condensed series of reforms. A social transformation and a legislative reform do not differ according to their duration but according to their content. The secret of historic change through the utilization of political power resides precisely in the transformation of simple quantitive modifications into a new quality or, to speak more concretely, in the passage of an historic period from one given form of society to another.

That is why people who pronounce themselves in favor of the method of legislative reform *in place of* and *in contradistinction to* the conquest of political power and social revolution, do not really choose a more tranquil, calmer, and slower road to the *same* goal, but a *different* goal. Instead of taking a stand for the establishment of a new society, they take a stand for surface modifications of the old society. If we follow the political conceptions of revisionism, we arrive at the same conclusion that is reached when we follow the economic theories of revisionism. Our program becomes not the realization of *socialism*, but the reform of *capitalism;* not the suppression of the system of wage labor, but the diminution of exploitation, that is, the suppression of the abuses of capitalism instead of the suppression of capitalism itself.

Does the reciprocal role of legislative reform and revolution apply only to the class struggles of the past? Is it possible that now, as a result of the development of the bourgeois juridical system, the function of moving society from one historic phase to another belongs to legislative reform and that the conquest of state power by the proletariat has really become "an empty phrase," as Bernstein put it?

The very opposite is true. What distinguishes bourgeois society from other class societies, from ancient society and from the social order of the Middle Ages? Precisely the fact that class domination does not rest on "acquired rights" but on *real economic relations*—the fact that wage labor is not a juridical relation but purely an economic relation. In our juridical system, there is not a single legal formula for the class domination of today. The few remaining traces of such formula of class domination are (as that concerning servants) survivals of feudal society.

How can wage slavery be suppressed the "legislative way" if wage slavery is not expressed in laws? Bernstein, who would do away with capitalism by means of legislative reform, finds himself in the same situation as Ouspensky's Russian policeman who tells: "Quickly I seized the rascal by the collar! But what do I see? The confounded fellow has no collar!" And that is precisely Bernstein's difficulty.

"All previous societies were based on an antagonism between an oppressing class and an oppressed class" *(Communist Manifesto)*. But in the preceding phases of modern society, this antagonism was expressed in distinctly determined juridical relations and could, especially because of that, accord, to a certain extent, a place to new relations within the framework of the old. "In the midst of serfdom, the serf raised himself to the rank of a member of the town community" *(Communist Manifesto)*. How was that made possible? It was made possible by the progressive suppression of all feudal privileges in the environs of the city: the corvée, the right to special dress, the inheritance tax, the lord's claim to the best cattle, the personal levy, marriage under duress, the right to succession, and the like which altogether constituted serfdom.

In the same way, the small bourgeoisie of the Middle Ages succeeded in raising itself, while it was still under the yoke of feudal absolutism, to the rank of bourgeoisie (*Communist Manifesto*). By what means? By means of the formal partial suppression or complete loosening of the corporative bonds, by the progressive transformation of the fiscal administration and of the army.

Consequently, when we consider the question from the abstract viewpoint, not from the historic viewpoint, we can *imagine* (in view of the former class relations) a legal passage, according to the reformist method, from feudal society to bourgeois society. But what do we see in reality? In reality, we see that legal reforms not only did not obviate the seizure of political power by the bourgeoisie but have, on the contrary, prepared for it and led to it. A formal social-political transformation was indispensable for the abolition of slavery as well as for the complete suppression of feudalism.

But the situation is entirely different now. No law obliges the proletariat to submit itself to the yoke of capitalism. Poverty, the lack of means of production, obliges the proletariat to submit itself to the yoke of capitalism. And no law in the world can give to the proletariat the means of production while it remains in the framework of bourgeois society, for not laws but economic development have torn the means of production from the producers' possession.

And neither is the exploitation inside the system of wage labor based on laws. The level of wages is not fixed by legislation, but by economic factors. The phenomenon of capitalist exploitation does not rest on a legal disposition, but on the purely economic fact that labor power plays in this exploitation the role of a merchandise possessing, among other characteristics, the agreeable quality of producing value—*more* than the value it consumes in the form of the laborer's means of subsistence. In short, the fundamental relations of the domination of the capitalist class cannot be transformed by means of legislative reforms, on the basis of capitalist society, because these relations have not been introduced by bourgeois laws nor have they received the form of such laws. Apparently Bernstein is not aware of this, for he speaks of "socialist reforms." On the other hand, he seems to express implicit recognition of this when he writes that "the economic motive acts freely today, while formerly it was masked by all kinds of relations of domination, by all sorts of ideology."

It is one of the peculiarities of the capitalist order that within it all the elements of the future society first assume, in their development, a form not approaching socialism but, on the contrary, a form moving more and more away from socialism. Production takes on a progressively increasing social character. But under what form is the social character of capitalist production expressed? It is expressed in the form of the large enterprise, in the form of the share-holding concern, the cartel, within which the capitalist antagonisms, capitalist exploitation, the oppression of labor power are augmented to the extreme.

In the army, capitalist development leads to the extension of obligatory military service, to the reduction of the time of service, and consequently, to a material approach to a popular militia. But all of this takes place under the form of modern militarism, in which the domination of the people by the militarist state and the class character of the state manifest themselves most clearly.

In the field of political relations, the development of democracy brings—in the measure that it finds a favorable soil—the participation of all popular strata in political life and, consequently, some sort of "people's state." But this participation takes the form of bourgeois parliamentarism, in which class antagonisms and class domination are not done away with but are, on the contrary, displayed in the open. Exactly because capitalist development moves through these contradictions, it is necessary to extract the kernel of socialist from its capitalist shell. Exactly for this reason must the proletariat seize political power and suppress completely the capitalist system.

Of course, Bernstein draws other conclusions. If the development of democracy leads to the aggravation and not to the lessening of capitalist antagonisms, "the Social

Democracy," he answers us, "in order not to render its task more difficult, must not hinder social reform and the working of democratic institutions." Indeed, that would be the right thing to do if the Social Democracy found to its taste, in the petty-bourgeois manner, the futile task of picking for itself all the good sides of history and rejecting the bad sides of history. However, in that case it should, at the same time, "try to stop" capitalism in general, for there is no doubt that the latter is the rascal placing all these obstacles in the way of socialism. But, capitalism furnishes besides the *obstacles* also the only *possibilities* of realizing the socialist program. The same can be said about democracy.

If democracy has become superfluous or annoying to the bourgeoisie, it is on the contrary necessary and indispensable to the working class. It is necessary to the working class because it creates the political forms (autonomous administration, electoral rights, etc.) which will serve the proletariat as fulcrums in its task of transforming bourgeois society. Democracy is indispensable to the working class, because only through the exercise of its democratic rights, in the struggle for democracy, can the proletariat become aware of its class interests and its historic task.

In a word, democracy is indispensable not because it renders superfluous the conquest of political power by the proletariat, but because it renders this conquest of power both *necessary* and *possible*. When Engels in his preface to the *Class Struggles in France* revised the tactics of the modern labor movement and urged the legal struggle as opposed to the barricades, he did not have in mind—this comes out of every line of the preface—the question of a definite conquest of political power, but the contemporary daily struggle. He did not have in mind the attitude that the proletariat must take toward the capitalist state at the time of seizure of power, but the attitude of the proletariat while in the bounds of the capitalist state. Engels was giving directions to the proletariat *oppressed*, and not to the proletariat victorious.

On the other hand, Marx's well-known sentence on the agrarian question in England (Bernstein leans on it heavily), in which he says: "We shall probably succeed easier

by buying the estates of the landlords," does not refer to
the stand of the proletariat *before*, but *after* its victory.
For there evidently can be a question of buying the property of the old dominant class only when the workers are
in power. The possibility envisaged by Marx is that of the
pacific exercise of the dictatorship of the proletariat and
not the replacement of the dictatorship with capitalist
social reforms. There was no doubt for Marx and Engels
about the necessity of having the proletariat conquer political power. It is left to Bernstein to consider the poultry
yard of bourgeois parliamentarism as the organ by means
of which we are to realize the most formidable social
transformation of history, *the passage from capitalist society to socialism.*

The Problem of Dictatorship

Lenin says: the bourgeois state is an instrument of oppression of the working class; the socialist state, of the bourgeoisie. To a certain extent, he says, it is only the capitalist state stood on its head. This simplified view misses the most essential thing: bourgeois class rule has no need of the political training and education of the entire mass of the people, at least not beyond certain narrow limits. But for the proletarian dictatorship, that is the life element, the very air without which it is not able to exist.

"Thanks to the open and direct struggle for governmental power," writes Trotsky, "the laboring masses accumulate in the shortest time a considerable amount of political experience and advance quickly from one stage to another of their development."

Here Trotsky refutes himself and his own friends. Just because this is so, they have blocked up the fountain of political experience and the source of this rising development by their suppression of public life! Or else we would have to assume that experience and development were necessary up to the seizure of power by the Bolsheviks, and then, having reached their highest peak, became superfluous thereafter.

In reality, the opposite is true! It is the very giant tasks which the Bolsheviks have undertaken with courage and determination that demand the most intensive political training of the masses and the accumulation of experience.

Freedom only for the supporters of the government, only for the members of one party, however numerous they may be, is no freedom at all. Freedom is always and exclusively freedom for the one who thinks differently.

Not because of any fanatical concept of "justice" but because all that is instructive, wholesome, and purifying in political freedom depends on this essential characteristic, and its effectiveness vanishes when "freedom" becomes a special privilege.

The Bolsheviks themselves will not want, with hand on heart, to deny that, step by step, they have to feel out the ground, try out, experiment, test now one way now another, and that a good many of their measures do not represent priceless pearls of wisdom. Thus it must and will be with all of us when we get to the same point, even if the same difficult circumstances may not prevail everywhere.

The tacit assumption underlying the Lenin-Trotsky theory of the dictatorship is this: that the socialist transformation is something for which a ready-made formula lies completed in the pocket of the revolutionary party, which needs only to be carried out energetically in practise. This is, unfortunately—or perhaps fortunately—not the case. Far from being a sum of ready-made prescriptions which have only to be applied, the practical realization of socialism as an economic, social, and juridical system is something which lies completely hidden in the mists of the future. What we possess in our program is nothing but a few main signposts which indicate the general direction in which to look for the necessary measures, and the indications are mainly negative in character, at that. Thus we know more or less what we must eliminate at the outset in order to free the road for a socialist economy. But when it comes to the nature of the thousand concrete, practical measures, large and small, necessary to introduce socialist principles into economy, law, and all social relationships, there is no key in any socialist party program or textbook. That is not a shortcoming but rather the very thing that makes scientific socialism superior to the utopian varieties. The socialist system of society should only be, and can only be, an historical product, born out of the school of its own experiences, born in the course of its realization, as a result of the developments of living history, which—just like organic nature, of which, in the last analysis, it forms a part—has the fine habit of always producing along with any real social need the means to its satisfaction, along with the task simultaneously the solution.

If such is the case, however, than it is clear that socialism by its very nature cannot be decreed or introduced by ukase. It has as its prerequisite a number of measures of force against property, etc. The negative, the tearing down, can be decreed; the building up, the positive, cannot. New territory. A thousand problems. Only experience is capable of correcting and opening new ways. Only unobstructed, effervescing life falls into a thousand new forms and improvisations, brings to light creative force, itself corrects all mistaken attempts. The public life of countries with limited freedom is so poverty stricken, so miserable, so rigid, so unfruitful, precisely because, through the exclusion of democracy, it cuts off the living sources of all spiritual riches and progress (proof: the year 1905 and the months from February to October 1917). There it was political in character; the same thing applies to economic and social life also. The whole mass of the people must take part in it. Otherwise, socialism will be decreed from behind a few official desks by a dozen intellectuals.

Public control is indispensably necessary. Otherwise the exchange of experiences remains only with the closed circle of the officials of the new regime. Corruption becomes inevitable. Lenin's words, Bulletin No. 29: Socialism in life demands a complete spiritual transformation in the masses degraded by centuries of bourgeois class rule. Social instincts in place of egotistical ones, mass initiative in place of inertia, idealism which conquers all suffering, etc., etc. No one knows this better, describes it more penetratingly, repeats it more stubbornly than Lenin. But he is completely mistaken in the means he employs. Decree, dictatorial force of the factory overseer, draconic penalties, rule by terror—all these things are but palliatives. The only way to a rebirth is the school of public life itself, the most unlimited, the broadest democracy and public opinion. It is rule by terror which demoralizes.

When all this is eliminated, what really remains? In place of the representative bodies created by general, popular elections, Lenin and Trotsky have laid down the soviets as the only true representation of the laboring masses. But with the repression of political life in the land as a whole, life in the soviets must also become more and more crippled. Without general elections, without unrestricted freedom of press and assembly, without a free struggle of opinion, life dies out in every public institution, becomes a mere semblance of life, in which only the bureaucracy remains as the active element. Public life gradually falls asleep, a few dozen party leaders of inexhaustible energy and boundless experience direct and rule. Among them, in reality only a dozen outstanding heads do the leading, and an elite of the working class is invited from time to time to meetings where they are to applaud the speeches of the leaders and to approve proposed resolutions unanimously—at bottom, then, a clique affair—a dictatorship, to be sure, not the dictatorship of the proletariat, however, but only the dictatorship of a handful of politicians, that is a dictatorship in the bourgeois sense, in the sense of the rule of the Jacobins (the postponement of the Soviet Congress from three-month periods to six-month periods!). Yes, we can go even further: such conditions must inevitably cause a brutalization of public life: attempted assassinations, shooting of hostages, and other violence.

Julian Martov

Dictatorship of the Minority

Julian Martov (1873–1923), one of the most interesting and poignant figures of Russian socialism, became a radical in his youth, worked briefly as a collaborator with Lenin at the turn of the century, and then became a spokesman for the left wing of Menshevism (Russian social democracy). During the First World War and then during the Revolution, Martov took a strongly left-wing position: he opposed the war as imperialist and objected to the participation of his Menshevik colleagues in the Kerensky government, which briefly ruled Russia in 1917. After the Bolshevik seizure of power, Martov tried for a while to serve as a loyal opposition, cutting himself off from those who advocated the forcible overthrow of the Bolshevik regime yet fiercely criticizing that regime for its steady encroachment on political liberties. In 1920, he left for exile in Germany.

The following selection is taken from his pamphlet The State and the Socialist Revolution, *written in 1921 and 1922, a harsh polemic against Lenin's authoritarianism.*

Popular revolutions of the preceding historic period had the following characteristics. The role of active factor in the overturn belonged to *minorities* of the social classes in whose interest the revolution developed. These minorities exploited the confused discontent and the sporadic explosions of anger arising among scattered and socially inconsistent elements within the revolutionary class. They guided the latter in the destruction of the old social forms. In certain cases, the active leader minorities had to use the power of their concentrated energy in order to shatter the inertia of the elements they tried to wield for revolutionary purposes. Therefore, these active, leader minorities sometimes made efforts—often successful efforts—to repress the passive resistance of the manipulated elements, when the latter refused to move forward toward the broadening and deepening of the revolution. The dictatorship of an active revolutionary minority, a dictatorship that tended to be terrorist, was the normal coming-to-a-head of the situation in which the old social order had confined the popular mass, now called on by the revolutionaries to forge their own destiny. Where the active revolutionary minority was not able to organize such a dictatorship or to maintain it for some time, as was the case in Germany, Austria, and France in 1848, we observed the miscarriage of the revolutionary process, a collapse of the revolution.

Engels said that the revolutions of the past historic period were the work of conscious minorities exploiting the spontaneous revolt of unconscious majorities. It is understood that the word *conscious* should be taken here in a relative sense. It was a question of pursuing political and social aims that were quite definite, though at the same time quite contradictory and utopian. The ideology of the Jacobins of 1793–1794 was thoroughly utopian. It cannot be considered to have been the product of an objective conception of the process of historic evolution. But in relation to the mass of peasants, small producers, and workers in whose name they demolished the old regime, the Jacobins represented a conscious vanguard whose destructive work was subordinated to positive problems.

In the last decade of the nineteenth century, Engels arrived at the conclusion that the epoch of revolutions effected by conscious minorities heading unknowing masses had closed for ever. From then on, he said, revolution would be prepared by long years of political propaganda, organization, education, and would be realized directly and consciously by the interested masses themselves. To such a degree has this idea become the conception of the great majority of modern socialists that the slogan: "All power to the soviets!" was originally launched as an answer to the need of assuring, during the revolutionary period, the maximum of active, conscious participation and the maximum of initiative by the masses in the task of social creation.

Read again Lenin's articles and speeches of 1917, and you will discover that their master thought "all power to the soviets" amounted then to the following: (1) the direct and active participation of the masses in the management of production and public affairs; (2) the obliteration of all gaps between the directors and the directed, that is, the suppression of any social hierarchy; (3) the greatest possible unification of the legislative and executive powers, of the production apparatus and the administrative apparatus, of the state machinery and the machinery of local administration; (4) the maximum of activity by the mass and the minimum of liberty for its elected representatives; (5) the total suppression of all bureaucracy. Parliamentarism was repudiated not only as the arena where two enemy classes collaborate politically and engage in "pacific" combats, but also as a mechanism of public administration. And this repudiation was motivated, above all, by the antagonism arising between this mechanism and the unbounded revolutionary activity of the mass, intervening directly in administration and production.

In August, 1917, Lenin wrote:

Having conquered political power, the workers will break up the old bureaucratic apparatus; they will shatter it to its very foundations until not one stone is left upon another: and they will replace it with a new one consisting of the same workers and employees, *against* whose transformation into bureaucrats will at once be undertaken, as pointed out in detail by Marx and Engels 1) not only electiveness, but also instant recall; 2) payment no higher than that of ordinary workers; 3) immediate transition to a state of things when *all* fulfill the functions of control and superintendence, so that *all* become "bureaucrats for a time, and *no one*, therefore can become a bureaucrat."*

He wrote of the *"substitution of a universal popular militia for the police,"* of the "electiveness and recall at any moment of all functionaries and commanding ranks,"

---

* *The State and Revolution.*

of "workers' control in its primitive sense, direct participation of the people at the courts, not only in the shape
of a jury but also by the suppression of specializing pros-
ecutors and defense counsels and by the vote of all present on the question of guilt." That is how the replacement of the old bourgeois democracy with the soviet
regime was interpreted in theory—and sometimes in
practice.

It was this conception of "all power to the soviets" that
was presented in the first Constitution adopted at the
third Soviet Congress on the initiative of V. Troutovsky.
It recognized the complete power of the communal soviet
within the limits of the *volost*, the power of the district
soviet within the bounds of the *ouyezd*, that of the provincial soviet within the limits of the *gubernia*, while the
unifying functions of each of the higher soviet organs
expressed themselves in the leveling of the differences
arising among the organs subordinated to it. Anticipating
the argument that such extreme federalism might undermine national unity, Lenin wrote in the same brochure:

Only people full of petty-bourgeois "superstitious faith" in the
state can mistake the destruction of the bourgeois state for the destruction of centralism. But will it not be centralism if the proletariat and poorest peasantry take the power of the state in their
own hands, organize themselves freely into communes, and unite
the action of all the communes in striking at capital, in crushing
the resistance of the capitalists, in the transfer of private property
in railways, factories, land, and so forth, to the entire nation, to
the whole of society? Will that not be centralism?*

Reality has cruelly shattered all these illusions. The
"Soviet state" has not established in any instance electiveness and recall of public officials and the commanding
staff. It has not suppressed the professional police. It has
not assimilated the courts in direct jurisdiction by the
masses. It has not done away with social hierarchy in
production. It has not lessened the total subjection of the
local community to the power of the state. On the contrary, in proportion to its evolution, the Soviet state
shows a tendency in the opposite direction. It shows a

---

* Lenin, *op. cit.*

tendency toward intensified centralism of the state, a tendency toward the utmost possible strengthening of the principles of hierarchy and compulsion. It shows a tendency toward the development of a more specialized apparatus of repression than before. It shows a tendency toward the greater independence of the usually elective functions and the annihilation of the control of these functions by the elector masses. It shows a tendency toward the total freedom of the executive organisms from the tutelage of the electors. In the crucible of reality, the "power of the soviets" has become the "soviet power," *a power that originally issued from the soviets* but has steadily become independent from the soviets.

We must believe that the Russian ideologists of the soviet system have not renounced entirely their notion of a nonstatist social order, the *aim* of the revolution. But as they see matters now, the road to this nonstatist social order no longer lies in the progressive atrophy of the functions and institutions that have been forged by the bourgeois state, as they said they saw things in 1917. Now it appears that their way to a social order that would be free from the state lies in the hypertrophy—the excessive development—of these functions and in the resurrection under an altered aspect, of most state institutions typical of the bourgeois era. The shrewd people continue to repudiate democratic parliamentarism. But they no longer repudiate, at the same time, those instruments of state power to *which parliamentarism is a counterweight within bourgeois society*: bureaucracy, police, a permanent army with commanding cadres that are independent of the soldiers, courts that are above control by the community, etc.

In contrast to the bourgeois state, the state of the transitional revolutionary period ought to be an apparatus for the "repression of the minority by the majority." Theoretically, it should be a governmental apparatus resting in the hands of the majority. In reality, the Soviet state continues to be, as the state of the past, a government apparatus resting in the hands of a minority (of another minority, of course). Little by little, the "power of the soviets" is being replaced with the power of a certain party. Little by little the party becomes the essential state institution, the framework and axis of the entire system of "soviet republics."

The evolution traversed by the idea of the "soviet state" in Russia ought to help us to understand the psychological basis of this idea in countries where the revolutionary process of today is yet in its initial phase. The "soviet regime" becomes the means of bringing into power and maintaining in power a revolutionary minority which claims to defend the interests of a majority, though the latter has not recognized these interests as its own, though this majority has not attached itself sufficiently to these interests to defend them with all its energy and determination. This is demonstrated by the fact that in many countries—it happened also in Russia—the slogan "all power to the soviets" is launched in opposition to the already existing soviets, created during the first manifestations of the revolution. The slogan is directed, in the first place, against the majority of the working class, against the political tendencies which dominated the masses at the beginning of the revolution. The slogan "all power to the soviets" becomes a pseudonym for the dictatorship of a minority. So that when the failure of July 3, 1917, had brought to the surface the obstinate resistance of the soviets to Bolshevik pressure, Lenin tore off the disguise in his pamphlet: *On the Subject of Slogans* and proclaimed that the cry "all power to the soviets!" was thenceforward out of date and had to be replaced with the slogan, "All power to the Bolshevik Party!" But this "materialization" of the symbol, this revelation of its true content, was only a moment in the development of the perfect political form, "finally discovered" and exclusively possessing the "capacity of bringing out the social substance of the proletarian revolution."

The retention of political power by the minority of a class (or classes), by a minority organized as a party and exercising its power in the interests of the class (or classes), is a fact arising from antagonisms typical of the most recent phase of capitalism. It thus offers a difference between the old revolutions and the new. On the other hand, the fact that it is a dictatorship by a minority constitutes a *bond of kinship* between the present revolution and those of the preceding historic period. If that is the basic principle of the governmental mechanism in question, it hardly matters if the exigency of given historic circumstances have made this principle assume the particular form of soviets.

The events of 1792–1794 in France offer an example of a revolution that was realized by means of a minority dictatorship set up as a party: the Jacobin dictatorship. The Jacobin party embraced the most active, the most "leftward," elements of the petty bourgeoisie, proletariat, and declassed intellectuals. It exercised its dictatorship through a network of multiple institutions: communes, sections, clubs, revolutionary committees. In this network, producers' organizations on the style of our workers' soviets were completely absent. Otherwise, there is a striking similarity and a number of perfect analogies, between the institutions used by the Jacobins and those serving the contemporary dictatorship. The party cells of today differ in no way from the Jacobin clubs. The revolutionary committees in 1794 and 1919 are entirely alike. The committees of poor peasants of today bear comparison with the committees and clubs, composed especially of poor elements, on which the Jacobin dictatorship based itself in the villages. Today, workers' soviets, factory committees, trade union centers mark the revolution with their stamp and give it its specific character. Here is where the influence of the proletariat in the large industries of today makes itself felt. Nevertheless, we see that such specifically class organisms, such specially proletarian formations, issuing from the millieu of modern industry, are as much reduced to the role of mechanical instruments of a party minority dictatorship as were the auxiliaries of the Jacobin dictatorship in 1792–1794, though the social origins of the latter were entirely different.

Placed in the concrete conditions of contemporary Russia, the Bolshevik party dictatorship reflects, in the first place, the interests and aspirations of the proletarian elements of the population. This would be truer in the case of soviets than might have arisen in advanced industrial countries. But the nature of the soviets, their adaptation to producers' organizations, is not the decisive factor here. We saw that after the 3rd of July, 1917, Lenin envisaged the *direct* dictatorship of the Bolshevik party, outside of the soviets. We see now that in certain places such a dictatorship is fully realized through the channel of revolutionary committees and party cells. All of this does not stop the party dictatorship (direct or indirect) from preserving in its class policy a primordial lien with the proletariat and reflecting above all, the interests and aspirations of the city laboring population.

On the other hand, as organizational cadres, the soviets may find themselves filled with elements that have a different class character. At the side of the workers' soviets, rise soviets of soldiers and peasants. So that in countries that are even more backward economically than Russia, the power of the soviets may represent something other than a proletarian minority. It may represent there a peasant minority or any other nonproletarian section of the population. The mystery of the "soviet regime" is now deciphered. We see now how an organism that is supposedly created by the specific peculiarities of a labor movement corresponding to the highest development of capitalism is revealed to be, at the same time suitable to the needs of countries knowing neither large capitalist production, nor a powerful bourgeoisie, nor a proletariat that has evolved through the experience of the class struggle. In other words, in the advanced countries, the proletariat resorts, we are told, to the soviet form of the dictatorship as soon as its élan toward the social revolution strikes against the impossibility of realizing its power in any other way than through the *dictatorship of a minority*, a minority within the proletariat itself.

The thesis of the "finally discovered form," the thesis of the political form that, belonging to the specific circumstances of the imperialist phase of capitalism is said to be the only form that can realize the social enfranchisement of the proletariat, constitutes the *historically* necessary illusion by whose effect the revolutionary section of the proletariat renounces its belief in its ability to draw behind it the majority of the population of the country and resuscitates the idea of the minority dictatorship of the Jacobins in the very form used by the bourgeois revolution of the eighteenth century. Must we recall here that this revolutionary method has been repudiated by the working class to the extent that it has freed itself from its heritage of petty-bourgeois revolutionarism?

As soon as the slogan "soviet regime" begins to function as a pseudonym under the cover of which the Jacobin and Blanquist idea of a minority dictatorship is reborn in the ranks of the proletariat, then the soviet regime acquires a universal acceptation and is said to be adaptable to any kind of revolutionary overturn. In this new sense, the "soviet form" is necessarily devoid of the specific substance that bound it to a definite phase of capitalist development. *It now becomes a universal form, which is supposed to be suitable to any revolution accomplished in a situation of political confusion, when the popular masses are not united, while the bases of the old regime have been eaten away in the process of historical evolution.*

Otto Bauer

National Character and the Idea of the Nation*

Translated here into English for the first time, the following article is taken from Otto Bauer's Die Nationalitätenfrage und die Sozialdemokratie *(1907). Otto Bauer (1881–1938) was for many years the leading figure in the Austrian Social Democratic Party, a prolific writer, and, together with Max Adler and Rudolf Hilferding, spokesman for the strand of socialist thought known as Austro-Marxism. In the years between the wars, this group tried to find a programmatic basis for a left-wing social democratic politics, one that would be more militant than the dominant social democratic outlook, yet would reject Bolshevik authoritarianism. Bauer himself was best known in the socialist movement as an authority on "the national question," first the complex of relationships among nationality groups in central and southeast Europe, and then, the whole question as to whether socialists should support the aspirations of oppressed nations or insist that only an international socialist commonwealth could solve the problems of nationality conflict.*

My definition of the nation as a community of character arising out of a community of fate has met with strong resistance from the Marxist school. This resistance is rooted in its strong distrust of the notion of national character, a distrust easily explainable by the constant abuse of that notion by nationalism, most shamefully during the war [World War I]. . . .

---

* Title supplied by editor.

The French physicist, Pierre Duhem, describes in his very stimulating book, *Purposes and Structure of Physical Theory*, the methods of English and French scientists. He notes some curious differences in the work of the most important physicists of the two nations. The French are very much concerned to have their systems unified, clear, and without contradiction; their need to understand is not satisfied until they reach experimentally verifiable laws from basic hypotheses through cogent deductions. The English lack that need. Their imagination is satisfied only when they have illustrated every complex of empirical laws by a mechanical model; it does not worry them that the hypotheses which they used to construct individual models are not connected, or even contradict each other.

The two nations try to satisfy two quite different spiritual needs in constructing an "exact" science: the French the need of reason for order and clarity, the English the need of imagination for conceivability, comprehensibility, and concreteness. And the scientists of the two nations use very different talents in developing physical systems. The French excel in abstract generalization, the English in the capacity to conceive complex groupings vividly and represent them graphically.

Duhem notes these differences where the layman would least suspect them: in the use of mathematics to develop physical systems. To the French, he says, a physical theory is a logical system, the algebraic calculation merely a subordinate aid to represent the chain of conclusions from the basic hypotheses to the last inferences as simply as possible. Therefore, they always want to have, at each point in the train of thought, a possibility of replacing calculation by the logical deduction which is its abbreviated expression and always try to obtain the strictest possible agreement between the hypotheses and the equations in which they are expressed.

The English lack this need. To them, algebraic calculation plays the role of a mechanical model which makes the phenomena easier to grasp because the transformations of the algebraic symbols in the course of calculations imitate the laws of motions of the phenomena under observation. The English physicists do not bother to attain a strict agreement between the idea and its algebraic symbol; they leave it to their intuition to bridge the two. But they do make use of their superior talent to grasp very complicated combinations quickly and vividly through condensed methods of calculation. The French prefer the operations of classical algebra, which knows only a few elementary operations; the English like the newer algebraic symbolism, which saves the many intermediate calculations of classical algebra but must use very many different symbols and handle them in accordance with very complicated rules.

Duhem asks whether these differences in the development of physical theories do not point to two different national spirits, which also manifest themselves in other branches of intellectual life. He does, indeed, note such a difference in philosophy, when he compares English philosophy since Bacon with the French since Descartes. He also discovers a closely linked difference in literature, through a comparison between Corneille and Shakespeare.

Let us take, a hero of Corneille: Auguste, hesitating between vengeance and leniency, or Rodrigue, confronting his respect with his love. Two feelings struggle in his heart, but what a magnificent order in their conflict! First the one, then the other, speaks in its proper turn, like two lawyers presenting their arguments to the court in elegantly constructed pleas. And, after both sides have presented their decisions, the will ends the debate with a decision as exact as a court judgment or a mathematical conclusion.

Duhem contrasts these characters with Lady Macbeth and Hamlet. Here, there is no conceptual analysis which dissects man into his elements, but a man in all his contradiction, in his terrifying unity and indivisibility!

Finally, Duhem uncovers a related difference by comparing French and English law. French law is collected into a few codes, systematically ordered and developed from clearly defined abstract concepts. In England, law is a heap of superimposed, disconnected, and contradictory legislation and common law, gathered in the course of centuries, never codified or systematized, but developed in the living practice of the courts according to everchanging needs. Here, too, as in physics, philosophy, and literature, the French show a need for systems and strict deductions from clearly defined abstract concepts. The English again exhibit a superior talent to survey the organically grown, in its contradictory diversity; to see their way clearly through the most complicated combinations, and not try to simplify or analyze; to make contradictions serve, in practical ways, practical needs.

Modern capitalism has leveled the cultural contents of the various national cultures. But even in this leveling process, national peculiarities affect the ways in which these cultural contents are adopted, represented, connected, evaluated, and developed. The same theory of relativity penetrates the physics of all nations. But it must overcome quite different intellectual inhibitions in Germany and in England; also, German and English scientists view it in very different spiritual contexts and therefore present it differently. The same literary fashions move writers of all countries; and yet a Russian expressionist tells the same story differently from a French one. The same workers' movement arises in all industrial countries; but the Italian working class reacts to the facts of capitalist exploitation differently from the Scandinavian.

This is what I have in mind when I speak of "national character." It has nothing to do with the fantasies of nationalist demagogy. For me, national character consists of differences, accessible only to a very fine psychological analysis, in the basic structure of the national mind, intellectual and esthetic taste, and reactions to the same stimuli; differences of which we become aware when we compare the cultural life of the nations, their science and philosophy, their poetry, music, and arts, their political and social life, their customs and way of life.

The nationalist school of historians presents "national character" as if it were a national substance whose attractions and repulsions are the real content of history. We cannot overcome this interpretation of history by disputing the undeniable existence of national peculiarities. We can do it only by stripping "national character" of its appearance of substance and showing that it is nothing but the precipitation of past historical processes, which is then changed by subsequent historical processes. My definition of the nation, as a community of character arising

out of a community of fate, implies nothing but the task
of deriving national character from national history.

In seventeenth- and eighteenth-century France, the
king's court was the model of manners and the source of
good taste for the educated upper classes. A court nobility, bound by the rigid but pleasing forms of courtly
etiquette, not doing a day's work even in administering
the state, living a useless life of refined enjoyment, was
the strongest influence on the development of French
culture. The culture of a courtly society can only be a
highly formal culture: it takes pleasure in the beauty and
solemnity of language, the elegance of presentation, of
the wit and grace of expression, the clarity and order of
thought. The taste of this powerful and brilliant court
influenced a culture which became, first, the common
property of the French nobility and then the cultural
heritage of the French bourgeoisie.

In England the king's court exercised no such dominating influence on the development of taste and life style
even under the Tudors, let alone in the seventeenth and
eighteenth centuries. The bearers of English culture were
the country aristocracy and the urban patriciate. The
English country nobility, descendants of the usurpers of
feudal and ecclesiastical estates, living on their properties, busy in an agriculture organized even then on purely
capitalist lines, active in the aristocratic self-government
of counties, perforce developed a very different esthetic
taste from that of the French court nobility. Not bound
by the strict forms of courtly manners and given to much
rougher pleasures, they simply could not become the
bearers of the sort of highly formal culture that pleased
the French court. Much closer to nature than the French,
they could see nature and men in their living individuality, and, since they were used to making economic and
administrative decisions, they developed a much more
practical outlook.

Next to the country nobility, the urban patriciate—
merchants, bankers, ship owners, manufacturers—gained
an ever stronger influence on the cultural development of
the nation. "The industrialist," says Duhem, "very often
has a broad mind. The need to combine arrangements, to
conduct affairs, to handle people, quickly develops in him

the capacity to grasp tangled arrangements of concrete things. He is, however, a very weak thinker: his daily work keeps him away from abstract concepts and general principles." Aren't we on the way towards understanding the cultural differences between the French and the English of today through the fact that the taste of different classes shaped the two cultures which the two nations inherited in the age of modern capitalism?

The great struggle between royal power and the landlord class was won by the king in France and by the landlords in England. In England, parliamentary and local government institutions based on the estates were never destroyed. What the barons had wrested from the Plantagenets later became the heritage of the gentry, the bourgeoisie, and, finally, the working class. As each new class rose, it did not destroy the political institutions of the state but took them over and adapted them. This continuity in the development of the English state explains English traditionalism: each rising class inherited the traditions of the institutions it took over.

Things were quite different in France. There, the royal power shattered the feudal institutions by force and erected an absolute monarchy on their ruins. This is why the bourgeois revolution had to shatter the state and build on its ruins a very different kind of state. In England, ever new parties entered the old house and made themselves at home in it; in France, the old house was torn down time and again, and new ones built from scratch.

The successive class struggles were therefore reflected quite differently in the cultural life of the two nations. In England, where the class struggle dissolved into a struggle for individual reform measures, the ideology of the rising class was linked with the ideology of the traditional class. As long as the new ideology satisfied the needs of the rising class and proved itself in practice, it did not matter that the elements of the new synthesis were of diverse origin and hence contradictory. But in France, where the contending classes were in all-round antagonism, abstract principle faced abstract principle, closed system faced closed system. And so, history bred different talents in the two nations: here, a talent to grasp soberly a concrete situation in all its individuality and diversity and to find practical solutions for the problems it created; there, a trend towards abstraction, generalization, systematization, and logical rigor.

In France absolutism crushed the Reformation. Cultural life remained under the influence of the Catholic Church, with the grandiose logical consistency of its dogma and the splendor of its worship to satisfy esthetic needs. In England, culture fell under the powerful influence of a Puritanism that distrusted everything esthetic and directed men towards a practical testing in their professional work. In France, the struggle of the bourgeoisie for its spiritual emancipation could be fought only against the claim of the Church to absolute spiritual superiority; its closed system of dogmas could be challenged only by an equally philosophical system of the Enlightenment, entirely freed from traditional Christianity. In England, religious toleration within Protestantism was won as early as the seventeenth century; personal emotional needs could seek satisfaction in a number of Christian churches and sects; the individual could very well combine modern science, which fed his need for knowledge, with a personal and undogmatic Christianity that would appease his emotional needs. In France, modern science had, from its very beginning, joined an ideological struggle against the Catholic dogma; its attention was thus centered upon the ultimate and most general abstractions and hypotheses, upon systems serving ideological purposes. In England, where the need of a systematic confrontation with the local, less ambitious varieties of Christianity was weaker and less general, science could concentrate its attention much more upon the search for empirical natural laws that would give a practical dominion over nature. It could view general abstractions and hypotheses, much earlier than in France, as mere tools for the presentation and recapitulation of empirical natural laws.

Are we now in a position to derive the cultural difference between the two nations from their different histories? Not quite. To gain a fuller understanding, we would have to go back much further into history and make a much deeper analysis. But this is not our task here. I want merely to show, by way of an example, how a "community of character" can be explained by a "community of fate." The meaning of my definition of a nation can now be grasped. It is nothing but a methodological postulate, intended to offer science an assignment: to gain an understanding of the national phenomenon by explaining the entire particularity of each nation through its characteristic history and the nationality of each individual through his personal historical component. Science must gain an understanding of the individual peculiarities of nations and the national peculiarities of individuals by using the tools of the Marxist conception of history. It will thus dissolve the deceptive appearance of the substantiality of nations to which all nationalist conceptions of history succumb.

My theory of the nation is not centered upon the definition of the nation but on the description of the integrative process that has produced the modern nation. If this theory can claim a merit, it is because it is the first to derive this process from economic development, changing social structures, and the class system. I have shown that, in the feudal and early capitalist periods, this process of integration could link only the governing classes into a national cultural community, and it could not occur at all with peoples who had an alien ruling class. I have further shown that this process could embrace the masses only when capitalism reached the next stage. It took two forms: in the "historical nations," integration meant the extension of the cultural community, originally confined to the governing classes, to the masses. But in "unhistorical nations," which lived under alien ruling classes, it was the very beginning of a national cultural community, a true "awakening." This derivation of the national integration process from economic and social development is, I feel, of more than theoretical interest to us.

For the workers' movement is one of the powerful levers for widening the national cultural community to include the masses. The greater the share of the cultural goods that the working class conquers for itself, the more it is influenced by the national cultural tradition and heritage of its country. In each country, the socialist ideology merges with its peculiar cultural tradition and becomes nationally differentiated. The cultural character of each nation stamps itself on its socialism. As the Catholic Church has acquired clear and definite national characteristics despite the uniformity of its Roman leadership, the rigidity of its self-contained system of dogmas, and the common Latin language of its clergy throughout the world, so the international socialist movement cannot escape this process of national differentiation. Any one who compares German Marxism, English Laborism, and Russian Bolshevism cannot overlook the fact that the national cultural heritage impresses a national form upon the international socialist ideology. The nearer the working class of a country comes to taking power, the more must it adapt its practices and methods of struggle to the national peculiarities of its battlefield. Similarly, the socialist ideology of the working class becomes more closely linked with the national cultural heritage, as it absorbs more culture.

We cannot overcome this national differentiation of socialism by subjecting all the national working class parties to the dictatorship of one of them, which would then impose upon them its own fighting tactics, without any reference to their national battlefields, and force upon them its canonized system of dogmas, without any regard for their own cultural traditions. It would only be a utopian attempt to impose one kind of socialism, itself the historical product of a peculiar national character, upon workers' movements with a quite different history and of a quite different character.

International socialism should rather understand the national differentiation of its ideology and tactics as the result of an external and internal growth. It must accept the national diversity of practical methods and theoretical ideas. . . . Our task must not be to stamp out national peculiarities but to bring about international unity in national diversity.

TRANSLATED BY I. A. LANGNAS

III

The Bolshevik Tradition

V. I. Lenin

The Bourgeois Revolution*

> Vladimir Lenin (1870–1924), one of the major rev-
> olutionary figures of the twentieth century, was the
> practical and theoretical leader of the revolutionary
> Marxist tendency which developed among the Rus-
> sian social democracy during the early 1900's and
> soon became known as Bolshevism. At the center of
> his thought Lenin developed the idea of the revolu-
> tionary vanguard party, composed in its leading
> cadres of full-time professional revolutionists. This
> kind of party, he believed, could alone educate, prod,
> and lead the workers beyond mere trade-union con-
> sciousness and into revolutionary action. What he
> had intended mainly as a strategy for the special
> conditions of revolutionary work under Czarism, be-
> came in the years following the Russian Revolution
> a model for Communist parties throughout the world.
> Lenin regarded himself as an orthodox Marxist ap-
> plying the general postulates of Western socialist
> thought to the particular conditions of backward
> Russia; his critics have argued that, in the course of
> this application, he radically transformed Marxism in
> accordance with the outlook created in him and his
> colleagues by the experience of living under Czarist
> autocracy.
>   The following selection is taken from his work
> Two Tactics of Social Democracy in the Democratic
> Revolution (1905; Selected Works, Vol. 1, Bk. 2).
> Here Lenin discusses the problem that vexed all Rus-
> sian radicals: What would be the nature of the forth-

---

* Title supplied by the editor.

coming Russian revolution? Would it be a traditional kind of bourgeois revolution leading to the creation of a democratic republic? Was the bourgeoisie in Russia, weak and pusillanimous, capable of such a revolution? Could Russia bypass capitalism and make a leap directly from social backwardness to advanced socialism? What relations could be foreseen between the Russian bourgeoisie and the Russian peasants, on the one hand, and the revolutionary socialist movement, on the other? Lenin treats these matters with his customary shrewdness, and it may help the reader to connect what he says here with Marx's Address to the Communist League (p. 48 *and Trotsky's* Three Concepts of the Russian Revolution *(p. 340).*

. . . It is entirely absurd to think that a bourgeois revolution does not express the interests of the proletariat at all. This absurd idea boils down either to the hoary Narodnik [Populist] theory that a bourgeois revolution runs counter to the interests of the proletariat and that therefore we do not need bourgeois political liberty, or to anarchism, which rejects all participation of the proletariat in bourgeois politics, in a bourgeois revolution, and in bourgeois parlimentarism. From the standpoint of theory, this idea disregards the elementary propositions of Marxism concerning the inevitability of capitalist development where commodity production exists. Marxism teaches that a society which is based on commodity production, and which has commercial intercourse with civilized capitalist nations, at a certain stage of its development itself inevitably takes the road of capitalism. Marxism has irrevocably broken with the ravings of the Narodniks and the anarchists to the effect that Russia, for instance, can avoid capitalist development, jump out of capitalism, or skip over it and proceed along some path other than the path of the class struggle on the basis and within the framework of this capitalism.

All these principles of Marxism have been proved and explained over and over again in minute detail in general and with regard to Russia in particular. And from these principles it follows that the idea of seeking salvation for the working class in anything save the further development of capitalism is *reactionary*. In countries like Russia, the working class suffers not so much from capitalism as from the insufficient development of capitalism. The working class is therefore *decidedly interested* in the broadest, freest, and most rapid development of capitalism. The removal of all remnants of the old order which are hampering the broad, free, and rapid development of capitalism is of decided *advantage* to the working class. The bourgeois revolution is precisely a revolution that most resolutely sweeps away the survivals of the past, the remnants of serfdom (which include not only autocracy but monarchy as well), and most fully guarantees the broadest, freest, and most rapid development of capitalism.

That is why a *bourgeois* revolution is *in the highest degree advantageous to the proletariat*. A bourgeois revolution is *absolutely* necessary in the interests of the proletariat. The more complete and determined, the more consistent the bourgeois revolution, the more assured will be the proletarian struggle against the bourgeoisie for socialism. Only those who are ignorant of the rudiments of scientific socialism can regard this conclusion as new or strange, paradoxical. . . .

On the other hand, it is more advantageous for the working class if the necessary changes in the direction of bourgeois democracy take place by way of revolution and not by way of reform; for the way of reform is the way of delay, of procrastination, of the painfully slow decomposition of the putrid parts of the national organism. It is the proletariat and the peasantry that suffer first of all and most of all from their putrefaction. The revolutionary way is the way of quick amputation, which is the least painful to the proletariat, the way of the direct removal of the decomposing parts, the way of fewest concessions to and least consideration for the monarchy and the disgusting, vile, rotten, and contaminating institutions which go with it. . . .

Marxism teaches the proletarian not to keep aloof from the bourgeois revolution, not to be indifferent to it, not to allow the leadership of the revolution to be assumed by the bourgeoisie but, on the contrary, to take a most energetic part in it, to fight most resolutely for consistent proletarian democracy, for carrying the revolution to its conclusion. We cannot jump out of the bourgeois-democratic boundaries of the Russian revolution, but we can vastly extend these boundaries, and within these boundaries we can and must fight for the interests of the proletariat, for its immediate needs, and for the conditions that will make it possible to prepare its forces for the future complete victory. . . .

The basic idea here is the one that the *Vperiod** has repeatedly formulated, stating that we must not be afraid of a complete victory for social democracy in a democratic revolution, i.e., of a revolutionary-democratic dictatorship of the proletariat and the peasantry, for such a victory will enable us to rouse Europe, and the socialist proletariat of Europe, after throwing off the yoke of the bourgeoisie, will in its turn help us to accomplish the socialist revolution. . . .

The *Vperiod* quite definitely stated wherein lies the real "possibility of holding power"—namely, in the revolutionary-democratic dictatorship of the proletariat and the peasantry, in their joint mass strength, which is capable of outweighing all the forces of counterrevolution, in the inevitable concurrence of their interests in *democratic* changes. . . . If in our fight for a republic and democracy we could not rely upon the peasantry as well as on the proletariat, the prospect of our "holding power" would be hopeless. But if it is not hopeless, if a "decisive victory of the revolution over Czarism" opens up such a possibility, then we must point to it, we must actively call for its transformation into reality and issue practical slogans, not only for *the contingency* of the revolution being carried into Europe, but also *for the purpose* of carrying it there. . . . Beyond the bounds of democracy, there can

---

* *Forward*, Lenin's paper, 1904/5.

be no question of the proletariat and the peasant bourgeoisie having a single will. Class struggle between them is inevitable; but it is in a democratic republic that this struggle will be the most thorough-going and widespread struggle of the people *for socialism*. Like everything else in the world, the revolutionary-democratic dictatorship of the proletariat and the peasantry has a past and a future. Its past is autocracy, serfdom, monarchy and privilege. In the struggle against this past, in the struggle against counterrevolution, a "single will" of the proletariat and the peasantry is possible, for here there is unity of interests.

Its future is the struggle against private property, the struggle of the wage worker against the employer, the struggle for socialism. Here singleness of will is impossible. Here our path lies not from autocracy to a republic but from a petty-bourgeois democratic republic to socialism. . . .

A social democrat must never for a moment forget that the proletariat will inevitably have to wage the class struggle for socialism even against the most democratic and republican bourgeoisie and petty bourgeoisie. This is beyond doubt. Hence the absolute necessity of a separate, independent, strictly class Party of Social Democracy. Hence the temporary nature of our tactics of "striking jointly" with the bourgeoisie and the duty of keeping a strict watch "over our ally, as over an enemy," etc. All this is also beyond the slightest doubt. But it would be ridiculous and reactionary to deduce from this that we must forget, ignore or neglect these tasks, which, although transient and temporary, are vital at the present time. The fight against the autocracy is a temporary and transient task of the socialists, but to ignore or neglect this task in any way would be tantamount to betraying socialism and rendering a service to reaction. The revolutionary-democratic dictatorship of the proletariat and the peasantry is unquestionably only a transient, temporary aim of the socialists, but to ignore this aim in the period of a democratic revolution would be downright reactionary. . . .

. . . We Marxists all know . . . that the bourgeoisie is inconsistent, self-seeking, and cowardly in its support of the revolution. The bourgeoisie, in the mass, will inevitably turn toward counterrevolution, toward the autocracy, against the revolution, and against the people immediately its narrow, selfish interests are met, immediately it "recoils" from consistent democracy (*and it is already recoiling from it!*). There remains the "people," that is, the proletariat and the peasantry; the proletariat alone can be relied on to march to the end, for it is going far beyond the democratic revolution. That is why the proletariat fights in the front ranks for a republic and contemptuously rejects silly and unworthy advice to take care not to frighten away the bourgeoisie. The peasantry includes a great number of semiproletarian as well as petty-bourgeois elements. This causes it also to be unstable and compels the proletariat to unite in a strictly class party. But the instability of the peasantry differs radically from the instability of the bourgeoisie, for at the present time the peasantry is interested, not so much in the absolute preservation of private property, as in the confiscation of the landed estates, one of the principal forms of private property. While this does not make the peasantry become socialist or cease to be petty bourgeois, it is capable of becoming a whole-hearted and most radical adherent of the democratic revolution. . . .

. . . The Russian revolution will begin to assume its real sweep, will really assume the widest revolutionary sweep possible in the epoch of bourgeois-democratic revolution, only when the bourgeoisie recoils from it and when the masses of the peasantry come out as active revolutionaries side by side with the proletariat. In order that it may be consistently carried to its conclusion, our democratic revolution must rely on such forces as are capable of paralyzing the inevitable inconsistency of the bourgeoisie (i.e., capable precisely of "causing it to recoil from the revolution," which the Caucasian adherents of *Iskra* fear so much because of their lack of judgment).

The proletariat must carry out to completion the democratic revolution, by allying to itself the mass of the peas-

antry in order to crush by force the resistance of the autocracy and to paralyze the instability of the bourgeoisie. The proletariat must accomplish the socialist revolution, by allying itself to the mass of the semiproletarian elements of the population, in order to crush by force the resistance of the bourgeoisie and to paralyze the instability of the peasantry and the petty bourgeoisie. . . .

V. I. Lenin

The Vanguard Party*

> *In 1902, Lenin published his famous pamphlet* What
> Is to Be Done? *the first systematic development of
> his views concerning the nature of the revolutionary
> party. Though it had only a limited immediate im-
> pact among Russian socialists and was virtually un-
> known in the West, where the social democrats were
> building mass working-class parties on lines utterly
> at variance with Lenin's proposals,* What Is to Be
> Done? *must in retrospect be judged one of the most
> influential political documents of our century.*

We have seen that the organisation of wide political agitation, and consequently, of all-sided political exposures
are an absolutely necessary *and paramount* task of activity, that is, if that activity is to be truly social democratic.
We arrived at this conclusion *solely* on the grounds of the
pressing needs of the working class for political knowledge and political training. But this ground by itself is
too narrow for the presentation of the question, for it
ignores the general democratic tasks of social democracy
as a whole, and of modern, Russian social democracy in
particular. In order to explain the situation more concretely we shall approach the subject from an aspect
that is "nearer" to the economist, namely, from the
practical aspect. "Every one agrees" that it is necessary to develop the political consciousness of the working
class. But the question arises: How is that to be done?
What must be done to bring this about? The economic

---

* Title supplied by editor.

struggle merely brings the workers "up against" questions concerning the attitude of the government toward the working class. Consequently, *however much we may try to "give to the economic struggle itself a political character," we shall never be able* to develop the political consciousness of the workers (to the degree of social-democratic consciousness) by confining ourselves to the economic struggle, for *the limits of this task are too narrow.* . . .

The workers can acquire class political consciousness *only from without*, that is, only outside of the economic struggle, outside of the sphere of relations between workers and employers. The sphere from which alone it is possible to obtain this knowledge is the sphere of relationships between *all* classes and the state and the government—the sphere of the interrelations between *all* classes. For that reason, the reply to the question: "What must be done in order that the workers may acquire political knowledge?" cannot be merely the one which, in the majority of cases, the practical workers, especially those who are inclined towards economism, usually content themselves with, i.e., "go among the workers." To bring political knowledge to the workers, the social democrats must *go among all classes of the population*, must despatch units of their army *in all directions*.

We deliberately select this awkward formula, we deliberately express ourselves in a simple, forcible way, not because we desire to indulge in paradoxes, but in order to "stimulate" the economists to take up their tasks which they unpardonably ignore, to make them understand the difference between trade-union and social-democratic politics, which they refuse to understand. Therefore, we beg the reader not to get excited, but to hear us patiently to the end.

Take the type of social-democratic circle that has been most widespread during the past few years, and examine its work. It has "contact with the workers," it issues leaflets—in which abuses in the factories, the government's partiality toward the capitalists, and the tyranny of the police are strongly condemned—and rests content with this. At meetings of workers, there are either no discussions, or they do not extend beyond such subjects. Lectures and discussions, on the history of the revolutionary movement, on questions of the home and foreign policy of our government, on questions of the economic evolution of Russia and of Europe, and the position of the various classes in modern society, etc., are extremely rare. Of systematically acquiring and extending contact with other classes of society, no one even dreams. The ideal leader, as the majority of the members of such circles picture him, is something more in the nature of a trade-union secretary than a socialist political leader. Any trade-union secretary, an English one, for instance, helps the workers to conduct the economic struggle, helps to expose factory abuses, explains the injustice of the laws and of measures which hamper the freedom of strikes and the freedom to picket, to warn all and sundry that a strike is proceeding at a certain factory, explains the partiality of arbitration courts which are in the hands of the bourgeois classes, etc., etc. In a word, every trade-union secretary conducts and helps to conduct "the economic struggle against the employers and the government." It cannot be too strongly insisted that *this is not* enough to constitute social democracy. The social democrat's ideal should not be a trade-union secretary, but *a tribune of the people*, able to react to every manifestation of tyranny and oppression, no matter where it takes place, no matter what stratum or class of the people it affects; he must be able to group all these manifestations into a single picture of police violence and capitalist exploitation; he must be able to take advantage of every petty event in order to explain his socialistic convictions and his social democratic demands *to all*, in order to explain to *all* and every one the world historical significance of the struggle for the emancipation of the proletariat. . . .

I assert: 1) that no movement can be durable without a stable organisation of leaders to maintain continuity; 2) that the more widely the masses are drawn into the struggle and form the basis of the movement, the more necessary is it to have such an organisation and the more stable must it be (for it is much easier then for demagogues to sidetrack the more backward sections of the masses); 3) that the organisation must consist chiefly of persons engaged in revolution as a profession; 4) that in a country with a despotic government, the more we *restrict* the membership of this organisation to persons who are engaged in revolution as a profession and who have been professionally trained in the art of combating the political police, the more difficult will it be to catch the organisation; and 5) the *wider* will be the circle of men and women of the working class or of other classes of society able to join the movement and perform active work in it. . . .

The question in the last analysis, amounts to the question we have considered above, namely, whether it is possible to have a mass *organisation* when the maintenance of strict secrecy is essential. We can never give a mass organisation that degree of secrecy which is essential for the persistent and continuous struggle against the government. But to concentrate all secret functions in the hands of as small a number of professional revolutionists as possible, does not mean that the latter will "do the thinking for all" and that the crowd will not take an active part in the movement. On the contrary, the crowd will advance from its ranks increasing numbers of professional revolutionists, for it will know that it is not enough for a few students and workingmen waging economic war to gather together and form a "committee," but that professional revolutionists must be trained for years; the crowd will "think" not of primitive ways but of training professional revolutionists. The centralisation of the secret functions of the *organisation* does not mean the concentration of all the functions of the *movement*. The active participation of the greatest masses in the dissemination of illegal literature will not diminish because a dozen professional revolutionists concentrate in their hands the secret part of the work; on the contrary, it will *increase tenfold*. Only in this way will the reading of illegal literature, the contribution to illegal literature, and to some extent even the distribution of illegal literature *almost cease to be secret work*, for the police will soon come to realise the folly and futility of setting the whole judicial and administrative machine into motion to intercept every copy of a publication that is being broadcast in thousands. This applies not only to the press, but to every function of the movement, even to demonstrations. The active and widespread participation of the masses will not suffer; on the contrary, it will benefit by the fact that a "dozen" experienced revolutionists, no less professionally trained than the police, will concentrate all the secret side of the work in their hands—prepare leaflets, work out approximate plans, and appoint bodies of leaders for each town district, for each factory district, and for each educational institution (I know that exception will be taken to my "undemocratic" views, but I shall reply to this altogether unintelligent objection later on). The centralisation of the more secret functions in an organisation of revolutionists will not diminish, but rather increase the extent and the quality of the activity of a large number of other organisations intended for wide membership and which, therefore, can be as loose and as public as possible, for example, trade unions, workers' circles for self-education, and the reading of illegal literature, and socialist, and also democratic, circles for *all other sections of the population,* etc., etc. We must have *as large a number as possible* of such organisations having the widest possible variety of functions, but it is absurd and dangerous to *confuse these with organisations of revolutionists,* to erase the line of demarcation between them, to dim still more the already incredibly hazy appreciation by the masses that to "serve" the mass movement we must have people who will devote themselves exclusively to social-democratic activities, and that such people must *train* themselves patiently and steadfastly to be professional revolutionists. . . .

V. I. Lenin

On Imperialism*

First published in 1917, Imperialism: The Highest Stage of Capitalism *is one of Lenin's most ambitious theoretical works. It attempts to demonstrate that imperialism is a "direct continuation of the fundamental properties of capitalism in general" and a central attribute of capitalism in its late stages. Lenin traces imperialist ventures and conflicts to an inner crisis of capitalist economy: the need of competing national economies to find new sources of raw material and more important, new possibilities for the investment of surplus capital during "the monopoly stage of capitalism." Thereby, argued Lenin, imperialism is basically not the result of political decisions made by enlightened or benighted governments, but rather a tendency inherent in the workings of developed capitalism.*

Imperialism emerged as the development and direct continuation of the fundamental attributes of capitalism in general. But capitalism only became capitalist imperialism at a definite and very high stage of its development, when certain of its fundamental attributes began to be transformed into their opposites, when the features of a period of transition from capitalism to a higher social and economic system began to take shape and reveal themselves all along the line. Economically, the main thing in this process is the substitution of capitalist monopolies for capitalist free competition. Free competition is the fundamental attribute of capitalism and of commodity produc-

---

* Title added by editor.

tion generally. Monopoly is exactly the opposite of free competition; but we have seen the latter being transformed into monopoly before our eyes, creating large-scale industry and eliminating small industry, replacing large-scale industry by still larger-scale industry, finally leading to such a concentration of production and capital that monopoly has been and is the result: cartels, syndicates, and trusts, and merging with them, the capital of a dozen or so banks manipulating thousands of millions. At the same time monopoly, which has grown out of free competition, does not abolish the latter, but exists over it and alongside of it, and thereby gives rise to a number of very acute, intense antagonisms, friction, and conflicts. Monopoly is the transition from capitalism to a higher system.

If it were necessary to give the briefest possible definition of imperialism, we should have to say that imperialism is the monopoly stage of capitalism. Such a definition would include what is most important, for, on the one hand, finance capital is the bank capital of a few big monopolist banks, merged with the capital of the monopolist combines of manufacturers; and, on the other hand, the division of the world is the transition from a colonial policy that was extended without hindrance to territories unoccupied by any capitalist power to a colonial policy of monopolistic possession of the territory of the world, which has been completely divided up.

But very brief definitions, although convenient, for they sum up the main points, are nevertheless, inadequate, because very important features of the phenomenon that has to be defined have to be especially deduced. And so, without forgetting the conditional and relative value of all definitions, which can never include all the concatenations of a phenomenon in its complete development, we must give a definition of imperialism that will embrace the following five essential features:

1 The concentration of production and capital developed to such a high stage that it created monopolies, which play a decisive role in economic life.

2 The merging of bank capital with industrial capital, and the creation, on the basis of this "finance capital," of a financial oligarchy.

3 The export of capital, which has become extremely important, as distinguished from the export of commodities.

4 The formation of international capitalist monopolies which share the world among themselves.

5 The territorial division of the whole world among the greatest capitalist powers is completed.

Imperialism is capitalism in that stage of development in which the dominance of monopolies and finance capital have established themselves; in which the export of capital has acquired pronounced importance; in which the division of the world among the international trusts has begun; in which the division of all territories of the globe among the great capitalist powers has been completed.

We shall see later that imperialism can and must be defined differently if consideration is to be given, not only to the basic, purely economic factors—to which the above definition is limited—but also to the historical place of this stage of capitalism in relation to capitalism in general, or in the relations between imperialism and the two main trends in the working-class movement. The point to be noted just now is that imperialism, as interpreted above, undoubtedly represents a special stage in the development of capitalism. In order to enable the reader to obtain as well grounded an idea of imperialism as possible, we deliberately quoted largely from bourgeois economists who are obliged to admit the particularly incontrovertible facts regarding modern capitalist economy. With the same object in view, we have produced detailed statistics which reveal the extent to which bank capital, etc., have developed, showing how the transformation of quantity into quality, of developed capitalism into imperialism, has expressed itself. Needless to say, all boundaries in nature and in society are conditional and changeable, and, consequently, it would be absurd to discuss the exact year or the decade in which imperialism "definitely" became established.

In this matter of defining imperialism, however, we have to enter into controversy, primarily, with Karl Kautsky, the principal Marxian theoretician of the epoch of the so-called Second International—that is, of the twenty-five years between 1889 and 1914.

Kautsky, in 1915 and even in November, 1914, very emphatically attacked the fundamental ideas expressed in our definition of imperialism. Kautsky said that imperialism must not be regarded as a "phase" or stage of economy, but as a policy; a definite policy "preferred" by finance capital; that imperialism cannot be "identified" with "contemporary capitalism"; that if imperialism is to be understood to mean "all the phenomena of contemporary capitalism"—cartels, protection, the domination of the financiers and colonial policy—then the question as to whether imperialism is necessary to capitalism becomes reduced to the "flattest tautology"; because, in that case, "imperialism is naturally a vital necessity for capitalism," and so on. The best way to present Kautsky's ideas is to quote his own definition of imperialism, which is diametrically opposed to the substance of the ideas which we have set forth (for the objections coming from the camp of the German Marxists, who have been advocating such ideas for many years already, have been long known to Kautsky as the objections of a definite trend in Marxism).

Kautsky's definition is as follows:

Imperialism is a product of highly developed industrial capitalism. It consists in the striving of every industrial capitalist nation to bring under its control or to annex increasingly big *agrarian* [Kautsky's italics] regions irrespective of what nations inhabit those regions.

This definition is utterly worthless because it one-sidedly, i.e., arbitrarily, brings out the national question alone (although this is extremely important in itself as well as in its relation to imperialism), it arbitrarily and *inaccurately* relates this question *only* to industrial capital in the countries that annex other nations, and in an equally arbitrary and inaccurate manner brings out the annexation of agrarian regions.

Imperialism is a striving for annexations—this is what the *political* part of Kautsky's definition amounts to. It is correct, but very incomplete, for politically, imperialism is, in general, a striving toward violence and reaction. For the moment, however, we are interested in the *economic* aspect of the question, which Kautsky *himself* introduced into his definition. The inaccuracy of Kautsky's definition is strikingly obvious. The characteristic feature of imperialism is *not* industrial capital, *but* finance capital. It is not an accident that in France it was precisely the extraordinarily rapid development of *finance* capital, and the weakening of industrial capital, that, from 1830 onward, gave rise to the extreme extension of annexationist (colonial) policy. The characteristic feature of imperialism is precisely that it strives to annex *not* only agricultural regions, but even highly industrialized regions (German appetite for Belgium; French appetite for Lorraine), 1) because the fact that the world is already divided up obliges those contemplating a *new* division to reach out for *any kind* of territory, and 2) because an essential feature of imperialism is the rivalry between a number of great powers in the striving for hegemony, i.e., for the conquest of territory, not so much directly for themselves as to weaken the adversary and undermine *his* hegemony. (Belgium is chiefly necessary to Germany as a base for operations against England; England needs Baghdad as a base for operations against Germany, etc.)

Kautsky refers especially—and repeatedly—to English writers who, he alleges, have given a purely political meaning to the word *imperialism* in the sense that Kautsky understands it. We take up the work by the Englishman Hobson, *Imperialism*, which appeared in 1902, and therein we read:

The new imperialism differs from the older, first, in substituting for the ambition of a single growing empire the theory and the practice of competing empires, each motivated by similar lusts of political aggrandisement and commercial gain; secondly, in the dominance of financial or investing over mercantile interests.

We see, therefore, that Kautsky is absolutely wrong in referring to English writers generally (unless he meant the vulgar English imperialist writers or the avowed apologists for imperialism). We see that Kautsky, while claiming that he continues to defend Marxism, as a matter of fact takes a step backward compared with the *social-liberal* Hobson, who *more correctly* takes into account two "historically concrete" (Kautsky's definition is a mockery of historical concreteness) features of modern imperialism: 1) the competition between *several* imperialisms, and 2) the predominance of the financier over the merchant. If it were chiefly a question of the annexation of agrarian countries by industrial countries, the role of the merchant would be predominant.

Kautsky's definition is not only wrong and un-Marxian. It serves as a basis for a whole system of views which run counter to Marxian theory and Marxian practice all along the line. We shall refer to this again later. The argument about words which Kautsky raises as to whether the modern stage of capitalism should be called "imperialism" or "the stage of finance capital" is of no importance. Call it what you will, it matters little. The fact of the matter is that Kautsky detaches the politics of imperialism from its economics, speaks of annexations as being a policy "preferred" by finance capital and opposes to it another bourgeois policy which, he alleges, is possible on this very basis of finance capital. According to his argument, monopolies in economics are compatible with nonmonopolistic, nonviolent, nonannexationist methods in politics. According to his argument, the territorial division of the world, which was completed precisely during the period of finance capital and which constitutes the basis of the present peculiar forms of rivalry between the biggest capitalist states, is compatible with a nonimperialist policy. The result is a slurring over and a blunting of the most profound contradictions of the latest stage of capitalism, instead of an exposure of their depth; the result is bourgeois reformism instead of Marxism.

Kautsky enters into controversy with the German apologist of imperialism and annexations, Cunow, who clumsily and cynically argues that imperialism is modern capitalism: the development of capitalism is inevitable and progressive; therefore imperialism is progressive; therefore, we should cringe before and eulogize it. This is something like the caricature of Russian Marxism which the Narodniks drew in 1894/95. They used to argue as follows: if the Marxists believe that capitalism is inevitable in Russia, that it is progressive, then they ought to open a public house and begin to implant capitalism! Kautsky's reply to Cunow is as follows: imperialism is not modern capitalism. It is only one of the forms of the policy of modern capitalism. This policy we can and should fight; we can and should fight against imperialism, annexations, etc.

The reply seems quite plausible, but in effect it is a more subtle and more disguised (and therefore more dangerous) propaganda of conciliation with imperialism; for unless it strikes at the economic basis of the trusts and banks, the "struggle" against the policy of the trusts and banks reduces itself to bourgeois reformism and pacifism, to an innocent and benevolent expression of pious hopes. Kautsky's theory means refraining from mentioning existing contradictions, forgetting the most important of them, instead of revealing them in their full depth; it is a theory that has nothing in common with Marxism. . . .

Kautsky writes:

from the purely economic point of view, it is not impossible that capitalism will yet go through a new phase, that of the extension of the policy of the cartels to foreign policy, the phase of ultra-imperialism,

i.e., of a superimperialism, a union of world imperialism and not struggles among imperialisms; a phase when wars shall cease under capitalism, a phase of "the joint exploitation of the world by internationally combined finance capital."

We shall have to deal with this "theory of ultraimperialism" later on in order to show in detail how definitely and utterly it departs from Marxism. In keeping with the plan of the present work, we shall examine the exact economic data on this question. Is "ultraimperialism" possible "from the purely economic point of view" or is it ultranonsense?

If by purely economic point of view, a "pure" abstraction is meant, then all that can be said reduces itself to the following proposition: evolution is proceeding toward monopoly; therefore the trend is toward a single world monopoly, to a universal trust. This is indisputable, but it is also as completely meaningless as is the statement that "evolution is proceeding" toward the manufacture of foodstuffs in laboratories. In this sense the "theory" of ultraimperialism is no less absurd than a "theory of ultraagriculture" would be.

If, on the other hand, we are discussing the "purely economic" conditions of the epoch of finance capital as a historically concrete epoch, which opened at the beginning of the twentieth century, then the best reply that one can make to the lifeless abstractions of "ultraimperialism" (which serve an exclusively reactionary aim: that of diverting attention from the depth of *existing* antagonisms) is to contrast them with the concrete economic realities of present-day world economy. Kautsky's utterly meaningless talk about ultraimperialism encourages, among other things, that profoundly mistaken idea which only brings grist to the mill of the apologists of imperialism, viz., that the rule of finance capital *lessens* the unevenness and contradictions inherent in world economy, whereas in reality it *increases* them. . . .

We notice three areas of highly developed capitalism with a high development of means of transport, of trade and of industry: the Central European, the British, and the American areas. Among these are three states which dominate the world: Germany, Great Britain, the United States. Imperialist rivalry and the struggle between these countries have become very keen because Germany has only a restricted area and few colonies (the creation of "Central Europe" is still a matter for the future; it is being born in the midst of desperate struggles). For the moment the distinctive feature of Europe is political disintegration. In the British and American areas, on the other hand, political concentration is very highly developed, but there is a tremendous disparity between the immense colonies of the one and the insignificant colonies of the other. In the colonies, capitalism is only beginning to develop. The struggle for South America is becoming more and more acute.

There are two areas where capitalism is not developed: Russia and Eastern Asia. In the former, the density of population is very low, in the latter it is very high; in the former political concentration is very high, in the latter it does not exist. The partition of China is only beginning, and the struggle between Japan, U.S.A., etc., in connection therewith is continually gaining in intensity.

Compare this reality, the vast diversity of economic and political conditions, the extreme disparity in the rate of development of the various countries, etc., and the violent struggles of the imperialist states, with Kautsky's silly little fable about "peaceful" ultraimperialism. Is this not the reactionary attempt of a frightened philistine to hide from stern reality? Are not the international cartels which Kautsky imagines are the embryos of "ultraimperialism" (with as much reason as one would have for describing the manufacture of tabloids in a laboratory as ultraagriculture in embryo) an example of the division *and the redivision* of the world, the transition from peaceful division to nonpeaceful division and vice versa? Is not American and other finance capital, which divided the whole world peacefully, with Germany's participation, for example, in the international rail syndicate, or in the international mercantile shipping trust, now engaged in *redividing* the world on the basis of a new relation of forces, which is being changed by methods *by no means* peaceful?

Finance capital and the trusts are increasing instead of diminishing the differences in the rate of development of the various parts of the world economy. When the relation of forces is changed, how else, *under capitalism*, can the solution of contradictions be found, except by resorting to *violence*?

V. I. Lenin

The State and Revolution

The State and Revolution, first published in 1918, expresses the very core of Lenin's thought. It was written three months before the October Revolution and interrupted by the Bolshevik seizure of power. "It is more pleasant and useful to go through the 'experience of the revolution' than to write about it," remarked Lenin.

While always basing himself on lengthy quotations from Marx and Engels, whom he proposed to rescue from social democratic interpreters, Lenin here develops in some detail his views on the nature of the state as an instrument of class oppression; the necessity for revolution as the means of establishing a new, proletarian state; the concept of the "dictatorship of the proletariat" as the new ruling power; and the stages of transition from capitalism to communism. The State and Revolution brings together in startling juxtaposition both the democratic and authoritarian components of Lenin's thought. Cf. the comments in Howe and Coser, Images of Socialism, p. 835

The State as the Product of the Irreconcilability of Class Antagonism

What is now happening to Marx's doctrine has, in the course of history, often happened to the doctrines of other revolutionary thinkers and leaders of oppressed classes struggling for emancipation. During the lifetime of great revolutionaries, the oppressing classes have visited relentless persecution on them and received their teaching with the most savage hostility, the most furious hatred, the most ruthless campaign of lies and slanders. After their death, attempts are made to turn them into harmless icons, canonise them, and surround their *names* with a certain halo for the "consolation" of the oppressed classes and with the object of duping them, while at the same time emasculating and vulgarising the *real essence* of their revolutionary theories and blunting their revolutionary edge. At the present time, the bourgeoisie and the opportunists within the labour movement are cooperating in this work of adulterating Marxism. They omit, obliterate, and distort the revolutionary side of its teaching, its revolutionary soul. They push to the foreground and extol what is, or seems, acceptable to the bourgeoisie. . . .

In such circumstances, the distortion of Marxism being so widespread, it is our first task to *resuscitate* the real teachings of Marx on the state. For this purpose it will be necessary to quote at length from the works of Marx and Engels themselves. Of course, long quotations will make the text cumbersome and in no way help to make it popular reading, but we cannot possibly avoid them. All, or at any rate, all the most essential passages in the works of Marx and Engels on the subject of the state must necessarily be given as fully as possible, in order that the reader may form an independent opinion of all the views of the founders of scientific socialism and of the development of those views, and in order that their distortions by the present predominant "Kautskyism" may be proved in black and white and rendered plain to all. . . .

Summarising his historical analysis Engels says:

The state is therefore by no means a power imposed on society from the outside; just as little is it "the reality of the moral idea," "the image and reality of reason," as Hegel asserted. Rather, it is a product of society at a certain stage of development; it is the admission that this society has become entangled in an insoluble contradiction with itself, that it is cleft into irreconcilable antagonisms which it is powerless to dispel. But in order that these antagonisms, classes with conflicting economic interests, may not consume themselves and society in sterile struggle, a power apparently standing above society becomes necessary, whose purpose is to moderate the conflict and keep it within the bounds of "order"; and this power arising out of society, but placing itself above it, and increasingly separating itself from it, is the state.

Here we have, expressed in all its clearness, the basic idea of Marxism on the question of the historical rôle and meaning of the state. The state is the product and the manifestation of the *irreconcilability* of class antagonisms. The state arises when, where, and to the extent that the class antagonisms *cannot* be objectively reconciled. And, conversely, the existence of the state proves that the class antagonisms *are* irreconcilable.

It is precisely on this most important and fundamental point that distortions of Marxisms arise along two main lines.

On the one hand, the bourgeois, and particularly the petty bourgeois ideologists, compelled under the pressure of indisputable historical facts to admit that the state only exists where there are class antagonisms and the class struggle, "correct" Marx in such a way as to make it appear that the state is an organ for *reconciling* the classes. According to Marx, the state could neither arise nor maintain itself if a reconciliation of classes were possible. But with the petty bourgeois and philistine professors and publicists, the state—and this frequently on the strength of benevolent references to Marx!—becomes a conciliator of the classes. According to Marx, the state is an organ of class *domination*, an organ of *oppression* of one class by another; its aim is the creation of "order" which legalises and perpetuates this oppression by moderating the collisions between the classes. But in the opinion of the petty-bourgeois politicians, order means reconciliation of the classes, and not oppression of one class by another; to moderate collisions does not mean, they say, to deprive the oppressed classes of certain definite means and methods of struggle for overthrowing the oppressors, but to practise reconciliation.

For instance, when, in the Revolution of 1917, the question of the real meaning and rôle of the state arose in all its vastness as a practical question demanding immediate action on a wide mass scale, all the Socialist revolutionaries and Mensheviks suddenly and completely sank to the petty-bourgeois theory of "reconciliation" of the classes by the "state." Innumerable resolutions and articles by politicians of both these parties are saturated through and through with this purely petty-bourgeois and philistine theory of "reconciliation." That the state is an organ of domination of a definite class which *cannot* be reconciled with its antipode (the class opposed to it) —this petty-bourgeois democracy is never able to understand. Its attitude towards the state is one of the most telling proofs that our Socialist Revolutionaries and Mensheviks are not socialists at all (which we Bolsheviks have always maintained), but petty-bourgeois democrats with a near-Socialist phraseology.

On the other hand, the "Kautskyist" distortion of Marx is far more subtle. "Theoretically," there is no denying that the state is the organ of class domination, or that class antagonisms are irreconcilable. But what is forgotten or glossed over is this: if the state is the product of the irreconcilable character of class antagonisms, if it is a force standing *above* society and "increasingly separating itself from it," then it is clear that the liberation of the oppressed class is impossible not only without a violent revolution, *but also without the destruction* of the apparatus of state power, which was created by the ruling class and in which this "separation" is embodied. As we shall see later Marx drew his theoretically self-evident conclusion from a concrete historical analysis of the problems of revolution. And it is exactly this conclusion which Kautsky—as we shall show fully in our subsequent remarks—has "forgotten" and distorted.

Special Bodies of Armed Men, Prisons, etc.

Engels continues:

In contrast with the ancient organisation of the *gens*, the first distinguishing characteristic of the state is the grouping of the subjects of the state *on a territorial basis*. . . .

Such a grouping seems "natural" to us, but it came after a prolonged and costly struggle against the old form of tribal or gentilic society.

. . . The second is the establishment of a *public force*, which is no longer absolutely identical with the population organising itself as an armed power. This special public force is necessary, because a self-acting armed organisation of the population has become impossible since the cleavage of society into classes. . . . This public force exists in every state; it consists not merely of armed men, but of material appendages, prisons and repressive institutions of all kinds, of which gentilic society knew nothing. . . .

Engels develops the conception of that "power" which is termed the state—a power arising from society, but placing itself above it and becoming more and more separated from it. What does this power mainly consist of? It consists of special bodies of armed men who have at their disposal prisons, etc.

We are justified in speaking of special bodies of armed men, because the public power peculiar to every state is not "absolutely identical" with the armed population, with its "self-acting armed organisation."

Like all the great revolutionary thinkers, Engels tries to draw the attention of the class-conscious workers to that very fact which to prevailing philistinism appears least of all worthy of attention, most common and sanctified by solid, indeed, one might say, petrified prejudices. A standing army and police are the chief instruments of state power. But can this be otherwise?

From the point of view of the vast majority of Europeans at the end of the nineteenth century whom Engels was addressing, and who had neither lived through nor closely observed a single great revolution, this cannot be otherwise. They cannot understand at all what this "self-acting armed organisation of the population" means. To the question, whence arose the need for special bodies of armed men, standing above society and becoming separated from it (police and standing army), the Western European and Russian philistines are inclined to answer with a few phrases borrowed from Spencer or Mikhailovsky, by reference to the complexity of social life, the differentiation of functions, and so forth.

Such a reference seems "scientific" and effectively dulls the senses of the average man, obscuring the most important and basic fact, namely, the break-up of society into irreconcilably antagonistic classes.

Without such a break-up, the "self-acting armed organisation of the population" might have differed from the primitive organisation of a herd of monkeys grasping sticks, or of primitive men, or men united in a tribal form of society, by its complexity, its high technique, and so forth, but would still have been possible.

It is impossible now, because society, in the period of civilisation, is broken up into antagonistic, and, indeed, irreconcilably antagonistic classes, which, if armed in a "self-acting" manner, would come into armed struggle with each other. A state is formed, a special power is created in the form of special bodies of armed men, and every revolution, by shattering the state apparatus, demonstrates to us how the ruling class aims at the restoration of the special bodies of armed men at *its* service, and how the oppressed class tries to create a new organisation of this kind, capable of serving not the exploiters, but the exploited.

In the above observation, Engels raises theoretically the very same question which every great revolution raises practically, palpably, and on a mass scale of action, namely, the question of the relation between special bodies of armed men and the "self-acting armed organisation of the population." We shall see how this is concretely illustrated by the experience of the European and Russian revolutions.

But let us return to Engels' discourse.

He points out that sometimes, for instance, here and there in North America, this public power is weak (he has in mind an exception that is rare in capitalist society, and he speaks about parts of North America in its preimperialist days, where the free colonist predominated), but that in general it tends to become stronger:

It [the public power] grows stronger, however, in proportion as the class antagonisms within the state grow sharper and with the growth in size and population of the adjacent states. We have only to look at our present-day Europe, where class struggle and rivalry in conquest have screwed up the public power to such a pitch that it threatens to devour the whole of society and even the state itself.

This was written as early as the beginning of the nineties of last century, Engels' last preface being dated June 16, 1891. The turn towards imperialism, understood to mean complete domination of the trusts, full sway of the large banks, and a colonial policy on a grand scale, and so forth, was only just beginning in France, and was even weaker in North America and in Germany. Since then the "rivalry in conquest" has made gigantic progress—especially as, by the beginning of the second decade of the twentieth century, the whole world had been finally divided up between these "rivals in conquest," i.e., between the great predatory powers. Military and naval armaments since then have grown to monstrous proportions, and the predatory war of 1914–1917 for the domination of the world by England or Germany, for the division of the spoils, has brought the "swallowing up" of all the forces of society by the rapacious state power nearer to a complete catastrophe.

As early as 1891 Engels was able to point to "rivalry in conquest" as one of the most important features of the foreign policy of the great powers, but in 1914–1917, when this rivalry, many times intensified, has given birth to an imperialist war, the rascally social chauvinists cover up their defence of the predatory policy of "their" capitalist classes by phrases about the "defence of the fatherland," or the "defence of the republic and the revolution," etc.1

The State as an Instrument for the Exploitation of the Oppressed Class

For the maintenance of a special public force standing above society, taxes and state loans are needed.

Having at their disposal the public force and the right to exact taxes, the officials now stand as organs of society *above* society. The free, voluntary respect which was accorded to the organs of the gentilic form of government does not satisfy them, even if they could have it. . . .

Special laws are enacted regarding the sanctity and the inviolability of the officials. "The shabbiest police servant

. . . has more authority" than the representative of the
clan, but even the head of the military power of a civilised state "may well envy the least among the chiefs of
the clan the unconstrained and uncontested respect
which is paid to him."

Here the question regarding the privileged position of
the officials as organs of state power is clearly stated. The
main point is indicated as follows: what is it that places
them *above* society? We shall see how this theoretical
problem was solved in practice by the Paris Commune in
1871 and how it was slurred over in a reactionary manner
by Kautsky in 1912:

As the state arose out of the need to hold class antagonisms in
check, but as it, at the same time, arose in the midst of the conflict of these classes, it is, as a rule, the state of the most powerful,
economically dominant class, which by virtue thereof becomes also
the dominant class politically, and thus acquires new means of
holding down and exploiting the oppressed class. . . .

Not only the ancient and feudal states were organs of
exploitation of the slaves and serfs, but

the modern representative state is the instrument of the exploitation of wage-labour by capital. By way of exception, however,
there are periods when the warring classes so nearly attain equilibrium that the state power, ostensibly appearing as a mediator,
assumes for the moment a certain independence in relation to
both. . . .

Such were, for instance, the absolute monarchies of the
seventeenth and eighteenth centuries, the Bonapartism of
the First and Second Empires in France, and the Bismarck regime in Germany.

Such, we may add, is now the Kerensky government in
republican Russia after its shift to persecuting the revolutionary proletariat, at a moment when the soviets, thanks
to the leadership of the petty-bourgeois democrats, have
already become impotent, while the bourgeoisie is *not yet*
strong enough to disperse them outright.

In a democratic republic, Engels continues, "wealth
wields its power indirectly, but all the more effectively,"
first, by means of "direct corruption of the officials"

(America); second, by means of "the alliance of the government with the stock exchange" (France and America). . . .

The omnipotence of "wealth" is thus more *secure* in a democratic republic, since it does not depend on the poor political shell of capitalism. A democratic republic is the best possible political shell for capitalism, and therefore, once capital has gained control (through the Palchinskys, Chernovs, Tseretelis and Co.) of this very best shell, it establishes its power so securely, so firmly, that *no* change, either of persons, or institutions, or parties in the bourgeois republic can shake it.

We must also note that Engels quite definitely regards universal suffrage as a means of bourgeois domination. Universal suffrage, he says, obviously summing up the long experience of German Social Democracy, is "an index of the maturity of the working class; it cannot, and never will, be anything else but that in the modern state."

The petty-bourgeois democrats, such as our socialist revolutionaries and Mensheviks, and also their twin brothers, the social chauvinists and opportunists of Western Europe, all expect "more" from universal suffrage. They themselves share, and instill into the minds of the people, the wrong idea, that universal suffrage "in the *modern* state" is really capable of expressing the will of the majority of the toilers and of assuring its realisation. . . .

The "Withering Away" of the State and Violent Revolution

Engels' words regarding the "withering away" of the state enjoy such popularity, they are so often quoted, and they show so clearly the essence of the usual adulteration by means of which Marxism is made to look like opportunism, that we must dwell on them in detail. Let us quote the whole passage from which they are taken:

The proletariat seizes state power, and then transforms the means of production into state property. But in doing this, it puts an end to itself as the proletariat, it puts an end to all class differences and class antagonisms, it puts an end also to the state as the state. Former society, moving in class antagonisms, had need of the state, that is, an organisation of the exploiting class at each period for the maintenance of its external conditions of production; therefore, in particular, for the forcible holding down of the exploited class in the conditions of oppression (slavery, bondage or serfdom, wage labour) determined by the existing mode of production. The state was the official representative of society as a whole, its embodiment in a visible corporate body; but it was this only in so far as it was the state of that class which itself, in its epoch, represented society as a whole: in ancient times, the State of the slave-owning citizens; in the Middle Ages, of the feudal nobility; in our epoch, of the bourgeoisie. When ultimately it becomes really representative of society as a whole, it makes itself superfluous. As soon as there is no longer any class of society to be held in subjection; as soon as, along with class domination and the struggle for individual existence based on the former anarchy of production, the collisions and excesses arising from these have also been abolished, there is nothing more to be repressed, and a special repressive force, a state, is no longer necessary. The first act in which the state really comes forward as the representative of society as a whole—the seizure of the means of production in the name of society—is at the same time its last independent act as a state. The interference of a state power in social relations becomes superfluous in one sphere after another, and then becomes dormant of itself. Government over persons is replaced by the administration of things and the direction of the processes of production. The state is not "abolished," *it withers away*. It is from this standpoint that we must appraise the phrase "people's free state"—both its justification at times for agitational purposes, and its ultimate scientific inadequacy—and also the demand of the so-called anarchists that the state should be abolished overnight.

Without fear of committing an error, it may be said that of this argument by Engels so singularly rich in ideas, only one point has become an integral part of socialist thought among modern socialist parties, namely, that, unlike the anarchist doctrine of the "abolition" of the state, according to Marx the state "withers away." To emasculate Marxism in such a manner is to reduce it to opportunism, for such an "interpretation" only leaves the hazy conception of a slow, even, gradual change, free from leaps and storms, free from revolution. The current popular conception, if one may say so, of the "withering away" of the state undoubtedly means a slurring over, if not a negation, of revolution.

Yet, such an "interpretation" is the crudest distortion of Marxism, which is advantageous only to the bourgeoisie; in point of theory, it is based on a disregard for the most important circumstances and considerations pointed out in the very passage summarising Engels' idea, which we have just quoted in full.

In the first place, Engels at the very outset of his argument says that, in assuming state power, the proletariat by that very act "puts an end to the state as the state." One is "not accustomed" to reflect on what this really means. Generally, it is either ignored altogether, or it is considered as a piece of "Hegelian weakness" on Engels' part. As a matter of fact, however, these words express succinctly the experience of one of the greatest proletarian revolutions—the Paris Commune of 1871, of which we shall speak in greater detail in its proper place. As a matter of fact, Engels speaks here of the destruction of the bourgeois state by the proletarian revolution, while the words about its withering away refer to the remains of *proletarian* statehood *after* the socialist revolution. The bourgeois state does not "wither away," according to Engels but is "put an end to" by the proletariat in the course of the revolution. What withers away after the revolution is the proletarian state or semistate.

Secondly, the state is a "special repressive force." This splendid and extremely profound definition of Engels' is given by him here with complete lucidity. It follows from this that the "special repressive force" of the bourgeoisie for the suppression of the proletariat, of the millions of workers by a handful of the rich, must be replaced by a "special repressive force" of the proletariat for the suppression of the bourgeoisie (the dictatorship of the proletariat). It is just this that constitutes the destruction of "the state as the state." It is just this that constitutes the "act" of "the seizure of the means of production in the name of society." And it is obvious that such a substitution of one (proletarian) "special repressive force" for another (bourgeois) "special repressive force" can in no way take place in the form of a "withering away"

Thirdly, as to the "withering away" or, more expressively and colourfully, as to the state "becoming dormant,"

Engels refers quite clearly and definitely to the period *after* "the seizure of the means of production (by the state) in the name of society," that is, *after* the socialist revolution. We all know that the political form of the "state" at that time is complete democracy. But it never enters the head of any of the opportunists who shamelessly distort Marx that when Engels speaks here of the state "withering away," or "becoming dormant," he speaks of *democracy*. At first sight this seems very strange. But it is "unintelligible" only to one who has not reflected on the fact that democracy is *also* a state and that, consequently, democracy will *also* disappear when the state disappears. The bourgeois state can only be "put an end to" by a revolution. The state in general, i.e., most complete democracy, can only "wither away."

Fourthly, having formulated his famous proposition that "the state withers away," Engels at once explains concretely that this proposition is directed equally against the opportunists and the anarchists. In doing this, however, Engels puts in the first place that conclusion from his proposition about the "withering away" of the state which is directed against the opportunists.

One can wager that out of every 10,000 persons who have read or heard about the "withering away" of the state, 9,990 do not know at all, or do not remember, that Engels did not direct his conclusions from this proposition against the anarchists *alone*. And out of the remaining ten, probably nine do not know the meaning of a "people's free state" nor the reason why an attack on this watchword contains an attack on the opportunists. This is how history is written! This is how a great revolutionary doctrine is imperceptibly adulterated and adapted to current philistinism! The conclusion drawn against the anarchists has been repeated thousands of times, vulgarised, harangued about in the crudest fashion possible until it has acquired the strength of a prejudice, whereas the conclusion drawn against the opportunists has been hushed up and "forgotten"!

The "people's free state" was a demand in the programme of the German Social Democrats and their current slogan in the seventies. There is no political substance in this slogan other than a pompous middle-class circumlocution of the idea of democracy. In so far as it referred in a lawful manner to a democratic republic, Engels was prepared to "justify" its use "at times" from a propaganda point of view. But this slogan was opportunist, for it not only expressed an exaggerated view of the attractiveness of bourgeois democracy, but also a lack of understanding of the socialist criticism of every state in general. We are in favour of a democratic republic as the best form of the state for the proletariat under capitalism, but we have no right to forget that wage slavery is the lot of the people even in the most democratic bourgeois republic. Furthermore, every state is a "special repressive force" for the suppression of the oppressed class. Consequently, *no* state is either a "free" or "people's state." Marx and Engels explained this repeatedly to their party comrades in the seventies.

Fifthly, in the same work of Engels, from which every one remembers his argument on the "withering away" of the state, there is also a disquisition on the significance of a violent revolution. The historical analysis of its role becomes, with Engels, a veritable panegyric on violent revolution. This, of course, "no one remembers"; to talk or even to think of the importance of this idea is not considered good form by contemporary socialist parties, and in the daily propaganda and agitation among the masses it plays no part whatever. Yet it is indissolubly bound up with the "withering away" of the state in one harmonious whole.

Here is Engels' argument:

. . . That force, however, plays another role (other than that of a diabolical power) in history, a revolutionary role; that, in the words of Marx, it is the midwife of every old society which is pregnant with the new; that it is the instrument with whose aid social movement forces its way through and shatters the dead, fossilised political forms—of this there is not a word in Herr Dühring. It is only with sighs and groans that he admits the possibility that force will perhaps be necessary for the overthrow of the economic system of exploitation—unfortunately! because all use of force, forsooth, demoralises the person who uses it. And this in spite of the immense moral and spiritual impetus which has resulted from every victorious revolution! And this in Germany, where a violent collision—which indeed may be forced on the people—would at least have the advantage of wiping out the servility which has permeated the national consciousness as a result of the humiliation of the Thirty Years' War. And this parson's mode of thought—lifeless, insipid and impotent—claims to impose itself on the most revolutionary party which history has known?

How can this panegyric on violent revolution, which Engels insistently brought to the attention of the German Social Democrats between 1878 and 1894, i.e., right to the time of his death, be combined with the theory of the "withering away" of the state to form one doctrine?

Usually the two views are combined by means of eclecticism, by an unprincipled, sophistic, arbitrary selection (to oblige the powers that be) of either one or the other argument, and in ninety-nine cases out of a hundred (if not more often), it is the idea of the "withering away" that is specially emphasised. Eclecticism is substituted for dialectics—this is the most usual, the most widespread phenomenon to be met with in the official Social-Democratic literature of our day in relation to Marxism. Such a substitution is, of course, nothing new; it may be observed even in the history of classic Greek philosophy. When Marxism is adulterated to become opportunism, the substitution of eclecticism for dialectics is the best method of deceiving the masses; it gives an illusory satisfaction; it seems to take into account all sides of the process, all the tendencies of development, all the contradictory factors and so forth, whereas in reality it offers no consistent and revolutionary view of the process of social development at all.

We have already said above, and shall show more fully later, that the teaching of Marx and Engels regarding the inevitability of a violent revolution refers to the bourgeois state. It *cannot* be replaced by the proletarian state (the dictatorship of the proletariat) through "withering away," but, as a general rule, only through a violent revolution. The panegyric sung in its honour by Engels and fully corresponding to the repeated declarations of Marx (remember the concluding passages of the *Poverty of Philosophy* and *The Communist Manifesto*, with its proud and open declaration of the inevitability of a violent revolution; remember Marx's *Critique of the Gotha Programme* of 1875 in which, almost thirty years later, he mercilessly castigates the opportunist character of that programme), this praise is by no means a mere "impulse," a mere declamation, or a polemical sally. The necessity of systematically fostering among the masses *this* and just this point of view about violent revolution lies at the root of the *whole* of Marx's and Engels' teaching. The neglect of such propaganda and agitation by both the present predominant social-chauvinist and the Kautskyist currents brings their betrayal of Marx's and Engels' teaching into prominent relief.

The replacement of the bourgeois by the proletarian state is impossible without a violent revolution. The abolition of the proletarian state, i.e., of all states, is only possible through "withering away." . . .

Transition from Capitalism to Communism

Between capitalist and communist society—Marx continues—lies the period of the revolutionary transformation of the former into the latter. To this also corresponds a political transition period, in which the state can be no other than *the revolutionary dictatorship of the proletariat.*

This conclusion Marx bases on an analysis of the role played by the proletariat in modern capitalist society, on the data concerning the development of this society, and on the irreconcilability of the opposing interests of the proletariat and the bourgeoisie.

Earlier the question was put thus: to attain its emancipation, the proletariat must overthrow the bourgeoisie, conquer political power and establish its own revolutionary dictatorship.

Now the question is put somewhat differently: the transition from capitalist society, developing towards communism, towards a communist society, is impossible without a "political transition period," and the state in this period can only be the revolutionary dictatorship of the proletariat.

What, then, is the relation of this dictatorship to democracy?

We have seen that *The Communist Manifesto* simply places side by side the two ideas: the "transformation of the proletariat into the ruling class" and the "establishment of democracy." On the basis of all that has been said above, one can define more exactly how democracy changes in the transition from capitalism to communism.

In capitalist society, under the conditions most favourable to its development, we have more or less complete democracy in the democratic republic. But this democracy is always bound by the narrow framework of capitalist exploitation, and consequently, always remains, in reality, a democracy for the minority, only for the possessing classes, only for the rich. Freedom in capitalist society always remains just about the same as it was in the ancient Greek republics: freedom for the slave owners. The modern wage slaves, owing to the conditions of capitalist exploitation, are so much crushed by want and poverty that "democracy is nothing to them," "politics is nothing to them"; that, in the ordinary peaceful course of events, the majority of the population is barred from participating in social and political life.

The correctness of this statement is perhaps most clearly proved by Germany, just because in this state constitutional legality lasted and remained stable for a remarkably long time—for nearly half a century (1871–1914)—and because Social Democracy in Germany during that time was able to achieve far more than in other countries in "utilising legality" and was able to organise into a political party a larger proportion of the working class than anywhere else in the world.

What, then, is this largest proportion of politically conscious and active wage slaves that has so far been observed in capitalist society? One million members of the Social Democratic Party—out of fifteen million wage workers! Three million organised in trade unions—out of fifteen million!

Democracy for an insignificant minority, democracy for the rich—that is the democracy of capitalist society. If we look more closely into the mechanism of capitalist democracy, everywhere, both in the "petty"—so-called petty—details of the suffrage (residential qualification, exclusion of women, etc.), and in the technique of the representative institutions, in the actual obstacles to the right of assembly (public buildings are not for "beggars"!), in the purely capitalist organisation of the daily press, etc., etc. —on all sides we see restriction after restriction upon democracy. These restrictions, exceptions, exclusions, obstacles for the poor, seem slight, especially in the eyes of one who has himself never known want and has never been in close contact with the oppressed classes in their mass life (and nine-tenths, if not ninety-nine hundredths, of the bourgeois publicists and politicians are of this class), but in their sum total these restrictions exclude and squeeze out the poor from politics and from an active share in democracy.

Marx splendidly grasped this *essence* of capitalist democracy, when, in analysing the experience of the Commune, he said that the oppressed were allowed, once every few years, to decide which particular representatives of the oppressing class should be in parliament to represent and repress them!

But from this capitalist democracy—inevitably narrow, subtly rejecting the poor, and therefore hypocritical and false to the core—progress does not march onward, simply, smoothly, and directly, to "greater and greater democracy," as the liberal professors and petty-bourgeois opportunists would have us believe. No, progress marches onward, i.e., toward communism, through the dictatorship of the proletariat: it cannot do otherwise, for there is no one else and no other way to *break the resistance* of the capitalist exploiters.

But the dictatorship of the proletariat, i.e., the organisation of the vanguard of the oppressed as the ruling class for the purpose of crushing the oppressors—cannot produce merely an expansion of democracy. *Together* with an immense expansion of democracy which *for the first time* becomes democracy for the poor, democracy for the people, and not democracy for the rich folk, the dictatorship of the proletariat produces a series of restrictions of liberty in the case of the oppressors, the exploiters, the capitalists. We must crush them in order to free humanity from wage slavery; their resistance must be broken by force; it is clear that where there is suppression there is also violence, there is no liberty, no democracy.

Engels expressed this splendidly in his letter to Bebel when he said, as the reader will remember, that "as long as the proletariat still *needs* the state, it needs it not in the interests of freedom, but for the purpose of crushing its antagonists; and as soon as it becomes possible to speak of freedom, then the state, as such, ceases to exist."

Democracy for the vast majority of the people, and suppression by force, i.e., exclusion from democracy, of the exploiters and oppressors of the people—this is the modification of democracy during the *transition* from capitalism to communism.

Only in communist society, when the resistance of the capitalists has been completely broken, when the capitalists have disappeared, when there are no classes (i.e., there is no difference between the members of society in their relation to the social means of production), *only then* "the state ceases to exist," and "*it becomes possible to speak of freedom.*" Only then a really full democracy, a democracy without any exceptions, will be possible and will be realised. And only then will democracy itself begin to *wither away* due to the simple fact that, freed from capitalist slavery, from the untold horrors, savagery, absurdities, and infamies of capitalist exploitation, people will gradually *become accustomed* to the observation of the elementary rules of social life that have been known for centuries and repeated for thousands of years in all school books; they will become accustomed to observing them without force, without compulsion, without subordination, without the *special apparatus* for compulsion which is called the state.

The expression "the state *withers away*" is very well chosen, for it indicates both the gradual and the elemental nature of the process. Only habit can, and undoubt-

edly will, have such an effect; for we see around us millions of times how readily people get accustomed to
observe the necessary rules of life in common if there is no
exploitation, if there is nothing that causes indignation,
that calls forth protest and revolt and has to be *suppressed*.

V. I. Lenin

No Compromises?

The following two selections are taken from "Left-Wing" Communism: An Infantile Disorder, first published in 1920 and composed by Lenin as a polemic against certain groups, especially Dutch and British, within the newly formed Third International. It was prepared especially for the Second Congress of the International, held in August, 1920, where issues of strategy and tactics were vigorously debated. The ultraleft communists in Western Europe, most of them belonging to small sects, had developed theories opposing work in trade unions, and declaring that Marxists should not run for office or take posts in bourgeois parliaments. Lenin's brilliant polemic against them can be appreciated even by those on the left who do not share all his premises. Its obvious relevance to the politics of the 1960's and 1970's is a prime example of the way old theoretical disputes can take on renewed interest with the passage of time.

In the quotation from the Frankfurt pamphlet, we saw how emphatically the "Lefts" advance this slogan. It is sad to see people who doubtless consider themselves Marxists and want to be Marxists forgetting the fundamental truths of Marxism. This is what Engels—who, like Marx, was one of those rarest of authors whose every sentence in every one of their great works contains remarkably profound meaning—wrote in 1874 in opposition to the manifesto of the Blanquist Communards:

"We are communists," [wrote the Blanquist Communards in their manifesto] "because we want to attain our goal without stopping at intermediate stations, without any compromises, which only postpone the day of victory and prolong the period of slavery."

The German communists are communists because through all the intermediate stations and all compromises, created, not by them, but by the course of historical development, they clearly perceive and constantly pursue the final aim, viz., the abolition of classes and the creation of a society in which there will no longer be private ownership of land or of the means of production. The thirty-three Blanquists are communists because they imagine that merely because *they* want to skip the intermediate stations and compromises, that settles the matter, and if "it begins" in the next few days—which they take for granted—and they come to the helm, "communism will be introduced" the day after tomorrow. If that is not immediately possible, they are not communists.

What childish innocence it is to present impatience as a theoretically convincing argument!*

In the same article, Engels expresses his profound esteem for Vaillant and speaks of the "undeniable merits" of the latter (who, like Guesde, was one of the most prominent leaders of international socialism up to August, 1914, when they both turned traitor to socialism). But Engels does not allow an obvious mistake to pass without a detailed analysis. Of course, to very young and inexperienced revolutionaries, as well as to petty-bourgeois revolutionaries of even a very respectable age and very experienced, it seems exceedingly "dangerous," incomprehensible, and incorrect to "allow compromises." And many sophists (being unusually or excessively "experienced" politicians) reason exactly in the same way as the British leaders of opportunism mentioned by Comrade Lansbury: "If the Bolsheviks may make a certain compromise, why may we not make any kind of compromise?" But proletarians schooled in numerous strikes (to take only this manifestation of the class struggle) usually understand quite well the very profound (philosophical, historical, political, and psychological) truth expounded

---

* Engels, "Program of the Blanquist Communards," from the German Social-Democratic newspaper *Volksstaat*, 1874, No. 73, given in the Russian translation of *Articles, 1871–1875*, Petrograd, 1919, pp. 52–53.

by Engels. Every proletarian has been through strikes and has experienced "compromises" with the hated oppressors and exploiters, when the workers had to go back to work either without having achieved anything or agreeing to only a partial satisfaction of their demands. Every proletarian—owing to the conditions of the mass struggle and the sharp intensification of class antagonisms in which he lives—notices the difference between a compromise enforced by objective conditions (such as lack of strike funds, no outside support, extreme hunger and exhaustion), a compromise which in no way diminishes the revolutionary devotion and readiness for further struggle on the part of the workers who have agreed to such a compromise, and a compromise by traitors, who try to ascribe to outside causes their own selfishness (strikebreakers also enter into "compromises"!), cowardice, desire to toady to the capitalists, and readiness to yield to intimidation, sometimes to persuasion, sometimes to sops, and sometimes to flattery on the part of the capitalists. . . .

Naturally, there are individual cases of exceptional difficulty and intricacy when the real character of this or that "compromise" can be correctly determined only with the greatest difficulty; just as there are cases of homicide where it is by no means easy to decide whether the homicide was fully justified and even necessary (as for example legitimate self-defence), or due to unpardonable negligence, or even to a cunningly executed, perfidious plan. Of course, in politics, where it is sometimes a matter of extremely complicated—national and international —relations between classes and parties, very many cases will arise that will be much more difficult than the questions of legitimate "compromise" in a strike, or the treacherous "compromise" of a strikebreaker, traitor leader, etc. It would be absurd to formulate a recipe or general rule ("No Compromises!") to serve all cases. One must use one's own brains and be able to find one's bearings in each separate case. That, in fact, is one of the functions of a party organization and of party leaders worthy of the title, namely, through the prolonged, persistent, variegated, and comprehensive efforts of all thinking representatives of the given class,* to evolve the knowledge, the experience and—in addition to knowledge and experience—the political instinct necessary for the speedy and correct solution of intricate political problems.

Naive and utterly inexperienced people imagine that it is sufficient to admit the permissibility of compromises *in general* in order to obliterate the dividing line between opportunism, against which we wage and must wage an irreconcilable struggle, and revolutionary Marxism, or communism. But if such people do not yet know that *all* dividing lines in nature and in society are mutable and to a certain extent conventional, they cannot be assisted otherwise than by a long process of training, education, enlightenment, and by political and everyday experience. It is important to single out from the practical questions of the politics of each separate or specific historical moment those which reveal the principal type of impermissible, treacherous compromises, compromises embodying the opportunism that is fatal to the revolutionary class, and to exert all efforts to explain them and combat them. During the imperialist war of 1914–1918 between two groups of equally predatory and rapacious countries, the principal, fundamental type of opportunism was social chauvinism, that is, support of "defence of the fatherland," which, in *such* a war, was really equivalent to defence of the predatory interests of one's "own" bourgeoisie. After the war, the defence of the robber "League of Nations," the defence of direct or indirect alliances with the bourgeoisie of one's own country against the revolutionary proletariat and the "soviet" movement, and the defence of bourgeois democracy and bourgeois parliamentarism against "soviet power" became the principal manifestations of those impermissible and treacherous compromises, the sum total

---

* Within every class, even in the most enlightened countries, even prevailing within the most advanced class, and even when the circumstances of the moment have roused all its spiritual forces to an exceptional degree, there always are—and inevitably *will be* as long as classes exist, as long as classless society has not fully entrenched and consolidated itself and has not developed on its own foundations —representatives of the class who do *not* think and are incapable of thinking. Were this not so, capitalism would not be the oppressor of the masses it is.

of which constituted the opportunism that is fatal to the revolutionary proletariat and its cause.

". . . One must emphatically reject all compromise with other parties . . . all policy of manoeuvring and compromise," write the German Lefts in the Frankfurt pamphlet.

It is a wonder that, holding such views, these Lefts do not emphatically condemn Bolshevism! For the German Lefts must know that the whole history of Bolshevism, both before and after the October Revolution is *full* of instances of manoeuvring, temporizing, and compromising with other parties, bourgeois parties included!

To carry on a war for the overthrow of the international bourgeoisie, a war which is a hundred times more difficult, protracted, and complicated than the most stubborn of ordinary wars between states, and to refuse beforehand to manoeuvre, to utilize the conflict of interests (even though temporary) among one's enemies, to refuse to temporize and compromise with possible (even though temporary, unstable, vacillating and conditional) allies—is not this ridiculous in the extreme? Is it not as though, when making a difficult ascent of an unexplored and hitherto inaccessible mountain, we were to refuse beforehand ever to move in zigzags, ever to retrace our steps, ever to abandon the course once selected to try others? And yet people who are so ignorant and inexperienced (if youth were the explanation, it would not be so bad; young people are ordained by God himself to talk such nonsense for a period), could meet with the support—whether direct or indirect, open or covert, whole or partial, does not matter—of certain members of the Dutch Communist Party!!

After the first Socialist revolution of the proletariat, after the overthrow of the bourgeoisie in one country, the proletariat of that country *for a long time* remains *weaker* than the bourgeoisie, simply because of the latter's extensive international connections, and also because of the spontaneous and continuous restoration and regeneration of capitalism and the bourgeoisie by the small commodity-producers of the country which has overthrown the bourgeoisie. The more powerful enemy can be conquered only by exerting the utmost effort, and by *necessarily*, thoroughly, carefully, attentively and skilfully taking advantage of every, even the smallest, "rift" among the enemies, of every antagonism of interest among the bourgeoisie of the various countries and among the various groups or types of bourgeoisie within the various countries, by taking advantage of every, even the smallest, opportunity of gaining a mass ally, even though this ally be temporary, vacillating, unstable, unreliable and conditional. Those who do not understand this do not understand even a particle of Marxism, or of scientific, modern Socialism *in general*. Those who have not proved by *deeds* over a fairly considerable period of time, and in fairly varied political situations, their ability to apply this truth in practice have not yet learned to assist the revolutionary class in its struggle for the emancipation of toiling humanity from the exploiters. And this applies equally to the period before and to the period after the conquest of political power by the proletariat. . . .

Capitalism would not be capitalism if the "pure" proletariat were not surrounded by a large number of exceedingly motley types intermediate between the proletarian and the semiproletarian (who earns his livelihood in part by the sale of his labour power), between the semiproletarian and the small peasant (and petty artisan, handicraft worker, and small master in general), between the small peasant and the middle peasant, and so on, and if the proletariat itself were not divided into more developed and less developed strata, if it were not divided according to territorial origin, trade, sometimes according to religion, and so on. And from all this follows the necessity, the absolute necessity, for the vanguard of the proletariat, for its class-conscious section, for the Communist Party, to resort to manoeuvres, arrangements, and compromises with the various groups of proletarians, with the various parties of the workers and small masters. The whole point lies in *knowing how* to apply these tactics in order to *raise*, and not lower, the *general* level of proletarian class consciousness, revolutionary spirit, and ability to fight and win. . . .

Working in Parliament?*

The surest way of discrediting and damaging a new political (and not only political) idea is to reduce it to absurdity on the plea of defending it. For every truth, if "overdone," if exaggerated, if carried beyond the limits of its actual applicability, can be reduced to absurdity and is even bound to become an absurdity under these conditions. That is just the kind of backhanded service the Dutch and German Lefts are rendering the new truth that the soviet form of government is superior to bourgeois-democratic parliaments. It stands to reason that any one who subscribed to the old view, or in general maintained that refusal to participate in bourgeois parliaments is impermissible under any circumstances, would be wrong. I cannot attempt to formulate here the conditions under which a boycott is useful, for the object of this pamphlet is far more modest, namely, to study Russian experience in connection with certain topical questions of international communist tactics. Russian experience has given us one successful and correct (1905) and one incorrect (1906) example of the application of the boycott by the Bolsheviks. Analyzing the first case, we see that we succeeded in *preventing the convocation* of a reactionary parliament by a reactionary government in a situation in which extraparliamentary, revolutionary mass action (strikes in particular) was mounting with exceptional rapidity, when not a single section of the proletariat and of the peasantry could support the reactionary government in any way, when the revolutionary proletariat was acquiring influence over the broad, backward masses through the strike struggle and the agrarian movement.

---

* Title supplied by editor.

In Western Europe and America, parliament has become especially abhorrent to the advanced revolutionary members of the working class. That is incontestable. It is quite comprehensible, for it is difficult to imagine anything more vile, abominable and treacherous than the behavior of the vast majority of the Socialist and Social Democratic parliamentary deputies during and after the war. But it would be not only unreasonable, but actually criminal to yield to this mood when deciding *how* this generally recognized evil should be fought. In many countries of Western Europe, the revolutionary mood, we might say, is at present a "novelty," or a "rarity," which had been all too long waited for vainly and impatiently; and perhaps that is why the mood is so easily succumbed to. Certainly, without a revolutionary mood among the masses, and without conditions facilitating the growth of this mood, revolutionary tactics would never be converted into action; but we in Russia have become convinced by very long, painful, and bloody experience of the truth that revolutionary tactics cannot be built on revolutionary moods alone. Tactics must be based on a sober and strictly objective appraisal of *all* the class forces of the particular state (and of the states that surround it, and of all states the world over) as well as of the experience of revolutionary movements. To show how "revolutionary" one is solely by hurling abuse at parliamentary opportunism, solely by repudiating participation in parliaments, is very easy; but just because it is too easy, it is not the solution for a difficult, a very difficult problem. It is much more difficult to create a really revolutionary parliamentary group in a European parliament than it was in Russia. Of course. But that is only a particular expression of the general truth that it was easy for Russia, in the specific, historically very unique situation of 1917, to *start* the socialist revolution, but it will be more difficult for Russia than for the European countries to *continue* the revolution and bring it to its consummation.

I had occasion to point this out already at the beginning of 1918, and our experience of the past two years has entirely confirmed the correctness of this view. Certain specific conditions, viz., 1) the possibility of linking up the Soviet revolution with the ending, as a consequence of this revolution, of the imperialist war, which had exhausted the workers and peasants to an incredible degree; 2) the possibility of taking advantage for a certain time of the mortal conflict between two world-powerful groups of imperialist robbers, who were unable to unite against their Soviet enemy; 3) the possibility of enduring a comparatively lengthy civil war, partly owing to the enormous size of the country and to the poor means of communications; 4) the existence of such a profound bourgeois-democratic revolutionary movement among the peasantry that the party of the proletariat was able to take the revolutionary demands of the peasant party (the Socialist Revolutionary Party, the majority of the members of which were definitely hostile to Bolshevism) and realize them at once, thanks to the conquest of political power by the proletariat—these specific conditions do not exist in Western Europe at present; and a repetition of such or similar conditions will not come so easily. That, by the way, apart from a number of other causes, is why it will be more difficult for Western Europe to *start* a socialist revolution than it was for us. To attempt to "circumvent" this difficulty by "skipping" the difficult job of utilizing reactionary parliaments for revolutionary purposes is absolutely childish. You want to create a new society, yet you fear the difficulties involved in forming a good parliamentary group, made up of convinced, devoted, heroic Communists, in a reactionary parliament! Is that not childish? If Karl Liebknecht in Germany and Z. Höglund in Sweden were able, even without mass support from below, to set examples in the truly revolutionary utilization of reactionary parliaments, how can one say that a rapidly growing revolutionary, mass party, in the midst of the postwar disillusionment and embitterment of the masses, cannot *hammer out* a communist group in the worst of parliaments?! Precisely because the backward masses of the workers and—to an even greater degree—of the small peasants are in Western Europe much more imbued with bourgeois-demo-

cratic and parliamentary prejudices than they were in
Russia, precisely because of that, it is *only* from within
such institutions as bourgeois parliaments that Communists can (and must) wage a long and persistent struggle,
undaunted by any difficulties, to expose, dissipate and
overcome these prejudices.

Leon Trotsky

Dual Power

> Leon Trotsky was born in Russia in 1879; he was
> murdered by an agent of the Russian secret police
> in Mexico in 1940. During the sixty years of his life,
> he remained a dedicated revolutionary. He worked
> as an underground organizer and writer for the Rus-
> sian revolutionary movement; he was the main practi-
> cal leader of the Bolshevik revolution and the or-
> ganizer of the Red Army during the civil war in
> Russia. He served as Foreign Minister in Lenin's cab-
> inet and became, after Lenin's death, the leader of
> the Left Opposition, struggling in vain to halt the
> Stalinist deformation of the Soviet state. When he
> was driven into exile, he set about trying to organize
> a new revolutionary movement, the Fourth Interna-
> tional, and wrote a large number of historical, politi-
> cal, and cultural works, all of them marked by range
> of mind, brilliance of style, and faithfulness to Marx-
> ist precepts.
>
> Dual Power is a chapter in Volume 1 of Trotsky's
> History of the Russian Revolution, published in
> 1932. In this essay Trotsky investigates the moment
> of historical tension when two powers stand poised
> against each other: that of the faltering state which
> represents the declining classes and that of the revo-
> lutionary institutions which speak in the name of the
> new.

What constitutes the essence of a dual power?* We must
pause upon this question, for an illumination of it has

---

* [*Dual power* is the phrase settled upon in Communist literature as
an English rendering of *dvoevlastie*. The term is untranslatable both

never appeared in historic literature. And yet this dual power is a distinct condition of social crisis, by no means peculiar to the Russian Revolution of 1917, although there most clearly marked out.

Antagonistic classes exist in society everywhere, and a class deprived of power inevitably strives to some extent to swerve the governmental course in its favor. This does not as yet mean, however, that two or more powers are ruling in society. The character of a political structure is directly determined by the relation of the oppressed classes to the ruling class. A single government, the necessary condition of stability in any regime, is preserved so long as the ruling class succeeds in putting over its economic and political forms upon the whole of society as the only forms possible.

The simultaneous dominion of the German Junkers and the bourgeoisie—whether in the Hohenzollern form or the republic—is not a double government, no matter how sharp at times may be the conflict between the two participating powers. They have a common social basis, therefore their clash does not threaten to split the state apparatus. The two-power regime arises only out of irreconcilable class conflict—is possible, therefore, only in a revolutionary epoch, and constitutes one of its fundamental elements.

The political mechanism of revolution consists of the transfer of power from one class to another. The forcible overturn is usually accomplsihed in a brief time. But no historic class lifts itself from a subject position to a position of rulership suddenly in one night, even though a night of revolution. It must already on the eve of revolution have assumed a very independent attitude towards the official ruling class; moreover, it must have focused upon itself the hopes of intermediate classes and layers, dissatisfied with the existing state of affairs, but not capable of playing an independent role. The historic preparation of a revolution brings about in the prerevolutionary

---

because of its form—twin-power-dom—and because the stem, *vlast,* means *sovereignty* as well as *power. Vlast* is also used as an equivalent of *government,* and in the plural corresponds to our phrase *the authorities.* In view of this, I have employed some other terms besides *dual power: double sovereignty, two-power regime,* etc. Tr.]

period, a situation in which the class which is called to realize the new social system, although not yet master of the country, has actually concentrated in its hands a significant share of the state power, while the official apparatus of the government is still in the hands of the old lords. That is the initial dual power in every revolution.

But that is not its only form. If the new class, placed in power by a revolution which it did not want, is in essence an already old, historically belated, class; if it was already worn out before it was officially crowned; if on coming to power it encounters an antagonist already sufficiently mature and reaching out its hand toward the helm of state, then instead of one unstable two-power equilibrium, the political revolution produces another, still less stable. To overcome the "anarchy" of this twofold sovereignty becomes at every new step the task of the revolution—or the counterrevolution.

This double sovereignty does not presuppose—generally speaking, indeed, it excludes—the possibility of a division of the power into two equal halves, or indeed any formal equilibrium of forces whatever. It is not a constitutional, but a revolutionary fact. It implies that a destruction of the social equilibrium has already split the state superstructure. It arises where the hostile classes are already each relying upon essentially imcompatible governmental organizations—the one outlived, the other in process of formation—which jostle against each other at every step in the sphere of government. The amount of power which falls to each of these struggling classes in such a situation is determined by the correlation of forces in the course of the struggle.

By its very nature such a state of affairs cannot be stable. Society needs a concentration of power, and in the person of the ruling class—or, in the situation we are discussing, the two half-ruling classes—irresistibly strives to get it. The splitting of sovereignty foretells nothing less than a civil war. But before the competing classes and parties will go to that extreme—especially in case they dread the interference of a third force—they may feel compelled for quite a long time to endure, and even to sanction, a two-power system. This system will nevertheless inevitably explode. Civil war gives to this double sovereignty its most visible, because territorial, expression. Each of the powers, having created its own fortified drill ground, fights for possession of the rest of the territory, which often has to endure the double sovereignty in the form of successive invasions by the two fighting powers, until one of them decisively installs itself.

The English revolution of the seventeenth century, exactly because it was a great revolution shattering the nation to the bottom, affords a clear example of this alternating dual power, with sharp transitions in the form of civil war.

At first the royal power, resting upon the privileged classes or the upper circles of these classes, the aristocrats and bishops, is opposed by the bourgeoisie and the circles of the squirarchy that are close to it. The government of the bourgeoisie is the Presbyterian Parliament supported by the City of London. The protracted conflict between these two regimes is finally settled in open civil war. The two governmental centers, London and Oxford, create their own armies. Here the dual power takes a territorial form, although, as always in civil war, the boundaries are very shifting. Parliament conquers. The king is captured and awaits his fate.

It would seem that the conditions are now created for the single rule of the Presbyterian bourgeoisie. But before the royal power can be broken, the parliamentary army has converted itself into an independent political force. It has concentrated in its ranks the Independents, the pious and resolute petty bourgeoisie, the craftsmen and farmers. This army powerfully interferes in the social life, not merely as an armed force, but as a Praetorian Guard, and as the political representative of a new class opposing the prosperous and rich bourgeoisie. Correspondingly the army creates a new state organ rising above the military command: a council of soldiers' and officers' deputies ("agitators"). A new period of double sovereignty has thus arrived: that of the Presbyterian Parliament and the Independents' army. This leads to open conflicts. The bourgeoisie proves powerless to oppose, with its own army the "model army" or Cromwell—that is, the armed plebeians. The conflict ends with a purgation of the Presbyterian Parliament by the sword of the Independents. There remains but the rump of a parliament; the dictatorship of Cromwell is established. The lower ranks of the army, under the leadership of the Levellers, the extreme left wing of the revolution, try to oppose the rule of the upper military levels, the patricians of the army, their own veritably plebeian regime. But this new two-power system does not succeed in developing: the Levellers, the lowest depths of the petty bourgeoisie, have not yet, nor can have, their own historic path. Cromwell soon settles accounts with his enemies. A new political equilibrium, and still by no means a stable one, is established for a period of years.

In the great French Revolution, the Constituent Assembly, the backbone of which was the upper levels of the Third Estate, concentrated the power in its hands, without, however, fully annulling the prerogatives of the king. The period of the Constituent Assembly is a clearly marked period of dual power, which ends with the flight of the king to Varennes, and is formally liquidated with the founding of the Republic.

The first French constitution (1791), based upon the fiction of a complete independence of the legislative and executive powers, in reality concealed from the people, or tried to conceal, a double sovereignty: that of the bourgeoisie, firmly entrenched in the National Assembly after the people's capture of the Bastille, and that of the old monarchy, still relying upon the upper circles of the priesthood, the clergy, the bureaucracy, and the military, to say nothing of their hopes of foreign intervention. In this self-contradictory regime lay the germs of its inevitable destruction. A way out could be found only in the abolition of bourgeois representation by the powers of European reaction or in the guillotine for the king and the monarchy. Paris and Coblenz must measure their forces.

But before it comes to war and the guillotine, the Paris Commune enters the scene, supported by the lowest city layers of the Third Estate, and with increasing boldness contests the power with the official representatives of the national bourgeoisie. A new double sovereignty is thus inaugurated, the first manifestation of which we observe as early as 1790, when the big and medium bourgeoisie are still firmly seated in the administration and in the municipalities. How striking is the picture—and how vilely it has been slandered!—of the efforts of the plebeian levels to raise themselves up out of the social cellars and catacombs and stand forth in the forbidden arena where people in wigs and silk breeches are settling the fate of the nation. It seemed as though the very foundation of society, tramped underfoot by the cultured bourgeoisie, was stirring and coming to life. Human heads lifted themselves above the solid mass, horny hands stretched aloft, hoarse but courageous voices shouted! The districts of Paris, bastards of the revolution, began to live a life of their own. They were recognized —it was impossible not to recognize them!—and transformed into sections. But they kept continually breaking the boundaries of legality and receiving a current of fresh blood from below, opening their ranks in spite of the law to those with no rights, the destitute *sans-culottes*. At the same time the rural municipalities were becoming a screen for a peasant uprising against that bourgeois legality which was defending the feudal property system. Thus from under the second nation arises a third.

The Parisian sections at first stood opposed to the Commune, which was still dominated by the respectable bourgeoisie. In the bold outbreak of August 10, 1792, the sections gained control of the Commune. From then on the revolutionary Commune opposed the Legislative Assembly, and subsequently the Convention, which failed to keep up with the problems and progress of the revolution, registering its events, but not performing them, because it did not possess the energy, audacity and unanimity of that new class which had raised itself up from the depths of the Parisian districts and found support in the most backward villages. As the sections gained control of the Commune, so the Commune, by way of a new insurrection, gained control of the Convention. Each of the stages was characterized by a sharply marked double sovereignty, each wing of which was trying to establish a single and strong government—the right by a defensive struggle, the left by an offensive. Thus, characteristically for both revolutions and counterrevolutions, the demand for a dictatorship results from the intolerable contradictions of the double sovereignty. The transition from one of its forms to the other is accomplished through civil war. The great stages of a revolution—that is, the passing of power to new classes or layers—do not at all coincide in this process with the succession of representative institutions, which march along after the dynamic of the revolution like a belated shadow. In the long run, to be sure, the revolutionary dictatorship of the *sans-culottes* unites with the dictatorship of the Convention. But with what Convention? A Convention purged of the Girondists, who yesterday ruled it with the hand of the Terror, a Convention abridged and adapted to the dominion of new social forces. Thus by the steps of the dual power the French Revolution rises in the course of four years to its culmination. After the ninth of Thermidor it begins, again by the steps of the dual power, to descend. And again civil war precedes every downward step, just as before it had accompanied every rise. In this way the new society seeks a new equilibrium of forces.

The Russian bourgeoisie, fighting with and cooperating with the Rasputin bureaucracy, had enormously strengthened its political position during the war. Exploiting the defeat of Czarism, it had concentrated in its hands, by means of the Country and Town unions and the Military-Industrial Committees, a great power. It had at its independent disposition enormous state resources and was in the essence of the matter a parallel government. During the war the Czar's ministers complained that Prince Lvov was furnishing supplies to the army, feeding it, medicating it, even establishing barber shops for the soldiers. "We must either put an end to this, or give the whole power into his hands," said Minister Krivoshein in 1915. He never imagined that a year and a half later, Lvov would receive "the whole power" only not from the Czar, but from the hands of Kerensky, Cheidze, and Sukhanov. But on the second day after he received it, there began a new double sovereignty: alongside of yesterday's liberal half-government, today formally legalized, there arose an unofficial, but so much the more actual government of the toiling masses in the form of the soviets. From the moment the Russian Revolution began to grow up into an event of world-historic significance.

What, then, is the peculiarity of this dual power as it appeared in the February Revolution? In the events of the seventeenth and eighteenth centuries, the dual power was in each case a natural stage in a struggle imposed upon its participants by a temporary correlation of forces, and each side strove to replace the dual power with its own single power. In the Revolution of 1917, we see the official democracy consciously and intentionally creating a two-power system, dodging with all its might the transfer of power into its own hands. The double sovereignty is created, or so it seems at a glance, not as a result of a struggle of classes for power, but as the result of a voluntary "yielding" of power by one class to another. In so far as the Russian "democracy" sought for an escape from the two-power regime, it could find one only in its own removal from power. It is just this that we have called the paradox of the February Revolution.

A certain analogy can be found in 1848, in the conduct of the German bourgeoisie with relation to the monarchy. But the analogy is not complete. The German bourgeoisie did try earnestly to divide the power with the monarchy on the basis of an agreement. But the bourgeoisie neither had the full power in its hands, nor by any means gave it over wholly to the monarchy. "The Prussian bourgeoisie nominally possessed the power, it did not for a moment doubt that the forces of the old government would place themselves unreservedly at its disposition and convert themselves into loyal adherents of its own omnipotence" (Marx and Engels).

The Russian democracy of 1917, having captured the power from the very moment of insurrection, tried not only to divide it with the bougeoisie, but to give the state over to the bourgeoisie absolutely. This means, if you please, that in the first quarter of the twentieth century the official Russian democracy had succeeded in decaying politically more completely than the German liberal bourgeoisie of the nineteenth century. And that is entirely according to the laws of history, for it is merely the reverse aspect of the upgrowth in those same decades of the proletariat, which now occupied the place of the craftsmen of Cromwell and the *sans-culottes* of Robespierre.

If you look deeper, the twofold rule of the Provisional Government and the Executive Committee had the character of a mere reflection. Only the proletariat could advance a claim to the new power. Relying distrustfully upon the workers and soldiers, the Compromisers were compelled to continue the double bookkeeping—of the kings and prophets. The twofold government of the liberals and the democrats only reflected the still concealed double sovereignty of the bourgeoisie and the proletariat. When the Bolsheviks displace the Compromisers at the head of the Soviet—and this will happen within a few months—then that concealed double sovereignty will come to the surface, and this will be the eve of the October Revolution. Until that moment the revolution will live in a world of political reflections. Refracted through the rationalizations of the socialist intelligentsia, the double sovereignty, from being a stage in the class struggle, became a regulative principle. It was just for this reason that it occupied the center of all theoretical discussions. Every thing has its uses: the mirrorlike character of the February double government has enabled us better to understand those epochs in history when the same thing appears as a full-blooded episode in a struggle between two regimes. The feeble and reflected light of the moon makes possible important conclusions about the sunlight.

In the immeasurably greater maturity of the Russian proletariat in comparison with the town masses of the older revolutions lies the basic peculiarity of the Russian Revolution. This first led to the paradox of a half-spectral double government and afterwards prevented the real one from being resolved in favor of the bourgeoisie. For the question stood thus: Either the bourgeoisie will actually dominate the old state apparatus, altering it a little for its purposes, in which case the soviets will come to nothing, or the soviets will form the foundation of a new state, liquidating not only the old governmental apparatus but also the dominion of those classes which it served. The Mensheviks and the Social Revolutionaries were steering toward the first solution, the Bolsheviks toward the second. The oppressed classes, who, as Marat observed, did not possess in the past the knowledge, or skill, or leadership to carry through what they had begun, were armed in the Russian Revolution of the twentieth century with all three. The Bolsheviks were victorious.

A year after their victory the same situation was repeated in Germany, with a different correlation of forces. The social democracy was steering for the establishment of a democratic government of the bourgeoisie and the liquidation of the soviets. Luxemburg and Liebknecht steered toward the dictatorship of the soviets. The Social Democrats won. Hilferding and Kautsky in Germany, Max Adler in Austria, proposed that they should "combine" democracy with the soviet system, including the workers' soviet in the constitution. That would have meant making potential or open civil war a constituent part of the state regime. It would be impossible to imagine a more curious utopia. Its sole justification on German soil is perhaps an old tradition: the Württemberg democrats of '48 wanted a republic with a duke at the head.

Does this phenomenon of the dual power, heretofore not sufficiently appreciated, contradict the Marxian theory of the state, which regards government as an executive committee of the ruling class? This is just the same as asking: Does the fluctuation of prices under the influence of supply and demand contradict the labor theory of value? Does the self-sacrifice of a female protecting her offspring refute the theory of a struggle for existence? No, in these phenomena we have a more complicated combination of the same laws. If the state is an organization of class rule, and a revolution is the overthrow of the ruling class, then the transfer of power from the one class to the other must necessarily create self-contradictory state conditions, and first of all in the form of the dual power. The relation of class forces is not a mathematical quantity permitting *a priori* computations. When the old regime is thrown out of equilibrium, a new correlation of forces can be established only as the result of a trial by battle. That is revolution.

It may seem as though this theoretical inquiry had led us away from the events of 1917. In reality it leads right into the heart of them. It was precisely around this problem of twofold power that the dramatic struggle of parties and classes turned. Only from a theoretical height is it possible to observe it fully and correctly understand it.

TRANSLATED BY MAX EASTMAN

Leon Trotsky

Three Concepts of the Russian Revolution

The following essay was written by Trotsky as an appendix to his biography of Stalin, published in 1946. It is a retrospective consideration of the opinions held by the various strands of the Russian socialist movement concerning a problem endlessly debated during the early years of the century and extremely relevant again in view of developments within the "Third World": What is the nature of the revolution that occurs in a backward country, such as Russia, and what is the relationship of the social forces —bourgeoisie, peasantry, working class—within that revolution? Here, from his own standpoint, but also with some objectivity, Trotsky delineates the differences between Plekhanov, Lenin, and himself. In the course of his exposition he also discusses briefly his own theory of "the permanent revolution."

Russia's development is first of all notable for its backwardness. But historical backwardness does not mean a mere retracing of the course of the advanced countries a hundred or two hundred years late. Rather, it gives rise to an utterly different "combined" social formation, in which the most highly developed achievements of capitalist technique and structure are integrated into the social relations of feudal and prefeudal barbarism, transforming and dominating them, fashioning a unique relationship of classes. The same is true of ideas. Precisely because of its historical tardiness, Russia proved to be the only European country in which Marxism, as a doctrine, and the Social Democracy, as a party, enjoyed a powerful development even prior to the bourgeois revolution—and naturally so, because the problem of the relation between the struggle for democracy and the struggle for socialism was subjected to the most profound theoretical examination in Russia.

The idealistic democrats—for the most part, the Populists—superstitiously refused to recognize the advancing revolution as a bourgeois revolution. They called it "democratic," attempting to hide under that neutral political label—not only from others, but from themselves as well—its social content. But Plekhanov, the founder of Russian Marxism, in his fight against Populism, showed as far back as the eighties of the past century that Russia had no reason whatsoever to rely on preferential ways of development; that, like the "profane" nations, it would have to go through the purgatory of capitalism; and that on this very path it would wrest political freedom, which was indispensable to the proletariat in its continuing fight for socialism. Plekhanov not only segregated the bourgeois revolution, as the immediate task, from the socialist revolution, which he in turn relegated to the vague future, but he foresaw distinct combinations of forces for each of them. The proletariat would secure political freedom jointly with the liberal bourgeoisie; then, after many decades, on a high level of capitalist development, the proletariat would proceed with the socialist revolution in direct conflict against the bourgeoisie.

To the Russian intellectual . . . [Lenin wrote toward the end of 1904], it always seems that to recognize our revolution as bourgeois means to make it colorless, to humiliate it, to vulgarize it. . . . The struggle for political freedom and the democratic republic in bourgeois society is to the proletarian merely one of the necessary stages in the struggle for the social revolution.

The Marxists are thoroughly convinced [he wrote in 1905] of the bourgeois character of the Russian Revolution. What does that mean? It means that those democratic transformations . . . which became indispensable for Russia not only do not signify in themselves the undermining of capitalism, the undermining of the domination of the bourgeoisie, but, on the contrary, they will be the first to really clear the ground for a widespread and rapid, a European rather than an Asiatic, development of capitalism;

they will be the first to make possible the rule of the bourgeoisie
as a class. We cannot jump out of the bourgeois-democratic framework of the Russian Revolution [he insisted], but we can considerably broaden that framework. . . .

In other words, we must create within the bourgeois society more favorable conditions for the further struggle of
the proletariat. To that extent Lenin followed in the foot-
steps of Plekhanov. The bourgeois character of the revolution was the meeting of the crossroads for the two
factions of the Russian social democracy.

For Plekhanov, Axelrod, and the leaders of Menshevism generally, the characterization of the revolution as
bourgeois had, above all, the political value of avoiding
the premature taunting of the bourgeoisie with the red
specter of socialism and thus "frightening it away" into
the camp of reaction. Said Axelrod, the chief tactician of
Menshevism, at the Unification Congress:

> The social relations of Russia have ripened only for a bourgeois
> revolution. While this general political lawlessness persists, we must
> not even so much as mention the direct fight of the proletariat
> against other classes for political power. . . . It is fighting for the
> conditions of bourgeois development. Objective historical condi-
> tions doom our proletariat to an inevitable collaboration with the
> bourgeoisie in the struggle against our common enemy.

The content of the Russian Revolution was thus confined beforehand to changes that were compatible with
the interests and the views of the liberal bourgeoisie.

This was the starting point for the fundamental divergence between the two factions. Bolshevism resolutely
refused to acknowledge that the Russian bourgeoisie was
capable of consummating its own revolution. With immeasurably greater force and consistency than Plekhanov, Lenin advanced the agrarian question as the central problem of the democratic revolution in Russia:

> The crux of the Russian Revolution is the agrarian [the land]
> question. We must make up our minds about the defeat or victory
> of the revolution . . . on the basis of accounting for the condition
> of the masses in their struggle for land.

At one with Plekhanov, Lenin regarded the peasantry as a petty-bourgeois class and the peasant land program as the program of bourgeois progressivism.

Nationalization is a bourgeois measure [he insisted at the Unification Congress]. It will give impetus to the development of capitalism by intensifying the class struggle, by strengthening the mobilization of land and the investment of capital in agriculture, by lowering the prices on grain.

Notwithstanding the admitted bourgeois character of the agrarian revolution, the Russian bourgeoisie was nevertheless hostile to the expropriation of the land owned by the landed gentry, and precisely for that reason strove for a compromise with the monarchy on the basis of a constitution after the Prussian model. To the Plekhanovite idea of union between the proletariat and the liberal bourgeoisie, Lenin counterposed the idea of union between the proletariat and the peasantry. He proclaimed the task of the revolutionary collaboration of these two classes to be the establishment of a "democratic dictatorship," as the only means for radically purging Russia of its feudal refuse, creating a free class of farmers and opening the way for the development of capitalism after the American rather than the Prussian model.

The victory of the revolution, he wrote, can be attained

only through dictatorship, because the realization of the transformations immediately and unconditionally necessary for the proletariat and the peasantry will call forth the desperate resistance of the landlords, of the big bourgeoisie, and of Czarism. Without dictatorship, it would be impossible to break that resistance, it would be impossible to defeat counter-revolutionary efforts. That would be, needless to say, not a socialist, but a democratic dictatorship. It would not be able to dispose of (without a whole series of intermediary stages in revolutionary development) the foundations of capitalism. At best, it would be able to introduce a radical redistribution of land ownership for the benefit of the peasantry, carry out a consistent and complete democratization, including a republic; uproot all the oppressive Asiatic characteristics in the life of the factory as well as the village; lay down the beginnings of important improvements in the condition of the workers; raise their standard of living; and finally, last but not least, carry the revolutionary conflagration into Europe.

Lenin's conception represented a tremendous step forward, proceeding as it did from the agrarian revolution rather than from constitutional reforms as the central task of the revolution, and indicating the only realistic combination of social forces that could fulfill that task. The weak point of Lenin's concept was its inherently contradictory notion, "the democratic dictatorship of the proletariat and the peasantry." Lenin himself, emphasized the basic limitations of that "dictatorship" when he openly called it *bourgeois*. He was thus implying that, for the sake of maintaining unity with the peasantry, the proletariat would be obliged to forego posing the socialist task directly during the impending revolution. But that would have meant the repudiation by the proletariat of its *own* dictatorship. The dictatorship was consequently, in essence, of the peasantry, although with the workers participating. On certain occasions that was precisely how Lenin spoke; for example, at the Stockholm Congress, when he replied to Plekhanov, who had rebelled against the "utopia" of seizing power: "What program are we talking about? About an agrarian program. Who in that program is supposed to seize the government? The revolutionary peasantry. Is Lenin confounding the government of the proletariat with that of the peasantry?" No, he said with reference to himself: Lenin sharply differentiated between the socialist government of the proletariat and the bourgeois-democratic government of the peasantry. "And how is a victorious peasant revolution possible," he exclaimed again, "without seizure of power by the revolutionary peasantry?" In that polemical formulation Lenin very clearly exposed the vulnerability of his position.

The peasantry was dispersed over the surface of an immense country, with cities as points of contact. By itself the peasantry was incapable even of formulating its own interests, for in each region they were differently conceived. Economic contact between provinces was established by the market and by the railroads; but both the market and the railroads were in the city's hands. In trying to break through the confines of the village and pool their interests, the peasantry necessarily succumbed to political dependence on the city. Neither was the peasantry homogeneous in its social relations: its *kulak* stratum naturally strove to entice it to unite with the city bourgeoisie, while the lower strata of the village pulled in the direction of the city workers. Under these circumstances, the peasantry as a whole was utterly incapable of assuming the reins of government.

True, in ancient China revolutions brought the peasantry to power, or rather, the military leaders of peasant insurrections. That led each time to a redivision of the land and the establishment of a new "peasant" dynasty, after which history began all over again: new concentration of lands, a new aristocracy, new usury, new uprisings. So long as the revolution maintained its purely peasant character, society did not emerge from these hopeless rotations. Such was the basis of ancient Asiatic, including ancient Russian, history. In Europe, beginning with the emergence of the Middle Ages, each victorious peasant uprising did not place a peasant government in power but a leftist burgher party. More precisely, a peasant uprising proved victorious only to the extent that it managed to establish the position of the city population's revolutionary sector. Seizure of power by a revolutionary peasantry was out of the question in twentieth-century bourgeois Russia.

The attitude toward the liberal bourgeoisie thus became the touchstone in the divergence between revolutionists and opportunists among Social Democrats. How far the Russian Revolution could venture, what character would be assumed by the future provisional revolutionary government, what tasks would confront it, and in what order it would dispose of them—these questions could be correctly posed in all their importance only in reference to the basic character of the proletariat's politics, and that character was determined, above all, by its relation to the liberal bourgeoisie. Plekhanov demonstratively and stubbornly shut his eyes to the fundamental object-lesson of nineteenth-century political history: wherever the proletariat appeared as an independent force, the bourgeoisie shifted to the camp of the counterrevolution. The bolder the struggle of the masses, the quicker the reactionary transformation of liberalism. No one has yet invented a way to paralyze the workings of the law of the class struggle.

"We must prize the support of the nonproletarian parties," Plekhanov was wont to repeat during the years of the First Revolution, "and not drive them away from us by tactless behavior." With such monotonous moralizings the sage of Marxism demonstrated that he was unable to grasp the living dynamics of society. "Tactlessness" might drive away an occasional oversensitive intellectual. But classes and parties are drawn or repelled by their social interests. "It may be safely said," Lenin retorted to Plekhanov, "that the liberals among the landed gentry will forgive you millions of 'tactless' acts, but they will never forgive incitements to take away their land." And not only the landed gentry: the upper crust of the bourgeoisie, bound to the landowners by identity of property interests and even more closely by the banking system as well as the upper crust of the petty bourgeoisie and of the intellectuals, materially and morally dependent on the large and middling property owners, dreaded the independent movement of the masses. Yet in order to overthrow Czarism, it was necessary to arouse scores upon scores of millions of the oppressed for a heroic, self-sacrificing, reckless, supreme revolutionary onslaught. The masses could be aroused to this uprising only under the banner of their own interests; hence, in the spirit of unreconcilable hostility toward the exploiting classes, and first of all, the landlords, the "frightening away" of the oppositional bourgeoisie from the revolutionary peasants and workers was therefore the immanent law of the revolution itself and could not be forestalled by "tactfulness" or diplomacy.

Each new month confined Lenin's estimate of liberalism. Notwithstanding the fondest hopes of the Mensheviks, the *Kadets* not only made no move to lead the "bourgeois" revolution but, on the contrary, more and more found their historic mission in fighting it. After the crushing defeat of the December Insurrection, the liberals, who, thanks to the ephemeral Duma, stepped out before the political footlights, strove with all their might to explain to the monarchy their insufficiently active counter-revolutionary behavior in the autumn of 1905, when the holiest pillars of "culture" were in danger. The leader of the liberals, Miliukov, who carried on *sub-rosa* negotiations with the Winter Palace, argued quite properly in the press that by the end of 1905 the *Kadets* were unable even to appear before the masses.

Those who now blame the [*Kadet*] party [he wrote] for not protesting then, by convoking meetings, against the revolutionary illusions of Trotskyism . . . simply do not understand or do not remember the moods then prevalent among the democratic public that attended these meetings.

By the "illusions of Trotskyism" the liberal leader meant the independent policy of the proletariat, which attracted to the soviets the sympathies of the cities' lower classes, soldiers, peasants, and of all the oppressed, thus alienating "cultivated" society. The evolution of the Mensheviks developed along parallel lines. Time and again they had to give alibis to the liberals for having found themselves in a bloc with Trotsky after October, 1905. The explanations of that talented publicist of the Mensheviks, Martov, came to this—that it was necessary to make concessions to the "revolutionary illusions" of the masses.

Populists regarded all workers and peasants as simply "toilers" and "exploited ones," who were equally interested in socialism, while to Marxists a peasant was a petty bourgeois, capable of becoming a socialist only to the extent that he either materially or spiritually ceased being a peasant. With a sentimentality characteristic of them, Populists saw in that sociological characterization a dire insult to the peasantry. Along that line was fought for two generations the principal battle between the revolutionary tendencies of Russia. In order to understand the subsequent conflict between Stalinism and Trotskyism, it is necessary to emphasize that, in consonance with all Marxist tradition, Lenin never regarded the peasant as a socialist ally of the proletariat; on the contrary, it was the overwhelming preponderance of the peasantry which had led Lenin to conclude that a socialist revolution was impossible in Russia. That idea recurs time and again in all his articles that directly or indirectly touch upon the agrarian question.

"We support the peasant movement," wrote Lenin in September, 1905, "insofar as it is revolutionary and democratic. We are preparing (at once, immediately preparing) to fight against it insofar as it asserts itself as a reactionary, antiproletarian movement. The whole essence of Marxism is in that twofold task. . . ." Lenin saw the Western proletariat and to some extent the semiproletarians of the Russian village as socialist allies, but never the whole of the peasantry. "At first, we support to the very end, with all means, including confiscation," he repeated with persistence typical of him, "the peasant in general against the landed proprietor, but later (and not even later, but at the very same time) we support the proletariat against the peasant in general."

"The peasantry will win in a bourgeois democratic revolution," he wrote in March, 1906, "and thereby will completely exhaust its revolutionism as a peasantry. The proletariat will win in a bourgeois democratic revolution, and thereby will only begin really to unfold its true socialist revolutionism." "The movement of the peasantry," he repeated in May of the same year, "is the movement of another class; it is a struggle not against the foundations of capitalism but for their purging of all the remnants of serfdom." That view may be traced in Lenin from article to article, from year to year, from volume to volume. Expressions and illustrations vary, but the basic thought is unalterable. Nor could it have been otherwise. Had Lenin seen a *socialist* ally in the peasantry, he would not have had the slightest basis for insisting upon the *bourgeois* character of the revolution and limiting it to "the dictatorship of the proletariat and the peasantry," to purely democratic tasks. On the occasions when Lenin accused me of "underestimating" the peasantry, he did not have in mind my failure to recognize the socialist tendencies of the peasantry but rather my failure to realize sufficiently, from Lenin's point of view, the bourgeois-democratic independence of the peasantry, its capacity to create its *own* power and through it impede the establishment of the socialist dictatorship of the proletariat.

The revaluation of that question commenced only during the years of the Thermidorian reaction, the beginning of which coincided by and large with Lenin's illness and death. From then on the union of Russian workers and peasants was declared to be in itself sufficient guaranty against the dangers of restoration and a firm pledge that socialism would be achieved within the borders of the Soviet Union. Having substituted the theory of socialism in a separate country for the theory of international revolution, Stalin began to call the Marxist evaluation of the peasantry "Trotskyism," and moreover not only with reference to the present but retroactively to the entire past.

It is, of course, possible to ask whether the classical Marxist view of the peasantry had not proved erroneous. That theme would lead us far beyond the limits of this essay. Suffice it to say for the present that Marxism never ascribed an absolute and immutable character to its estimation of the peasantry as a nonsocialist class. Marx said long ago that the peasant is capable of judgment as well as prejudgment. The very nature of the peasantry is altered under altered conditions. The regime of the dictatorship of the proletariat discovered very great possibilities for influencing the peasantry and for reeducating it. History has not yet plumbed to the bottom the limits of these possibilities. But it is already clear that the growing role of state compulsion in the U.S.S.R. has, far from refuting, basically confirmed the very view of the peasantry that distinguished Russian Marxists from Populists. Yet, whatever the situation on that score today, after twenty-odd years of the new regime, the fact remains that prior to the October Revolution, or rather prior to the year 1924, no one in the Marxist camp, and least of all Lenin, had regarded the peasantry as a factor of socialist development. Without the aid of a proletarian revolution in the West, he reiterated time and again, restoration is unavoidable in Russia. He was not mistaken: the Stalinist bureaucracy is nothing else than the first stage of bourgeois restoration.

Such were the divergent positions of the two main

factions of the Russian social democracy. But alongside them, as early as the dawn of the First Revolution, a third position was formulated, which met with practically no recognition in those days, but which we must explain —not only because it was confirmed by the events of 1917, but particularly because seven years after the revolution, after being turned upside down, it began to play an utterly unforeseen role in the political evolution of Stalin and of the entire Soviet bureaucracy.

Early in 1905 I published in Geneva a pamphlet which analyzed the political situation as it existed around the winter of 1904. I came to the conclusion that the independent campaign of liberal petitions and banquets had exhausted its possibilities; that the radical intellectuals, who had shifted their hopes to the liberals, had found themselves in a blind alley together with the latter; that the peasant movement was creating conditions favorable for victory yet incapable of assuring it; that the showdown could be brought about only through an armed insurrection of the proletariat; that the very next stage along that way must be the general strike. This pamphlet, called "Until the Ninth of January," had been written prior to the Bloody Sunday in Petersburg. The powerful wave of strikes which began that day, together with the first armed clashes that supplemented it, was an unequivocal confirmation of the pamphlet's strategic prognosis.

The preface to my work was written by Parvus, a Russian émigré, who had already become by then a prominent German writer. Parvus was an extraordinarily creative personality, capable of becoming infected with the ideas of others as well as enriching others with his ideas. He lacked the inward balance and application necessary to contribute anything worthy of his talents as a thinker and writer to the labor movement. There is no doubt that he exerted considerable influence on my personal development, especially with respect to the social-revolutionary understanding of our epoch. A few years before our first meeting, Parvus passionately defended the idea of a general strike in Germany; but the country was passing through prolonged industrial prosperity, the Social Democracy was adjusting itself to the Hohenzollern regime, and foreigners' revolutionary propaganda met nothing but ironical indifference. Having read my pamphlet in manuscript, the very next day after the bloody events in Petersburg, Parvus was overwhelmed with the thought of the exceptional role which the proletariat of backward Russia was called upon to play. Several days spent jointly in Munich were filled with conversations that clarified much to both of us and brought us personally close together. The preface Parvus then wrote to the pamphlet entered permanently into the history of the Russian Revolution. In a few pages he shed light on those social pecularities of backward Russia, which, true enough, were already well known, but from which no one before him had drawn all the necessary inferences:

Political radicalism throughout western Europe [wrote Parvus], as everybody knows, depended primarily on the petty bourgeoisie. These were artisans and generally all of that part of the bourgeoisie which was caught up by the industrial development but which at the same time was superseded by the class of capitalists. . . . In Russia of the precapitalist period, cities developed on the Chinese rather than on the European model. These were administrative centers, purely official and bureaucratic in character, devoid of any political significance, while in the economic sense they were trade bazaars for the landlord and peasant milieu of its environs. Their development was still rather inconsiderable, when it was terminated by the capitalist process, which began to establish large cities in its own image, that is, factory towns and centers of world trade. . . . That which had hindered the development of petty-bourgeois democracy came to benefit the class consciousness of the proletariat in Russia—the weak development of the artisan form of production. The proletariat was immediately concentrated in the factories. . . .

Greater and greater masses of peasants will be drawn into the movement. But all they can do is to aggravate the political anarchy rampant in the country and thus weaken the government; they cannot become a compact revolutionary army. Hence, as the revolution develops, an even greater portion of political work will fall to the lot of the proletariat. At the same time, its political awareness will be enhanced and its political energy will grow apace. . . .

The Social Democracy will be confronted with this dilemma: to assume responsibility for the provisional government or to stand aloof from the labor movement. The workers will regard that government as their own, no matter what the attitude of the

Social Democracy. . . . In Russia only workers can accomplish a revolutionary insurrection. In Russia the revolutionary provisional government will be a government of the *workers' democracy*. That government will be social democratic, should the Social Democracy be at the head of the revolutionary movement of the Russian proletariat. . . .

The Social Democratic provisional government cannot accomplish a socialist insurrection in Russia, but the very process of liquidating the autocracy and establishing a democratic republic will provide it with fertile ground for political activity.

In the heyday of revolutionary events in the autumn of 1905, I met Parvus again, this time in Petersburg. Remaining organizationally independent of both factions, we jointly edited *Russkoye Slovo* (The Russian World), a newspaper for the working-class masses, and, in coalition with the Mensheviks, the important political neswpaper *Nachalo* (The Beginning). The theory of permanent revolution was usually associated with the names of "Parvus and Trotsky." That was only partially correct. Parvus attained revolutionary maturity at the end of the preceding century, when he marched at the head of the forces that fought so-called Revisionism, i.e., the opportunistic distortions of Marx's theory. But his optimism was undermined by the failure of all his efforts to push the German Social Democracy in the direction of a more resolute policy. Parvus grew increasingly more reserved about the perspectives of a socialist revolution in the West. At the same time he felt that "the Social-Democratic provisional government cannot accomplish a socialist insurrection in Russia." Hence, his prognosis indicated, instead of the transformation of the democratic into the socialist revolution, merely the establishment in Russia of a regime of workers' democracy, more or less as in Australia, where the first labor government, resting on a farmerist foundation, did not venture beyond the limits of the bourgeois regime.

I did not share that conclusion. Australian democracy, maturing organically on the virgin soil of a new continent, immediately assumed a conservative character and dominated the youthful yet rather privileged proletariat. Russian democracy, on the contrary, could come about only in consequence of a large-scale revolutionary insurrection, the dynamics of which would never permit the labor government to maintain itself within the framework of bourgeois democracy. Our differences of opinion, which began soon after the Revolution of 1905, led to a complete break at the beginning of the war, when Parvus, in whom the skeptic had completely killed the revolutionist, proved to be on the side of German imperialism and subsequently became the counselor and inspirer of the first President of the German Republic, Ebert.

After writing my pamphlet, "Until the Ninth of January," I repeatedly returned to the development and the grounding of the theory of permanent revolution. In view of the significance it subsequently acquired in the intellectual evolution of the hero of this biography [Stalin], it is necessary to present it here in the form of exact quotations from my works of the years 1905 and 1906.

The nucleus of population in a contemporary city—at least, in a city of economic and political significance—is the sharply differentiated class of hired labor. It is this class, essentially unknown to the Great French Revolution, which is fated to play the decisive role in our revolution. . . . In an economically more backward country the proletariat may come to power sooner than in a country more advanced capitalistically. The conception of a kind of automatic dependence of the proletarian dictatorship on a country's technical forces and means is a prejudice of extremely simplified "economic" materialism. Such a view has nothing in common with Marxism. . . . Notwithstanding the fact that the productive forces of United States industry are ten times greater than ours, the political role of the Russian proletariat, its influence on the politics of its own country and the possibility that it may soon influence world politics are incomparably greater than the role of significance of the American proletariat. . . .

It seems to me that the Russian Revolution will create such conditions that the power may (in the event of victory, *must*) pass into the hands of the proletariat before the politicians of bourgeois liberalism will find it possible fully to unfold their genius for statecraft. . . . The Russian bourgeoisie will surrender all the revolutionary positions to the proletariat. It will also have to surrender revolutionary hegemony over the peasantry. The proletariat in power will come to the peasantry as the class liberator. . . . The proletariat, leaning on the peasantry, will bring into motion all the forces for raising the cultural level of the village and for developing political consciousness in the peasantry. . . .

But will not perhaps the peasantry itself drive the proletariat away and supersede it? That is impossible. All historic experience repudiates that supposition. It shows that the peasantry is utterly incapable of an *independent* political role. . . . From the aforesaid it is clear how I look upon the idea of the "dictatorship of the proletariat and the peasantry." The point is not whether I deem it admissible in principle, whether I "want" or "do not want" such a form of political cooperation. I deem it unrealizable—at least, in the direct and immediate sense.

The foregoing already shows how incorrect is the assertion that the conception here expounded "jumped over the bourgeois revolution," as has been subsequently reiterated without end. "The struggle for the democratic renovation of Russia, . . ." I wrote at the same time, "is in its entirety derived from capitalism, is being conducted by forces formed on the basis of capitalism, and *immediately, in the first place,* is directed against the feudal and vassal obstacles that stand in the way of developing a capitalist society." But the substance of the question was with what forces and by which methods these obstacles could be overcome.

The framework of all the questions of the revolution may be limited by the assertion that our revolution is *bourgeois* in its objective goals and consequently, in all its inevitable results, and it is possible at the same time to close one's eyes to the fact that the principal active force of that bourgeois revolution is the proletariat which is pushing itself toward power with all the impact of the revolution. . . . One may comfort himself with the thought that Russia's social conditions have not yet ripened for a socialist economy—and at the same time overlook the thought that, upon coming to power, the proletariat would inevitably, with all the logic of its situation, push itself toward the management of the economy at the expense of the state. . . . Coming into the government not as helpless hostages but as the leading force, the representatives of the proletariat will by virtue of that alone smash the demarcation between the minimal and maximal program, i.e., *place collectivism on the order of the day*. At what point in that tendency the proletariat would be stopped will depend on the interrelation of forces, but certainly not on the initial intentions of the proletariat's party. . . .

But we may already ask ourselves: must the dictatorship of the proletariat inevitably smash itself against the framework of the bourgeois revolution or can it, on the basis of the existing histori-

cal situation of the *world*, look forward to the perspective of victory, after smashing this limiting framework? . . . One thing may
be said with certainty: without the direct governmental support
of the European proletariat, the working class of Russia will not
be able to maintain itself in power and transform its temporary
reign into an enduring socialist dictatorship.

But this does not necessarily lead to a pessimistic prognosis:

The political liberation, led by the working class of Russia, will
raise the leader to a height unprecedented in history, transmit to
him colossal forces and means, and make him the initiator of the
worldwide liquidation of capitalism, for which history has created
all the objective prerequisites.

As to the extent to which international social democracy will prove capable of fulfilling its revolutionary task,
I wrote in 1906:

The European socialist parties—and in the first place, the mightiest of them, the German party—have developed their conservatism, which grows stronger in proportion to the size of the masses
embraced by socialism and the effectiveness of the organization
and the discipline of these masses. Because of that, the Social
Democracy, as the organization that embodies the political experience of the proletariat, may at a given moment become the
immediate obstacle on the path of an open clash between the
workers and the bourgeois reaction.

Yet I concluded my analysis by expressing the assurance that

the Eastern revolution will infect the Western proletariat with revolutionary idealism and arouse in it the desire to start talking
"Russian" with its enemy . . .

To sum up. Populism, like Slavophilism, proceeded
from illusions that Russia's course of development would
be utterly unique, escaping capitalism and the bourgeois
republic. Plekhanov's Marxism concentrated on proving
the identity in principle of Russia's historical course with
that of the West. The program that grew out of that
ignored the very real and far from mystical peculiarities

of Russia's social structure and revolutionary development. The Menshevik view of the revolution, purged of its episodic stratifications and individual deviations, was tantamount to the following: the victory of the Russian bourgeois revolution was possible only under the leadership of the liberal bourgeoisie and must put the latter in power. Later the democratic regime would let the Russian proletariat, with incomparably greater success than heretofore, catch up with its elder Western brothers on the road of the struggle for socialism.

Lenin's perspective may be briefly expressed in the following words: the backward Russian bourgeoisie is incapable of completing its own revolution! The complete victory of the revolution, through the intermediacy of the "democratic dictatorship of the proletariat and the peasantry," would purge the land of medievalism, invest the development of Russian capitalism with American tempo, strengthen the proletariat in city and village, and make really possible the struggle for socialism. On the other hand, the victory of the Russian Revolution would give tremendous impetus to the socialist revolution in the West, while the latter would not only protect the Russian from the dangers of restoration but would also enable the Russian proletariat to come to the conquest of power in a comparatively brief historical period.

The perspective of permanent revolution may be summarized in the following way: the complete victory of the democratic revolution in Russia is conceivable only in the form of the dictatorship of the proletariat, leaning on the peasantry. The dictatorship of the proletariat, which would inevitably place on the order of the day not only democratic but socialistic tasks as well, would at the same time give a powerful impetus to the international socialist revolution. Only the victory of the proletariat in the West could protect Russia from bourgeois restoration and assure it the possibility of rounding out the establishment of socialism.

That compact formula discloses with equal distinctness the similarity of the latter two concepts in their irreconcilable differentiation from the liberal Menshevik perspective as well as their extremely essential distinction from each other on the question of the social character and the tasks of the "dictatorship" which must grow out of the revolution. The not infrequent complaint in the writings of the present Moscow theoreticians that the program of the dictatorship of the proletariat was "premature" in 1905 is beside the point. In an empirical sense, the program of the democratic dictatorship of the proletariat and the peasantry proved equally "premature." The unfavorable combination of forces at the time of the First Revolution did not so much preclude the dictatorship of the proletariat as the victory of the revolution in general. Yet all the revolutionary groups were based on the hope of complete victory; the supreme revolutionary struggle would have been impossible without such a hope. The differences of opinion dealt with the general perspective of the revolution and the strategy arising from that. The perspective of Menshevism was false to the core: it pointed out the wrong road to the proletariat. The perspective of Bolshevism was not complete: it correctly pointed out the general direction of the struggle, but characterized its stages incorrectly. The insufficiency in the perspective of Bolshevism did not become apparent in 1905 only because the revolution itself did not undergo further development. But then at the beginning of 1917 Lenin was obliged to alter his perspective, in direct conflict with the old cadres of his party.

No political prognosis can pretend to be mathematically exact; suffice it if it correctly indicates the general line of development and helps to orient the actual course of events, which inevitably bends the main line right and left. In that sense it is impossible not to see that the concept of permanent revolution has completely passed the test of history. During the initial years of the Soviet regime no one denied that; on the contrary, that fact found acknowledgment in a number of official publications. But when the bureaucratic reaction against October opened up in the calmed and cooled upper crust of Soviet society, it was at once directed against the theory which reflected the first proletarian revolution more completely than anything else, while at the same time openly exposing its unfinished, limited, and partial character. Thus, by way of repulsion, originated the theory of socialism in a separate country, the basic dogma of Stalinism.

TRANSLATED BY CHARLES MALAMUTH

Leon Trotsky

Stalinism and Bolshevism

> *Toward the end of his career, Trotsky felt obliged to counter the criticisms made by various socialists and liberals that both the degeneration of the Bolshevik regime in Russia and the rise of Stalinist totalitarianism were the result—some said inevitable, others probable—of earlier failures on the part of the Bolsheviks or of an authoritarian potential in the Bolshevik outlook. Some critics traced the causes of Stalinism back to the Bolshevik conception of "the vanguard party" and others to the decision of Lenin to ban opposition parties after the revolution. In 1937, Trotsky wrote an essay called "Stalinism and Bolshevism" in which he argued vigorously against the identification of the two or the causal attribution of the first to the second. The bulk of this essay appears below.*

Is Bolshevism Responsible for Stalinism?

Is it true that Stalinism represents the legitimate product of Bolshevism, as all reactionaries maintain, as Stalin himself avows, as the Mensheviks, the anarchists, and certain left doctrinaires considering themselves Marxist, believe? "We have always predicted this," they say. "Having started with the prohibition of the other socialist parties, the repression of the anarchists, and the setting up of the Bolshevik dictatorship in the soviets, the October revolution could end only in the dictatorship of the bureaucracy. Stalin is the continuation and also the bankruptcy of Leninism."

The flaw in this reasoning begins in the tacit identification of Bolshevism, October Revolution, and Soviet Union. The historical process of the struggle of hostile forces is replaced by the evolution of Bolshevism in a vacuum. Bolshevism, however, is only a political tendency, closely fused with the working class but not identical with it. And aside from the working class there exist in the Soviet Union a hundred million peasants, various nationalities, and a heritage of oppression, misery, and ignorance. The state built up by the Bolsheviks reflects not only the thought and will of Bolshevism but also the cultural level of the country, the social composition of the population, the pressure of a barbaric past and of no less barbaric world imperialism. To represent the process of degeneration of the Soviet state as the evolution of pure Bolshevism is to ignore social reality in the name of only one of its elements, isolated by pure logic. One has only to call this elementary mistake by its real name to do away with every trace of it.

Bolshevism, at any rate, never identified itself either with the October Revolution nor with the Soviet state that issued from it. Bolshevism considered itself as one of the factors of history, the "conscious" factor—a very important but not the decisive one. We never sinned in historical subjectivism. We saw the decisive factor, on the existing basis of productive forces, in the class struggle, not only on a national but on an international scale.

When the Bolsheviks made concessions to the peasant tendency to private ownership, set up strict rules for membership in the party, purged the party of alien elements, prohibited other parties, introduced the NEP, granted enterprises as concessions, or concluded diplomatic agreements with imperialist governments, they were drawing partial conclusions from the basic fact that had been theoretically clear to them from the beginning: that the conquest of power, however important it may be in itself, by no means transforms the party into a sovereign ruler of the historical process. Having taken over the state, the party is able, certainly, to influence the development of society with a power inaccessible to it before; but in return it submits itself to ten times greater influence from all other elements of society. It can, by the direct attack of hostile forces, be thrown out of power. Given a more dragging tempo of development, it can degenerate internally while maintaining itself in power. It is precisely this dialectic of the historical process that is not understood by those sectarian logicians who try to find in the decay of the Stalinist bureaucracy an annihilating argument against Bolshevism.

In essence these gentlemen say: the revolutionary party that contains in itself no guarantee against its own degeneration is bad. By such a criterion Bolshevism is naturally condemned: it has no talisman. But the criterion itself is wrong. Scientific thinking demands a concrete analysis: how and why did the party degenerate? No one but the Bolsheviks themselves has up to the present time given such an analysis. To do this they had no need to break with Bolshevism. On the contrary, they found in its arsenal all they needed for the clarification of its fate. They drew this conclusion: certainly Stalinism "grew out" of Bolshevism, not logically, however, but dialectically; not as a revolutionary affirmation but as a Thermidorian negation. They are by no means the same.

The Fundamental Prognosis of Bolshevism

The Bolsheviks, however, did not have to wait for the Moscow trials to explain the reasons for the disintegration of the governing party of the U.S.S.R. Long ago they foresaw and spoke of the theoretical possibility of this development. Let us remember the prognosis of the Bolsheviks, not only on the eve of the October Revolution but years before. The specific alignment of forces in the national and international field can enable the proletariat to seize power first in a backward country such as Russia. But the same alignment of forces proves beforehand that *without a more or less rapid victory of the proletariat in the advanced countries* the workers' government in Russia will not survive. Left to itself, the Soviet regime must either fall or degenerate. More exactly: it will first degenerate and then fall. I myself have written about this more than once, beginning in 1905. In my *History of the Rus-*

sian Revolution (cf. the Appendix to the last volume: "Socialism in One Country") are collected all the statements on this question made by the Bolshevik leaders from 1917 until 1923. They all lead to one conclusion: without a revolution in the West, Bolshevism will be liquidated either by internal counterrevolution, or by external intervention, or by a combination of both. Lenin stressed again and again that the bureaucratization of the Soviet regime was not a technical or organizational question, but the potential beginning of the degeneration of the workers' state.

At the Eleventh Party Congress in March, 1923, Lenin spoke of the support offered to Soviet Russia at the time of the NEP by certain bourgeois politicians, particularly the liberal professor Ustrialov. "I am for the support of the Soviet power in Russia," said Ustrialov, although he was a *Kadet,* a bourgeois, a supporter of intervention, "because on its present course it is sliding back into an ordinary bourgeois power." Lenin prefers the cynical voice of the enemy to "sugary communistic babble." Soberly and harshly he warns the party of the danger:

> What Ustrialov says is possible; one must say it openly. History knows transformations of all kinds; it is absolutely trivial in politics to put one's faith in conviction, devotion, and other excellent moral qualities. A small number of people have excellent moral qualities. The historical outcome is decided by gigantic masses who, if they are not pleased with this small number of people, will treat them none too politely.

In a word, the party is not the only factor of development and, on a larger historical scale, is not the decisive one.

> One nation conquers another [continued Lenin at the same congress, the last in which he participated]. This is quite simple and understandable to everyone. But what of the culture of these nations? That is not so simple. If the conquering nation has a higher culture than the defeated, it imposes its culture on the latter, but if the contrary is true then the defeated nation imposes its culture on the conqueror. Did not something like this occur in the capital of the RSFSR and was it not in this way that 4,700 communists (almost a whole division and all of them the best) were submitted to an alien culture?

This was said in the beginning of 1923, and not for the first time. History is not made by a few people, even "the best"; and not only that: these "best" can degenerate in the spirit of an alien, that is a bourgeois culture. Not only can the Soviet state abandon the ways of socialism, but the Bolshevik party can, under favorable historic conditions, lose its Bolshevism.

From the clear understanding of this danger issued the Left Opposition, definitely formed in 1923. Recording day by day the symptoms of degeneration, it tried to oppose to the growing Thermidor the conscious will of the proletarian vanguard. However, this subjective factor proved to be insufficient. The "gigantic masses" which, according to Lenin, decide the outcome of the struggle, became tired of internal privations and of waiting too long for the world revolution. The mood of the masses declined. The bureaucracy won the upper hand. It cowed the revolutionary vanguard, trampled upon Marxism, prostituted the Bolshevik party. Stalinism conquered. In the form of the Left Opposition, Bolshevism broke with the Soviet bureaucracy and its Comintern. This was the real course of development.

To be sure, in a formal sense Stalinism did issue from Bolshevism. Even today the Moscow bureaucracy continues to call itself the Bolshevik party. It is simply using the old label of Bolshevism the better to fool the masses. So much the more pitiful are those theoreticians who take the shell for the kernel and the appearance for the reality. In the identification of Bolshevism and Stalinism, they render the best possible service to the Thermidorians and precisely thereby play a clearly reactionary role.

In view of the elimination of all other parties from the political field the antagonistic interests and tendencies of the various strata of the population must, to a greater or lesser degree, find their expression in the governing party. To the extent that the political center of gravity has shifted from the proletarian vanguard to the bureaucracy, the party has changed in its social structure as well as in its ideology. Owing to the impetuous course of its development, it has suffered in the last fifteen years a far more radical degeneration than did the social democracy in half a century. The present purge draws between Bolshevism and Stalinism not simply a bloody line but a whole river of blood. The annihilation of all the old generation which participated in the civil war, and that part of the youth which took seriously the Bolshevik traditions shows not only a political but a thoroughly physical incompatibility between Bolshevism and Stalinism. How can this be ignored?

Stalinism and "State Socialism"

The anarchists, for their part, try to see in Stalinism the organic product not only of Bolshevism and Marxism but of "state socialism" in general. They are willing to replace Bakunin's patriarchal "federation of free communes" by the more modern federation of free soviets. But, as formerly, they are against centralized state power. In fact, one branch of "state" Marxism, social democracy, after coming to power, became an open agent of capitalism; the other gave birth to a new privileged caste. It is obvious that the source of the evil lies in the state. From a wide historical viewpoint, there is a grain of truth in this reasoning. The state as an apparatus of constraint is undoubtedly a source of political and moral infection. This also applies, as experience has shown, to the workers' state. Consequently, it can be said that Stalinism is a product of a condition of society in which society was still unable to tear itself out of the straitjacket of the state. But this situation, containing nothing for the evaluation of Bolshevism or Marxism, characterizes only the general cultural level of mankind, and above all, the relation of forces between proletariat and bourgeoisie. Having agreed with the anarchists that the state, even the workers' state, is the offspring of class barbarism and that real human history will begin with the abolition of the state, we have still before us in full force the question: what ways and methods will lead, *ultimately*, to the abolition of the state? Recent experience proves that they are certainly not the methods of anarchism.

The leaders of the CNT, the only important anarchist organization in the world, became, in the critical hour,

bourgeois ministers. They explained their open betrayal
of the theory of anarchism by the pressure of "exceptional
circumstances." But did not the leaders of German social
democracy invoke, in their time, the same excuse? Naturally, civil war is not a peaceful and ordinary but an
"exceptional" circumstance. Every serious revolutionary
organization, however, prepares precisely for "exceptional
circumstances." The experience of Spain has shown once
again that the state can be "denied" in booklets published
in "normal circumstances" by permission of the bourgeois
state, but that the conditions of revolution leave no room
for "denial" of the state; they demand, on the contrary,
the conquest of the state. We have not the slightest intention of blaming the anarchists for not having liquidated
the state by a mere stroke of the pen. A revolutionary
party, even after having seized power (of which the anarchist leaders were incapable in spite of the heroism of
the anarchist workers) is still by no means the sovereign
ruler of society. But we do severely blame the anarchist
theory, which seemed to be wholly suitable for times of
peace, but which had to be dropped rapidly as soon as
the "exceptional circumstances" of the . . . revolution had
begun. In the old days there were—and probably are
now—certain generals who considered that the most
harmful thing for an army was war. In the same class are
those revolutionaries who claim that their doctrine is destroyed by revolution.

Marxists are wholly in agreement with the anarchists in
regard to the final goal: the liquidation of the state.
Marxists are "stateist" only to the extent that one cannot
achieve the liquidation of the state simply by ignoring it.
The experience of Stalinism does not refute the teaching
of Marxism but confirms it by inversion. The revolutionary doctrine, which teaches the proletariat to orient itself
correctly in situations, and to profit actively by them,
contains, of course, no automatic guarantee of victory.
But victory is possible only through the application of
this doctrine. Moreover, the victory must not be thought
of as a single event. It must be considered in the perspective of an historic epoch. The first workers' state—on a
lower economic basis and surrounded by imperialism—

was transformed into the *gendarmerie* of Stalinism. But genuine Bolshevism launched a life and death struggle against that *gendarmerie*. To maintain itself, Stalinism is now forced to conduct a direct *civil war* against Bolshevism, under the name of "Trotskyism," not only in the U.S.S.R., but also in Spain. The old Bolshevik party is dead, but Bolshevism is raising its head everywhere.

To deduce Stalinism from Bolshevism or from Marxism is the same as to deduce, in a larger sense, counterrevolution from revolution. Liberal-conservative and later reformist thinking has always been characterized by this cliché. Due to the class structure of society, revolutions have always produced counterrevolutions. Does this not indicate, asks the logician, that there is some inner flaw in the revolutionary method? However, neither the liberals nor the reformists have succeeded, as yet, in inventing a more "economical" method. But if it is not easy to rationalize the living historical process, it is not at all difficult to give a rational interpretation of the alternation of its waves, and thus by pure logic to deduce Stalinism from "state socialism," fascism from Marxism, reaction from revolution, in a word, the antithesis from the thesis. In this domain as in many others anarchist thought is the prisoner of liberal rationalism. Real revolutionary thinking is not possible without dialectics.

The Political "Sins" of Bolshevism as the Source of Stalinism

The arguments of the rationalists assume at times, at least in their outer form, a more concrete character. They do not deduce Stalinism from Bolshevism as a whole but from its political sins. The Bolsheviks, according to Gorter, Pannekoek, certain German "spartacists," and others, replaced the dictatorship of the party; Stalin replaced the dictatorship of the party with the dictatorship of the bureaucracy. The Bolsheviks destroyed all parties but their own; Stalin strangled the Bolshevik party in the interest of a Bonapartist clique. The Bolsheviks made compromises with the bourgeoisie; Stalin became its ally and support. The Bolsheviks preached the necessity of participation in the old trade unions and in the bourgeois parliament; Stalin made friends with the trade union bureaucracy and bourgeois democracy. One can make such comparisons at will. For all their apparent effectiveness they are entirely empty.

The proletariat can take power only through its vanguard. In itself the necessity for state power arises from an insufficient cultural level of the masses and their heterogeneity. In the revolutionary vanguard, organized in a party, is crystallized the aspiration of the masses to obtain their freedom. Without the confidence of the class in the vanguard, without the support of the vanguard by the class, there can be no talk of the conquest of power. In this sense, the proletarian revolution and dictatorship are the work of the whole class, but only under the leadership of the vanguard. The soviets are only the organized form of the tie between the vanguard and the class. A revolutionary content can be given to this form only by the party. This is proved by the positive experience of the October Revolution and by the negative experience of other countries (Germany, Austria, finally Spain). No one has either shown in practice or tried to explain articulately on paper how the proletariat can seize power without the political leadership of a party that knows what it wants. The fact that this party subordinates the soviets politically to its leaders has, in itself, abolished the soviet system no more than the domination of the conservative majority has abolished the British parliamentary system.

As far as the *prohibition* of the other soviet parties is concerned, it did not flow from any "theory" of Bolshevism but was a measure of defense of the dictatorship in a backward and devastated country, surrounded by enemies on all sides. For the Bolsheviks, it was clear from the beginning that this measure, later completed by the prohibition of factions inside the governing party itself, signalized a tremendous danger. However, the root of the danger lay not in the doctrine or in the tactics but in the material weakness of the dictatorship, in the difficulties of its internal and international situation. If the revolution had triumphed, even if only in Germany, the need of prohibiting the other soviet parties would immediately have fallen away. It is absolutely indisputable that the domination of a single party served as the juridical point of departure for the Stalinist totalitarian system. But the reason for this development lies neither in Bolshevism nor in the prohibition of other parties as a temporary war measure, but in the number of defeats of the proletariat in Europe and Asia.

The same applies to the struggle with anarchism. In the heroic epoch of the revolution, the Bolsheviks went hand in hand with the genuinely revolutionary anarchists. Many of them were drawn into the ranks of the party. The author of these lines discussed with Lenin more than once the possibility of allotting to the anarchists certain territories where, with the consent of the local population, they would carry out their stateless experiment. But civil war, blockade, and hunger left no room for such plans. The Kronstadt insurrection? But the revolutionary government naturally could not "present" to the insurrectionary sailors the fortress which protected the capital only because the reactionary peasant-soldier rebellion was joined by a few doubtful anarchists. A concrete historical analysis of the events leaves not the slightest room for the legends, built up on ignorance and sentimentality, concerning Kronstadt, Makhno, and other episodes of the revolution.

There remains only the fact that the Bolsheviks from the beginning applied not only conviction but also compulsion, often to a most brutal degree. It is also indisputable that later the bureaucracy that grew out of the revolution monopolized the system of compulsion for its own use. Every state of development, even such catastrophic states as revolution and counterrevolution, flows from the preceding stage, is rooted in it and takes on some of its features. Liberals, including the Webbs, have always maintained that the Bolshevik dictatorship was only a new version of Czarism. They close their eyes to such "details" as the abolition of the monarchy and the nobility, the handing over of the land to the peasants, the expropriation of capital, the introduction of planned economy, atheist education, etc. In the same way liberal-anarchistic thought closes its eyes to the fact that the

Bolshevik revolution, with all its repressions, meant an upheaval of social relations in the interest of the masses, whereas the Stalinist Thermidorian upheaval accompanies the transformation of Soviet society in the interest of a privileged minority. It is clear that in the identification of Stalinism with Bolshevism there is not a trace of socialist criteria.

Christian Rakovsky

Bureaucracy and the Soviet State*

Christian Rakovsky (1873–?) began his political
career in the Russian revolutionary movement, soon
adhering to the Bolshevik wing. After the revolution
he served as prime minister of the Ukraine and as
Ambassador to Great Britain. During the mid-twen-
ties he was one of the most articulate spokesmen for
the Trotskyist opposition, and somewhat later was
exiled by the Stalin regime to Astrakhan. In 1933,
he recanted his opposition. In 1938, he was sen-
tenced to twenty years imprisonment. His subsequent
fate is uncertain.

The article that follows was written in 1928 as a
letter to Valentinov, another exiled oppositionist. Going beyond the usual Trotskyist analysis of why the
Bolshevik regime had degenerated—the economic
and cultural backwardness of Russia, the disastrous
aftereffects of the civil war, the smallness of the
working class in relation to the Russian population as
a whole—Rakovsky entered an area of analysis that
Marxists had either shunned or been unaware of. He
discussed the effects of power as such, power even
under the most favorable circumstances, upon a class
and a party that had never before exercised it. Not
only did he thereby venture upon a sociological investigation of bureaucracy as a problem affecting all
modern societies; he also—again going beyond Trotsky—anticipated the view (see the later essays by
Hilferding and Shachtman) that the bureaucratic

---

* From "Power and the Russian Worker," *The New International*, November, 1934, pp. 105–109. Title supplied by editor.

rulers of the Stalinist dictatorship were coalescing into a new ruling class.

Two years after writing this article, Rakovsky developed his argument with still greater boldness:

From the workers' state with bureaucratic perversions—*as Lenin defined our form of government—we have developed into* a bureaucratic state with proletarian-communist survivals.

Before our eyes, a great class of rulers has been taking shape *and is continuing to develop. . . . The unifying factor of this unique class is that unique form of private property, governmental power.* "The bureaucracy has the state in its possession," wrote Marx, "as rights of private property."

Dear Comrade Valentinov:

. . . What characterizes the flood of scandals that have just been exposed, what is most dangerous in it, is precisely this passivity of the masses (a passivity which is still greater in the Communist mass than among those not in the party) towards the unprecedented manifestations of despotism which have taken place. Workers witnessed them, but passed them off without protesting or contended themselves with grumbling a little out of fear of those who were in power, or simply out of political indifference. . . .

The question of the causes of this indifference and the means calculated to eliminate it, proves to be essential. . . .

The explanations which you give of this fact are, without a doubt, correct; every one of us has already presented them in his speeches; they have, in part, already found their reflection in our platform. Nevertheless these interpretations and the remedies proposed for getting out of this painful situation, have had and still have an empirical character; they relate to each particular case and do not settle the essence of the question.

In my opinion, this has happened because the question in itself is a new one. Up to now, we have witnessed plenty of examples of the spirit of activity of the working class sinking and declining until it even reached the point of political reaction. But these examples appeared to us, both here and abroad, during a period when the proletariat was still fighting for the conquest of political power. We could not have an example of the spirit of decline in the proletariat at a time when it had power in its hands, for the simple reason that ours is the first case in history where the working class has held the power for so long a time. Up to now we have known what could happen to the proletariat, that is, what oscillations could take place in its state of mind, when it is an oppressed and exploited class; but it is only now that we can evaluate on the basis of facts the changes occurring in the state of mind of the working class when it takes over *the leadership*.

This political position (of ruling class) is not devoid of dangers; they are, on the contrary, quite great. I do not have in mind here the objective difficulties due to the whole ensemble of historical circumstances; capitalist encirclement outside and petty bourgeois encirclement inside the country. No, it is a question of the difficulties inherent in every new ruling class, which are the consequence of the conquest and the exercise of the power itself, of the aptitude or the inaptitude to utilize it.

You understand that these difficulties would continue to exist up to a certain point even if we were to suppose for a moment that the country was populated only by proletarian masses and if, on the outside, only proletarian states existed. These difficulties might be called *the professional risks* of power. Indeed, the position of a class fighting for the conquest of power and that of a class which holds it in its hands, are different. I repeat that in speaking of dangers I do not have in mind the relationships which exist with the other classes, but rather those which are created in the ranks of the triumphant class.

What does a class taking the offensive represent? A maximum of unity and of cohesion. All craft and group, to say nothing of individual interests, retire to the background. All the initiative is in the hands of the militant mass itself and of its revolutionary vanguard, connected with this mass in the most intimately organic fashion.

When a class seizes power, one of its sections becomes the agent of this power. Thus the bureaucracy comes forward. In a socialist state, where capitalist accumulation is forbidden by the members of the ruling party, this differentiation commences by being functional; then it becomes social. I am thinking here of the social position of a communist who has at his disposal an automobile, a good apartment, a regular vacation, who receives the maximum wage authorized by the party—a position which differs from that of the communist working in the coal mines and receiving from 50 to 60 rubles a month. As to the workers and employees, you know that they are divided into eighteen different categories. . . .

Another consequence is that part of the functions formerly performed by the whole party, by the whole class, now become attributes of power, that is, only of a certain quantity of persons in this party and in this class. The unity and the cohesion which were formerly the natural consequence of the revolutionary class struggle can now be maintained only thanks to a whole system of measures having as their aim the preservation of the equilibrium between the various groupings of this class and party, their subordination to the fundamental goal. But that is a long and delicate process. It consists in politically educating the dominant class to the skill which it must acquire in order to keep hold of the state apparatus, the party, and the trade unions, to control and direct them.

I repeat: it is a matter of education. No class ever came into the world possessing the art of administration. It is acquired only thanks to experience, to mistakes committed, that is, by drawing the lessons from the mistakes one commits himself. A Soviet constitution, however ideal, cannot assure the working class the application, without obstacles, of its dictatorship and its governmental control, if the proletariat does not know how to utilize the rights which the constitution accords it. The lack of harmony existing between the political capacities of a given class, its administrative skill, and the constitutional juridical forms which it works out for its use when it conquers power, is an historical fact. It can be observed in the evolution of all classes, in part also in the history of the bourgeoisie. The English bourgeoisie, for example, fought a good many battles, not only to recast the constitution after its own interests, but also in order to be able to profit by its rights and, in particular, by its right to vote, fully and without obstacles. The novel by Charles Dickens, *Pickwick Papers*, contains many of those scenes of the epoch of English Constitutionalism, when the ruling group, assisted by the administrative apparatus, overturned into the ditches the coaches bearing the opposition voters, so that they would not arrive in time to the ballot boxes.

This process of differentiation is perfectly natural with the bourgeoisie which has triumphed or is about to triumph. Indeed, taken in the broadest sense of the term, it constitutes a series of economic and even of class groupings. We know the existence of the big, the middle, and the petty bourgeoisie; we know that there are financial, commercial, industrial, and agrarian bourgeoisies. As a result of certain events, like wars and revolutions, regroupings occur within the ranks of the bourgeoisie itself; new strata appear, beginning to play a role proper to them, as, for example, proprietors, purchasers of national wealth, or the *nouveaux riches,* as they are called, who come forward after every war that lasts for any length of time. During the French Revolution, at the period of the Directory, these *nouveaux riches* constituted one of the factors of the reaction.

In general, the history of the Third Estate triumphing in France in 1789 is extremely instructive. In the first place, this Third Estate was itself extremely variegated. It extended over everybody who was not a part of the nobility or the clergy; thus, it comprised not only all the varieties of the bourgeoisie, but also the workers and the poverty-stricken peasants. It is only gradually, after a long fight, after armed interventions, repeated on numerous occasions, that the legal possibility for the whole of the Third Estate to participate in the administration of the country was realized in 1792. The political reaction which began even before Thermidor consists in that *the power began to pass, both formally and in fact, into the hands of an increasingly restricted number of citizens.* Little by little, first by the fact of the situation and then by law, the masses of the people were eliminated from the government of the country.

It is true that here the pressure of the reaction made itself felt primarily along the seams and edges, joining together the scraps of classes which comprised the Third Estate. It is also true that if one examines a distinct grouping of the bourgeoisie, it does not present class contours as clearcut as those which, for example, separate the bourgeoisie and the proletariat, that is, two classes playing an entirely different role in production.

Furthermore, in the course of the French Revolution, during the period of its decline, the power not only acted to eliminate social groups which only yesterday marched together by agreement and were united by the same revolutionary aim, but it also disintegrated more or less homogeneous social masses. Functional specialization, the given class bringing forth out of its ranks the upper circles of functionaries—that is the result of the fissures which were converted, thanks to the pressure of the counterrevolution, into yawning gaps. It is as a result of this that the dominant class itself produced the contradictions during the struggle.

The contemporaries of the French Revolution, those who participated in it, and even more so the historians of the epoch that followed, occupied themselves with the question of the causes that promoted the degeneration of the Jacobin Party. On more than one occasion, Robespierre put his supporters on guard against the consequences that the *intoxication of power* might involve. He warned them that, having it in their hands, they ought not to be *too self-presumptive*, "get puffed up," he said, or as we would say now, not allow oneself to be infected by "Jacobin vanity." But as we shall see later, Robespierre himself contributed a good deal to letting the power slip out of the hands of the petty bourgeoisie leaning upon the Parisian workers.

We shall not quote here the indications supplied by the contemporaries concerning the various causes for the decomposition of the Jacobins, as for example the tendency to enrich themselves, the participation in contract awards, supplies, etc. Rather let us point to a strange and well-known fact: the opinion of Babeuf that the fall of the Jacobins was greatly facilitated by the noble dames with whom they were so deeply smitten. He addressed himself to the Jacobins in these terms: "What are you doing, pusillanimous plebeians? Today they hold you in their arms, tomorrow they will strangle you!" (If automobiles had existed at the time of the French Revolution, we would have had the factor of the "automobile harem," pointed to by comrade Sosnovsky as having played a fairly important role in shaping the ideology of our Soviet and party bureaucracy.) But what played the most important role in the isolation of Robespierre and the Jacobin Club, what separated them sharply from the masses (workers and petty bourgeoisie), was, besides the liquidation of all the elements of the left, beginning with the Enragés, the Hébertists, and the Chaumists (in general the whole Paris Commune), the gradual elimination of the elective principle and its replacement by the *principle of appointments*.

The dispatch of commissioners to the armies or to the towns where the counterrevolution was raising its head, was not only a legitimate but an indispensable job. But when, little by little, Robespierre began to replace the judges and the commissioners of the various sections of Paris who, up to then, had been elected in the same way as the judges; when he began to appoint the chairmen of the revolutionary committees and reached the point of substituting functionaries for the whole leadership of the Commune, he could thereby only reinforce the bureaucracy and kill off popular initiative. Thus, the regime of Robespierre, instead of raising the spirit of activity of the masses, who were already oppressed by the economic crisis, only aggravated the evil and facilitated the work of the antidemocratic forces. Dumas, the chairman of the revolutionary tribunal, complained to Robespierre that he was unable to find any jurors for the tribunal, for nobody wanted to fill this function. But Robespierre experienced this indifference of the Parisian masses in his own case when, on the 10th of Thermidor, he was marched through the streets of Paris, wounded and bleeding, without anyone fearing that the popular masses might intervene in behalf of the dictator of yesterday.

Obviously, it would be ridiculous to attribute the fall

of Robespierre as well as the defeat of the revolutionary democracy to the *principle of appointments*. But without a doubt, it accelerated the action of the other factors. Among them the decisive role was played by the difficulties of provisionment, caused in large part by two years of bad harvest (as well as by the disturbances connected with the passing of the large agrarian property of the nobility to the small scale cultivation of the land by the peasants), by the constant rise of the price of bread and meat, by the fact that the Jacobins did not, at the outset, want to resort to administrative measures to curb the avidity of the rich peasants and the speculators. When the Jacobins finally decided, under the violent pressure of the masses, to adopt the law on the maximum, this law, operating under conditions of a free market and capitalist production, could act inevitably only as a palliative.

Let us now pass to the reality in which we live. I believe that it is necessary first of all to point out that when we use expressions like *party* and *masses,* we should not lose sight of the content which the history of the last ten years has introduced into these terms. The working class and the party—no longer *physically* but *morally*—are no longer what they were ten years ago. I am not exaggerating when I say that the militant of 1917 would hardly recognize himself in the person of the militant of 1928. A profound change has taken place in the anatomy and the physiology of the working class. . . .

In speaking of the working class it is necessary to find a reply to a whole series of questions, for example:

- What is the percentage of workers now engaged in our industry who entered it after the revolution and the percentage which worked there before it?
- What is the proportion of those who formerly participated in the revolutionary movement, took part in strikes, were deported or imprisoned, took part in the civil war or the Red army?
- What is the percentage of workers engaged in industry who work there without interruption? How many of them work there only occasionally?
- What is the proportion in industry of semiproletarian, semipeasant elements, etc.?

If we penetrate to the very depths of the proletarian, semiproletarian, and in general the toiling masses, we will encounter whole sections of the population about whom very little is said among us. I do not have in mind here only the unemployed, who constitute an ever growing danger which was, however, clearly indicated by the opposition. I am thinking of the mendicant or half-pauperized masses, who, thanks to the tiny subsidies granted by the state, are encamped on the outskirts of pauperism, thievery, and prostitution.

We cannot imagine how people sometimes live a bare few steps away form us. It occasionally happens that one collides with phenomena whose existence in a Soviet state could not even be suspected and which leave the impression of a suddenly discovered abyss. It is not a question of pleading the cause of the Soviet power by invoking the fact that it has not yet been able to rid itself of the painful heritage left it by the Czarist and capitalist regime. No, but in our epoch, under our regime we record the existence in the body of the working class of crevices into which the bourgeoisie could drive a wedge.

At one time, under the bourgeois power, the conscious part of the working class drew this great mass, including the semivagabonds, behind it. The fall of the capitalist regime was to bring about the liberation of the *entire proletariat*. The semivagabond elements rendered the bourgeoisie and the capitalist state responsible for their situation; they looked to the revolution to bring about a change in their conditions. At the present time, these circles are not content: their position has not improved, or only barely. They begin to look with hostility upon the Soviet power as well as that part of the working class which labors in industry. They become particularly the enemies of the Soviet party and trade union functionaries. Sometimes you hear them speak of the summits of the working class as the "new nobility."

I will now dwell here on the differentiation which the power has introduced into the proletariat and which I designated above as "functional." The function has modified the organ itself, that is, the psychology of those who are charged with the various tasks of management in the administration and the economy of the state, has changed to such a point that not only objectively but subjectively, not only materially but morally, they have ceased to be a part of this same working class. Thus, for example, the manager of a factory playing at being a "satrap," in spite of the fact that he is a communist, despite his proletarian origin, despite the fact that he was still at the bench a few years ago, will not embody in the eyes of the workers the best qualities that the proletariat possesses. Molotov can, to his heart's content, put an equal sign between the dictatorship of the proletariat and our state with its bureaucratic degenerations. By this he only discredits the dictatorship without disarming the legitimate discontentment of the workers.

If we pass over to the party itself, in addition to all the nuances that we encounter in the working class, it is necessary to add the turncoats from other classes. The social structure of the party is much more heterogeneous than that of the proletariat. This was always the case, naturally with this difference, that while the party lived an intense ideological life, it fused this social amalgam into a single alloy, thanks to the struggle of the active revolutionary class. But the power is a cause, in the party as well as in the working class, of the same differentiation which reveals the seams existing between the various social layers. The bureaucracy of the soviets and the party is a fact of a new order. It is not a question here of isolated cases, of hitches in the conduct of some comrade, but rather of a new social category to which a whole treatise ought to be devoted. . . .

You ask what has become of the spirit of activity of the party and of our proletariat? Where has their revolutionary initiative gone to? Where are their ideological interests, their revolutionary valor, their proletarian pride? You are astonished at there being so much sluggishness, cowardice, pusillanimity, arrivism, and so many other things that I would have added on my own account? How does it happen that men having a valorous revolutionary past, whose personal honesty is beyond question, who on more than one occasion gave examples of devotion to the revolution, should have been transformed into piteous bureaucrats?

Saddest of all is the fact that no reflex takes place on

the part of the party and the mass. For two years, an especially bitter struggle developed between the opposition and the upper circles of the party: in the course of the last two months events took place that ought to have opened the eyes of the blindest. Still, one does not yet feel that the party masses have intervened. Also comprehensible is the pessimism displayed by certain comrades and which I feel peering out of your questions too.

Babeuf, after coming out of the prison of l'Abbaye and casting a glance about him, began to ask what had become of the people of Paris, the workers of the Saint-Antoine and Saint-Marceau suburbs, those who took the Bastille on July 14, 1789, the Tuileries Palace on August 10, 1792, who besieged the Convention on May 30, 1793, to say nothing of their numerous other armed actions. He summed up his observations in a single phrase, in which one feels the bitterness of the revolutionist: "It is harder to reeducate the people in an attachment to liberty than to conquer it."

We have seen why the people of Paris forgot the allure of liberty: the famine, unemployment, the suppression of the revolutionary cadres (many of the leaders had been guillotined), the removal of the masses from the management of the country. All this brought about such a great physical and moral exhaustion of the masses that the people of Paris and the rest of France required thirty-seven years of respite before beginning a new revolution. Babeuf formulated his program in two words (I speak here of his 1794 program): "Liberty and an elected Commune."

I must make a confession here: I have never let myself be swayed by the hope that it would suffice for the leaders to appear in the party meetings and the workers' gatherings for them to win over the masses to the side of the opposition. I always considered such hopes, which came from the side of the Leningrad leaders, as being a certain survival from the period when they took the official ovations and applause for the expression of the true sentiment of the masses, attributing them to their imaginary popularity. . . . However, the point of departure, the premise should have been that the job of educating the party and the working class is a difficult and long-term job, all the more so because the mind must first be cleared of all the impurities introduced into it by the practice of the soviets and the party and the bureaucracy of these institutions.

It must not be lost sight of that the majority of the party members (to say nothing of the young communists) have the most erroneous conception of the tasks, the functions, and the structure of the party, namely: the conception that the bureaucracy teaches them by its example, its practical conduct, and its stereotyped formulae. All the workers who joined the party after the civil war came in, in most cases, after 1923 (the Lenin enrollment): they have no idea of what the regime of the party once was. The majority of them is devoid of that revolutionary class education which is acquired in the struggle, in life, in conscious practice. At one time, this class consciousness was obtained in the struggle against capitalism; today, it must take shape in participating in the building up of socialism. But our bureaucracy, having made a hollow phrase of this participation, the workers nowhere acquire such an education. I exclude, of course —as being an abnormal means of educating the class— the fact that our bureaucracy, by reducing real wages, by aggravating the working conditions, by promoting the development of unemployment, provokes the workers to struggle and arouses class consciousness; but then, it is hostile to the socialist state.

In the conception of Lenin and of all of us, the task of the party leadership lies precisely in preserving the party and the working class from the corruptive influence of privileges, of favors, and of tolerations inherent in the power by reason of its contact with the debris of the old nobility and the petty bourgeoisie; the perverse influence of the NEP, the temptation of bourgeois morals and ideology, should have been forestalled. At the same time we had the hope that the party leadership would create a new proletarian, and new morals in daily life. . . .

In my opinion, the first condition to enable our party leadership to exercise an educative role is to reduce the magnitude and the functions of this leadership. Three-fourths of the apparatus ought to be disbanded. The tasks of the remaining fourth ought to receive strictly determined limitations. This would also apply to the tasks, functions, and rights of the central organs. The party members must regain their rights, which have been trampled underfoot, by having themselves accorded sure guarantees against the despotism to which the upper circles have accustomed us.

It is hard to imagine what is taking place in the lower ranks of the party. It is especially in the struggle against the opposition that the ideological mediocrity of these cadres was manifested, as well as the corruptive influence which they exercise over the proletarian masses of the party. If at its summit there was still a certain ideological line, an erroneous and sophistic line, at the lower rungs, mixed, it is true, with a strong dose of bad faith, on the other hand, the most unrestrained demogoguery was employed against the opposition. The agents of the party did not hesitate to exploit anti-Semitism, the phobia against foreigners, hatred of intellectuals, etc. I believe that any reform of the party that bases itself upon the party bureaucracy, will prove utopian. . . .

Nikolai Bukharin

Imperialism and World Economy

> Nikolai Bukharin (1888–1938) was, from his student
> days, an active participant in the Russian revolution-
> ary movement, adhering to the Leninist wing, al-
> though, at various times before and after the revolu-
> tion, he temporarily opposed Lenin from the Left.
> After the Revolution, he served as editor of Pravda,
> was a leading figure in the Communist International,
> and the author of numerous books expounding Marx-
> ism-Leninism. He allied himself with Stalin against
> Trotsky, but then, in the late twenties, found him-
> self under assault by the victorious Stalin. In the
> terminology of the Russian Communists during the
> twenties, Bukharin was a "right communist": that is,
> he opposed forced collectivization and terror in the
> countryside and urged a more moderate regime
> within the ruling party. After expulsion from the
> party and recantation, he was finally made one of
> the victims in the third Moscow Trial and, after this
> frame-up, was killed.
>
> The selection below is taken from Bukharin's book,
> Imperialism and World Economy (1929), in which
> he analyzes the direction of modern capitalist econ-
> omy, the tendency toward stratification of economy,
> and allied trends.

Imperialism is the policy of finance capitalism, i.e., a
highly developed capitalism implying a considerable
ripeness of the organisation of production; in other
words, imperialist policies by their very existence be-
speak the ripeness of the objective conditions for a new

socioeconomic form; consequently, all talk about the "necessity" of imperialism as a limit to action is liberalism, is in itself semi-imperialism. The further existence of capitalism and imperialism becomes nothing more nor less than a question of the interrelation between mutually struggling class forces.

There exists, however, the danger of another opportunist deviation that is outwardly opposed to fatalism, a theory now being most assiduously developed in literature by Karl Kautsky. Starting from the correct notion that the further existence of imperialism depends upon the interrelation of social forces, Kautsky proceeds along the following line.

Imperialism, he says, is a definite method of capitalist politics; the latter can exist even without forcible methods, in the same way as capitalism can exist with an eight-hour work day instead of a ten- or twelve-hour day. As far as the work day is concerned, the proletariat meets the bourgeois tendency toward increasing the labour day with its proletarian tendency to shorten the number of labour hours, doing so within the framework of capitalism. In the very same manner, says Kautsky, it is necessary to meet the bourgeois violent tendencies of imperialism with the peaceful tendencies of the proletariat. Thus, Kautsky asserts, the question can be solved within the framework of capitalism. Radical as this theory may seem at first glance, it is in fact a thoroughly reformist one.

Later we shall deal at length with the analysis of the possibility of "peaceful capitalism" *à la* Kautsky ("ultraimperialism"). At present we wish to advance only a formal argument. We assert, namely, that from the fact that imperialism is a problem of the interrelation of forces, it does not at all follow that it can disappear within the framework of capitalism, just as the fifteen-hour work day or unregulated wages, etc., disappeared. If the problem were to be solved so simply, it would be possible to "map out" also the following perspective: it is known that capitalism implies the acquisition of surplus value by the capitalists; all the new value n is divided into two parts, $n = v + s$; this distribution, looked upon from its quantitative side, depends upon the interrelation of social forces (the antagonism of interests was early formulated by Ricardo). With the growth of resistance on the part of the working class, it is perfectly thinkable that v will increase at the expense of s, and that n will be distributed in a proportion more favorable for the workers. Since, however, the gradual increase of the proletariat's share is determined by the interrelation of forces, and since there is no limit set for this increase, the working class, having reduced the share of the capitalist to the size of mere salaries, peacefully "drains" capitalism in turning the capitalists into mere employees or—at worst —into pensioners of the collective body. This idyllic picture is obviously a reformist Utopia. No less of a Utopia is Kautsky's "ultraimperialism."

Kautsky and his followers assert that the very process of capitalist development is favorable to the growth of elements that can serve as a support for ultraimperialism. The growth of international interdependence of capital, they say, creates a tendency towards eliminating competition among the various "national" capitalist groups. This "peaceful" tendency, they say, is strengthened by pressure from below, and in this way rapacious imperialism is replaced by gentle ultraimperialism.

Let us analyse the question on its merits. Speaking economically, the question must be formulated as follows: how is an agreement (or a merger) of the state capitalist trusts possible? For imperialism, as we all know, is nothing but the expression of competition between state capitalist trusts. Once this competition disappears, the ground for the policy of imperialism disappears also, and capital divided into many "national" groups is transformed into a single world organisation, a universal world trust opposed by the world proletariat.

Speaking in an abstract, theoretical way, such a trust is perfectly thinkable, for, generally speaking, there is no economic limit to the process of cartelisation. In our opinion, Hilferding is perfectly right when, in his *Finanzkapital,* he says:

The question arises as to where the limits of cartelisation can actually be drawn. The question must be answered in the sense that there is no absolute limit to cartelisation. On the contrary, the tendency towards a continuous widening of the scope of cartelisation may be observed. Independent industries are becoming more and more dependent upon the cartelised ones and finally join them. As a result of this process, a universal cartel ought to emerge. Here all capital production would be consciously regulated from one centre, which determines the size of production in all its spheres. . . . This would be a consciously regulated society in an antagonistic form. This antagonism, however, is the antagonism of distribution. . . . The tendency toward creating such a universal cartel, and the tendency toward establishing a central bank coincide, and out of their unification grows the great concentrating power of finance capital.

This abstract economic possibility, however, by no means signifies its actual probability. The same Hilferding is perfectly right when he says in another place:

Economically, a universal cartel to guide all production and thus to eliminate crises, would be possible; such a cartel would be thinkable economically, although socially and politically such a state appears unrealisable, for the antagonism of interests, strained to the last possible limits, would necessarily bring about its collapse.

In reality, however, the sociopolitical causes would not even admit the formation of such an all-embracing trust. In the following we shall attempt to prove this thesis.

Comparative equality of positions in the world market is the first condition for the formation of a more or less stable compact. Where there is no such equality, the group occupying a more favourable position in the world market has no reason for joining a compact: on the contrary, it sees an advantage in continuing the struggle, for it has grown to hope that the competitor will be defeated. This is a general rule for the formation of compacts. It is just as applicable to state capitalist trusts, with which we are dealing here, as it is in other cases. Two series of conditions, however, have to be taken into consideration here.

First of all, purely economic equality. This includes equality in the cost of production. Equality in the cost of production, however, reduces itself in the final analysis to equality in labour values and therefore to a relatively equal level of development of productive forces. Thus equality of economic structure is a condition for the formation of agreements. Where the difference in economic structure is considerable, where there is, as a consequence, inequality in the cost of production, there the state capitalist trust that possesses a higher technique finds it unprofitable to enter into an agreement. This is why the highly developed industry of Germany—to take as an example the practice of agreements as we find it in the various production branches—prefers to appear isolated in the world market as far as its main lines are concerned. Of course, when we deal with a state capitalist trust, we take into account a certain mean figure relative to all the production branches; we then proceed, not from the interests of the capitalist groups owning one or the other production branch but from the interests of "organised industry," where after all the dominant note is being struck by the large-scale capitalists of heavy industry, whose relative economic importance keeps on growing. Transportation cost is added to production cost proper.

Aside from this "purely economic" equality, a necessary condition for the formation of stable agreements is equality of economic policies. We have seen above that capital's connection with the state is transformed into an additional economic force. The stronger state secures for its industries the most advantageous trade treaties, and establishes high tariffs that are disadvantageous for the competitors. It helps its finance capital to monopolise the sales markets, the markets for raw materials, and particularly the spheres of capital investment. It is therefore easily understood why, when conditions of the struggle are being taken stock of in the world market, the state capitalist trusts reckon, not only with the purely economic conditions of the struggle, but also with the economic policies of the respective states. This is why even where there are relatively equal economic structures, but the military powers of the state capitalist trusts differ considerably, it is better for the stronger to continue the struggle rather than to enter into a compact or to merge with the others. If we view the situation of the struggling "nations" from this point of vantage, we realise that there is no reason to expect, at least in the more or less near future, an agreement or a merging of the state capitalist trusts and their transformation into a single world trust. It is sufficient to compare the economic structure of France and Germany, of England and America, of the developed countries in general, with such countries as Russia (the latter, though not belonging to the category of state capitalist trusts, nevertheless add to the establishment of certain relations in the world market) to realise how far we are from a world capitalist organisation.* The same may be said also as regards military power. If the present war has shown (at least so far) a comparative equality of the opposing groups, one must not forget that we deal here with combinations of forces, each of which is by no means a stable entity.

The question of equality must be considered not only statically, but mainly dynamically. The "national" groups of the bourgeoisie build their plans not only on what "is" but also on what "will probably be." They take into strict account every possibility of development which may allow a certain group to become superior to all the others in due time, although at the present moment it may be economically and politically equal to its competitor. This circumstance makes the lack of equilibrium still more acute.† The great stimulus to the formation of an international state capitalist trust is given by the internationalisation of capitalist interest as described in the first

---

* To avoid misunderstandings, we must emphasize that this assertion of ours by no means contradicts another one which says that the economic development of the foremost countries has created "objective prerequisites" for the social organisation of production. As far as the possibility of social production is concerned, the foremost countries are all on a comparatively equal level. There is no contradiction between those assertions, because the basis of differentiation is not the same.

† The bourgeoisie understands this perfectly well. Thus, a German professor, Max Krahmann (in his book, *Krieg und Montanindustrie*, Berlin, 1915, first volume of the series *Krieg und Volkswirtschaft*) says: "As in the present small [!] World War, so in the future great war, where North America and Eastern Asia will also have their word to say, it is entirely impossible for the group of agricultural states to fight the union of industrial states. . . . Thus, universal peace [*der Weltfrieden*] could be secured were the industrial states able to come to terms [*sich vertragen könnten*]. Since this is excluded for the time being, then . . ." etc. (p. 15).

section of our work (participation in and financing of international enterprises, international cartels, trusts, etc.). Significant as this process may be in itself, it is, however, counteracted by a still stronger tendency of capital toward nationalisation and toward remaining secluded within state boundaries. The benefits accruing to a "national" group of the bourgeoisie from a continuation of the struggle are much greater than the losses sustained in consequence of that struggle. By no means must we overestimate the significance of the already existing international industrial agreements. As we have noted above, many of them are very unstable, representing as they do businessman's organisations of a relatively low type with a comparatively small centralisation, and often embracing highly specialised production branches (the bottle syndicate). Only companies formed in such spheres of production as are based on a natural monopoly (oil) possess comparative stability. Of course, the tendency towards internationalisation would none the less triumph "in the last analysis," but it would do so after a considerable period of very stubborn struggles between the state and capitalist trusts.

But are not the costs of the struggle, i.e., military expenditures, perchance so large that it does not pay for the bourgeoisie to continue in this way? Is not such a plan as the proposed militarisation of England an expression of bourgeois "stupidity" which is blind to its own interests? Alas, it is not so. We must attribute this quality rather to the naïve pacifists than to the bourgeoisie. The latter keeps its balance sheet in perfect shape. The truth of the matter is that those who make such arguments ordinarily lose sight of all the complex functions of military power. Such power, as we have seen above, functions not only in times of war, but also in times of peace to back up its finance capital in "peaceful competition." The pacifists forget that the war burdens, due to the incidence of taxation, etc., are borne mainly by the working class, partly by the intermediary economic groupings which are being expropriated during the war (which means in the process of the greatest centralisation of production).

It follows from the above that the actual process of

economic development will proceed in the midst of a sharpened struggle between the state capitalist trusts and the backward economic formations. A series of wars is unavoidable. In the historic process which we are to witness in the near future, world capitalism will move in the direction of a universal state capitalist trust by absorbing the weaker formations. Once the present war is over, new problems will have to be "solved" by the sword. Partial agreements are, of course, possible here and there (e.g., the fusion of Germany and Austria is quite probable). Every agreement or fusion, however, will only reproduce the bloody struggle on a new scale. Were Central Europe to unite according to the plans of the German imperialists, the situation would remain comparatively the same; but even were *all* of Europe to unite, it would not yet signify "disarmament." It would signify an unheard of rise of militarism, because the problem to be solved would be a colossal struggle between Europe on the one hand, America and Asia on the other. The struggle among small (small!) state capitalist trusts would be replaced by a struggle between still more colossal trusts. To attempt to eliminate this struggle by "home remedies" and rose water is tantamount to bombarding an elephant with peas, for imperialism is not only a system most intimately connected with modern capitalism, it is also the most essential element of the latter.

We have seen in the second section the peculiarities in the structure of modern capitalism and the formation of state capitalist trusts. This economic structure, however, is connected with a certain policy, namely, the imperialist policy. This not only in the sense that imperialism is a product of finance capitalism, but also in the sense that finance capital cannot pursue any other policy than an imperialist one, as we characterised it above. The state capitalist trust cannot become an adherent of free trade, for thereby it would lose a considerable part of its capitalist *raison d'être*. We have already pointed out that protectionism allows the acquisition of additional profits on the one hand, facilitates competition in the world market on the other. In the same way finance capital, expressing as it does capitalist monoply organisations, cannot

relinquish the policy of monopolising "spheres of influence," of seizing sales markets and markets for raw materials or spheres of capital investment. If one state capitalist trust fails to get hold of an unoccupied territory, it will
be occupied by another.

Peaceful rivalry, which corresponded to the epoch of
free competition and of the absence of any organisation
of production at home, is absolutely inconceivable in the
epoch of an entirely different production structure and of
the struggle among state capitalist trusts. Those imperialist interests are of such magnitude for the finance capitalist groups, and they are so connected with the very foundations of their existence, that the governments do not
shrink before the most colossal military expenditures just
to secure for themselves a stable position in the world
market. The idea of "disarmament" within the framework
of capitalism is particularly absurd as far as the state
capitalist trusts that occupy the foremost positions in the
world market are concerned. Before their eyes there always shines the picture of subjugating the whole world,
of acquiring an unheard-of field for exploitation—a thing
termed by the French imperialists *l'organisation
d'économie mondiale* and by the German imperialists *Or-
ganisierung der Weltwirtschaft*.

Would the bourgeoisie exchange this "high" ideal for
the pot of porridge of disarmament? Where is the guarantee for a given state capitalist trust that a pernicious
rival will not continue the "abandoned" policy in spite of
all formal agreements and guarantees? Everyone acquainted with the history of the struggle among cartels
even within the boundaries of one country knows how
often, when the situation changed, when the market conditions changed, agreements dissolved like soap bubbles.
Imagine a strong state capitalist trust like the U.S. waging war against a union of all other trusts—the "agreement" will then be shattered to pieces in no time. (In the
latter case we would have a tremendous formation constructed after the type of an ordinary syndicate and having the state capitalist trusts as its component parts.
Such an agreement between the state capitalist trusts
would not be able at once to skip all intermediary stages,

to become a real centralised trust. A type of agreement, however, that implies intense internal struggle is easily amenable to the influence of changing conditions.) We have taken a hypothetical case where formal unification is a fact. However, this unification cannot take place because the bourgeoisie of every country is by no means as naïve as many of its *bona fide* pacifists who wish nothing more than to persuade the bourgeoisie and to "prove" to it that it does not understand its own advantages. . . .

But, one may argue, this is exactly what Kautsky and his friends assume, namely, that the bourgeoisie will relinquish its imperialistic methods when it is compelled to do so by pressure from below. Our reply is that two possibilities are open in this case: either the pressure is weak, then everything remains as before; or the pressure is stronger than the "resistance," then we have before us not a new era of ultra-imperialism but a new era of nonantagonistic social development.

The entire structure of world economy in our times forces the bourgeoisie to pursue an imperialist policy. As the colonial policy is inevitably connected with violent methods, so every capitalist expansion leads sooner or later to a bloody climax. Hilferding says:

Violent methods are inseparably bound up with the very essence of colonial policy, which without them would lose its capitalist meaning; they are so much an integral element of the colonial policy as the existence of a proletariat divorced from all ownership is generally a *conditio sine qua non* of capitalism. To be in favour of a colonial policy and at the same time to talk about eliminating its violent methods is a dream which cannot be treated with more earnestness than the illusion that one can eliminate the proletariat while retaining capitalism.

The same thing may be said about imperialism. It is an integral element of finance capitalism without which the latter would lose its capitalist meaning. To imagine that the trusts, this embodiment of monopoly, have become the bearers of the free trade policy, of peaceful expansion, is a deeply harmful Utopian fantasy.

But is not the epoch of "ultraimperialism" a real possibility after all, can it not be affected by the centralisation process? Will not the state capitalist trusts devour one another gradually until there comes into existence an all-embracing power which has conquered all the others? This possibility would be thinkable if we were to look at the social process as a purely mechanical one, without counting the forces that are hostile to the policy of imperialism. In reality, however, the wars that will follow each other on an ever larger scale must inevitably result in a shifting of the social forces. The centralisation process, looked at from the capitalist angle, will inevitably clash with a sociopolitical tendency that is antagonistic to the former. Therefore it can by no means reach its logical end; it suffers collapse and achieves completion only in a new, purified, noncapitalist form. It is for this reason that Kautsky's theory is by no means realisable. It looks upon imperialism not as an inevitable accompaniment of capitalist development, but as one of the "dark sides" of capitalist development. Like Proudhon, whose philistine Utopia Marx fought so bitterly, Kautsky wishes to eliminate "dark" imperialism leaving intact the "sunny" sides of the capitalist order. His concept implies a slurring over of the gigantic contradictions which rend asunder modern society, and in this respect it is a reformist concept. It is a characteristic feature of theorising reformism that it takes pains to point out all the elements of capitalism's adaptation to conditions without seeing its contradictions. For a consistent Marxist, the entire development of capitalism is nothing but a process of a continuous reproduction of the contradictions of capitalism on an ever wider scale. The future of world economy, as far as it is a capitalist economy, will not overcome its inherent lack of adaptation; on the contrary, it will keep on reproducing this lack of adapation on an ever wider scale. These contradictions are actually harmonised in another production structure of the social organism—through a well-planned socialist organisation of economic activities.

Nikolai Bukharin

Organized Mismanagement in Modern Society

In Pravda, June 30, 1929 Nikolai Bukharin——by then no longer the ally of Stalin, but, like Trotsky a few years earlier, the victim of the Stalinist drive toward totalitarianism——published a seemingly routine exercise in Marxist polemic. It was a long review of a book by a German theorist, Hermann Bente, in which a description had been advanced of the increasing bureaucratization of modern economy, and the postulate suggested that this bureaucratization is the dominant social trend of our time. By now forced to employ an Aesopian vocabulary, Bukharin was obviously fascinated by Bente's material. In his review, he quoted at length from Bente, apparently feeling that what he could not freely say himself he could quote from an opponent——so as, finally, to refute him.

At the outset, Bukharin advances an idea profoundly heretical in the Soviet context: there are "two parallel developments" in the movement of capitalist economy and that of the Soviet economy. After several pages of standard Marxist refutation of Bente's theory (in the course of which Bukharin notes that Bente fails to consider the class correlation of bureaucratism in different societies, as well as the ways in which the "organized mismanagement" of bureaucratism intensifies the crises of capitalism), Bukharin then approaches his explosive sentence: "The Soviet reader may be startled to find a certain formal resemblance between some of the organizational problems posed and solved by Bente and the problems raised and settled in Soviet practice." And though Bukharin then hastens to muffle this dangerous observation, it is clear that he has made two major points which the attentive Russian reader was likely to grasp: (1) that in modern society there may be forms of bureaucratic degeneration that are not limited to capitalism and indeed are characteristic of all societies; (2) that many of the harsh descriptions Bente offers of the "organized mismanagement" of advanced capitalism also apply to the totalitarian collectivism of the Stalinist regime.

The result is an essay which, in an opaque and tangential style, approaches the idea that Stalinism is a new social phenomenon and gives a series of signs that, perhaps too late, Bukharin, yesterday's defender of Marxist orthodoxy, is beginning to be drawn to heterodox notions about the possible convergence of modern societies. Later, socialist thinkers in the West, enjoying freedom of expression, will develop similar ideas in a more systematic way.

Bukharin's essay, here translated into English for the first time, appears below in condensed form. Some of the illustrative material from Bente, by now familiar to Western readers, has been omitted; so too has Bukharin's lengthy refutation of Bente's underlying theories.

The latest forms taken by capitalism, the deep internal and structural changes they reveal, and, above all, the sharply rising trend toward state capitalism pose a number of new problems. For the second time in the last decade, "controlled economy" is being subjected to analysis. The first time was during the war. The drastic increase in state intervention, manifested in its most consistent form in blockaded Germany, whose economy was transformed into an isolated and planned military-capitalist economy, led to the publication of a great deal of theoretical literature. But today state capitalism is rising on a different foundation. Tentatively, and making every reservation about the incompleteness of the analogy, it may be said that contemporary state capitalism in the "advanced" capitalist countries stands in the same relationship to the "state capitalism" of 1914–1918 as the present system of the growing socialist economy in the U.S.S.R., with its planning in key areas, does to the economy of military communism.

Obviously, each of these two parallel developments owes something to the past. But what needs stressing is that there is a basic difference, a difference of principle, between the military economic systems (military state capitalism and military communism) and the "peaceful" economic systems being built in capitalism and socialism with the aid of the "New Economic Policy." The military systems are geared to consumption, but not in the sense in which "normal" socialist economy is geared to the satisfaction of the needs of the masses and likewise in contrast to the capitalist concentration on profits and the capitalist principle of "production for the sake of production."

To begin with, the military systems are geared to a very special type of consumption, primarily unproductive military consumption, the "satisfaction of war needs." Secondly, this is relatively short-term consumption, which is worlds away from the growing—steadily growing—consumption by the masses. Thirdly, and for that very reason, it is to a large extent rational consumption of a "given supply of goods." Fourthly, precisely because it involves the rational devouring of goods in short periods of time, this consumption occurs at the expense of production, is damaging to production, and is consequently damaging to the long-term development of consumption itself. Accordingly, under the system of military state capitalism, capitalist production stimuli were suppressed, while the system of military communism suppressed both the initiative of the ordinary producer and, to some extent, the production stimuli of the socialist sector which could not be adequately utilized for lack of direct contact with the small producer—the peasant.

Capitalist economy is "production for the sake of production"; to some extent, it is production at the expense of consumption. Military capitalist economy is consumption at the expense of production (and, within the consumption sector, it represents military consumption at the expense of mass consumption). Socialist economy is production for consumption, and the development of mass demand is a powerful stimulus to the development of production. In the final analysis, capitalist economy, precisely because it embodies the principle of "production for the sake of production," hampers the development of production (for example, low wages and the consequent low level of mass consumption act as a brake on technical progress: it has been found that, where wages are low, certain new and technically improved machines are not "economical"). Socialist economy, for the very reason that it must be geared to satisfying the growing needs of the masses, comes closest to perfection as regards the rates of development.

The capitalist and the socialist military economic systems, of course, reflect class approaches which are diametrically opposed and are in deadly conflict, and their historical significance is therefore entirely different. But they have this in common: *in both cases, the primary concern is with military consumption and the rationalization of military consumption, even at the expense of production.* It follows that the "second cycle" of state capitalism is quite different from the first, military cycle. Similarly, the problems of theory which are under scrutiny today are very different from those of the era of military economy. What is being discussed in the capitalist countries is not the theory of planned economy of the beleaguered capitalist fortress ("military state capitalism"); rather, the trend toward state capitalism growing up as a *"normal"* capitalist system is being analyzed. . . .

Out of the wealth of the literature on this subject, Hermann Bente's book, *Organized Mismangement. Economic forms of bureaucratized economy and their changes in the era of collectivized capitalism,* * calls for detailed comment. This work represents an attempt to construct an abstract theory of organization, with special emphasis on the nature of unproductive expenditure

---

* Dr. Hermann Bente. *Organisierte Unwirtschaftlichkeit. Die oekonomische Gestalt verbeamteter Wirtschaft und ihre Wandlung im Zeitalter des gesamtwirtschaftlichen Kapitalismus.* Jena, Gustav Fischer, 1929.

caused by the very structure of "bureaucratized economy." This is the first abstract theoretical *generalization* of its kind, and for this reason it deserves serious attention.

In his introduction, the author states outright that the transition to organized capitalism is the most salient feature of our times. This new system is accompanied by a form of "mismanagement" which, according to him, is the inevitable concomitant of the very principle of organization. Hitherto, all economic theories have been theories of "management." But it can readily be shown that what is rational in organizational terms may not be rational in terms of management of the economy, in precisely the same way that the requirements of management and technology do not always coincide.

The essence of organizational "mismanagement" is that the links in the organizational chain which should be means for attaining the goal of economic management are transformed into an end in themselves.

This development takes a number of different forms. These include: leveling different problems and people down to the same bureaucratic standard, so that they are then regarded as being of equal "value" and are dealt with in the same way. Regulations, orders, records, and reports—documents of every kind—become the crux of work, an end in themselves. In public enterprises, circulars and various formal documents play an enormous part; in cartels, too, the more profitable and the less viable concerns are deemed to be of equal value; records and reports are piled up high, and statistics, too, are often accumulated to the point of absurdity. The number of intermediary steps is excessive; sometimes the same piece of business must travel twice along that path, and the profits are eaten up by the cost of the control system. And while that path is being traveled, the problem itself may have been superseded by events. Work distribution is ossified (an official sitting at one window has nothing to do, while long lines form at another window, where some other "specialized" service is being provided); the quotas (for participation in production) in cartels are similarly frozen. . . .

The noneconomic criteria in the system of "organized mismanagement" include assigning primary importance to physical size as a classification principle: economic evaluation is replaced by "the grouping of objects according to their magnitude in space or time." Here are a few examples: scientific work is undervalued and mechanical work overestimated, because it can be seen in terms of "amounts"; the qualitative essence of the creative function is not understood—at the top will be found the diligent plodders, the bureaucracy of science, and not original thinkers who raise new problems and stimulate the young to choose new paths. Such people often "strive to prove their importance and significance in that . . . they are extremely touchy when it comes to defending their field of competence; they expand their office as much as possible, so that the greater number of their subordinates would make it necessary to raise their own rank." . . . Yet another example of the means becoming an end in itself is the formalistic approach, which reigns supreme. "Wherever the formal element is raised above the factual, the letter above the spirit, the order above a free decision, the report above actual experience, procedure above action, and the law above life, a perverted relationship ensues." *Fiat justitia, pereat mundus* (let justice triumph though the world perish). The bureaucrat views his work as consisting wholly in "squeezing all objects and all relations of public and, where possible, private life into certain formulas, regulations, and paragraphs. . . . He has no conception whatever of the value of time." A petrified, dead "procedure" becomes the chief yardstick; rational division of labor is frustrated by the official's refusal to make the slightest move which is not "in his sphere"; personnel policy is aimed not at "putting the right person in the right place," but rather at encouraging people who do not make trouble for the enterprise; men who would like to introduce reforms are denied access everywhere. Such a situation—typical of "late capitalism"—contains the germs of its own destruction. Characteristically, the official and his field of work are both set apart from economic struggle: "the official because of his permanent tenure, and his activity because it is monopolistic in nature." Dead "questions," "the regulation," "the order," strangle living business. . . .

This "mismanagement" results from three kinds of causes: natural–technical, organizational, and psychological. "The over-all reason for mismanagement is its remoteness from reality." In economics, a distinction must be drawn between two spheres of human activity: the realm of the inorganic, or phenomena relating to *things;* and the realm of the organic, or phenomena relating to *living beings.* Each of these two categories of phenomena is subject to its own laws. Where mechanical operations are concerned (the working of a piston, technology generally), the purpose of rationalization is to eliminate differences, inequalities, and multiplicity of methods and to introduce instead the highest possible degree of uniformity. In the realm of living phenomena, the growth of multiformity is the law (compare the *per capita* tax and the modern differentiated forms of taxation, the Ten Commandments and the modern codes of law, the "budget" of the savage and the budget of the contemporary worker). The kingdom of "organized mismanagement" deals with the "organization" of living phenomena. Natural–technical remoteness from living reality occurs when 1) the subject dealt with is removed from "living reality" in time or space, and 2) when the service provided is so removed. The first type is common where the economic governing bodies are out of contact with the market, so that the market can bring pressure to bear on them only through a number of intermediary stages, and the orders they issue must go back through those same stages. The pressure of reality (in this case, of the market) "loses its original force and does not introduce corrections where they are needed." In other words, it affects not the organizationally or technically weakest links in the chain, but rather those managed by the less clever tacticians or the less privileged among the directors of the enterprise or department.

Still more important than this "remoteness from reality" is the case of monopolies and publicly managed enterprises. Monopolies can be quite "economically" operated, but since they wholly dominate the market there is no

pressing need for them to be economical; they are therefore readily subject to ossification and bureaucratism.
Any policy that eliminates competition has the same effect. The fields in which "organized mismanagement"
really flourishes are the various publicly managed enterprises, cultural institutions, etc., where efficiency is generally not measured in terms of price. In such cases, economic criteria are virtually absent. Lastly, mention must
be made of the intermediary authorities within the enterprise, who are doubly removed from reality, both as regards the external role of the enterprise and its internal
functions. All these forms of remoteness from reality develop along with the growth of industrial concentration. . . . Bureaucratization of the economy is the fate
of capitalism. Centralized bureaucratic organization
operates through "directives" on the one hand and "reports" on the other, the directives generally being drawn
up on the basis of the reports. The source of information is not actual experience, but documents, reports,
accounts. It is on the basis of these that a directive is
issued, and it bears no relation to actual individual "occurrences"; and even if it should, it hardens into a formula which will soon be in contradiction with current
reality; it is not longer a means but an end in itself, and
the master of living people.

The reasons for bureaucratic centralization are the
complexity and the enormous size of economic enterprises, which makes direct personal supervision impossible. At the same time, the longer the chain of command,
the more difficult it is to set the entire machine in motion.
Consequently, "past a certain point, it is better to renounce the advantages of absolutely autonomous administration and to replace the artificial links by live ones, i.e.,
directives by men." Life is varied, and responses to it
must be varied, too. . . . Directives from the center
should be confined to stating the problem in general
terms, and specific action should be worked out by the
subordinate agencies, which operate in accordance with,
and in response to, actual conditions.

The psychological causes of "organized mismanagement" are 1) insufficient development of the economic

approach, e.g., the pacifist ideology in the economic, political, religious, and other spheres is a symptom of fatigue, of a lack of the will to live, while thinking nowadays is "antieconomic," "sociopolitical" (Alfred Weber says that the "hero of our day" is the "hero in bedroom slippers," the "professional Philistine"); and 2) veneration of form (not surprisingly, the economic apparatus of Germany is full of former army men, with their drill-sergeant mentality and their stress on obedience), fanatic love of "procedure," fear of independent thought or action, fear of responsibility. . . .

The consequence of "organized mismanagement" includes first, material waste. In the sphere of organization, the technical ideal is the maximum of order; but the economic ideal is maximum efficiency. The two do not necessarily coincide. . . . The second consequence is perversion of work relations. Since the means to an end becomes an end in itself, a whole chain of perverted relations results: "the form of organization is not determined by the optimum effect, but it itself determines to what extent economic needs will be satisfied. . . ." In a word, the people are there for the official and not the official for the people. Add to this, superfluous occupations created to provide posts; duplication of work; and separate and unrelated types of work being handled in the same department. The result is perversion of the distribution of labor, unnecessary overhead, overlapping of functions, lack of a sense of responsibility, impossibility of getting an over-all picture of the work performed—unnecessary labor on the one hand, and under-utilization of staff on the other. . . . Bureaucratism is economic arteriosclerosis, which hinders circulation; it usually appears in old age and is a symptom of decline. Organized mismanagement heralds the coming death of individualistic capitalism, rather than of capitalism in general. With bureaucratism, economic leaders fall by the wayside, and creative thinkers with them; the creation collapses with its creators. . . .

The Soviet reader may be startled to find a certain formal resemblance between some of the organizational problems posed and solved by Bente and the problems raised and settled in Soviet practice. We must make it clear that even those questions that Bente on the whole solves correctly arise in a different form in our country: thus, for example, the problem of bureaucratism in our case is not "purely organizational," but is also one of class, since our apparatus is not staffed by members of one class only; the problem of "centralization versus decentralization," like the problem of bureaucratism, is closely linked with the problem of the masses; while the problems of competition and of stagnation caused by monopoly are linked with the problem of raising the standard of living of the masses on the one hand and the problem of socialist competition on the other. And we omit a number of highly important problems having to do with the relations between town and village. Nevertheless, Bente's attempt deserves our attention: it gives us a full-scale picture of the problem of economic machinery as a scientific problem. It shows us clearly that this problem has become urgent for "them." Our own experience of socialist construction raises similar problems for us with even greater urgency. It has become essential for us to analyze them.

TRANSLATED BY VALERIE ROSEN

IV

Non-Marxian Socialism

John Stuart Mill

Socialism and Liberty*

John Stuart Mill (1806–1873) is, of course, the great nineteenth-century English liberal, author of On Liberty, On Representative Government, *and other classics of political thought. In his mature years, Mill moved beyond traditional liberalism; indeed, it was his liberal values which led him to seek a more humane society than nineteenth-century English capitalism seemed likely to provide. Mill became a kind of liberal-socialist, anticipating many of the problems that would trouble socialists in the mid-twentieth century.*

The selection below is taken from Mill's Principles of Political Economy, Book II, Chapter I (1867).

Private property, in every defense made of it, is supposed to mean the guarantee of individuals of the fruits of their own labor and abstinence. The guarantee to them of the fruits of the labor and abstinence of others, transmitted to them without any merit or exertion of their own, is not of the essence of the institution, but a mere incidental consequence, which when it reaches a certain height, does not promote, but conflicts with the ends which render private property legitimate. To judge of the final destination of the institution of property, we must suppose everything rectified, which causes the institution to work in a manner opposed to that equitable principle, of proportion between remuneration and exertion, on which in every vindication of it that will bear the light, it is assumed to

---

* Title supplied by editor.

be grounded. We must also suppose two conditions realized, without which neither Communism nor any other laws or institutions could make the condition of the mass of mankind other than degraded and miserable. One of these conditions is universal education; the other, a due limitation of the numbers of the community. With these, there could be no poverty even under the present social institutions; and these being supposed, the question of Socialism is not, as generally stated by Socialists, a question of flying to the sole refuge against the evils which now bear down humanity, but a mere question of comparative advantages, which futurity must determine. We are too ignorant either of what individual agency in its best form, or Socialism in its best form, can accomplish, to be qualified to decide which of the two will be the ultimate form of human society.

If a conjecture may be hazarded, the decision will probably depend mainly on one consideration, viz., which of the two systems is consistent with the greatest amount of human liberty and spontaneity. After the means of subsistence are assured, the next in strength of the personal wants of human beings is liberty; and (unlike the physical wants, which as civilization advances become more moderate and more amenable to control) it increases instead of diminishing in intensity as the intelligence and the moral faculties are more developed. The perfection both of social arrangements and of practical morality would be to secure to all persons complete independence and freedom of action, subject to no restriction but that of not doing injury to others; and the education which taught or the social institutions which required them to exchange the control of their own actions for any amount of comfort or affluence, or to renounce liberty for the sake of equality, would deprive them of one of the most elevated characteristics of human nature. It remains to be discovered how far the preservation of this characteristic would be found compatible with the Communistic organization of society. No doubt, this, like all the other objections to the Socialist schemes, is vastly exaggerated. The members of the association need not be required to live together more than they do now, nor need they be controlled in the disposal of their individual share of the produce, and of the probably large amount of leisure which, if they limited their production to things really worth producing, they would possess. Individuals need not be chained to an occupation, or to a particular locality. The restraints of Communism would be freedom in comparison with the present condition of the majority of the human race. The generality of laborers in this and most other countries have as little choice of occupation or freedom of locomotion, are practically as dependent on fixed rules and on the will of others as they could be on any system short of actual slavery, to say nothing of the entire domestic subjection of one half the species, to which it is the signal honor of . . . Socialism that they assign equal rights, in all respects, with those of the hitherto dominant sex. But it is not by comparison with the present bad state of society that the claims of Communism can be estimated; nor is it sufficient that it should promise greater personal and mental freedom than is now enjoyed by those who have not enough of either to deserve the name. The question is whether there would be any asylum left for individuality of character; whether public opinion would not be a tyrannical yoke; whether the absolute dependence of each on all, and surveillance of each by all, would not grind all down into a tame uniformity of thoughts, feelings, and actions. This is already one of the glaring evils of the existing state of society, notwithstanding a much greater diversity of education and pursuits, and a much less absolute dependence of the individual on the mass, than would exist in the Communistic regime. No society in which eccentricity is a matter of reproach, can be in a wholesome state. It is yet to be ascertained whether the Communistic scheme would be consistent with that multiform development of human nature, those manifold unlikenesses, that diversity of tastes and talents, and variety of intellectual points of view, which not only form a great part of the interest of human life, but by bringing intellects into a stimulating collision, and by presenting to each innumerable notions that he would not have conceived of himself, are the mainspring of mental and moral progression.

I have thus far confined my observations to the Communistic doctrine, which forms the extreme limit of Socialism, according to which not only the instruments of production, the land and capital, are the joint property of the community, but the produce is divided and the labor apportioned, as far as possible, equally. The objections, whether well or ill grounded, to which Socialism is liable, apply to this form of it in their greatest force. The other varieties of Socialism mainly differ from Communism in not relying solely on what M. Louis Blanc calls the point of honor of industry, but retaining more or less of the incentives to labor derived from private pecuniary interest. Thus it is already a modification of the strict theory of Communism, when the principle is professed of proportioning remuneration to labor. The attempts which have been made in France to carry Socialism into practical effect, by associations of workmen manufacturing on their own account, mostly began by sharing the remuneration equally, without regard to the quantity of work done by the individual; but in almost every case this plan was after a short time abandoned and recourse was had to working by the piece. The original principle appeals to a higher standard of justice and is adapted to a much higher moral condition of human nature. The proportioning of remuneration to work done is really just only in so far as the more or less of the work is a matter of choice; when it depends on natural difference of strength of capacity, this principle of remuneration is in itself an injustice; it is giving to those who have, assigning most to those who are already most favored by nature. Considered, however, as a compromise with the selfish type of character formed by the present standard of morality, and fostered by the existing social institutions, it is highly expedient, and until education shall have been entirely regenerated, is far more likely to prove immediately successful than an attempt at a higher ideal.

Oscar Wilde

The Soul of Man Under Socialism

The name of Oscar Wilde (1854–1900) is seldom associated with politics, let alone socialist politics; yet this poet, playwright, and epigrammatist wrote one of the most brilliant documents in the non-Marxist tradition of socialist thought. The Soul of Man Under Socialism *(1891) contains trenchant criticisms of the conventional utilitarian arguments in behalf of socialism; it anticipates many ideas concerning the relation of the individual to the powerful state that later socialist revisionists would develop. Only the first part of Wilde's essay appears here, since the second part wanders away from the theme of socialism toward problems of art and culture.*

The chief advantage that would result from the establishment of Socialism is, undoubtedly, the fact that Socialism would relieve us from that sordid necessity of living for others which, in the present condition of things, presses so hardly upon almost everybody. In fact, scarcely any one at all escapes.

Now and then, in the course of the century, a great man of science, like Darwin; a great poet, like Keats; a fine critical spirit, like M. Renan; a supreme artist, like Flaubert, has been able to isolate himself, to keep himself out of reach of the clamorous claims of others, to stand "under the shelter of the wall," as Plato puts it, and so to realise the perfection of what was in him, to his own incomparable gain, and to the incomparable and lasting gain of the whole world. These, however, are exceptions. The majority of people spoil their lives by an unhealthy

411

and exaggerated altruism—are forced, indeed, so to spoil them. They find themselves surrounded by hideous poverty, by hideous ugliness, by hideous starvation. It is inevitable that they should be strongly moved by all this. The emotions of man are stirred more quickly than man's intelligence; and, as I pointed out some time ago in an article on the function of criticism, it is much more easy to have sympathy with suffering that it is to have sympathy with thought. Accordingly, with admirable though misdirected intentions, they very seriously and very sentimentally set themselves to the task of remedying the evils that they see. But their remedies do not cure the disease; they merely prolong it. Indeed, their remedies are part of the disease.

They try to solve the problem of poverty, for instance, by keeping the poor alive; or, in the case of a very advanced school, by amusing the poor.

But this is not a solution: it is an aggravation of the difficulty. *The proper aim is to try and reconstruct society on such a basis that poverty will be impossible.* And the altruistic virtues have really prevented the carrying out of this aim. Just as the worst slave-owners were those who were kind to their slaves and so prevented the horror of the system being realised by those who suffered from it and understood by those who contemplated it, so, in the present state of things in England, the people who do most harm are the people who try to do most good; and at last we have had the spectacle of men who have really studied the problem and know the life—educated men who live in the East End—coming forward and imploring the community to restrain its altruistic impulses of charity, benevolence, and the like. They do so on the ground that such charity degrades and demoralises. They are perfectly right. Charity creates a multitude of sins.

There is also this to be said. It is immoral to use private property in order to alleviate the horrible evils that result from the institution of private property. It is both immoral and unfair.

Under Socialism all this will, of course, be altered. There will be no people living in fetid dens and fetid rags and bringing up unhealthy, hunger-pinched children in the midst of impossible and absolutely repulsive surroundings. The security of society will not depend, as it does now, on the state of the weather. If a frost comes we shall not have a hundred thousand men out of work, tramping about the streets in a state of disgusting misery, or whining to their neighbours for alms, or crowding round the doors of loathsome shelters to try and secure a hunch of bread and a night's unclean lodging. Each member of the society will share in the general property and happiness of the society, and if a frost comes no one will practically be anything the worse. Upon the other hand, *Socialism itself will be of value simply because it will lead to Individualism.*

Socialism, Communism, or whatever one chooses to call it, by converting private property into public wealth, and substituting cooperation for competition, will restore society to its proper condition of a thoroughly healthy organism, and insure the material well-being of each member of the community. It will, in fact, give Life its proper basis and its proper environment. But for the full development of Life to its highest mode of perfection, something more is needed. What is needed is Individualism. If the Socialism is Authoritarian; if there are Governments armed with economic power as they are now with political power; if, in a word, we are to have Industrial Tyrannies, then the last state of man will be worse than the first. At present, in consequence of the existence of private property, a great many people are enabled to develop a certain very limited amount of Individualism. They are either under no necessity to work for their living or are enabled to choose the sphere of activity that is really congenial to them and gives them pleasure. These are the poets, the philosophers, the men of science, the men of culture—in a word, the real men, the men who have realised themselves and in whom all Humanity gains a partial realisation. Upon the other hand, there are a great many people who, having no private property of their own, and being always on the brink of sheer starvation, are compelled to do the work of beasts of burden, to do work that is quite uncongenial to them and to which they are forced by the peremptory, unreasonable, degrading Tyranny of want. These are the poor, and amongst them there is no grace of manner, or charm of speech, or civilisation, or culture, or refinement in pleasures, or joy of life. From their collective force Humanity gains much in material prosperity. But it is only the material result that it gains, and the man who is poor is in himself absolutely of no importance. He is merely the infinitesimal atom of a force that, so far from regarding him, crushes him—indeed, prefers him crushed, as in that case he is far more obedient.

Of course, it might be said that the Individualism generated under conditions of private property is not always, or even as a rule, of a fine or wonderful type, and that the poor, if they have not culture and charm, have still many virtues. Both these statements would be quite true. The possession of private property is very often extremely demoralising, and that is, of course, one of the reasons why Socialism wants to get rid of the institution. In fact, property is really a nuisance. Some years ago people went about the country saying that property has duties. They said it so often and so tediously that, at last, the Church has begun to say it. One hears it now from every pulpit. It is perfectly true. Property not merely has duties, but has so many duties that its possession to any large extent is a bore. It involves endless claims upon one, endless attention to business, endless bother. If property had simply pleasures, we could stand it; but its duties make it unbearable. In the interest of the rich we must get rid of it. The virtues of the poor may be readily admitted and are much to be regretted. We are often told that the poor are grateful for charity. Some of them are, no doubt, *but the best amongst the poor are never grateful*. They are ungrateful, discontented, disobedient, and rebellious. They are quite right to be so. Charity they feel to be a ridiculously inadequate mode of partial restitution, or a sentimental dole, usually accompanied by some impertinent attempt on the part of the sentimentalist to tyrannise over their private lives. Why should they be grateful for the crumbs that fall from the rich man's table? They should be seated at the board and are beginning to know it. As for being discontented, a man who would not be discontented with such surroundings and such a low mode of life would be a perfect brute. Disobedience, in the eyes of any one who has read history, is man's original virtue. It is through disobedience that progress has been made, through disobedience and through rebellion. Sometimes the poor are praised for being thrifty. But to recommend thrift to the poor is both grotesque and insulting. It is like advising a man who is starving to eat less. For a town or country labourer to practise thrift would be absolutely immoral. Man should not be ready to show that he can live like a badly fed animal. He should decline to live like that and should either steal or go on the rates, which is considered by many to be a form of stealing. As for begging, it is safer to beg than to take, but it is finer to take than to beg. No; a poor man who is ungrateful, unthrifty, discontented, and rebellious is probably a real personality and has much in him. He is at any rate a healthy protest. As for the virtuous poor, one can pity them, of course, but one cannot possibly admire them. They have made private terms with the enemy and sold their birthright for very bad pottage. They must also be extraordinarily stupid. I can quite understand a man accepting laws that protect private property, and admit of its accumulation, as long as he himself is able under these conditions to realise some form of beautiful and intellectual life. But is is almost incredible to me how a man whose life is marred and made hideous by such laws can possibly acquiesce in their continuance.

However, the explanation is not really so difficult to find. It is simply this. Misery and poverty are so absolutely degrading, and exercise such a paralysing effect over the nature of men, that no class is ever really conscious of its own suffering. They have to be told of it by other people, and they often entirely disbelieve them. What is said by great employers of labour against agitators is unquestionably true. Agitators are a set of interfering, meddling people, who come down to some perfectly contented class of the community and sow the seeds of discontent amongst them. That is the reason why agitators are so absolutely necessary. Without them, in our incomplete state, there would be no advance towards civilisation. Slavery was put down in America, not in consequence of any action on the part of the slaves, or even any express desire on their part that they should be free. It was put down entirely through the grossly illegal conduct of certain agitators in Boston and elsewhere, who were not slaves themselves, nor owners of slaves, nor had anything to do with the question really. It was, undoubtedly, the Abolitionists who set the torch alight, who began the whole thing. And it is curious to note that from the slaves themselves they received, not merely very little assistance, but hardly any sympathy even; and when at the close of the war the slaves found themselves free, found themselves indeed so absolutely free that they were free to starve, many of them bitterly regretted the new state of things. To the thinker, the most tragic fact in the whole of the French Revolution is not that Marie Antoinette was killed for being a queen, but that the starved peasant of the Vendée voluntarily went out to die for the hideous cause of feudalism.

It is clear, then, that no Authoritarian Socialism will do. For while under the present system a very large number of people can lead lives of a certain amount of freedom and expression and happiness, under an industrial barrack system, or a system of economic tyranny, nobody would be able to have any such freedom at all. It is to be regretted that a portion of our community should be practically in slavery, but to propose to solve the problem by enslaving the entire community is childish. Every man must be left quite free to choose his own work. No form of compulsion must be exercised over him. If there is, his work will not be good for him, will not be good in itself, and will not be good for others. And by work I simply mean activity of any kind.

I hardly think that any Socialist, nowadays, would seriously propose that an inspector should call every morning at each house to see that each citizen rose up and did manual labour for eight hours. Humanity has got beyond that stage and reserves such a form of life for the people whom, in a very arbitrary manner, it chooses to call criminals. But I confess that many of the Socialistic views that I have come across seem to me to be tainted with ideas of authority, if not of actual compulsion. Of course, authority and compulsion are out of the question. All association must be quite voluntary. *It is only in voluntary associations that man is fine.*

But it may be asked how Individualism, which is now more or less dependent on the existence of private property for its development, will benefit by the abolition of such private property. The answer is very simple. It is true that, under existing conditions, a few men who have had private means of their own, such as Byron, Shelley, Browning, Victor Hugo, Baudelaire, and others, have been able to realise their personality more or less completely. Not one of these men ever did a single day's work for hire. They were relieved from poverty. They had an immense advantage. The question is whether it would be for the good of Individualism that such an advantage should be taken away. Let us suppose that it is taken away. What happens then to Individualism? How will it benefit?

It will benefit in this way. Under the new conditions Individualism will be far freer, far finer, and far more intensified than it is now. I am not talking of the great imaginatively realised Individualism of such poets as I have mentioned, but of the great actual Individualism latent and potential in mankind generally. For the recognition of private property has really harmed Individualism, and obscured it, by confusing a man with what he possesses. It has led Individualism entirely astray. It has made gain not growth its aim. So that man thought that the important thing was to have and did not know that the important thing is to be. *The true perfection of man lies, not in what man has, but in what man is.* Private property has crushed true Individualism and set up an Individualism that is false. It has debarred one part of the community from being individual by starving them. It has debarred the other part of the community from being individual by putting them on the wrong road and encumbering them. Indeed, so completely has man's personality been absorbed by his possessions that the English law has always treated offences against a man's property with far more severity than offences against his person, and property is still the test of complete citizenship. The industry necessary for the making of money is also very demoralising. In a community like ours, where property confers immense distinction, social position, honour, respect, titles, and other pleasant things of the kind, man, being naturally ambitious, makes it his aim to accumulate this property, and goes on wearily and tediously accumulating it long after he has got far more than he wants, or can use, or enjoy, or perhaps even know of. Man will kill himself by overwork in order to secure property, and really, considering the enormous advantages that property brings, one is hardly surprised. One's regret is that society should be constructed on such a basis that man has been forced into a groove in which he cannot freely develop what is wonderful, and fascinating, and delightful in him—in which, in fact, he misses the true pleasure and joy of living. He is also, under existing conditions, very insecure. An enormously wealthy merchant may be —often is—at every moment of his life at the mercy of things that are not under his control. If the wind blows an extra point or so, or the weather suddenly changes, or some trivial thing happens, his ship may go down, his speculations may go wrong, and he finds himself a poor man, with his social position quite gone. Now, nothing should be able to harm a man except himself. Nothing should be able to rob a man at all. What a man really has, is what is in him. What is outside of him should be a matter of no importance.

With the abolition of private property, then, we shall have true, beautiful, healthy Individualism. Nobody will waste his life in accumulating things and the symbols for things. One will live. To live is the rarest thing in the world. Most people exist, that is all.

It is a question whether we have ever seen the full expression of a personality, except on the imaginative plane of art. In action, we never have. Cæsar, says Mommsen, was the complete and perfect man. But how tragically insecure was Cæsar! Wherever there is a man who exercises authority, there is a man who resists authority. Cæsar was very perfect, but his perfection traveled by too dangerous a road. Marcus Aurelius was the perfect man, says Renan. Yes; the great emperor was a perfect man. But how intolerable were the endless claims upon him! He staggered under the burden of the empire. He was conscious how inadequate one man was to bear the weight of that Titan and too vast orb. What I mean by a perfect man is one who develops under perfect conditions; one who is not wounded, or worried, or maimed, or in danger. *Most personalities have been obliged to be rebels. Half their strength has been wasted in friction.* Byron's personality, for instance, was terribly wasted in its battle with the stupidity, and hyprocrisy, and Philistinism of the English. Such battles do not always intensify strength; they often exaggerate weakness. Byron was never able to give us what he might have given us. Shelley escaped better. Like Byron, he got out of England as soon as possible. But he was not so well known. If the English had had any idea of what a great poet he really was, they would have fallen on him with tooth and nail and made his life as unbearable for him as they possibly could. But he was not a remarkable figure in society, and consequently he escaped, to a certain degree. Still, even in Shelley the note of rebellion is sometimes too strong. The note of the perfect personality is not rebellion, but peace.

It will be a marvellous thing—the true personality of man—when we see it. It will grow naturally and simply, flower-like, or as a tree grows. It will not be at discord. It will never argue or dispute. It will not prove things. It will know everything. And yet it will not busy itself about knowledge. It will have wisdom. Its value will not be measured by material things. It will have nothing. And yet it will have everything, and whatever one takes from it, it will still have, so rich will it be. It will not be always meddling with others, or asking them to be like itself. It will love them because they will be different. And yet, while it will not meddle with others, it will help all, as a beautiful thing helps us by being what it is. The personality of man will very wonderful. It will be as wonderful as the personality of a child.

In its development it will be assisted by Christianity, if men desire that; but if men do not desire that, it will develop none the less surely. For it will not worry itself about the past, nor care whether things happened or did not happen. Nor will it admit any laws but its own laws; nor any authority but its own authority. Yet it will love those who sought to intensify it, and speak often of them. And of these Christ was one.

"Know Thyself" was written over the portal of the antique world. Over the portal of the new world, "Be Thyself" shall be written. And the message of Christ to man was simply "Be Thyself." That is the secret of Christ.

When Jesus talks about the poor He simply means personalities, just as when He talks about the rich He simply means people who have not developed their personalities. Jesus moved in a community that allowed the accumulation of private property just as ours does, and the gospel that He preached was not that in such a community it is an advantage for a man to live on scanty, unwholesome food, to wear ragged, unwholesome clothes, to sleep in horrid, unwholesome dwellings, and a disadvantage for a man to live under healthy, pleasant, and decent conditions. Such a view would have been wrong there and then, and would, of course, be still more wrong now and in England; for as man moves northwards the material necessities of life become of more vital importance, and our society is infinitely more complex, and displays far greater extremes of luxury and pauperism than any society of the antique world. What Jesus meant was this. He said to man, "You have a wonderful personality. Develop it. Be yourself. Don't imagine that your perfection lies in accumulating or possessing external things. Your perfection is inside of you. If only you could realise that, you would not want to be rich. Ordinary riches can be stolen from a man. Real riches cannot. In the treasury house of your soul there are infinitely precious things that may not be taken from you. And so, try to so shape your life that external things will not harm you. And try also to get rid of personal property. It involves sordid preoccupation, endless industry, continual wrong. Personal property hinders individualism at every step." It is to be noted that Jesus never says that impoverished people are necessarily good, or wealthy people necessarily bad. That would not have been true. Wealthy people are, as a class, better than impoverished people, more moral, more intellectual, more well-behaved. *There is only one class in the community that thinks more about money than the rich, and that is the poor.* The poor can think of nothing else. That is the misery of being poor. What Jesus does say is that man reaches his perfection, not through what he has, not even through what he does, but entirely through what he is. And so the wealthy young man who comes to Jesus is represented as a thoroughly good citizen, who has broken none of the laws of his state, none of the commandments of his religion. He is quite respectable, in the ordinary sense of that extraordinary word. Jesus says to him, "You should give up private property. It hinders you from realising your perfection. It is a drag upon you. It is a burden. Your personality does not need it. It is within you, and not outside of you, that you will find what you really are, and what you really want." To His own friends He says the same thing. He tells them to be themselves, and not to be always worrying about other things. What do other things matter? Man is complete in himself. When they go into the world, the world will disagree with them. That is inevitable. The world hates Individualism. But this is not to trouble them. They are to be calm and self-centered. If a man takes their cloak, they are to give him their coat, just to show that material things are of no importance. If people abuse them, they are not to answer back. What does it signify? The things people say of a man do not alter a man. He is what he is. Public opinion is of no value whatsoever. Even if people employ actual violence, they are not to be violent in turn. That would be to fall to the same low level. After all, even in prison, a man can be quite free. His soul can be free. His personality can be untroubled. He can be at peace. And, above all things, they are not to interfere with other people or judge them in any way. Personality is a very mysterious thing. A man cannot always be estimated by what he does. He may keep the law, and yet be worthless. He may break the law, and yet be fine. He may be bad, without ever doing anything bad. He may commit a sin against society, and yet realise through that sin his true perfection.

There was a woman who was taken in adultery. We are not told the history of her love, but that love must have been very great; for Jesus said that her sins were forgiven her, not because she had repented, but because her love was so intense and wonderful. Later on, a short time before His death, as He sat at a feast, the woman came in and poured costly perfumes on His hair. His friends tried to interfere with her, and said that it was an extravagance, and that the money that the perfume cost should have been expended on charitable relief of people in want, or something of that kind. Jesus did not accept that view. He pointed out that the material needs of Man were great and very permanent, but that the spiritual needs of Man were greater still, and that in one divine moment, and by selecting its own mode of expression, a personality might make itself perfect. The world worships the woman, even now, as a saint.

Yes, there are suggestive things in Individualism. Socialism annihilates family life, for instance. With the abolition of private property, marriage in its present form must disappear. This is part of the program. Individualism accepts this and makes it fine. It converts the abolition of legal restraint into a form of freedom that will help the full development of personality and make the love of man and woman more wonderful, more beautiful, and more ennobling. Jesus knew this. He rejected the claims of family life, although they existed in His day and community in a very marked form. "Who is my mother? Who are my brothers?" He said, when He was told that they wished to speak to Him. When one of His followers asked leave to go and bury his father, "Let the dead bury the dead," was His terrible answer. He would allow no claim whatsoever to be made on personality.

And so he who would lead a Christ-like life is he who is perfectly and absolutely himself. He may be a great poet, or a great man of science; or a young student at a University, or one who watches sheep upon a moor; or a maker of dramas, like Shakespeare, or a thinker about God, like Spinoza; or a child who plays in a garden, or a fisherman who throws his nets into the sea. It does not matter what he is, as long as he realises the perfection of the soul that is within him. All imitation in morals and in life is wrong. Through the streets of Jerusalem at the present day crawls one who is mad and carries a wooden cross on his shoulders. He is a symbol of the lives that are marred by imitation. Father Damien was Christ-like when he went out to live with the lepers, because in such service he realised fully what was best in him. But he was not more Christ-like than Wagner, when he realised his soul in music; or than Shelley, when he realised his soul in song. There is no one type for man. There are as many perfections as there are imperfect men. And while to the claims of charity a man may yield and yet be free, to the claims of conformity no man may yield and remain free at all.

Individualism, then, is what through Socialism we are to attain to. As a natural result the State must give up all idea of government. It must give it up because, as a wise man once said many centuries before Christ, there is such a thing as leaving mankind alone; there is no such thing as governing mankind. *All modes of government are failures.* Despotism is unjust to everybody, including the despot, who was probably made for better things. Oligarchies are unjust to the many, and ochlocracies are unjust to the few. High hopes were once formed of democracy; but democracy means simply the bludgeoning of the people by the people for the people. It has been found out. I must say that it was high time, for all authority is quite degrading. It degrades those who exercise it and degrades those over whom it is exercised. When it is violently, grossly, and cruelly used, it produces a good effect, by creating, or at any rate bringing out, the spirit of revolt and individualism that is to kill it. When it is used with a certain amount of kindness, and accompanied by prizes and rewards, it is dreadfully demoralising. People, in that case, are less conscious of the horrible pressure that is being put on them, and so go through their lives in a sort of coarse comfort, like petted animals, without ever realising that they are probably thinking other people's thoughts, living by other people's standards, wearing practically what one may call other people's second-hand clothes, and never being themselves for a single moment. "He who would be free," says a fine thinker, "must not conform." And authority, by bribing people to conform, produces a very gross kind of overfed barbarism amongst us.

With authority, punishment will pass away. This will be a great gain—a gain, in fact, of incalculable value. As one reads history, not in the expurgated editions written for schoolboys and passmen, but in the original authorities of each time, one is absolutely sickened, not by the crimes that the wicked have committed, but by the punishments that the good have inflicted; *and a community is infinitely more brutalised by the habitual employment of punishment than it is by the occasional occurrence of crime.* It obviously follows that the more punishment is inflicted the more crime is produced, and most modern legislation has recognised this and has made it its task to diminish punishment as far as it thinks it can. Wherever it has really diminished it the results have always been extremely good. The less punishment the less crime. When there is no punishment at all, crime will either cease to exists, or, if it occurs, will be treated by physicians as a very distressing form of dementia, to be cured by care and kindness. For what are called criminals nowadays are not criminals at all. Starvation, and not sin, is the parent of modern crime. That indeed is the reason why our criminals are, as a class, so absolutely uninteresting from any psychological point of view. They are not marvellous Macbeths and terrible Vautrins. They are merely what ordinary, respectable, commonplace people would be if they had not got enough to eat. When private property is abolished there will be no necessity for crime, no demand for it; it will cease to exist. Of course, all crimes are not crimes against property, though such are the crimes that the English law, valuing what a man has more than what a man is, punishes with the harshest and most horrible severity, if we except the crime of murder, and regard death as worse than penal servitude, a point on which our criminals, I believe, disagree. But though a crime may not be against property, it may spring from the misery and rage and depression produced by our wrong system of property holding, and so, when that system is abolished, will disappear. When each member of the community has sufficient for his wants and is not interfered with by his neighbour, it will not be an object of any interest to him to interfere with any one else. Jealousy, which is an extraordinary source of crime in modern life, is an emotion closely bound up with our conceptions of property, and under Socialism and Individualism will die out. It is remarkable that in communistic tribes jealousy is entirely unknown.

Now, as the State is not to govern, it may be asked what the State is to do. The State is to be a voluntary association that will organise labour and be the manufacturer and distributor of necessary commodities. *The State is to make what is useful. The individual is to make what is beautiful.* And as I have mentioned the word labour, I cannot help saying that a great deal of nonsense is being written and talked nowadays about the dignity of manual labour. There is nothing necessarily dignified about manual labour at all, and most of it is absolutely degrading. It is mentally and morally injurious to man to do anything in which he does not find pleasure, and many forms of labour are quite pleasureless activities and should be regarded as such. To sweep a slushy crossing for eight hours on a day when the east wind is blowing is a disgusting occupation. To sweep it with mental, moral, or physical dignity seems to me to be impossible. To sweep it with joy would be appalling. Man is made for something better than disturbing dirt. All work of that kind should be done by a machine.

And I have no doubt that it will be so. Up to the present, man has been, to a certain extent, the slave of machinery, and there is something tragic in the fact that as soon as man had invented a machine to do his work he began to starve. This, however, is, of course, the result of our property system and our system of competition. One man owns a machine which does the work of five hundred men. Five hundred men are, in consequence, thrown out of employment, and, having no work to do, become hungry and take to thieving. The one man secures the produce of the machine and keeps it, and has five hundred times as much as he should have, and probably, which is of much more importance, a great deal more than he really wants. Were that machine the property of all, everyone would benefit by it. It would be an immense advantage to the community. All unintellectual labour, all monotonous, dull labour, all labour that deals with dreadful things, and involves unpleasant conditions, must be done by machinery. Machinery must work for us in the coal mines, and do all sanitary services, and be the stokers of steamers, and clean the streets, and run messages on wet days, and do anything that is tedious or distressing. *At present machinery competes against man. Under proper conditions machinery will serve man.* There is no doubt at all that this is the future of machinery, and just as trees grow while the country gentleman is asleep, so while Humanity will be amusing itself, or enjoying cultivated leisure—which, and not labour, is the aim of man—or making beautiful things, or reading beautiful things, or simply contemplating the world with admiration and delight, machinery will be doing all the necessary and unpleasant work. The fact is, that civilisation requires slaves. The Greeks were quite right there. Unless there are slaves to do the ugly, horrible, uninteresting work, culture and contemplation become almost impossible. Human slavery is wrong, insecure, and demoralising. On mechanical slavery, on the slavery of the machine, the future of the world depends. And when scientific men are no longer called upon to go down to a depressing East End and distribute bad cocoa and worse blankets to starving people, they will have delightful leisure in which to devise wonderful and marvellous things for their own joy and the joy of every one else. There will be great storages of force for every city, and for every house if required, and this force man will convert into heat, light, or motion, according to his needs. Is this Utopia? A map of the world that does not include Utopia is not worth even glancing at, for it leaves out the one country at which Humanity is always landing. And when Humanity lands there, it looks out, and seeing a better country, sets sail. . . .

George Orwell

A Footnote to Wilde*

> *George Orwell (1903–1950) was one of the major English writers of the twentieth century: essayist, novelist, political commentator, and life-long socialist. The following piece appeared first in the London Observer in 1948 as a review of a reprint of Oscar Wilde's* The Soul of Man Under Socialism.

Oscar Wilde's work is being much revived now on stage and screen, and it is well to be reminded that Salome and Lady Windermere were not his only creations. Wilde's *The Soul of Man under Socialism*, for example, first published nearly sixty years ago, has worn remarkably well. Its author was not in any active sense a Socialist himself, but he was a sympathetic and intelligent observer; although his prophecies have not been fulfilled, they have not been made simply irrelevant by the passage of time.

Wilde's vision of Socialism, which at that date was probably shared by many people less articulate than himself, is Utopian and anarchistic. The abolition of private property, he says, will make possible the full development of the individual and set us free from "the sordid necessity of living for others." In the Socialist future there will not only be no want and no insecurity, there will also be no drudgery, no disease, no ugliness, no wastage of the human spirit in futile enmities and rivalries.

Pain will cease to be important; indeed, for the first time in his history, Man will be able to realise his person-

---

* Title supplied by editor.

ality through joy instead of through suffering. Crime will disappear, since there will be no economic reason for it. The State will cease to govern and will survive merely as an agency for the distribution of necessary commodities. All the disagreeable jobs will be done by machinery, and everyone will be completely free to choose his own work and his own manner of life. In effect, the world will be populated by artists, each striving after perfection in the way that seems best to him.

Today, these optimistic forecasts make rather painful reading. Wilde realised, of course, that there were authoritarian tendencies in the Socialist movement, but he did not believe they would prevail, and with a sort of prophetic irony he wrote: "I hardly think that any Socialist, nowadays, would seriously propose that an inspector should call every morning at each house to see that each citizen rose up and did manual labour for eight hours"—which, unfortunately, is just the kind of thing that countless modern Socialists would propose. Evidently something has gone wrong. Socialism, in the sense of economic collectivism, is conquering the earth at a speed that would hardly have seemed possible sixty years ago, and yet Utopia, at any rate Wilde's Utopia, is no nearer. Where, then, does the fallacy lie?

If one looks more closely one sees that Wilde makes two common but unjustified assumptions. One is that the world is immensely rich and is suffering chiefly from maldistribution. Even things out between the millionaire and the crossing-sweeper, he seems to say, and there will be plenty of everything for everybody. Until the Russian Revolution, this belief was very widely held—"starving in the midst of plenty" was a favourite phrase—but it was quite false, and it survived only because Socialists thought always of the highly developed Western countries and ignored the fearful poverty of Asia and Africa. Actually, the problem for the world as a whole is not how to distribute such wealth as exists but how to increase production, without which economic equality merely means common misery.

Secondly, Wilde assumes that it is a simple matter to arrange that all the unpleasant kinds of work shall be done by machinery. The machines, he says, are our new race of slaves: a tempting metaphor, but a misleading one, since there is a vast range of jobs—roughly speaking, any job needing great flexibility—that no machine is able to do. In practice, even in the most highly mechanised countries, an enormous amount of dull and exhausting work has to be done by unwilling human muscles. But this at once implies direction of labour, fixed working hours, differential wage rates, and all the regimentation that Wilde abhors. Wilde's version of Socialism could only be realised in a world not only far richer but also technically far more advanced than the present one. The abolition of private property does not of itself put food into anyone's mouth. It is merely the first step in a transitional period that is bound to be laborious, uncomfortable, and long.

But that is not to say that Wilde is altogether wrong. The trouble with transitional periods is that the harsh outlook which they generate tends to become permanent. To all appearances this is what has happened in Soviet Russia. A dictatorship supposedly established for a limited purpose has dug itself in, and Socialism comes to be thought of as meaning concentration camps and secret police forces. Wilde's pamphlet and other kindred writings—*News from Nowhere*, for instance—consequently have their value. They may demand the impossible, and they may—since a Utopia necessarily reflects the aesthetic ideas of its own period—sometimes seem "dated" and ridiculous, but they do at least look beyond the era of food queues and party squabbles, and remind the Socialist movement of its original half-forgotten objective of human brotherhood.

William Morris

Art and Socialism

The distinguished nineteenth-century poet William Morris (1834–1896) was one of the first major converts to socialism among English literary and intellectual people. He worked actively in the nascent socialist movement of his day and wrote a number of significant essays on the relationship between socialism and culture. The one below was first given in 1884 as a lecture to the Secular Society of Leicester; it appears in this volume with some local and topical references omitted.

. . . I put forward a claim on behalf of labour enslaved by Commerce, which I know no thinking man can deny is reasonable, but which if acted on would involve such a change as would defeat Commerce, that is, would put Association instead of Competition, Social Order instead of Individualist Anarchy. Yet I have looked at this claim by the light of history and my own conscience, and it seems to me so looked at to be a most just claim and that resistance to it means nothing short of a denial of the hope of civilization. This then is the claim: *It is right and necessary that all men should have work to do which shall be worth doing, and be of itself pleasant do to, and which should be done under such conditions as would make it neither over-wearisome nor over-anxious.* Turn that claim about as I may, think of it as long as I can, I cannot find that it is an exorbitant claim; yet again I say if Society would or could admit it, the face of the world would be changed; discontent and strife and dishonesty would be ended. To feel that we were doing work useful to others and pleasant to ourselves and that such work and its due reward could not fail us! What serious harm could happen to us then? And the price to be paid for so making the world happy is Revolution: Socialism instead of *Laissez faire*.

How can we of the middle classes help to bring such a state of things about, a state of things as nearly as possible the reverse of the present state of things? The reverse; no less than that. For first, THE WORK MUST BE WORTH DOING; think what a change that would make in the world! I tell you I feel dazed at the thought of the immensity of work which is undergone for the making of useless things. It would be an instructive day's work for any one of us who is strong enough to walk through two or three of the principal streets of London on a weekday and take accurate note of everything in the shop windows which is embarrassing or superfluous to the daily life of a serious man. Nay, the most of these things no one, serious or unserious, wants at all; only a foolish habit makes even the lightest-minded of us suppose that he wants them, and to many people even of those who buy them they are obvious encumbrances to real work, thought, and pleasure. But I beg you to think of the enormous mass of men who are occupied with this miserable trumpery, from the engineers who have had to make the machines for making them, down to the hapless clerks who sit daylong year after year in the horrible dens wherein the wholesale exchange of them is transacted, and the shopmen who, not daring to call their souls their own, retail them amidst numberless insults which they must not resent, to the idle public which doesn't want them, but buys them to be bored by them and sick to death of them. I am talking of the merely useless things; but there are other matters not merely useless, but actively destructive and poisonous, which command a good price in the market; for instance, adulterated food and drink. Vast is the number of slaves whom competitive Commerce employs in turning out infamies such as these. But quite apart from them there is an enormous mass of labour which is just merely wasted; many thousands of men and women making Nothing with terrible and inhuman toil which deadens the soul and shortens mere animal life itself.

All these are the slaves of what is called luxury, which in the modern sense of the word comprises a mass of sham wealth, the invention of competitive Commerce, and enslaves not only the poor people who are compelled to work at its production, but also the foolish and not over-happy people who buy it to harass themselves with its encumbrance. Now if we are to have popular Art, or indeed Art of any kind, we must at once and for all be done with this luxury; it is the supplanter, the changeling of Art; so much so that by those who know of nothing better it has been taken for Art, the divine solace of human labour, the romance of each day's hard practice of the difficult art of living. But I say Art cannot live beside it, nor self-respect in any class of life. Effeminacy and brutality are its companions on the right hand and the left. This, first of all, we of the well-to-do classes must get rid of if we are serious in desiring the new birth of Art: and if not, then corruption is digging a terrible pit of perdition for society, from which indeed the new birth may come, but surely from terror, violence, and misery. Indeed if it were but ridding ourselves, the well-to-do people, of this mountain of rubbish, that would be something worth doing: things which everybody knows are of no use; the very capitalists know well that there is no genuine healthy demand for them, and they are compelled to foist them off on the public by stirring up a strange feverish desire for petty excitement, the outward token of which is known by the conventional name of fashion, a strange monster born of the vacancy of the lives of rich people, and the eagerness of competitive Commerce to make the most of the huge crowd of workmen whom it breeds as unregarded instruments for what is called the making of money.

Do not think it a little matter to resist this monster of folly; to think for yourselves what you yourselves really desire will not only make men and women of you so far, but may also set you thinking of the due desires of other people, since you will soon find when you get to know a work of art, that slavish work is undesirable. And here

furthermore is at least a little sign whereby to distinguish
between a rag of fashion and a work of art: whereas the
toys of fashion when the first gloss is worn off them do
become obviously worthless even to the frivolous, a work
of art, be it never so humble, is long-lived; we never tire
of it; as long as a scrap hangs together it is valuable and
instructive to each new generation. All works of art in
short have the property of becoming venerable amidst
decay; and reason good, for from the first there was a
soul in them, the thought of man, which will be visible in
them so long as the body exists in which they were im-
planted.

And that last sentence brings me to consider the other
side of the necessity for labour only occupying itself in
making goods that are worth making. Hitherto we have
been thinking of it only from the user's point of view;
even so looked at it was surely important enough; yet
from the other side, as to the producer, it is far more
important still. For I say again that in buying these
things

'Tis the lives of men you buy!

Will you from mere folly and thoughtlessness make
yourselves partakers of the guilt of those who compel
their fellowmen to labour uselessly? For when I said it
was necessary for all things made to be worth making, I
set up that claim chiefly on behalf of Labour; since the
waste of making useless things grieves the workman doubly. As part of the public he is forced into buying them,
and the more part of his miserable wages, is squeezed out
of him by an universal kind of truck system; as one of the
producers he is forced into making them, and so into
losing the very foundations of that pleasure in daily work
which I claim as his birthright; he is compelled to labour
joylessly at making the poison which the truck system
compels him to buy. So that the huge mass of men who
are compelled by folly and greed to make harmful and
useless things are sacrificed to Society. I say that this
would be terrible and unendurable even though they
were sacrificed to the good of Society if that were possi-

ble; but if they are sacrificed not for the welfare of Society but for its whims, to add to its degradation, what do luxury and fashion look like then? On one side ruinous and wearisome waste leading through corruption to corruption on to complete cynicism at last, and the disintegration of all Society; and on the other side implacable oppression destructive of all pleasure and hope in life, and leading—whitherward?

Here then is one thing for us of the middle classes to do before we can clear the ground for the new birth of Art, before we can clear our own consciences of the guilt of enslaving men by their labour. One thing; and if we could do it perhaps that one thing would be enough, and all other healthy changes would follow it: but can we do it? Can we escape from the corruption of Society which threatens us? Can the middle classes regenerate themselves? At first sight one would say that a body of people so powerful, who have built up the gigantic edifice of modern Commerce, whose science, invention, and energy have subdued the forces of nature to serve their everyday purposes, and who guide the organization that keeps these natural powers in subjection in a way almost miraculous; at first sight one would say surely such a mighty mass of wealthy men could do anything they please. And yet I doubt it: their own creation, the Commerce they are so proud of, has become their master; and all we of the well-to-do classes, some of us with triumphant glee, some with dull satisfaction, and some with sadness of heart, are compelled to admit not that Commerce was made for man, but that man was made for Commerce.

On all sides we are forced to admit it. There are of the English middle class today, for instance, men of the highest aspirations towards Art, and of the strongest will; men who are most deeply convinced of the necessity to civilization of surrounding men's lives with beauty; and many lesser men, thousands for what I know, refined and cultivated, follow them and praise their opinions. But both the leaders and the led are incapable of saving so much as half-a-dozen commons from the grasp of inexorable Commerce; they are as helpless in spite of their culture and their genius as if they were just so many over-worked

shoe-makers. Less lucky than King Midas, our green
fields and clear waters, nay, the very air we breathe, are
turned not to gold (which might please some of us for an
hour maybe) but to dirt; and to speak plainly we know
full well that under the present gospel of Capital not only
there is no hope of bettering it, but that things grow
worse year by year, day by day. Let us eat and drink, for
tomorrow we die, choked by filth. . . .

Meanwhile, if otherwise that oppression has left us
scarce any work to do worth doing, one thing at least is
left us to strive for, the raising of the standard of life
where it is lowest, where it is low: that will put a spoke
in the wheel of the triumphant car of competitive Commerce. Nor can I conceive of anything more likely to
raise the standard of life than the convincing some thousands of those who live by labour of the necessity of their
supporting the second part of the claim I have made for
Labour; namely, THAT THEIR WORK SHOULD BE
OF ITSELF PLEASANT TO DO. If we could but convince them that such a strange revolution in Labour as
this would be of infinite benefit not to them only, but to
all men and that it is so right and natural that for the
reverse to be the case, that most men's work should be
grievous to them, is a mere monstrosity of these latter
days, which must in the long run bring ruin and confusion on the society that allows it—if we could but convince them, then indeed there would be chance of the
phrase Art of the People being something more than a
mere word. At first sight, indeed, it would seem impossible
to make men born under the present system of Commerce understand that labour may be a blessing to them,
not in the sense in which the phrase is sometimes
preached to them by those whose labour is light and
easily evaded; not as a necessary task laid by nature on
the poor for the benefit of the rich, not as an opiate to
dull their sense of right and wrong, to make them sit
down quietly under their burdens to the end of time,
blessing the squire and his relations: all this they could
understand our saying to them easily enough, and sometimes would listen to it I fear with at least a show of
complacency, if they thought there were anything to be

made out of us thereby. But the true doctrine that labour should be a real tangible blessing in itself to the working man, a pleasure even as sleep and strong drink are to him now, this one might think it hard indeed for him to understand, so different as it is from anything which he has found labour to be.

Nevertheless, though most men's work is only borne as a necessary evil like sickness, my experience as far as it goes is, that whether it be from a certain sacredness in handiwork which does cleave to it even under the worst circumstances, or whether it be that the poor man who is driven by necessity to deal with things which are terribly real, when he thinks at all on such matters, thinks less conventionally than the rich—whatever it may be, my experience so far is that the working-man finds it easier to understand the doctrine of the claim of Labour to pleasure in the work itself than the rich or well-to-do man does. . . .

Now once more I will say that we well-to-do people, those of us who love Art, not as a toy, but as a thing necessary to the life of man, as a token of his freedom and happiness, have for our best work the raising of the standard of life among the people, or in other words, establishing the claim I made for Labour, which I will now put in a different form, that we may try to see what chiefly hinders us from making that claim good and what are the enemies to be attacked. Thus then I put the claim again: *Nothing should be made by man's labour which is not worth making or which must be made by labour degrading to the makers.*

Simple as the proposition is, and obviously right as I am sure it must seem to you, you will find, when you come to consider the matter, that it is a direct challenge to the death to the present system of labour in civilized countries. That system, which I have called competitive Commerce, is distinctly a system of war; that is, of waste and destruction, or you may call it gambling if you will; the point of it being that under it whatever a man gains he gains at the expense of some other man's loss. Such a system does not and cannot heed whether the matters it makes are worth making; it does not and cannot heed whether those who make them are degraded by their work: it heeds one thing and only one, namely what it calls making a profit, which word has come to be used so conventionally that I must explain to you what it really means, to wit, the plunder of the weak by the strong. Now I say of this system, that it is of its very nature destructive of Art, that is to say of the happiness of life. Whatever consideration is shown for the life of the people in these days, whatever is done which is worth doing, is done in spite of the system and in the teeth of its maxims; and most true it is that we do all of us tacitly at least admit that it is opposed to all the highest aspirations of mankind.

Do we not know, for instance, how those men of genius work who are the salt of the earth, without whom the corruption of Society would long ago have become unendurable? The poet, the artist, the man of science, is it not true that in their fresh and glorious days, when they are in the heyday of their faith and enthusiasm, they are thwarted at every turn by Commercial War with its sneering question, "Will it pay?" Is it not true that when they begin to win worldly success, when they become comparatively rich, in spite of ourselves they seem to us tainted by the contact with the commercial world? Need I speak of great schemes that hang about neglected, of things most necessary to be done, and so confessed by all men, that no one can seriously set a hand to because of the lack of money; while if it be a question of creating or stimulating some foolish whim in the public mind, the satisfaction of which will breed a profit, the money will come in by the ton? Nay, you know what an old story it is of the wars bred by Commerce in search of new markets, which not even the most peaceable of statesmen can resist, an old story and still it seems forever new, and now becomes a kind of grim joke, at which I would rather not laugh if I could help it, but am even forced to laugh from a soul laden with anger.

And all that mastery over the powers of nature which the last hundred years or less have given us: what has it done for us under this system? In the opinion of John Stuart Mill, it was doubtful if all the mechanical inventions of modern times have done anything to lighten the toil of labour; be sure there is no doubt that they were not made for that end, but to make a profit. Those almost miraculous machines, which if orderly forethought had dealt with them might even now be speedily extinguishing all irksome and unintelligent labour, leaving us free to raise the standard of skill of hand and energy of mind in our workmen and to produce afresh that loveliness and order which only the hand of man guided by his soul can produce: what have they done for us now? Those machines of which the civilized world is so proud, has it any right to be proud of the use they have been put to by commercial war and waste?

I do not think exultation can have a place here: commercial war has made a profit of these wonders; that is to say it has by their means bred for itself millions of unhappy workers, unintelligent machines as far as their daily work goes, in order to get cheap labour, to keep up its exciting but deadly game forever. Indeed that labour would have been cheap enough, cheap to the commercial war generals, and deadly dear to the rest of us, but for the seeds of freedom which valiant men of old have sowed amongst us to spring up in our own day into Chartism and Trade Unionism and Socialism, for the defence of order and a decent life. Terrible would have been our slavery, and not of the working classes alone, but for these germs of the change which must be. Even as it is, by the reckless aggregation of machine workers and their adjoints in the great cities and the manufacturing districts, it has kept down life amongst us and keeps it down to a miserably low standard, so low that any standpoint for improvement is hard even to think of. By the means of speedy communication which it has created, and which should have raised the standard of life by spreading intelligence from town to country, and widely creating modest centres of freedom of thought and habits of culture, by the means of the railways and the like, it has gathered to itself fresh recruits for the reserve army of competing lack-alls on which its gambling gains so much depend, stripping the countryside of its population and extinguishing all reasonable hope and life in the lesser towns.

Nor can I, an artist, think last or least of the outward

effects which betoken this rule of the wretched anarchy
of commercial war. Think of the spreading sore of London swallowing up with its loathsomeness field and wood
and heath without mercy and without hope, mocking our
feeble efforts to deal even with its minor evils of smoke-
laden sky and befouled river; the black horror and reckless squalor of our manufacturing districts, so dreadful to
the senses which are unused to them that it is ominous
for the future of the race that any man can live among it
in tolerable cheerfulness; nay, in the open country itself
the thrusting aside by miserable jerry-built brick and
slate of the solid grey dwellings that are still scattered
about, fit emblems in their cheery but beautiful simplicity
of the yeomen of the English field, whose destruction at
the hands of the as yet young commercial war was la-
mented so touchingly by the high-minded More and the
valiant Latimer. Everywhere in short the change from old
to new involves one certainty, whatever else may be
doubtful, a worsening of the aspect of the country.

This is the condition of England, of England the country of order, peace, and stability, the land of common
sense and practicality, the country to which all eyes are
turned of those whose hope is for the continuance and
perfection of modern progress. There are countries in
Europe whose aspect is not so ruined outwardly, though
they may have less of material prosperity, less widespread middle-class wealth to balance the squalor and
disagrace I have mentioned; but if they are members of
the great commercial whole, through the same mill they
have got to go, unless something should happen to turn
aside the triumphant march of War Commercial before it
reaches the end. That is what three centuries of Commerce have brought that hope to, which sprang up when
feudalism began to fall to pieces. What can give us the
dayspring of a new hope? What, save general revolt
against the tryranny of commercial war? The palliatives
over which many worthy people are busying themselves
now are useless, because they are but unorganized partial
revolts against a vast, wide-spreading, grasping organization which will, with the unconscious instinct of a
plant, meet every attempt at bettering the condition of

the people with an attack on a fresh side; new machines, new markets, wholesale emigration, the revival of grovelling supersititions, preachments of thrift to lack-alls, of temperance to the wretched—such things as these will baffle at every turn all partial revolts against the monster we of the middle classes have created for our own undoing.

I will speak quite plainly on this matter, though I must say an ugly word in the end if I am to say what I think. The one thing to be done is to set people far and wide to think it possible to raise the standard of life. If you think of it, you will see clearly that this means stirring up general discontent. And now to illustrate that I turn back to my blended claim for Art and Labour, that I may deal with the third clause in it; here is the claim again: *It is right and necessary that all men should have work to do: first, Work worth doing; second, Work of itself pleasant to do; third, Work done under such conditions as would make it neither over-wearisome nor overanxious . . . .*

These are the days of combat: who can doubt that as he hears all round him the sounds that betoken discontent and hope and fear in high and low, the sounds of awakening courage and awakening conscience?

These, I say, are the days of combat, when there is no external peace possible to an honest man; but when for that very reason the internal peace of a good conscience founded on settled convictions is the easier to win, since action for the cause is offered us.

Or will you say that here in this quiet, constitutionally governed country of England there is no opportunity for action offered to us? If we were in gagged Germany, gagged in Austria, or in Russia where a word or two might land us in Siberia or the prison of the fortress of Peter and Paul, why then, indeed—Ah! my friends, it is but a poor tribute to offer on the tombs of the martyrs of liberty, this refusal to take the torch from their dying hands! Is it not of Goethe it is told, that on hearing one say he was going to America to begin life again, he replied: "Here is America, or nowhere"? So for my part I say: "Here is Russia, or nowhere." To say the governing classes of England are not afraid of freedom of speech, therefore let us abstain from speaking freely, is a strange paradox to me. Let us on the contrary press in through the breach which valiant men have made for us; if we hang back we make their labours, their sufferings, their deaths, of no account. Believe me, we shall be shown that it is all or nothing; or will any one here tell me that a Russian moujik is in a worse case than a sweating tailor's wage slave? Do not let us deceive ourselves, the class of victims exists here as in Russia. There are fewer of them? Maybe; then are they of themselves more helpless, and so have more need of our help.

And how can we of the middle classes, we the capital-ists, and our hangers-on, help them? By renouncing our class, and on all occasions when antagonism rises up be-tween the classes casting in our lot with the victims, with those who are condemned at the best to lack of educa-tion, refinement, leisure, pleasure, and renown and at the worst to a life lower than that of the most brutal of savages in order that the system of competitive Com-merce may endure. There is no other way, and this way, I tell you plainly, will in the long run give us plentiful occasion for self-sacrifice without going to Russia. I feel sure that in this assembly there are some who are steeped in discontent with the miserable anarchy of the century of Commerce; to them I offer a means of renouncing their class by supporting Socialist propaganda . . .

This to my mind is opportunity enough for those of us who are discontented with the present state of things and long for an opportunity of renunciation; and it is very certain that in accepting the opportunity you will have at once to undergo some of the inconveniences of martyr-dom, though without gaining its dignity at present. You will at least be mocked and laughed at by those whose mockery is a token of honour to an honest man, but you will, I don't doubt it, be looked on coldly by many excel-lent people, not all of whom will be quite stupid. You will run the risk of losing position, reputation, money, friends even: losses which are certainly pinpricks to the serious martyrdom I have spoken of, but which none the less do try the stuff a man is made of, all the more as he can escape them with little other reproach of cowardice than that which his own conscience cries out at him. Nor can I assure you that you will forever escape scot-free from the attacks of open tyranny. It is true that at present capitalist society only looks on Socialism in England with dry grins. But remember that the body of people who have, for instance, ruined India, starved and gagged Ireland, and tortured Egypt have capacities in them, some ominous signs of which they have lately shown, for openly playing the tyrants' game nearer home. So on all sides I can offer you a position which involves sacrifice, a position which will give you your America at home and make you inwardly sure that you are at least of some use to the cause; and I earnestly beg you, those of you who are convinced of the justice of our cause, not to hang back from active participation in a struggle which, whoever helps or whoever abstains from helping, must beyond all doubt end at last in Victory!

George Bernard Shaw

Socialism and Liberty

Playwright and pamphleteer, George Bernard Shaw (1856–1950) was for many years an active spokesman for the English Fabian Society, a distinguished group of intellectuals who spread the doctrine of reformist socialism. Written in his usual brisk and amusing style, this chapter from Shaw's The Intelligent Woman's Guide to Socialism, published in 1928, discusses problems of snobbery, conventionality, and social coercion. The language is far from that of most socialist theoreticians, but the points raised by Shaw have had to be considered, sometimes too late, by socialists less witty than he.

The dread of Socialism by nervous people who do not understand it, on the ground that there would be too much law under it, and that every act of our lives would be regulated by the police, is more plausible than the terrors of the ignorant people who think it would mean the end of all law, because under Capitalism we have been forced to impose restrictions that in a socialized nation would have no sense, in order to save the proletariat from extermination, or at least from extremities that would have provoked it to rebellion. Here is a little example. A friend of mine who employed some girls in an artistic business in which there was not competition enough to compel him to do his worst in the way of sweating them, took a nice old riverside house, and decorated it very prettily with Morris wallpapers, furnishing it in such a way that the girls could have their tea comfortably in their workrooms, which he made as homelike as possible. All went well until one day a gentleman walked in and announced himself to my friend as the factory inspector. He looked round him, evidently much puzzled, and asked where the women worked. "Here" replied my friend, with justifiable pride, confident that the inspector had never seen anything so creditable in the way of a factory before. But what the inspector said was, "Where is the copy of the factory regulations which you are obliged by law to post up on your walls in full view of your employees?" "Surely you don't expect me to stick up a beastly ugly thing like that in a room furnished like a drawing room," said my friend. "Why, that paper on the wall is a Morris paper; I can't disfigure it by pasting up a big placard on it." "You are liable to severe penalties," replied the inspector, "for having not only omitted to post the regulations, but for putting paper on your walls instead of having them limewashed at the intervals prescribed by law." "But hang it all!" my friend remonstrated, "I want to make the place homely and beautiful. You forget that the girls are not always working. They take their tea here." "For allowing your employees to take their meals in the room where they work you have incurred an additional penalty," said the inspector. "It is a gross breach of the Factory Acts." And he walked out, leaving my friend an abashed criminal caught redhanded.

As it happened, the inspector was a man of sense. He did not return; the penalties were not exacted; the Morris wallpapers remained; and the illicit teas continued; but the incident illustrates the extent to which individual liberty has been cut down under Capitalism for good as well as for evil. Where women are concerned it is assumed that they must be protected to a degree that is unnecessary for men (as if men were any more free in a factory than women); consequently the regulations are so much stricter that women are often kept out of employments to which men are welcomed. Besides the factory inspector, there are the Commissioners of Inland Revenue inquiring into your income and making you disgorge a lot of it, the school attendance visitors taking possession of your children, the local government inspectors making you build and drain your house not as you please but as they order, the Poor Law officers, the unemployment insurance officers, the vaccination officers, and others whom I cannot think of just at present. And the tendency is to have more and more of them as we become less tolerant of the abuses of our capitalist system. But if you study these interferences with our liberties closely you will find that in practice they are virtually suspended in the case of people well enough off to be able to take care of themselves: for instance, the school attendance officer never calls at houses valued above a certain figure, though the education of the children in them is often disgracefully neglected or mishandled. Poor Law officers would not exist if there were no poor, nor unemployment insurance officers if we all got incomes whether we were employed or not. If nobody could make profits by sweating, nor compel us to work in uncomfortable, unsafe, insanitary factories and workshops, a great deal of our factory regulations would become not only superfluous but unbearably obstructive.

Then consider the police: the friends of the honest woman and the enemies and hunters of thieves, tramps, swindlers, rioters, confidence tricksters, drunkards, and prostitutes. The police officer, like the soldier who stands behind him, is mainly occupied today in enforcing the legalized robbery of the poor which takes place whenever the wealth produced by the labor of a productive worker is transferred as rent or interest to the pockets of an idler or an idler's parasite. They are even given powers to arrest us for "sleeping out," which means sleeping in the open air without paying a landlord for permission to do so. Get rid of this part of their duties, and at the same time of the poverty which it enforces, with the mass of corruption, thieving, rioting, swindling, and prostitution which poverty produces as surely as insanitary squalor produces smallpox and typhus, and you get rid of the least agreeable part of our present police activity, with all that it involves in prisons, criminal courts, and jury duties.

As to the mass of oppressive and unjust laws that protect property at the expense of humanity, and enable proprietors to drive whole populations off the land because sheep or deer are more profitable, we have said enough about them already. Naturally we shall get rid of them when we get rid of private property.

Now, however, I must come to one respect in which official interference with personal liberty would be carried under Socialism to lengths undreamed of at present. We may be as idle as we please if only we have money in our pockets; and the more we look as if we had never done a day's work in our lives and never intend to, the more we are respected by every official we come in contact with, and the more we are envied, courted, and deferred to by everybody. If we enter a village school the children all rise and stand respectfully to receive us, whereas the entrance of a plumber or carpenter leaves them unmoved. The mother who secures a rich idler as a husband for her daughter is proud of it; the father who makes a million uses it to make rich idlers of his children. That work is a curse is part of our religion; that it is a disgrace is the first article in our social code. To carry a parcel through the streets is not only a trouble, but a derogation from one's rank. Where there are blacks to carry them, as in South Africa, it is virtually impossible for a white to be seen doing such a thing. In London we condemn these colonial extremes of snobbery; but how many ladies could we persuade to carry a jug of milk down Bond Street on a May afternoon, even for a bet?

Now it is not likely, human laziness being what it is, that under Socialism anyone will carry a parcel or a jug if she can induce somebody else (her husband, say) to carry it for her. But nobody will think it disgraceful to carry a parcel because carrying a parcel is work. The idler will be treated not only as a rogue and a vagabond, but as an embezzler of the national funds, the meanest sort of thief. The police will not have much trouble in detecting such offenders. They will be denounced by everybody, because there will be a very marked jealousy of slackers who take their share without "doing their bit." The real lady will be the woman who does more than her bit, and thereby leaves her country richer than she found it. Today nobody knows what a real lady is; but the dignity is assumed most confidently by the women who ostentatiously take as much and give as nearly nothing as they can.

The snobbery that exists at present among workers will also disappear. Our ridiculous social distinctions between manual labor and brain work, between wholesale business and retail business, are really class distinctions. If a doctor considers it beneath his dignity to carry a scuttle of coals from one room to another, but is proud of his skill in performing some unpleasantly messy operation, it is clearly not because the one is any more or less manual than the other, but solely because surgical operations are associated with descent through younger sons from the propertied class and carrying coals with proletarian descent. If the petty ironmonger's daughter is not considered eligible for marriage with the ironmaster's son, it is not because selling steel by the ounce and selling it by the ton are attributes of two different species, but because petty ironmongers have usually been poor and ironmasters rich. When there are no rich and no poor, and descent from the proprietary class will be described as "criminal antecedents," people will turn their hands to anything, and indeed rebel against any division of labor that deprives them of physical exercise. My own excessively sedentary occupation makes me long to be a half-time navvy. I find myself begging my gardener, who is a glutton for work, to leave me a few rough jobs to do when I have written myself to a standstill; for I cannot go out and take a hand with the navvies, because I should be taking the bread out of a poor man's mouth; nor should we be very comfortable company for one another with our different habits and speech and bringing up, all produced by differences in our parents' incomes and class. But with all these obstacles swept away by Socialism I could lend a hand at any job within my strength and skill, and help my mates instead of hurting them, besides being as good company for them as I am now for professional persons or rich folk. Even as it is, a good deal of haymaking is done for fun; and I am persuaded (having some imagination, thank Heaven!) that under Socialism open-air workers would have plenty of voluntary help, female as well as male, without the trouble of whistling for it. Laws might have to be made to deal with officiousness. Everything would make for activity and against idleness; indeed it would probably be much harder to be an idler than it is now to be a pick-pocket. Anyhow, as idleness would be not only a criminal offense, but unladylike and ungentlemanly in the lowest degree, nobody would resent the laws against it as infringements of natural liberty.

Lest anyone should at this point try to muddle you with the inveterate delusion that because capital can increase wealth people can live on capital without working, let me go back just for a moment to the way in which capital becomes productive.

Let us take those cases in which capital is used, not for destructive purposes, as in war, but for increasing production, that is, saving time and trouble in future work. When all the merchandise in a country has to be brought from the makers to the users on packhorses or carts over bad roads, the cost in time and trouble and labor of man and beast is so great that most things have to be made and consumed on the spot. There may be a famine in one village and a glut in another a hundred miles off because of the difficulty of sending food from one to the other. Now if there is enough spare subsistence (capital) to support gangs of navvies and engineers and other workers whilst they cover the country with railways, canals, and metaled roads, and build engines and trains, barges and motor cars to travel on them, to say nothing of aeroplanes, then all sorts of goods can be sent long distances quickly and cheaply; so that the village which formerly could not get a cartload of bread and a few cans of milk from a hundred miles off to save its life is able to buy quite cheaply grain grown in Russia or America and domestic articles made in Germany or Japan. The spare subsistence will be entirely consumed in the operation; there will be no more left of it than of the capital lent for the war, but it will leave behind it the roadways and waterways and machinery by which labor can do a great deal more in a given time than it could without them. The destruction of these aids to labor would be a very different matter from our annual confiscations of the National Debt by taxation. It would leave us much poorer and less civilized, in fact most of us would starve, because big modern populations cannot support themselves without elaborate machinery and railways and so forth.

Still, roadways and machines can produce nothing by themselves. They can only assist labor. And they have to be continually repaired and renewed by labor. A country crammed with factories and machines, traversed in all directions by roadways, tramways, and railways, dotted with aerodromes and hangars and garages, each crowded with aeroplanes and airships and motor cars would produce absolutely nothing at all except ruin and rust and decay if the inhabitants ceased to work. We should starve in the midst of all the triumphs of civilization because we could not breakfast on the clay of the railway embankments, lunch on boiled aeroplanes, and dine on toasted steam-hammers. Nature inexorably denies to us the possibility of living without labor or of hoarding its most vital products. We may be helped by past labor; but we must live by present labor. By telling off one set of workers to produce more than they consume, and telling off another set to live on the surplus while the first set makes roads and machines, we may make our labor much more productive, and take out the gain either in shorter hours of work or bigger returns from the same number of hours of work as before; but we cannot stop working and sit down and look on while the roads and machines make and fetch and carry for us without anyone lifting a finger. We may reduce our working hours to two a day, or increase our income tenfold, or even conceivably do both at once; but by no magic on earth can any of us honestly become an idler. When you see a person who does no productive or serviceable work, you may conclude with absolute certainty that she or he is spunging on the labor of other people. It may or may not be expedient to allow certain persons this privilege for a time: sometimes it is; and sometimes it is not. I have already described how we offer at present, to anyone who can invent a labor-saving machine, what is called a patent, that is, a right to take a share of what the workers produce with the help of that machine for fourteen years. When a man writes a book or a play, we give him, by what is called copyright, the power to make everybody who reads the book or sees the play performed pay him and his heirs something during his lifetime and fifty years afterwards. This is our way of encouraging people to invent machines and to write books and plays instead of being content with the old handiwork, and with the Bible and Shakespeare; and as we do it with our eyes open and with a definite purpose, and the privilege lasts no longer than enough to accomplish its purpose, there is a good deal to be said for it. But to allow the descendants of a man who invested a few hundred pounds in the New River Water Company in the reign of James I to go on forever and ever living in idleness on the incessant daily labor of the London rate-payers is senseless and mischievous. If they actually did the daily work of supplying London with water, they might reasonably claim either to work for less time or receive more for their work than a water carrier in Elizabeth's time; but for doing no work at all they have not a shadow of excuse. To consider Socialism a tyranny because it will compel everyone to share the daily work of the world is to confess to the brain of an idiot and the instinct of a tramp.

Speaking generally, it is a mistake to suppose that the absence of law means the absence of tyranny. Take, for example, the tyranny of fashion. The only law concerned in this is the law that we must all wear something in the presence of other people. It does not prescribe what a woman shall wear; it only says that in public she shall be a draped figure and not a nude one. But does this mean that a woman can wear what she likes? Legally she can; but socially her slavery is more complete than any sumptuary law could make it. If she is a waitress or a parlor-maid there is no question about it: she must wear a uniform or lose her employment and starve. If she is a duchess she must dress in the fashion or be ridiculous. In the case of the duchess nothing worse than ridicule is the penalty of unfashionable dressing. But any woman who has to earn her living outside her own house finds that if she is to keep her employment she must also keep up appearances, which means that she must dress in the fashion, even when it is not at all becoming to her, and her wardrobe contains servicable dresses a couple of years out of date. And the better her class of employment the tighter her bonds. The ragpicker has the melancholy privilege of being less particular about her working clothes than the manageress of a hotel; but she would be very glad to exchange that freedom for the obligation of the manageress to be always well dressed. In fact the most enviable women in this respect are nuns and police-women, who, like gentlemen at evening parties and military officers on parade, never have to think of what they will wear, as it is all settled for them by regulation and custom.

This dress question is only one familiar example of the extent to which the private employment of today imposes regulations on us which are quite outside the law, but which are none the less enforced by private employers on pain of destitution. The husband in public employment, the socialized husband, is much freer than the unsocial-ized one in private employment. He may travel third class, wearing a lounge suit and soft hat, living in the suburbs, and spending his Sundays as he pleases, whilst the others must travel first class, wear a frock coat and tall hat, live at a fashionable address, and go to church regularly. Their wives have to do as they do; and the single women who have escaped from the limitations of the home into independent activity find just the same difference between public work and private: in public employment their livelihood is never at the mercy of a private irresponsible person as it is in private. The lengths to which women are sometimes forced to go to please their private employers are much more revolting than, for instance, the petty dishonesties in which clerks are forced to become accomplices.

Then there are estate rules, that is to say, edicts drawn up by private estate owners and imposed on their tenants without any legal sanction. These often prohibit the building on the estate of any place of worship except an Anglican church or of any public house. They refuse houses to practitioners of the many kinds that are now not registered by the General Medical Council. In fact they exercise a tyranny which would lead to a revolution if it were attempted by the King, and which did actually provoke us to cut off a king's head in the seventeenth century. We have to submit to these tyrannies because the people who can refuse us employment or the use of land have powers of life and death over us and can therefore make us do what they like, law or no law. Socialism would transfer this power of life and death from private hands to the hands of the constitutional authorities and regulate it by public law. The result would be a great increase of independence, self-respect, freedom from interference with our tastes and ways of living, and, generally, all the liberty we really care about.

Childish people, we saw, want to have all their lives regulated for them, with occasional holiday outbursts of naughtiness to relieve the monotony; and we admitted that the able-bodied ones make good soldiers and steady conventional employees. When they are left to themselves they make laws of fashions, customs, points of etiquette, and "what other people will say," hardly daring to call their souls their own, though they may be rich enough to do as they please. Money as a means of freedom is thrown away on these people. It is funny to hear them declaring, as they often do, that Socialism would be unendurable because it would dictate to them what they should eat and drink and wear, leaving them no choice in the matter, when they are cowering under a social tyranny which regulates their meals, their clothes, their hours, their religion and politics, so ruthlessly that they dare no more walk down a fashionable street in an unfashionable hat, which there is no law to prevent them doing, than to walk down it naked, which would be stopped by the police. They regard with dread and abhorrence the emancipated spirits who, within the limits of legality and cleanliness and convenience, do not care what they wear, and boldly spend their free time as their fancy dictates.

But do not undervalue the sheepish wisdom of the conventional. Nobody can live in society without conventions. The reason why sensible people are as conventional as they can bear to be is that conventionality saves so much time and thought and trouble and social friction of one sort or another that it leaves them much more leisure for freedom than unconventionality does. Believe me, unless you intend to devote your life to preaching unconventionality, and thus make it your profession, the more conventional you are, short of being silly or slavish or miserable, the easier life will be for you. Even as a professional reformer you had better be content to preach one form of unconventionality at a time. For instance, if you rebel against high-heeled shoes, take care to do it in a very smart hat.

Bertrand Russell

Science and Art Under Socialism

Bertrand Russell (1872–1970), one of the towering minds of our century, wrote, in addition to his works in philosophy and mathematics, a number of more popular books concerned with social problems. "Science and Art Under Socialism" is taken from his Proposed Roads to Freedom *(1919); it is notable for having advanced ideas once regarded as utopian but now being seriously discussed in Western society.*

Socialism has been advocated by most of its champions chiefly as a means of increasing the welfare of the wage-earning classes, and more particularly their material welfare. It has seemed, accordingly, to some men whose aims are not material, as if it has nothing to offer toward the general advancement of civilization in the way of art and thought. Some of its advocates, moreover—and among these Marx must be included—have written, no doubt not deliberately, as if with the socialist revolution the millennium would have arrived, and there would be no need of further progress for the human race. I do not know whether our age is more restless than that which preceded it, or whether it has merely become more impregnated with the idea of evolution, but, for whatever reason, we have grown incapable of believing in a state of static perfection, and we demand, of any social system, which is to have our approval, that it shall contain within itself a stimulus and opportunity for progress toward something still better. The doubts thus raised by socialist writers make it necessary to inquire whether socialism

455

would in fact be hostile to art and science, and whether it would be likely to produce a stereotyped society in which progress would become difficult and slow.

It is not enough that men and women should be made comfortable in a material sense. Many members of the well-to-do classes at present, in spite of opportunity, contribute nothing of value to the life of the world and do not even succeed in securing for themselves any personal happiness worthy to be so called. The multiplication of such individuals would be an achievement of the very minutest value; and if socialism were merely to bestow upon all the kind of life and outlook which is now enjoyed by the more apathetic among the well-to-do, it would offer little that could inspire enthusiasm in any generous spirit.

> The true role of collective existence says M. Naquet . . . is to learn, to discover, to know. Eating, drinking, sleeping, living, in a word, is a mere accessory. In this respect, we are not distinguished from the brute. Knowledge is the goal. If I were condemned to choose between a humanity materially happy, glutted after the manner of a flock of sheep in a field, and a humanity existing in misery, but from which emanated, here and there, some eternal truth, it is in the latter that my choice would fall.*

This statement puts the alternative in a very extreme form in which it is somewhat unreal. It may be said in reply that for those who have had the leisure and the opportunity to enjoy "eternal truths" it is easy to exalt their importance at the expense of sufferings which fall on others. This is true; but, if it is taken as disposing of the question, it leaves out of account the importance of thought for progress. Viewing the life of mankind as a whole, in the future as well as in the present, there can be no question that a society in which some men pursue knowledge while others endure great poverty offers more hope of ultimate good than a society in which all are sunk in slothful comfort. It is true that poverty is a great evil, but it is not true that material prosperity is in itself a great good. If it is to have any real value to society, it

---

* L'Anarchie et le Collectivisme, p. 114.

must be made a means to the advancement of those higher goods that belong to the life of the mind. But the life of the mind does not consist of thought and knowledge alone, nor can it be completely healthy unless it has some instinctive contact, however deeply buried, with the general life of the community. Divorced from the social instinct, thought, like art, tends to become finicky and precious. It is the position of such art and thought as is imbued with the instinctive sense of service to mankind that we wish to consider, for it is this alone that makes up the life of the mind in the sense in which it is a vital part of the life of the community. Will the life of the mind in this sense be helped or hindered by socialism? And will there still be a sufficient spur to progress to prevent a condition of Byzantine immobility?

In considering this question we are, in a certain sense, passing outside the atmosphere of democracy. The general good of the community is realized only in individuals, but it is realized much more fully in some individuals than in others. Some men have a comprehensive and penetrating intellect, enabling them to appreciate and remember what has been thought and known by their predecessors and to discover new regions in which they enjoy all the high delights of the mental explorer. Others have the power of creating beauty, giving bodily form to impalpable visions out of which joy comes to many. Such men are more fortunate than the mass, and also more important for the collective life. A larger share of the general sum of good is concentrated in them than in the ordinary man and woman; but also their contribution to the general good is greater. They stand out among men and cannot be wholly fitted into the framework of democratic equality. A social system which would render them unproductive would stand condemned, whatever other merits it might have.

The first thing to realize—though it is difficult in a commercial age—is that what is best in creative mental activity cannot be produced by any system of monetary rewards. Opportunity and the stimulus of an invigorating spiritual atmosphere are important, but, if they are present, no financial inducements will be required, while if they are absent, material compensations will be of no avail. Recognition, even if it takes the form of money, can bring a certain pleasure in old age to the man of science who has battled all his life against academic prejudice or to the artist who has endured years of ridicule for not painting in the manner of his predecessors; but it is not by the remote hope of such pleasures that their work has been inspired. All the most important work springs from an uncalculating impulse and is best promoted, not by rewards after the event, but by circumstances which keep the impulsive alive and afford scope for the activities which it inspires. In the creation of such circumstances our present system is much at fault. Will socialism be better?

I do not think this question can be answered without specifying the kind of socialism that is intended: some forms of socialism would, I believe, be even more destructive in this respect than the present capitalist regime, while others would be immeasurably better. Three things which a social system can provide or withhold are helpful to mental creation: first, technical training; second, liberty to follow the creative impulse; third, at least the possibility of ultimate appreciation by some public, whether large or small. We may leave out of our discussion both individual genius and those intangible conditions which make some ages great and others sterile in art and science—not because these are unimportant, but because they are too little understood to be taken account of in economic or political organization. The three conditions we have mentioned seem to cover most of what can be *seen* to be useful or harmful from our present point of view, and it is therefore to them that we shall confine ourselves.

1. *Technical training.* Technical training at present, whether in science or art, requires one or other of two conditions. Either a boy must be the son of well-to-do parents who can afford to keep him while he acquires his education, or he must show so much ability at an early age as to enable him to subsist on scholarships until he is ready to earn his living. The former condition is, of course, a mere matter of luck, and could not be preserved

in its present form under any kind of socialism or communism. This loss is emphasized by defenders of the present system, and no doubt it would be, to some extent, a real loss. But the well-to-do are a small proportion of the population, and presumably on the average no more talented by nature than their less fortunate contemporaries. If the advantages which are enjoyed now by those few among them who are capable of good work in science or art could be extended, even in a slightly attenuated form, to all who are similarly gifted, the result would almost infallibly be a gain, and much ability which is now wasted would be rendered fruitful. But how is this to be effected?

The system of scholarships obtained by competition, though better than nothing, is objectionable from many points of view. It introduces the competitive spirit into the work of the very young; it makes them regard knowledge from the standpoint of what is useful in examinations rather than in the light of its intrinsic interest or importance; it places a premium upon that sort of ability which is displayed precociously in glib answers to set questions rather than upon the kind that broods on difficulties and remains for a time rather dumb. What is perhaps worse than any of these defects is the tendency to cause overwork in youth, leading to lack of vigor and interest when manhood has been reached. It can hardly be doubted that by this cause, at present, many fine minds have their edge blunted and their keenness destroyed.

State socialism might easily universalize the system of scholarships obtained by competitive examination, and if it did so it is to be feared that it would be very harmful. State socialists at present tend to be enamored of the system, which is exactly of the kind that every bureaucrat loves: orderly, neat, giving a stimulus to industrious habits, and involving no waste of a sort that could be tabulated in statistics or accounts of public expenditure. Such men will argue that free higher education is expensive to the community, and only useful in the case of those who have exceptional abilities; it ought, therefore, they will say, not to be given to all but only to those who will become more useful members of society through receiving it. Such arguments make a great appeal to what are called "practical" men, and the answers to them are of a sort which it is difficult to render widely convincing. Revolt against the evils of competition is, however, part of the very essence of the socialist's protest against the existing order, and on this ground, if on no other, those who favor socialism may be summoned to look for some better solution.

Much the simplest solution, and the only really effective one, is to make every kind of education free up to the age of twenty-one for all boys and girls who desire it. The majority will be tired of education before that age and will prefer to begin other work sooner; this will lead to a natural selection of those with strong interests in some pursuit requiring a long training. Among those selected in this way by their own inclinations, probably almost all who have marked abilities of the kind in question will be included. It is true that there will also be many who have very little ability: the desire to become a painter, for example, is by no means confined to those who can paint. But this degree of waste could well be borne by the community; it would be immeasurably less than that now entailed by the support of the idle rich. Any system which aims at avoiding this kind of waste must entail the far more serious waste of rejecting or spoiling some of the best ability in each generation. The system of free education up to any grade for all who desire it is the only system which is consistent with the principles of liberty, and the only one which gives a reasonable hope of affording full scope for talent. This system is equally compatible with all forms of socialism and anarchism. Theoretically, it is compatible with capitalism, but practically it is so opposite in spirit that it would hardly be feasible without a complete economic reconstruction. The fact that socialism would facilitate it must be reckoned a very powerful argument in favor of change, for the waste of talent at present in the poorer classes of society must be stupendous.

2. *Liberty to follow the creative impulse.* When a man's training has been completed, if he is possessed of really

great abilities, he will do his best work if he is completely free to follow his bent, creating what seems good to him, regardless of the judgment of "experts." At present this is only possible for two classes of people: those who have private means, and those who can earn a living by an occupation that does not absorb their whole energies. Under socialism, there will be no one with private means, and if there is to be no loss as regards art and science, the opportunity which now comes by accident to a few will have to be provided deliberately for a much larger number. The men who have used private means as an opportunity for creative work have been few but important: one might mention Milton, Shelley, Keats, and Darwin as examples. Probably none of these would have produced as good work if they had had to earn their livelihood. If Darwin had been a university teacher, he would of course have been dismissed from his post by the influence of the clerics on account of his scandalous theories.

Nevertheless, the bulk of the creative work of the world is done at present by men who subsist by some other occupation. Science, and research generally, are usually done in their spare time by men who live by teaching. There is no great objection to this in the case of science, provided the number of hours devoted to teaching is not excessive. It is partly because science and teaching are so easily combined that science is vigorous in the present age. In music, a composer who is also a performer enjoys similar advantages, but one who is not a performer must starve, unless he is rich or willing to pander to the public taste. In the fine arts, as a rule, it is not easy in the modern world either to make a living by really good work or to find a subsidiary profession which leaves enough leisure for creation. This is presumably one reason, though by no means the only one, why art is less flourishing than science.

The bureaucratic state socialist will have a simple solution for these difficulties. He will appoint a body consisting of the most eminent celebrities in an art or a science, whose business it shall be to judge the work of young men and to issue licenses to those whose productions find favor in their eyes. A licensed artist shall be considered to have performed duty to the community by producing

works of art. But of course he will have to prove his
industry by never failing to produce in reasonable quantities, and his continued ability by never failing to please
his eminent judges—until, in the fullness of time, he becomes a judge himself. In this way, the authorities will
insure that the artist shall be competent, regular, and
obedient to the best traditions of his art. Those who fail
to fulfil these condtions will be compelled by the withdrawal of their license to seek some less dubious mode of
earning their living. Such will be the ideal of the state
socialist.

In such a world all that makes life tolerable to the
lover of beauty would perish. Art springs from a wild and
anarchic side of human nature; between the artist and
the bureaucrat there must always be a profound mutual
antagonism, an age-long battle in which the artist, always
outwardly worsted, wins in the end through the gratitude
of mankind for the joy that he puts into their lives. If the
wild side of human nature is to be permanently subjected to the orderly rules of the benevolent, uncompre-
hending bureaucrat, the joy of life will perish out of the
earth, and the very impulse to live will gradually wither
and die. Better a thousandfold the present world with all
its horrors than such a dead mummy of a world. Better
anarchism, with all its risks, than a state socialism that
subjects to rule what must be spontaneous and free if it is
to have any value. It is this nightmare that makes artists,
and lovers of beauty generally, so often suspicious of
socialism. But there is nothing in the essence of socialism
to make art impossible: only certain forms of socialism
would entail this danger. William Morris was a socialist
and was a socialist very largely because he was an artist.
And in this he was not irrational.

It is impossible for art, or any of the higher creative
activities, to flourish under any system which requires
that the artist shall prove his competence to some body of
authorities before he is allowed to follow his impulse.
Any really great artist is almost sure to be thought incompetent by those among his seniors who would be generally regarded as best qualified to form an opinion. And
the mere fact of having to produce work which will

please older men is hostile to a free spirit and to bold innovation. Apart from this difficulty, selection by older men would lead to jealousy and intrigue and backbiting, producing a poisonous atmosphere of underground competition. The only effect of such a plan would be to eliminate the few who now slip through owing to some fortunate accident. It is not by any system, but by freedom alone, that art can flourish.

There are two ways by which the artist could secure freedom under socialism of the right kind. He might undertake regular work outside his art, doing only a few hours' work a day and receiving proportionately less pay than those who do a full day's work. He ought, in that case, to be at liberty to sell his pictures if he could find purchasers. Such a system would have many advantages. It would leave absolutely every man free to become an artist, provided he were willing to suffer a certain economic loss. This would not deter those in whom the impulse was strong and genuine, but would tend to exclude the dilettante. Many young artists at present endure voluntarily much greater poverty than need be entailed by only doing half the usual day's work in a well-organized socialist community; and some degree of hardship is not objectionable, as a test of the strength of the creative impulse, and as an offset to the peculiar joys of the creative life.

The other possibility would be that the necessaries of life should be free, as anarchists desire, to all equally, regardless of whether they work or not. Under this plan, every man could live without work: there would be what might be called a "vagabond's wage," sufficient for existence but not for luxury. The artist who preferred to have his whole time for art and enjoyment might live on the "vagabond's wage"—travelling on foot when the humour seized him to see foreign countries, enjoying the air and the sun, as free as the birds, and perhaps scarcely less happy. Such men would bring color and diversity into the life of the community; their outlook would be different from that of steady, stay-at-home workers, and would keep alive a much-needed element of light-heartedness which our sober, serious civilization tends to kill. If they became very numerous, they might be too great an economic burden on the workers; but I doubt if there are many with enough capacity for simple enjoyments to choose poverty and freedom in preference to the comparatively light and pleasant work which will be usual in those days.

By either of these methods, freedom can be preserved for the artist in a socialistic commonwealth—far more complete freedom, and far more widespread, than any that now exists except for the possessors of capital. . . .

3. *Possibility of appreciation.* This condition is one which is not necessary to all who do creative work, but in the sense in which I mean it the great majority find it very nearly indispensable. I do not mean widespread public recognition, nor that ignorant, half-sincere respect which is commonly accorded to artists who have achieved success. Neither of these serves much purpose. What I mean is rather understanding, and a spontaneous feeling that things of beauty are important. In a thoroughly commercialized society, an artist is respected if he makes money, and because he makes money, but there is no genuine respect for the works of art by which his money has been made. A millionaire whose fortune has been made in button hooks or chewing gum is regarded with awe, but none of this feeling is bestowed on the articles from which his wealth is derived. In a society which measures all things by money the same tends to be true of the artist. If he has become rich he is respected, though of course less than the millionaire, but his pictures or books or music are regarded as the chewing gum or the button hooks are regarded, merely as a means to money. In such an atmosphere it is very difficult for the artist to preserve his creative impulse pure: either he is contaminated by his surroundings, or he becomes embittered through lack of appreciation for the object of his endeavor.

It is not appreciation of the artist that is necessary so much as appreciation of the art. It is difficult for an artist to live in an environment in which everything is judged by its utility, rather than by its intrinsic quality. The whole side of life of which art is the flower requires something which may be called disinterestedness, a capacity for direct enjoyment without thought of tomorrow's problems and difficulties. When people are amused by a joke they do not need to be persuaded that it will serve some important purpose. The same kind of direct pleasure is involved in any genuine appreciation of art. The struggle for life, the serious work of a trade or profession, is apt to make people too solemn for jokes and too preoccupied for art. The easing of the struggle, the diminution in the hours of work, and the lightening of the burden of existence, which would result from a better economic system, could hardly fail to increase the joy of life and the vital energy available for sheer delight in the world. And if this were achieved there would inevitably be more spontaneous pleasure in beautiful things, and more enjoyment of the work of artists. But none of these good results are to be expected from the mere removal of poverty: they all require also a diffused sense of freedom, and the absence of that feeling of oppression by a vast machine which now weighs down the individual spirit. I do not think state socialism can give this sense of freedom, but some other forms of socialism, which have absorbed what is true in anarchist teaching, can give it to a degree of which capitalism is wholly incapable. . . .

V

Recent Socialist Thought

Ignazio Silone

Why Fascism Won*

> *Ignazio Silone (b. 1900), the distinguished Italian novelist and author of* Fontamara *and* Bread and Wine, *has been a life-long socialist, more and more of the nonideological and humanist variety. In 1938, he published a brilliant book,* The School for Dictators, *written as a series of dialogues among Mr. W., a would-be American dictator, Professor Pickup, a comic and pedantic American sociologist, and Thomas the Cynic, a veteran European socialist who has abandoned his earlier dogmas but retains his animating convictions. We may assume that in these conversations Thomas speaks largely for Silone himself. The discussions concern the politics of dictatorship and the unique characteristics of fascism. Here is a section concerning "the peculiar conditions which have made fascism and Nazism possible in our time."*

Thomas the Cynic   I should like to correct the erroneous impression that it was fascism that defeated socialism, either in Italy or Germany. The truth is that in both countries fascism was born from the socialist defeat.

Mr. W. and Professor Pickup   Who did defeat socialism in Italy and Germany?

Thomas the Cynic   Socialism defeated itself. In the postwar crisis of Italian and German society, in the months immediately following the armistice, socialism appeared to the masses as the only force capable of giving a new form to society and satisfying their human

---

* Title supplied by editor.

aspirations. In both countries the socialist movement was hopelessly divided. On the one hand there were the revolutionaries, whose aim was the immediate expropriation of the possessing classes and the setting up of the dictatorship of the proletariat; on the other the reformists, whose aim was legal and democratic development toward their socialist goal. In Italy, the reformists and the revolutionaries neutralized each other, with the result that the former carried out no reforms and the latter never attempted a revolution. In Germany, the Social Democrats actively helped to crush the Spartakist movement, and so far from attempting to substitute a socialist economy for the moribund German capitalist economy, never even made a bold or serious effort to democratize the country. What happened instead was that, as has been aptly said, "the Kaiser departed but the generals remained." A revolutionary situation does not last for many years, and if the revolutionary party does not seize its chance the disappointed masses turn against it and raise the opposite party to power. In Italy, the turning point came after the occupation of the factories, the evacuation of which broke the *élan* of the workers and demoralized them, and showed them that the party upon whom they had rested their hopes was capable of nothing but verbiage. Up to 1923, the German socialists still had a chance of decisive intervention in the reorganization of the country, but they, too, capitulated without a struggle. The Italian and German working classes had to face the first violent onslaughts of fascism after their own organizations had begun a disorderly retreat and had abandoned the advanced position hurriedly occupied, more by surprise than by force, in the months immediately after the armistice. The new situation was exploited by the capitalists, who took the opportunity of shifting the greater part of the burden of economic and financial distress to the backs of the masses and reduced wages in order to be able to meet foreign competition.

When the revolutionary danger was exhausted because of the internal deficiencies of the socialist movement itself, and even before fascism was a real political force, the bourgeoisie backed Mussolini and Hitler, in order to transform the working-class retreat into a rout and strike a decisive blow at social reformism, which had grown too expensive. This aspect of the struggle could be observed more plainly in Italy, where the situation developed extremely rapidly under the guidance of a fascist leader possessing the most realistic political vision. There is no doubt whatever that fascism rose and developed as a reaction against social reformism rather than against revolutionary or communist-socialism. The rich peasants, the merchants, the petty industrialists who joined Mussolini's *fasci en masse* in 1921, did so to find arms to fight the inconvenient reformist institutions which had reduced the profit of their labor and their capital to a minimum. Fascist reaction was most bloodthirsty in the Po Valley provinces, where, in the course of forty years of peaceful activity, the reformists had built up a vast network of leagues, cooperatives, benefit societies, and credit institutions, controlling the whole of local economic life and in some areas actually exercising a monopoly. The noisy and ineffectual "revolutionism" of the left-wingers imperiled nothing but the public street lamps and occasionally the bones of an unlucky policeman, but the patient, methodical and legal work of the reformists threatened something far more sacred: the profits of private enterprise; and more particularly, not the profits of the big banks, to which the reformist institutions themselves had to apply for credits, but the profits of the small business man.

The laws of the state provide a sufficient defense for the bourgeoisie against revolutionism of the windbag variety; even if existing laws are inadequate, it is easy enough to make new ones. But when faced with the advance of peaceful, democratic reformism the bourgeoisie appealed for aid to the terrorist gangs of fascism and themselves broke the laws by which they felt themselves no longer protected. Later fascist violence also descended upon the revolutionary socialists and communists just when, their hopes of an immediate revolution having faded, they were concentrating upon a campaign to maintain workers' wages and conditions, in order to prevent themselves from being isolated from the masses; and they introduced a combative spirit into this campaign that upset the opportunist calculations of many reformist leaders, who were terror-stricken by the fascist onslaught and were inclined to compromise. Subsequent developments and complications must not cause us to overlook the essential fact that fascism is a counter-revolution against a revolution that never took place.

Will history repeat itself in this way in other countries? I believe it to be essential if they are to have fascism. Let me state my meaning in this way. The birth of fascism presupposes the following conditions: in the first place the state must be in a state of crisis, that is to say, radical social changes must have taken place which are utterly irreconcilable with the old political system; in the second place the crisis of the state must be of such a nature as to be of most immediate benefit to the socialist movement, to which the masses must be irresistibly drawn, feeling it to be the only movement capable of creating a new world; in the third place, the socialists, when confronted with their responsibilities, must turn out to be utterly inadequate to the arduous task before them and do nothing but increase the general confusion, completely failing to fulfill the hopes reposed in them. When these three conditions are fulfilled, fascism appears on the scene as *tertius gaudens*, the interloper who steals the plum. Unless its leader is a complete idiot, its prospects are excellent.

Mr. W.   It is not easy to translate what you have been saying into the language of American politics, because a socialist movement in the European sense does not exist in our country, Mr. Cynic. But as I am anxious to gain a better understanding of what is happening in Europe, I should like to ask you why the failure of socialism did not help democracy instead of fascism?

Professor Pickup   I foresee the usual reply: that the democratic class is weak, devoid of will, and incapable of adapting itself to the new forms of struggle, which are somewhat crude and plebeian and not entirely averse to the use of force. That is a very superficial reply in the eyes of anyone who knows history and remembers the courage and heroism of those who fought for democracy in past centuries. According to my way of thinking, the explanation of the inferiority of democracy as against fascism must be sought in the inadequacy of the democratic idea.

Thomas the Cynic It must not be forgotten that so far fascism has only been established in countries where democracy has never had deep roots; in these countries the democratic idea has therefore had less chance than elsewhere of demonstrating what you call its inadequacy, professor. But even if fascism is one day established in a country where democracy is older and much more firmly rooted (I do not wish to discourage Mr. W.), that will certainly not mean that the democratic idea is exploded. It will only mean the political defeat of one definite historical form of democracy. I believe the democratic idea will survive all the political forms with which it has so far been identified. When men have succeeded in overthrowing the present exceptional regimes represented by fascism and Bolshevism, they will return to the democratic idea with the joy of the prisoner returning to freedom and create new and, it is to be hoped, less fictitious forms of democracy than those we have hitherto known. Whenever, for the sake of brevity, we talk of the crisis of democracy or of the defeat of democracy we should make it clear that the democratic principle is not in question, but only the peculiar historical form of political democracy commonly called *bourgeois democracy*. There are many signs that the latter is now in decline.

The difference between the democrats of the present day and their ancestors, who fought in past centuries for popular liberties, for equality before the law, for political liberties, and risked their lives on the barricades, in civil wars and wars of independence, is very great indeed, professor, and it has nothing whatever to do with individual psychological properties. The idea of political and legal equality used to be a novelty, an ideal, that kindled all minds of quality and caused men to espouse the cause of the people and take part in the struggle against the court, the nobility, the clergy, and foreign domination. But the democrats of the present day no longer have an ideal to realize. They are traditionalists, conservatives. They live on the yield of their ancestors' conquests. A class in the ascendant, a class fulfilling a revolutionary function, increases the stature of its representatives, gives them the preeminence of Cromwell, Jefferson, Mazzini, Lenin. But a democracy in decline, maintaining itself by compromises and retreats, can only be represented by such people as Giolitti, Brüning, Laval, Chamberlain; and it is to be feared that the more time passes the steeper is the decline. You know that among the politicians of the left in France there are some who pose as neo-Jacobins, but in their imitation of the Mountain, all they achieve is some extravagance of clothing and a certain way of doing their hair. It is not a question of good or bad will. Bourgeois democracy may yet find worthy representatives, but I think this most likely to happen in countries in which democracy has never existed, in feudal, semifeudal, colonial countries that have only just reached the threshold of the bourgeois revolution. Think of men like Sun-Yat-Sen and Gandhi, and compare them to the democratic ministers of France and England. They belong to the same historical movement, but the former face the dawn and the latter the sunset. In short, the leaders of European democracy show all the characteristic signs of a political class that has exhausted its mission.

Professor Pickup Goebbels has stated that the success of National Socialism depended in great measure "on the stupidity of its opponents."

Our opponents [he wrote] were in possession of the power; the army, the police, the bureaucratic apparatus, the parties, and the parliamentary majority were theirs. They controlled public opinion, the press, the wireless, in short everything that can be summed up under the term "power." If a small group that began with seven men possessing only the right of criticism succeeded in the space of fourteen years in wresting this right, together with the power itself, from their opponents, there can be no question as to which was the cleverer. Had our opponents been the cleverer, they could not have failed to find ways and means to prevent us from dispossessing them in view of the gross disproportion of our resources.

Thomas the Cynic From that point of view, every change of regime looks like the result of stupidity on the part of the old ruling class; it looks as if they allowed themselves to be taken by surprise. There are plenty of historians who try to prove that if Louis XVI had acted differently, or if Tsarist circles had done this or that in

1917, neither the French nor the Russian Revolution would have taken place. The same thing might be said of all other revolutions, about all of which there is something incomprehensible in the eyes of the superficial. And it is perfectly true. A governing class, up to the very day of its downfall, possesses all the material means for defending itself, but it lacks the will, the capacity, the courage to use them; and it is the latter which are the essentials of government. Before being beaten and dispossessed physically it has long been morally beaten. It maintains itself by force of shortsighted, supine, will-less inertia. It is affected by the senile diseases of formalism and legalitarianism in their most grotesque forms, and, though utterly devoid of its former democratic spirit, continues to pay lip service to formulas and entrenches itself behind respect for laws and procedure which benefit the opponents of democracy instead of democracy itself and have the opposite effect to that for which they were devised.

Professor Pickup The fascists and the Nazis certainly succeeded brilliantly in using democracy in order to destroy it. "Democracy," Hitler wrote in *Mein Kampf*, "is at best a means to an end, which one uses to cripple one's opponent and leave the road clear for one's own actions." After the 1928 elections, Goebbels wrote:

We enter the Reichstag to provide ourselves with arms in democracy's own arsenal. We become Reichstag deputies in order to lay the Weimar mentality low with its own staff and props. If democracy is stupid enough to give us free passes and assistance in doing it this evil service, that is its own affair.

Two years later he added: "The legal conquest of the Republic is in full swing." No one could accuse him of lacking candor. In 1935, two years after the conquest of power, he declared:

We National Socialists have never stated we were democrats. On the contrary, we publicly stated that we only used democratic means to win power, and that after the seizure of power we would ruthlessly deny our opponents all the facilities that were granted us when we were in opposition.

And they have kept their word.

Thomas the Cynic A governing class in decline lives by half-measures, from day to day, always postponing the examination of vital questions until tomorrow. If it is forced to make a stand it appoints committees and sub-committees, and by the time these have completed their labors the situation has changed. Being late means slamming the stable door after the horse has been stolen. It also means self-deception on the part of statesmen and evasion of their responsibilities; they wash their hands, so to speak, to show them white and clean for the benefit of future historians. The height of the art of government for our contemporary democratic statesmen seems to consist in accepting smacks in the face to avoid having their posteriors kicked; in putting up with the lesser evil, in everlastingly thinking out new compromises in order to smooth over conflicts and trying to reconcile the irreconcilable.

The opponents of democracy take advantage of this and become ever more impudent. They plot and conspire in open daylight, establish arms dumps, march their supporters through the streets in military formation, beat up the most hated democratic leaders. The government, "measuring its words carefully in order not to aggravate the situation," deplores all these things, and hopes that "for the country's good name" they were "not premeditated," and makes heartrending appeals to the nation to return to a calmer mood. The most important thing in the government's eyes is to avoid any word or action that might irritate the fascists and aggravate the situation. If the police discover that political and military leaders are implicated in the organization of sedition and have taken a direct and active part in preparing arms dumps, for instance, the government becomes bold, and a few secondary figures are arrested as a warning. But the leaders are not arrested, because that would mean precipitating an irreparable crisis. The democratic leaders know that they have everything to lose and nothing to gain from the embitterment of political relations. They fondly delude themselves that by their ostrich policy they are gaining time. Thus the young Spanish Republic pardoned Sanjurjo and retained the monarchical generals at the head of the army, even though everybody knew they were preparing a *coup d'état*. In Italy the *fasci* who perpetrated acts of violence throughout the country acknowledged Mussolini as their leader and took their orders from him, but Mussolini himself was never touched; and the officers and generals who were members of the *fasci* were retained on the active list. Similarly, "to contribute to the pacification of the country," the German Republic pardoned Ludendorff after the failure of the Kapp *putsch* in 1920 and of the Hitler *putsch* in 1923 and left unpunished the leaders of the terrorist "Consul" organization, who ordered the assassination of Erzberger and Rathenau, although there was no doubt about their identity or responsibility for the crimes.

Mr. W.   In Berlin, we met Baron von Killinger and the Duke of Koburg, president of the German Red Cross, who were both members of the "Consul" organization from the first. They boast publicly now of the assassinations for which they were responsible, and they told us in detail how they were organized. They told us how little trouble they had to take, even in the democratic days, to conceal their own participation in these affairs. Their boldness, in fact, was on a par with the cowardice of the republican authorities.

Professor Pickup   In his book *Kampf um Berlin*, Goebbels wrote: "The cowardice of the bourgeois parties is unexampled in political history"; and elsewhere: "We learned once and for all that it was useless to have any hopes of the political bourgeoisie. The political bourgeoisie is cowardly."

Mr. W.   Nevertheless there are democrats who are not cowardly and do not contemplate the development of the crisis passively but try to remedy it, if necessary with new laws and bold reforms.

Thomas the Cynic   It is true that there are democrats who realize the utter futility of such methods of government and propose an extension of the democratic principle to spheres of social life from which it has hitherto been excluded, by means of control over a part of private economy, for example. There have been such democrats even in countries where fascism is now triumphant, and they suffered the same fate as the reformist socialists, of whom they are a variation. But the application, even the most kid-gloved application, of control of private economy, when it has been tried in times of acute crisis, has hitherto invariably served only to bring social conflicts to a head, with results, even in the economic sphere, exactly opposite to what was hoped. I confess I am far from being an authority on the subject, but I believe it to be easier to kill a person outright than to hold a knife under his ribs for any length of time. I mean everyone prefers death to prolonged torture. Similarly it is intelligible that capitalists, when their profits are already reduced or uncertain, should prefer sudden expropriation, equivalent to their social death, to the slow torture of continued reforms and controls that leave them neither alive nor dead. Capitalists live in holy terror of the Communists, but they hate the reformists more. A capitalist on whom a new tax is imposed becomes as blasphemous as an "anarchist" or "atheist." He need not even be a big capitalist. Peasants, artisans, professional men behave in exactly the same way, and in Italy and Germany they were among the first to abandon the democratic parties and join the fascist fold. The democrats of whom we spoke can count neither on the richer nor the poorer bourgeoisie to support them in their reforms; nor can they appeal to the active support of the working class, because the latter, being imbued with the Marxist spirit, if they started moving at all, would pass far beyond the limits of partial reforms and would undoubtedly try to shake the very foundations of bourgeois society. Thus the democratic reformers are condemned to the sterile role of prophets in the wilderness. That is the sum total of circumstances that make fascism possible.

Mr. W. Don't you think that Italian and German experience has taught the democrats of other countries anything?

Thomas the Cynic It is difficult to learn from other people's experience, Mr. W. Generally one learns in one's youth and from one's own experience, but bourgeois democracy is no longer young, and the experience of past centuries is not of very much use. A still sadder spectacle is provided by those democratic politicians who really try to understand what is happening and do not look upon present-day events with the weary skepticism of men who have lost all real interest. With the best will in the world, they do not succeed in understanding. Their culture is nineteenth-century culture, evolutionist or positivist. They believe in the slow, gradual, inevitable Progress of the human race. How could they understand what is happening before their eyes today? Other people may try to explain, but that does not help, because a declining political class suffers from all the afflictions of old age, including deafness. Fénelon sent advice and warnings to his king, indirectly in *Télémaque* and directly in his *Lettre à Louis XIV*, but they were useless. How many warnings did Tsar Nicholas II receive? To have understood them he would have had not to have been the Tsar. A declining political class not only lacks the strength, the capacity, the courage to use the material means at its disposal to govern and to defend itself against the foes that assail it; it even lacks the intelligence to understand the continually changing situation. It understands neither what is happening nor what is brewing. That is why bourgeois democracy in Italy and Germany (it was not very old in either country, but in both it was afflicted with precocious senility) was incapable of profiting by the failure of the socialist revolution to reinforce its own position. Thus the working-class parties had shown themselves incapable of achieving power, and the old democratic leaders were no longer capable of holding it. Since nature abhors a vacuum, society was forced to create a substitute—fascism.

Otto Bauer

The Essence of Fascism

In 1939, during the last weeks of his life, Otto Bauer, the exiled leader of Austrian socialism (see note, p. 267), began to write an essay on the nature of fascism. Like other investigators, both socialist and nonsocialist, he was concerned with the problem of the extent to which fascism constitutes still another stage in the development of capitalist society and the extent to which it can usefully be seen as a new mode of social organization. Bauer did not complete his work, but here are some sections from it.

In what way is fascist state control distinguished from the earlier phases of capitalist development? All capitalist production is production for the sake of profit. The movement of the rate of profit has therefore hitherto regulated capitalist economy. It determined the distribution of capital funds and thereby also the distribution of labor power in the individual branches of production. Capital avoided branches of production with lower rates of profit and flowed towards the branches of production in which the rate of profit was highest. The movement of the rates of profit determined the change in the course of the markets. As the rate of profit rose, the capitalists enlarged the existing plants and created new ones; the industries manufacturing the means of production prospered at a rapid pace; from them prosperity spread itself over the entire national economy. As the rate of profit fell, stock prices tumbled; with the crash of the exchange, investment ceased; the production goods industries became idle; the entire national economy fell into a state of depression. This controlling function of the automatic movement of the rate of profit is abolished by fascist state control. No longer the rate of profit in the individual branches of production but the dictate of the state decides in which branches of production new capital accumulation shall be invested. No longer the fluctuations of the general average rate of profit but the will of the state decides on the extent of a new industrial investment and therefore on the course of the market.

It was capitalism's greatest triumph that the unprecedented development of the social productive forces occurred in a society in which the domination of these forces was left exclusively to the individual striving for profit. Since capital now seeks refuge in fascist state control, the capitalist profit economy can no longer be regulated by the automatic movement of the rates of profit and can no longer be governed by the individual striving for profit, but needs social regulation administered by the state. It thus happens that the development of the productive forces of society has come into glaring conflict with the social order based on private ownership of the means of production and, for that reason, governed by individual striving for profit.

In reality the development of the fascist states shows the superiority of the social organization of the economy over capitalist anarchy that leaves the development of production to the sway of the profit motive. The rapid elimination of unemployment in the Third Reich, the precipitate development of new branches of production under the dictate of the fascist regime, the exceedingly rapid economic and therefore also military and political strengthening of Germany, the shifting of the balance of power to the advantage of the fascist states proves nothing else than the superiority of planned social organization over capitalist anarchy.

But as great as the efficiency of fascist state control proves itself to be, it places its increased efficiency, however, exclusively at the service of military and economic preparation for war. It throttles the importation for foreign foodstuffs in order to use the foreign currency for raw materials essential for war. It limits the development of the consumer goods industries by capital accumulation and investment bans and by its regulation of the import of raw materials in order to concentrate the entire social force on the development of the war industries. For that reason it plunges society into peculiar crises. The normal crises of capitalist economy are crises of superabundance; the purchasing power of the masses, having fallen behind the development of their production, does not suffice to acquire the increasing mass of the products of their own labor. Fascist state control, on the contrary, evokes crises of scarcity: even though all the workers are employed, the working class is working feverishly, and the means of production are used to their full capacity, there is a shortage of essential foodstuffs and raw materials. Though the number of employed workers and their productivity is increasing, a rapidly rising proportion of their work serves, not to produce consumer goods for their own needs, but to enlarge the war industries and produce implements of war. It thus diminishes the share of the working class in the product of its own labor. Exploitation of the workers becomes intensified. The intensified exploitation is enforced by fascism's peculiar system of labor organization.

The free wage earner is not, like a slave, the property of a master. He is not, like a serf, compelled to perform forced labor for a feudal master. He disposes freely of his own labor power. Yet, without possessing the means of production, he is forced to sell his labor power to an employer or starve to death. He is a serf, not of a single employer, but of a whole class of employers. It is, however, left to his own decision to which employer he will hire himself and if he will sell his labor power for the wage offered by the employer. He can dissolve the labor contract and leave his place of work, when he hopes to be able to sell his labor power more advantageously somewhere else.

A result of the legal freedom of the worker is his right to organize. If the worker is free to decide for himself at what price he is ready to sell his labor power, then the workers have also the right to agree among themselves that they will refuse their labor to the employers in order to prevent a lowering of or to achieve a betterment of the working conditions, and to form unions to lead these wage struggles and help workers who are engaged in them. The workers' right to strike, the development of unions and of collective agreements are the results of the legal freedom of the worker to dispose of his own labor power.

Fascism has completely demolished this whole structure of rules for labor relations of the private capitalist society. Fascism has dissolved the unions and replaced them with its own organizations. These organizations do not serve the interests of the workers, but are instruments of the state for ruling them. Fascism has abolished the right to strike, has reorganized the relation between employers and workers on military lines, resembling the relation between the officer and his command. Fascism has replaced the shop committees, representing the interests of the workers against the employers, with its committees of trustees, representing the "shops," i.e., the employers against the workers. The freely signed agreement between employers and workers has been replaced by the official decree of wages and working conditions through the labor trustees. The worker is no longer free to decide under what conditions he will sell his labor power. He can no longer refuse his labor in order to prevent a lowering of the working conditions or to achieve a bettering of them. The state tells him at what price he must sell his labor power.

The fascist state has decreed that a large section of the working class—particularly the youth—cannot be employed in important branches of production without a special official permit. It has also decreed that no worker in the metal and building industries as well as in agriculture can leave his work and seek new employment without an official permit in each individual case. The worker can then no longer freely decide to which employer he will hire himself. As the feudal serf was legally compelled to render statute labor to the feudal lord to whom he was bound, so is the worker, in the fascist state, compelled to work for the employer assigned him by the officials of the state. Being bound to this employer's shop, as the feudal serf to his native region, he is in fact his employer's serf.

The fascist state has finally made it the duty of every citizen, without any exception, to take such work as the state's labor officials may assign him. It has in this way generally and basically abolished the freedom of the worker to move, choose his own vocation and conclude labor contracts.

Since German fascism came into power, the number of employed workers in Germany has risen tremendously. The eight-hour-day was shot to pieces; the working day made longer; the methods of work rationalized and intensified. The output of work of the German working class has risen much faster than the number of employed workers. Formerly, in times of rising need for labor, wages rose because the demand for labor was greater; thus the unions could achieve better wages and working conditions. The fascist state, on the other hand, has forbidden and prevented any rise in wages during a time of the fastest rise of the need for labor power. The state's labor trustees have not allowed collective higher wages. Higher wages for the individual were prevented by forbidding workers to change their place of employment in order to obtain higher wages by utilizing the competition amongst the employers for experienced labor. Furthermore, the money wages were lowered through higher taxes, higher premiums for social insurance, and through "voluntary" contributions. The real wages were to a still greater extent lowered through higher prices for the most important necessities of life. The result is, that the total income of the German working class has risen much more slowly than the amount, intensity, and productivity of the labor produced by this working class.

The fascist rules for labor relations form the basis for the corporative economic structure of fascism. The fascist state can decree the imposition of the social labor contracts upon capital and labor only if fascism abolishes the freedom of labor agreements; if it does not leave the settling of wages to the free agreement between employers and workers; but through its own apparatus itself fixes the wages as well as the commodity prices. The fascist rules for labor relations presume the totalitarian political system of suppression and domination by fascism. Only under the terror of the totalitarian system of domination is the working class so intimidated, that it bears without resistance this system of exploitation which is against its own vital interests. The fascist rules for labor relations serve the aggressive imperialism of the fascist state. Only the substantially more severe exploitation of labor enables the fascist state to strengthen its armaments and develop its war industry with extreme rapidity.

Fascism consolidates the power of the state into unbridled totalitarian power. It forcibly and effectively suppresses all resistance of the exploited classes against capitalist exploitation, which it intensifies to the highest degree possible. It subjects the capitalist process of production to its decrees and thereby raises its level of productivity. Fascism thus appears to be the utmost in capitalist victory over proletarian socialism. In spite of this, however, fascism is the product of the deterioration of capitalism. It appears first when the capitalist bourgeoisie no longer can keep the mass of people obedient through moral leadership under democratic forms but only through a dictatorship of terror. It appears first when the economic machinery can no longer be effectively regulated by the desire for profit of individual capitalists but requires the social direction provided by the state.

Under the fascist dictatorship, the social direction of economic life is based upon private ownership of the means of production and transportation. The state leaves the means of production with the private owners who operate only for the sake of profit. It will not, however, allow the operators to dispose of the profits, which it regulates by direct decree. It subordinates all special interests of the individual group of employers to the interests of war armaments, claiming this to be for the common good. The bureaucracy which directs the economic life comes hereby inevitably into conflict with one special interest after the other. These conflicts multiply. This struggle represents the conflict between the social direction of the economic processes and the private ownership of the means of production.

Revolutionary tendencies are inherent in fascist society even though they are hidden by the terror of the fascist dictatorship. These tendencies, however, are themselves full of inner conflicts. The conflict which exists between the social direction of the processes of production and the private ownership of the means of production can be solved in two ways:

Private ownership can shatter the chains of the social direction of the processes of production. Thus society relapses into the form of liberal capitalism. Or the social direction of the processes of production can remove the barriers of private ownership of the means of production. Society thus changes from the social direction of capitalist economy, in the interest of imperialism, into a social organization of economy in the interest of the satisfaction of social needs. In the revolutionary tendencies, inherent in fascist society, is therefore hidden the conflict between liberal and socialist tendencies. This conflict can only be liquidated through a historical process in which the antifascist revolution crushes the fascist corporation and then evolves into the socialist revolution, which rebuilds the organization of society and the direction of the economic life on a higher plane, for a higher purpose.

Paul Sering

Notes on Fascism*

*Paul Sering (b. 1908) was for a while the pen name
of one of the most gifted political analysts of our
time, Richard Lowenthal. A veteran of the German
socialist movement, Lowenthal went into exile directly after Hitler's seizure of power and became associated with a left-socialist refugee group called The
New Beginning. In 1946, Lowenthal wrote a book
on fascism called* Beyond Capitalism, *from which the
following excerpt has been translated into English
for the first time. It provides a remarkably cogent
analysis of Nazism in terms that show both a continuation of the Marxist approach and a readiness to
go beyond its limitations. Lowenthal has since
worked as a journalist in England and is at present
a professor at the Free University in Berlin. Among
his publications is* World Communism: The Disintegration of a Secular Faith *(1964).*

Capitalist planning tends by its very nature towards armaments and imperialist expansion. The monopolistic
trusts which, under capitalist planning, renounce their
sovereign freedom of action in exchange for a decisive
influence on the contents of the plan, consciously push in
this direction as it corresponds to their interests. But this
tendency of "planned capitalism," this pressure of big
capital, does not prevail automatically. Only the outcome
of political struggles among the most diverse interests for
the control of planning can settle the question whether a

---

* Title supplied by editor.

(technically successful) imperialist type of planning or a (necessarily imperfect) policy of planning for welfare is actually adopted in any given situation.

Fascism as a Political Movement

To label the National Socialist regime in Germany as *fascist* and to define fascism as the rule of the most aggressive and reactionary sections of monopoly capital is, therefore, no explanation of the Nazi victory of 1933 and the twelve years of Nazi rule that followed it. It is not even a satisfactory description of the forces behind Nazism. To realize this, one need only consider the fact that Italian fascism governed between 1922 and 1934 with an economic policy quite different from that later followed by the Nazis: the Fascist economy in Italy was not, until 1934, a planned economy as defined here. Mussolini's economic policy in that period did not essentially go beyond the policy of subsidies traditionally practised by capitalist governments; nor could it protect the Italian economy from being surprised and severely shaken by the Great Depression, just as was the economy of every capitalist country. Italy took planning measures only under the pressure of the economic sanctions imposed by the League of Nations during the Ethiopian War and under the inspiration of the model offered by Hitler Germany. From then on, developments in the two countries did indeed run parallel—though with Germany, thanks to her modern economic structure and her heavy-industry base, always in the van.

Nonetheless, to call the Hitler regime *fascist* is scientifically justified from the *political* viewpoint. For these two regimes—and they alone—shared decisive features in their forms of political rule and in the forces on which they relied. We must now attempt to discover the specific character of those new political systems, and the precise nature of their affinity with imperialist planning.

Its Social Base

Both Italian fascism and German National Socialism were organized mass movements before they seized power, in contrast to authoritarian regimes of the traditional type, which share with them their oppressive character but not their active harnessing of mass movements. In both cases, the appeal of those mass movements rested upon three main slogans: nationalism; attack on parliamentary democracy; and struggle against the workers' movement. In both Italy and Germany, fascism, unlike all earlier political movements, was not representative of one particular unchanging class or group interest. Both fascism and National Socialism were products of a crisis; both gathered in their ranks the victims of political and economic instability from all classes: bankrupt employers and intellectuals without jobs; *déclassé* officers and debt-ridden peasants; artisans and shopkeepers crushed by competition; workers made desperate by long-term unemployment; front-line veterans unable to find their way back into a disorganized civilian life; and youths deprived of the chance to find a normal occupation. These elements could no longer draw hope from their role in the productive process; they looked for salvation to the state—a "strong" national state.

In Italy, the nationalist wave arose from disappointment with the results of victory in World War I, in Germany from the effects of defeat. Italy lacked democratic experience because her prewar parliament had been little more than an arena for narrow cliques of professional politicians, with no participation of the masses; Germany, because the Reichstag had no constitutional control over the government until 1918. It Italy, believing Catholics did not participate in political life until World War I, while the workers' movement had no hope of winning government responsibility. In the Kaiser's Germany, the two largest mass movements, the Catholics and the Social Democrats, had been barred from effective access to governmental power. In Italy, the young democracy fell into a mortal crisis because the class problems of a semifeudal society required a revolutionary solution, but the workers' movement was neither prepared to take power by democratic nor by violent means. By a combination of negative radicalism and lack of a positive sense of purpose, it helped to paralyze the untried democratic institutions, yet disappointed those who hoped that it would replace them by a "proletarian dictatorship." Germany's young democracy barely survived the postwar crisis, but failed to destroy the traditional power bases of antidemocratic groups in the state machine and economic life: it fell a victim to the Great Depression, because the struggle between incompatible interests paralyzed the parliamentary machine, and because both wings of the workers' movement proved equally incapable of convincing the masses that they could show a way out.

The Centralized Party

The economic crisis in which fascism seized power thus offered abundant food for antiparliamentary and antisocialist propaganda, in both Italy and Germany. But the Fascist parties were more than mere engines of propaganda geared to the exploitation of mass despair: they were terroristic fighting organizations with a centralized military structure, adapted for demonstrating their strength, intimidating their enemies, and taking over the state apparatus as soon as the party entered the government. The acts of violence committed by the *squadristi,* the SA, and the SS were not just expressions of natural brutality but part of a well-planned system, aimed at impressing people with the strongest of all propaganda arguments in a situation of desperate political and economic insecurity: "We want power—and are strong enough to conquer it." The *"Fuehrer* principle," i.e., the centralist design of the party, copied from military models, was a necessity both for this form of the struggle for power and for the next step, the merging of the fascist party machine with the equally centralized machine of the state bureaucracy. For the technique of the fascist struggle for power is illegal, but not revolutionary. It does not shrink from any crime, yet does not aim to overthrow the state apparatus, only to take it over in "strictly legal" fashion.

The Total State

The system of government set up by Italian fascism and German National Socialism after their victory shows the same crucial parallels as their situations of origin and their political and organizational techniques. It is the system of the "total state," the centralised one-party state, in which the ruling party holds a monopoly control of all forms of social organization, as well as of information and propaganda. Italian fascism gropingly developed the "Fuehrer principle" in its own party and the transition to the one-party state; German National Socialism, having learned the lessons of its model, accomplished in months what the latter had done in years. It started by crushing the workers' movement; it went on to ban all other parties, including its former coalition partners; finally, it subjected all other organizations, from the newly created compulsory organizations of workers and peasants down to the last sports club and savings association, to the control of imposed Nazi *Fuehrers*. It began by forbidding the press of the opposition parties; it went on to a *Gleichschaltung* (forced coordination) of the nonparty press; it ended by subjecting all sources of information not only to negative censorship but to positive directives, thus turning them into tools of government propaganda. This network of all-pervasive propaganda and all-embracing organizations, intended not merely to suppress critical opinions and opposing organizations in the manner of old-fashioned police states, but to get the very last subject into its propagandist and organizational grip and mobilize him for the goals of the regime, is the true hallmark of the twentieth-century total state.

Dictatorship is the abolition of all legal restraints on the power of the state. Total dictatorship is the total abolition of the rights of the individual, not only for the duration of an emergency but on principle: such rights exist only as long as they do not conflict with the purposes of the state; in a totalitarian regime there exist no rights against the state. Protective custody and concentration camps, special tribunals and judgments rendered on instruction from the political authorities in accordance with *gesundes Volksempfinden* (literally "the healthy instinct of the people"), arbitrary murders, arrests and confiscations justified by a freely interpreted "reason of state," all these are consequences that flow inevitably from the fundamental principle of total dictatorship.

Fascism and Capitalist Property

The arbitrary violation of all rights in particular cases contrasts conspicuously with another essential trait of fascist dictatorship: the maintenance of the right of property in principle. Under fascism the individual can be deprived of his property at any time, because he belongs to the political opposition, because he is a Jew, because he belongs to a subject nation, or, even in the case of a big capitalist, because he fails to conform to the economic plan. But capitalist property as the basis of the traditional class structure is preserved, and the composition of the economic oligarchy remains, on the whole, intact; it is merely supplemented by rising elements from the fascist party. Not only did the Nazis fail to nationalize a single privately owned industry; while carrying out their economic planning, they actually returned to private ownership majority blocks of shares of vital capitalist groups which the German government had taken over during the Great Depression. They did not do so out of respect for legal titles, which meant nothing to them, nor from a belief in free enterprise, which they subjected to their plan, but because they realized that the political and social hierarchies are naturally linked: he who wants to establish the authority of the state as unassailable would only make his task more difficult if he undermined the authority of the exploiting class. When the Nazis bestowed upon the employers the title of *Betriebsfuehrer* (*Fuehrer* of the enterprise), they gave this awareness conscious expression by translating into their jargon the traditional principle that the owner should be "master in his house."

On the basis of the Italian and German examples, we have described the fascist movement and the fascist state as political phenomena, and not as mere products of economic developments. A fascist movement cannot be produced at will by monopoly capital; its birth presupposes a crisis of democracy, its victory a failure of the workers' movement. The fascist movement, its leaders included, is a product of decomposition, arising from the crisis of free capitalism and from the crisis of democratic institutions conditioned by it. But once such a movement develops, it becomes a natural ally of the aggressive-imperialist groups of monopoly capital. It is therefore immaterial whether the individual fascist leader honestly believes in his ideas or is paid from the beginning to spread them: sooner or later he is bound to be supported by monopoly capital.

Fascism and Planned Imperialism

To realize this, we need only reflect for a moment on the political requirements of planned imperialism. Imperialist planning, the subordination of the entire economy to the needs of nonproductive armaments and expansion, is the form of planning least compatible with the free representation of interests in general and with a free workers' movement in particular. Imperialist planning means that, in time of peace and without any external compulsion, productive forces are systematically diverted from the production of goods that would be useful for raising the standard of living. It requires that the resistance of the workers against this policy be broken, and this in a situation where planning leads to full employment, so that the natural economic position of the workers is strong. Imperialist planning demands that the labor market be replaced by direction of labor, the reserve army of unemployed workers by a reserve army of labor slaves. This is impossible as long as democratic freedoms exist. But neither is it possible for a reactionary police state which thinks it can break the labor unions simply by forbidding them. Total preparation for war demands a total organizational integration and a total propagandistic remodeling of the masses by the total state; and only a regime that can rely, over and above the state apparatus, on the voluntary support of a mass movement which provides it with cadres for the leadership and control of all mass organizations, can solve this task. Fascism is therefore, we repeat, not the automatic result of the wishes of monopoly capital and of the economic tendency toward planned imperialism; it is a product of the capitalist crisis, which makes its appearance only under certain *politi-*

cal circumstances. But the existence of such circumstances and the victory of fascism are *preconditions* for the possibility of consistent imperialist planning; in that sense fascism is the classic political form of planned imperialism.

Historical Background of German Nazism

It is evident that the political conditions for the victory of fascism include those rooted in the entire national history and way of life of the peoples concerned. We have already referred to some of the more obvious factors of political and social history, e.g., the lack of a well-developed democratic tradition in Italy and Germany, the existence of semifeudal landlordism in southern Italy and of an essentially antidemocratic state apparatus, taken over from the Empire, in Germany. Another such factor was the young nationalism of two peoples that, owing to an unfortunate history, achieved national unity only in the nineteenth century and therefore came at the end of the line when the earth was shared out among the nations of Europe.

The Revolt Against Europe

But the role of history in shaping the conditions for the origin and victory of fascism far transcends the contribution of particular economic, social, and political institutions, of the tangible remains of a predemocratic past. German National Socialism for one has unleashed such an explosive force of destruction, such a berserk fury in its denial of the recognized values of the European tradition, that its roots must be sought in a different dimension of historical and social causation. The bestial conception of human existence, consistently carried through from theoretical racism via the "destruction of biologically unworthy lives" to the extermination of millions of human beings by methods hitherto reserved for noxious insects, was more than an epiphenomenon of a total war economy or a consequence of total dictatorship. It reflected a more profound historical process: the nihilist revolt against Europe.

This revolt has a general European and a specific German side. The humanist tradition which, in its Christian, liberal, or socialist form, has been the foundation of any civilized society in Europe is, like any achievement of civilization, forever threatened by the return of chaos. The forms of social organization change; the cultural values retain their binding force only if their practical meaning for the rules of conduct is ever interpreted anew in the light of the changing needs of society, without a break in their continuity. Every age of acute social transformation is an age of acute danger to civilization. Every new social formation, every movement or institution which becomes a focus for human devotion and self-sacrifice, may become the factor that breaks up an entire system of values, unless it can find its place within it.

Cracks in the Humanist Tradition

The development of national consciousness and the rise of sovereign states in Europe have always implied such a danger: the danger of an hypostasis of the nation state as an absolute that would destroy civilization. The development of the market economy and the penetration of a society based on the division of labor by the egoistic rationality of economic liberalism have always carried the danger that human society would degenerate into a war of all against all, only externally regulated by the rules of the market game.

The attempt to deal with human and social problems in terms of biological, i.e., zoological, analogies became an intellectual fashion in the nineteenth century, starting from the parallel drawn between Darwin's "natural selection" and liberal economic competition. The shock administered to the social order by the French Revolution produced, in the Frenchman Gobineau, an ancestor of Hitler's and Rosenberg's racial theory. Rosenberg explains the Russian Revolution in the same way as Gobineau had explained the French: he was the first to see the revolt of the masses as an uprising of *Untermenschen* (subhuman creatures) against the "higher" race.

The "achievement" of the Nazis lies in combining all these elements of disintegration: the counter-revolution-

ary theory of the biologically given upper class with the
liberal belief in the inevitable victory of the stronger, and
with the nationalist identification of one's own people
with the highest racial heritage, at once most creative
and predestined to rule all others. For the understanding
of history and society, as much value as a magic formula.
But when this formula was recited over the witches'
cauldron of postwar Germany, all hell broke loose.

The Crisis Point of a Value System

A cultural community, a value system are always put in
jeopardy when their values fail to be applied to the main
social problems of the hour. The discrepancy between the
accepted moral norms and actual human behavior, always
present in any society, becomes unbearable in such crises;
values which have lost their relevance in real life come to
be regarded by the masses as mere upper class hypocrisy,
and thus lose their binding force.

Such a failure became visible in several ways in the
European crisis that started with World War I. The old
economic, political, and social elites proved unable to
show a way out of the crisis of capitalism. The liberal
spokesmen denied the existence of a fundamental crisis
and the need to take new paths. The Christian churches
spoke of a moral crisis, but were not prepared to apply
Christian ethics to the concrete problems of the time; at
best they recommended palliatives and shrunk from basic
economic and social changes. Defense of the continuity
of property rights that had lost their content and of the
authority of the failing political and economic elites
seemed more important to them than preservation of the
continuity of humanistic values through a renewal of
their practical content. And the democratic socialists,
who alone advocated a basic institutional transformation
within the European tradition, failed to demonstrate, in
the critical fifteen years between 1918 and 1933, an effective method for achieving their objectives.

. . . And International Causes

The failure to tackle the task of economic and social
reform was matched by an equally fatal failure to reorder

international relations. World War I had been fought and won by the Western Allies in the name of democracy, the right of national self-determination, and the need for a supranational order; it had ended with the founding of democratic states throughout Europe, with national self-determination applied to a higher degree than ever before, and with the first attempt to create a League of Nations. But the new political order for the old continent was constructed without regard for its economic necessities; it was linked to a ruinous system of war debts and reparations; it was backed by a group of powers that, with revolutionary Russia kept out and America withdrawing into isolation, was not, in the long run, strong enough to give it stability even in terms of mere power politics.

Germany as Focus of the Crisis

The revolt against declining capitalism, against the domination of Europe by the Western powers, and against the democratic and humanist ideals preached but not practised by "Western capitalism," thus became fused in the minds, passions, and actions of millions of people; and nowhere did it find a more fertile soil than in Germany, defeated on the battlefield and in a state of social upheaval. Here, the ideology and practice of economic liberalism had always appeared as Western imports to be kept out by protective tariffs in the national interest. Here, too, the national idea had come into conflict with the democratic ever since national unity had been achieved, not by a democratic popular movement, but by the military power of Bismarck's Prussia. Here, the bourgeois way of life had never struck deep roots; and the uncertainties of the rapid transition from the patriarchal norms and habits of a semifeudal absolutism into the unknown future of an organized industrial society were reflected in the intense historical consciousness of Germany as a "wanderer between two worlds" and in the readiness to believe in the unique historical mission of the German people.

In choosing its name, National Socialism proclaimed its intention to fuse the two sources of revolutionary energy, the demands for national and for social justice, into the stream of a single mass movement. Yet it directed the explosive energies that were latent in the unstable German situation to a wholly destructive goal, the denial of any binding moral order. The Marxian prophecy that the alternative to socialism would be a decline into barbarism became terrible reality in the nihilism of the Third Reich. The wanderer between two worlds became a wanderer into nothingness.

TRANSLATED BY I. A. LANGNAS

Lucien Laurat

Collectivism, Modern Technique, and Democracy*

Lucien Laurat (b. 1898) is a veteran of the French radical movement, whose book Marxism and Democracy, *published in England in 1940, deserves to be better known than it is. Laurat was intensely aware that the growth of the modern state as a seemingly autonomous and uncontainable social power raises urgent problems for socialists who had previously tended to assume that a mere transfer of political authority from "them" to "us" would solve most problems. Here he examines the relationship between the growth of industrial bureaucracy, massive technique, and the state machine, on the one hand, and efforts to establish popular democratic control, on the other.*

We have already pointed to the striking analogies to be observed in the economic structures of all the principal industrial countries. Whether it is the United States, Great Britain, Germany, France, Italy, or Russia, their economic systems develop in the same general direction and their points in common may be summed up as follows:

1. The increasing organic fusion between the state and the economic system; the development, at first spontaneous and then more and more deliberate, of "control levers"; the rapidly increasing centralization of all economic activity; the development of decentralized control

---

* Title supplied by editor.

lacking coordination in the direction of centralized and coordinated control.

2. The development of property towards more and more collectivist forms (increase in the numbers of the shareholding public, the decline of the private sector of the economic system before the advance of the public sector); the broadening of social legislation; the development of increasingly collectivist legal forms.

3. However, this process of centralization and collectivization is taking place on a basis of contradictions: the control levers and such property as has already been collectivized are not in the hands of society as a whole; a small minority controls these levers and administers this collectivized property exclusively in its own interests. In the totalitarian countries, the people are prevented by violence from expressing their will, and in the democratic countries they still passively tolerate this situation.

4. This small minority occupying all the commanding positions is recruited from all social classes. Originally they appeared in the guise of a monopolist and finance plutocracy, the master of organized capitalism and the immediate beneficiary of the fascist movement. However, in the fascist countries it has to give ground under the pressure of the bureau-technocracy it has raised to power, and it risks having to abdicate before it altogether. In the democratic countries, this plutocracy seeks to utilize the technicians, but there as elsewhere these technicians are beginning to turn against them. In Russia, where the November Revolution overthrew all the old forms, the plutocracy was destroyed and replaced by a bureaucracy, which is now beginning to develop more and more into a technocracy. The development towards a more and more controlled economy creates, together with the necessary control organs, the technicians capable of using them.

The economic and social characteristics we have just sketched are common to all the countries mentioned. The varying political regimes and the nature of the upheavals which gave rise to some of them have obviously given special characteristics to the economic framework of each country, but these are only of superficial interest when compared with their fundamental resemblances. We see no cause to be surprised at the existence of such differences. The development of capitalism also took on many and varied forms; in one country the development was uninterrupted, in another it proceeded by revolutionary fits and starts; in one country it adapted itself to a relatively democratic regime, and in another it passed through periods of terrorist dictatorship. However, despite all this the fact remains that these widely varying surface differences, which have been interpreted in so many different ways, were all expressions of one and the same process of development. In every case the final result was the triumph of nineteenth-century capitalism, whose fundamental traits are characteristic of all the advanced countries of our day.

We are faced with the same situation again. The new economic structure which is arising out of the convulsions of decadent capitalism is taking shape under varying conditions, and is developing in various countries within the framework of capitalism, more vigorous or more mature in some countries, less vigorous or less mature in others. The political convulsions may provoke a premature delivery (in Germany and Italy) or lead to a caesarian operation (in Russia). We must decide once and for all not to let ourselves be hypnotized by this or that particular feature of this or that regime or political event, but to keep our minds fixed on those factors which are generally valid and common to the fundamental economic evolution of them all. If, instead of studying the general economic characteristics of adolescent capitalism, Marx had confined himself to enumerating the differences between the *political* regimes of Great Britain, France, and Germany, he would never have been able to provide us with the indispensable key for the understanding of modern social development.

To a certain extent the totalitarian countries show us what is likely to be the future of Western Europe and the United States, though not necessarily the future of their *political institutions*. We categorically reject the absurd idea that all countries must in any case and under all circumstances pass through a fascist or Bolshevist dictatorship. However, from the standpoint of the *economic structure*, it appears quite certain to us that the "intermediary forms" to which British, French, and American capitalism will ultimately give birth will be a more and more controlled economic system with increasingly collectivist forms. Seeing that not everyone is qualified to control economy, those who do so will inevitably be the specialists, or, if you like, the technicians, and it is here that the *technocratic menace* looms up because we must make a clear distinction between the technician pure and simple and the technocrat.

For a long time the great majority of the technicians were absolutely hostile to the idea of socialism and to trade-union organization and action. They thought themselves better able to defend their own interests by making common cause with the capitalists against the working class. This mental attitude corresponded to the social relations existing throughout the past century. In a period when the shareholding public was still comparatively restricted in numbers, and when the employers owned and directed their businesses themselves, the technicians collaborated closely with their employers, and they enjoyed an income which allowed them a reasonable hope of one day rising into the ranks of the possessing classes.

Today the situation is different. The great spread of polytechnical institutions has led to the overcrowding of all the technical professions, to widespread unemployment amongst technicians (even before the great economic crisis), and to the great deterioration of their conditions. Industrial concentration and the gradual elimination of smaller undertakings now deprive the great majority of the technicians of all hope of one day rising into the ranks of a higher social class. The fact that joint-stock companies have become the dominant form in modern economic life has created new relations between the technicians and their employers. Instead of an employer directing his own business, there is now a plutocratic oligarchy which commands without working, and rules without in reality directing the business. Formerly the close collaborators of their employers, today the technicians have become the mere servants of the plutocratic administrators. Today the technicians are becoming more and more conscious of their situation, and they are beginning to rebel against the humiliating way in which they are being treated by people who they are gradually recognizing as mere parasites.

The technocratic doctrine, which arose a few years ago in the United States, was to a great extent the expression of that revolt. In proclaiming that the economic system was in reality directed by technicians, the technocrats expressed their opposition to the dictatorship of the monopolist and finance plutocracy, but at the same time they opposed the aspirations of the working class, which they regarded as nothing but a passive instrument for the execution of their orders. We must not seek to hide the fact that such a mentality is extremely dangerous.

In face of the universal crisis, an expression of the decadence of capitalism, the working-class movement and the technocracy are in agreement in their belief that a radical transformation, both political and economic, is urgently necessary, and that the anarchical economy of our day must be disciplined and controlled. However, whilst the technocrats aspire to substitute their own rule (hence the word "technocracy") for that of the monopolist and finance plutocracy, socialism and trade unionism seek to place the general interests of the community as a whole above all particular interests, including that of the technicians. In short, they believe that it is not a question of replacing one set of privileges by another, but of abolishing privileges altogether. It was not by accident that the doctrine of technocracy arose in the United States, a new and young country, where the revolt against privilege takes on utopian forms just as it did a century ago in this old Europe of ours. A few years back we described technocracy as "the utopian socialism of the twentieth century." It might also be described as Saint-Simonism on a Yankee scale—which would amount to much the same thing.

We know very well that a growing section of the technicians, particularly in France, is abandoning this technocratic mentality and that it is giving disinterested devotion to the organizations of the working class, to which in any case the technicians belong both socially and economically. However, we also know that the technicians perform a directing function in the economic process and that under certain circumstances they might develop into a new privileged caste, as we can see more and more clearly in Russia today. This danger will even grow as the state penetrates further and further into the economic system, and we have already seen that a state which increasingly assumes economic functions may easily develop into a forcing house for a new class of exploiters.

The technicians are members of the wage-earning class, but those amongst them who occupy directive positions come under that particular category of variable capital, which Marx has called "wages of superintendence" and which we have designated by vs (value surplus). During the course of capitalist development and parallel with the impersonalization of capital, vs has separated itself from p (profits), and now approximates to v (value). However, this development towards a generalized wage-earning class has not effaced the difference between v and vs. This new relation between v and vs is still concealed both under organized capitalism and in the fascist economic system. It is cloaked by the fact that by far the greater part of p is seized by the plutocracy and that the domination of v and vs by p is much greater than the domination of v by vs. This cloak falls altogether in the soviet economic system in which the revenue of the bureaucratic oligarchy presents itself in the form of vs and includes also p.

Thus we must ask ourselves seriously whether the transitional economic system which is developing is not characterized, at least to a certain extent, by the preponderance, not to say the predominance, of the technicians, the term technicians embracing not only engineers, but all those who occupy directive positions. In view of the increasing penetration of the state into the economic system —a penetration which is particularly deep in the totalitarian countries—a growing number of administrative functions are becoming economic functions. The bureaucrats themselves are beginning to appear as the technicians of administration. In this way the question arises of whether the relation between v and vs conceals *a new class antagonism* destined to develop during the period of transition, whether this presents itself in the form of an economic autocracy (Germany, Italy, and Russia) or in the form of a "mixed economy" as provided for in the Labour Plan of the French C.G.T.

Class antagonism is another way of saying the exploitation of man by man. This exploitation of man by man has taken on many different forms throughout the ages, its three principal forms being slavery, serfdom, and wage slavery. The first two were based on oppression *legally sanctioned*. The last category is based on the liberty of the worker, the exploitation of the wage worker being accomplished *solely by economic laws*, and not by any written law whatever. However, one condition is necessary to bring about this state of affairs: the masses of the people must be prevented from obtaining possession of the instruments of production. The mechanism of capitalism undertakes to do this on its own, and only where it proves too weak to do so does written law intervene to make good the deficiency. Compared with slavery and serfdom, modern capitalism represents a great step forward. Under capitalism, exploitation is no longer founded on a legal basis but exists purely as the result of economic factors.

The totalitarian economic systems seem to be a relapse into forced labour, into precapitalist forms of exploitation. However, on examining the relation between v and vs we observe that this constraint is merely superimposed on an already existing inequality not caused by it. The fact that the technocracy appropriates a disproportionate share of the national revenue, that the magnitude of vs is disproportionate as compared with v (a fact particularly obvious in Russia, where there is no plutocracy) is due to *economic causes*. In short, this constraint does nothing but reinforce an already existing inequality.

Nevertheless, we must not lose sight of the fact that this new antagonism, between v and vs, reflects *a difference of degree and not of kind*. The labour of superintendence and direction is better paid because it is more highly qualified labour, and it will remain so even without constraint and without dictatorship as long as the requisite qualifications are rare. All attempts at excessive leveling in this respect would endanger the smooth working of the economic system so long as there is not a sufficient number of competent technicians available, that is to say, as long as the requisite qualifications have not been obtained by a growing number of people, thereby losing their rarity.

Only the higher education of the masses can remedy a state of affairs in which vs is greater than the remuneration of unqualified labour. The quantitative discrepancy between v and vs will disappear only when a leveling is brought about by raising the general cultural standards of the people. Here we have the famous "apprenticeship fees" of which Lenin spoke and which the workers are obliged to pay to their specialists as long as the latter succeed in maintaining their cultural monopoly.

It is a different matter altogether with category p, which belongs by right to society as a whole once the plutocracy has been expelled from its positions. After the liquidation of the plutocracy, the receivers of vs, now established at the commanding points of circulation abandoned by the plutocracy, will quite naturally tend to seize p, or as much of it as they can. This is the danger which we regard as one of the fundamental characteristics of our epoch and of the intermediate economic forms.

The best antidote to this danger appears to us to be democracy. Under the leaden cloak of dictatorship, the bureau-technocracy is free to dispose of p just as it likes. Only the existence of democracy can prevent this. Democracy certainly cannot do away with the necessity of paying "apprenticeship fees," but it can confine these fees to vs, and prevent their becoming larger at the expense of any considerable part of what was s-v.

Democracy—in other words, public control—is the condition *sina qua non* for any collectivist economic system. Without democracy, and unless the community as a whole enjoys an absolute right of control and decision, collective property is an empty phrase. It is not sufficient that a dictatorial clique should proclaim that property is collective. Property cannot be collective until the community as a whole is free to dispose of it as it wishes.

The untrammelled exercise of these public liberties is an indispensable condition for the smooth functioning of an economic system, of which an important, and even vital, sector is withdrawn from the influence of the automatic laws of the liberal economic system. The rentability of this sector, in which competition no longer operates, cannot be assured except by democratic control exercised by the community as a whole. In an economic system more and more penetrated by the state, democracy becomes an economic factor of the greatest importance, whereas in the epoch of economic liberalism the democratic or dictatorial character of a political regime was of secondary importance for economic life. On the other hand, a democratic organization of economic life becomes a more and more indispensable condition for political democracy today. Political democracy is threatened and weakened by economic oligarchies whether they originate in the category p or the category vs. Political democracy and economic democracy are becoming more and more interdependent. One cannot exist without the other.

In any case, democracy is nothing but a mold, a written law. The existence of this mold, as necessary as it is, is far from being sufficient in itself. This democratic mold offers immense possibilities, but these possibilities can become realities only if the following conditions are fulfilled:

1. The *democratic will* of the majority of the people; without this democratic will the first dictator who comes along can overthrow the democratic regime without striking a blow.

2. The *competence* of the masses of the people; it is useless to have wonderful democratic machinery if the masses of the people do not know how to use it.*

In other words, if democracy is to have any real vitality

---

* One can only laugh at the grandiloquent phrases of certain frothy individuals who shriek of "total democracy" at the tops of their voices, but wisely refrain from telling us exactly what they mean by it. In those countries which enjoy wide public liberties and which possess representative institutions based on universal suffrage, the greater or lesser degree of perfection of democracy depends on the maturity and the ability of the masses of the people. "Total" democracy cannot be conceived of except on the basis of a maturity equally "total" of the masses of the people, and unfortunately we have not yet arrived at that stage.

it must be based on the *competence and maturity* of the masses of the people. The degree of emancipation of labour possible of attainment in a given historical epoch is directly dependent on the degree of maturity and competence of the workers and on their ability to control the collectivist forms which are developing more or less automatically before their eyes.

Alas, democracy appears greatly discredited in our day! If it were only a question of the thunderous speeches of dictators periodically proclaiming "the bankruptcy of democracy," we could easily console ourselves, but even in the ranks of socialists there are antidemocratic tendencies whose spokesmen assure us that democracy has had its day. We humbly proclaim ourselves old-fashioned enough to reject this point of view completely.

The enemies of democracy make the undoubted weaknesses of parliamentarianism a pretext for recommending systems either frankly dictatorial or camouflaged with the name "direct democracy." We agree entirely that the referendum is an excellent democratic instrument, and we should like to see it introduced in France to settle important questions. However, when, under the pretext of "correcting" and "improving" democracy, people try to take us back to antediluvian democratic forms, we are compelled to protest vigorously.

Where we find that democracy is imperfect, the cause is generally a lack of sufficient parliamentarianism rather than the contrary. Like all human institutions, parliamentarianism is obviously not perfect, but like other human institutions, it is also open to amendment and improvement. However, in order to improve it we must first obtain as clear an idea as possible of its real shortcomings. Above all, we must take care not to blame it for faults for which it is not responsible.

Providing it is accompanied by all those liberties which are the essence of democracy, parliament may be called the mirror of public opinion. If a man looks at himself in a mirror and finds the reflected image rather depressing, that may be the fault of the mirror; on the other hand it may be that the features of the beholder are far from perfect. What we are now calling "the crisis of parliamentarianism" is due to a little of both. Parliament reflects the image of society as it is, with all its divisions and hostilities. The fact that today many parliaments exhaust themselves in sterile palaver and find their capacity for action greatly reduced, is often because the opposing political forces are more or less equal in strength and mutually paralyse each other in the representative assemblies. In this case it is not the mirror we must blame but the ugliness of capitalist society in its decadence, and there is no point whatever in breaking the mirror.

The parliamentary system certainly has its defects. In other words, the mirror is not at all what it should be. In this connection the essential defect of parliamentarianism today arises from the fact that the state is taking over an increasing number of economic tasks. Parliament, which is the backbone of the modern democratic state, is being called upon more and more frequently to deal with economic questions of vital importance. Unfortunately members of parliament are almost always elected on pure and simple political programs (only socialist parties represent an exception to this rule and have done for the past fifty years) and they are plainly incompetent to discuss such matters fruitfully.

The tendency to organic fusion of the state and the economic system has given rise in certain quarters to the idea of reforming parliamentarianism on the basis of two assemblies, the one political and the other economic. This idea, in itself quite an excellent one, will nevertheless prove impossible of useful realization, unless such an economic assembly is the expression of *economic democracy*. If, on the other hand, its realization were left in the hands of a privileged clique, democracy would have nothing whatever to gain from it.

However, in our opinion the time has come to consider seriously a reform of parliamentarianism. This reform should be carried out by extending public liberties, developing economic democracy, and adapting the parliamentary regime to those new and ever more pressing economic necessities which are arising in our day.* At the same time we should like to point out to the socialist

---

* See my book, *Economie dirigée et socialisation*, Part IV, Chap. 4, where we deal more thoroughly with this question.

detractors of parliamentarianism: (1) up to the present, no democratic form has been found which provides the masses of the people with a better expression of their will; (2) the best way to repair the defects of the parliamentary system, and to save it from the paralysis which results from a general equilibrium of opposing forces, would be to send more socialists to parliament.

As far as democracy itself is concerned, together with Marx and Engels we consider it the condition *sine qua non* of all fruitful socialist activity, because without it collective property would be inconceivable. We believe, with Karl Kautsky, that "to doubt democracy is in reality to doubt the proletariat itself," and that, in general, the existence of a dictatorial and authoritarian government at a given moment proves, for this moment at least, "the inability of the proletariat to emancipate itself, because no proletariat capable of doing so would tolerate for one moment any government determining what it should read, what it should hear, and what it should do."*

---

* Karl Kautsky, *Die materialistische Geschichtsauffassung,*Vol. II, pp. 469–470.

Rudolf Hilferding

State Capitalism or Totalitarian State Economy

*One of the two or three most distinguished econo-
mists produced by European Social Democracy, Rudolf Hilferding (1877–1941), along with Otto Bauer,
was a leading spokesman of "Austro-Marxism." Hilferding's major work was Das Finanzkapital, 1910,
a detailed and ambitious Marxist analysis of modern
capitalism. Forced to go into exile by the advent of
Nazism, Hilferding spent his last years in Paris. During the war he was betrayed by the Vichy regime
and murdered by the Gestapo.*

*The following article, first printed in 1940, ap-
peared in a Russian-language journal, the Socialist
Courier, issued in Paris. It was written as a discussion of the views advanced by a British socialist,
R. L. Worrall, who had posed the theory that the economic system of Stalinist Russia was "state capitalism." Hilferding's article is notable as an early statement of the view that in the totalitarian society
established in Russia, neither capitalist nor socialist
norms apply. Instead, argues Hilferding, a new social order, "a totalitarian state economy," has
emerged.*

The concept of "state capitalism" can scarcely pass the
test of serious economic analysis. Once the state becomes
the exclusive owner of all means of production, the functioning of a capitalist economy is rendered impossible by
destruction of the mechanism which keeps the life-blood
of such a system circulating. A capitalist economy is a
market economy. Prices, which result from competition

among capitalist owners (it is this competition that "in the last instance" gives rise to the law of value), determine what and how much is produced, what fraction of the profit is accumulated, and in what particular branches of production this accumulation occurs. They also determine how in an economy, which has to overcome crises again and again, proportionate relations among the various branches of production are reestablished whether in the case of simple or expanded reproduction.

A capitalist economy is governed by the laws of the market (analyzed by Marx) and the autonomy of these laws constitutes the decisive symptom of the capitalist system of production. A state economy, however, eliminates precisely the autonomy of economic laws. It represents not a market but a consumers' economy. It is no longer price but rather a state planning commission that now determines what is produced and how. Formally, prices and wages still exist, but their function is no longer the same; they no longer determine the process of production, which is now controlled by a central power that fixes prices and wages. Prices and wages become means of distribution which determine the share that the individual receives out of the sum total of products that the central power places at the disposal of society. They now constitute a technical form of distribution which is simpler than direct individual allotment of products, which no longer can be classed as merchandise. Prices have become symbols of distribution and no longer comprise a regulating factor in the economy. While maintaining the form, a complete transformation of function has occurred.

Both the "stimulating fire of competition" and the passionate striving for profit, which provide the basic incentive of capitalist production, die out. Profit means individual appropriation of surplus products and is therefore possible only on the basis of private ownership. But, objects Mr. Worrall, did Marx not consider accumulation as an essential earmark of capitalism, and does not accumulation play a decisive role in the Russian economy? Is that not state capitalism?

Mr. Worrall has overlooked one slight detail; namely,

that Marx refers to the accumulation of *capital*, of an ever-increasing amount of the means of production which produce profit and the appropriation of which supplies the driving force to capitalist production. In other words, he refers to the accumulation of value which creates surplus value, i.e., a specifically *capitalist* process of expanding economic activity.

On the other hand, the accumulation of means of production and of products is so far from being a specific feature of capitalism that it plays a decisive part in all economic systems, except perhaps in the most primitive collecting of food. In a consumer economy, in an economy organized by the state, there is not accumulation of values but of consumers' goods, products that the central power wants in order to satisfy consumers' needs. The mere fact that the Russian state economy accumulates does not make it a capitalist economy, for it is not capital that is being accumulated. Mr. Worrall's argument is based on a gross confusion between value and use-value. And he really believes that a socialist economy could do without accumulation!

But what then (and here we come to the basic question) is that central power that rules over the Russian economy? Trotsky and Worrall reply: "Bureaucracy." But while Trotsky refuses to consider the bureaucracy as a class (according to Marx a class is characterized by the place it occupies in the process of production), Worrall makes an amazing discovery. Soviet bureaucracy in its structure (which unfortunately he does not analyze) differs "basically" from any other bourgeoisie, but its function remains the same—the accumulation of capital. The fact that, despite great structural differences, the function can remain unchanged is, of course, a miracle that cannot occur in nature but seems (according to Worrall) possible in human society.

In any case, Worrall accepts this as evidence that Russia is dominated by a bourgeois class and thus by state capitalism. He clings obstinately to his confusion of capital and the means of production and seems unable to conceive of any form of accumulation other than capitalist accumulation. He fails to understand that accumulation (i.e., the expansion of production) in any economic system is the task of the managers of production; that even in an ideal socialist system this accumulation can result only from the surplus product (which only under capitalism takes the form of surplus value), and that the fact of accumulation in itself does not prove the capitalist nature of an economy.

But does the "bureaucracy" really "rule" the economy and consequently the people? Bureaucracy everywhere, and particularly in the Soviet Union, is composed of a conglomeration of the most varied elements. To it belong not only government officials in the narrow sense of the word (i.e., from minor employees up to the generals and even Stalin himself) but also the directors of all branches of industry and such functionaries as, for example, the postal and railway employees. How could this variegated lot possibly achieve a unified rule? Who are its representatives? How does it adopt decisions? What organs are at its disposal?

In reality, the "bureaucracy" is not an independent bearer of power. In accordance with its structure as well as its function, it is only an instrument in the hands of the real rulers. It is organized as an hierarchy and subordinated to the commanding power. It receives but does not give orders. Any functionary, as Trotsky justly puts it, "can be sacrificed by his superior in the hierarchical system in order to decrease any kind of dissatisfaction." And these are the new masters of production, the substitute for capitalists! Stalin thoroughly exploded this myth when, during the last purges, he ordered shot, among others, thousands of industrial managers.

It is not the bureaucracy that rules, but he who gives orders to the bureaucracy. And it is Stalin who gives orders to the Russian bureaucracy. Lenin and Trotsky with a select group of followers who were never able to come to independent decisions as a party but always remained an instrument in the hands of the leaders (the same was true later with the Fascist and National Socialist Parties) seized power at a time when the old state apparatus was collapsing. They changed the state apparatus to suit their needs as rulers, eliminating democracy and establishing their own dictatorship which in their ideology, but by no means in practice, was identified with the "dictatorship of the proletariat." Thus they created the first *totalitarian state*, even before the name was invented. Stalin carried on with the job, removing his rivals through the instrument of the state apparatus and establishing an unlimited personal dictatorship.

This is the reality which should not be obscured by construing alleged domination by a "bureaucracy," which is in fact subordinate to the government to the same extent as are the rest of the people. This is true even though some modest crumbs from the master's table may be doled out to it—without, of course, a guarantee that other crumbs are to follow and at the price of constant danger to their very lives. Their material share does not constitute any important portion of the social product. Nevertheless, the psychological effect of such a differentiation may be quite considerable.

Important economic consequences flow from this fact. It is the essence of a totalitarian state that it subjects the economy to its aims. The economy is deprived of its own laws, it becomes a controlled economy. Once this control is effected, it transforms the market economy into a consumers' economy. The character and extent of needs are then determined by the state. The German and Italian economies provide evidence of the fact that such control, once initiated in a totalitarian state, spreads rapidly and tends to become all-embracing, as was the case in Russia from the very beginning.* Despite great differences in their points of departure, the economic systems of totalitarian states are drawing close to each other. In Germany, too, the state, striving to maintain and strengthen its power, determines the character of production and accumulation. Prices lose their regulating function and become merely means of distribution. The economy, and with it the exponents of economic activity, are more or less subjected to the state, becoming its subordinates. The economy loses the primacy which it held under bourgeois

---

* Writing in 1940, Hilferding is referring to the German Nazi and Italian Fascist economies at this point.

society. This does not mean, however, that economic circles do not have great influence on the ruling power in Germany as well as in Russia. But their influence is conditional, has limits and is not decisive in relation to the essense of policy. Policy is actually determined by a small circle of those who are in power. It is their interests, their ideas as to what is required to maintain, exploit, and strengthen their own power that determines the policy which they impose as law upon the subordinated economy. This is why the subjective factor, the "unforeseeable," "irrational" character of political development has gained such importance in politics.

The faithful believe only in heaven and hell as determining forces; the Marxist sectarian only in capitalism and socialism, in classes—bourgeoisie and proletariat. The Marxist sectarian cannot grasp the idea that present-day state power, having achieved independence, is unfolding its enormous strength according to its own laws, subjecting social forces and compelling them to serve its ends for a short or long period of time.

Therefore neither the Russian nor the totalitarian system in general is determined by the character of the economy. On the contrary, it is the economy that is determined by the policy of the ruling power and subjected to the aims and purposes of this power. The totalitarian power lives by the economy, but not for the economy or even for the class ruling the economy—as is the case of the bourgeois state, though the latter (as any student of foreign policy can demonstrate) may occasionally pursue aims of its own. An analogy to the totalitarian state may be found in the era of the late Roman Empire in the regime of the Praetorians and their emperors.

Of course, from a social-democratic viewpoint the Bolshevik economy can hardly be called "socialist," for to us socialism is indissolubly linked to democracy. According to our concept, socialization of the means of production implies freeing the economy from the rule of one class and vesting it in society as a whole, a society which is democratically self-governed. We never imagined that the political form of that "managed economy" that was to replace capitalist production for a free market could be unrestricted absolutism. The correlation between the economic basis and the political structure seemed to us a very definite one: namely, that the socialist society would inaugurate the highest realization of democracy. Even those among us who believed that the strictest application of centralized power would be necessary or inevitable for the period of transition, considered this period only temporary and bound to end after the suppression of the propertied classes. Together with the disappearance of classes, class rule was also to vanish, that class rule which we considered the only possible form of political rule in general. "The state is withering away. . . ."

But history, this "best of all Marxists," has taught us differently. It has taught us that "administering of things," despite Engels' expectations, may turn into unlimited "administering of people," and thus not only lead to the emancipation of the state from the economy but even to the subjection of the economy to the state.

Once subjected to the state, the economy secures the continued existence of this form of government. The fact that such a result flows from a unique situation primarily brought about by war does not exclude a Marxist analysis, but it alters somewhat our rather simplified and schematic conception of the correlation between economy and state and between economy and politics which developed in a completely different period. The emergence of the state as an independent power greatly complicates the economic characterization of a society in which politics (i.e., the state) plays a determining and decisive role.

For this reason the controversy as to whether the economic system of the Soviet Union is "capitalist" or "socialist" seems to me rather pointless. It is neither. It represents a *totalitarian state economy*, i.e., a system to which the economics of Germany and Italy are drawing closer and closer.

TRANSLATED BY NINA STEIN

Milovan Djilas

The New Class in Communist Society

> *Milovan Djilas (b. 1911) began his political career in the Yugoslav Communist movement, served as a partisan with Tito in the Second World War, held a number of major posts in the Tito regime (including that of Vice President of the country), and then, in 1953, began to develop heretical views which would soon bring him close to the position of democratic socialism. For these views Djilas was twice imprisoned by the Tito government, spending a total of nine years in jail. He emerged unbroken in mind and spirit, one of the moral heroes of our time. The selection below is taken from his book* The Unperfect Society *(1969) which continues the critique of Communist society begun in his earlier volume* The New Class, *as a new form of social exploitation different in kind from capitalism and socialism. His views on this topic are similar to those expressed in this anthology by Rudolf Hilferding, Lucien Laurat, and Max Shachtman.*

May Marx forgive me one last dereliction: the crisis in Communism is not brought about by economic, so-called objective factors, but almost exclusively by human, so-called subjective factors. Strangely enough, these subjective factors are not ideas that grip the masses and so lead to material power. Rather, they are individual acts, a human defiance of coercion, whether that coercion takes the form of brute force or of spiritual domination or, as is most frequently the case, of a mixture of the two. The unfortunate human race, the wretched human being, will endure all evils, even coercion, for as long as it can and must; it will never submit to them.

Long ago Aristotle discovered that every human community is a community of diverse aspirations. This confirms that no system ever can be good for, and acceptable to, all men. No objection can be made even to Communism on the score that it is no better than other systems, although that it is happens to be precisely its own illusion. Similarly, the collapse of despotisms is never caused by the degree of their harshness; the collapse comes when human consciousness is ready to accept that the despotism is absurd and irrational, i.e., no longer capable of justifying its existence as a satisfaction of human needs.

Because of this, the intellectually fastidious person, as well as the man in the street (if such a person exists), puts up with Communism in spite of its seeming to be "unnatural" to him. At the same time, for its part, Communism, however brutally, does resolve vital problems of some nations which other social systems, for one reason or another, have been incapable of doing.

From its very inception as an idea, Communism has been accompanied by doubts as to its practicability; from the first moment of its establishment, there has been, within its own ranks, discontent over a gulf between its promises and its practices. The reason is that Communism, like every other revolutionary despotism, has failed to bring itself into harmony, let alone identify itself, with unidealized, natural desires, and with the ordinary everyday life of the people. Sooner or later a "more natural" unidealized system has to be substituted for Communism's violent revolutionary role. This is not to say that the revolutionary role is eccentric—it is a role for which certain societies and nations in our time have had a need, as have other societies and nations at other times, each with a different pattern of violent revolutionary movements and coups. There is an inevitability imposed by the very nature and historical role of every revolutionary doctrine and every revolution. A way of life without any determinable ultimate objective but that of keeping alive will eventually abandon Communism as a revolutionary doctrine and form of government, having no regard for Communism's idealistic objectives and still less for the good intentions and qualities of its leaders.

The economic and social relationships introduced by Communism, although they are a hotbed of new ideas and prototypes, are not in themselves the cause of its conflict with the currents of life. There may be no cause at all, at least not in a single and unmistakable form. It may simply be that with time a store of knowledge is accumulated and social circumstances are shifted, so that even the Communists themselves no longer believe in Communism, while in ordinary workaday life there persist abominable stereotypes—the imprints of Marxist ideology, as it were—that provide the leaders of Communist society with their pattern of reference. Today the most egregious and deep-rooted failures of Communism are neither the result of resistance by the "class enemy," since he hardly exists any longer, nor the result of the aggressive intentions of the "imperialists," since the Communists accept "imperialists," as equal partners in the era of "nuclear holocaust" or, at the least, manage to live in peace and cooperation with them.

The failures spring from inside Communism itself, which is why, it would seem, they become the harder to reverse the more that Communism is left to its own resources. Communism is hard pressed by the very forces of life. Its gravediggers are its own more or less doctrinaire pragmatists; in one generation the same leaders turn from revolutionaries into despots, and then from despots into "liberals" who use Communist ideas as a coinage for settling their bills. The Communist leaders' frequent changes of doctrinal clothing, together with their stupid resistance to superficial life styles, no less than their deluded resistance to the facts of life, make Communism—once the hope and the beacon for millions of fighters who sacrificed everything for it—ugly in its disintegration, uglier than any other outdated system in the past. In betokening reality, the poets already sense that Communism is about to decimate its sacred cows.

The playwright and satirist Matija Bećković, using a

pseudonym, wrote of Yugoslav society in 1967 in this vein:

In 1945, many of today's ordinary everyday occurrences would have been unlikely, inconceivable. At that time no one could possibly have believed that within twenty years, tens of thousands of Yugoslavs would be working abroad. Only reactionaries could possibly have believed that Communist partisans, the war veterans of Yugoslavia, would in some cases be working under the direction of German war veterans. No one ever imagined that students would go on working as milk deliverymen, or that the children of revolutionaries would have separate schooling. Arguments like these had been very effective in compromising the bourgeoisie. Who was to know at that time that there would be progressive monarchs in the world, and that we should be on friendly terms with many of them? Not even people with the most idiosyncratic imaginations, for whom nothing is sacred, ever dreamed that the Nazi war criminal Erih Rajaković would come to Yugoslavia with his family for a holiday. Few people knew that churches and palaces were part of our cultural heritage, a priceless historical treasure. There were people who had returned from the future to give their impressions to the nation. They maintained, and people believed them, that there would be none of these things: prostitutes, night clubs, gambling casinos, strip-tease clubs, corruption, financial disparities, wages or salaries, civil servants, domestic help, fashions, mistresses and servants, or even road sweepers.

Only the most incorrigible could possibly have believed that we should close schools in mourning for American presidents, smoke American cigarettes, drink American liquor, chew American gum, wear Italian shoes, drink Spanish wine, eagerly buy German cars, sing cowboy songs. . . .

Who would have believed that German war veterans would marry our daughters and sisters and would become welcome and valued tourists?

All these things are commonplace today. It was inevitable. At one time there has been one lot of fallacies to come to terms with, at another time there has been another. The impossible has become the probable. . . . *

That kind of irony constitutes a piece from the jigsaw of Yugoslavia today, where the disintegration and transformation of Communism seems to be more multifarious

---

* Dr. Janez Pacuk, "The Cinema as a Refrigerator for Illusions," *Svet*, Belgrade, No. 577, November 11, 1967, p. 20.

and conspicuous than in any other East European country or in Communism as a world movement. There are differences, of course, because of different conditions and different openings, available to the party bureaucracies —in other words, "different roads to socialism" that can be taken by separate countries. All Communist parties and systems are now caught at the same time in the decline of the classical revolutionary pattern and in the birth of a new peacetime one. In Yugoslavia this manifests itself in the form of an economic crisis that may be insuperable, as well as in an ideational withering away of the party; in Poland, in the form of a conflict between the hard-core, doctrinaire pro-Soviet bureaucrats and the nationalist, democratic intellectuals in the party; in Czechoslovakia, in the form of a showdown that the freedom-seeking people, led by democratic Communists, are having with the remnants of Stalinism; in Rumania, in the form of nationalist resistance by both the top party leaders and the people to Soviet hegemony—and so on. In international Communism, "separatism" is taking place in the form of a deepening conflict between the two Communist superpowers, the Soviet Union and China, and a further estrangement of other Communist parties from both of them.

Thus the circle of interparty and intergovernment contradictions is closed: first the Soviet Union and then China, since they could not help being great powers, were forced to exert their hegemony over the weaker and unprotected Communist parties, and these were precisely the parties that defected, one after the other, for the sake of their own survival. Every state, every social group, for that matter, always has a natural desire for the status of equality. With the establishment of more and more Communist regimes, the time was bound to come when the once-accepted world center could no longer command unquestioning obedience, when it would become enfeebled, and when internationalism would end in formal dissolution. There, quickening in the womb of national frameworks, were the embryos of the heresies.

This historical development is, incidentally, further evidence that Communism is not a religion but a political movement, or, rather, a political authority of a special type: wherever it was first and foremost an ideology and thus endowed with many of the characteristics of a religion, it was possible, indeed essential, for it to have a definite center, but as soon as it became transformed into a number of different states, the process of dissolution was bound to take place. This invites comparisons. The origins of the schism in the Catholic Church at the beginning of the sixteenth century lay in the opposition to papal secular authority by increasingly powerful princes, rather than in differing interpretations of dogma. But Catholicism purged itself as a religion in the Counter-Reformation, and the gradual weakening of the Vatican's secular power resulted in an actual strengthening of its role as a religious world center. For the same reasons, if a logical forecast of history does not go awry, Communism is not threatened by internecine wars similar to those between Catholics and Protestants in the Seventeenth century. Yet, because of the impending circumstances both inside and outside Communist countries, it is not out of the question that there may be all kinds of conflicts, even wars, between Communist countries—and these could become part of a wider area of conflict, on a world scale, if not the actual cause of such a conflict.

So the national and international differences and dissensions in the Communist world reflect and complement each other, with a steady tendency toward national emancipation and ideological diversity—in other words, toward the diminution of dogmatism. Disintegration or change in Communism is both a vertical and a horizontal process: vertical in that it is taking place in the Communist idea itself, in the movement on a world scale and in each party separately; and horizontal in that is it undergoing a steady multilateral breakaway, with the national parties separating from each other as well as from the Communist superpowers.

These upheavals in Communism are accompanied, and partly conditioned, by the restratification taking place in society itself and by the change in the balance of its forces. Thus, in the whole of the East European Communist world, in each East European country in a different guise and with varying intensity, *ground has already been covered for the creation of a new social stratum*—a special middle class recruited from all present-day strata, from the top of the party oligarchy itself to skilled workers and well-to-do peasants. The sum and substance of this new stratum of society and *specialists* of all kinds—artists, engineers, teachers, technicians, managers, and skilled political people. The new stratum is forming an undoctrinaire, even antidoctrinaire, class that is bent on raising its standard of living and keen on advancing technical capability and profitable business. It came into being spontaneously as a result of industrialization, and it grew from the environment and social relationships that industrial technology creates. As yet this social group, this emerging class, has thus far no ideology of its own, no organized pattern, although suggestions of both are beginning to show even among its Communist members. Among its members, more and more, are to be found independent-thinking theoreticians and democratic sympathizers. The party bureaucracy has been unable to check the emergence of this class because its members are indispensable to the bureaucracy's own survival. The bureaucracy cannot maintain power without the material advances provided by the industrial and cultural transformation that the members of this class alone can carry out. Moreover, the bureaucracy has been forced to accord recognition and to make concessions to members of this class and to prospective members of it. Today, now that these people are established in their own right as a force in society, all that the bureaucracy can do is chide them for their "deficiencies" in social awareness or for their "unsocialist" ethics, or make them a target of political campaigns and administrative trickery to curb their efforts to organize themselves. The very fact that the growing strength of this class cannot now be restrained—and that the growth of its privileges in society will result in better living standards for the rest of the nation as well—means that this is the class of the future. . . . And although I do not expect this class to improve immediately the freedoms of choice to any great extent, I feel that I am in a sense its spokesman, because I can at least envisage the inevitability of its progress. . . . In my view, a man's nature cannot be divorced today from the actual historical frame it occupies, and the destiny of nations is expressed within that frame. . . .

Because this sort of development has gone farthest in Yugoslavia, and because Yugoslavia is a multinational state, it is undoubtedly an excellent example of the vertical and horizontal disintegration of Communism and the restratification of society. Yugoslavia is also a living proof of Communism's unsuitability for contemporary life, an unsuitability that has a regular pattern everywhere, and of which Yugoslavia displays certain aspects—ideological, nationalistic, social. Sometimes one aspect is more in evidence, at other times another, but never is any divorced from the whole.

Max Shachtman

Stalinism: A New Social Order*

> Max Shachtman (b. 1903) was for some years the
> leading American spokesman for Trotskyism; in the
> 1950's he moved toward a version of democratic so-
> cialism. The essay which appears below was written
> in 1940, shortly after a factional dispute in which
> Shachtman broke from Trotsky on the matter of
> political attitude toward Stalinist Russia. Though
> couched in an "internal" idiom, that is, as an effort
> at collective self-clarification within the radical move-
> ment, this essay raises some of the central sociologi-
> cal, political, and moral problems which both social-
> ists and nonsocialists have encountered in trying to
> analyze Communist totalitarianism as an historically
> unique social system. The essay is taken from the
> author's book, The Bureaucratic Revolution (1962).

. . . Our investigation aims to reevaluate the character
and significance of the period of the degeneration of the
Russian Revolution and the Soviet state, marked by the
rise and triumph of the Stalinist bureaucracy. Its results
call for a revision of the theory that the Soviet Union is a
workers' state.

In our analysis, we must necessarily take issue with
Leon Trotsky, yet, at the same time, base ourselves
largely upon his studies. Nobody has even approached
him in the scope and depth of his contribution to understanding the problem of the Soviet Union. . . .

---

* Title supplied by editor.

Briefly stated, this has been our traditional view of the character of the Soviet Union:

The character of the social regime is determined first of all by the property relations. The nationalization of land, of the means of industrial production and exchange, with the monopoly of foreign trade in the hands of the state, constitute the bases of the social order in the U.S.S.R. The classes expropriated by the October Revolution, as well as the elements of the bourgeoisie and the bourgeois section of the bureaucracy being newly formed, could reestablish private ownership of land, banks, factories, mills, railroads, etc., only by means of a counterrevolutionary overthrow. By these property relations, lying at the basis of the class relations is determined for us the nature of the Soviet Union as a proletarian state.*

But it is not a workers' state in the abstract. It is a degenerated, a sick, an internally imperilled workers' state. Its degeneration is represented by the usurpation of all political power in the state by a reactionary, totalitarian bureaucracy, headed by Stalin. But while *politically* you have an anti-Soviet Bonapartist dictatorship of the bureaucracy, according to Trotsky, it nevertheless defends, in its own and very bad way, the *social* rule of the working class. This rule is expressed in the preservation of nationalized property. In bourgeois society, we have had cases where the social rule of capitalism is preserved by all sorts of political regimes—democratic and dictatorial, parliamentary and monarchial, Bonapartist and fascist. Yes, even under fascism, the bureaucracy is not a separate ruling class, no matter how irritating to the bourgeoisie its rule may be. Similarly in the Soviet Union. The bureaucracy is a caste, not a class. It serves, as all bureaucracies do, a class. In this case, it serves—again, badly—to maintain the social rule of the proletariat. At the same time, however, it weakens and undermines this rule. To assure the sanitation and progress of the workers' state toward socialism, the bureaucracy must be overthrown. Its totalitarian regime excludes its removal by means of more or less peaceful reform. It can be elimi-

* Trotsky, *Problems of the Development of the U.S.S.R.*, 1931, p. 3.

nated, therefore, only by means of a revolution. The revolution, however, will be, in its decisive respects, not social but political. It will restore and extend workers' democracy, but it will not produce any fundamental social changes, no fundamental changes in property relations. Property will remain state property.

Omitting for the time being Trotsky's analysis of the origin and rise of the Stalinist bureaucracy, which is elaborated in detail in *The Revolution Betrayed,* we have given above a summary of the basic position held by us jointly up to now. So far as characterizing the class nature of the Soviet Union is concerned, this position might be summed up even more briefly as follows:

To guarantee progress towards socialism, the existence of nationalized property is necessary but not sufficient, a revolutionary proletarian regime is needed in the country, plus favorable international conditions (victory of the proletariat in more advanced capitalist countries). To characterize the Soviet Union as a workers' state, the existence of nationalized property is necessary and sufficient. The Stalinist bureaucracy is a caste. To become a ruling class, it must establish new property forms.

Except for the slogan of revolution, as against reform, this was substantially the position vigorously defended by Trotsky and the Trotskyist movement for almost fifteen years. The big article on Russia written by Trotsky right after the war broke out, marked, in our opinion, the first —and a truly enormous—contradiction of this position. Not that Trotsky abandoned the theory that the Soviet Union is a degenerated workers' state. Quite the contrary, he reaffirmed it. But at the same time, he advanced a theoretical possibility which fundamentally negated his theory—more accurately, the motivation for his theory— of the class character of the Soviet state.

If the proletariat does not come to power in the coming period, and civilization declines further, the immanent collectivist tendencies in capitalist society may be brought to fruition in the form of a new exploiting society ruled by a new bureaucratic class, neither proletarian nor bourgeois. Or, if the proletariat takes power in a series of countries and then relinquishes it to a privileged bureaucracy, like the Stalinist, it will show that the proletariat is congenitally unable to become a ruling class and then "it will be necessary in retrospect to establish that in its fundamental traits the present U.S.S.R. was the precursor of a new exploiting regime on an international scale."

The historic alternative, carried to the end, is as follows: either the Stalin regime is an abhorrent relapse in the process of transforming bourgeois society into a socialist society, or the Stalin regime is the first stage of a new exploiting society. If the second prognosis proves to be correct, then, of course, the bureaucracy will become a new exploiting class. However onerous the second perspective may be, if the world proletariat should actually prove incapable of fulfilling the mission placed upon it by the course of development, nothing else would remain except openly to recognize that the socialist program based on the internal contradictions of capitalist society, ended as a Utopia. It is self-evident that a new "minimum" program would be required—for the defense of the interests of the slaves of the totalitarian bureaucratic society.

But are there such incontrovertible or even impressive objective data as would compel us today to renounce the prospect of the socialist revolution? That is the whole question.*

That is not the whole question. To that question, we give no less vigorously negative a reply than Trotsky. There is no data of sufficient weight to warrant abandoning the revolutionary socialist perspective. On that score, Trotsky was and remains quite correct. The essence of the question, however, relates not to the perspective, but to the theoretical characterization of the Soviet state and its bureaucracy.

Up to the time of this article, Trotsky insisted on the following two propositions: (1) nationalized property, so long as it continues to be the economic basis of the Soviet Union, makes the latter a workers' state, regardless of the political regime in power; and, (2) so long as it does not create new property forms, unique to itself, and so long as it rests on nationalized property, the bureaucracy is not a new or an old ruling class, but a caste. In "The

---

* Trotsky, "The U.S.S.R. in War," *The New International*, Nov. 1939, p. 327.

U.S.S.R. in War," Trotsky declared it *theoretically possible* (we repeat: not probable, but nevertheless theoretically possible) (1) for the property forms and relations now existing in the Soviet Union to continue existing and yet represent not a workers' state but a new exploiting society; and (2) for the bureaucracy now existing in the Soviet Union to become a new exploiting and ruling class without changing the property forms and relations it now rests upon.

To allow such a theoretical *possibility*, does not eliminate the revolutionary perspective, but it does destroy, at one blow, so to speak, the *theoretical* basis for our past characterization of Russia as a workers' state. . . .

In his writings on the Soviet Union, and particularly in *The Revolution Betrayed*, Trotsky speaks interchangeably of the "property forms" and the "property relations" in the country as if he were referring to one and the same thing. Speaking of the new political revolution against the bureaucracy, he says: "So far as concerns property relations, the new power would not have to resort to revolutionary measures." Speaking of the capitalist counterrevolution he says: "Notwithstanding that the Soviet bureaucracy has gone far toward preparing a bourgeois restoration, the new regime would have to introduce into the matter of forms of property and methods of industry not a reform, but a social revolution."

When refering to property forms in the Soviet Union, Trotsky obviously means nationalized property, that is, state ownership of the means of production and exchange. It is just as obvious that, no matter what has been changed and how much it has been changed in the Soviet Union by Stalinism, state ownership of the means of production and exchange continues to exist. It is further obvious that when the proletariat takes the helm again in Russia it will maintain state property.

However, what is crucial are not the property forms, i.e., nationalized property, whose existence cannot be denied, but precisely the relations of the various social groups in the Soviet Union to this property, i.e., *property relations*! If we can speak of nationalized property in the Soviet Union, this does not yet establish what the property relations are.

Under capitalism, the ownership of land and the means of production and exchange is in private (individual or corporate) hands. The distribution of the means of instruments of production under capitalism puts the possessors of capital in command of society and of the proletariat, which is divorced from property and has only its own labor power at its disposal. The relations to property of these classes, and consequently the social relations into which they necessarily enter in the process of production, are clear to all intelligent persons.

Now, the state is the product of irreconcilable social contradictions. Disposing of a force separate from the people, it intervenes in the raging struggle between the classes in order to prevent their mutual destruction and to preserve the social order. "But having arisen amid these conflicts, it is as a rule the state of the most powerful economic class that by force of its economic supremacy becomes also the ruling political class and thus acquires new means of subduing and exploiting the oppressed masses," writes Engels. Under capitalism, "the most powerful economic class" is represented by its capitalist class state.

What is important to note here is that the social power of the capitalist class derives from its "economic supremacy," that is, from its direct ownership of the instruments of production; and that this power is reflected in or supplemented by its political rule of the state machine, of the "public power of coercion." The two are not identical, let it be noted further, for a Bonapartist or fascist regime may and has deprived the capitalist class of its political rule only to leave its social rule, if not completely intact, then at least fundamentally unshaken.

Two other characteristics of bourgeois property relations and the bourgeois state are worth keeping in mind.

Bourgeois property relations and precapitalist property relations are not as incompatible with each other, as either of them are with socialist property relations. The first two not only have lived together in *relative* peace for long periods of time but, especially in the period of imperialism on a world scale, still live together today. An example of the first was the almost one-century-old cohabitation of the capitalist North and the Southern slaveocracy in the United States; an outstanding example of the second is British imperialism in India. But more important than this is a key distinction between the bourgeoisie and the proletariat. The capitalist class already has wide economic power before it overthrows feudal society and, by doing so, it acquires the necessary political and social power which establishes it as *the* ruling class.

Finally, the bourgeois state solemnly recognizes the right of private property, that is, it establishes juridically (and defends accordingly) that which is already established in fact by the bourgeoisie's ownership of capital. The social power of the capitalist class lies fundamentally in its actual ownership of the instruments of production, that is, in that which gives it its "economic supremacy," and *therefore* its control of the state.

How do matters stand with the proletariat, with its state, and the property forms and property relations unique to it? The young bourgeoisie was able to develop (within the objective limits established by feudalism) its specific property relations even under feudalism; at times, as we have seen, it could even share political power with a precapitalist class. The proletariat cannot do anything of the kind under capitalism, unless you accept those utopians who still dream of developing socialism right in the heart of capitalism by means of "producers' co-operatives." By its very position in the old society, the proletariat has no property under capitalism. The working class acquires economic supremacy *only after* it has seized political power.

We have already seen [said *The Communist Manifesto*] that the first step in the workers' revolution is to make the proletariat the ruling class, to establish democracy. The proletariat will use its political supremacy in order, by degrees, to wrest all capital from the bourgeoisie, to centralize all the means of production into the hands of the state [This meaning the proletariat organized as ruling class], and, as rapidly as possible, to increase the total mass of productive forces.

Thus by its very position in the new society, the proletariat still has no property, that is, it does not own property in the sense that the feudal lord or the capitalist did. It was and remains a property-less class! It seizes state power. The new state is simply the proletariat organized as the ruling class. The state expropriates the private owners of land and capital, and ownership of land and the means of production and exchange becomes vested in the *state*. By its action, the state established new property forms—nationalized, or state-ified, or collectivized property. It has also established new property relations. So far as the proletariat is concerned, it has a fundamentally new relationship to property. The essence of the change lies in the fact that the working class is in command of that state-owned property *because* the state is the proletariat organized as the ruling class (through its soviets, its army, its courts, and institutions like the party, the unions, the factory committees, etc.). There is the nub of the question.

The economic supremacy of the bourgeoisie under capitalism is based upon its ownership of the decisive instruments of producton and exchange. Hence, its social power; hence, the bourgeois state. The social rule of the proletariat cannot express itself in private ownership of capital, but only in its "ownership" of the state in whose hands is concentrated all the decisive economic power. *Hence, its social power lies in its political power.* In bourgeois society, the two can be and are divorced; in the proletarian state, they are inseparable. Much of the same thing is said by Trotsky when he points out that in contrast to private property, "the property relations which issued from the socialist revolution are indivisibly bound up with the new state as their repository" (*The Revolution Betrayed*). But from this follows in reality what does not follow in Trotsky's analysis. The proletariat's relations to property, to the new, collectivist property, are indivisibly bound up with its relation to the state, that is, to the political power.

We do not even begin to approach the heart of the problem by dealing with its juridical aspects, however. That suffices, more or less, in a bourgeois state. There, let us remember, the juridical acknowledgment by the state of private ownership corresponds exactly with the palpable economic and social reality. Ford and Du Pont own their plants . . . and their congressmen; Krupp and Schroeder own their plants . . . and their deputies. In the Soviet Union, the proletarian is master of property only if he is master of the state which is its repository. That mastery alone can distinguish it as the ruling class. "The transfer of the factories to the state changed the situation of the worker only juridically," Trotsky points out quite aptly. And further: "From the point of view of property in the means of production, the differences between a marshal and a servant girl, the head of a trust and a day laborer, the son of a people's commissar and a homeless child, seem not to exist at all."

Precisely! And why not? Under capitalism, the difference in the relations to property of the trust head and the day laborer is determined and clearly evidenced by the fact that the former is the owner of capital and the latter owns merely his labor power. In the Soviet Union, the difference in the relations to property of the six persons Trotsky mentions is not determined or visible by virtue of ownership of basic property but precisely by the degree to which any and all of them "own" the state to which all social property belongs.

The state is a political institution, a weapon of organized coercion to uphold the supremacy of a class. It is not owned like a pair of socks or a factory; it is controlled. No class—no modern class—controls it directly, among other reasons because the modern state is too complicated and all-pervading to manipulate like a seventeenth-century New England town meeting. A class controls the state indirectly, through its representatives, its authorized delegates.

The Bolshevik Revolution lifted the working class to the position of ruling class in the country. As Marx and Engels and Lenin had foreseen, the conquest of state power by the proletariat immediately revealed itself as "something which is no longer really a form of the state." In place of "special bodies of armed men" divorced from the people, there rose the armed people. In place of a corrupted and bureaucratized parliamentary machine, the democratic soviets embracing tens of millions. In the most difficult days, in the rigorous period of War Communism, the state was the "proletariat organized as the ruling class," organized through the soviets, through the trade unions, through the living, revolutionary proletarian Communist Party.

The Stalinist reaction, the causes and course of which have been traced so brilliantly by Trotsky above all others, meant the systematic hacking away of every finger of control the working class had over its state. And with the triumph of the bureaucratic counterrevolution came the end of rule of the working class. Workers' control in the factories went a dozen years ago. The people were forbidden to bear arms, even nonexplosive weapons—it was the possession of arms by the people that Lenin qualified as the very essence of the question of the state! The militia system gave way decisively to the army separated from the people. The Communist Youth were formally prohibited from participating in politics, i.e., from concerning themselves with the state. The Communist Party was gutted, and the Bolsheviks in it broken in two, imprisoned, exiled, and finally shot. How absurd are the lamentations about the "one-party dictatorship" in light of this analysis! It was precisely this party, while it lived, which was the last channel through which the Soviet working class exercised its political power.

The recognition of the present Soviet state as a workers' state [wrote Trotsky in his thesis on Russia in 1931] not only signifies that the bourgeoisie can conquer power in no other way than by an armed uprising but also that the proletariat of the U.S.S.R. has not forfeited the possibility of submitting the bureaucracy to it, of reviving the party again, and of mending the regime of the dictatorship—without a new revolution, with the methods and on the road of *reform*.

Quite right. And conversely: when the Soviet proletariat finally lost the possibility of submitting the bureaucracy to itself by methods of reform and was left with the weapons of revolution, we should have abandoned our characterization of the U.S.S.R. as a workers' state. Even if belatedly, it is necessary to do that now.

That political expropriation of the proletariat which is defined in Trotsky's analysis—that is nothing more nor less than the destruction of the class rule of the workers, the end of the Soviet Union as a workers' state.

A change in class rule, a revolution or counterrevolution, without violence, without civil war, gradually? Trotsky has reproached defenders of such a conception with "reformism-in-reverse." The reproach might hold in our case, too, but for the fact that the Stalinist counterrevolution was violent and bloody enough. The seizure of power by the Bolsheviks was virtually bloodless and non-violent. The breadth and duration of the civil war that followed were determined by the strength, the virility, and not least of all by the international imperialist aid furnished to the overturned classes.

The comparative *one-sidedness* of the civil war attending the Stalinist counterrevolution was determined by the oft-noted passivity of the masses, their weariness, their failure to receive international support. In spite of this, Stalin's road to power lay through rivers of blood and over a mountain of skulls. Neither the Stalinist counterrevolution nor the Bolshevik revolution was effected by Fabian gradualist reforms.

The conquest of state power by the bureaucracy spelled the destruction of the property relations established by the Bolshevik revolution.

If the workers are no longer the ruling class and the Soviet Union no longer a workers' state, and if there is no private-property-owning capitalist class ruling Russia, what is the class nature of the state and what exactly is the bureaucracy that dominates it?

Hitherto we called the Stalinist bureaucracy a caste and denied it the attributes of a class. Yet, Trotsky admitted that the definition of the Russian bureaucracy as a caste has not "a strictly scientific character. Its relative superiority lies in this, that the makeshift character of the term is clear to everybody, since it would enter nobody's mind to identify the Moscow oligarchy with the Hindu caste of Brahmins." In résumé, it is called a caste not because it is a caste—the old Marxian definition of a caste would scarcely fit Stalin & Co.—but because it is not a class. Without letting the dispute "degenerate into sterile toying with words," let us see if we cannot come closer to a scientific characterization than we have in the past.

Bukharin defined a class as "the aggregate of persons playing the same part in production, standing in the same relation toward the other persons in the production process, these relations being also expressed in things (instruments of labor)." According to Trotsky, a class is defined "by its independent role in the general structure of economy and by its independent roots in the economic foundation of society. Each class . . . works out its own special forms of property. The bureaucracy lacks all these social traits."

In general, either definition would serve. But not as an absolutely infallible test for all classes in all class societies. The Marxian definition of a class is obviously widened by Engels to include a social group "that did not take part in production" but which made itself "the indispensable mediator between the two producers," exploiting them both. The merchants characterized by Engels as a class are neither more nor less encompassed by Trotsky's definition, given above, or in Bukharin's than is the Stalinist bureaucracy (except in so far as this bureaucracy most definitely takes part in the process of production). But the indubitable fact that the bureaucracy has not abolished state property is not sufficient ground for withholding from it the qualification of a class, although, as we shall see, within certain limits. But, it has been objected:

If the Bonapartist riffraff is a class, this means that it is not an abortion but a viable child of history. If its marauding parasitism is "exploitation" in the scientific sense of the term, this means that the bureaucracy possesses a historical future as the ruling class indispensable to the given system of economy.[*]

Is or is not the Stalinist bureaucracy "a ruling class indispensable" to the system of economy in the Soviet

---

[*] Trotsky, "Again and Once More Again on the Nature of the U.S.S.R.," *The New International*, Feb., 1940, p. 14.

Union? The question is precisely: what is the given system of economy? For the *given* system, the property relations established by the counterrevolution, the Stalinist bureaucracy is the indispensable ruling class. As for the economic system and the property relations established by the Bolshevik Revolution (under which the Stalinist bureaucracy was by no means the indispensable ruling class), these are just what the bureaucratic counterrevolution destroyed! To the question, is the bureaucracy indispensable to "Soviet economy," one can therefore answer, yes and no.

To the same question put somewhat differently, is the bureaucracy an "historical accident," an abortion, or viable and a necessity, the answer must be given in the same spirit. It is an historical necessity, "a result of the iron necessity to give birth to and support a privileged minority so long as it is impossible to guarantee genuine equality" (*The Revolution Betrayed*). It is not an "historical accident" for the good reason that it has well-established historical causes. It is not inherent in a society resting upon collective property in the means of production and exchange, as the capitalist class is inherent in a society resting upon capitalist property. Rather, it is the product of a conjunction of circumstances, primarily that the proletarian revolution broke out in *backward* Russia and was not supplemented and thereby saved by the victory of the revolution in the *advanced* countries. Hence, while its concrete characteristics do not permit us to qualify it as a viable or indispensable ruling class in the same sense as this historical capitalist class, we may and do speak of it as a ruling class whose complete control of the state now guarantees its political and economic supremacy in the country.

It is interesting to note that the evolution and transformation of the Soviet bureaucracy in the workers' state, the state of Lenin and Trotsky is quite different and even contrary to the evolution of the capitalist class in its state. Speaking of the separation of the capitalist manager into capitalists *and* managers of the process of production, Marx writes:

The labor of superintendence and management arising out of the antagonistic character and rule of capital over labor, which all modes of production based on class antagonisms have in common with the capitalist mode, is directly and inseparably connected, also under the capitalist system, with those productive functions, which all combined social labor assigns to individuals as their special tasks. . . . Compared to the money capitalists, the industrial capitalist is a laborer, but a laboring capitalist, an exploiter of the labor of others. The wages which he claims and pockets for this labor amount exactly to the appropriated quantity of another's labor and depend directly upon the rate of exploitation of this labor, so far as he takes the trouble to assume the necessary burdens of exploitation. They do not depend upon the degree of his exertions in carrying on this exploitation. He can easily shift this burden to the shoulders of a superintendent for moderate pay. . . . Stock companies in general, developed with the credit system, have a tendency to separate this labor of management as a function more and more from the ownership of capital, whether it be self-owned or borrowed.[*]

Even though this tendency to separate out of the capitalist class (or the upper ranks of the working class) a group of managers and superintendents is constantly accentuated under capitalism, this group does not develop into an independent class. Why? Because to the extent that the manager (i.e., a highly paid superintendent-worker) changes his "relations to property" and becomes an owner of capital, he merely enters into the already existing capitalist class. He need not and does not create new property relations.

The evolution has been distinctly different in Russia. The proletariat in control of the state, and therefore of economy, soon found itself unable directly to organize economy, expand the productive forces, and raise labor productivity because of a whole series of circumstances: its own lack of training in management and superintendence, in bookkeeping and strict accounting; the absence of help from the technologically more advanced countries, etc. As with the building of the Red Army, so in industry, the Russian proletariat was urged by Lenin to call upon, and it did call upon, a whole host and variety of experts, some from its own ranks, some from the ranks of the class enemy, some from the ranks of the band-

---

[*] *Capital*, Vol. III.

wagon-jumpers, constituting in all a considerable bureaucracy.

Given the revolutionary party, given the soviets, given
the trade unions, given the factory committees, that is,
given those concrete means by which the workers ruled
the state, *their* state, this bureaucracy, however perilous,
remained within the limitations of "hired hands" in the
service of the workers' state. In political or economic life
—the bureaucracies in both tended to and did merge—
the bureaucracy was subject to the criticism, control, recall, or discharge of the "working class organized as a
ruling class."

The whole history of the struggle of the Trotskyist
movement in Russia against the bureaucracy signified, at
bottom, a struggle to prevent the crushing of the workers'
state by the growing monster of a bureaucracy which was
becoming increasingly different in *quality* from the "hired
hands" of the workers' state as well as from any kind of
bureaucratic group under capitalism. What we have
called the consummated usurpation of power by the
Stalinist bureaucracy was, in reality, nothing but the self-
realization of the bureaucracy as a class and its seizure
of state power from the proletariat, the establishment of
its own state power and its own rule.

The *qualitative* difference lies precisely in this: the bureaucracy is no longer the controlled and revocable "managers and superintendents" employed by the workers'
state in the party, the state apparatus, the industries, the
army, the unions, the fields, but the owners and controllers of the state, which is in turn the repository of collectivized property and thereby the employer of all hired
hands, the masses of the workers, above all, included.

The situation of the young Soviet republic (the historical circumstances surrounding its birth and evolution)
imposed upon it the "division of labor" described above,
and often commented on by Lenin. Where a similar division of labor under capitalism does not transform the
economic or political agents of the ruling class into a new
class, for the reasons given above (primarily, the relations
to capitalist private property), it does tend to create a
new class in a state reposing on collectivized property,

that is, in a state which is itself the repository of *all* social property.

Trotsky is entirely right when he speaks of "dynamic social formations [in Russia] which have had no precedent and have no analogies." It is even more to the point when he writes that "the very fact of its [the bureaucracy's] appropriation of political power in a country where the principal means of production are in the hands of the state, creates a new and hitherto unknown relation between the bureaucracy and the riches of the nation." For what is unprecedented and new, hitherto unknown, one cannot find a sufficiently illuminating analogy in the bureaucracies in other societies which did not develop into a class but remained class-serving bureaucracies.

What Trotsky calls the indispensable theoretical key to an understanding of the situation in Russia is the remarkable passage from Marx which he quotes in *The Revolution Betrayed*: "A development of the productive forces is the absolutely necessary practical premise [of communism], because without it want is generalized, and with want the struggle for necessities begins again and that means that all the old crap must revive."

Both Lenin and Trotsky kept repeating in the early years: in backward Russia, socialism cannot be built without the aid of the more advanced countries. Before the Revolution, in 1915, Trotsky made clear his opinion —for which Stalinism never forgave him—that without state aid of the Western proletariat, the workers of Russia could not hope to remain in power for long. That state aid did not come, thanks to the international social democracy, later ably supplemented by the Stalinists. But the prediction of Lenin and Trotsky did come true. The workers of the Soviet Union were unable to hold power. That they lost it in a peculiar, unforeseen, and even unforeseeable way—not because of a bourgeois restoration, but in the form of the seizure of power by a counterrevolutionary bureaucracy which retained and based itself on the new, collectivist form of property—is true. But they did lose power. The old crap was revived, in a new, unprecedented, hitherto unknown form, the rule of a *new bureaucratic class*. A class that always was, that always will be? Not at all. *"Class,"* Lenin pointed out in April, 1920, *"is a concept that takes shape in struggle and in the course of development."*

Can this new class look forward to a social life span as long as that enjoyed, for example, by the capitalist class? We see no reason to believe that it can. Throughout modern capitalist society, ripped apart so violently by its contradictions, there is clearly discernible the irrepressible tendency towards collectivism, the only means whereby the productive forces of mankind can be expanded and thereby provide that ample satisfaction of human needs, which is the precondition to the blooming of a new civilization and culture. But there is no adequate ground for believing that this tendency will materialize in the form of a universal "bureaucratic collectivism." . . .

What has already been said should serve to indicate the similarities between the Stalinist and fascist bureaucracies, but above all to indicate the profound social and historical difference between them. Following our analysis, the animadversions of all species of rationalizers on the identity of Stalinism and fascism remain just as superficial as ever.

Trotsky's characterization of the two bureaucracies as "symmetrical" is incontrovertible but only within the limits with which he surrounds the term, namely, they are both products of the same failure of the Western proletariat to solve the social crisis by social revolution. To go further, they are identical, but again within well-defined limits. The political regime, the technique of rule, the highly developed social demagogy, the system of terror without end—these are essential features of Hitlerite and Stalinist totalitarianism, some of them more fully developed under the latter than under the former. At this point, however, the similarity ceases. . . .

Fascism, resting on the mass basis of the petty bourgeoisie gone mad under the horrors of the social crisis, *was called to power deliberately* by the big bourgeoisie in order to preserve its social rule, the system of private property. Writers who argue that fascism put an end to capitalism and inaugurated a new social order, with a new class rule, are guilty of an abstract and static conception of capitalism, more accurately, of an idealization of capitalism as permanently identical with what it was in its halcyon period of organic upward development, its "democratic" phase.

Faced with the imminent prospect of the proletarian revolution putting an end both to the contradictions of capitalism and to capitalist rule, the bourgeoisie preferred the annoyance of a fascist regime which would suppress (not abolish!) these contradictions and preserve capitalist rule. In other words, at a given stage of its *degeneration*, the *only* way to preserve the capitalist system in any form is by means of the totalitarian dictatorship. As all historians agree, calling fascism to political power, the abandonment of political rule by the bourgeoisie, was the conscious act of the bourgeoisie itself.

But, it is argued, *after* it came to political power, the fascist bureaucracy completely dispossessed the bourgeoisie and itself became the ruling class—which is precisely what needs to be but has not been proved. The system of private ownership of socially operated property *remains basically intact*. After being in power in Italy for over eighteen years, and in Germany for almost eight, fascism has yet to nationalize industry, to say nothing of expropriating the bourgeoisie (the expropriation of small sections of the bourgeoisie, the Jewish, is done in the interests of the bourgeoisie as a whole). Why does Hitler, who is so bold in all other spheres, suddenly turn timid when he confronts the "juridical detail" represented by the private (or corporate) ownership of the means of production? Because the two cannot be counterposed: his boldness and "radicalism" in all spheres is directed towards maintaining and reinforcing that "juridical detail," that is, capitalist society, to the extent to which it is at all possible to maintain it *in the period of its decay*.

But doesn't fascism control the bourgeoisie? Yes, in a sense. That kind of control was foreseen long ago. In January, 1916, Lenin and the Zimmerwald left wrote: "At the end of the war a gigantic universal economic upheaval will manifest itself with all its force, when, under a general exhaustion, unemployment, and lack of capital, industry will have to be regulated anew, when the terrific indebtedness of all states will drive them to tremendous taxation, and when state socialism—militarization of the economic life—will seem to be the only way out of financial difficulties." Fascist control means precisely this new regulation of industry, the militarization of economic life in its sharpest form. It controls, it restricts, it regulates, it plunders, but with all that it maintains and even strengthens the capitalist profit system, leaves the bourgeoisie intact as the class owning property. It *assures* the profits of the owning class, taking from it that portion which is required to maintain a bureaucracy and police-spy system needed to keep down labor (which threatens to take away *all* profits and *all* capital, let us not forget) and to maintain a highly modernized military establishment to defend the German bourgeoisie from attacks at home and abroad and to acquire for it new fields of exploitation outside its own frontiers.

But isn't the fascist bureaucracy, too, becoming a class? In a sense, yes, but not a new class with a new class rule. By virtue of their control of the state power, any number of fascist bureaucrats, of high and low estate, have used coercion and intimidation to become board directors and stockholders in various enterprises. This is especially true of those bureaucrats assigned to industry as commissars of all kinds. On the other side, the bourgeoisie acquires the "good will" of Nazi bureaucrats, employed either in the state or the economic machinery, by bribes of stocks and positions on directing boards. There is, if you wish, a certain process of fusion between sections of the bureaucracy and the bourgeoisie. But the bureaucrats who become stockholders and board directors do not thereby become a new class, they enter as integral parts of the industrial or financial bourgeoisie class which we have known for quite some time.

Private ownership of capital, that "juridical detail" before which Hitler comes to a halt, is a social reality of the profoundest importance. With all its political power, the Nazi bureaucracy remains a bureaucracy; sections of it fuse with the bourgeoisie, but as a social aggregation, it is not developing into a new class. Here, control of the state power is not enough. The bureaucracy, in so far as its development into a new class with a new class rule of its own is concerned, *is itself controlled* by the objective reality of the private ownership of capital.

How different it is with the Stalinist bureaucracy! Both bureaucracies "devour, waste, and embezzle a considerable portion of the national income"; both have an income above that of the people and privileges which correspond to their position in society. But similarity of income is not a definition of a social class. In Germany, the Nazis are not more than a bureaucracy—extremely powerful, to be sure, but still only a bureaucracy. In the Soviet Union, the bureaucracy is the ruling class, because it possesses as its own the state power which, in this country, is the owner of all social property.

In Germany, the Nazis have attained a great degree of independence by their control of the state, but it continues to be "the state of the most powerful economic class," the bourgeoisie. In the Soviet Union, control of the state, sole owner of social property, makes the bureaucracy the most powerful economic class. Therein lies the fundamental difference between the Soviet state, even under Stalinism, and all other *precollectivist* states. The difference is of epochal historical importance.

The difference is between increased state intervention to preserve capitalist property and the collective ownership of property by the bureaucratic state. How express the difference summarily and in conventional terms? People buying canned goods want and are entitled to have labels affixed that will enable them to distinguish at a glance pears from peaches from peas. "We often seek salvation from unfamiliar phenomena in familiar terms," Trotsky observed. But what is to be done with unprecedented, new, hitherto unknown phenomena, how label them in such a way as to describe at once their origin, their present state, their more than one future prospect, and wherein they resemble and differ from other phenomena? The task is not easy. Yet, life and politics demand some conventional, summary terms for social phenomena; one cannot answer the question, "What is the Soviet state?" by repeating in detail a long and complex analysis. The demand must be met as satisfactorily as is possible in the nature of the case.

The early Soviet state we would call, with Lenin, a bureaucratically deformed workers' state. The Soviet state today we would call—bureaucratic collectivism, a characterization which attempts to embrace both its historical origin and its distinction from capitalism as well as its current diversion under Stalinism. The German state today we would call, in distinction from the Soviet state, bureaucratic or totalitarian state capitalism. These terms are neither elegant nor absolutely precise, but they will have to do for want of any others more precise or even half as precise.

Ivan Svitak

The Czech Revolution and After

*Ivan Svitak (b. 1925) is a Czech philosopher who was
extremely active during the democratization struggle
that took place in his country in 1968. His articles
were among the most forthright expressions in the
Prague journals demanding the creation of a democratic socialist society. Previously he had lectured in
philosophy at various Czech universities, had been
forbidden several times to continue lecturing or writing because of his "revisionist" views, and in 1964
had been expelled from the Czech Communist Party.
He is at present an exile living in the United States.*

1. Dictatorships are as old as mankind. The essence of
dictatorship consists in the unchallenged rule over the
state by a single person, clique, or power group, and it is
of merely secondary importance whether or not parliaments exist, elections are held, and various forms of state
agencies and posts are established. Moreover, modern
dictatorships do not merely represent a tighter form of
the old features of autocracy, despotism, and tyranny;
they have also other, new features. Modern dictatorships
—that is to say, totalitarian dictatorships—are the government monopoly of a ruling minority, but in contrast
and in addition to the historical forms of dictatorship,
they have at their disposal a mass movement and a mass
ideology, they govern the whole state by commands, and
they intervene in every sphere of the life of the citizens,
including their private life. Not only do the totalitarian
dictatorships and their ideology offer to their citizens a

higher standard of living or a better form of government but they also offer solutions for every problem in the life of the individual and thus become a temporal substitute for religion, a message of redemption through a new faith in ideology, the party, and the leader.

2. Totalitarian dictatorship is a new form of absolutism, a modern type of despotism. The essence of totalitarian dictatorship is the reduction of the individual to a tool of the power apparatus. For this reason, every totalitarian dictatorship must destroy personality and individuality, not because the leading politicians are sadists (although there are sadists too), but because this orientation arises from the character of absolute, centralized, and unchallenged power. Propaganda and terror, the control of the mass information media, and the secret police are the most important instruments for the automation of the individual.

3. Totalitarian dictatorship does not know the methods of indirect government; it rules by terror, fear, and indirect action. Because of this, the common-interest organizations which were originally formed in the interest of their founders, also became bureaucratic mechanisms for the purpose of ruling over broad sections of the population, the workers, the young, etc. This power is exercised under the assumption that everything is permitted in the interest of the race, class, or nation, and that humanistic considerations are a mere sign of weakness. The dictatorships of the Metternich or Bach (Austrian prime minister in the first years of the reign of Emperor Francis Joseph I) type, and of the emperors and tsars, were regimes far more humane than the modern dictatorships.

4. A totalitarian dictatorship is a compact and uncontrollable system of power which is used by people who are convinced that only they know what is good for the race, nation, or class; what progress is and the interest of mankind—in fact, what is good for the whole world—and who, in their fanaticism, believe that they have the right to impose their program on the masses. Conflicts within the ruling elite are settled by means of dialectical orthodoxy, and heresy is dealt with in periodical purges and through

tricks, since they cannot be dealt with in any other manner where there is no control. The people, the masses, the classes do not participate in decision-making, but they are encouraged to offer their thanks to the party and government.

5. Totalitarian dictatorship is based on terror and it cannot retain power without terror. This terror is not an expedient resorted to only in exceptional circumstances in order to attain specific ends; this terror is a specific form of government of totalitarian dictatorships. The basic function of terror consists in ensuring the automation of the citizen and in turning him into a pliable political tool of the power elite. Even when a totalitarian dictatorship is tottering, its secret police—the chief instrument of terror—continue to function reliably. The result is the complete subjugation of life to politics and power.

6. A totalitarian dictatorship finds its support in the emotionalism of the masses and in the disintegration of the rational attitudes and standards of value of modern times. It is supposed to be able to deal with phenomena of crisis; it ensures its effects through absolute control over the opinions and attitudes of the population, and through propaganda spread by the mass information media. Cliches and stereotyped oversimplifications which become the generally accepted truth through constant repetition, are not subject to verification or to criticism.

7. Totalitarian dictatorships operate with the *a priori* assumption of unity of the people, nation, party, bloc; that is, with the postulate of moral political unity, although this unity does not really exist. Therefore, differences of opinion are regarded as heresy and those holding them are regarded as enemies and traitors. Not only are the liberties of the individual and civil rights thrown overboard, but this very suppression of freedom is extolled as a triumph of progress and as the hallmark of a higher social order.

8. Establishment of the function of an individual in a totalitarian dictatorship is, in addition to terror, ensured chiefly by means of propaganda in the media of mass information. The constantly repeated allegations regard-

ing a fictitious enemy create a psychosis about a constant exceptional threat to the achievements of the revolution, race, nation, or class, a danger which justifies the permanent state of martial law, affecting ideas and people. If the citizen is to be permanently confused, it is necessary to operate with the fiction of an enemy (the Jews, the imperialists, another nation, the whites, the blacks, the Chinese, the Europeans, etc.) who constitute a danger to the citizen from which the dictatorship protects him.

9. Totalitarian dictatorships arise from the internal weakness of democratic orders, the disintegration of which is a precondition for the rise of dictatorships just as the establishment of democracy is the precondition for the fall of a dictatorship. Totalitarian dictatorships, mass movements, and the party apparatus undergo substantial functional changes after assuming power. In the struggle for power, the movement usually changes into a bureaucratic machinery of government, power is institutionalized, and a separate totalitarian organization is established. The spontaneous movement and its motives are replaced by the monopolistic system of party views, a party surrounded by a system of satellite organizations. The state turns into an instrument of the totalitarian elite, which preserves through its own political institution—the party—a decisive influence; this is the origin of the dual government of state and party, so typical of every dictatorship.

10. As soon as the ruling elite constitutes itself after the takeover of power, it begins to govern autocratically and to influence public opinion in its own interest, which is presented as the interest of the masses. The trend toward an accumulation of power leads inevitably to the fact that power is uncontrollable and becomes an apparatus of suppression, turned also against those very classes which enthroned the new elite. In practice, the totalitarian state is based on violence against both people and ideas, on a functioning and effective violence. The totalitarian states have been and are the biggest threat to humanity throughout its history; they constitute a total threat to human values, to European culture, and to the meaning of human freedom.

The Nature of the Czechoslovak Dictatorship

1. The nature of the totalitarian dictatorship, under which we have lived for the past twenty years, had some national characteristics. An outstanding advantage of the regime was the fact that it was headed by full-blooded Bohemians, with their Austrian tradition of joviality combined with the muddled inefficiency of a concierge (for which there is such a good German word, *Schlamperei*). A more detailed definition of this specific quality would require a team of geniuses familiar with the great thoughts of C. N. Parkinson on the natural growth of inefficiency.

2. The measure of the Czechoslovak type of totalitarian dictatorship was its chaos; this dictatorship was rather a comic paradox. Apart from some murders, the government was as helpless in the handling of absolute power as a baby would be with a slide rule. The occasional fits of democracy, periodically installed and dethroned, never succeeded in bringing about fundamental changes, and the foundations of this system were undermined again and again by aggressive stupidity.

3. The spontaneously spouting geyser of this stupidity, tirelessly gushing for twenty years in the official and the tolerated cultural press, in declarations made by statesmen and pioneer leaders, has not in spite of all the extreme efforts been able to undermine the foundations of the socialist order. The natural intelligence of these good-hearted Slovak, Moravian, and to some extent also, Czech people, always corrected the worst excesses and reduced them to a tolerable measure.

4. Thus our history of the last twenty years may be likened to a phase of marking time; sometimes we would lift our feet as if marching, sometimes as if running—yet we did not move from the spot. Under such circumstances, one must ask one's compatriots what the purpose of the "march" might be. It is like the question which a naughty girl friend of mine used to put to soldiers confined to barracks, when she asked them over the fence whether they liked the service. When they said "no" she

asked them why they did not leave. To voice this kind of question has now become one of our duties.

5.   Another characteristic of this totalitarian dictatorship was that for twenty years it kept itself free of any inner political shocks because in the critical year 1956/57 it was able to reduce the price of Hungarian salami, and to blacken the critics as intellectuals. It repeated this method in every critical situation before and after. The political philosophy of the statesmen of this period was based on the scapegoats—the capitalists, kulaks, Jews, and intellectuals—and Hungarian sausage. Therefore if a politician was unable to reduce the price of Hungarian salami it might have fatal consequences for him.

6.   The salami realism in politics was effective until such time as there was something else of which the price could be reduced; it must be admitted that both our nations were satisfied with this state of affairs. This realism was pursued at the expense of economic efficiency, for it made possible less work for more money, and ensured actual, legal, and economic equality between the laborer and the university professor. Thanks to this *consensus gentium* there has never been any political opposition worth talking about in Czecholovakia, not even in the past ten years, marked as they were by growing economic difficulties. The country has been ushered toward collapse with the tacit discipline of subjugated but thrifty citizens whose hopes have not been pinned to freedom but to an MB (type of Skoda car).

7.   The cemetery-like quiet of this dictatorship and its well-functioning, truncheon-assured respectability seemed to be unassailable from within. Suddenly, the resources, which made possible the grand policy of bribing the nation by a higher standard of living, failed —actually it was the economics of the high consumer standard that failed. The sudden failure of the economic structure—by no means incurable—was sufficient to bring about a state of insecurity and to provoke a remarkable change of political orientation.

8.   Still another fundamental feature of the Czechoslovak totalitarian dictatorship was its extraordinarily conservative character, conflicting with the ineradicable tra-

dition of elementary freedoms of a European state. In Poland, they did not execute their Gomulka, in Bulgaria and Hungary they executed one minister each, but the crop of Czechoslovak Stalinism was the richest of all.

9. In every important question concerning the socialist bloc, the Czechoslovak foreign policy has stuck most persistently to the hard line. The gradual emancipation of Yugoslavia, Poland, Hungary, Albania, China, Rumania, and Cuba from the Soviet example was followed grudgingly, and any attempt at copying these examples was always condemned. The reason given was always the same —the lower standard of living in these countries, in other words the pocket of Mr. Cehona (Mr. Smith).

10. The conservative foreign-political aspect of state policy was by no means platonic and the sincere statements of support for the fascist-like Arab regimes of Nasser's type were not empty words. The supplies of war material, financed so readily by irretrievable credits, directly served the Arab imperialist policies. The characteristic features of the dictatorship, i.e., its realistic and conservative Czech nature, must be taken into consideration when we attempt to understand the possible further development of this totalitarian dictatorship.

The Nature of the Present Changes

1. Are we witnessing a revolution or a revolt? A revolution means structural social changes in class relations, in the relations between economy and policy, and in the structure of the mechanism of power. A revolt (putsch) is an exchange of teams and does not affect structural relations and questions. It is up to us to decide which of the two we witness—the game is open.

2. We are completely apathetic to the latter possibility. We have no reason to be enthusiastic about an exchange of persons. The sociologists and philosophers know that "institutions are stronger than people," and that without the control mechanism of public opinion every member of the elite must degenerate. There is no exception to this rule. Antonin Novotny started as an exponent of the liberalizing trend. Today young people

must barricade themselves in the university grounds against the Polish national hero of 1956.

3. The possibility of structural changes is, on the contrary, of the greatest interest to us because it opens the way to an open socialist society, i.e., to socialist democracy. However, this is still far off, although it appears at the moment as an illusion embracing the whole nation, based on the resignation of a few persons. The students have little reason to support this illusion; on the contrary, they have every reason to be on the watch for false cards which may yet appear on the table in the course of this game, the result of which is to decide the nature of the state in which we are to live.

4. If we observe realistically and critically the results of the three-months-old process of regeneration, we must come to the conclusion that so far there have been no structural changes in the mechanism of the totalitarian dictatorship, with the sole exception of the temporary nonexistence of censorship. The monopoly of a single party has been unaffected; so far, there is no machinery for forming a political will of the people.

5. The hierarchic concept of state bodies and social organizations, directed from a single center, remains unchanged. It is incompatible with democracy, of which an essential ingredient is the fact that the political will is the result of certain social processes, in which the various factors play a relatively independent role. On the ideological level the ideological values and political programs compete with each other, while on the level of state power the legislative, the executive, and the judiciary (i.e., parliament, government, and the independent judiciary) check one another, and finally on the level of the economic and civic activities of the citizenry, the special-interest groups, the bureaucracy, and public opinion play their independent roles.

6. There is only one aspect at the present time which justifies hopes in the process of democratization—the free expression of public opinion. It is therefore in this area that the counterattacks of the conservative forces must be expected in the near future. These forces will call for

restraint; they will offer new economic programs and new persons instead of fundamental political changes. We, on the other hand, must attempt to make the best use of the tolerated freedom with a view to making possible democratic elections as the next step on our way toward establishing a European socialist state.

7. This process is possible only if the fundamental conflict of the present Czechoslovak state is solved: this conflict is by no means to be found only in the relationship of two nations but in the mechanism of the totalitarian dictatorship. The bureaucracy of this dictatorship did do away with the Stalinist cult, but it has kept without change the power structure of Stalinism, including the bureaucratic apparatus and the policy of a cultural whip. We must liquidate this dictatorship or it will liquidate us.

8. The liquidation of the mechanisms of totalitarian dictatorship and the totalitarian way of thinking is a condition for achieving democratic socialism. Totalitarian dictatorship is our enemy No. 1. We have enough brains and hands for the program of socialist freedom, but we also have a large number of resistant elements. If the question is posed: "From where, with whom, and where to?" it may be answered briefly: "From Asia to Europe, alone."

9. This means, from totalitarian dictatorship to an open society, to the liquidation of the monopoly of power, and to an effective control of the elite in power by a free press and public opinion. From the bureaucratic management of society and culture by "the cutthroats of the official line" (term used by Wright Mills) to the employment of the basic human and civil rights, at least in the degree known to bourgeois democratic Czechoslovakia. With the workers' movement minus its *apparatchiks*, with the middle classes minus the groups of willing collaborators, and with the intelligentsia in the front. The intellectuals of this country must raise their claim to the leadership of a democratic socialist society open to democracy and humanism if there is to be an end to the irrational dialectic of abuse and tyranny.

10.　The remarkable element of the presents changes is the fact that, until now, no substantial changes have taken place, that the mechanisms of totalitarian dictatorship have been untouched. Only the freedom of the press exists and a hope that there may be democratic elections and that the functions of power in the state may be rearranged. We are not interested in a change of the cadres, nominated by a grossly undemocratic system; what we want is a lasting process of democratization, in other words a permanent transformation of the totalitarian dictatorship into a European system with a democratic form of government.

Evan Durbin

A Socialist View of Democracy*

> *Though virtually unknown on this side of the Atlantic, Evan Durbin (1906–1948) has exerted considerable influence on the political leaders and intellectual spokesmen of the British Labor Party. His special interest was in reconciling the perspective of socialism with a strict adherence to democratic methods and norms. His writings are notable for the candor with which he recognized the difficulties such an effort might involve. The following selection is taken from* The Politics of Democratic Socialism (1940).

If the method of dictatorship is an unlikely way to secure social justice, what alternative method is open to us? I wish to argue that the only conceivable route to a better social order lies in the pathway of democracy and that the political method of democratic government is an essential principle, not an accidental accompaniment of any just society.

If by the "socialist commonwealth" we mean a society in which a larger measure of social justice has been established thorough the instrumentality of a planned economy, then I believe that the democratic method is an inherent part of socialism and cannot be separated from it, any more than batting can be separated from cricket or love from life. They are all necessary parts of a complex whole.

I am now concerned to argue the validity of this contention; but before I do so, it is necessary to make clear

---

* Title supplied by editor.

the sense in which I use the term *democracy*. Democracy is an ambiguous term in political discussion. Many people use it in such a way as to make it synonymous with the phrase "the good society." A community is a "true" democracy only if all causes for sighing and weeping have passed away. Before such persons will call any society a democracy, it must be completely free from social inequalities and economic insecurity. J. A. Hobson uses the term in this sense when he says "effective political democracy is unattainable without economic equality." In this use the term *democracy* becomes identified with the conception of social justice itself and is therefore remote from the political practice of any present society.

By using the word in this way it is possible to say, quite rightly, that we have not got "democracy" in Britain, or America, or France, or Sweden. In none of these countries has inequality, or insecurity, or class antagonism, passed wholly away. Democracy, in its utopian sense, does not exist within these nations. They only possess "capitalist democracy," or "*political* democracy." They do not possess "economic democracy," or "true democracy," or "real democracy."

Now it is perfectly open to anyone to use terms as they please. If some people choose to mean by *democracy* what other people mean by *Utopia* there is nothing to stop them doing so. The moon will still be the moon even if we call it the sun. Utopia by any other name will smell as sweet and look as remote. But it is not in Utopia, nor in the perfect society, that I am, for the moment, interested. I wish to discuss a narrower thing, a single political habit, a method of taking political decisions, a practicable and actual condition of certain societies. In short, what I want to consider is the significance or value of what the Utopian "democrats" would call "mere political democracy." In what does that consist? Of what value is it? By what arguments can it be justified or criticized?

It is obvious that the institution of "mere political democracy" must exist in some real sense, even in a capitalist society, since it is possible to distinguish "capitalist democracies" from "capitalist dictatorships." Even in his most fanatical moments, the communist has not denied the *possibility* of making the distinction, although he used to deny the *importance* of making it. There must be therefore some sense in which democracy is compatible with capitalism and consequently with economic inequality. It is with this limited form of political democracy, its meaning and value, that I am here concerned.

In what does "democracy" in this sense consist? I believe the correct answer to this question to be that political democracy consists in the possession by any society of *three* characteristic habits or institutions:

1 The *first* and most typical of these characteristics is the ability of the people to choose a government.

Disagreement between individuals is of the very essence of human personality. As long as we are different persons, there will be some of us who like one thing and some who do not, some who desire one order of society and some another, some who believe justice to be realized in one set of circumstances and some who disagree with that judgment.

Now the course of action taken at any moment, and the form of society thus brought slowly into existence, are determined largely by the decisions of the government. The government has its hands upon the controls of the "apparatus of coercion" and is therefore the *immediate* authority determining social policy. The nature of the decisions taken by the government will depend upon the character of the persons forming it. Consequently there can be no control of the form of society by us, the common people, unless it is possible to change the personnel of the government and of the legislature. That is the first and most obvious characteristic of political democracy: the existence of a government responsible to the people, and the dependence of it and of the membership of the legislative assembly upon the free vote of the people.

In our own history we have found that the essential thing to attain and preserve is the power of the people to *dismiss* a government from office. This negative power is in reality an important positive power, because ordinary men and women are moved more deeply by the disapproval of measures they dislike in practice, than by their less definite conception of what they desire in the future.

Political change in democracies is more frequently induced by a slow accumulation of resentment against an existing government or institution, than by the growth of a positive idea of new social forms. Experience is more real than imagination, to unimaginative people.

Every practising politician appreciates this fact. The enthusiasts composing the party machine through which he has to work may be animated by the clear vision of a new society; but they are, at the best, a small minority of the surrounding electoral masses, and the masses are rarely inspired by Christian's clear vision, from a great distance, of the Celestial City. This is not to say that constructive social imagination is not powerful in the affairs of men, but only that democracies proceed to realize the prophets' vision by careful processes of empirical test. By the slow testing of ideas and of institutional experiments, by rejecting all those of which they disapprove and insisting upon the gradual extension of the things they find by experience that they like, an intelligent electorate unconsciously constructs a society that in large measure contents it. Little as we reformists of the left may like it, the absence of a reforming or revolutionary zeal in our communities is a tribute to the fundamental, and often unrecognizable, ways in which society has been adapted to suit the unconscious, but essential, requirements of the people composing it.

Of this I shall have more to say presently. For the moment I wish only to insist upon the importance of the negative power to destroy a government as part of the broader right to choose a government. It is the continuous retention of this power that I shall call the "maintenance of democracy."

2 But the continued existence of this right implies and requires the existence of a *second*, and less obvious, political institution. If liberty is to exist, if the dependence of government upon the will of the people is to be real, there must always be a real choice before the people. This implies the steady maintenance of a critical and essential institution—that of *freedom to oppose the government of the day*. Unless the electorate has more than one possible government before it; unless there is more

than one party able to place its views before the country; unless, that is to say, the opposition is free to prepare itself to take over power and the government to surrender it peacefully after an electoral decision against it, there is no choice before the people. Their choice is Hobson's choice: they may walk or go upon their legs, they may die or cease to live, they may eat bread or bread. The range of choice is no greater.

This obvious reflection reveals at once the sharp absurdity of the electoral practices of modern dictatorships. Modern dictatorships pay to the institutions of democracy the sincerest form of flattery, that of imitation. They copy the device of the general election. But is is an empty and silly imitation, like that of an ape reading a newspaper or a baboon playing on a violin. It deceives no one, except those who wish to be deceived. Of course, no amount of electoral machinery, nor platform eloquence, nor secret balloting, nor "equal voting" has the slightest real significance if there is finally nothing to vote about, no choice before the voters. The contemporary German and Russian elections, in which one party receives 98 percent or 99 percent of the votes polled, may be a tribute to the efficiency of the terror by which these unfortunate peoples are governed; but they have no more political significance than the jabbering of a school of marmosets or the senseless and uniform hissing of a gaggle of geese.

This we can see at once by asking the critical question: *What is the choice before the German or Russian electorate?* There is only one party in the election. There is only one government that can be formed. There may be a choice of individuals, but there is no choice of policy. The alternative before the German people is the choice between Führer Hitler or Führer Hitler; before the Russian people Comrade Stalin or Comrade Stalin. They may choose in the one country, the National Socialist Party or the National Socialist Party; in the other, the Communist Party or the Communist Party. As Herr Goebbels said, "All we National Socialists are convinced that we are right, and we cannot bear with anyone who maintains that he is right. For either, if he is right, he must be a

National Socialist, or, if he is not a National Socialist then he is not right."* Comrade Stalin thinks very much the same. It is only odd that both these self-righteous regimes consider it worth while to spend so much time and money in marching the adult population mechanically and idiotically through the polling booths to affirm a meaningless slogan.†

Here then is the acid test of democracy. Democracy may be defined by the toleration of opposition. In so far as it is tolerated, in so far as alternative governments are allowed to come into existence and into office, democracy, in my sense, exists. In so far as opposition is persecuted, rendered illegal, or stamped out of existence, democracy is not present, and either has never existed or is in process of being destroyed.

Obviously this is not a simple test. There are varying degrees of freedom permitted to those in opposition to the government of the day in the various political systems of the world. In the older democracies, like our own, there is complete legal freedom for parties in opposition to the government. Their rights in respect of political agitation are the *same* as those of the government. From this extreme there is an almost infinite gradation of liberty, through the milder dictatorships of Poland and even Italy, to the savage and ruthless insistence upon uniformity that characterizes Germany and Russia. There is no precise line at which it is possible to say that all the communities on this side of it are democracies and all on the other side of it are dictatorships. But, although the test is quantitative and complicated, it is nevertheless an acid test. The suppression of opposition, as distinct from

---

* Speech reported in *The Times*, October 6th, 1935.

† In point of fact, the external form and machinery of a general election has been converted by both types of dictatorship into a compulsory nationwide class in adult education and a compulsory exercise in the state religion. The campaign preceding the election is made an opportunity for lecturing—or rather shrieking—about the political questions of the moment, and the actual farce of balloting is a test of the efficiency and enthusiasm of the local parties. This horrible mimicry of democratic institutions has become an important part of the modern apparatus of tyranny.

sedition,* is the proof of dictatorial ambition. It is by our judgment of that condition in society that we shall judge democracy itself.†

3 But there is a *third*, and still less obvious, characteristic necessary to the existence of democracy. Both the previous characteristics—those of responsible government and of legal opposition—are the definitive properties of democracy, but they are not the causes of democracy. When these conditions are present in a society, democracy in my sense is present also; when they are absent democracy in my sense is dead. But they do not cause democracy to become present; they simply define democracy. What then *causes* democracy to appear? What is the substantial social condition guaranteeing its existence and continuance?

Now I shall go on to argue, before this part is finished, that the ultimate cause of stable democratic habits among a people is the possession by them of a certain type of emotional character. I shall argue that democracy is the epiphenomenon of a certain emotional balance in the individuals composing a nation, and I shall try to describe the kind of personality that, in my view, alone makes democracy possible. But there is a simpler and more immediate description of the *result* of the predominance of such persons in any society; and that is, in my submission, the most essential condition for the existence and maintenance of democracy. It is the existence of *an implicit undertaking between the parties contending for power in the state not to persecute each other.*‡ It is upon that agreement that I believe democracy can alone be securely founded. Mutual toleration is the keystone of the arch and the cornerstone of the building.

---

* The advocacy of the *violent* overthrow of the government.
† Of course I am not arguing the proposition that "the more parties there are the better." The institutions of democracy clearly work best with a very small number of parties.
‡ Or any other minority, such as a racial or religious minority within the state.

John Strachey

Accumulation, Democracy, and Equality

John Strachey (1901–1963) first became well-known as a political analyst and economist presenting the communist case in the English language. His most notable book in that period of his life is The Coming Struggle for Power. *Later, he broke sharply from the communist movement and ended his life as a leading spokesman for democratic socialism, active in the British Labor Party, and, for a time, serving in the Labor government. The following essay is taken from Strachey's book* Contemporary Capitalism *(1956); it deals with socioeconomic problems in what Strachey calls "late-stage capitalism."*

The Question of Accumulation

The question of the degree of equality or inequality in the distribution of the national income is bound up with the question of the rate at which capital will be accumulated. This is the question, to put the thing in physical terms, of the proportion of its productive energies which the community will devote to making consumers' goods for its here-and-now satisfaction, as against the proportion it will devote to making new means of production, with which to make still more consumers' goods later on. The experience of the last quarter century in particular goes to show that the whole stability—the very fate and fortune—of latest-stage capitalisms are bound up with this issue.

At this point a definition of the terms used becomes inevitable. We shall use the term *accumulation* to express the whole process of diverting some of the productive effort of the community from producing new consumers' goods for here-and-now consumption and devoting those resources to producing new means of production. It was one of the main, if largely tacit, assumptions of economics that it could be taken for granted that any productive resources so diverted, withheld, or saved, would almost automatically be used to make new means of production. For this act of making new means of production the economists usually used the term *investment*. (Note that this is itself a different and narrower sense of the word investment from the one in everyday use: for the act of "investing" 1,000 pounds in, say, government bonds has only a remote and indirect connection with making new means of production.) Therefore the economists assumed that the whole process of accumulation would always in practice be successfully accomplished. The idea that the negative side of accumulation, namely, the diverting of resources from here-and-now consumption, may happen without its resulting in the positive side of investing these resources in new means of production, did not occur to them. But it can happen. It has been proved that a capitalist community may divert or withhold a certain proportion of its productive potential from immediate consumption—and then simply let those resources lie idle. This will be an issue to which we shall have to return again and again. Nevertheless, at the outset of our argument we are not concerned with it. We are concerned with the complete act of accumulation, assuming for the moment that both sides of it are successfully accomplished.

The question of successfully accomplished accumulation has two aspects, each of which is of the highest importance. First, there is the strictly economic or quantitative aspect: what proportion of its productive capacity is society to withhold from immediate consumption, seeking to devote it to producing new means of production? How is this proportion to be settled? Is the contemporary danger that latest-stage capitalisms will devote too much or too little to accumulation? And what are the factors which will tend to increase or diminish this proportion?

Second, there is the sociological, or qualitative, aspect: what social *form* is to be taken by the resources which are set aside for this accumulative purpose? Are they to take the form of the private profits of a small class of rich men and women? This form of accumulation is closely identified with the private ownership of society's existing means of production, from the use of which the new funds derive. Or should the sums devoted to accumulation be owned by the community as a whole, so that they become a consciously set-aside deduction from the current national income—set aside for the purpose of increasing that income after the passage of time? This form of accumulation is, of course, closely identified with the public ownership of the means of production.

And, finally, which is it of these two aspects of the question which really matters, both to the standard of life and to the state of mind of the wage-earning population? Is what matters the proportion of its energies which society devotes, at the expense of immediate consumption, to creating new means of production? Or is the essence of the matter the social form taken by the resources which represent this share, i.e., whether they take the form of private profit or a socially owned fund?

Overaccumulation

To take the quantitative question first. It has been, as we have seen, common ground, explicitly for Marx, and implicitly for every school of orthodox economists, that under capitalism there would be a most unequal distribution of income, and it has been assumed that this would lead to a high rate of accumulation. Indeed Marx's diagram of capitalism depicted a society blindly and monomaniacally accumulative. He had no doubts of the power of the acquisitive drive of capitalism. This, as he said repeatedly, was the one true function of the system. But he foretold that capitalism would push what was in essence attempted overaccumulation so far that the system must break down; it would break down not only because of the political wrath of the workers reduced to subsistence, or below it, but also because of the economic nemesis which accumulation pushed to this point would bring upon it, for the wage-earning mass of the population would be left too poor to buy the consumers' goods, the only ultimate purpose of which the ever-growing stock of new means of production was, after all, to produce. (This was Marx's basic explanation of crisis and slump.) Thus Marx believed that attempted overaccumulation based on an ever more extreme degree of inequality was the nemesis of the system.

In any event, the democratic counterforces, pressing for greater equality, have, in such highly developed capitalist societies as Britain and America, prevented the system from rushing on to its fate in this way. But this, we concluded, did not mean that Marx's diagnosis of the innate tendencies of the system was unsound. Moreover we shall see that one clear-sighted school of non-Marxist economists have come substantially (and tacitly) to agree with him.

Underaccumulation

It is hardly too much to say, however, that all other orthodox economists, including even so progressive a figure as Schumpeter, have feared, and still fear, that the system will suffer from exactly the opposite tendency. They fear that the democratic counterpressures will make society too equalitarian to be able to save and accumulate sufficiently to keep it technically progressive. Even Keynes himself, in his earlier period, at the time of writing the *Economic Consequences of the Peace*, still shared, we saw, these opposite fears. At that time, before he had developed his general theory, he too feared, rather than hoped, that society would soon cease to be "so framed" as to produce the maximum degree of inequality, and consequently the maximum rate of accumulation. He had not then realised that the rate of accumulation which latter-day capitalist society, left to itself, would attempt would be so high as to be self-defeating. But by the nineteen-thirties Keynes had seen that the real danger was precisely that. To this day, however, almost every other economist is still "viewing with alarm" the effect of democratic pressures working towards equality, and, consequently, a relatively high rate of consumption and low rate of accumulation. They suppose that the flow of new capital will be cut off, that society will cease to accumulate, that the wage earners will waste society's assets by consuming its entire gross annual product on riotous living.

Can Democracy Do It?

In fact, it is most unlikely that the democratic counter-pressures upon capitalism will get *too* strong. They are most unlikely to make society too equalitarian and so to cut down the rate of accumulation too far. They have, indeed, disproved the prediction of ever-increasing misery. But it has taken them all their time to enable the wage earners to do not much more than hold their own—to hold, that is to say, their relative share in the total national product. The position of the holders of capital is too strong for the main "danger" to be that of the democratic pressures succeeding too well.* For in the latest stage of capitalism, especially, the limits set by competition to the growth of profits have largely collapsed. The tendency of the latest-stage capitalism really is towards ever-growing profits. Stalin's account of the system was false only because he failed to see that the system had been to some extent balanced—hitherto, at any rate—in Britain and America by democratic counter-pressures. For, as we shall see in later volumes, in the case of Germany, the most appalling consequences in fact ensue if the democratic counterpressure on the latest-stage capitalism is relaxed.

As soon as the conclusions of this part of our narrative are thus set out in summary form, we shall see what an immense role they give to democracy. Can democracy possibly sustain such a role? Is it realistic to believe that the mere exercise of the franchise, every three of four

---

* They face very difficult practical problems in applying their pressure; we shall be much concerned with this perplexing issue as our argument proceeds.

years, can modify the very structure of the economy in such a way that it will cease to be "so framed" that it drives blindly towards maximum accumulation, cost what it may? Put that way the proposition seems most unlikely. But this is too narrow a definition of democracy. Contemporary democracy is much more than the effective possession of the franchise. In order to exist effectively, contemporary democracy must include not only solidly organised and also genuinely democratic trade unionism, but also such things as the statutory buttressing of the agriculturalists, deeply entrenched traditions of free speech, free assembly, and personal liberty. Contemporary democracy must amount to a complex of institutions and social traditions, the whole producing an all-pervading climate of opinion, if it is to fulfil its momentous economic role. When we see it whole, in this way, its capacity to modify the economic structure of society does not seem so incredible. Its action may seem weak indeed in comparison with the iron compulsions of capitalism. But, like a living thing, so long as life is in it, democracy is immensely persistent and pervasive; it may yet save the day.

At this point in our study it is too early to do more than pose such questions as these. But one thing we may notice already and that is the folly of looking upon social development statically and absolutely. Everything economic and social is ceaselessly changing, and changing at varying speeds. In particular, the political and the economic factors are ceaselessly interacting and modifying each other's development. All is process and becoming. It was Marx who, above all, emphasised the necessity of this dynamic approach if any useful sociology was to emerge; it was Marx (and still more Engels) who inveighed constantly and eloquently against the rigid, antihistorical absolutism of the economic and political conceptions of their orthodox contemporaries. How bitter an irony it is, then, that contemporary Marxism has been put into a Stalinist straitjacket which renders it incapable of taking into account the flow and flux of mid-twentieth-century social development in the highly developed economies of the West. Common or garden British and American empiricism, for all its inadequacies and banalities, which Engels used to satirise so brilliantly, is now far less out of touch with reality.

In any event, what matters is not to attempt to predict whether the impact of democracy will prove sufficient to modify capitalism ultimately out of recognition; that none of us can confidently assert. The essential thing is to see that the struggle is being fought out above all in the field of democratic action. The essential thing is to see that the struggle is being fought out in terms of the attempt to preserve, extend, and make effective those democratic forces which impinge on capitalism. It is, above all, because the Stalinist in the West will not face that fact that he bars himself from taking effective part in the social contests of our Western time and place.

So much for the quantitative aspect of accumulation. The answer to the question of whether the danger is that accumulation will be too big or too small must be that under capitalism its innate tendency is to become so big as to be self-defeating. Nevertheless, as we shall see immediately, there may be social cross currents and eddies which will introduce important qualifications to that conclusion at particular times and places.

The Private Appropriation of Social Accumulation

We can now pass on to the second, the sociological, the qualitative, aspect of the matter. We must consider the social form under which accumulation takes place in capitalist societies. The form taken by accumulation in all capitalist societies, whether or not they have reached the latest stage, is private profit, or rather it is rent, interest, and profit; it is private appropriation.

We come here upon one of the main anomalies of contemporary capitalism. For, whatever may have been the case in the adolescence of the system, accumulation is today unquestionably the accumulation of a socially produced surplus. The old arguments that the surplus arises from the "abstinence" (or the "waitings") of individual private persons, are now seen to be largely curiosities. No one who has a grasp of the reality of contemporary large-scale industry can doubt that the surplus which society annually accumulates for reinvestment in new means of production is the result of a social process of production. In that process thousands, or rather millions —indeed in the last analysis the whole community—cooperate to produce. Nevertheless under capitalism this socially and cooperatively produced surplus still in the main takes the form of private profit, and consequently becomes the private property of a strictly limited number of people who cannot be reckoned as comprising more than 10 percent of the population. Moreover it remains as true as ever it was that in law (if not in fact) this socially produced surplus becomes the private property of the owners of existing capital, to do exactly what they like with. Legally they need not reinvest a penny of it. Legally they could distribute to themselves as shareholders, by way of dividends, the whole of the undistributed profits of companies instead of reinvesting them. True they would then have to pay back a substantial part of the surplus in tax. But again, legally, they could spend on themselves every penny which, by every kind of device, they could retain. And, as common observation will show, they do manage so to retain and spend a remarkable number of pennies. When all the qualifications have been made, the fact remains that the socially produced surplus is still privately appropriated, and always must be so, so long as the main body of the country's means of production is privately owned. This has far-reaching consequences.

The first of these consequences is that so long as this state of things exists the wage earners are bound to see the indispensable process of accumulation as the mere piling up of profits in the hands of the rich. Keynes may have told them that the rich are bees accumulating the honey of profits for the benefit of us all. The fact remains that the wage earners see that the social surplus passes, initially at least, into the hands of this small class of the rich as their absolute private property. And the rich are under no legal obligation to accumulate by reinvesting it, but can dissipate all of that part of it which they can retain, after a struggle with the tax gatherers, on luxuries, if they so wish. This one of those manifest scandals which, even if the economic loss involved is not so great as would at first sight appear, can hardly continue indefinitely once its existence is realised.

The Rights of Property

We brush here against the vast and vexed question of "the rights of property." Fortunately we need not embark, for our present purposes, on any enquiry as to the contemporary justification, or lack of it, for different categories of private property. We need not now distinguish, for example, between property in nondurable consumers' goods, such as clothing, the right to which no one disputes, property in dwelling houses lived in by their owners, the right to which only doctrinaires dispute, and property in means of production worked by their owners, the right to which it is foolish to dispute. We need not do more than differentiate all such forms of property from the form that chiefly concerns us here, namely, income-bearing property in means of production (whether land, capital, or equipment) with which the owner has no real working or managerial connection. It is this last form of property—and predominantly its sub-division of share-holding in large, oligopolistic companies—with which we are above all concerned.

The historical justification of the rights of property is that property is the creation of man's own labour; therefore to take it from him is to rob him of the fruits of his labour. This, for example, is how Locke puts it, archetypally, in the second *Essay on Civil Government:*

Thus the grass my horse has bit, the turfs my servant has cut, the ore I have digged in any place, where I have a right to them in common with others, become my property, without the assignation or consent of anybody. The labour that was mine, removing them out of that common state they were in, hath fixed my property in them. . . . Though the water running in the fountain be everyone's, yet who can doubt but that in the pitcher it is his only who drew it out? (Chapter V.)

Notice, however, that the grass which the philosopher's horse bit, and the turfs his servant cut, do not become the property of the horse or the servant; they become the philosopher's property. Already a social alchemy is at work transforming the right of property from being the assurance that a man will reap what he sowed into its opposite, into the assurance that one man of property will reap what many other men have sowed.

In the case of contemporary shareholding, almost the last dreg of reality has been drained out of this classic justification. The representative shareholder in a large modern company has had as much to do with the creation of either its plant, or its product, as he has had with the creation of the moon. He has usually never even seen the factories or mines the shares of which he had bought; for that matter he may have only a hazy idea of what they produce. He has usually put no more than a small fraction, a twentieth or a fiftieth part, of his total fortune in any one enterprise, and he is frequently "switching" his investments from one concern to another, so that he has only a quite mild interest in the fortunes of any particular firm. Yet this is the form of property which is still defended by the arguments which were, and are, applicable to the peasant's plot or the artisan's workshop. And so slow is society in adjusting its thinking to its own rapid development (especially, of course, when its most influential thinkers do not *want* to make the adjustment) that the wage earners themselves can often still be impressed by these arguments. Some of them at least can still be persuaded to suppose that the defence of the right of certain families to draw, generation after generation, great incomes from shares in the major oligopolies, with which they have no other connection at all than this extractive one, is the defence of the garage proprietor's, or the one-man shopkeeper's, or the peasant's right to the fruits of his labour in creating his garage, his shop, or his farm.

Socialists, for that matter, are much to blame for failing to make the all-important distinction between these different forms of property sufficiently clear. And in the course of this study we must settle accounts with this whole issue. In this chapter, however, all that we are considering is the economic and social consequences of the private appropriation of a socially produced surplus. And for this limited purpose the essential form of property is, I repeat, modern shareholding. So long as this form of property remains unmodified a moral poison is bound to permeate society. For its manifestation is unearned, property-derived income, which will become an increasingly indefensible economic category. In particular, it will become increasingly indefensible with the passing of each generation. For it is above all inheritance which cuts the last connection between property-derived income and any function in the process of social production. All arguments about the rewards of enterprise and the like, which may have force for a particular entrepreneur, become simply farcical when the enterprise which, it may be held, is being rewarded was that of an iron-master in the eighteen-sixties, and the reward is going to his great-grandchildren. For this reason, recent democratic socialist economists, notably Mr. Hugh Dalton and Mr. Hugh Gaitskell, have laid great emphasis on limiting more and more the right to inherit considerable quantities of income-bearing property. This is undoubtedly a sound view, so long as it is realised that income from inherited property is merely the most scandalous case of the general scandal of the private appropriation of the socially produced surplus by means of private property in the means of production.

How Much Does It Matter?

How much, however, does the continuance of this scandal matter economically? To Marxists it is, of course, all-important, for it is the essence of exploitation. But a more important question is this: how much does it matter in the minds and hearts of the Western wage earners themselves? The answer must surely be that it matters to them a good deal, but not overwhelmingly. Many wage earners do realise more or less clearly that they and the technicians and executives are the people who produce the social surplus, and resent bitterly the fact that, legally at any rate, it is appropriated by passive shareholders. So long as private shareholding in large, oligopolistic companies, which is now the economically decisive form of private property, persists, the wage earners can never feel that they are genuinely working either for themselves or for the community.

But we must not lose sight of the other side of the picture. The fact is that the *immediate* economic gain of abolishing the private appropriation of the socially accumulated surplus would be by no means so great as would appear at first sight. This is not to deny that the amount of social waste represented by the luxury expenditure of the rich in all latest-stage capitalisms is considerable. It is least important in Britain, more important in America, and more important still, in proportion to the national income, in Western Germany (and, for that matter, in France and Italy). But nevertheless it is not a very large factor in the standard of life which the wage-earning mass of the population of such societies can hope to achieve. For it must be agreed that the leaders of the national economy, the skilled technicians and the high executives (as contrasted with the functionless shareholders), must, at our stage of human development, receive very considerably higher incomes than the rank and file of the community. Moreover, it has now been discovered by trial and error that this must be so, in the contemporary stage of human development, in any form of society, whether capitalist or communist. Once this is recognised, the fact must be faced that, while the amounts, in latest-stage capitalisms, spent by idle and functionless property owners would provide a useful fund for raising the standard of life of the masses, yet they would be by no means sufficient suddenly to transform that standard. The real scandal is the existence of a category of persons deriving very large net incomes (in one way or another) from completely passive shareholding in the main productive enterprises of society, rather than the actual quantitative loss to the community which their expenditure represents.*

---

* Thus the differentials in *earned* income in contemporary Britain may well be on the low, rather than on the high, side. But this fact is habitually confused with the continued existence of very high *unearned*, property-derived incomes, the huge differential effect of which taxation can do no more than mitigate, as we have seen.

Nevertheless, the long-term, as opposed to the immediate, economic gain of abolishing, or even markedly diminishing, unearned property-derived income might be very great. This would be so if the resultant saving (in real terms, the productive effort thus released), instead of being distributed to the mass of the population, was used to increase investment. Let us say, purely for the sake of argument, that the rich are receiving (net) 10 percent of the gross national product by way of property-derived income, half of which they spend and half of which they save and reinvest. If, then, the 5 percent of the national product used by by the rich in the spending of their unearned incomes was added to investment, it would permit, over the years, of a rapid acceleration in the rate of growth of the national product. It would not indeed *double* the rate of investment, for, as we shall see immediately, the savings of the rich are today far from being the only source of investment. But it would, over, say, a decade, make a very useful difference. This, however, presupposes a way of making sure that the extra accumulation thus effected actually would be used, i.e., invested. Moreover it presumes a progressive *abolition* of the functionless, unearned, property-derived incomes of the rich, as distinct from their mere mitigation by taxation. And I for one cannot image any way of effecting that abolition except by the transference of their income-bearing property to society.

Semicollectivised Accumulation

Writing in the nineteen-fifties, it is necessary to add a further qualification to the classical socialist objection to the private appropriation of the socially produced surplus. In capitalist societies of the latest stage, such as Britain and America, an important part of the social surplus never in fact reaches the hands of the individual owners of capital, although it still nominally becomes their legal property. In the first place, a really considerable part is now taxed away again, pooled in the hands of the state, and used as society thinks best. On the whole this tax-diverted part of the surplus tends to be spent upon current consumption, usually by way of either social services or defence. And conservatively minded writers accordingly see in the taxation of profits and of large incomes in general a squandering of the seed corn of the community. But their arguments can never be taken on their merits so long as their suggestion for preserving the seed corn is—to continue the agricultural analogy—to let the landlords keep it as their absolute private property to do what they like with. Moreover, there is nothing inevitable about the state using its part of the social surplus for consumption after it has diverted it by tax. It can be, and in Britain recently on occasions has been, used, directly or indirectly, for accumulation, i.e., it has been used to add to the community's stock of productive resources.

Second, the great corporations, which have become the decisive units of production, are increasingly inclined to refrain from distributing a part of the remainder of their surpluses (after tax) to their individual shareholders. Increasingly they themselves use a part of their surpluses for developing their own means of production. This semicollectivised process of accumulation on the part of the great corporations may well become an even more important factor than the pooling of surpluses in the national budget by means of taxation. As these pages were being first drafted in May, 1954, the largest of all British privately owned companies, Imperial Chemical Industries, issued its annual report. It showed that in the years 1945 to 1952, I.C.I. had invested in new productive equipment, stock, etc., 213 million pounds. Of this 153 million pounds had been drawn from "sources within the company," i.e., from nondistributed surpluses of one kind or another. Only 60 million pounds had been raised from the market. Nor would it be true to say that all of this latter sum of 60 millions pounds represented the capital of individual rich men which they could have spent on luxuries instead of reinvesting in I.C.I. A great part of it unquestionably represented semicollectivised surpluses of another kind, i.e., funds of insurance companies and similar institutions. Or again, we can take a much more general illustration from America. In 1953, the profits of all corporations appear to have been some 43 billion dollars before tax. Of this sum 23 billion dollars went in corporate taxes, 10 billion dollars was held back by the corporations as undistributed profits and presumably reinvested, leaving only 10 billion dollars to be distributed to individual shareholders (*Economic Report of the President 1954*, Chart 23, p. 43). This is an account of an economy in which the function of accumulation is in a state of transition.

Such developments of the latest stage begin to point beyond the confines of the system itself. For example, we are at once prompted to ask why the directors of the boards of the oligopolies accumulate in this way, if the process benefits them, individually and financially, but remotely, if at all? The answer is no doubt complex, but in the main, surely, it must be that they accumulate in order to enhance the power and success of their organisations; they accumulate in order to be the directors of a concern of the first rather than the second magnitude. The accumulate for fear that their corporation will lag behind in the race for technical improvement and may thus ultimately be swallowed up by a rival. And if at first hearing these seem but weak motives compared to real, old-fashioned self-enrichment, the answer must be that they have not proved so. Our experience is that the oligopolies accumulate very determinedly. It evidently matters extremely to their directors that "their show" should expand and succeed even if they will continue to get much the same salaries, expense accounts, and privileges after it has done so. Old-fashioned competition has been metamorphosed into a complex kind of rivalry. Moreover, since their motive is the acquisition of prestige and power, rather than wealth, their motive for expansion is an unlimited one. "Keeping up with the Joneses" is a trivial matter compared with "keeping up with the I.C.I."— or with Duponts or Fords.

The Amount, Not the Form

For all these reasons it is becoming clear that what chiefly determines the standard of life of the mass of the population is not the social *form* taken by accumulation, e.g., whether it be private profit or a social fund, but its *amount*. In other words, at any given level of national productivity, what in the main determines the national standard of life is not whether accumulation takes the form of private property or a social fund, but whether the rate of accumulation is set high or low. The higher it is set, the lower will be the standard of life (other things being equal) at the given moment; but the higher (other things being equal) will be the standard of life attainable in the future. Conversely, the lower the rate of accumulation, the more of our products we shall be able to consume now, but the slower we shall enlarge our productive capacity.

The importance of the amount rather than the form of accumulation has been brought into our consciousness by the fact that the communist societies of our day, which have abolished the private appropriation of the social surplus, are nevertheless maintaining a higher rate of accumulation than any other societies of which we have evidence. Thus, if we ignore for a moment the form which accumulation takes, the communist societies undoubtedly deduct from their wage earners a larger proportion of their product than do the capitalist societies. Can it be said, then, that they "exploit" their workers even more than do the capitalists? That all depends on whether the question of the *form* or the *amount* of the deduction from possible present consumption is considered the main thing. To the Marxist, the decisive thing is that none of the vast sums deducted from possible consumption in Russia, for example, go into the pockets of Russian owners of the means of production in the form of private profit. They are all used to build new steel works, power stations, atom plants, etc., potentially at least for the ultimate benefit of the Russian people as a whole. On the other hand, a sceptically and conservatively minded Western wage earner might comment that in fact the considerably smaller proportionate deduction made in the form of private profit from *his* possible consumption was not, in the main, used for the luxury spending of the rich, but did get used for building new means of production;

that he was confident of getting his share of the final products of these new means of production, as a result of using his weapon of democratic pressure; that for his part he was more concerned with the *amount* of the deduction than the form; that he would rather have, say, 20 percent taken from him for private profit than 40 percent for a social fund.

Nevertheless, their tremendous rate of uninterrupted accumulation will undoubtedly stand the communist societies in immensely good stead in the long run, even though it means that they have hitherto had to hold down the standard of life of the mass of their populations more rigorously, and more tyrannously, perhaps than capitalist societies have ever done. This fact is illustrated not only by the forty years' history of Russia since the Revolution. The gigantic nations of Asia are, in the middle of the twentieth century, beginning the processes of industrialisation; China is engaging on that process in a predominantly socialist form; India in a semicapitalist form. And if, on the whole, many people fancy that China will succeed in industrialising herself more rapidly than India, that is precisely because they think that the communist dictatorship in China will squeeze a higher rate of accumulation out of the Chinese people than can be secured from the Indian people by a mixed process, which is partly capitalist and partly democratic socialist.

Paradoxical conclusions emerge from these considerations. On the one hand, bitter experience in the first half of the century has taught us that the innate tendency of latest-stage capitalism is to attempt to maintain an extreme degree of inequality, and, associated with it, so high a rate of accumulation as to lead to periodic slumps and crises.

But, as we have seen, the degree of inequality has now been somewhat mitigated, on balance by the pressure of the wage earners acting through democratic institutions. The wage earners, who have become conscious of what is happening, are now apt to grudge every penny put aside for accumulation, because it takes the form of totally unjustified unearned income. Thus the profound paradox might arise that, as the influence of the wage earners grows, and in spite of the fact that classical capitalism's supreme tendency was to accumulation *à l'outrance*, the contemporary democratic capitalisms might be, to some extent, immobilised by the play and balance of their own social forces. Under the pressure of wage earners resentful of the out-of-date social form taken by accumulation, namely, private profit, they might accumulate too intermittently or too sluggishly to hold their own in the race with the ruthlessly accumulative communist societies. In that case the ironic situation would have been reached that it was precisely the fact that accumulation took the sociologically indefensible form of private profit which was making adequate and successful accumulation difficult.

Before and After the Hump

Indeed it has been argued that democracies, even if they have become socialist democracies, will never be able to match the rate of accumulation of the dictatorships. For, it is suggested, their electors will always see to it that their governments devote a very high proportion of their gross national products to immediate consumption. I believe that this contention has force for societies in one stage of economic development, but that it has much less force for societies which have reached a more developed stage.

This brings us to a concept used by modern economists, particularly Dr. Thomas Balogh, the concept that there is a "hump" in the process of the industrialisation and general modernisation of a community, a "hump" which it is arduous and painful in the extreme to surmount. But once this hump is surmounted, and by whatever methods, the community will be able to develop, and in particular to accumulate, with far less difficulty. Till communities are "over the hump" the process of capital accumulation is both imperative, if appreciable progress is to be made, and at the same time extremely painful for the population. For the bitter truth is that in such circumstances accumulation, under no matter what kind of social system, can only take place at the direct expense of the existing standard of life of the mass of the population. The man-hours of labour necessary to build the initial, basic industrial equipment of the country in question must be diverted somehow from the task of providing the existing supply of consumers' goods and services. This must mean, unless circumstances are especially favourable, an initial fall in that standard. It would be asking much of an electorate to ask it to vote itself such a fall in its own, by hypothesis, meagre standards of life, however much the economists were to prove that this was the only way to raise those standards, at any speed, in the long run. Thus it may well prove to be true that it is very difficult to combine a socialist economy and democracy in communities which have not yet surmounted the "hump" in the process of industrialisation—in, that is, what are often now called undeveloped countries (and they comprise, let it not be forgotten, the larger parts of both the capitalist and the communist worlds). But then experience shows that it is also very hard to combine a capitalist economy and democracy at this "prehump" stage of economic development. After all, we never even tried to establish democracy in the contemporary sense in Britain until we were well over the hump, somewhere about the third quarter of the nineteenth century. It is the fact of underdevelopment, not the particular economic system, whether capitalist or socialist, which makes it difficult for democracy to function in a "prehump" society.

Once, however, the initial hump of industrialisation has been surmounted a very different situation arises. A high rate of accumulation becomes at once less imperative and far easier to achieve. The level which is achieved becomes a matter of social preference. If the level is set on the low side, all that will happen is that the present standard of life will be high, but its rate of growth over the decades relatively slow, and vice versa. Such countries as America, Britain, Australia and New Zealand, Western Germany, Sweden, Holland, Canada—and more precariously France—are over the hump. In the communist world Russia (and perhaps Eastern Germany and Czechoslovakia) alone has even approached it; but Russia may now (1956) be nearly over. It will be extremely interesting to see whether or not Russia begins to develop democratic institutions if and when she comes down the developed side.

On the whole, then, the prediction that democracies, once at any rate they have begun to transform the social form taken by accumulation into a consciously set-aside fund—once they have begun to become socialist, that is to say, for this is one way of defining the essence of the transition—will prove spendthrift, and so cause their countries to fall behind in the race of economic development, will, I believe, prove to have little force, at least in the case of highly developed communities. For all that the acceptance of a high rate of accumulation will do to their populations is to impose an initially slower increase of their standard of life than would otherwise have been possible; it need never mean an arrest of that rise or an initial fall. Once accumulation predominantly takes the form of a publicly accounted for, continually discussed, social fund, instead of the large unearned incomes of irresponsible individuals, the difficulty of securing support for a high rate of accumulation will become much less. After all, we are at present asking the wage earners to abstain from consumption in order to provide high incomes to the rich which they need not legally use for accumulation at all, but are quite free to dissipate in any form of luxury spending (and, after all, in some cases that is what does actually happen). After the transformation of the form and method of accumulation, it will not, I believe, prove difficult to convince modern electorates that a high rate of accumulation is in their long-run interest. Even the simplest peasant knows the necessity of putting aside the seed corn.

Evidence that this is so is provided by the example of Sweden. Sweden is by no means a fully socialist democracy. Nevertheless she has now (1956) been ruled by Social Democratic governments, with socialistic and equalitarian tendencies, virtually without interruption for twenty-five years. And yet in 1956 Sweden is accumulating at an exceedingly high per cent of her gross national product. Again, the rate of accumulation instinctively established by the British Labour Government in

1945–1951 was much higher instead of lower than that which British capitalism had established in the nineteen-thirties.

There is a final reason why the basic problem of accumulation should be manageable for socialist democracies. The wage earners learned by agonising experience in the interwar years that maintaining a relatively low rate of consumption, in order to make possible a high rate of accumulation, may not, under capitalism, result in a rapid growth of society's powers of production at all. It may produce, instead, chronic mass unemployment. For the resources "saved" from consumption may not get used after all for the creation of new means of production; they may simply be left idle. It is this monstrous contingency, even more than private profit, that "puts off" the present-day electorate from accepting a high rate of accumulation. As soon as this has ceased to be a possibility, the electorate will be much more favourable to a high rate of accumulation. On the other hand, it is this very characteristic of latest-stage capitalism which more than anything else complicates the problem of its transformation by democratic means into a predominantly socialist society.

Michael Harrington

A View of the "Third World"*

Michael Harrington (b. 1928), author of The Other America *and* Toward a Democratic Left, *is the National Chairman of the Socialist Party of the United States. The following essay, which offers a democratic socialist analysis of problems of development in the "Third World," is taken from Harrington's pamphlet* American Power in the Twentieth Century, *published by the League for Industrial Democracy, 1967.*

It has been said so often that the rich nations are getting richer and the poor nations poorer that the very enormity of the fact is lost in cliché.

In the middle of the "Development Decade," proclaimed by the U.N., the Food and Agricultural Organization (FAO) announced that the developing lands were more ill-nourished in 1965 than they had been before World War II, and the Organization for Economic Cooperation and Development (OECD) estimated in 1966 that the nourishment needs in these countries will grow twice as fast as the supply during the remaining years of the century. Also in 1966, the U.N. journal *World Economic Survey* reported that the purchasing power of the Third World had declined while its net outflow of interest and profit to the wealthy powers—the tribute the poor pay to the rich—had increased by 10 percent. This outrage has been repeatedly denounced by the Secretaries

---

* Title supplied by the editor.

General of the U.N., various Popes, the World Council of Churches, and the U.S. Secretary of Defense.

As Mr. McNamara summarized this anguished prospect in a Montreal speech in 1966, in the year 2000 half of the developing nations will have achieved a per capita income of 170 dollars a year, assuming a continuation of present trends; the American figure would be 4,500 dollars. This tragedy is utterly rational according to the economic "laws" of the world the West has carefully created in the last century.

When capitalism conquered the planet, it destroyed or corrupted the indigenous achievements it encountered. Native industry was broken up either by force or because it could not compete with cheap, manufactured goods; direct tribute, and sometimes slave labor, were required; and the "mother" country entered into an alliance with the most reactionary of the local leaders. These cruelties were much more sophisticated and effective than those of the pirates and freebooters; the triumphant entrepreneurs not only stole from their subjects but also integrated them into their economic system.

"You cannot continue to inundate a country with your manufactures," Karl Marx shrewdly observed at the time, "unless you enable it to give some produce in return." Thus, a new economy was created. The colony exported primary products from its fields and mines according to the needs of the metropolitan economy (the profits were shipped out, too). Then, with whatever pittance was left to them, the natives were allowed to buy manufactured goods from their exploiters and so provided them with still another profit. There was, to be sure, some economic progress and modernization in the colony; the French proclaimed it in most noble terms: they were engaged in *la mission civilatrice*.

According to the rationalizations of the time, the various countries were simply doing what they could do "best," submitting to the impersonal laws of economics. People somehow failed to realize that these "laws" were artificial constructions of Western power. Asia, Africa, and Latin America were carefully and systematically denied the benefits of the new industrialism; they were designated the hewers of wood and the drawers of water.

After World War II, a new indignity was in store for the Third World. Paradoxically, the new nations suffered because the advanced lands were now less interested in exploiting them. The new mid-century technology no longer required great quantities of traditional raw materials; synthetics now substituted for old imports, and subsidized, protected agricultural sectors took care of about 80 percent of the need for primary products. Ironically, the very success of the Western welfare state, and particularly of government policies to promote full employment, made profiteering in the backward areas less attractive. For now the wealthy powers had created such stable and enormous markets that they could make more money producing for one another's affluence than by investing in underdeveloped countries.

On the world market, the demand for manufactured goods zoomed while that for primary products declined. The First Committee of the U.N. Trade and Development Conference in 1964 reported the result: between 1950 and 1962 prices paid for the exports of the underdeveloped countries went down by 7 percent and prices paid for their imports from the industrialized countries went up by 27 percent. And whenever the Third World managed to attract some public or private capital from the great powers, they paid cash on the barrelhead. The result of these trends has been, in the words of Raul Prebisch, "a regressive redistribution of income . . . between the developed and developing countries."

As Gunnar Myrdal has pointed out, everyone knows that it is more profitable to invest in safe projects than in risky ones—in European and American affluence rather than in Third World poverty. Given the political and social outlook of private business, available funds will go to private rather than to public enterprises and to undertakings in the ex-colonies only when they promote a quick profit rather than balanced growth of the whole society. The priorities so skillfully built into the very structure of the international economy are often a more efficient, and subtle, way of keeping the world's poor in their unhappy place than were the gunboats and troops of the earlier imperialism. To do incalculable harm to the masses of the Third World, the Western politician or businessman need not be evil, but only reasonable and realistic.

The man-made logic of the international division of labor is so compelling that it directs the developing country to embrace the misfortune which has been visited upon it. And this is precisely what the Committee for Economic Development (CED), one of the most sophisticated and liberal business organizations in the U.S., advocated in a 1966 policy statement. The new nations, the CED said, must invest "where the increment in value of product promises to be greatest." This sounds quite sensible, and it leads to the conclusion that priority should be given to those export industries "that can earn substantial foreign exchange if they can compete with effective industries in other countries. . . ." Obviously, fledgling societies cannot compete with the advanced giant industries of Europe and America; it would be a waste to allocate resources to a modern technological sector which would, after all, only duplicate Western factories and at a much higher and noncompetitive cost.

In obedience to the "laws" of the world market, the developing country must find some export specialty that suits the needs of the big powers, for that is the only rational thing to do in a system created by, and for, these big powers. And this logic can easily override consideration of the needs of the people or the requirements for building a balanced, modern economy. But even a country that manages to escape from these inexorabilities of the inernational economy and invests in an advanced enterprise is victimized by the way the world is organized. Celso Furtado, a brilliant Latin-American economist, has vividly analyzed what this means:

Technology developed "organically" in the West. When the first factories needed semiskilled and unskilled operatives, peasants were expropriated and a working class was created. As mechanical ingenuity advanced, the workers were progressively withdrawn from primary and secondary occupations (agriculture, mining, and mass production) and channeled into the service and white-collar sector. At times, these transitions were accomplished by brute force; at times, mass action won concessions and ameliorations. In either case, economy and society grew up side by side with the machines and the new organization of work.

Thus, Furtado points out, the corporation is designed to fit the needs of profit making in an advanced economy, and when one tries to transplant its technology to impoverished, developing lands, furious contradictions result. The newest machines save manpower—a blessing in the U.S. and a curse in a country with rampant underemployment. Mass production requires a huge market nonexistent in an archaic agricultural society. So, Furtado concludes, the very structure of economic life in the new nations, forced upon them in the last century, makes it difficult for them to absorb the benefits of scientific and technical progress on those rare occasions when they might have the opportunity to do so.

Thus, the rich nations specialize in activities which make work easier, goods more abundant, leisure more widespread, and living standards higher. The poor nations are left with the grubby tasks of primary production and with a stagnant or declining market; they must sell cheap and buy dear from the booming factories. In such a world, the gap separating the impoverished from the affluent will grow no matter what the U.N. General Assembly decides....

East-West Entente— Rich North Against Poor South?

We have one foot in genesis and the other in apocalypse, and annihilation is always an option. The future could even conform to a half-truth found in the fantasies of Mao Tse-tung: the advanced communist societies can benefit from international injustice every bit as much as the corporations. This might lead to a deal between well-heeled commissars and executives to end the old-fashioned conflict between East and West, so that the industrialized North could get on with the serious work of exploiting the backward South without regard to race, class, or political creed. An extraordinary potential exists in the world of the late 1960's. The struggle between East and West, communism and capitalism, which has dominated international politics since the end of World War II, could now come to an end—and be replaced by this conflict between the North, both communist and capitalist, and the South, which is poor.

The following turgid piece of prose is from an article entitled "Cost Accounting in Economic Relations between Socialist Countries"; it appeared in the October, 1966, issue of the international organ of the pro-Moscow Communists, the *World Marxist Review*:

> The prices for which the socialist countries sell their goods are influenced mostly by the conditions of production in the capitalist lands, and for this reason the exchange proportions are not always commensurate with the proportion of the expenditure of socially necessary labor within the framework of the socialist world economy.

Che Guevara made the same point more bluntly. In a 1965 speech, Guevara said,

> We should not speak any more about developing mutually beneficial trade based on prices which are really disadvantageous to the underdeveloped countries because of the law of value and the unequal relations of international trade caused by that law. How can "mutual benefit" mean the selling at world market prices of raw materials that cost the underdeveloped countries unlimited sweat and suffering and the buying at world market prices of machines produced in large, modern, mechanized factories?

There is no way of evading this point. For world prices reflect, precisely, the cheapness of primary products and the great expense of industrial goods. And if the fat communists use these prices in their relations with the impoverished communists, then they are getting the same kind of unjust advantage as the fat capitalists.

Guevara followed his logic to its conclusion: "If we establish that type of relationship between two groups of nations, we must argue that the socialist countries are to a certain extent accomplices of imperialist exploitation." And this exactly is admitted in the convoluted phrases of the Russian *World Marxist Review*.

The strange notion of a non- and even anticapitalist imperialism was first put forward in the 1920's by one of the most brilliant of the Bolshevik economists, E. Preobrazhensky.* His analysis still casts a very real light upon the present relations between the Communists and the Third World. The essence of trade between a capitalist power and a colony, Preobrazhensky said, was that "the figures will always show an inequality in the expenditure of labor on the two masses of goods exchanged as equivalents." In Guevara's terms, sweat is cheap and machines are costly. But, Preobrazhensky continued, this "nonequivalence of exchange" would go on even *after* the victory of socialism in the capitalist countries for it was, in part at least, a function of the backwardness of peasant economies as compared to *any* industrialized economy, capitalist or socialist. Preobrazhensky advocated the abolition of this inequity as fast as possible through the modernization of the retrograde societies.

But the victorious socialist revolution in the "capitalist countries"—that socialism based upon the European working class and technology which all the original Bolsheviks anticipated—never came to pass, and Preobrazhensky's hypothesis was never tested. Yet, it follows from the record of communist totalitarianism (a system which is neither capitalist nor communist) that the Bolshevik theorist had divined one of the most important truths of the second half of the twentieth century: that the division between rich and poor, industrialized and backward, North and South, can transcend social systems. As the *World Marxist Review* shamefacedly admitted and Guevara boldly asserted, both the fat communist and the fat capitalist can benefit from the "nonequivalence of exchange" on the world market.

---

* *The New Economics*, by E. Preobrazhensky, translated by Brian Pearce. Oxford, Clarendon Press, 1965.

This fact has not escaped the notice of the Third World. Here is Julius Nyerere's observation:

> Socialist countries, no less than capitalist countries, are prepared to behave like the millionaire—to use millions to destroy the other "millionaire," and it need not be a capitalist millionaire—it is just as likely to be a socialist "millionaire." In other words, socialist wealth now tolerates poverty, which is an even more unforgiveable crime . . . don't forget that rich countries . . . may be found on either side of the division between the capitalist and socialist countries.

But this imperialist process on the communist side was not restricted to profiteering from world market prices; it was political as well. Thus, the pro-Castro editors of the *Monthly Review* in the U.S. rightly noted that Cuba, by specializing in sugar production for the "socialist" market, had become politically dependent on the Russians. There can be little doubt that this client relationship helped cause Fidel to opt for Moscow against Peking in the ideological Sino-Soviet dispute. On the other hand, the East European Communist countries have been openly fighting since 1956 to reject the "socialist" division of labor proposed by the Russians; for under Moscow's system of fraternal exploitation it was suggested that some of the East European states play the classic role of raw-materials and agricultural supplier to the industrialized Big Brother in the Soviet Union.

Acting again in classic capitalist fashion, the Russians have been quite willing to subordinate their ideology in order to make a killing on the international market. In the summer of 1966, for instance, Fidel Castro expressed outrage at the "criminal" idea that Moscow was going to sign a commercial pact with Brazil. Nikolai Patolichev replied for the Soviet Union in the pragmatic phrases of a good businessman who will let nothing interfere with a good deal:

> We believe that foreign trade cannot, and should not, acknowledge frontiers or ideology. My government attributes the utmost importance to commercial relations with countries in the course of economic development, like Brazil. . . . The continuous increase of

production in the Soviet economy permits us to accelerate the rhythm and volume of our exports. . . .

In this last sentence, the Russian spokesman clearly implied that his country, as it becomes more industrialized, will take advantage of the exploitative relationships which have been so conveniently designed by world capitalism.

At this point one encounters an element of truth in the Maoist fantasy of international politics and Communist betrayal. Practical reasons have already impelled the U.S. and Russia to a measure of détente—the armament race and the threat of nuclear holocaust. As Russia becomes more modernized, the two social systems seem to some of their proponents less at odds. If these trends continue, the old antagonists of the Cold War might make a *de facto*, worldwide gentleman's agreement in which each tacitly respects the right of the other to exploitation in its own economic and political sphere.

There is a concrete possibility of the development described by the Algerian delegate to the U.N. Economic and Social Council Meeting in Geneva, in July, 1966: "Even as the détente in the Cold War has permitted an attenuation of the conflict between blocs with different social systems, one must fear that the East-West opposition will revolve on its axis and become an antagonism of North against South."

Theories on the Fate of Old and New Nations

The theory that the advanced powers are inevitably committed to reaction implies that there is no hope of democracy in the new nations.

The various formulations of America's (or, more precisely, capitalism's) role and fate, from Lenin to Mao, have obvious deficiencies. Yet, it is true that America has displayed a vested interest in at least some of the misery and poverty of the globe, and the defense of such ill-gotten gains could be (and in the past has been) the basis of a world view and foreign policy. There is the tragic possibility that this view might lead America to continue to promote the gap between rich and poor nations. The exploitation of impoverished people, however, is not a necessity for the American economy but only a cruel convenience. The nation could make new international departures without undergoing a sweeping domestic transformation. There would be many motives for such a change, among them enlightened self-interest (the present trends hurry toward more instability and violence which could be disastrous for the wealthy as well as for the hungry) and that current of democratic idealism which still flows within American society.

So the U.S. embraces an *almost*-imperialism. America has the potential of positive change, of helping to create a new world; yet that course would require considerable radicalization of its political life. If, as Aldous Huxley once said pessimistically, a 99 percent pacifist is a 100 percent militarist, then one can optimistically hope that an *almost*-imperialist will become anti-imperialist.

Lenin's belief that capitalism's inability to resolve its internal contradiction drove it to seek imperium over the entire world has become one of the most influential ideas of the twentieth century. And not only those who submit to Communist orthodoxy give lip service to this analysis. (As for the Chinese Communists, it is only lip service; for they have made the most sweeping revisions of doctrine, albeit in a spirit of fanatic fundamentalism.) Beyond that, almost all the nationalist, noncommunist revolutionists and reformers of the ex-colonial world have affirmed one or another version of the Leninist thesis. And even in the advanced countries Lenin's idea has had a profound effect upon intellectual life.

On the whole, the postwar experience violates the letter of the Leninist argument at almost every point—yet leaves much of its spirit intact. Following Marx, Lenin held that capitalism was not simply interested in plunder and booty abroad. The struggle between the various Western powers "for the sources of raw materials . . . and for 'spheres of influence'" was also a fight to avoid crisis at home. Since 1945 and with the single but glaring exception of oil, this assertion has become less true with every passing day. Advances in technology, synthetics, the organization of the market, and a whole host of factors have reduced the importance of the ex-colonies for the big powers; paradoxically, in the short run, the Third World would perhaps be better off if the capitalists were more interested in exploiting it.*

But the heart of Lenin's argument was not the simple assertion that there was a greedy scramble for resources and markets. Lenin believed that capitalism was forced to export its capital because it could not invest it profitably within the limits of the advanced economy. As the system became mature and overorganized, the rate of profit fell, and business was thus driven overseas in search for capital outlets. Thus, imperialism was the distinctive and last historical stage of capitalism itself—a final, desperate attempt to postpone the crisis of the system. However, the same maturity that forced the capitalists to war among themselves over the division of global spoils also heightened the revolutionary consciousness of the working class. So, World War I signaled the beginning of the epoch of "imperialist war and proletarian revolution."

There is no need here to discuss the complex question of how much this analysis applied to events before 1945. Relevant here is that throughout the postwar period, the trend in the export of capital has been to accentuate investment by the affluent powers *in* the affluent powers, rather than competition among them for opportunities in the ex-colonial world. During this time, American "direct investment" abroad (where business set up a plant in a foreign country rather than exporting American goods to it) more than doubled—and England and Canada absorbed more than 60 percent of the increase. These movements of capital, leaving the oil industry aside for a moment, accounted for a smaller proportion of the national income than similar exports had for Britain in the nineteenth century.

---

* For relevant figures on the trends in international trade, see *Modern Capitalism*, by Andrew Schonfeld, Appendix I, pp. 428–429. For the most recent government figures, see the September, 1966, issue of *Survey of Current Business*.

In France, by the mid-sixties, this situation had become a key element in Gaullist economic thinking. The failure of the French computer industry had made that country dependent on American corporations—and allowed the U.S. State Department to veto the sale of machines which might have facilitated the development of the *force de frappe*. As a result, the French government launched a state-subsidized merger movement to create a corporate base large enough to sustain a modern computer technology. There were those on the left who criticized de Gaulle for not having acted earlier and more decisively in this area. The socialist Gaston Defferre, for instance, said that "Europe will be colonized by the United States unless we decide to pool our resources in order to create industrial concerns comparable in size to the American ones and able to compete with them on an equal footing." The British Labor government took much the same line when it reopened its bid for entry into the Common Market in 1966.

Now all of this has a familiar, Leninist ring to it and hardly shows that the world market has been turned into a charitable trust. Gigantic corporations, with the conscious political support of their governments, are engaged in a fierce competition for markets. But the setting is not at all Leninist, for the fight is not conducted so much in Asia, Africa, or Latin America as in Europe and America. Thus, Western business has preserved much of its old-fashioned Leninist spirit, though it has profoundly revised the letter of Lenin's law.

But there is a recalcitrant exception to these trends: oil. For the economy as a whole, the raw materials and capital export markets of the Third World have become less and less important. In economic terms, it is not *necessary* for the U.S. to promote international injustice in order to maintain domestic prosperity. But the huge and politically powerful oil industry thrives on these inequities.

In 1964, there were 44.3 billion dollars of direct U.S. investment overseas; in 1965, 49.2 billion. In both years, net foreign investment was only about 5 percent of gross private domestic investment (the percentage actually declined a bit from 1964 to 1965). In both years, the distribution of this capital was about the same. In 1964, for instance, 31.2 percent of the American money had gone to Canada, 27.2 percent to Europe, 20.1 percent to Latin America, 6.9 percent to Asia, and 3.5 percent to Africa. All these figures support the thesis that exploiting the Third World is a diminishing and noncrucial part of the American economy.

At the same time, however, the petroleum and mining industries accounted for around 40 percent of this total, about the same portion as that of manufacturing. More to the point, the income in 1964 on 14.3 billion dollars of petroleum investment was more than *twice* as great as that realized on the 16.8 billion of investment in manufacturing (1.9 billion as against .876 billion). This obviously is a superprofit and it depends on arrangements with countries that are either poor or rich in a distorted way (Kuwait, which has the second highest per capita income in the world, is a balkanized fief for oil and not, as it should be, a source of wealth for Mideast development generally).

In the process of accumulating this enormous wealth, the oil industry works hand in glove with the U.S. government, and vice versa. The companies benefit, of course, from direct production controls within America —the money made in this rigidly *dirigiste* sector of the economy paradoxically seems to create *laisser-faire* millionaires—and the princely benefits from the 27½ percent depletion allowance. Import controls are also designed to support the (costly, noncompetitive) American wells in the manner to which they are accustomed. Indeed, world oil prices are an ingenious and artificial creation; John Strachey once calculated that, were the Arabs to nationalize the petroleum operations in their countries and permit a "market" price to emerge, oil consumers in the West would be able to buy at a much cheaper price than now prevails. However, since a single decision of Royal Dutch Shell was reported by Elizabeth Jager to have affected the balance of payments position of both Britain and Italy, it is unlikely that any such experimentation will be allowed.

But oil politics have also affected American foreign

policy. The basic premise was stated in Harry Truman's reminiscences on the 1945 Mideast crisis: "If the Russians were to control Iran's oil, either directly or indirectly, the raw material balance of the world would undergo a serious change and it would be a serious loss for the economy of the Western world."

The oil industry's argument is, of course, that as the producer of a strategic fuel its interests must be protected precisely in the interest of America's common good. Recently, in a Senate speech in May, 1966, Senator Robert F. Kennedy gave an example of the kind of private self-interest dominating the policy of the nation. In Peru, Kennedy said, President Belaunde had asked for 16 million dollars for a domestic Peace Corps type project. The State Department held up these funds in order to "make the Peruvians more reasonable" in the negotiations which they were then carrying on with American oil companies. Kennedy added, "The same was true in Argentina." And, it should also be noted, when AID threatened to turn off food shipments unless India accepted American price-fixing for fertilizer, it acted as the agent of oil companies.

The oil industry, then, acts according to the classical Leninist scenario. It profiteers in the Third World, supports local reaction, opposes democratic and modernizing movements, and sometimes treats the U.S. government like a hired plant security guard. At almost every point, the result has been to make American foreign policy more reactionary. If the country's international actions were dedicated to reduce the gap between rich and poor nations, the oil industry would suffer. The resultant misery of various millionaires would hardly overturn the American economy; but the catch is, of course, political. Oil is powerful in Washington, and therefore any hope of a truly democratic foreign policy would require the defeat of its domestic influence.

With this very important caveat about oil, a general and un-Leninist proposition can be restated: the prosperity of the American economy need not depend on the exploitation of the Third World and, to a considerable measure, does not at this moment. The reactionary policies the country has followed in widening the international gap between the rich and the poor are thus not the inexorable expressions of economic and social structure. They are reasonable, businesslike evils perpetrated according to the rules of this world which was so carefully made for us; but these rules could be changed. And that is something which is not to be found in the philosophy of Lenin or his followers.

Lenin and Keynes

The crucial question is whether or not it is possible, without a revolution of the system itself, to substitute social for armaments spending. In their work *Monopoly Capital*, Baran and Sweezy curiously treat this most fundamental issue only in a footnote. Writing of the liberals who "postulate . . . a substitution of welfare spending for military spending," they comment: "We must say of such liberals what Marx said of the bourgeois reformers of his day: 'They all want the impossible, namely the conditions of bourgeois existence without the necessary consequences of those conditions.'" This argument, based on a Marxian generality (which arose out of a controversy with Proudhon), is hardly convincing proof of the state and tendency of the American economy in the late sixties and seventies. It is necessary to consult reality as well as authority.

This can best be done by examining the actual, living fate of a projection very similar to the one urged by Baran and Sweezy. The author was V. I. Lenin, the date, 1916, the text, *Imperialism*.

It goes without saying (Lenin wrote) that if capitalism could develop agriculture, which today lags far behind industry everywhere, it could raise the standard of living of the masses, who are everywhere still poverty-stricken and underfed; in spite of the amazing advance in technical knowledge, there could be no talk of a superabundance of capital. . . . But if capitalism did these things it would not be capitalism: for uneven development and wretched conditions of the masses are fundamental and inevitable conditions and premises of this mode of production.

Lenin's prediction certainly held up from 1916 to 1945. In the twenties, the purchasing power of the masses of

Americans was held down while the productive capacity of the society was vastly increased and there was an eventual collapse. In the thirties, Roosevelt's attempts to follow Keynes and to inject effective demand into the economy were half-hearted and ultimately ineffective. But from 1945 on, every one of the advanced capitalist powers pursued some variant of a full-employment policy. These efforts hardly created Utopia; they were consonant with the persistence of great poverty, increasing injustice in the distribution of wealth and, particularly in the U.S., a chronic and scandalous level of unemployment (but not general joblessness of the thirties type). Capitalism had remained capitalism, yet it had learned that improving the lot of the masses could be good business.

There is no point in picturing this development in idyllic terms. The version of Keynesianism embraced by the American businessman of the sixties did not involve the notion that a reduction in defense spending would be compensated by a corresponding, multibillion-dollar rise in social investments. The "reactionary Keynesians" favored tax cuts which would disproportionately benefit the rich, maximize private consumption, and keep the public sector on starvation rations. If American society has come to a certain consensus that the government must intervene to stave off depression and that intervention would certainly be needed in the case of peace, there is still a fierce debate as to how this shall be done. The conservatives propose to prime the pump by raising the living standard of the wealthy, the liberals and radicals by improving the lot of the poor and of society as a whole.

But the American economy does not correspond to the rigid simplicity of the Baran-Sweezy model. In 1916, Lenin had the excuse that he could not look thirty years ahead into the future; but we have now lived that future and cannot afford to ignore its reality.

Moreover, one cannot speak of a simple substitution of social spending for defense outlays. As John Kenneth Galbraith pointed out in *The New Industrial State*, the billions for armament go to a very specific sector of the economy, one that requires extensive research and development for the creation of a sophisticated and advanced technology. Some of these machine and human skills could be put to benevolent use—but some could not. There must therefore be, Galbraith argues, a public investment in a peacetime production which is technologically similar to the annihilation industry. . . .

There is a general American commitment to government intervention against depressions, and there is the possibility that, with a turn toward the democratic left, this commitment could take the form of a vast social investment which would substitute for the armament sector. Here too, as in the case of overseas exploitation, there are powerful vested interests in the prevailing order of injustice. These will not be easily defeated—but they can be. Cold war, imperialism, the accentuation of the chasm between rich and poor nations, all these are deep trends in both the national and international economy of the U.S.; but they are not inexorable fates.

Up and On from Almost-Imperialism

America, the *almost*-imperialist, could act to change the imperialist order of things. American (and Western) prosperity does not depend on the evil which is done in the international economy; this country—and the rest of the West—could actually benefit by acting humanely in the world. If the imperialist heritage of economic interest, ideology, and feeling of superiority were rooted in economic necessity, there would be no hope of overcoming it. Since it is not, there is hope—but so far, in the postwar period, this is a most modest and theoretical consolation. The statistical possibilities for doing global good require radicalized politics if they are ever to be realized. An America that cannot even provide decent housing for its own "well-off" poor is hardly going to lead in the bold measures needed to end the threat of starvation forever.

Indeed, noneconomic factors might keep America from doing anything decent for the world's poor. In his provocative, thoughtful article on "Counterrevolutionary America" in the April, 1967, issue of *Commentary*, Robert Heilbroner argued that this was necessarily so. In Heilbroner's view, the "social psychology" of the less devel-

oped countries is an even greater barrier to modernization than their low levels of production. The ancient
ways have to be rooted out, the social structure has to be
overturned, and this requires

> some shock treatment like that of Communism. . . . Only a cam-
> paign of an intensity and singlemindedness that must approach the
> ludicrous and the unbearable offers the chance to ride roughshod
> over the resistance of the rich and the poor alike and to open the
> way for the forcible implantation of those modern attitudes and
> techniques without which there will be no escape from the misery
> of underdevelopment.

Heilbroner concedes that an American economy with
1.3 trillion dollars in corporate assets could afford the loss
of 16 billion of capital in Asia, Africa, and Latin America
without facing an internal crisis. But he doubts that the
U.S. is politically able to tolerate the upheavals, the
smashing of the old oligarchies, the violence inherent in
the development process. Therefore, he concludes,
". . . Communism, which may indeed represent a retrogressive movement in the West where it should continue
to be resisted with full energies, may nonetheless represent
a progressive movement in the backward areas where its
advent may be the only chance these areas have of escaping misery."

There are two distinct parts of this thesis, one a description, the other a value judgment. The latter asserts
that if a coercive and even totalitarian accumulation of
capital is the only practical way out of the impoverished
past into a more just future, then one reluctantly endorses
the "progressiveness" of this tragic, but unavoidable, transition. There is a perpetual danger that this attitude will
lead to a surrender of morality in the name of the "wave
of the future." Mussolini made the trains run on time,
Hitler "solved" the problem of unemployment, South Africa has the highest per capita income for black men on
that continent, and Franco has recently presided over
growth rates to be envied by communist planners. Yet, no
one of the democratic left would propose political support for a fascist government, however economically successful.

But even supposing Heilbroner's descriptive analysis is correct and there is no way for developing nations to avoid the agony of totalitarian modernization, democratic leftists still cannot give their support to those who carry out this transformation. Even when they are only a tiny minority whose hour has not yet come, it is those who are struggling for justice rather than growth rates who are the political determinant of what is truly progressive. Sometimes they will even be found within the communist movement—or in the one, official and single party: wherever they are, these people represent their nation's most precious resource.

But Heilbroner's description is overly pessimistic. The gloomy pattern he outlines is a possibility, perhaps even a probability. But it is not absolutely fated to come true, and by thinking that it is, there is a danger of helping to fulfill a deplorable prophecy.

It is not clear to me that America must react with such hostility to the violence and turmoil of the developmental process. Senator J. W. Fulbright is a conservative in the old humane and humanist sense of the term; he believes that human nature will eventually assert itself in the communist world and produce a "Thermidor" which will make the revolution practical and realistic. He therefore favors a policy of watchful waiting and he is, of course, opposed to American intervention into every upheaval. I disagree with Fulbright's analysis—particularly in discussions of human nature and Thermidor—yet tend to share many of his conclusions. Relevant is the fact that the Senator from Arkansas has long recognized the reality described by Heilbroner and that he has not recoiled from it in horror.

In *Old Myths and New Realities*, Fulbright wrote, ". . . we must be under no illusions as to the extreme difficulty of uprooting long-established ruling oligarchies without disruptions involving lesser or greater degrees of violence. The historic odds are probably against the prospects of peaceful social revolution. . . ." The democratic left could be at least as candid as the conservative Senator; it is not at all precluded that the American people could come to accept these disturbing complexities of international politics.

But it is possible to tamper with the "historical odds" cited by Fulbright (and Heilbroner); for they are, to a degree, man-made. The American policy I have described sets in motion a vicious circle: the market transfers wealth from the poor to the rich—and foreign aid, far from off-setting this tendency, exacerbates it. Thus, the developing countries discover that they must accumulate capital from their own internal resources. They must create a coercive state, whether communist or not; thus, they suppress the opposition, not simply of the wealthy but of the mass of the people who now must work harder, eat less, and give up the consolation of their ancient superstitions. In the U.S. the attendant violence and impieties are viewed with alarm and their existence becomes one more reactionary argument for pursuing international policies that breed still more violence.

Toward a New World Economy

If, however, the direction of this spiral were reversed, hopeful factors would reinforce one another. If some wealth were actually transferred from the rich nations to the poor, at least some economic compulsion toward coercion and violence would be removed. Consumption could, for instance, be gradually increased without endangering the whole modernization program. And the marvelous fact of ex-colonial people rising out of their poverty should make it politically easier in the U.S. to argue for redoubled efforts. And so, the crucial issue is political, not economic, for trends do not create new societies; they only make them possible. . . .

First, there must be international economic planning which will allocate massive resources to the new nations on the basis of their needs and capacities. To accomplish this, economic aid must be freed from the priorities of generals, diplomats, corporation executives—and commissars. But this cannot be done while appropriations are subject to the vagaries of annual political review in donor countries. The advanced powers will have to agree to some long-term mechanism of international taxation which will automatically provide the required sums to create a *contrat social* for the planet....

Second, the present "laws" of the international economy must be repealed and turned upside down. Where the world market of the past century was designed to transfer wealth from poor to rich, we must now devote our ingenuity to the building of mechanisms with the exact opposite effect. This means understanding and applying Gunnar Myrdal's paradox: only a double standard can ensure fairness; for now it is obvious that free and equal trade between unequal nations leads to systematic injustice. In the name of equity and not of charity, trade policies must discriminate in favor of the developing countries.

To paraphrase Keynes, the pursuit of a just world economy will guarantee not civilization itself but its possibility. And to follow this course of action is our only chance to close the gap between the world's rich and poor.

Daniel Bell

Work, Alienation, and Social Control

Daniel Bell (b. 1919), professor of sociology at Harvard University, is the author of The End of Ideology *and* A History of Marxian Socialism in the United States. *The following essay, which first appeared in the Summer, 1959 issue of* Dissent, *discusses a topic which has since become a major concern among those seeking a revival of socialist thought.*

In recent years there has arisen a sophistication which understands that the abolition of private property alone will not guarantee the end of exploitation. The problem has been posed as: how does one check bureaucracy? The problem is a real one. In socialist thought the "new" answer is to raise again the theme of "workers' control." This has shaped the demand for *comités d'entreprise* in France, for *mitbestimmungsrecht* in Germany, and is emerging in Britain as the left-wing answer to the British Labor Party's plan, "Industry and Society." It underlay, of course, the demand for workers' councils in Poland and Yugoslavia. I have no quarrel with the demand *per se*, but it is often difficult to know what the concept means.

In communist theory and discussion on this concept (apart from the opportunistic absorption of syndicalist ideas), the slogan of "workers' control" was conceived of almost entirely in *political* terms, as one of the means of undercutting the economic power of the employer class under capitalism, as a means *to* power, but not as a technique of democratization or the administration of industry *in* a socialist society.*

At the other extreme there were the detailed, imaginative, but unworkable, blueprints pieced together by the medievalists, distributivists, and syndicalists who formed the Guild Socialist movement in Britain before and after World War I. The movement has been insufficiently appreciated, for the Guild Socialists wrestled, as did the earlier Fabians, with concrete problems of administration. Most of the questions which beset socialist and managerial societies today were anticipated and thrashed out in Guild Socialist debates. They were aware that nationalization of the means of production might result in the exploitation of the individual guilds by the state (e.g., the building of unwanted new investment at the expense of consumption or leisure, the setting of high work norms, etc.). On the other hand, syndicalism, or the ownership of production by the individual guilds, might lead to a separatism or "parochial imperialism" whereby a single guild might seek to benefit at the expense of others. The guildsmen "solved" the problem by vesting title to capital and land in the state, but leasing the property to the guilds at a rent (or interest) large enough to cover government expenses. Politically, the guild state was to be composed of a bicameral body, the one a geographical Parliament, the other made up of functional (i.e., vocational) representatives. The consumer, through Parliament, was to set the goals of production; the Council of Guild Representatives was responsible for the efficient conduct of industry. Each guild was to be a self-governing body, based on

---

* See, for example, the explicit statement by Trotsky, the 1931 letter entitled *Ueber Arbeiterkontrolle der Produktion*, reprinted in the *New International*, May–June, 1951, pp. 175–178. "For us," said Trotsky, "the concept of workers' control exists within the scope of a capitalist regime, under bourgeois domination. . . . [It] means a kind of economic dual power in the factory, banks, business enterprises, etc. . . . Thus a workers' control regime, by its very nature, can only be thought of as a provisional, transitional regime during the period of the shattering of the bourgeois state. . . ." For a discussion of the shifting attitudes of Lenin and of the Communist regime on workers' control shortly after the Russian Revolution, *see* my essay, "Two Roads from Marx," in *The End of Ideology*, Glencoe, The Free Press, 1960.

local councils; membership was to be open freely, but if jobs were unavailable the state was to support the waiting applicant until he could work. Each guild was set to its own condition of work—tempo, grievance procedures, etc. The guild would receive money in proportion to its membership but could distribute the shares in accordance with the wishes of the membership, either in equal shares or in differentials according to skills. In contrast to production, distribuion was to be under the control of the state, with Parliament determining wage and price levels and the general level of new investment. Foreign trade, inevitably, would be a government monopoly. But ordinary forms of property, homes, autos, etc., would be left to the individual.

As a compromise between statism and syndicalism, Guild Socialism has given us many useful guides. Its weakness is that it sought to grapple with too many problems and that it set forth too detailed a blueprint. It was, paradoxically, too rational. Human societies cannot be made over *de nuovo*. One has to begin, pragmatically, with existing structures and with the character, temperament, and traditions—and desires—of the people concerned.

If the slogan of "workers' control" is raised, the simple starting point, perhaps, is to ask: workers' control over *what*? Control over the entire economy? This is unfeasible. A syndicalist society is too much a single-interest affair, which, if extended with its own bureaucracy, would simply substitute one form of interest domination for another. In a single industry or enterprise? One can question, further, whether this, too, is a meaningful (realistic) concept.* The British T.U.C. report, in 1932, on *The Control of Industry*, which accepted the public cor-

---

* Hannah Arendt, the keenest student of totalitarianism, and a sympathetic critic of the idea of workers' councils, writes apropos of the Hungarian and Polish experiences of 1957: ". . . it is quite doubtful whether the political principle of equality and self-rule can be applied to the economic sphere of life as well. It may be that ancient political theory, which held that economics, since it was bound up with the necessities of life, needed the rule of masters to function well, was not so wrong after all." For her extraordinary discussion of the meaning

poration rather than guild structure as the form of nationalized property, and joint consultation rather than syndicalist organization as the form of social control, was a
hard-headed recognition of the limits of workers' control.
And the new British Labor Party program on "Industry
and Society," which extends the idea of social control,
through state ownership of shares in enterprises, although
increasing the risk of a new "managerial" class society, is,
in principle, a large step forward in creating "social ac-
countability" of corporations to society,† which is the aim,
too, of workers' control.

The major confusion in the idea of workers' control, as
it has been put forward by socialists and syndicalists, is
that the word "control" has always had a double meaning: as direction (e.g., to control the course of an automobile); and as a check (e.g., to control someone's rage).
Usually, in the debates on workers' control, the proponents have rarely singled out the different meanings.
Roughly speaking, socialists have talked of workers' control to mean direction, management of an enterprise by
the workers themselves, or the participation in management. This latter sense is the meaning of workers' control
as it is being tried in Yugoslavia. The difficulty inherent
in worker participation in management is that it tends to
minimize the separate interest of workers from management and to rob the workers of an independent status in
the plant. Historically, the trade union has been a restric-
tive and protective organization, acting to defend workers' interests. Where the union has become an instrument
to "control" the workers, in the interests of national unity
or for the state, workers have formed substitute bodies.

of the spontaneous emergence of workers' councils during the 1957
events, *see* her article "Totalitarian Imperialism," *Journal of Politics*,
Vol. 20, 1958, pp. 5–43.

† Even joint consultation, it should be pointed out, runs the risk of being a catchword. One can point out, wryly, that in practice joint consultation may simply become a "buck-passing" mechanism whereby
each of the parties, managers as well as works council representatives,
evades its own responsibilities. For a revealing picture of this, particularly for those who fear the specter of "managerialism," *see* the
study by Elliott Jaques, *The Changing Culture of a Factory*, London,
Tavistock Publications, 1951.

This was the history of the shop stewards movement in Britain during World War I, of the workers' councils in Poland in October 1956. In Yugoslavia today the Communist Party is in a dilemma. Because the workers have been brought into participation in management there seems to be no functional role for the union; and some theorists have gone so far as to say that the trade unions ought to be eliminated. In Britain, on the other hand, the unions in nationalized industries have consistently refused to participate on the boards of management or to take responsibility for production. The union continues to act as an independent, defensive institution *vis-à-vis* management.

Is there, then, no role at all for workers' control? If there is any meaning to the idea of workers' control, it is control—*in the shop*—over the things which directly affect his workaday life: the rhythms, pace, and demands of work; a voice in the setting of equitable standards of pay; a check on the demands of the hierarchy over him. These are perhaps "small" solutions to large problems, what Karl Popper has called "piecemeal technology," but look where the eschatological visions have led!

Let us separate out two things which are crucial, I believe, in affecting the worker in the plant: one is the question of equity in treatment; the other is the impact of technology and an engineering culture on the work process itself.

By *equity*, a worker wants a situation in which no supervisor should have arbitrary or capricious power over him and in which some channel exists whereby his own grievances find an impartial adjudication. And secondly, by equity, a worker wants to be assured that his wage, *relative to others in the plant or area*, is fair. The question of differentials in wages is a difficult one. In the past these differentials have been set by custom or by the supply-and-demand balances in the market. In recent years engineers have sought, through job evaluation schemes, to set up "impartial" intervals between classes of jobs. Often these have failed because the "ornery" workers refuse to believe that mechanical criteria, mechanically applied, constitute equity; and sometimes because "power" groups in a plant refuse to recognize a scheme which disadvantages them.* In the West, by and large, the functions of the unions (or of shop committees, since in Germany, for example, the unions deal with regional wage policies and have no roots in the shops) have been directed, with a large measure of success, to securing recognized standards of equity written into collective bargaining contracts. The principles of seniority, of arbitration and umpire procedures, of union determination of methods of sharing wage increases (e.g., through equal or across-the-board allocations, or through percentage increases), all attest to the victory of the workers' conception of equity, rather than the employers', in the matter of fair treatment in the plant.

But in the second aspect of control, in the challenge to the work process itself, the unions have failed. The most characteristic fact about the American factory worker today—and probably the worker in factories in other countries as well—is his lack of interest in work. Few individuals think of "the job" as a place to seek any fulfillment. There is quite often the camaraderie of the shop, the joking, gossip, and politicking of group life. But *work* itself, the daily tasks which the individual is called upon to perform, lacks any real challenge and is seen only as an irksome chore to be shirked, or to be finished as well as possible. Most workers, by and large, are not articulate about work. Questionnaires and surveys provide merely the muttered semiapprovals or disapprovals, the grudging assents, or the grunted displeasures which mask the "to-

---

* For an interesting attempt to set an "objective" standard of pay differentials, *see* the article by Elliott Jaques in the *New Scientist*, London, July 3, 1958, p. 313. Jaques believes that by measuring the "time-span" which an individual has to perform jobs on his own initiative, without review, he is able to elicit "an unrecognized system of norms of what constitutes fair payment for any given level of work," and that these norms are "intuitively recognized by the people at work themselves." This would lead, says Jaques, to "an empirical basis for a national wages and salary policy."

Dr. Jaques has elaborated his proposals in an important but neglected book, *Equitable Payment*, New York, John Wiley, 1961.

hell-with-it-all" attitude of the individual who feels his life space constricted.* But the behavior itself becomes a judgment. First and foremost, it appears in the constant evasion of thought about work, the obsessive reveries (often sexual) while on the job, the substitution of the glamor of leisure for the drudgeries of work. Yet the harsher aspects are present as well. It takes the form of crazy racings on the job or what the workers call the "make-out" game, i.e., the breakneck effort to fulfill one's quotas early in order to lounge for the rest of the hour or day (and it is striking to see how this pattern is recapitulated identically by the Soviet worker in his habit of "storming"), by the sullen war against production standards, and, most spectacularly, even if infrequently, by the eruption of "wildcat strikes."†

Contemporary sociology has come to the melancholy and defeatist conclusion that technology as "progress" cannot be reversed.‡ In a rational order one would *reduce* to as little time as possible the number of hours spent in irksome work, and then find respite in leisure.

---

* Some sociologists deny that workers in a plant tend to be unhappy, and point to survey data—much of it collected by management—to show that the workers are fairly well satisfied with the job. The argument misses two essential points: first, there may be other aspects than work itself which provide some satisfaction, e.g., the clique or the group; and, second, no questionnaire on satisfaction is meaningful unless the worker is aware of alternative possibilities of work. (This, I suppose, is the meaning of the old saw: How can you keep them down on the farm after they've seen Paree? A farmer never having seen or known Paree may be satisfied with his lot; but is he, once he knows wider horizons?) My quarrel with industrial sociology—*see* my article "Adjusting Men to Machines," *Commentary*, July, 1947, and my essay *Work and Its Discontents*—is that not only has industrial sociology accepted managerial biases in conceptualizing what is a problem (e.g., the idea of "restriction of output") but that it has failed to conceive of alternative methods of organization of work so as to provide real choices for a worker.

† The most comprehensive account of the effect of machine labor on human personality can be found in George Friedmann's *Où va le travail humaine?* Paris, 1951. Most of this is included in the translation by Harold Sheppard published in *Industrial Society*, Glencoe, Free Press, 1958. *See*, too, Alvin Gouldner, *Wildcat Strike*, Yellow Springs, Ohio, Antioch Press, 1954.

‡ *See* David Riesman, *The Lonely Crowd*, New Haven: Yale University Press, 1950, as a prime example.

But is this the case? Can we not do something about the nature of the work process itself?

Actually the root of alienation lies *not* in the *machine* —as romantics like William Morris or Friedrich Junger were prone to say—but in the concept of *efficiency* which underlies the organization of the work process. The idea of efficiency dictates a breakdown of work and a flow of work in accordance with engineering rationality. It seeks to increase output by erasing any "waste"; and waste is defined as those moments of time which are not subject to the impersonal control of the work process itself. Central to the idea of efficiency is a notion of measurement. Modern industry, in fact, began not with the factory—the factory had been known in ancient times—but with measurement. Through measurement we passed from the division of labor into the division of time. Through measurement, industry was able to establish a calculus of time and pay a worker on the basis of units of work performed. But the value of work itself could only be defined in terms of its cost to the user; and cost was—and is —conceived primarily in narrow market terms. Thus the psychological costs of indifference or neuroses, the social costs of road and transport, are charges all outside the interest and control of the enterprise. Thus such a consideration, for example, as the site of a factory is determined largely by the possibility of increasing output rather than by the costs involved in travel time for the worker, community crowding, etc. In these situations the human being is taken as one more variable in the process and quite often a very subordinate one. Our emphasis has been on economic growth and increased output, but not on what kind of men are being molded by the work process. Even the recent vogue of "human relations" has been considered a justified cost to management in terms not of increasing satisfaction in work but of increasing output. The assumption has been made, of course, that if a worker is more satisfied he will increase his output. But what if the costs of satisfaction, involved in reorganizing the work process, mean a *decreased* output? What then? Which "variable" does one seek to maximize: the satisfaction of the work group or the productivity of the enterprise?

I have tried to spell out in some detail elsewhere* the reasons why the cult of efficiency has been an unanalyzed assumption in the "logics" of modern industry. Some of it is due to a utilitarian rationality (one of the sources, too, for the practical British bent for seeing problems in "administrative" rather than ideological terms), much to early technological necessity, since the nature of early steam power required the bunching of work. Once the goal of efficiency was established, however, the rationalization of work began; so, in Taylorism, we have the detailed breakdown of time, and, with Gilbreth, the economizing of motion.

In the United States, apart from questions of production standards, the unions have failed to challenge the organization of work. To do so would require a radical challenge to society as a whole: to question the location of industry or size of plant is not only to challenge managerial prerogatives, it is to question the logic of a consumption economy whose prime consideration is lower costs and increasing output. Moreover, how could any single enterprise, in a competitive situation, increase its costs by reorganizing the flow of work, without falling behind its competitors?

But this is not only a failing of "capitalist" society. In the socialist societies, sadly, there has been almost no imaginative attempt to think through the meaning of the work process. In Britain this has been, in part, the heritage of the Webbs and their own concept of efficiency (capitalism for them was wasteful and anarchic; socialism would be a "tidy" society). But of equal weight is the fact that, with outmoded machinery and in a falling world market, British society has been forced to think primarily of productivity in order to compete in the world markets. And who, today, would challenge the God

---

* *See* my book *Work and Its Discontents*, Boston, Beacon Press, 1956, for a discussion of the relation of efficiency to the concepts of rationality, and the necessary relationship of meaningful work to meaningful play and leisure.

of Productivity, if it might mean a lowered standard of living?

In Communist countries, where minority dictatorship has sought to speed rapid industrialization, the effects on the workers have been even harsher. Lenin's solution for the disorganization of production, for example, in a famous speech in June, 1919, was to introduce piecework and Taylorism in order to discipline the workers.* In the West, at least, where dehumanized work results in increasing productivity, the fruits of that productivity are shared with the workers. In the Communist countries, not only is work dehumanized but the social surplus through "primitive accumulation" goes to enhance the power of the state.

For underdeveloped countries, where living standards are pitifully low, it is difficult to talk of sacrificing production in order to make work more meaningful to the worker. Yet these are not nor should they be put in either/or terms. Engineers have learned that if efficiency considerations are pushed too far—if work is broken down into the most minute parts and made completely monotonous—it becomes self-defeating. The question is always one of "how much." But the question must be stated and placed in the forefront of considerations.

One need not accept the fatalism of the machine process or create new Utopias in automation to see that changes are possible. These range from such large-scale changes as genuine decentralization, which brings work to the workers rather than transporting large masses of workers to the work place, to the relatively minute but important changes in the pace of work, such as extending job cycles, job enlargement, allowing natural rhythms of work.†

The specifics are there: what is needed is a change of fundamental attitude. If one is to say, for example, that

---

* "Scientific Management and the Dictatorship of the Proletariat," *Collected Works*, Vol. 7.

† *See*, for example, Charles A. Walker's *The Man on the Assembly Line* for a fascinating discussion of changes in time cycles and the effect on work.

the worker is not a commodity, then one should take the step of abolishing piecework and eliminating the distinction whereby one man gets paid on a weekly or annual salary, and another man is paid by the piece or the hour. If one accepts again the heritage of the old socialist and humanist tradition of worker protest, then the work place itself and not the market should be the center of determination of pace and tempo of work. The "flow of demand," to employ the sociological jargon, must come from the worker himself rather than from the constraints imposed from above. Even if costs were to rise, surely there is an important social gain in that the place where a man spends such a large part of his day becomes a place of meaning and satisfaction rather than of drudgery. Fifty years ago, few enterprises carried safety devices to protect workers' limbs and lives. Some protested that adoption of such devices would increase costs. Yet few firms today plead that they cannot "afford" to introduce safety devices. Is meaningfulness in work any less important?

R. H. S. Crossman

The Idea of Progress and the Fallacy of Materialism

> *R. H. S. Crossman (b. 1907) is a leading socialist intellectual in contemporary England, and recently a member of the Labor Party government. "The Idea of Progress and the Fallacy of Materialism" is Section 3 of his essay, "Towards a Philosophy of Socialism," which first appeared in* New Fabian Essays, *1952.*

. . . Do we assume that, with the usual setbacks, the world is steadily progressing towards unity and freedom; and that democratic socialism, or something like it, will eventually be the pattern of a world government? Or have we lost faith in the progress which was the almost universal belief, not only of the early Fabians, but of the whole civilised world at the beginning of this century?

A simple test of this is to take two extreme points of view, those of H. G. Wells and Arnold Toynbee. Wells writes in *The Outline of History*:

> Our history has traced a steady growth of the social and political units into which men have combined. In the brief period of ten thousand years these units have grown from the small family tribe of the early Neolithic culture to the vast united realms—vast, yet still too small and partial—of the present time. And this change in size of the state—a change manifestly incomplete—has been accompanied by profound changes in all its nature. Compulsion and servitude have given way to ideas of associated freedom, and the sovereignty that was once concentrated in an autocratic king and god has been widely diffused throughout the community.

In this passage, the whole illusion of automatic progress is concisely expressed. History is the story of the evolution of society from the small unit to the large unit, and from the unit based on compulsion to the unit based on voluntary association; and this process will go on until we reach a world state, with no compulsions.

Towards the end of his life Wells began to despair, because he realised the failure of his implicit principle, that *the enlargement of scientific knowledge, i.e., power to control nature and men, necessarily increases freedom.* Faced by the obvious failure of rationalism to rationalise human nature, he moved very near to the pessimistic position of Arnold Toynbee.

Primitive societies may be likened to people lying torpid upon a ledge on a mountain-side, with a precipice below and a precipice above; civilisations may be likened to companions of these sleepers who have just risen to their feet and have started to climb up the face of the cliff above; while we for our part may liken ourselves to observers whose field of vision is limited to the ledge and to the lower slopes of the upper precipice and who have come upon the scene at the moment when the different members of the party happen to be in these respective postures and positions. The recumbent figures, despite our first impression, cannot be paralytics in reality; for they cannot have been born on the ledge, and no human muscles except their own can have hoisted them to this halting place. On the other hand, their companions who are climbing at the moment have only just left the same ledge; and, since the next ledge is out of sight, we do not know how high or how arduous the next pitch may be. We only know that it is impossible to halt and rest.

Most of us would now agree that Toynbee's sense of direction was better than that of the early Wells. Yet until the 1930s Wells' illusions were shared by liberals, Marxists and early Fabians; they were, indeed, the climate of all progressive public opinion.

This materialist conception of progress was based on assumptions about human behavior which psychological research has shown to have no basis in reality, and on a theory of democratic politics which has been confuted by the facts of the last thirty years. There is neither a natural identity of interests nor yet an inherent contradiction in the economic system. The growth of science and popular education does not automatically produce an "upward" evolution in society, if by "upward" is meant from servile to democratic forms; and the apocalyptic assumption that, after a period of dictatorship, a proletarian revolution must achieve a free and equal society is equally invalid. *The evolutionary and the revolutionary philosophies of progress have both proved false.* Judging by the facts, there is far more to be said for the Christian doctrine of original sin than for Rousseau's fantasy of the noble savage, or Marx's vision of the classless society.

Our first task, therefore, is to redefine progress. In what sense can we speak of it at all? Is there, as every communist, as well as every liberal and socialist, has believed, any upward movement in human history, or is it merely a story without plot or meaning?

To begin with, we must accept the fact that, in the strictest sense of the words, there is no such thing as moral progress. For morality consists in the decision to do good, and there is no evidence that more men decide more often to do what they believe to be their duty in a civilised society than do so in a primitive society. From the aspect of *individual* morality, modern civilisation merely faces men with different choices from those presented at earlier stages of our history. It enlarges the area of free choice. It enables us to cure sickness on a huge scale—and to destroy each other on a huge scale. It enables us to liberate each other on a huge scale—and to tyrannise each other on a huge scale. Men do, of course, "behave better" to each other in a society which forbids slavery than in one which tolerates it. But, in terms of individual morality, there are just as many opportunities for a slave owner to be a saint as for a citizen of a free democracy. Civilisation does not *make* us morally better, any more than democracy *makes* us use our liberty. The only continuous lines which we can trace in human history, and even these sag sometimes for hundreds of years at a time, are (1) the social accumulation of knowledge, and (2) the enlargement, through this accumulation, of men's power to control both nature and one another.

But both these lines of progress are morally neutral.

The individual and the society that possess more knowledge and power are not necessarily better than their backward ancestors. Here is one point where Toynbee's picture is more acceptable than that of Wells or Marx— its rejection of any moral determinism in history. There is no automatic progress or improvement in human nature, but there is an almost automatic accumulation of knowledge and power, which we can use equally for self-destruction or for self-emancipation.

Of course, it would be absurd to deny the existence in history of periods of *social* progress. Athenian democracy was an advance on the Solonian system, just as our own Welfare State is an improvement on the social morality of the 1840s. *The socialist measures this progress of social morality by the degree of equality and respect for individual personality expressed in the distribution of power and in the institutions of law and property within a state. This standard, indeed, is what we mean by the socialist ideal.*

It is important to observe, however, that there is no evidence of any continuous upward line of social progress. Free societies, in the sense we have given to the world, have existed at various times in recorded history and probably in prehistory as well. They have grown and they have perished, to be replaced by despotism and exploitation. Once we understand the nature of human freedom, this will not seem surprising, nor will it depress us unduly. For the social accumulation of knowledge and power does not make it any *easier* for men to build a free society. Knowledge can be used to enslave much more easily than to liberate; and destruction is as natural to man as construction. T. H. Huxley was right when, in a famous essay, he compared a free society to a garden. Nature produces either a wilderness of weeds or an arid patch of ground. Left to itself, a garden runs wild, and the gardener spends far more time in rooting out weeds than in planting flowers. Social morality, freedom, and equality do not grow by any law of economics or politics, but only with the most careful cultivation. So far, therefore, from viewing history as steady advance towards freedom, we should regard exploitation and slavery as the normal state of man and view the brief epochs of liberty as tremendous achievements. They could only be preserved for a few generations by constant cultivation, and they cannot be expected to become the general rule.

This is the point of departure for a modern theory of socialism. Instead of regarding social change as tending towards the enlargement of freedom, we must assume that increased concentration of power, whether in the form of technological development or social organisation, will always produce exploitation, injustice, and inequality in a society, unless the community possesses a social conscience strong enough to civilise them. Human institutions will always be not merely amoral but immoral, as Reinhold Niebuhr showed in his famous book, unless they are moralised by individual men and women aware of this proclivity and waging unceasing war against it. Every economic system, whether capitalist or socialist, degenerates into a system of privilege and exploitation unless it is policed by a social morality, which can only reside in a minority of citizens. Every political party degenerates into office-seeking, unless its leaders are faced by an opposition within the ranks. Every Church becomes a vested interest without its heretics, and every political system, including democracy, ossifies into an oligarchy. Freedom is always in danger, and the majority of mankind will always acquiesce in its loss, unless a minority is willing to challenge the privileges of the few and the apathy of the masses.

In the nineteenth century, this challenge was the task of liberalism. Today it has fallen to socialism. But we cannot fulfil it so long as we base our policy on the materialist fallacy that material progress *makes* men either free or equal. One particularly vicious form of this fallacy is the belief that economics are the determinant factors in social change and that, if we achieve economic justice, we automatically secure human freedom.

Unfortunately, man molds not only nature to his use, but also his fellow men: if he is a tool-using animal, as Marx declared, one of the handiest tools is his neighbour. The school, the press, the radio, the party machine, the army, the factory, are all instruments through which man, unless checked by a social conscience armed with sanctions, will exert power over the minds of his fellow men. The Political Revolution, which has concentrated coercive power and thought control in a few hands, is just as important a historical fact as the Industrial Revolution. Yet since Graham Wallas, almost nothing has been written by socialists about the Political Revolution, although it was the techniques of thought control and centralised coercion which frustrated the apocalyptic visions of liberals and Marxists and made possible both the modern Western democracy and the totalitarian state. Without these, it might have been possible, as the liberals hoped, for the nation state to wither away into economic brotherhood of man, or for the Leninist dictatorship of the proletariat to develop into a peaceful anarchy, in which coercive authority was scarcely apparent. But actually those who control the media of mass communication and the means of destruction (propaganda and the armed forces) are far more powerful today than the owners of the means of production. The state is no longer the executive committee of the bourgeoisie: the bourgeoisie are becoming the managers working for the state.

Marx saw that, though capitalism was the enemy, the Industrial Revolution was "objectively progressive," a stage in social development. Yet, as soon as capitalism reached maturity, it became a system of privilege and exploitation. Today the enemy of human freedom is the managerial society and the central coercive power which goes with it. And yet the Political Revolution has been "objectively progressive," in the sense that the instruments of mass communication and coercion, if restrained by social morality, *can* be used to enlarge freedom. Just as capitalism *could* be civilised into the Welfare State, so the managerial society *can* be civilised into democratic socialism.

The Soviet Union is the most extreme example of managerialism, because its Stalinist rulers consciously repudiate the primacy of morality over expediency and so destroy the possibility of an active social conscience, which could save them from the corruption of power. The capitalist class never did that, and this is why capitalist development did not fulfil the prophecies of Marx. No capitalist country was ever so theoretically and methodically capitalist as Russia is Stalinite today. This is also the reason why, judged by European standards, the U.S.A. is a better form of society than the U.S.S.R. In America, a liberal and Christian morality, and a Constitution and political tradition derived from it, have frustrated the full development of capitalism and still put up strong resistance against totalitarian tendencies. To reject America as a capitalist country and to treat the Soviet Empire as an example of socialist planning is to make nonsense of every one of our ideals. In reality, they are the two great examples of the modern managerial state, the one consciously and systematically managerial, the other moving towards the same end under the pressure of the Cold War. But whereas, in the U.S.A., totalitarianism and aggressiveness can still be checked by social conscience, in Russia they cannot. We can cooperate with the Americans as allies, influencing their policies despite their superior strength. It would be folly to expect such a relationship with the Soviet Union. Coexistence, yes. Mutually beneficial agreements, yes. But never cooperation.

One factor which has prevented many British socialists from accepting this obvious fact is the belief that in some sense the Soviet Union is a "workers' state." In fact, like all totalitarian states, it is an elite society, created by a revolutionary intelligentsia, which admittedly merely used the working-class movement, such as it was, in order to engineer its own capture of power. Indeed, the appeal of the communist philosophy, as distinct from communist slogans, has always been to the disillusioned intelligentsia. It offers them the power of which they are deprived, and a theory to justify its ruthless use; and it provides them with a scientific philosophy which satisfies their religious cravings while permitting them to feel modern and up-to-date.

It is noteworthy that the chief successes of communism since the Russian Revolution have been in backward countries, where popular education scarcely exists and a genuine working-class movement has for that reason failed to develop. In such countries, democracy must be a sham, since power is held in a few hands and public opinion consists of a few thousand people. *The carriers of communism in Asia are a tiny, educated minority, who form the social conscience and who have been personally wounded by the insolence of Western imperialism and white ascendancy.* The coolie in Malaya, or for that matter the tribesman in Nigeria, does not want *either* liberty, equality, and fraternity, *or* the dictatorship of the proletariat. He is below the level of such political aspirations. Not so the minor civil servant, the university professor, and the lawyer. The affronts perpetrated by the white man on this social conscience are a far more important communist lever than the economic condition of the masses.* Communism enlists the conscience and idealism of this elite and offers it a "career open to the talents" in its totalitarian society. In the twentieth century, democracy is no longer, as it was in the period of Marx, a *necessary* stage on the way to industrialisation. Unless trained in the Western tradition, as the Indians were, the elite does not desire it: and the masses do not require it, since they can be modernised (taught to drive tractors, fly aeroplanes, and worship Stalin) without any democratic liberation. For fighting a modern war, for working on a collective farm, or for repetitive work in a factory, the Chinese coolie is more malleable material and more expendable than a Western European worker or a New England farmer. So too, the colonial intelligentsia are more suitable members of a communist managerial class than Westerners, imbued with democratic traditions. Totalitarianism may well be the normal state of twentieth-century man, unless he has the good fortune to belong to a society which was either modernised before the century began, or indoctrinated with Western standards by a colonial power.

The recognition that progress does not necessarily bring freedom has led a considerable number of socialist intellectuals to accept defeat and to withdraw from poli-

---

* The success of the Labour Party's Indian policy confirms this view. It brought no economic benefit to the masses. But it has cured the anti-British resentment of the educated minority, which detests racial inequality and demands power and status for itself.

tics into mysticism or quietism. But this is not the only conclusion which can be drawn. Facing the century of totalitarianism, we can choose between two philosophies, symbolised by the figures of Buddha and Prometheus. Buddha represents the withdrawal from the struggle for freedom. For the Oriental Buddhist or for the Western defeatist, intellectual humility is the greatest virtue; the good man is not involved, but detached; he accepts this world as a vale of woe and seeks realisation in a transcendental eternity. The other philosophy, that of the sceptical humanist, is symbolised by Prometheus, chained to his Caucasian peak, with the eagle pecking out his liver. Prometheus stole fire from the gods in order to help his fellow men. He did not believe that any law of nature or divine purpose would automatically give freedom and happiness to his fellow men. Neither God nor history was on his side. It was his duty to steal fire, in defiance of law and order, and to prefer eternal agony to the denial of truth. He was surrounded by mysteries, but he recognised that they were veils to be pierced, not divine realities to be worshipped. So too the humanist today knows that we are surrounded by misery and injustice and that it is quite possible that all we have achieved in Western Europe may be destroyed. But he also knows that it is man's destiny to struggle against this natural process, and that there is no more justification for pessimism in politics than there is for a gardener to say, "I'll give up weeding because it's a wet summer."

By rejecting the automatism of Wells and Marx and the defeatism of Koestler or Aldous Huxley, we purify our socialist philosophy of illusions, which for many years have been sapping its strength. To realise that the socialist society is not the norm, evolved by material conditions, but the exception, imposed on immoral society by human will and social conscience, is not to emasculate our socialism, but to set ourselves a challenge.

Moreover, it shows us another difference between socialism and communism. The communist, like the Calvinist, derives this self-confidence from the sense that history is on his side and that his victory is predestined by forces largely outside his control. The democratic socialist draws his inspiration from the belief that nothing but human will and social conscience can liberate men from a historical process which, if left to itself, leads to slavery, exploitation, and war. The test of communism is the statistical success of each Five Year Plan and the size and strength of the Russian Empire. The test of socialism is the extent to which it shapes a people's institutions to the moral standards of freedom—even at the cost of a lower standard of living or the surrender of an empire.

Martin Buber

Marx and the Renewal of Society

Though best-known as a Jewish philosopher and theologian, Martin Buber (1878–1965) was also a social thinker, what might be called a humanistic socialist. His book Paths in Utopia *(1950) is a stimulating discussion of the various kinds of socialist expectation. He shows the way the images of the socialist society of the future held by pre-Marxist, Marxist, and post-Marxist thinkers also reveal the ethical quality of their thought. The essay below is a chapter from this book, criticizing the traditional Marxist view that to trouble very much about pictures of socialism would be to succumb to wilful fantasies and blueprints.*

We have seen that it is the goal of Utopian socialism so-called to substitute society for state to the greatest degree possible, moreover a society that is "genuine" and not a state in disguise. The prime conditions for a genuine society can be summed up as follows: it is not an aggregate of essentially unrelated individuals, for such an aggregate could only be held together by a "political," i.e., a coercive principle of government; it must be built up of little societies on the basis of communal life and of the associations of these societies; and the mutual relations of the societies and their associations must be determined to the greatest possible extent by the social principle—the principle of inner cohesion, collaboration, and mutual stimulation. In other words: only a structurally rich society can claim the inheritance of the state. This goal can be attained neither by a change in the order of government, i.e., those who dispose of the means of power, alone; nor by a change in the order of ownership, i.e., those who dispose of the means of production, alone; nor yet by any laws and institutions governing the forms of social life from outside, alone; nor by a combination of all these. All these things are necessary at certain stages of the transformation, with the restriction, of course, that no coercive order shall result which would standardize the whole and not tolerate the emergence of those elements of spontaneity, internal dynamism, and diversity so indispensable to the evolution of a genuine society. What, however, is essential, so essential that all these phases should only subserve its full implementation, is the growth of the genuine society itself, partly from already existing societies to be renewed in form and meaning, partly from societies to be built anew. The more such a society is actually or potentially in being at the time of the changes, the more it will be possible to realize socialism as an actuality in the changed order, that is, to obviate the danger of the power principle, be it in political or economic form or both, finding entry again, and of the human relations, the real life of society, remaining, underneath the changed surface of laws and institutions, as hopelessly out of joint and askew as ever they were under the capitalist regime. Those changes in the economic and political order inevitably imply, as regards the realization of socialism, the necessary removal of obstacles, but no more and no less. Without such a change the realization of socialism remains nothing but an idea, an impulse, and an isolated experiment; but without the actual restructuring of society the change of order is only a facade. It is not to be supposed that the change comes first and the restructuring afterwards; a society in transformation may well create for itself the instruments it needs for its maintenance, for its defence, for the removal of obstacles, but changed power relations do not of themselves create a new society capable of overcoming the power principle. Utopian socialism regards the various forms of cooperative society as being the most important cells for social restructure; and the more utopianism clarifies its ideas the more patently does the leading role seem to fall to the

producer-cum-consumer cooperative. The cooperative is
not an end in itself for the utopian, not even when a large
measure of socialism has been successfully realized
within it; the point is rather to produce the substance
which will then be released by the new order, established
in its own right so as to unify the multifarious cells.
Genuine utopian socialism can be termed "topical" socialism in a specific sense: it is not without *topographical*
character, it seeks to realize itself in a given place and
under given conditions, that is, "here and now," and to
the greatest degree possible here and now. But it regards
the local realization (and this has become increasingly
clear as the idea has developed) as nothing but a point of
departure, a beginning, something that must be there for
the big realization to join itself on to; that must be there
if this realization is to fight for its freedom and win universal validity; that must be there if the new society is to
arise out of it, out of all its cells and those they make in
their likeness.

Let us, at this juncture, put the decisive questions of
means and ends to Marx and Marxism.

Right from his earliest socialistic formulations up to the
full maturity of his thought, Marx conceived the end in a
way that comes very close to utopian socialism. As early
as in August, 1844, he was writing (in his essay *Critical
Glosses*):

Revolution as such—the overthrow of existing power and the
dissolution of the old conditions—is a political act. But without
revolution, socialism cannot carry on. Socialism needs this political
act in so far as it needs destruction and dissolution. But when its
organizing activity begins, when its ultimate purpose, its soul
emerges, socialism will throw the political husk away.

We must read this in conjunction with the following
passage written earlier on in the same year (*On the Jewish Question*):

Only when man has reorganized and organized his *forces propres*
as *social* forces [it is therefore not necessary, as Rousseau thinks, to
change man's nature, to deprive him of his *forces propres* and give
him new ones of a social character] and, consequently, no longer

cuts off his social power from himself in the form of political power (i.e., no longer establishes the state as the sphere of organized rule) only then will the emancipation of mankind be achieved.

Since Marx is known even in his early days to have regarded politics as obviously nothing but the expression and elaboration of class rule, politics must accordingly be abolished with the abolition of the latter: the man who is no longer "sundered from his fellowman, and from the community" is no longer a political being. This, however, is not regarded as the first consequence of some postrevolutionary development. Rather, as is clearly stated in both the above passages, revolution as such, i.e., revolution in its purely negative, "dissolvent" capacity, is the last political act. As soon as the organizing activity begins on the terrain prepared by the overthrow, as soon as the positive function of socialism starts, the political principle will be superseded by the social. The sphere in which this function is exercised is no longer the sphere of the political rulership of man by man. Marx's dialectical formulation leaves no doubt as to what the sequence of events actually is in his opinion; first the political act of *social* revolution will annihilate not merely the class state, but the state as a power formation altogether, whereas the *political* revolution was the very thing that "constituted the state as a public concern, that is, as the real state." On the other hand, "the organizing activity" will begin, i.e., the reconstruction of society, only after the complete overthrow of existing power, whatever organizing activity preceded the revolution was only organization for the struggle. From this we can see with the greatest clarity what it is that connects Marx with utopian socialism: the will to supersede the political principle by the social principle; and what divides him from it: his opinion that this supersession can be effected by exclusively political means, hence by way of sheer suicide, so to speak, on the part of the political principle.

This opinion is rooted deep in Marx's dialectical view of history, which found classical formulation fifteen years later in the preface to his book, *A Critique of Political Economy*.

Yet, in the concluding section of his polemic against Proudhon, we encounter what appears to be a not inconsiderable limitation. "The working class," he says, "will, in the course of its development (*dans le cours de son développement*), replace the old bourgeois society by an association which will exclude classes and their antagonisms, and there will no longer be any political power in its proper sense (*il n'y aura plus de pouvoir politique, proprement dit*), since political power is nothing but the official sum (*le résumé officiel*) of the antagonisms obtaining in bourgeois society." "No political power in its proper sense"—that means: no political power in the sense of an expression and elaboration of class rule, which is quite self-evident if class rule really has been abolished. Let us leave aside for the moment the question which obviously never entered into Marx's field of vision, namely, whether in those circumstances the proletariat would really be the "last" class, with whose accession to power class rule would collapse altogether, that is, whether a new social differentiation would not arise within the victorious proletariat itself, one which, even though the class designation might not apply, might very well lead to a new system of domination.

There still remains, however, the no less momentous question as to the nature and extent of political power in the "improper" sense, that is to say, the political power that no longer rests on class rule but persists after the classes have been abolished. Might it not be possible for such power to make itself no less felt, indeed more felt, than that based on class rule, especially so long as it was a matter of "defending the revolution"—so long, in fact, as humanity as a whole had not abolished class rule, or even, perhaps, so long as humanity had not adopted the view or the realization of socialism prevailing in that particular state in which the victory of the proletariat had been won?

But the thing that concerns us most of all is this: so long, in such a state or states, as this fixed point of view prevails, and prevails with all the technique and instruments of power at the disposal of our age, how can that spontaneity, that free social form seeking and form giving, that unfettered power of social experimentation and decision so indispensable to the realization of socialism and the emergence of a socialist form of society, how can they possibly get to work? By omitting to draw a clear line of demarcation between power in its proper and improper senses Marx opens the door to a type of political principle which, in his opinion, does not and cannot exist: a type which is not the expression and elaboration of class-rule, but is rather the expression and elaboration of power tendencies and power struggles not characterized by class, on the part of groups and individuals. Political power in the improper sense would accordingly be "the official sum of antagonisms" either within the proletarian class itself or, more precisely, within the nation in which "class rule has been abolished."

His impressions of the problematical Revolution of 1848 served to sharpen Marx's critical attitude to experiments in social restructure. If the "little experiments, inevitably abortive" had already been censured in the *Manifesto*, now (in the report *The Class War in France* of 1850) "doctrinaire socialism" was accused of "wishing away the revolutionary conflict of the classes and the need for it by means of petty artifices and gross sentimentalities," and (in the *Eighteenth Brumaire* of 1852) the French proletariat was reprobated for having partly committed itself to "doctrinaire experiments, exchange banks, and workers' associations," and thus to a "movement which, having given up the struggle to overthrow the old world despite all the means at its disposal, prefers to seek its own salvation behind society's back, privately, inside the narrow framework of its existence, and which will thus necessarily come to grief."

Marx's faith in the impending revolution was still unshaken at that time, but his confidence in an impending world revolution in the full sense of the word began to waver. In 1858 he wrote to Engels: "The difficult question for us is this. On the continent, the revolution is imminent and will immediately assume a socialist form. But will it not necessarily be crushed in this small corner of the earth [meaning the continent of Europe!], seeing that over a far greater area the movement of bourgeois society is still in the ascendant?" His doubts seem to have deepened still more in the following years. On the other hand he became more and more impressed with the significance of the extrarevolutionary political struggle. After another six years this was worked out *inter alia* in the "Inaugural Address to the International Workers' Association." Having praised the Ten-Hour Law as the "triumph of a principle," he went on to call the rise of the Cooperative Movement "a still greater triumph for the political economy of labour over the political economy of capital." The value of these great social experiments, he said, could not be overestimated; for the workers, who had set up cooperative factories without any help at all, had thereby proved that wage labour "is destined to give way to associated labour." The cooperative system, however, if it was to free the masses, needed "developing on a national scale and consequently promoting by national means," hence precisely what Louis Blanc and Lassalle had hoped and striven for. But such a thing would not be conceded by the big landed proprietors and the capitalists of their own free will. "Therefore," he ends, it is "the great duty of the working class" to seize political power.

We must give this word "therefore" our full attention. Labour is to win political power in the parliaments in order to sweep the obstacles out of the way of the cooperative movement. Marx is here ascribing a central significance to cooperation, and in particular to the producer cooperatives. Although it is stressed, as also in Resolutions Marx drew up for the Geneva Congress of 1866, that the cooperative movement was not capable of remodeling capitalist society of itself, it is none the less acknowledged as the proper way to remodel it, save that for this to succeed the acquisition of state power by the workers was essential. At this point Marx comes remarkably close to restructural thinking in practice without accepting it in principle. Worthy of mention in this connection is the fact that he clearly recognizes the danger of the cooperatives degenerating into ordinary bourgeois joint-stock companies, and even recommends the right remedy: that all the workers employed should receive the same share.

But less than three months before the opening of the Geneva Congress for which he drew up this Resolution, Marx wrote to Engels about the tendencies expressed by the French in a debate of the General Council of the International: "Proudhonized Stirnerism. Splitting everything up into little 'groups' or 'communes' and then making a 'company' of them, but not a state." It is here that the undercurrent of state centralism creeps unmistakably into Marx's ideas, if only by implication. The federalism of Proudhon he is attacking has not the slightest wish to split everything up into communes, it only wants to confer relatively extensive autonomy on the existing communes and combine them into units, whose own combination would represent a more organic form of community than the existing state. As against this Marx once more holds fast to the state as such.

But now, another five years later, a revolutionary event exerted a new influence on Marx's views, an event stronger than any preceding it and tending in another direction: the Paris Commune. In one of his most significant writings, the address to the General Council of the International on the civil war in France, he sketched a picture of the growth, activities and aims of the Commune. The historical reliability of this picture has been disputed, but that does not concern us here: the picture is a confession and one that is of great importance for our theme, which is the variations in Marx's views concerning the evolution of a new society.

What distinguished the Commune in Marx's eyes *toto genere* from all earlier endeavours, "its true secret," is that it was "essentially a working-class government." That is to be understood literally: Marx means a government not merely appointed by the working class but also actually and factually exercised by it. The Commune is "the self-government of the producers." Born of universal suffrage and elected by the Parisians themselves, representation of this kind, consisting as it does of members who can be replaced at any time and who are bound by the definite instructions of their electors—such representation

"should not be a parliamentary but a working body, executive and legislative at the same time." The same form of
organization was to be provided for every commune in
France right down to the smallest village. The provincial
communes were to administer their common affairs in the
district parliament and the district assemblies in their
turn were to send deputies to the national delegation. In
place of centralized state power originating from the era
of absolute monarchy, "with its omnipresent organs,"
there would consequently emerge a largely decentralized
community. "The few, but important, functions still left
over for a central government were to be transferred to
communal, i.e., strictly answerable, officials." The decentralization, however, would not be a fragmentation but a
reconstitution of national unity on an organic basis and
would mean a reactivating of the nation's forces and
therefore of the national organism as a whole. "The communal constitution would have rendered up to the body
social all the powers which have hitherto been devoured
by the parasitic excrescence of the 'state,' which battens
on society and inhibits its free movement. By this deed
alone it would have brought about the regeneration of
France." It is obvious that Marx is speaking here not of
certain historical state forms but of the state in general.
By becoming something "self-evident," local self-government renders state-power "superfluous." Never did any
utopian socialist express himself more radically on this
point.

But the political structure of the Commune is, for
Marx, only a prelude to the real and decisive thing—the
great social transformation to which, with its plans and
its dispositions, it would inevitably have led had it not
been destroyed. He sees in the Commune "the finally
discovered political form, in whose sign the economic
liberation of labour can march forward." The Commune
wanted "to make individual property a truth, by converting the means of production, land, and capital into the
mere tools of free and associated labour," and labour
amalgamated in producer cooperatives at that. "If cooperative production," Marx cries, "is not to remain a snare
and a delusion, if it is to oust the capitalist system, if the

cooperatives as a whole are to regulate national production according to a common plan and thereby take it under their own control—what else would that be, gentlemen, but communism, and a communism that is *possible?*" That is, a communism that proves its possibility in the teeth of the widespread notion of its "impossibility." A federalism of communes and cooperatives—for that is precisely what this picture sketches—is thus acknowledged by Marx as genuine communism. To be sure, he still sets his face against all utopianism. The working class "has no cut-and-dried Utopias to introduce by a plebiscite." The communal and cooperative system which it wants to build up into a new community and a new society is not a contrivance of the mind: only out of the reality of the association of old and new generations, the reality that is gradually emerging from the nation itself, out of these things alone can the working class build its work and its house. "It has no ideals to realize, it has only to set free those elements of the new society which have already developed in the womb of the collapsing bourgeois society." Here we have that notion of "development" again, dating from 1847; but this time it is completely unequivocal and indubitably meant in the sense of a prerevolutionary process, one, moreover, whose nature consists in the formation of small, federable units of men's work and life together, of communes and cooperatives, in respect to which it is the sole task of the revolution to set them free, to unite them and endow them with authority. This certainly accords at all points with the famous formula given in the *Critique of Political Economy* twelve years previously, as regards the new and higher conditions of production, which, however, will never supplant the old "until the material conditions for their existence have been gestated in the womb of the old society itself." But it is nowhere hinted in the report of the General Council that the Paris Commune miscarried because the gestation had not been completed. And the "elements of the new society" that had developed in the womb of the old, collapsing one—they were for the most part those very cooperatives which had been formed in France under the influence of utopian socialism, just as the political federalism of the communes Marx described had been formed under the influence of Proudhon. These cooperatives it was that were characterized as "little experiments, inevitably abortive" in *The Communist Manifesto;* but had the Commune triumphed—and everything in the report indicates that it could have triumphed but for this or that particular circumstance—then they would have become the cell-substance of the new society.

From this standpoint, i.e., of Marxist *politics of revolution,* statements like the following one by Engels in 1873 can therefore be understood: "Had the autonomists been content to say that the social organization of the future would admit authority only within the bounds unavoidably set by the conditions of production themselves, then we could have agreed with them." As if Proudhon had not time and again emphasized the necessity of constantly setting boundaries between possible decentralization and necessary centralization! Another time (1874) Engels says, adhering strictly to the formulation Marx gave in the Report of the Commission set up by the Hauge Congress in 1872 to examine the activities of the Bakuninists, that all socialists were agreed that the state would wither away as a result of the social revolution-to-be, and political authority with it; but that the "antiauthoritarians" were wrong to demand "that the political state should be abolished at a blow *before* the social conditions producing it were abolished." "They demand," Engels continues, "that the first act of the social revolution should be the abolition of authority." In actual fact no prudent antiauthoritarian socialist had ever demanded anything but that the revolution should begin by curing the *hypertrophy* of authority, its proliferation, and from then on concentrate on reducing it to proportions that would correspond to the circumstances given at any time. Engels answers the alleged demand as follows: "Have you ever seen a revolution, gentlemen? A revolution is certainly the most authoritarian thing there is." If that means that the revolutionary struggle as such must proceed under far-sighted leadership and strict discipline, so much cannot be doubted; but if it means that in the revolutionary epoch (of which nobody can say when it

will end), the whole population is to be limitlessly determined in all branches of its life and thought by one
central authoritarian will, then it is inconceivable how
such a stage can ever evolve into socialism.

Four years after his paper on the Commune, Marx, in a
letter sharply criticizing the program sketched for the
Unification Congress of Gotha, set out afresh his misgiv-
ings about the cooperatives, with the obvious political
intent of bringing one of the chief points in the program
of the Lassallites into question and thus undermining the
possibility of any compromise with them. Certainly Marx
was only setting his face against the "establishment of
cooperative societies with state aid," though allowing cooperative production to stand as the socialist goal; but
expressions like "specific miracle-cure," "sectarian movement," and even "reactionary workers" in connexion with
Buchez' program are clear enough. Despite that, however, the paragraph dealing with Producer Associations
financed out of state credit was accepted by the Congress.

But nothing affords us a deeper insight into Marx's
ambivalent attitude to the question of the internal transformation of society and the conditions for it than his
correspondence with Vera Zasulitch in 1881.

The publication of these documents by Ryazanov is
therefore particularly valuable, because they acquaint us
with Marx's drafts, some of them very detailed, for his
answering letter; as published the drafts run to more than
900 lines, with innumerable deletions, emendations, am-
plifications; the letter itself runs only to about 40.

Vera Zasulitch, "the woman of the moment, the woman
with a mission," as Stepniak calls her, had written to
Marx from Geneva to ask him, as author of *Capital*, the
first volume of which was "enjoying great popularity in
Russia" and was also playing a part particularly in discussions on the agrarian question and the Russian village
community, to ask him what he thought about the prospects of the village community in the future. It was, she
said, "a question of life and death" for the Russian Socialist Party, and on it also depended the personal fate of the
revolutionary Socialists. For, either the village communi-

ties, once free of the excessive taxes and tributes as well
as of the government's arbitrary dealings, were capable in
themselves of developing in a socialist direction, i.e., of
gradually organizing the production and distribution of
goods on a collective basis, in which case the revolutionary Socialist would have to "devote all his powers to the
freeing of the communities and their development," or
else, as many people who called themselves Marxists declared, basing themselves on Marx, the village community was an "archaic form" condemned by history and
scientific socialism alike to perdition. In that case the
Socialists, who would seek in vain to calculate in how
many decades the land would pass out of the hands of
the Russian peasants into those of the bourgeoisie and in
how many centuries capitalism in Russia might conceivably reach a stage of development similar to that in Western Europe, would have to restrict themselves to propaganda among the urban workers, propaganda which
"will continue to pour into the masses of the peasants
who, as a result of the dissolution of the village community, will be thrown on to the streets of the great
cities in their search for wages." One can see that as a
matter of fact it is nothing less than the decision whether
or not the work of the Socialists in Russia could have any
assured future for the next few generations. Must Russia
go the way of Western Europe, where, with the rise of
advanced capitalism, the "archaic" forms of community
necessarily dissolve of themselves, and is there no alternative but to prepare a class-conscious core of urban
proletariat for the still distant time of industrialization?
On the other hand, if there exists, by reason of her
special agrarian institutions, a special way for Russia,
quite apart, as it were, from the general dialectics of
history, a way by which to imbue the traditional pattern
of communal ownership and production with socialist
spirit; if one could, by developing this pattern from
within and obtaining a better position for it externally,
create an organic social reality which would ripen into
the revolution, and, liberated by the latter and established in full freedom and right, which would thereupon
constitute itself as the backbone of the new society—if

all this, then there is indeed a great and immediate constructive-revolutionary task which may lead quite soon, perhaps, to the realization of socialism. The decision as to which of the two was the historical truth was left in Marx's hands.

His exertions to give the right answer are of a thoroughness and scrupulosity worthy of admiration. Already before this he had occupied himself with the same knotty problem, and now he attacked it afresh with especial intensity. Again and again we see him canceling one formulation of great delicacy and precision only to seek another still more adequate. Although but a series of fragmentary sketches these notes seem to me the most important attempt that has been made to grasp synthetically the theme of the Russian village community.

Owing to the paucity of historical material, the village community is still one of the least understood departments of ethnic sociology, within which the Russian type, whose development is extremely poorly documented, forms a perplexing chapter. In accordance with the prevailing scientific opinion of his time, Marx was inclined to attribute a very early origin to it. Today we are wont to regard it as rather late in origin and as an outcome of Russia's fiscal policy. But this is surely not the final word. Research will, I think (as important works of our own day indicate) establish that Marx was not so wrong as people assumed and that the fiscal system did not create new social forms, but made use of old ones. But here we have to concern ourselves not so much with historical inquiry as with an inquiry into the socialist prospects of the village community, as Marx saw them.

Marx declared in his drafts, in connexion with a remark of the ethnologist Morgan, that the present crisis of capitalism would end by modern society returning to a higher form of the archaic type of communal ownership and production, that is, by its going over to the communist pattern. Hence we were not to let the word *archaic* alarm us, for in this direction lay the golden opportunity for the Russian village community. It had a big advantage over all other archaic communities of the same type: it alone in Europe had maintained itself on a wide national scale.

It would not, therefore, as had been the fate of communal ownership in Western Europe, disappear with social progress. Rather, it might "gradually slough off its primitive characteristics and develop as the direct basis of collective production on a national scale." Marx points out that he had, in his *Capital,* confined the "historical fatality" of the accumulation of capital which progressively expropriates all property accruing from personal labour, expressly to Western Europe. Since the land in the hands of the Russian peasants had never been their private property, such a line of development was inapplicable to them. Instead, one needed simply to replace the government institution of the *Volost,* which "links a fair number of villages together," by a "peasant assembly elected by the commune itself and serving as the economic and administrative organ of their interests." The transition from work in allotments to full cooperative work would easily be accomplished then, in which connexion Marx stresses the familiarity of the peasants with the communal work contracts of the *Artel* as an added inducement to this. The inevitable economic need for such a process would make itself felt as soon as the village community, freed of its burdens and with more land at its disposal, was in normal circumstances; and as for the necessary material conditions, Russian society, having lived so long at the expense of the peasant, surely owed him the requisite wherewithal for such a transition.

It is clear that Marx is thinking of a change that can actually be accomplished in the circumstances given. But on the other hand he draws emphatic attention to a peculiarity of the Russian village community which afflicts it with impotence and makes all historical initiative impossible for it. By this he means its isolation; it is a "localized microcosm," and no connexion exists between the life of one commune and that of the others. In other words, what Marx is really missing without consciously making use of the idea, is the trend towards *federation.* This peculiarity, he says, is not to be found everywhere as the characteristic of this type of community; but "wherever it is found, it has given rise to a more or less centralized despotism over the communes." Only by means of a general revolt can the isolation of the Russian village community be broken. Its present state is (for reasons which Marx does not specify) economically untenable; "for the Russian communes to be saved, a Russian revolution is needed." But the revolution must come in time and it must "concentrate all its powers on securing the free rise of the village community." Then the latter will soon develop "comme élément régénérateur de la société russe et comme élément de supériorité sur les pays asservis par le régime capitaliste."

In the short letter that Marx actually sent to Vera Zasulitch, a single sentence follows the reference to the relevant passages in his *Capital*. The sentence runs: "The analysis given in my *Capital* offers, therefore, no reasons either for or against the viability of the village commune; however, the special study I have devoted to it and the material for which I have sought in the original source convince me that the commune is the mainstay of social regeneration in Russia, but that, if it is to function as such, one must first of all eliminate the injurious influences which work upon it from all sides, and then secure for it the normal conditions of spontaneous development."

The basis of the argument is so enormously compressed that even the message it manages to convey can hardly be grasped in its proper significance. Evidently this process of compression was inevitable, since in the drafts the pros and cons confronted one another in such a manner as to be irreconcilable in fact if not in appearance. In theory Marx affirmed the possibility of a prerevolutionary development of the commune in the direction desired, but in practice he made its "salvation" dependent on the timely appearance of the revolution. Here as elsewhere the determining factor is clearly the political element: the fear lest constructive work should sap the strength of the revolutionary impetus. Since, however, the political element in Marx was not offset by any insight into the significance of social restructure, the pros and cons had ultimately to be replaced by a sentence which could hardly appear to Vera Zasulitch as an answer to her fateful question. Even in his own lifetime Marx, as Tönnies says, was something of an oracle, who, on account of the ambiguity of his answers, was often petitioned in vain. At any rate Vera Zasulitch, in the answer to her question as to whether the revolutionary socialist should devote all his strength to the freeing and developing of the communes, could have heard no "yes" echoing out of Marx's letter, which for her was of the highest authority.

Not long afterwards, she wrote (in the preface to the Russian translation of Engels' *Evolution of Socialism from Utopia to Science*, published in 1884) a few passages on the village community which draw the conclusion from Marx's oracle that the gradual liquidation of communal ownership was inevitable; that Russia's immediate future belonged to capitalism, but that the socialist revolution in the West would put a term to capitalism in the East as well, "and then the remnants of the institution of communal ownership would render a great service to Russia." In his Foreword to the Russian translation (also by Vera Zasulitch) of *The Communist Manifesto* in 1882, Engels had given a somewhat different answer to the question he himself formulated obviously under the influence of Marx. "Can the Russian village community," he asked, "which is already an extremely corrupt form of the original communal ownership of land, pass over *direct* to a higher, communist form of ownership—or must it first of all go through the process of liquidation familiar to us in the historical development of the West?" His answer (as usual, less equivocal and more massive than Marx's, but also less regardful of the profundity of the problem) is as follows: "Should the Russian Revolution become the signal for a workers' revolution in the West, so that both complement one another, then the Russian communal ownership of today might serve as the starting point for communist development." Later he seems to have grown more sceptical, but he avoided (so Gustav Mayer reports) "getting involved in the internal struggles between those Russian Socialists who trusted more to the peasants and those who trusted more to the rise of an industrial proletariat."

As against Eduard Bernstein, who rightly pointed out the similarity between the program of the Paris Commune as reported by Marx and Proudhon's federalism,

Lenin declared emphatically that Marx was a centralist and that his statements in the *Civil War in France* show "no trace of a deviation from centralism." Stated in such general terms this view is untenable. When Marx says that the few functions "which will then remain for centralization" should be handed over to communal officials, he means without a doubt: decentralize as many state functions as possible and change those that must remain centralized into administrative functions, not, however, only *after* some postrevolutionary development lasting an indefinite time, but *inside* the revolutionary action itself —thus realizing what, according to Engels' well-known criticism of the draft to the Erfurt program, "every French department, every parish possessed—complete self-administration." Nevertheless, Lenin was not wrong; Marx always remained a centralist at heart. For him the communes were essentially political units, battle organs of the revolution. Lenin asks, "If the proletariat were to organize itself absolutely freely into communes, and were to unite the activities of these communes in a common front against capital . . . would that not be . . . proletarian centralism?" Of course it would, and to this extent Lenin and not Bernstein is Marx's faithful interpreter. But that is true merely of the revolution as such, which —in the sense of Marx's definition of the commune—is not a "development" spread out over several generations, but a coherent historical *act*, the act of smashing capitalism and placing the means of production in the hands of the proletariat.

But in the French program for the communes, each individual commune with its "local self-government" is by no means a mere cog in the great apparatus of revolution, or, to put it less mechanically, not merely an isolated muscle within the revolutionary exertions of the body politic; on the contrary it is destined to outlast the upheaval as an independent unit equipped with the maximum of autonomy. During the act, the commune's particular will merges spontaneously in the great impulse of the whole, but afterwards it is to acquire its own sphere of decision and action, so that the really vital functions are discharged "below" and the general administrative functions "at the top." Each commune is already invested in principle with its own proper powers and rights within the revolutionary process, but it is only after the accomplishment of the common act that they can come into actuality. Marx accepted these essential components of the commune-idea but without weighing them up against his own centralism and deciding between them. That he apparently did not see the profound problem that this opens out is due to the hegemony of the political point of view; a hegemony which persisted everywhere for him as far as concerned the revolution, its preparation, and its effects. Of the three modes of thinking in public matters —the economic, the social, and the political—Marx exercised the first with methodical mastery, devoted himself with passion to the third, but—absurd as it may sound in the ears of the unqualified Marxist—only very seldom did he come into more intimate contact with the second, and it never became a deciding factor for him.

To the question of the elements of social restructure, a fateful question indeed, Marx and Engels never gave a positive answer, because they had no inner relation to this idea. Marx might occasionally allude to "the elements of the new society which have already developed in the womb of the collapsing bourgeois society" and which the revolution had only "to set free"; but he could not make up his mind to foster these elements, to promote them and sponsor them. The political act of revolution remained the one thing worth striving for; the political preparation for it—at first the direct preparation, afterwards the parliamentary and trades unionist preparation —the one task worth doing, and thus the political principle became the supreme determinant; every concrete decision about the practical attitude to such restructural elements as were actually present, in the process of formation or to be constituted anew, was reached only from the standpoint of political expediency. . . .

This zigzag line may well serve as a symbol of the tragic misdevelopment of the socialist movement. With all the powerful forces of propaganda and planning it had gathered the proletariat about itself; in the political and economic field it had acted with great aggressive aplomb in attack and defence, but the very thing for which, ultimately, it had made propaganda and planned and fought—the evolution of the new social form—was neither the real object of its thought nor the real goal of its action. What Marx praised the Paris Commune for, the Marxist movement neither wanted nor achieved. It did not look to the lineaments of the new society which were there for all to see; it made no serious effort to promote, influence, direct, coordinate, and federate the experiments that were in being or about to be; never by consistent work did it of its own accord call any cell groups and associations of cell groups of living community into existence. With all its great powers it lent no hand to shaping the new social life for mankind which was to be set free by the revolution.

Harold Rosenberg

The Pathos of the Proletariat

*Though known mainly as an art and literary critic,
Harold Rosenberg (b. 1906) has also written a series
of extremely suggestive essays on the problems of
Marxian socialism. One of these, which was first
printed in* Kenyon Review, Autumn, 1949, *appears
below.*

"And he himself must speak through [the mask] saying thus . . .
'If you think I come hither as a lion, it were pity of my life: no, I
am no such thing; I am a man as other men are:'—and there, indeed, let him name his name, and tell them plainly he is Snug the
joiner."

A Midsummer Night's Dream

"The working class is either revolutionary or it is nothing."

Karl Marx

The hero of Marx's drama of history is, of course, the
proletariat. It is the action of this "character" that is to
resolve the tragic conflict and introduce the quiet order
of comprehended events. To be sure, there will still be
conflict under communism—the clash of individuals affirming themselves against one another and against the
whole will not cease. But the antagonisms of that order
will not be bloody struggles like those bred in the imagination of the dramatic poet. Conflicts rather like the
themes in the mind of the philosopher, stirring the entire
thought and enriching it with novelties. Through the socialist revolution, the world of Aeschylus and Shakespeare, whom Marx reread each year, will "rise" to the
world of Hegel, the teacher whom he refused to abandon.

What is this actor that is to "realize philosophy," as

Macbeth his ambition or Orestes his revenge? And, by making reality to be as something thought, to release mankind from the consequences of the opacity of facts—the excessive act, the hypnosis of the past, estrangement from one's actual self?

The hero of history was to be a social class, a special kind of collective person. *The German Ideology* describes a class in general terms. As distinguished from other unions, "there exists," says Marx, "a materialistic connection of men with one another." Founded on the physical relations among individuals and things, the class is formed for combat, "to carry on a common battle against another class." Yet, though it is the basic bond among men, the class is not a mere collection of human beings. "The class in its turn achieves an independent existence over against the individuals." Corporeal and combative, the class stands apart from them and impresses them into an adventure of its own.

The class, not the individual, has character and an historical physiognomy. The real relations in which the individual has existed until now have not permitted him to be himself. His conditions of labor and the menace of others have linked him to his class; to the extent that he is thus joined, he is an "abstract individual." The class "subsumes" him under itself and "subjects him to all kinds of ideas, etc." The class is identical with that in the life of the individual which prevents him from being an individual. It is the non-self of the individual appearing as a positive shape, as when the empty space between two objects in a painting forms the outline of a face. The class is inescapably present to the individual as another self—it is the reality of his unreality.*

History for Marx is the history of just such separated nonhuman entities. It is neither the history of individuals nor the history of ideas.

---

* Other thinkers conceive the modern individual's non-self as the void or nothingness; for Marx it appears to have features more clearly drawn than the self, since it is made up of the social material from which alone the self makes its existence concrete. It would seem to follow from Marx that our unhappy consciousness is owing not so much to our being haunted by emptiness as that we are accompanied by an *alter ego* which we can neither become nor refuse to become.

> This [materialistic] connection is ever taking on new forms, and thus presents a "history" independently of any political or religious nonsense that would hold men together on its own.

Precisely because it is the history of the nonhuman classes must history be brought to an end. And for the same reason, only the class "character" can perform the act that will terminate it.

From *The German Ideology* we derive only the most general notions about the proletariat. It is as if we wanted to know Socrates and were told that Socrates is a man (in this case, that the proletariat is not a man). In *Capital* we come somewhat closer to his image.

> The principal agents of this [capitalist] mode of production, the capitalist and the wage worker, are to that extent merely personifications of capital and wage labor. They are definite social characters assigned to individuals by the process of social production. They are the products of these definite social conditions of production.

Here the specific "materialistic connections" of capitalism have produced two "definite social characters," the capitalist and the wage worker. Having imposed themselves upon individual human beings and made them identical with one another, these seem prepared to play their historical parts.

Upon closer consideration, however, we note that these "mere personifications" are not, as such, historical actors but metaphors of political economy. They represent what Marx calls in the same passage the "peculiar traits" of capitalist production. They are like those little figures that illustrate statistical charts. Dramatically, they belong to the order of *types* in melodrama or the morality play. Like First Murdered or Sir Avarice, their lives are but reflections of the behavior or status which they exemplify. It is the plot, not they themselves as collective persons, that is responsible for all their movements.

In the Preface to *Capital*, Marx makes it quite clear that the personification lacks human choice:

> I paint the capitalist and the landlord in no sense *couleur de rose*. But here individuals are dealt with only in so far as they are person-

ifications of economic categories, embodiments of particular class relations and class interests. My standpoint can . . . less than any other make the individual responsible for relations whose creature he socially remains, however much he may subjectively raise himself above them.

As in *The German Ideology*, the class as personification is but a mass of persons who have been minted into an abstraction which forms part of a system of relations. It is without human motivation, whether individual or collective. If it struggles with other classes, it is not in order to affirm a common self or desire but because it is moved by the "contradictions" of the system of which it is an "agent."

Were history the struggle of such characters, how could Marx maintain that "men make their own history"? A history made by personifications would be history made not by human beings, even human beings stirred by their own unreality, but by embodied Ideas or elements of a process. Devoid of pathos, the conflict of these categories hardly deserves Marx's description as "the great historical tragedy." Philosophy would have been realized all too soon.

Nor, if the class man is a personification, does it have meaning to speak of a class as *revolutionary*. The personification represents or incarnates—how can it overthrow that of which it is the sign? To personify labor, the worker need only work for wages; of itself that makes him a proletarian, nothing more is required. The assigned character does not forbid him to act politically as a reactionary or a Buddhist. A worker so defined might be sufficient for economists of other schools, concerned with calculations of things as they are. But it is the peculiarity of Marx's "political economy" that he sees this class as destined to alter completely the conditions that created it. Such an active role cannot be attributed to a character that is but an embodiment of existing relations. For revolution an actor different from a personification is needed.

It would appear that Marx saw something more in the class character: it is, he says, a personification only "to that extent" that it is an agent of the production process.

In his historical and polemical writings he speaks of the classes as full-fledged persons, with egos that strive, dream, become conscious of themselves. The bourgeoisie in the opening pages of *The Eighteenth Brumaire* is a hero disguised as a Roman; the proletariat of *The Class Struggles in France* is "scarred, irreconcilable, unconquerable." There, beyond personifying, the class possesses a collective personality, and acts according to its own intelligence and spirit. That this spirit is the essence of the class is implicit in Marx's statement: "The working class is either revolutionary or it is nothing." Without being revolutionary the class would still represent "materialistic connections," yet lacking the impulse of the historical actor the economic identity is nothing.

Are such references to the subjectivity of a class merely examples of political rhetoric, like the femininity of France or the perfidiousness of Albion? Or does its specific inner character belong to the full definition of a class? Unless we know if consciousness of itself is essential to its historical existence, and what the nature of that consciousness is, the concept of the proletariat is not clear. In our day this question has taken on immense practical importance. If the working class is but an embodied economic category, socialism, the presumed next historical situation, can be brought about through the manipulation of the class by bands of ideologists, reformist or revolutionary. If, however, the very existence of the proletariat presupposes the development in it of a consciousness and will, only its direct decisions and acts have any relevance to the socialist outcome of the Marxist drama—action by others in its name would be action in a void. Thus the entire meaning of Marx's theory turns on his conception of that mysterious social and metaphysical entity, which is at once an Idea that is a character and a community of struggling human beings that has the form of an Idea. If there is to be socialism, who is to create it, and *what* is that *who*?

With some eagerness we pass from Marx's definition of the class as a personification to the next chapter of *Capital*, the last of Volume 3. Having devoted his immense study to the impersonal processes by which modern man lives and falsifies himself, Marx now proposes to analyze "the great classes of modern society resting upon the capitalist mode of production." Says he, "The first question to be answered is this: What constitutes a class?" He is about to isolate the single substance of the economic and historical, to exhibit the organisms that we inhabit, that make us what we are, and by which we shall be carried into the future. We turn the page quickly—and are met by that classic declaration of mystery documents: HERE THE MANUSCRIPT ENDS.

> All that is solid melts into the air, all that is holy is pro-faned. . . .
>
> *The Communist Manifesto*

Capital breaks off without having merged into a single figure the wretched personification of wage labor, that flesh and blood machine part fitted into modern production, and the future hero of history.* We are left with the dialectics of the earlier writings and with Marx's historical and programmatic works.

Dialectically, the mechanically impelled personification *must* turn into the conscious hero, since it is, as it were, but the physical aspect of a being who thinks and acts. The status of the working class results automatically in its "self-activity," and the inevitable awakening of the proletariat is both the means and the end of socialism. Thus the working class is revolutionary by definition: it is formed "over against" another class; "with its birth," declares *The Communist Manifesto*, "begins its struggle with the bourgeoisie." The Buddhism of a workingman may therefore be disregarded, for he becomes a revolutionist in becoming altogether himself.

Accepting revolutionary consciousness as immanent in the proletariat, Marx's dialectics overleaps, however, its emergence as an historical fact. This is confirmed by Eng-

---

* The projected fourth volume of *Capital*, which Marx described to Engels as "the historical-literary one," might have undertaken to do this.

els in a letter to Mehring eleven years after Marx's death:

> We all laid and were bound to lay the main emphasis on the derivation of political, juridical, and other ideological notions, and of the actions arising through the medium of these notions, from basic economic facts. But in so doing we neglected the formal side —the way in which these notions come about—for the sake of the content.

If not in Marx's analysis of capitalism, nor in the Marxian "materialist" method, where shall one discover his conception of the classes as makers of history? Would it not be at those points where he sees them involved in actual revolutionary situations? There, it is no longer enough to refer to the classes in terms of the general development of society. And indeed when he writes of the ideas and images dominating the revolutions of his day, Marx does not "neglect the way in which these notions come about." Directed at the self-consciousness and passions of human groups in action, his method combines with his intuition to produce shaded Hegelianisms and other concepts peculiar to him, though often thoroughly "un-Marxian." These take their place in his thought through the coherence of his metaphors and the recurrence of certain dramatic formulas, such as the resurrection of the dead (theme of *The Eighteenth Brumaire*), the integrating effects of defeat (theme of *The Class Struggles in France*), the spontaneous accuracy of the revolutionary act (*The Civil War in France*), the revelation through conflict of historical "secrets" (several works). Here, too, are signs of a "method"—a method, a cast rather, of the imagination. What its connection is with Marxian materialism I shall not attempt to say. Suffice it that when the materialism of Marxist writings lacks the inspiration of this order of "rhetoric" its alienation from the historical insight of the master is evident at once.

The self-consciousness that converts the class from economic personification into historical actor is not an intellectual comprehension of class interests and relations but is part of the revolutionary act itself. The class engages itself in the drama of history by its passionate and willful *poetry* of the event.*

The poetry of its action constitutes the portrait of the class as an historical actor. Marx's image of the proletarian hero of history thus becomes visible in his characterization of the poetry of working-class upheaval. As befits the actor who is to terminate the drama, this poetry has a different relation to history from that of all previous actors:

> The social revolution cannot draw its poetry from the past but only from the future. It cannot begin with itself before it has stripped off all superstitions in regard to the past. Earlier revolutions required world-historical recollections in order to drug themselves concerning their own content. In order to arrive at their own content, the revolution of the 19th century must let the dead bury the dead. There the phrase went beyond the content; here the content goes beyond the phrase. (*The Eighteenth Brumaire*)

The proletarian revolution is to be characterized by its total abandonment of the past. It is to owe nothing to that repertory of heroic forms out of which history had furnished earlier revolutionists with the subjective means for meeting their situation. Other historical mass actors —peoples, cults, bands, classes, including the "unheroic"

---

* The following point has been raised by several readers of "The Resurrected Romans" (*The Kenyon Review*, Autumn, 1948): that in speaking of the Roman "disguise" of the bourgeoisie and their interests, Marx crudely represented the poetry of the revolution as a *falsification* of "reality." This criticism is largely justified by the language Marx uses in describing the psychological function of revolutionary rhetoric and costumes—"self-deceptions," "conceal from themselves," "drugs," etc. Yet, taking into account his notion as a whole, I am inclined to believe that he regards the Roman identity not as a falsification of the bourgeois reality but as its humanization. It is not that the French revolutionists were "really" businessmen posing as Romans, but that in donning this costume and assuming this "illusory" self, members of a mere economic category were changed into citizens of an historical community. True, this involved concealment and a mistake; without these, however, the real bourgeoisie could not have made their historical appearance. Hence, in relation to the total event, "poetry" does not mean for Marx "untrue"; it means the subjective form of the historical, which in a genuine revolution is bound to correspond with the demands of the situation and thus to constitute historical truth.

bourgeoisie—had, when bent on remaking the world, presented themselves on the stage in ancestral costume and with transcendental allies. The proletariat alone is to perform its part in everyday clothes and without sacrament. It is not to make itself capable of revolution by displacing itself with sublime models. Its revolution is to begin internally not with a myth but with a "stripping off"; it is to become in its mind and in its imagination exactly what it in fact is, the personification of wage labor. With the working class, for the first time, human beings living under more or less common conditions are to coalesce into a conscious active community without the aid of god or hero, prophet or leader, without rite of initiation or founding miracle, with visions, without ideals, without "the phrase that goes beyond the content."

The pastlessness of the proletarian revolution is the key to the character of the working class and its role. In a toast "to the proletarians of Europe," Marx declared:

For our part we do not mistake the shape of the shrewd spirit that continues to mark all these contradictions [between the productive forces and the social relations of our epoch]. We know that if the newfangled forces of society are to work satisfactorily they need only be mastered by newfangled men—and such are the working men. They are as much the invention of modern time as machinery itself. In the signs that bewilder the middle class, the aristocracy, and the poor prophets of regression, we recognize our old friend Robin Goodfellow, the old mole that can work in the earth so fast, that worthy pioneer—the revolution.

The proletarians are new men, an "invention of modern time." The spirit that agitates them is not Hamlet's old mole and worthy pioneer, his father's ghost. This hero never had a father; he sprang from the same source as the factory. The shrewd spirit that informs him of his situation and prompts him to his act is no ghost from the grave. He lets the dead bury the dead. The spirit that speaks to him is the spirit of the future. The revolution *will* father the working class by giving birth to it as a human community. Without this inner animation the workers are machines and have no other historical status;

by it they achieve an identity and are converted into men.

An utterly new invention, the proletariat is alien to the ancestral spirit. But in this alienation its subjective condition is an exact reflection of its external situation. For the mark of our era is that in it the past has lost its power to define men and to move them.

Constant revolutionizing of production, uninterrupted disturbance of all social conditions, everlasting uncertainty and agitation, distinguish the bourgeois epoch from all earlier ones. All fixed, fast-frozen relations, with their train of ancient and venerable prejudices and opinions, are swept away, all new-formed ones become antiquated before they can ossify. All that is solid melts into the air, all that is holy is profaned, and man is at last compelled to face with sober senses his real conditions of life and his relations with his kind. (*The Communist Manifesto*)

The middle class has inaugurated The Modern. Its sign is the release of time into all human situations. What is not altered is swept away. No longer does history resemble a succession of friezes with the old standing intact behind the new. The whole historical substance is in motion. No *deus ex machina* remains to step forward in historical crises to rescue the frustrated mass-hero through the conversion of businessmen into Romans, farmers into Old Testament prophets. No more Caesars, no more John Browns. Revolution through repetition has become impossible.* If, like their predecessors, proletarian revolutionists "engaged in revolutionizing themselves and things, in creating something entirely new . . . anxiously conjure up the spirits of the past to their service," their conjuring is fated to be met with silence. The past will neither communicate with these children of the machine nor provide them with heroic masks. One spirit alone remains to move the workers, the shrewd spirit that challenges "the real conditions."

In that its own pastlessness corresponds to that of the

---

* Marx, and of course the Marxists after him, obviously underestimated the power of the past to initiate historical actions. It has by no means been exhausted even now. But Marx seems correct as to the loss of its *creative* power, in that revived forms no longer appear capable of moving society forward, as they once were.

modern world, the proletariat becomes the protagonist of present-day mankind. To it is put the question of creative action deprived of the guidance of tradition. The liquefaction of the past gives the word "pioneer" a literal application. From the emptiness of their time relation, this class, laboring in the very core of urban society, is to derive the subjective characteristics of a community isolated in a desert of space. Like that of Rimbaud, contemporary of the Commune, the mind of Marx's working class exists in the *as if* of an American or African wilderness. For it, as for him, Europe is strewn with "poetic old junk"; no more than the poet of deliberate self-estrangement can this mass, produced entirely by the content of the historical and stranger to its forms, hope to achieve its human "other self" through appropriating an existing poetry. Rimbaud's banner: "It is necessary to be absolutely modern," is raised over the revolution of newfangled men which is to take place without recourse to the higher powers of the dead. With everything solid melted into the air, only what they themselves create can have reality for them. The everlasting uncertainty of capitalist society has with them given rise to human beings whose normal life is uncertainty, and which is therefore consistent only with "the revolution in permanence" through which they endlessly change their own natures as they remake the conditions of their lives.

"I enter the true kingdom of the sons of Ham," announces Rimbaud. For his part Marx does not hesitate to designate as "barbarian" his hero of the modern for whom the past has no gifts. The proletariat is barbarian in exactly the same sense that the American has long been Europe's barbarian. Estranged from that continent's accumulations of time, both appear as tossing in Rimbaud's drunken boat toward who knows what "incredible Floridas" of the future. Like an American, an American object, the proletarian and the "commodity" he produces lack that saturation with the years that for Europe is synonymous with cultural meaning and spiritual presence.

To our grandparents, [said Rilke] a "house," a "well," a tower familiar to them, even their own dress, their cloak, was still infinitely more, infinitely more intimate; almost each thing, a vessel in which they found something human and into which they set aside something human. Now, from America, empty indifferent things are crowding over to us, sham things, *life decoys.* . . . A house, in the American understanding, an American apple or a grapevine there, has nothing in common with the house, the fruit, the grape into which went the hopes and meditations of our forefathers. . . . We are perhaps the last still to have known such things.

The proletariat is of this "American" sphere, in which persons, places, things, human relations, exist without the time dimension.* "To detach a fact from its origin," recently said the French philosopher Levinas, "is precisely to live in the modern world."

For Rilke the world had formerly been made human by meditation. The American does not meditate, he acts. So, too, the proletariat, whose self-consciousness arises through the "practical movement." These heirs of the bourgeois principle of uninterrupted activity seem therefore cast for the same role: the annihilation of culture. The dissolution by capitalism of all sacred and human relations has been carried to its extreme by the Americans and awaits completion by the proletarian hordes.†

If stability, authority, sacrament are needed to make men human, what but civilization's doom is the American-proletarian world? Between the old subjectivity, born of a lengthy intimacy among people and things, and the spirit of change that rules the newfangled men, rages a deadly conflict, which liberalism, insensible of dramatic

---

* Naturally, Americans resent being called barbarians, especially in the false-aristocratic ideology of European reaction. But this justified indignation should not cause us to miss the suggestiveness of the term, understood as describing not a moral or intellectual inferiority but an historical difference in spiritual form. As new men, Americans can hardly hope to define themselves unless they assert their subjective difference from Europeans and refuse to seek inspiration in the past, even in an American past.

† From Flaubert's plan for the conclusion of *Bouvard et Pécuchet:*
Pécuchet sees the future of humanity in dark colors.
The modern man is lessened, and has become a machine. . . .
There will be no longer ideal, religion, morality.
The United States will have conquered the earth.
Universal greed. There will be no longer anything but a debauch of
    workmen.

issues in a state of development, obscures by its pragmatic proposals. Placing his bet for the future on the proletarian revolution which "cannot draw its poetry from the past," Marx brushes aside the liberal veil and squarely proclaims himself the foe of the pastist spirituality of Europe. America, democracy, the proletariat will triumph, yet civilization will not perish. In the world denuded by ceaseless activity, a new humanism has become possible, that of soberly facing the real conditions and relations of men. In place of the sacred sentiments found or secreted in things, a secular spirituality will recreate itself from moment to moment out of man's conscious grapple with his historical situation. Its poetry will flow not from the stillness of the past but from the movement toward the future, not from time come to rest but from time as change, not from the dead but from what is being born, not from the human as heritage but from the needs of humanity.

As the potential embodiment of the spirit of the modern, the proletariat derives from its position an advantage over the American.* In his action the latter is unquestionably the living model of the newfangled—revolutionists from Marx to Lenin have drawn upon his practices. Free of traditional auras, the American stakes everything on the value of his deed. Nothing "in" objects or men checks him from changing or replacing them. Transforming landscapes, materials, memories, he "takes things in his stride," "finds the right man for the right job." He converts the past itself to his needs;† to a significant degree

---

* In comparing the American and the proletariat, we think of them, of course, not as categories, where they overlap, but as subjectively defined communities performing as historical actors.

† The Americans, said Goebbels, with rare comic envy, "have the ability of taking their relatively small stock of culture and by a modernized version making of it something that is a very à propos for the present time. We are loaded down altogether too much with tradition and piety. We hesitate to clothe our cultural heritage in modern dress. It therefore remains purely historical or museum-like and is at best understood by groups within the Party, the Hitler Youth, or the Labor Service. The cultural heritage of our past can be rendered fruitful for the present on a large scale only if we present it with modern means. The Americans are masters at this sort of thing. I suppose because they are not weighted down as much as we with historical ballast. Nevertheless we shall have to do something about it." (The Goebbels Diaries)

he realizes Marx's vision of communism as a society in which "the present dominates the past."

But though he is the natural representative of the modern, the American exists in a situation that does not impel him to make himself its hero. Pioneering is not forced upon him as a continual and total demand. His accomplishments provide him with room in which to rest; his history has been one of setting limits to his revolutionizing. For all the audacity of his behavior the American does not place himself in open opposition to the past nor challenge tradition as the champion of a new conception of spirit based on ceaseless activity.* He refuses to will, and make himself responsible for, his destruction of the sanctity of time. The American acts in silence, so to speak, permitting his consciousness and his conscience to remain bounded by the spirituality of Europe. In America, Marx pointed out, "the feverishly youthful movement of material production, that has a new world to make its own, has left neither time nor opportunity for abolishing the old spirit world." Like nature, the American accepts with equanimity whatever of the old succeeds in surviving his processes.

The proletariat, however, is not permitted by its situation to give a limited expression to its modernity. Severed from the past, alien to the various poetries of contemplation by which other participants in the everlasting agitation to rediscover their original humanity, the workingman can conceive the human only as an undertaking of projects. Yet, though to him action is the very essence of being a man, he may not act, for his movements are controlled by others. He is in the center of the transforming process, yet he neither decides what is to be transformed nor stamps his likeness on the finished thing. As a pioneer, he could be a man; actually, he is bound to the machine and can initiate nothing and make nothing his. In this exclusion from the beginning and end of his ac-

---

* America was closer to delivering such a challenge a century ago (e.g., as expressed in Whitman's Prefaces) than it is at present, when, its past-destroying action having expanded to world scale, it hesitates to attack *any* tradition.

tion, the proletarian must recognize himself as a tool deprived of humanity.

As the American is the free man and master of the
industrial epoch, even when he refuses his freedom and
his mastery, the proletarian is its inherent victim. He
represents the internal flaw of the modern, its original sin.
While everything about him is revolutionized, he alone
remains in a fixed relation. The ceaseless conversion of
everything into presentness has other victims—the proletariat stands apart from them all. Aristocrats, priestly
casts, ancient races, clinging to their pasts or prevented
from abandoning them, are plunged into crisis by "pro-
faning" capitalism. Yet these can be saved for the modern
world (and this is the struggle of liberalism) by the removal of their time stigma, by being brought up to date
and given "a new start." The misery of the workingman
alone cannot be ameliorated through equalizing him with
his epoch. He suffers *in* his presentness as one totally
involved in this hour's affirmation of itself. Stemming entirely from his part in it, his discontent is central to the
movement of modern history. *The proletariat is the modern itself experienced as misery.*

For the American, action is a fact. For the worker it is
but a possibility, the anguishing possibility of transforming himself into a man. Hemmed in on the stripped functional stage, altogether *there*, without past or paradise,
he is, except for this possibility, a mere prop, a thing
that personifies. Speaking half-figuratively,* to become
human the proletariat must "Americanize" itself, that is,
become a character who, living in a present devoid of the
aura of memory, joins itself to human history through
the freedom of its action.

---

* Only half-figuratively, since becoming an American has been the actual
salvation of millions of workingmen. With the proletariat there is more
to the impulse to become an American than the desire for economic
opportunity, flight from oppression, etc. Primarily, it is a will to enter a
world where the past no longer dominates, and where therefore that
creature of the present, the workingman, can merge himself into the
whole. Thus proletarians emigrate to America in a different spirit from
middle-class people or peasants, who from the moment they enter "American time" experience it as something disconcerting and even immoral,
and whose nostalgia for their homelands and customs often lasts for

Yet all existing relations—and in the core of these its own existence as proletariat—forbid the working class to act. Hence its revolution can set itself no limits but must subdue "all existing conditions" (*The Communist Manifesto*). The proletarian victim of the modern cannot enter the historical drama as an actor without becoming its hero. In "the indefinite prodigiousness of their aims" (*The Eighteenth Brumaire*) the workers signify that with them revolution is a need of the spirit, a means of redemption. Before Marx's internal pioneer opens a frontier without end.

Communism . . . turns existing conditions into conditions of unity. (*The German Ideology*)

The figure of the permanent pioneer is created by the implications of the union of men in action through their response to actual conditions and without reference to the past. All the high hopes and promises of socialism rest upon this supposed outcome of our mythless situation. The community to be founded by the featureless metaphors of wage labor, to whom everything human is but a possibility that needs to be brought to life through action, would be like no other community in history. Its existence itself would destroy the root of all known human miseries—the hallucinatory nature of social life itself.

The illusory community, in which individuals have up till now combined, always took on an independent existence in relation to them and was at the same time, since it was the combination of one class over against another, not only a completely illusory community, but a new fetter as well. In the real community the individuals obtained their freedom in and through their association. (*The German Ideology*)

generations. But America's thin timecrust, that seems so desolate to them, is precisely what satisfies the proletariat. Becoming an American is a kind of revolution for foreign proletarians; though it is a magical revolution rather than a revolutionary act. It alters the workingman's consciousness of himself; like a religious conversion it supplies him with a new identity. But this change does not extinguish his previous situation. He is still in the realm of personifications. As an American, too, a social character will be assigned to him: worker, farmer, capitalist. The elimination of these continues to call for a transformation of the historical plot.

The community as the supremely fantastic "being" renders us incommensurate* with reality and generates those false selves which make of our lives comedies and tragedies of mistaken identity. A community that is nothing else than the united action of its members in their common situation must cause the phantoms that beset us to disappear.

The reality which communism creates is precisely the real basis for rendering it impossible that anything should exist independently of individuals. (*The German Ideology*)

No institutions, idols, programs, none of Blake's "mental Deities" to be above the human being and driving him. No longer is each individual haunted by an alien "I" detached from his daily life and bringing to it threats or salvation. The historical stage ceases to be invaded by the banners and uniforms of unpredictable messengers called into being by prophets or heroes. In place of battling cults, states, classes, a single actor mediates his next creation. This actor is Man, released from his past as Frenchman or Russian, Jew or Hindu.

Through having been submitted by capitalism to uniform conditions, and through having turned those conditions into "conditions of unity," society recaptures the organic coherence it has lacked since primitive times. Yet this unseparated state is experienced by the individual as absolute freedom. No longer an independent entity, the community has become the individual himself in his real situation; individual existence corresponds exactly to that of the collectivity. Each is equivalent to the all; for each is joined to the all, not through surrender to its symbols, but by the concrete extension of his own being. A sponta-

---

* Like Kierkegaard, Marx recognizes that man takes up the slack between himself and historical reality by creating illusory selves. To this fate Kierkegaard responded with the Christian-romantic "movement" of "becoming infinitely subjective"—the individual resigns himself to the incommensurability and puts it behind him through withdrawing from the social and historical in the direction of the self in its "god-relation." The classicist Marx sees an opposite "movement," an external one harmonizing man and the world by changing the world into something altogether human.

neous communion and togetherness, as in invasions,
floods, celebrations, becomes the normal state. With solidarity insured by genuine self-interest, the drama of
choice between revolt and submission becomes an anachronism and with it the poetries of worship and blas-
phemy. In the language of *Capital*, the life process of
society strips off its mystical veil.

No longer pastist or futurist, altogether in his moment,
man has at last gained a capacity for the historical—with
a kind of Renaissance zest, yet unmotivated to violence,
he revels in it as his proper medium: "A touch of your
finger on the drum sets loose all the sounds and begins
the new harmony" (Rimbaud, *Illuminations*). The individual conceives his existence in terms of creations which
in totally satisfying him are serviceable to all mankind,
whether undertaken alone or in collaboration with others.
Connoisseur of time, he commits himself entirely to these
Grand Coulees with an inwardness that draws from death
the true savor of each instant. His daily life is an enact-
ment of Hegelian dialectic as summarized by Marx:

> It concludes in its comprehension an affirmative recognition of the
> existing state of things, at the same time also, the recognition of
> the negation of that state, of its inevitable breaking up.

This utterly human and universal community springs
up readily in the mind of the analyst of the conditions,
material and cultural, of our epoch. Its appearance in
actuality, however, faces awesome obstacles. We have
seen that proletarian revolution calls for the inner alteration of men on a mass scale. That a transformation of this
order shall take place under the inspiration of "the real
conditions," problems of creation never coped with before must be surmounted. In the birth of the time-gifted
"I" of the proletariat as the collective self of the working
class lies the drama of the socialist revolution—and its
pathos.

It is a drama of self-creation. Its anguish arises, ironically, from the same source as its potential grandeur: that
the revoluntionary community has no existence independently of the action of its members. The working class is

not something the worker can *join*, like a church or a nation. Only when he enters a concrete struggle is he inwardly identified as a proletarian. As it lacks anchorage in the past, his class also lacks it in the ideal.

Communism is for us not a stable state which is to be established, an ideal to which reality will have to adjust itself. We call communism the *real* movement which abolishes the present state of things. The conditions of this movement result from the premises now in existence. (*The German Ideology*)

The proletariat must make itself and continue to make itself in revolutionary action; at rest it has no identity.

The unhinging of the consciousness of the proletariat from the past or imagined future causes its action to take on, Marx repeatedly reminds us, a singular historical style —it is soberly realistic. Making oneself would seem to be a different process from recognizing oneself as an already existing, if hidden, "I." Self-recognition takes place in an ecstatic leap which overwhelms all time distinctions. Having discovered their identity in antiquity,

bourgeois revolutions storm ever more swiftly from success to success; their dramatic effects outdo each other; men and things seem set in sparkling brilliants; ecstasy is the everyday spirit. (*The Eighteenth Brumaire*)

Realistic self-creation involves action immeasurably more arduous.

Proletarian revolutions, on the other hand, criticise themselves constantly, interrupt themselves continually in their own course, come back to the apparently accomplished in order to recommence it afresh, deride with unmerciful thoroughness the inadequacies, weaknesses, and paltrinesses of their first attempts, seem to throw down their adversary only in order that he may draw new strength from the earth and rise again more gigantic before them, recoil ever and anon from the indefinite prodigiousness of their own aims, until the situation has been created which makes all turning back impossible, and the conditions themselves cry out: *Hic Rhodus, hic salta! Hier ist die Rose, hier tanze!* (*The Eighteenth Brumaire*)

Liberation from the poetry of the past has brought the proletariat sobriety; its realism cannot, however, supply it with inner continuity. So long as its situation fluctuates, its action must fluctuate with it; but since its action alone causes it to be, its existence is an oscillation between struggle and nothingness. Thus constant self-scrutiny marks its revolutionary style—Baudelairian in contrast to the Hugoesque enthusiasm of the bourgeoisie—for without persistent criticism how can it be sure that its action is its own and not in the service of another? At all points it betrays a sense of inner incompletion, a doubt with respect to its identity and its motives. With its "indefinitely prodigious" aims, it starts again and again from the beginning, as if confessing its own nullity between one effort and the next.

Controlled by the historical plot, the proletariat can be rescued from its lunar periodicity (appropriate to its role as a "force of nature") only in being subjected by events to an even pressure within a constantly narrowing area, "until the situation has been created that makes all turning back impossible." The primary condition therefore for the conversion of the proletariat from a personification into an actor is the "growing mass of misery" predicted by Marx. A constantly worsening crisis is needed to keep the working class present upon the stage and to bring coherence to its movements.

Yet even if the situation of the workers were to reach the vanishing point of human endurance (by what measure?), the socialist revolution could not begin unless the proletariat, preserving the immediacy of its response to its conditions, and resisting in impermeable sobriety the rise of new myths, could recognize that the time had come for its final assault. According to Marx, however, it is precisely those conditions that make living in the actual world intolerable that cause people to project other worlds and to live in them. The growing misery of the proletariat must tend to plunge it into increasing fantasy. But should the workers, intoxicated with visions, surrender themselves to "alien bonds," the class would break up and abandon its rôle. Hardship can be the basis of unity only if the workers succeed in remaining stripped of whatever might subjectively soften their situation or carry them beyond it. To achieve immediacy as its mode of consciousness, the proletariat must have "nothing to lose but its chains," in the intellectual and emotional as well as in the economic and social sense. Accompanying the "asceticizing" of their physical existence by the hostile process in which they are caught, a disciplined asceticism of the imagination must reduce them to the severity of a category. The growing mass of misery must be matched by a growing mass of emptiness. In order that the mask become human the man must have willed to become nothing but the mask.

Hence, as Lenin insisted, though with a different conclusion, *the most extreme conditions cannot guarantee the revolutionary unification of the workers*. It must begin in an inner undertaking: that of willing to make themselves the suffering abstraction which their role implies that they are.

Before the proletariat lies the pathetic choice, either to become historically nothing as a class through inactivity, or to become humanly nothing in order to be equal to its historical situation. Either to be individuals without a role, members of a passive economic category, and susceptible of being captured in every crisis by some alien collectivity; or to form a collectivity of their own, throwing themselves as in a trance into the limitless adventure of the revolution in permanence. To realize philosophy, the proletariat must tragically endure the dialectics of history by its readiness to sacrifice itself for the moment alone, thus affirming the identity of the lives of its members with the historical role of the class.

They have no ideals to realize but to set free the elements of the new society with which old collapsing bourgeois society is itself pregnant. . . . The great social measure of the Commune was its own working existence. (*The Civil War in France*)

The proletariat must be prepared to die in order to exist and for nothing else. Such appears to be the impasse of truly secular (without ideologies, as well as without myths) historical creation.

When shall we . . . salute the birth of the new labor, the new
wisdom, the flight of tyrants and demons? (*Rimbaud*)

The mythless proletariat, suffering with naked consciousness the trials of its position, is a tragic concept in
heroic style. One understands why Marx criticized Lassalle's historical tragedy, *Franz von Sickingen,* for making
"political unity its chief idea." "You should have *Shake-
spearized* more," Marx wrote. "As it is, I consider your
greatest fault to be *Schillerization,* the transformation of
individuals into mere mouthpieces of the spirit of the
age." Against the romantic bourgeois revolution, with its
rhetoric, its gestures, its costumes he himself had placed
a figure that had yet to define itself. As with Aristotle, the
plot comes before the hero. A sober Sophoclean victim of
the facts, he is trapped and pushed toward his doom by
contradictions from which nothing can save him, for the
concrete means for their solution do not yet exist.* The
struggles induced by his misery are, however, not in vain.
Constituting his existence itself, they bring about a ripen-
ing of his situation and a clarification of his consciousness. In the descending scale of his fortunes his illusions
fall away one by one until, when his true identity stands
revealed, not by thought but by an unavoidable act, the
tragedy is resolved in a transcendence.

To the extent that its plot conforms to our actual historical situation, this grand drama is a profound hypothesis. Before it is actually performed, however, it cannot be
more than an hypothesis, since its outcome depends upon
the subjective capacity of its proletarian hero to perform
its role, upon the immediacy of its consciousness, and
upon its will to endure. Marx, however, refuses to regard
proletarian action as an *if* of creative hazard. For him the
revolution is an historical certainty. From this translation
of the dramatic into the "scientific" arise the essential

---

* "Historical action is to yield to their personal inventive action," Marx
wrote contemptuously of the utopians; "historically created conditions of
emancipation to fantastic ones; and the gradual, spontaneous class organization of the proletariat to an organization of society specially con-
trived by these inventors. Future history resolves itself in their eyes
into the propaganda and practical carrying out of their social plans."
(*The Communist Manifesto*)

ambiguities of Marxism. Accepting the revolutionary proletariat as an hypothesis, we should look for the emergence of this heroic image in the finite struggles of the
working class, in its poetry. Each such struggle would
then appear as laden with suspense and pathos. Of more
practical importance, we could be aware whether the
values attached to this image were in the way of being
realized. But with Marx all finite efforts of the workers
are subsumed under the *concept* of the class-conscious
proletariat. Thus, though he thinks of the revolution as a
tragedy, he does not behold its incidents as tragic, and
his work lacks the pathetic tonality appropriate to its
notion of the workers transforming themselves through
constant risk of their lives. The rationalism of Marx's
prose favorites wins against his beloved Shakespeare and
Aeschylus. An optimism with respect to the historical
drama as a whole subdues the anguish of the hero's striving against utter defeat through which the happy resolution is to be reached. Even in his description of the Commune and its executioners, the peak of his revolutionary
eloquence, it is the *foes* of the revolution that he most
vividly evokes. Concerning the peculiar state of consciousness of the Paris "pioneers," so strangely isolated in
time and space, of their relations with one another, of
their sense of what lay ahead, he takes no notice. To the
pathos of the momentary foreshadowing of communism
in flesh and blood, he responds only with moral passion
and historical prophecy. For him the Commune is a single lost battle in a war that can have but one conclusion.
Thus Marx himself prepares the shallow trust of Marxism
in rationalistic formulas.

Marx attempts to guarantee the appearance of the proletariat as actor in two ways. The first is through metaphysics. In his Introduction to *The Living Thoughts of
Karl Marx*, Trotsky summarizes this position:

The productive forces need a new organizer and a new master,
and, *since existence determines consciousness*, Marx had no doubt
that the working class, at the cost of errors and defeats, will
come to understand the actual situation, and sooner or later, will
draw the imperative practical conclusions [my italics].

Assuming that the proposition, existence determines consciousness, is correct, can it be relied upon to produce the *particular* kind of consciousness (revolutionary) anticipated by Marx? If Marx could be aware in advance of the situation and of its necessary effect on the mind of the workers, the consciousness of Marx would have preceded existence, which is in violation of the proposition. It might be answered that the capitalist situation already existed in Marx's time and that it is the development of that situation, first understood by him, that the workers will come to grasp. But this would be to detach the situation from the human beings in it and to conceive it as unaffected by changes in mankind. Within the movement of capitalism Marx might predict the general direction of certain processes—concentration of capital, accelerated crises, etc.—but he cannot predict the total historical situation of the masses, which includes the history of their consciousness of themselves in their situation, or their lack of it. Yet nothing less than this total situation can be meant by "existence" in its determination of consciousness.*

Marxism must therefore admit that it can predict nothing concerning the consciousness of the proletariat and hence of its action, in which case the proletariat remains an hypothesis and not a certainty; or it must reduce the situation to a given number of external elements, definable in advance, and thus become identical with what is known as "vulgar materialism" or "Mechanical Marxism."

The failure of the situation to give rise to revolutionary consciousness leads Marx and Marxists to a second type of effort to guarantee the revolution: through politics and propaganda. In his letter to Mehring quoted above, Engels recognized the failure of "the basic economic facts" to explain "the way in which these ["political, juridical, ideological"] notions come about." In the same year (1893) he exhibits more concretely the consequences of

---

* Trotsky does not seem to realize that for the workers "to understand the actual situation" means not only a consciousness of objective relations and "practical conclusions" but self-consciousness. Had he been aware of this, his acceptance of the Bolshevik theory of the relation between the party and masses would have been even more difficult.

this failure for Marxism. In the revolution of 1848, he recalls in his Introduction to *The Class Struggles in France*, Marx relied upon the masses' understanding of their situation to sustain their revolutionary spirit:

The proletarian masses themselves, even in Paris, after the victory, were still absolutely in the dark as to the path to be taken. And yet the movement was there, instinctive, spontaneous, irrepressible. Was not this just the situation in which a revolution had to succeed? . . . If, in all the longer revolutionary periods, it was so easy to win the great masses of the people by the merely plausible and delusive views of the minorities thrusting themselves forward, how could they be less susceptible to *ideas which were the truest reflex of their economic position, which were nothing but the clear, comprehensible expression of their needs, of needs not yet understood by themselves, but only vaguely felt*. To be sure, this revolutionary mood of the masses had almost always, and usually very speedily, given way to lassitude or even to a revulsion to its opposite, as soon as illusion evaporated and disappointment set in. But here it was not a question of delusive views . . . [my italics].

His social-economic analysis had convinced Marx that the proletariat was objectively powerful enough to overcome the government. Since existence determines consciousness, the workers had already "vaguely" grasped the truth of their position. All that was needed was to clarify this awareness with ideas which were nothing else than what they already knew. The "instinctive movement" would thereupon be sustained against a collapse into disillusioned apathy; and "the proletariat grown wise by experience must become the decisive factor."

The "ideas which were the truest reflex" failed, however, to produce this steadying effect. "History," Engels goes on to say, "has proved us, and all who thought like us, wrong." Not wrong in relying on the truth, but wrong, he explains, in estimating the situation—it was not ripe for proletarian revolution. This mistake raises numerous questions regarding the determination of consciousness which Engels ignores. Does the diminishing of the fervor of the masses in 1850 signify that they were more conscious than Marx of their situation, instinctively aware of its unripeness? So it would seem, since their abandonment of revolution conformed to the real position rather than to Marx's erroneous notion of it. But if the masses acted correctly without the Marxian "reflex," and even in opposition to it, what is the function of the reflex? Also, should it not be admitted that the mood of the masses is a better measure of the situation than the Marxian analysis? Another question: had Marx correctly estimated the "unripe" situation of 1848, would his truth then have had the effect of maintaining revolutionary fervor? We know that in such a situation Marx counsels wary support of a bourgeois revolution for the sake of progress and warns the proletariat that the fruit of their struggle will be taken from them. He strives to check fervor by criticism rather than to heighten and maintain it. Must not this dispelling of illusion have the same effect as the bitter awakening described by Engels, depleting the masses' revolutionary energy?

At any rate, Engels' confession of error would have been more magnanimous if, giving full weight to the fatal consequences of misleading the workers even on one occasion, he had inquired into the dangers of Marxian certainty and of its tendency in political practice to convert its philosophy into its opposite and to ascribe to its own program the finality of existence itself. Instead, Engels proceeds with a demonstration that in 1893 history has corrected its earlier deficiencies and that the situation is now prepared for proletarian revolution. Evidence of this is the triumph among the workers of "the theory of Marx, sharply formulating the final aims of the struggle." Apparently, existence and consciousness have been firmly welded together:

At that time the masses, sundered and differing according to locality and nationality, linked only by the feeling of common suffering, undeveloped, tossed to and fro in their perplexity from enthusiasm to despair; today a great international army of socialists, marching irresistibly on and daily growing in number, organization, discipline, insight and assurance of victory.

The collective "I" of the proletariat finally defined itself —it has become the Party. Proletarian unity and action, conceived as an anguished response to the real conditions and "having no ideals to realize," has become a disci-

plined, self-assured "march" toward defined aims. Proletarian consciousness, once consisting of "the content and
material of its revolutionary activity," has become Marxist
theory.°

Engels seems unaware that what he is describing as an
historical development is to an equal degree a decisive
shift in Marxist philosophy, that its reliance upon existence to supply the proletariat with a self and an intelligence is being quietly abandoned in favour of party
ideology and discipline. His contention that the rise of a
marching party is a reflection of the changed position of
the proletariat cannot eliminate the qualitative difference
between the kind of concrete intelligence that arises out
of a spontaneous movement and the stratagems which the
Marxist brain will deduce from its outline of the situation
and its place in the scenario of history.

For Engels in 1893, the continuity of the revolutionary
movement no longer depends upon the reflexes of a proletariat that has been forced into revolt; it is no longer
subject to the intermittences of the heart and mind of the
working class.

In order that the masses may understand what is to be done,
long, persistent work is required, and it is just this work which
we are now pursuing, and with a success which drives the enemy
to despair.

Instead of learning in action, the working class is put to
school by the Party; it marches with its will in the secure
custody of the leadership. Marching has indeed replaced
revolutionary action, the movement which was to have
been the source itself of the "alteration" of the workers.†

° Contrast Engels' *Introduction* to the following passage in Marx's text
of four decades earlier: "A class in which the revolutionary interests
of society are concentrated, so soon as it has risen up, finds directly in
its own situation the content and material of its revolutionary activity;
foes to be laid low; measures, dictated by the needs of the struggle, to
be taken; the consequences of its own deeds drive it on. It makes no
theoretical inquiries into its own task."

† "Both for the production on a mass scale of this communist consciousness, and for the success of the cause itself, the alteration of men
on a mass scale is necessary, an alteration which can only take place in
a practical movement, a revolution." (*The German Ideology*)

The "decisive shock force of the international proletarian army" has become, says Engels, the two million voters of the German Social Democracy and their allies. "We, the "revolutionaries," the "rebels," he observes complacently —noting that "the irony of world history turns everything upside down"—"we are thriving far better on legal methods than on illegal methods and revolt." With the military language—"shock troops," "army," and "revolutionaries" in quotes—what has become of the shrewd spirit and the notion that the working class makes itself human only through revolt?

Was Engels' conversion of Marx's drama of history from an order assumed to be inherent in events into a didactic fable of socialist politics a betrayal of the master's thought a decade after his death? In no respect. Marx, too, had attempted to overcome by political means the laggardness of existence in producing revolutionary consciousness.

If this country [England] is the classic seat of landlordism and capitalism, by virtue of that fact it is also here that the material conditions of their destruction are most highly developed. The General Council [dominated by Marx] being at present placed in the happy position of having its hand directly on this great level of the proletarian revolution . . . it would be sheer folly, we would almost say it would be an outright crime, to allow that hold to fall into purely English hands!

The English have all the material requisites necessary for the social revolution. What they lack is the spirit of generalization and revolutionary ardor. *It is only the General Council which can supply this deficiency*, which can thus accelerate the truly revolutionary movement in this country and consequently everywhere. . . . As the General Council we can initiate measures which later, in the public execution of their tasks, appear as spontaneous movements of the English working class [my italics]. (Resolution of the General Council of the International Workingmen's Association, January 1, 1870)

Somehow the material conditions have failed in England to transform themselves into intellect and ardor, and Marx holds it to be criminal folly to depend upon them to do so. Nor will a true reflex "suffice." He proposes to substitute himself for the mass "I" of the British proletariat by originating its acts. Yet he has no intention of formally rejecting his doctrine of immanence and self-emancipation. He wishes his acts to "appear as spontaneous movements of the English working class." And if accused of Machiavellianism, he has already replied that he is but "accelerating the truly revolutionary movement" called for by his script of history.

Marx's passage from philosophy to instigation seems rather a vacillation following the course of events than a final step. Actual upheavals, like the Commune or the American Civil War, restore his perspective of spectator and prompter of an historical drama developing through the concrete consciousness and actions of class actors inspired by their situation. The laws of history then appear to assert themselves ironically against *all* political programs. Engels, too, confronted by revolutionary action, but without the "greater lever" to tempt him, rests his expectations on dramatic irony; in 1885 he writes to Zasulich concerning Russia, where no Marxist organisation existed:

People who boasted that they had *made* a revolution have always seen the next day that they had no idea what they were doing, that the revolution they *made* did not in the least resemble the one they would have liked to make. That is what Hegel calls the irony of history, an irony that few historic personalities escape.

When the drama is being physically enacted, Hegel reenters "materialism."

What proves unendurable to the philosopher of class conflict is the apparent discontinuity of the drama, the long intermissions in which the proletarian protagonist fails to appear on the stage. Theoretically, the revolution is always in progress, with an ever-present proletariat growing more class conscious and more active. In actuality, Marx is painfully aware, the action on the stage is not continuous, and the "contradictory" process of development fails to translate itself into human conflict. Revolts are far apart and when they do occur prove to be but moments lacking in extension. Even worse than the discontinuity of the action is the discontinuity of the hero.

Social peace, dissolving the working class into individuals with nonclass identifications, causes the proletariat to fade again into the metaphor on which it was founded and to become an historical nothing. This makes normal political activity extremely difficult for the working class as Marx conceived it.

To establish the proletarian hypothesis as a fact Marx originates, at least in embryo, a new kind of politics, which goes beyond support of the working class and development of socialist theory, as in *The Communist Manifesto* and *Capital*. In response to the prolonged quiescence of the proletariat he assigns to his theory the function of the material conditions as the source of proletarian consciousness and action—he seeks *to create* the proletariat as a revolutionary class. Out of this effort arises Marxist politics, in which union and intelligence are born not from the total pathetic experience of those who endure the situation but from the detached brain that has analysed it.

As philosopher and historian, Marx attacks the utopians and "Marxists" for their dogmatism and their dreams of making history according to their plans; as a politician he himself is a Marxist. The intuition of history as a tragedy which, with the elimination of myth, may come to its close through a saving catastrophe is submerged under a programmatic optimism. Its existence and its action centered in the Marxist organization, the proletariat seems to lose its hypothetical character. The semblance of moving toward the goal appears to relieve the workers of the pathos of choosing between permanent revolution and nothingness. In time the human "recoil" before the "indefinite prodigiousness" of socialist revolution ceases to play any part in the writings of the movement (except with Georges Sorel and Rosa Luxemburg), or is used as a justification for techniques of discipline.

But having translated class consciousness from tragic self-recognition into political tutoring, Marxism is haunted by its philosophical premises. If its analysis is the consciousness of the socialist revolution, whose existence determines this consciousness? The class's? Or the Party's? Or is it undermined by both? So long as Marx could say, "The great social measure of the Commune [which was not a Marxist creation] was its own working existence," it was clear that theory was subordinate to the concrete action of the class and that communism was in truth attempting to be the intelligence of "the real movement that abolishes the present state of things." Once, however, class spontaneity has yielded to steady marching at the heels of the Party, the latter must look to itself as the source of historical consciousness, since it is it that experiences while the masses are undergoing the "long, persistent work" of learning. But if its own existence guides it, the Marxist Party is "an independent being" and its theory a mere ideology.* In that case, the high claims of socialism for the release of human individuals into unlimited creativity through the "self-activity" of the proletariat are no longer legitimate. Those hopes rested upon the origin of the collective act in history itself, in the reflex of the individuals of the class to their concrete situation, rather than, as formerly, in a separated community or ideal; but now socialism has produced its own illusory community and independently existing creation of the mind.

Thus in the heart of Marxism a conflict prevails between metaphysics (existence determines consciousness and defeats all preconceptions) and politics ("we can initiate measures"). The "dialectical" overcoming of this conflict through combining its messianism of total liberation with guidance of the masses as an "army" results logically in a politics of hallucination. In Marx's "we can initiate measures which will later appear as spontaneous movements"—this sentence shows the actual content of the synthesis of spontaneity and control—a new principle is making its appearance, though dimly. It is neither the materialist principle of the primacy of existence nor the idealist one that action has its source in thought. It suggests that actions can release a revealed destiny which both dominates existence and precedes thought. With the

---

* The mark of an "ideologist," says Engels, is that "every act, since it is transmitted by thought, also seems to him in the last analysis to be *founded* on thought." Is not the act of the proletarian who is undergoing Party instruction *founded* on Marxism?

affirmation of this power we stand at the verge of twentieth-century political irrationalism.

Primarily, destiny-politics consists of a demonic displacement of the ego of the historical collectivity (class, nation, race) by the party of action, so that the party motivates the community and lays claim to identity with its fate and to its privileges as a creature of history. In *What Is To Be Done*, Lenin begins by denying that the proletariat can be an independent historical actor; for him it is a collective character with a role but without the revolutionary ego and consciousness necessary to play its part. Its struggles are but reflexes of economic contradictions which can never of themselves result in revolution. The giant figure of the proletariat is doomed to remain a personification of exploitation and misery until it is possessed by an alien subject that will send it hurtling along its predestined path. This conscious and active ego is the Bolshevik Party of "scientific" (destiny-knowing) professional revolutionaries. In the most literal sense the Party's relation to the class is demonical; after a series of paroxysms the collective body of the class is inhabited and violently moved by a separate will which is that of another group or even of one man. Lenin used the word "subjectivity" to mean precisely the Party and its decisions.

If the revolutionary violence of the proletariat resulted from its historical situation, the class would bear no moral responsibility—it will be recalled that Marx accorded to the capitalists, too, immunity from class guilt. The class exists "outside" the individual and compels him, while its own acts are necessary in the sense that necessity exists in the physical world. Besides, even if the class were responsible, who could judge it? Only history itself, whose creature and "agent" it is. "History is the judge," says Marx, "the proletariat its executioner." Hence so long as its hero is actually the revolutionary working class of Europe, Marxism need not concern itself with the morality of its means—the truth itself and its revelation, through which the instinctive movement of the victim-hero is transformed into a conscious act, is its sole and exclusive means.

Political Marxism demands for itself the metaphysical privileges of class action. The violence of the "vanguard," having become "dialectically" the act of the proletariat, justifies itself by the existence of the workers as victims of the wage system. Any attack upon that system by Marxist intellectuals and wielders of power becomes a liberating movement on the part of the class. Thus the Party need not account for the means it employs—all the more so since its program is taken to be identical with the reality which is the ground of all future values. It even denies that the form of its organization is a "principled question" —to be totally authoritarian does not prevent its being totally democratic, since its acts are the acts of the proletariat and the proletariat is, by definition, the demos.

As it attributes to the class the subjectivity of the Party, without regard to the actual will or consciousness of the workingman, it also attributes subjectivity to the "embodiments of particular class interests." Capitalists and members of other classes are held automatically guilty of historical crimes, despite the unwillingness of Marx to "make the individual responsible for relations whose creature he socially remains." Thus dictatorship and terror exercised by the proletarian *alter ego* go hand in hand with bringing the social categories artificially to life.

Morally bewildered by assuming for itself the role of the class, Marxism destroys by the same means the basis for the historical insight that was the genius of its author. The Party wishes to analyse events in class terms; standing in the place of the proletariat it can see only itself. Traditional parties are aware that they represent specific configurations of interest and desires. The party of action does not feel itself *in the presence of* any social body. The featureless mass of laborers exists historically only in that the Party creates it; the Party program is the true expression of the workers' interests and their own demands are but errors to be eliminated or exploited. The Party is an absolute with regard to the class, and through it an absolute with regard to history. Referring to the "lag" of workers behind the Party of the most advanced, Engels asserts:

and this alone explains why it is that actually the "solidarity of the proletariat" is everywhere realized in different party groupings which carry on life and death feuds with one another, as the Christian sects in the Roman Empire did amidst the worst persecutions. (Letter to Bebel, 1873)

As a liberating program, Marxism founders on the subjectivity of the proletariat. So soon as it declares itself, rather than their common situation, to be the inspiration of men's revolutionary unity and ardor—how else can it offer itself simultaneously to the French working class and to nonindustrial French colonials?—Marxism becomes an ideology competing with others. When fascism asserted the revolutionary working class to be an invention of Marxism, it was but echoing the Marxist parties themselves. If the class as actor is a physical extension of the Party, fascism was justified in claiming that a magical contest in creating mass-egos could decide which collectivities are to exist and dominate history. Moreover, it proved that heroic pantomime, symbolism, ritual, bribes, appeals to the past, could overwhelm Marxist class consciousness. What choice was there for the workers between the fascist costume drama and a socialism that urged them to regard their own working clothes as a costume? In Germany and Italy the working class was driven off the stage of history by the defeat of the Party —in Russia it was driven off by its victory.

The elimination of the illusory community has proved to be far more difficult than Marx imagined. Though released from the sacred, the consciousness of the workingmen has not become an infallible reflection of their bare material condition. Their pastless barbarism has failed to immunize them to heroes and ideals. In moments of crisis the newfangled men seem as susceptible to self-surrender as their tradition-bound predecessors. They have neither chosen nor been compelled to change themselves into the inhuman "character assigned to them by the process of production."

Yet the proletarian personification remains. A single external character imposes itself upon the human mass of wage workers. And the presence of the mask continues *to imply* action on its part, no matter how many times it

shows itself to be in fact incapable of it. Neither theory
nor events can refute the hypothesis of the revolutionary
working class. So long as the category exists the possibility cannot be excluded that it will recognize itself as a
separate human community and revolutionize everything
by affirming itself and its traditionless interests.

In this proletarian category the twentieth century has
concentrated a unique power. No modern government
can survive against the expressed will of its workers;
decades ago Sorel pointed out that trading on the
chances of that expression is the main feature of contemporary politics. Whatever be concluded about history as an epic of class struggle, the potent effects in our
time of the *likelihood* of class struggle cannot be denied.
On the one hand, the present social order is permanently
menaced by the workers' tremendous potential power;
on the other, the fact that this power rests with an
anonymous category, an historical "nothing," tempts all
modern myth-makers to seize upon the class as raw material for new collectivities by which society can be
subjugated. Cannot the history-less proletariat be converted into *anything* as readily as into itself? Keeping the drama in suspense between revolution by the
working class on its own behalf and revolution as a tool
for others, the pathos of the proletariat dominates modern history.

Leszek Kolakowski

The Concept of the Left

Leszek Kolakowski (b. 1927) is one of the leading "revisionist" thinkers in contemporary Poland. During the mid-fifties, he was one of the editors of Po Prostu, a weekly which sharply criticized "the new class" of Communist bureaucrats and which was suspended in 1957. Among his books are Toward a Marxist Humanism, 1968, a collection of his theoretical essays in English translation. A brilliant and courageous fighter against authoritarian dogmatism in Poland, Kolakowski has been expelled from the Communist Party and deprived of certain professional rights at the University of Warsaw. The idea of a democratic and humanist socialism finds powerful confirmation in his work.

Every work of man is a compromise between the material and the tool. Tools are never quite equal to their tasks, and none is beyond improvement. Aside from differences in human skill, the tool's imperfection and the material's resistance together set the limits that determine the end product. But the tool must fit the material, no matter how remotely, if it isn't to produce a monstrosity. You cannot properly clean teeth with an oil drill or perform brain operations with a pencil. Whenever such attempts have been made, the results have always been less than satisfactory.

The Left as Negation

Social revolutions are a compromise between utopia and historical reality. The tool of the revolution is utopia, and the material is the social reality on which one wants to impose a new form. The tool must to some degree fit the substance if the results are not to become ludicrous.

There is, however, an essential difference between work on physical objects and work on history; for the latter, which is the substance, also creates the tools used to give this substance shape. Utopias which try to give history a new form are themselves a product of history, while history itself remains anonymous. That is why even when the tools turn out to be grossly unsuited to the material, no one is to blame, and it would be senseless to hold anyone responsible.

On the other hand, history is a human product. Although no individual is responsible for the results of the historical process, still each is responsible for his personal involvement in it. Therefore each is also responsible for his role in fashioning the intellectual tools used upon reality in order to change it—for accepting or rejecting a given utopia and the means employed to realize it.

To construct a utopia is always an act of negation toward an existing reality, a desire to transform it. But *negation is not the opposite of construction—it is only the opposite of affirming existing conditions*. That is why it makes little sense to reproach someone for committing a destructive rather than a constructive act, because every act of construction is necessarily a negation of the existing order. At most, you may reproach him for not supporting the reality that exists and for wanting to change it; or, on the other hand, for accepting it without qualification, without seeking change; or, finally, for seeking harmful changes. But a negative position is only the opposite of a conservative attitude toward the world, negation in itself being merely a desire for change. The difference between destructive and constructive work lies in a verbal mystification stemming from the adjectives used to describe the changes, which are considered either good or bad. Every change is, in fact, an act both negative and positive at one and the same time, and the opposite only of an affirmation of things as they are. To blow up a house is just as constructive as to build one—and at the same time just as negative. Of course, this does not mean that it is all the same whether one destroys or builds a house. The difference between the two acts is that the first, in most instances, works to the detriment of the people involved, and the second is almost always to their benefit. The opposite of blowing up a house is not to build a new house but to retain the existing one.

This observation will serve to lead to conclusions whose aim is to define more closely the meaning we give to the concept of the social Left.

The Left—and this is its unchangeable and indispensable quality, though by no means its only one—is a movement of negation toward the existent world. For this very reason it is, as we have seen, a constructive force. It is, simply, a quest for change.

That is why *the Left rejects the objection that its program is only a negative and not a constructive one.*

The Left can cope with reproaches directed at the potential harm or utility that may arise from its negations. It can also contend with the conservative attitude that wants to perpetuate things as they are. It will not defend itself, however, against the accusation of being purely negative, because every constructive program is negative, and vice versa. A Left without a constructive program cannot, by that token, have a negative one, since these two terms are synonymous. If there is no program, there is at the same time no negation, that is, no opposite of the Left—in other words, conservativism.

Utopia and the Left

But the act of negation does not in itself define the Left, for there are movements with retrogressive goals. Hitlerism was the negation of the Weimar Republic, but this does not make it leftist. In countries not controlled by the Right, an extreme counter-revolutionary movement is always a negation of the existing order. Thus the Left is defined by its negation, *but not only by this;* it is also defined by the direction of this negation, in fact, by the nature of its utopia.

I use the word *utopia* deliberately and not in the derogatory sense that expresses the absurd notion that all social changes are pipe dreams. By utopia I mean a state of social consciousness, a mental counterpart to the social movement striving for radical change in the world—a counterpart itself inadequate to these changes and merely reflecting them in an idealized and obscure form. It endows the real movement with the sense of realizing an ideal born in the realm of pure spirit and not in *current* historical experience. Utopia is, therefore, a mysterious consciousness of an actual historical tendency. As long as this tendency lives only a clandestine existence, without finding expression in mass social movements, it gives birth to utopias in the narrower sense, that is, to individually constructed models of the world, as it *should* be. But in time utopia becomes actual social consciousness; it invades the consciousness of a mass movement and becomes one of its essential driving forces. Utopia, then, crosses over from the domain of theoretical and moral thought into the field of practical thinking, and itself begins to govern human action.

Still, this does not make it realizable. Utopia always remains a phenomenon of the world of thought; even when backed by the power of a social movement and, more importantly, even when it enters its consciousness, it is inadequate, going far beyond the movement's potentials. It is, in a way, "pathological" (in a loose sense of the word, for utopian consciousness is in fact a natural social phenomenon). It is a warped attempt to impose upon a historically realistic movement goals that are beyond history.

However—and this is fundamental to an understanding of the internal contradictions of left-wing movements— the Left cannot do without a utopia. The Left gives forth utopias just as the pancreas discharges insulin—by virtue of an innate law. Utopia is the striving for changes which "realistically" cannot be brought about by immediate action, which lie beyond the foreseeable future and defy planning. Still, utopia is a tool of action upon reality and of planning social activity.

A utopia, if it proves so remote from reality that the wish to enforce it would be grotesque, would lead to a monstrous deformation, to socially harmful changes threatening the freedom of man. The Left, if it succeeds, would then turn into its opposite—the Right. But then, too, the utopia would cease to be a utopia and become a slogan justifying every current practice.

On the other hand, the Left cannot renounce utopia; it cannot give up goals that are, for the time being, unattainable, but that impart meaning to social changes. I am speaking of the social Left as a whole, for though the concept of the Left is relative—one is a leftist only in comparison with something, and not in absolute terms—still the extreme element of every Left is a revolutionary movement. The revolutionary movement is a catch-all for all the ultimate demands made upon existing society. It is a total negation of the existing system and, therefore, also a total program. A total program is, in fact, a utopia. A utopia is a necessary component of the revolutionary Left, and the latter is a necessary product of the social Left as a whole.

Yet why is a utopia a condition of all revolutionary movements? Because much historical experience, more or less buried in the social consciousness, tells us that goals unattainable now will never be reached unless they are articulated when they are still unattainable. It may well be that the impossible at a given moment can become possible only by being stated at a time when it is impossible. To cite an example, a series of reforms will never attain the goals of revolution, a consistent reform party will never imperceptibly be transformed into the fulfillment of a revolution. *The existence of a utopia as a utopia is the necessary prerequisite for its eventually ceasing to be a utopia.*

A revolutionary movement cannot be born simultaneously with the act of revolution, for without a revolutionary movement to precede it the revolution could never come about. As long as the revolutionary act has not been accomplished, or is not indisputably and clearly evident, it is a utopia. For today's Spanish proletariat a social revolution is a utopia; but the Spanish proletariat will never achieve a revolution if it does not proclaim it when it is impossible. This is why tradition plays such an important role in the revolutionary movement: the movement would never know any victories if it had not in previous phases suffered inevitable defeats—if it had not initiated revolutionary activity when the historical situation precluded success.

The desire for revolution cannot be born only when the situation is ripe, because among the conditions for this ripeness are the revolutionary demands made of an unripe reality. The continuous influence of social consciousness is one of the necessary conditions for the maturation of history to the point of radical change; utopia is a prerequisite of social upheavals, just as unrealistic efforts are the precondition of realistic ones. That is the reason why revolutionary consciousness cannot be satisfied with mere participation in changes already taking place; it cannot merely follow events, but must precede them at a time when they are neither planned nor anticipated.

Therefore—and this is an elementary practical conclusion—*the Left doesn't mind being reproached for striving for a utopia.* It may have to defend itself against the accusation that the content of its utopia is damaging to society, but it need not defend itself against the charge of being utopian.

The Right, as a conservative force, needs no utopia; its essence is the affirmation of existing conditions—a fact and not a utopia—or else the desire to revert to a state which was once an accomplished fact. The Right strives to idealize actual conditions, not to change them. What it needs is fraud, not utopia.

The Left cannot give up utopia, because it is a real force even when it is merely a utopia. The sixteenth-century revolt of the German peasants, the Babouvist movement, and the Paris Commune were all utopian. As it turned out, without such utopian activities no nonutopian, progressive social changes would have taken place. Obviously, it does not follow that the task of the Left is to undertake extreme actions in every historical situation. All we are saying is that to condemn utopia for the mere fact that it is a utopia is rightist, conservative, and hampers the prospects of ever creating a utopia. In any event, we are not at the moment formulating social tasks. We are considering the concept of the Left completely in the abstract, trying to ascertain and not to postulate. Since the Left is as "normal" a social phenomenon as the Right, and progressive social movements are as normal as reactionary ones, it is equally normal for the Left, which is a minority, to be persecuted by the Right.

The Left and Social Classes

The concept of the Left remains unclear to this day. Although only about a hundred and fifty years old, it has acquired universal historical dimensions and is applied to ancient history by virtue of a diffusion of meaning common to all languages. Broadly used, the term has a practical function, but its meaning becomes very obscure, more sensed than understood. One thing is certain: It is easier to say which movements, programs, and attitudes are Left in relation to others than to determine where the Left ends and the Right begins in the political power relationship within society's total structure. We speak of a Left within Hitler's party, but that does not, of course, mean that the German Right was restricted to the party Right and that everything else, including the left wing of that party, was the Left in an absolute sense. Society cannot be divided into a Right and a Left. A leftist attitude toward one movement can be linked with a rightist attitude toward another. It is only in their relative meanings that these words make sense.

But what do we mean when we say a movement or an attitude is Left in relation to another? More specifically, which aspect of the concept of the Left is valid in all social situations? For example, what do we mean when we speak of the Left in the Radical Party of France, or of the social-democratic, Catholic, or communist Left? Is there some common element in the word used in such varied contexts? Or are we simply stating that every political situation reveals some human activity we either approve or find to be the less repugnant, and which we therefore call "the Left"? (I say "we call" because the Left draws the dividing line between the Left and the Right, while the Right fights this division systematically —and in vain, for the Left's self-definition is strong enough to define the Right and, in any event, to establish the existence of the demarcation line.)

No doubt because it has taken on a positive aura, the term *Left* is often appropriated by reactionary groups. For example, there is the "European Left," a political annex of the European Coal and Steel Community. So the mere use of the word does not define the Left. We must look for other signposts to help us fix our position in this murky area. Slogans like "freedom" and "equality" belong, of course, to the tradition of the Left; but they lost their meaning once they became universal catch-words to which everyone attaches his own arbitrary interpretation. As time passes, the Left must define itself ever more precisely. For the more it influences social consciousness, the more its slogans take on a positive aura, the more they are appropriated by the Right and lose their defined meaning. Nobody today opposes such concepts as "freedom" and "equality"; that is why they can become implements of fraud, suspect unless they are explained. What is worse, the word *socialism* has also acquired many meanings.

Naturally, it is quite easy to define the Left in general terms, as we can define "progress." But general definitions are necessarily misleading and difficult to apply in concrete discussions. For example, we can say that "Leftness" is the degree of participation in the process of social development that strives to eliminate all conditions in which the possibility of satisfying human needs is obstructed by social relations. From such a definition we derive a certain number of equally general slogans that are too universally acceptable to be useful in fixing political demarcations. The concepts of the Left, of progress, and of freedom are full of internal contradictions; political disputes do not arise from the mere acceptance or rejection of the concepts.

Therefore, rather than construct an easy though ineffective general concept of the Left applicable to all eras, let us accept existing social reality as a fact and look for the basic conflicts that define current history. These are, first of all, class conflicts and, secondarily, political ones. However, the political battle is not completely identical with the pattern of class relations; it is not a carbon copy of them transposed to relations between political parties. This is so because class divisions are not the only kind, and classes themselves are becoming more, rather than less, complicated, because they are split from within by nationality or ideology. Finally, there are political divisions, in so far as they assume diverse forms of autonomy. Under these conditions political life cannot reflect class conflicts purely and directly but, on the contrary, ever more indirectly and confusedly. As a matter of fact, it was never otherwise—if it had been, all historical conflicts would have been resolved centuries ago. That is why the statement that it must be in the interest of the working class to belong to the Left does not always hold true. On the one hand, it is characteristic of the Left to try not to realize men's wishes against their will, nor to force them to accept benefits they do not desire. On the other hand, the working class of a given country may be greatly influenced by nationalism, yet the Left will not support nationalistic demands; elsewhere, the working class may have deep roots in a religious tradition, yet the Left is a secular movement. Even real immediate interests of the working class can be in opposition to the demands of the Left. For example, for a long time the English workers benefited from colonial exploitation— and yet the Left is an enemy of colonialism.

That is why the Left cannot be defined by saying it will always, in every case, support every demand of the working class, or that it is always on the side of the majority. The Left must define itself on the level of ideas, conceding that in many instances it will find itself in the minority. Even though in today's world there is no leftist attitude independent of the struggle for the rights of the working class, though no leftist position can be realized outside the class structure, and though only the struggle of the oppressed can make the Left a material force, nevertheless the Left must be defined in intellectual, and not class, terms. This presupposes that concrete intellectual life is not and cannot be an exact replica of class interests.

On this basis, we can set forth certain characteristics of the position of the Left in various social orders:

In capitalist countries, the fight of the Left is to abolish all social privilege. In noncapitalist countries, it is to remove privileges that have grown out of noncapitalist conditions.

In capitalist countries, the Left fights all forms of colonial oppression. In noncapitalist ones, it demands the abolition of inequalities, discrimination, and the exploitation of certain countries by others.

In capitalist countries, the Left struggles against limitations on freedom of speech and expression. It does so also in noncapitalist lands. In one and the other the Left fights all the contradictions of freedom that arise in *both kinds* of social conditions. How far can one push the demand for tolerance without turning against the idea of tolerance itself? How can one guarantee that tolerance will not lead to the victory of forces that will strangle the principle of tolerance? This is the great problem of all leftist movements. It is also true, obviously, that the Left can make mistakes and act ineffectively, and thus engender a situation that is inimical to itself. However, it is not faulty tactics that are the distinguishing feature of the Left, for, as we have said, its criteria are established on an ideological plane.

In capitalist countries, the Left strives to secularize social life. This is also true in noncapitalist countries.

In capitalist countries, the destruction of all racism is an essential part of the Left's position. This is so in noncapitalist lands as well.

Everywhere the Left fights against the encroachment of any type of obscurantism in social life; it fights for the victory of rational thought, which is by no means a luxury reserved for the intellectuals, but an integral component of social progress in this century. Without it, any form of progress becomes a parody of its own premises.

Finally, under both systems, the Left does not exclude the use of force when necessary, though the use of force is not an invention of the Left, but rather an unavoidable form of social existence. The Left accepts the antinomy of force, but only as an antinomy and not as a gift of fate. Everywhere the Left is ready to compromise with historical facts, but it rejects ideological compromises; that is, it does not abdicate the right to proclaim the basic tenets of its existence regardless of its political tactics.

The Left is free of sacred feelings; it has no sense of sanctity toward any existing historical situation. It takes a position of permanent revisionism toward reality, just as the Right assumes an attitude of opportunism in respect to the world as it is. The Right is the embodiment of the inertia of historical reality—that is why it is as eternal as the Left.

In both systems, the Left strives to base its prospects on the experience and evolutionary tendencies of history; whereas the Right is the expression of capitulation to the situation of the moment. For this reason the Left can have a political ideology, while the Right has nothing but tactics.

Within the context of both systems, the Left knows that every human freedom satisfies a specific need, but that there is also a need for freedom as such.

The Left does not fear history. It believes in the flexibility of social relations and of human nature—in the possibility of changing them. Within both camps it rejects all humility *vis-à-vis* existing situations, authorities, doctrines, the majority, prejudgments, or material pressures.

In both, the Left—not excluding the use of force, not ashamed of it, and not calling it "upbringing" or "benevolence" or "care for children," etc.—nevertheless rejects any means of political warfare that lead to moral consequences which contradict its premises.

All this time I have been describing the Left as a certain ideological and moral attitude. For the Left is not a single defined political movement, or party, or group of parties. The Left is a characteristic which to a greater or lesser degree can serve particular movements or parties, as well as given individuals of human activities, attitudes, and ideologies. One can be leftist from one point of view and not from another. There rarely occur political movements that are totally leftist in every aspect throughout the entire course of their existence. A man of the Left can participate in the political struggle and be a politician in a leftist party, but refuse to approve actions and opinions that are clearly inimical to a leftist attitude. Which does not mean, obviously, that the leftist position does not lead to internal conflicts and contradictions.

For these reasons the Left, as such and as a whole, cannot be an organized political movement. The Left is always to the left in certain respects with relation to some political movements. Every party has its left wing, a current which is farther to the left than the rest of the party in regard to some trait that can be cited as an example. Still, this does not mean that all the leftist elements of all parties taken together form a single movement, or that they are more closely allied to each other than they are to the party that gave birth to them. This would be so if they fulfilled all the requirements of being left in every aspect; but in that case they would not have been segments of so many diverse parties with such varied programs to begin with. The left wing of the Christian-democratic parties has, as a rule, infinitely more in common with them than with the socialist Left, yet it is the Christian-democratic Left on this very basis. Its "Leftness" may be shown by a stand on one or another actual political problem that, in the particular instance, brings it nearer the left of other parties—for example, a condemnation of colonialism or racism. On the other hand, the demands of the Left are met to varying degrees by different parties, which for this reason are called more or less leftist.

The Left and Communism in Poland

Can one speak of a pure party of the Left, and if so when? Is the Communist Party one? Since we cannot at this time define all the Communist parties, let us apply this question to the Polish Party.

For a long time the division into a Party Left and Right did not exist, although some members were more or less to the left. It did not exist because the Party was deprived of any real political life, because its ideology did not grow out of its own historical experience but was to a large degree imposed upon it regardless of experience. The division into a Left and a Right was drawn only when the political life of the Party came into being.

The split took place according to positions on the problems that always divide a movement into a Left and a Right. The Party Left was made up of those who fought to abolish all forms of privilege in social life, to recognize the principle of equality in dealings among nations, and to oppose local and foreign nationalism, reserving the right to call it by its real name of nationalism. The Left stands for the abolition, without chicanery, of all kinds of anti-Semitism in Poland, for freedom of speech and discussion, for *victory over dogma* and over dull, doctrinaire or else magical thinking in political life, for legality in public relations, for the maximum increase in the role of the working class within the system of government, for the liquidation of the lawlessness of the police. It fights against calling crimes "communism" and gangsters "communists"—and against a thousand other things.

I am listing these items summarily, without going into specifics, only to show that the direction of the changes intended to lead to the triumph of socialist democracy was inspired in the Party by its Left, whose demands on all vital points are included in what we call a leftist position. The Party Right consists of the forces of Stalinist inertia, defending a system based on a principles that renounce Polish sovereignty in favor of a foreign nationalism. It supports the dictatorship of doctrinaire schemas in intellectual life, the dictatorship of the police in public life, and military dictatorship in economic life. It suppresses freedom of speech and uses the terminology of government by the people to conceal government by a political apparatus that disregards both the opinion of the public and its needs. The forces of Stalinism within the Party were and are a concentration of all the basic characteristics that define the Right, conservatism, and reaction.

However, the Left in the Polish Communist Party finds itself in a peculiar position, in which political tendencies do not cover a single unbroken gamut "from left to right," but abound in complications. The forces of the Left stand between two rightist tendencies: the reaction within the Party, and traditional reaction. This is a new historical development, awareness of which has arisen only in the past few years. It is as yet a very restricted phenomenon, but its implications are international. We will refrain from describing the historical causes of this situation, which in a certain phase of its development created a crisis in the communist movement, and simply state that the new Left appeared within the movement when it became apparent that a new Right existed. We will not at this time take up the question of just how the old Left degenerated and survived in the form of a Right—a process of which the history of Stalinism furnishes an instructive example—but it does not seem that this process was caused by the mere fact of the Left's coming to power. That is, it does not seem that the Left can exist only in a position of opposition, or that the possession of power is incompatible with the nature of the Left and leads inevitably to its downfall.

For although the negation of reality is part of the nature of the Left, it does not follow necessarily that reality must always be contrary to the demands of the Left. History, it is true, provides countless experiences that seem to speak for such a view and tempt us to see the Left as condemned to be an "eternal opposition." Yet over the years history has witnessed many setbacks to demands (for example, equality before the law) that subsequently, after centuries of suffering and defeat, became reality. Love of martyrdom and heroics is as alien to the Left as opportunism in a current situation or renunciation of utopian goals. The Left protests against the existing world, but it does not long for a void. It is an explosive charge that disrupts the stability of social life, but it is not a movement toward nothingness.

The Weaknesses of the Left

The main weakness of the Left was not that it grew out of negation, but that its negation attained only the level of *moral protest* and not of practical thought. A leftist attitude that stops at the stage of moral experience has little practical effect. "Bleeding-heartism" is not a political position.

Another trait, one that was unavoidable in our circumstances, was that the Left could not be an organized movement but only an unclear, fragmented negative consciousness opposed to the Right, which was bound by no scruples of loyalty regarding the formation of splinter factions within the Party. Thus the Left did not become a political movement in the true sense, but merely the sum total of spontaneous moral positions.

One weakness of the Left arose from the regressive circumstances of the international situation, the details of which I won't go into but which distinctly favored rightist activities.

Other weaknesses of the Left were those elements of the immediate situation from which the efforts of the Right could draw strength. The Right has no scruples about using every kind of demagogy, every political and ideological slogan that will enable it to dominate the situation of the moment. When necessary, it makes use of anti-Semitism to gain a certain number of allies from the bigots within or outside the party. The Right is primarily after power. In the fight for power (which, for example, it does not possess in Poland today), it is prepared to advance any leftist slogans that can count on popular appeal. Let us speak openly: Contempt for ideology is the strength of the Right because it allows for greater flexibility in practice and for the arbitrary use of any verbal facade that will facilitate the seizure of power. The Right is backed not only by the inertia of old customs and institutions, but also by the power of the lie; true, only a little way, but far enough to enable it to master the situation. At a given moment these ideological slogans are exposed as tactical imposture; but the trick is to make sure this moment comes only after the situation is in hand and the police are at one's disposal. That is why it is important for the Left to have available at all times criteria of recognition in the form of attitudes toward those actual political matters which, for one reason or another, force the Right to reveal itself for what it is. Today such criteria exist chiefly in the domain of international affairs.

The Left was also weakened by the fact that the general social protest against the compromised methods of the government was too often linked with reactionary demands unacceptable to the Left. But at that stage of its development, the Left was not strong enough to assume leadership of this protest.

As a result of these circumstances, the Left (on an international scale) could not help but be defeated. Nevertheless, if it is to exist, the Left must above all be aware of the danger of its *ideological* position.

The danger lies in its double exposure to two forms of rightist pressure. The Left must be particularly alert to its need to define its special position as *constantly and simultaneously* opposed to both those forces. It must clearly and continuously proclaim its negative stand against both rightist currents, of which one is the expression of Stalinist inertia and the other of the inertia of capitalism in its most backward and obscurantist cast. The Left is in grave danger if it directs its criticism toward only one pressure, for it thus blurs its political demarcations. Its position must be expressed in simultaneous negation. The Left must oppose Polish nationalism as adamantly as it does foreign nationalisms that threaten Poland. It must take the same clear rational attitude toward both the sclerotic religiosity of the Stalinist version of Marxism and the obscurantism of the clergy. It must simultaneously reject socialist phraseology as a facade for police states and democratic phraseology as a disguise for bourgeois rule. Only thus can the Left retain its separate, distinct position, which is that of a minority. Nevertheless, the Left does not desire to become a majority at any price.

In the current situation, the Left's greatest claim is ideological. To be more precise, it is to differentiate exactly between ideology and *current political tactics*. The Left does not refuse to compromise with reality as long as compromises are so labeled. It will always counteract any attempt to bend ideology to the demands of the moment, to temporarily necessary concessions, to tactics. While the Left realizes that on occasion it is powerless in the face of crime, it refuses to call crime a "blessing."

This is definitely not a trivial or secondary matter. A political party that does not rely on an authentic ideological base can exist for a long time in a state of vegetation, but it will collapse like a house of cards if confronted by difficulties. A case in point is the Hungarian Party. A communist movement that subordinates its ideology to immediate tactics is destined for degeneration and defeat. It can exist only with the support of the power and the repressive capacity of the state. The intellectual and moral values of communism are not luxurious ornaments of its activity, but the conditions of its existence. That is why it is difficult to create leftist socialism in a reactionary country. A communist movement whose sole form of existence is sheer tactics and which permits the loss of its original intellectual and moral premises ceases to be a leftist movement. Hence the word *socialism* has come to have more than one meaning, and is no longer synonymous with the word *left*. And this is why a regeneration of the concept of the Left is necessary—also so that we can delimit the meaning of socialist slogans. We therefore propose the term *leftist socialism*.

Without surrendering any of the premises of its existence, the Left is obviously ready to make alliances with any groups, no matter how small, and with all "leftist foci" wherever they may be. But it must refuse to support rightist situations and activities; or if compelled to do so under duress, it must call this "duress" and refrain from seeking ideological justification for its actions.

The Left knows that these demands merely seem modest and realizes they may lead to new defeats—but such defeats are more fruitful than capitulation. For this reason, the Left is not afraid of being a minority, which is what it is on an international scale. It knows that history itself calls forth in every situation a leftist side which is as necessary a component of social life as its aspect of conservatism and inertia.

The contradictions of social life cannot be liquidated; this means that the history of man will exist as long as man himself. And the Left is the fermenting factor in even the most hardened mass of the historical present. Even though it is at times weak and invisible, it is nonetheless the dynamite of hope that blasts the dead load of ossified systems, institutions, customs, intellectual habits, and closed doctrines. The Left unites those dispersed and often hidden atoms whose movement is, in the last analysis, what we call progress.

Oskar Lange

The Economist's Case for Socialism

> *Oskar Lange (1904–1965), formerly professor of economics at the University of Chicago and during the later years of his life an official in the Gomulka government in Poland, was one of the more creative and undogmatic Marxian economists of the twentieth century. The essay below is taken from Lange and Taylor,* On the Economic Theory of Socialism, *1938; it presents a specialist's argument, yet one that should be accessible to the layman, concerning the economic problems of a socialist society.*

The rules of consistency of decisions and of efficiency in carrying them out in a socialist economy are exactly the same as those that govern the actual behavior of entrepreneurs on a purely competitive market.* Competition forces entrepreneurs to act much as they would have to

---

* There seems to exist an apparent exception: the rule which determines the output of an industry. Under free competition, the output of an industry is such that the price of the product is equal to the average cost of production, while the social optimum output (i.e., the output which best satisfies consumers' preferences) is obtained when the output of an industry is such that the price of the product is equal to the *marginal* cost incurred by the industry in producing that amount. When the industry works under constant returns there is no difference, for average and marginal costs incurred by the industry are equal. If, however, external economies or diseconomies of scale are present, there is a divergence which has already been noted by Marshall and explicitly recognized by Professor Pigou. *See* Alfred Marshall, *Principles of Economics* (London, 1930), pp. 472 and 474–475; also Pigou, *The Economics of Welfare*, pp. 223–225. But this exception can be interpreted as due to a difference in the comprehensiveness of the items that enter into the accounting of costs and benefits (discussed on page 704 below).

act were they managers of production in a socialist system. The fact that free competition tends to enforce rules of behavior similar to those in an ideal planned economy makes competition the pet idea of the economist. But if competition enforces the same rules of allocating resources as would have to be accepted in a rationally conducted socialist economy, what is the use of bothering about socialism? Why change the whole economic system if the same result can be attained within the present system, if only it could be forced to maintain the competitive standard?

But the analogy between the allocation of resources in a competitive capitalist and a socialist economy is only a purely formal one. The *formal* principles are the same, but the *actual* allocation may be quite different. This difference is due to two features* that distinguish a socialist economy from an economic system based on private ownership of the means of production and on private enterprise.

One feature is the distribution of incomes. Only a socialist economy can distribute incomes so as to attain the maximum social welfare. In any system with private ownership of the means of production, the distribution of incomes is determined by the distribution of ownership of the ultimate productive resources. This distribution is a historical datum which originates independently of the requirements of the maximization of social welfare. For instance, the distribution of landed property is different in countries where the big landed estates of the feudal epoch have been broken up by bourgeois and peasant revolutions from where they have been left intact. Under capitalism the distribution of the ownership of the ultimate productive resources is a very unequal one, a large part of the population owning only their labor power. Under such conditions demand price does not reflect the relative urgency of the needs of different persons† and the allocation of resources determined by the demand

---

* These two features, though without reference to a socialist economy, have been touched upon already by Marshall in discussing the doctrine of maximum satisfaction. *See Principles of Economics*, pp. 470–472.

† This criticism presupposes, of course, that the various utilities derived from a given income by different persons are comparable. The theory

price offered for consumer's goods is far from attaining
the maximum of social welfare. While some are starving
others are allowed to indulge in luxury. In a socialist
society the incomes of the consumers could be determined so as to maximize the total welfare of the whole
population.

Free choice in consumption and free choice of occupation being assumed, the distribution of incomes maximizing the total welfare of society has to satisfy the following
two conditions: (1) The distribution has to be such that
the same demand price offered by different consumers
represents an equal urgency of need. This is attained if
the marginal utility of income is the same for all consumers. (2) The distribution has to lead to such apportionment of the services of labor between the different occupations as to make the differences of the value of the
marginal product of labor in the various occupations
equal to the differences in the marginal disutility involved in their pursuit. Assuming the marginal utility
curves of income to be the same for all individuals, condition 1 is satisfied when all consumers have the same income. But condition 2 requires a differentiation of incomes, since, to secure the apportionment of labor ser-

---

of economic equilibrium does not need any such assumption, for being
an *explanation* of behavior under given conditions, it is concerned only
with individuals, each maximizing his utility separately. But the possibility of such comparison is a postulate necessary (except in a Robinson Crusoe economy) if different equilibrium positions are to be interpreted in terms of *human welfare*. And such intrepretation is required
for choosing different economic *policies*. If this possibility is denied,
any judgment as to the merits of economic policies, transcending the
question of purely formal consistency of decisions and of efficiency in
carrying them out, is impossible. In such cases also no reason can be
found why the allocation of resources ought to be based on the demand
prices resulting from the free consumers' choices, rather than on the
whim of a dictator. Any other preference scale chosen at random by the
Central Planning Board would do equally well. To deny the compara-
bility of the urgency of need of different persons and at the same time to
regard the allocation of resources based on demand prices as the only
one consistent with economic principles would be contradictory. It would
be, as Mr. Dobb has rightly observed, a maneuver which enables "the
scientific dignity of an ethical neutrality to be combined with an un-
diminished capacity to deliver judgments on practical affairs" (M. H.
Dobb, "Economic Theory and the Problem of a Socialist Economy,"
Economic Journal, December, 1933, p. 591). The logical fallacy of
such a trick is easily exposed.

vices required, differences in the marginal disutility of the various occupations have to be compensated by differences in incomes. The contradiction, however, is only apparent. By putting leisure, safety, agreeableness of work, etc., into the utility scales of the individuals, the disutility of any occupation can be represented as opportunity cost. The choice of an occupation offering a lower money income, but also a smaller disutility, may be interpreted as the purchase of leisure, safety, agreeableness of work, etc., at a price equal to the difference between the money income earned in that particular occupation and in others. Thus the differences of incomes required by condition 2 are only apparent. They represent prices paid by the individuals for different conditions of work. Instead of attaching different money incomes to the various occupations, the administration of a socialist economy might pay all citizens the same money income and charge a price for the pursuit of each occupation. It becomes obvious not only that there is no contradiction between both conditions, but that condition 2 is necessary to satisfy condition 1.*

Our argument holds strictly if the marginal utility curve of income is the same for all individuals.† Of

---

* Thus Mr. Dobb is wrong when he maintains that these conditions are contradictory. (*See op. cit.*, pp. 591–592.) Unless education and training for the different occupations are free, condition 1 is also necessary to satisfy condition 2, for if the marginal utility of income were not the same for all persons, the value of the marginal product of the services of labor (which is equal to wages) would be higher, relative to the disutility, in those occupations which have a higher cost of training. This happens in capitalist society where those who can afford expensive education and training are paid out of any proportion to the relative disutility of their work. Condition 2 would not work, however, in the case of exceptional talents (for instance, of prominent artists or surgeons), which form a natural monopoly. In such cases the value of the marginal product of the services of labor must be necessarily out of any proportion to the marginal disutility. If rewarded according to the value of the marginal product of their services such persons would form a privileged group drawing very high incomes (e.g., writers in the Soviet Union). But a socialist society might also pay them incomes which are far below the value of the marginal product of their services without affecting the supply of those services.

† This does *not* imply that all individuals have the same utility scales, although it would follow from such an assumption.

course, this does not correspond to reality, and one might think of taking into account the differences between the marginal utility curves of income of different individuals by granting higher incomes to the more "sensitive" persons. But since such differences as in "sensitiveness" cannot be measured, the scheme would be impracticable. Besides, the differences in "sensitiveness" existing in present society are chiefly due to the social barriers between classes, e.g., a Hungarian count being more "sensitive" than a Hungarian peasant. Such differences would disappear in the relatively homogeneous social stratification of a socialist society, and all differences as to "sensitiveness" would be of purely individual character. Such individual differences may be assumed to be distributed according to the normal law of error.* Thus, basing the distribution of incomes on the assumption that all individuals have the same marginal utility curve of income, a socialist society would strike the right average in estimating the relative urgency of the needs of different persons, leaving only random errors, while the distribution of income in capitalist society introduces a constant error—a class bias in favor of the rich.

The other feature which distinguishes a socialist economy from one based on private enterprise is the *comprehensiveness* of the items entering into the price system. What enters into the price system depends on the historically given set of institutions. As Professor Pigou has shown, there is frequently a divergence between the private cost borne by an entrepreneur and the social cost of production.† Into the cost account of the private entrepreneur only those items enter for which he has to pay a price, while such items as the maintenance of the unemployed created when he discharges workers, the provision for the victims of occupational diseases and industrial accidents, etc., do not enter, or, as Prof. J. M. Clark has

---

* Such differences in the marginal utility curves of income of different individuals as are not purely random but due to age, family status, infirmity, etc., would be easily recognized, and incomes could be differentiated accordingly.
† *The Economics of Welfare*, Pt. II, Chap. 9.

shown, are diverted into social overhead costs.* On the other side, there are the cases where private producers render services which are not included in the price of the product.

An economic system based on private enterprise can take but very imperfect account of the alternatives sacrificed and realized in production. Most important alternatives, like life, security, and health of the workers, are sacrificed without being accounted for as a cost of production. A socialist economy would be able to put *all* the alternatives into its economic accounting. Thus it would evaluate *all* the services rendered by production and take into the cost accounts *all* the alternatives sacrificed; as a result it would also be able to convert its social overhead costs into prime costs. By doing so it would avoid much of the social waste connected with private enterprise. As Professor Pigou has shown, much of this waste can be removed by proper legislation, taxation, and bounties also within the framework of the present economic system, but a socialist economy can do it with much greater thoroughness.

A very important case of benefits and costs which the private producer cannot consider arises when external economies or diseconomies of scale are present. In such cases the increase in output by one producer increases or diminishes the efficiency of the factors of production engaged by the other producers. Since the social benefit or cost which thus arises is not rewarded to or imposed upon the individual producer, he cannot take it into account in determining his output. And under free competition the number of firms producing a commodity is such that the price of the product is equal to the average cost borne by the private producers. Thus the social benefits and costs due to external economies or diseconomies are not accounted for. In a socialist economy this situation is taken care of automatically by the rule that each industry produce just enough to equalize the *marginal* cost incurred by the industry in producing that amount with the

---

* J. Maurice Clark, *Studies in the Economics of Overhead Costs*, Chicago, 1923, pp. 25–27, 397–403, 463–464.

price of the product. External economies and diseconomies arising from a change in the output of the industry appear in the form of a divergence between average and marginal cost incurred by the industry. They are taken care of by the rule to equalize not the average, but the marginal, cost of production with the price of the product.

As a result of the possibility of taking into account *all* the alternatives a socialist economy would not be subject to the fluctuations of the business cycle. Whatever the theoretical explanation of the business cycle, that cumulative shrinkage of demand and output caused by a cumulative reduction of purchasing power could be stopped in a socialist economy. In a socialist economy there can be, of course, grave mistakes and misdirection of investments and production. But such misdirection need not lead to shrinkage of output and unemployment of factors of production spreading over the whole economic system. A private entrepreneur *has* to close his plant when he incurs grave losses. In a socialist economy a mistake is a mistake, too, and has to be corrected. But in making the correction *all* the alternatives gained and sacrificed can be taken into account, and there is no need to correct losses in one part of the economic system by a procedure which creates still further losses by the secondary effect of a cumulative shrinkage of demand and of unemployment of factors of production. Mistakes can be *localized*, a partial overproduction does not need to turn into a general one.* Thus the business cycle theorist would lose his subject of study in a socialist economy, but the knowledge accumulated by him would still be useful in finding out ways of preventing mistakes and methods of correcting those made that would not lead to further losses.

The possibility of determining the distribution of in-

---

* The decision of the Central Planning Board being guided, not by the aim to secure a maximum profit on each separate investment, but by considerations of making the best use of all the productive resources available in the whole economic system, an amount of investment sufficient to provide full employment for all factors of production would be always maintained.

comes so as to maximize social welfare and of taking *all* the alternatives into the economic account makes a socialist economy, from the economist's point of view, superior to a competitive regime with private ownership of the means of production and with private enterprise,* but especially superior to a competitive capitalist economy where a large part of the participants in the economic system are deprived of any property of productive resources other than their labor. However, the actual capitalist system is not one of perfect competition; it is one where oligopoly and monopolistic competition prevail. This adds a much more powerful argument to the economist's case for socialism. The wastes of monopolistic competition have received so much attention in recent theoretical literature that there is no need to repeat the argument here. The capitalist system is far removed from the model of a competitive economy as elaborated by economic theory. And even if it conformed to it, it would be, as we have seen, far from maximizing social welfare. Only a socialist economy can fully satisfy the claim made by many economists with regard to the achievements of free competition. The *formal* analogy, however, between the principles of distribution of resources in a socialist and in a competitive regime of private enterprise makes the scientific technique of the theory of economic equilibrium which has been worked out for the latter also applicable to the former.

The actual capitalist system is much better described by the analysis of Mrs. Robinson and of Professor Chamberlin than by that of Walras and of Marshall. But the

---

* The deficiencies due to inequality of incomes would be absent in a competitive system where the private ownership of the means of production is equally distributed among the population. (Marx called such a system *einfache Warenproduktion.*) Such a system is incompatible with large-scale industry. But, on account of the approximate equality of incomes in such a system, a socialist economy could partly embody such a system in its own. Therefore, socialism does not need to abolish the private ownership of the means of production in small-scale industry and farming, provided large-scale production is not more economical in these particular fields. By appropriate legislation, taxes, and bounties, a socialist economy can induce those small-scale entrepreneurs to take *all* alternatives into consideration and avoid the danger of their causing serious business fluctuations.

work of the latter two will be more useful in solving the problems of a socialist system. As a result, Professor Chamberlin and Mrs. Robinson face the danger of losing their jobs under socialism, unless they agree to be transferred to the department of economic history to provide students of history with the theoretical apparatus necessary to understand what will appear to a future generation as the craze and folly of a past epoch.

Against these advantages of a socialist economy the economist might put the disadvantage resulting from the arbitrariness of the rate of capital accumulation, if accumulation is performed "corporately." A rate of accumulation which does not reflect the preferences of the consumers as to the time-shape of the flow of income may be regarded as a diminution of social welfare. But it seems that this deficiency may be regarded as overbalanced by the advantages enumerated. Besides, saving is also in the present economic order determined only partly by pure utility considerations, and *the rate of saving is affected much more by the distribution of incomes, which is irrational from the economist's point of view*. Further, as Mr. Robertson has already shown,[*] and Mr. Keynes has elaborated in his analysis of the factors determining the total volume of employment,[†] in a capitalist economy the public's attempt to save may be frustrated by not being followed by an appropriate rate of investment, with the result that poverty instead of increased wealth results from the people's propensity to save. Thus the rate of accumulation determined "corporately" in a socialist society may prove to be, from the economic point of view, much more rational than the actual rate of saving in capitalist society is.

There is also the argument which might be raised against socialism with regard to the efficiency of public officials as compared with private entrepreneurs as managers of production. Strictly speaking, these public officials must be compared with corporation officials

[*] D. H. Robertson, *Banking Policy and the Price Level*, London, 1926, pp. 45–47; *Money*, rev. ed., London, 1929, pp. 93–97.
[†] J. M. Keynes, *The General Theory of Employment, Interest, and Money*, London, 1936.

under capitalism, and not with private small-scale entrepreneurs. The argument thus loses much of its force. The
discussion of this argument belongs to the field of sociology rather than of economic theory and must therefore be
dispensed with here. By doing so we do not mean, however, to deny its great importance. It seems to us, indeed,
that *the real danger of socialism is that of a bureaucratization of economic life,* and not the impossibility of
coping with the problem of allocation of resources. Unfortunately, we do not see how the same, or even greater,
danger can be averted under monopolistic capitalism.
Officials subject to democratic control seem preferable to
private corporation executives who practically are responsible to nobody.

However, the really important point in discussing the
economic merits of socialism is not that of comparing the
equilibrium position of a socialist and of a capitalist economy with respect to social welfare. Interesting as such a
comparison is for the economic theorist, it is not the real
issue in the discussion of socialism. The real issue is
*whether the further maintenance of the capitalist system
is compatible with economic progress.*

That capitalism has been the carrier of the greatest
economic progress ever witnessed in the history of the
human race the socialists are the last to deny. Indeed,
there has scarcely ever been a more enthusiastic eulogy
of the revolutionizing achievements of the capitalist system than that contained in *The Communist Manifesto*.
The bourgeoisie, states the Manifesto,

has been the first to show what man's activity can bring about. It
has accomplished wonders far surpassing Egyptian pyramids, Roman aqueducts, and Gothic cathedrals; it has conducted expeditions that put in the shade all former exoduses of nations and
crusades. . . . The bourgeoisie, by the rapid improvement of all
instruments of production, by the immensely facilitated means of
communication, draws all, even the barbarian, nations into civilization. . . . The bourgeoisie, during its rule of scarce one hundred
years, has created more massive and more colossal productive
forces than have all preceding generations together. Subjection of
nature's forces to man, machinery, application of chemistry to industry and agriculture, steam navigation, railways, electric telegraphs, clearing of whole continents for cultivation, canalization of

rivers, whole populations conjured out of the ground—what earlier century had even a presentiment that such productive forces slumbered in the lap of social labor?

The question arises, however, whether the institutions of private property of the means of production and of private enterprise will continue indefinitely to foster economic progress, or whether, at a certain stage of technical development, they turn from being promoters into becoming shackles of further advance. The last is the contention of the socialists.

The unprecedented economic progress of the last two hundred years is due to innovations increasing the productivity of a given combination of factors of production, or creating new commodities and services. The effects of such innovations on the profits of private enterprise are twofold: 1) The entrepreneur introducing an innovation gains an immediate, though under free competition only temporary, profit or increase in profit. 2) The entrepreneurs using the antiquated means of production, or producing competing goods which are replaced by cheaper rivals, suffer losses which ultimately lead to a devaluation of the capital invested in their business; on the other side there may be entrepreneurs who profit by new demand created in consequence of the innovation. In any case, each innovation is necessarily connected with a loss of value of certain old investments.

In a competitive regime, with the parametric function of prices and with free entry of new firms into each industry, entrepreneurs and investors *have* to submit to the losses and devaluation of old investments resulting from innovations, for there is no possibility of counteracting these innovations. The only way for entrepreneurs to meet the situation is to try to introduce innovations in their own business, which, in turn, inflict losses on others. But when business units become so large as to make the parametric function of prices and the possibility of free entry of new firms (and investments) into the industry ineffective, there arises a tendency to avoid a devaluation of the capital invested. A private enterprise, unless forced by competition to do otherwise, will introduce innova-

tions only when the old capital invested is amortized, or
if the reduction of cost is so pronounced as to offset the
devaluation of the capital already invested, i.e., if the
average total cost becomes lower than the average prime
cost of producing with the old machinery or equipment.
But such slowing up of technical progress is against the
social interest.*

The tendency to maintain the value of existing investments becomes even more powerful when the ownership
of the capital invested is separated from the entrepreneurial function, as is increasingly the case in modern
so-called *financial capitalism*. For the industrial enterprise has to replace the full value of the capital invested
or fail. This is strictly true if the financing of the enterprise has been made through bond issues, but even if it
has been made by stock issues a pronounced decline of
stock quotations injures its financial prestige.

But the maintenance of the value of invested capital is
not compatible with cost-reducing innovations. This has
been pointed out very brilliantly by Professor Robbins:

The maintenance of the value of invested capital may very well
mean that producers who find prospects in one industry more attractive than the prospects in any others are prevented from entering it, that cost-reducing improvements of technique which would
greatly cheapen the commodity to consumers are held up, that the
"wasteful competition" of people who are content to serve the
consumer for lower returns than before is prevented from reducing prices. Every schoolboy knows that the cheapness which comes
from importing corn is incompatible with the maintenance of the
value of the corn lands which would be cultivated if import were

---

* It is in the interest of society that *any* improvement available be introduced, irrespective of what happens to the value of capital already
invested. If the improvement allows the commodity to be produced at an
average total cost which is lower than the average prime cost of producing it with the old machinery, a replacement of the old machinery
by the new is obviously in the interest of the public. But even if the
average total cost of the new method of production is not lower than the
average prime cost of producing with the old machinery, its introduction is in the interest of the public. In this case both the old and the
new machinery ought to be employed in production, the public getting
the benefit of lower prices. The loss of value of the old capital invested
is exactly compensated by the public's gain in consequence of price reduction. Cf. Pigou, *The Economics of Welfare*, pp. 190–192.

restricted. The platitudes of the theory of international trade do not lose any of their force if they are applied to domestic competition. The argument, for instance, that road transport diminishes the value of railway capital has just as much and just as little force as the argument that cheap food lowers the value of agricultural property. . . . Economic progress, in the sense of cheapening of commodities, is not compatible with the preservation of the value already invested in particular industries.*

Therefore, when the maintenance of the value of the capital already invested becomes the chief concern of the entrepreneurs, further economic progress has to stop, or, at least, to slow down considerably.

And in present capitalism the maintenance of the value of the particular investment has, indeed, become the chief concern. Accordingly, interventionism and restrictionism are the dominant economic policies.† But since innovations very frequently reduce the value of capital in other firms or industries rather than in that which introduces them, innovations cannot be stopped altogether. When the pressure of new innovations becomes so strong as to destroy the artificially preserved value of the old investments a frightful economic collapse is the result. The stability of the capitalist system is shaken by the alternation of attempts to stop economic progress in order to protect old investments and tremendous collapses when those attempts fail. The increasing instability of business conditions can be remedied only by either giving up the attempts to protect the value of old investments or successfully stopping innovations.

But holding back technical progress would involve the capitalist system in a new set of difficulties because there would be no profitable investment opportunities for capital accumulation. Without technical progress (of the labor-saving kind), discovery of new natural resources, or considerable increase in population (and the latter two are not sufficient in our day to outbalance a lack of the first), the marginal *net* productivity of capital is liable to

---

* *The Great Depression,* p. 141.
† The protection of monopoly privileges and of particular investments is also the chief source of the imperialist rivalries of the Great Powers.

fall to a level insufficient to compensate the liquidity preference of the capital holders. This result is even more accentuated when a part of the industries enjoy a monopoly position which enables them to protect the value of their investments, for the fact that new capital finds free entry only into those industries where free competition still prevails depresses the marginal *net* productivity of capital much more than would otherwise be the case. As substantiated by Mr. Keynes' brilliant analysis,* this would lead to a deflationary pressure resulting in chronic unemployment of the factors of production.

To prevent such chronic unemployment the state would have to undertake great public investments, thus replacing the private capitalist where the latter refuses to enter because of the low rate of return on the investment. Unless further capital accumulation is effectively prohibited, the state would have to replace the private capitalists more and more in their function as investors. Thus the capitalist system seems to face an unescapable dilemma: holding back technical progress leads, through the exhaustion of profitable investment opportunities, to a state of chronic unemployment which can be remedied only by a policy of public investments on an ever-increasing scale, while a continuance of technical progress leads to the instability due to the policy of protecting the value of old investments which has been previously described.

It seems to us that the tendency to maintain the value of old investments can be removed successfully only by the abolition of private enterprise and of the private ownership of capital and natural resources, at least in those industries where such tendency prevails. Two other ways of removing it are conceivable.

One way would be the return to free competition. This

---

* See *The General Theory of Employment*, pp. 217–221 and 308–309. It ought to be mentioned that the difficulties presented to the capitalist system through capital accumulation finding no outlet in profitable investment opportunities were discussed, though no definite conclusions were reached, by a long series of writers of the Marxist school; Tugan-Baranowski, Hilferding, Rosa Luxemburg. Otto Bauer, Bucharin, Sternberg, Grossmann, and Strachey are only the most important of them. These writers have, however, been much more successful in explaining the bearing of those difficulties on the imperialist policy of the capitalist states.

way, however, does not seem to be possible because of the large size of modern business units. In a system based on the pursuit of private profit each entrepreneur has the natural tendency to exploit all possibilities of increasing his profit. The tendency to restrict competition is as natural for private enterprise as the tendency to protect the value of old investments is natural for private ownership of capital. As Adam Smith long ago remarked: "The interest of dealers in any particular branch of trade or manufactures is always in some respect different from, or even opposite to, that of the public. To widen the market and to narrow the competition is always the interest of the dealers. To widen the market may frequently be agreeable enough to the interest of the public, but to narrow the competition must be always against it."* Or in another passage: "People of the same trade seldom meet together, even for merriment or diversion, but the conversation ends in a conspiracy against the public, or in some contrivance to raise prices."† No private entrepreneur or private capitalist can be expected to renounce voluntarily an opportunity to raise his profit or the value of his investment:

> *Al mondo non fur mai persone ratte*
> *a far lor pro ed a fuggir lor danno.*
> > Dante, Inferno, Canto II

The system of free competition is a rather peculiar one. Its mechanism is one of *fooling* entrepreneurs. It requires the pursuit of maximum profit in order to function, but it destroys profits when they are actually pursued by a larger number of people. However, this game of blindman's buff with the pursuit of maximum profit is possible only as long as the size of the business unit is small and the number of entrepreneurs is consequently large. But with the growth of large-scale industry and the centralization of financial control the pursuit of maximum profit destroys free competition.

The picture would not be complete without adding

---

* *Wealth of the Nations*, 3rd ed., London, 1922, Vol. I, p. 250.
† *Ibid.*, p. 130.

that political interference in economic life is frequently used to protect profits or investments.* This political intervention is also a result of the growing size of industrial and financial units. Small-scale enterprises are too small to be politically significant, but the economic power of big corporations and banking interests is too great not to have serious political consequences. As long as the maximization of profit is the basis of all business activities, it is unavoidable that industrial and financial corporations should try to use their economic power to increase profits or the value of their investments by proper state intervention.† And unless the executive and legislative organs of the state are abstract metaphysical entities beyond the reach of any earthly influence, they will yield to the pressure of those powers. A return to free competition could be accomplished only by splitting up the large-scale business units to destroy their economic and political power. This could be attained only at the cost of giving up large-scale production and the great economic achievements of mass production that are associated with it. Such an artificially maintained system of free competition would have to prohibit the use of advanced technology.

There is a second possible way of overcoming the tendency to maintain the value of old investments: the control of production and investments by the government with the purpose of preventing monopoly and restrictionism. Such control would signify planning of production and investment without removing private enterprise and private ownership of the means of production. However, such planning can scarcely be successful. The great economic power of corporations and banks being what it is,

---

* Much more frequently in Europe than in the United States.

† This has also an important influence on the selection of business leaders. Under free competition, the most successful leader of a business enterprise is he who is able to produce at the lowest cost. With interventionism and restrictionism the best businessman is he who best knows how to influence in his interest the decisions of the organs of the state (in regard to tariffs, government subsidies or orders, advantageous import quotas, etc.). A special ability in this direction may well compensate for the incapacity to produce at a low cost. The best lobbyist becomes the most successful business leader. What formerly was regarded as a special trait of the munitions industry becomes in interventionist capitalism the general rule.

it would be they who would control the public planning authorities rather than the reverse. The result would be planning for monopoly and restrictionism, the reverse of what was aimed at.

But even if this could be avoided, such control would be unsuccessful. To retain private property and private enterprise and to force them to do things different from those required by the pursuit of maximum profit would involve a terrific amount of regimentation of investment and enterprise. To realize this one has but to consider that government control preventing restrictionist preservation of the value of old investments would have to force producers to act in a way which imposes on them actual losses of capital. This would upset the financial structure of modern capitalist industry. The constant friction between capitalists and entrepreneurs on the one side and the controlling government authorities on the other side would paralyze business. Besides, the corporations and big banks could use their economic power to defy the government authorities (for instance, by closing their plants, withdrawing investments, or other kinds of economic sabotage). As a result the governments would have either to yield, and thus give up any effective interference with the pursuit of maximum profit, or transfer the defying corporations and banks into public ownership and management. The latter would lead straight to socialism.

Thus, monopoly, restrictionism, and interventionism can be done away with only together with private enterprise and the private ownership of the means of production, which, from being promoters, have turned into obstacles, of economic progress. This does not imply the necessity, or wisdom, of abolishing private enterprise and private property of the means of production in those fields where real competition still prevails, i.e., in small-scale industry and farming. In these fields, private property of the means of production and private enterprise may well continue to have a useful social function by being more efficient than a socialized industry might be. But the most important part of modern economic life is just as far removed from free competition as it is from socialism;* it is choked up with restrictionism of all sorts. When this state of things will have become unbearable, when its incompatibility with economic progress will have become obvious, and when it will be recognized that it is impossible to return to free competition, or to have successful public control of enterprise and of investment without taking them out of private hands, then socialism will remain as the only solution available. Of course, this solution will be opposed by those classes who have a vested interest in the *status quo*. The socialist solution can, therefore, be carried out only after the political power of those classes has been broken.

---

* According to the United States Senate report on *Industrial Prices and Their Relative Inflexibility*, 74th Congress, 1st Session, Document No. 13, p. 10, written by Prof. G. C. Means, in the United States "more than one-half of all manufacturing activity is carried on by two hundred big corporations, while big corporations dominate the railroad utility fields and play an important role in the fields of construction and distribution." *See also* A. A. Berle and G. C. Means, *The Modern Corporation and Private Property*, New York, 1933, Bk. 1, Chap. 3, and A. R. Burns, *The Decline of Competition*, New York, 1936.

Oskar Lange

Marxian Economics and Modern Economic Theory

The following essay by Oskar Lange, which first appeared in The Review of Economic Studies, *June, 1935, has become a classical statement of the case for a version of a free or "market" socialism.*

The Marxist's claim to superiority for his economics is that "bourgeois" economics has utterly failed to explain the fundamental tendencies of the development of the capitalist system. These tendencies are: 1) the constant increase of the scale of production which by substituting large-scale for small-scale production has led to the transition from the free-competitive capitalism of the nineteenth century to the present monopolistic (or rather oligopolistic) capitalism; 2) the substitution of interventionism and "planning" for *laissez-faire;* 3) the transition from free trade to high protectionism and economic nationalism in international relations; 4) the constant expansion of the capitalist method of production in noncapitalist countries, which as long as competition was free led to a relatively peaceful permeation of capitalist economy and Western civilization through the whole world, but which with oligopolistic and interventionist capitalism leads to imperialist rivalry among the principal capitalist powers; 5) the increase of economic instability in the capitalist system, which by destroying the economic and social security of the population of capitalist countries, causes them to rebel against the existing economic system, whatever the ideology and program underlying this rebellion (socialism or fascism).

The claim that "bourgeois" economists have failed to explain these tendencies in the development of capitalism and to formulate them into a theory of economic evolution seems to be justified indeed. How utterly they failed to do so is conspicuous from the fact that many of them denied this development until the phenomena apparently became so overwhelming as to be familiar to anybody but the professional economist who was always the last to recognize their existence. Thus the tendency towards the concentration of production was denied, or, if admitted, was regarded as of minor significance for the nature of the economic system, until the monopolistic (or oligopolistic) character of the basic industries became so obvious that a special theory of limited competition had to be developed to supplement orthodox economic theory. The transition from free trade to protectionism was mainly interpreted as an act of economic folly; its close connection with the transition from free competition to monopolistic control has as yet scarcely been realized by "bourgeois" economists. The imperialist rivalry of capitalist powers has mainly been explained in purely political terms, the connection between imperialist rivalry and the fight for monopolistic control scarcely being realized. It was very generally held among "bourgeois" economists both at the beginning of the twentieth century and in the years preceding 1929, that the economic stability of capitalism was increasing and that business fluctuations were becoming less and less intense. Thus the Marxian claim that "bourgeois" economists failed to grasp the fundamental tendencies of the evolution of the capitalist system proves to be true. They either denied the existence of these tendencies, or if they took account of them they never succeeded in explaining them by a consistent theory of economic evolution, but effectively offered no more than a historical description. On the other hand, Marxian economics must be admitted to have anticipated these tendencies correctly and to have developed a theory which investigates the causal mechanism of this evolution and thus shows its inevitability.

It may be contended, however, that ths lack of understanding of the basic phenomena of the evolution of capi-

talism by the professional economists was not a failure of
their science, but rather a personal failure due to their
middle-class social allegiance. They certainly could not
be expected to look with favour on a theory of evolution
which draws the conclusion that the middle-class will be
wiped out in the process of evolutions. If this were the
case, it would have been an *error artificis* rather than an
error artis, the psychological grounds of which are easily
explained. There are, however, reasons which seem to
suggest that the failure is more than a purely personal
one and that some *error artis* is involved. In order to
display this let us imagine two persons: one who has
learned his economics only from the Austrian School, Pareto and Marshall, without ever having seen or even heard
a sentence of Marx or his disciples; the other one who, on
the contrary, knows his economics exclusively from Marx
and the Marxists and does not even suspect that there
may have been economists outside the Marxist School.
Which of the two will be able to account better for the
fundamental tendencies of the evolution of capitalism?
To put the question is to answer it.

But this superiority of Marxian economics is only a
partial one. There are some problems before which
Marxian economics is quite powerless, while "bourgeois"
economics solves them easily. What can Marxian economics say about monopoly prices? What has it to say on the
fundamental problems of monetary and credit theory?
What apparatus has it to offer for analysing the incidence
of a tax, or the effect of a certain technical innovation on
wages? And (irony of Fate!) what can Marxian economics contribute to the problem of the optimum distribution
of productive resources in a socialist economy?

Clearly the relative merits of Marxian economics and
of modern "bourgeois" economic theory belong to different "ranges." Marxian economics can work the economic evolution of capitalist society into a consistent
theory from which its necessity is deduced, while "bourgeois" economists get no further than mere historical description. On the other hand, "bourgeois" economics is
able to grasp the phenomena of the everyday life of a
capitalist economy in a manner that is far superior to

anything the Marxist can produce.* Further, the anticipations which can be deduced from the two types of economic theory refer to a different range of time. If people want to anticipate the development of capitalism over a long period, a knowledge of Marx is a much more effective starting point than a knowledge of Wieser, Böhm-Bawerk, Pareto, or even Marshall (though the last-named is in this respect much superior). But Marxian economics would be a poor basis for running a central bank or anticipating the effects of a change in the rate of discount.

The difference between the explanatory value of Marxian and "bourgeois" economics respectively is easily accounted for if the essential features of modern economic theory are recalled. Economic theory as developed by the Austrian, Marshallian, and Lausanne schools is essentially a *static* theory of economic equilibrium analysing the economic process under a system of constant *data* and the mechanism by which prices and quantities produced adjust themselves to changes in these data. The data themselves, which are psychological (the preference scales of the consumers), technical (the production functions), and institutional (the forms and distribution of property of the factors of production, the monetary and banking system, etc.) are regarded as outside the scope of economic theory. The study of the data is a matter of descriptive and statistical investigation, the study of

---

* This difference is connected, of course, with the respective social functions of "bourgeois" and Marxian economics. The first has to provide a scientific basis for rational measures to be taken in the current administration of the capitalist economy, "monetary and credit policy, tariffs, localization, monopoly prices, etc.," the social function of the latter has been to provide a scientific basis for long-range anticipations guiding the rational activity of a revolutionary movement directed against the very institutional foundations of the capitalist system. But in providing a scientific basis for the current administration of the capitalist economy, "bourgeois" economics has developed a theory of equilibrium which can also serve as a basis for the current administration of a socialist economy. It is obvious that Marshallian economics offers more for the current administration of the economic system of Soviet Russia than Marxian economics does, though the latter is surely the more effective basis for anticipating the future of capitalism. In so far, modern economic theory, in spite of its undoubted "bourgeois" origin, has a universal significance.

changes in the data is the province of economic history. If there are any "laws" discoverable in the change of data, their study is outside the range of economic theory. Further, the institutional data of the theory are not specified. In so far as the theory of economic equilibrium is merely a theory of distribution of scarce resources between different uses it does not need any institutional data at all, for the relevant considerations can be deduced from the example of Robinson Crusoe. In so far as economics is not even a social science. When economic theory is concerned with the pricing process, the specification of institutional data is very general. All that is assumed is the existence of the institutions necessary for the functioning of an exchange economy. But the consequences of the additional institutional* datum which distinguishes capitalism from other forms of exchange economy, i.e., the existence of a class of people who do not possess any means of production, is scarcely examined.

Now, Marxian economics is distinguished by making the specification of this additional institutional datum the very cornerstone of its analysis, thus discovering the clue to the peculiarity of the capitalist system by which it differs from other forms of exchange economy. Another characteristic feature of Marxian economics (which will be shown to be closely connected with the former one) is that it provides not only a theory of economic equilibrium, but also a theory of economic evolution. For modern "bourgeois" economics, the problem of economic evolution belongs not to economic theory but to economic history. The study of changes in the data of the economic system is regarded as being beyond the scope of economic theory: for these changes are considered to be from the economists' point of view accidental, not results

---

* By calling the fact of division of society into proletarians and owners of means of production an institutional datum I do not mean to imply that it is imposed by law. It might be better, perhaps, to distinguish between institutional data, resulting from legal institutions, and other types of sociological data which are not expressed in the form of legal institutions, but as the term *institutional* is used generally in a very broad sense, there is no need to make such distinction for the purpose of this paper.

of the economic process.* In opposition to this point of view, Marxian economics provides further a *theory* of economic evolution.†

The Marxian theory of economic evolution is based on the contention that it is possible, in certain circumstances, to deduce the necessity for, and also the direction of a certain change of economic data, and that such a change follows, in a particular sense, from the very mechanism of the economic process in capitalist society. What this mechanism is and what the term *necessity* means in this connection will be seen later; here it is sufficient to mention that the fundamental change in data occurs in production (a change of the production function) and that the "necessity" of such change can be deduced only under the institutional set-up specific to capitalism. Thus a "law of development" of the capitalist system is established. Hence the anticipation of the future course of events deduced from the Marxian theory is not a mechanical extrapolation of a purely empirical trend, but an anticipation based on the recognition of a law of development and is, with certain reservations, not less stringent than an anticipation based on the static theory of economic equilibrium, such as, for instance, the anticipation that a rise in price leads, under certain circumstances, to a decline of the amount of a commodity demanded.

The economist whose horizon does not extend beyond

---

* Also H. L. Moore's theory of moving equilibrium explains only the reaction of the economic system to a given continuous change of data. The change of data itself is determined statistically but is not an object of theoretical analysis. The same is true of the "dynamic" theories which deduce the necessity of fluctuations from time lags in adjusting supply to change in price. These theories deduce the impossibility of an equilibrium in certain cases from the very nature of the adjustment mechanism, but they cannot deduce theoretically the changes of data responsible for the trend on which the fluctuations due to the process of adjustment are superimposed.

† The difference between a *theory* of economic evolution and a mere historical account of it is excellently explained in Chapter 2 of Schumpeter's *Theory of Economic Development*, Cambridge, Mass., Harvard University Press, 1934. Schumpeter is the only economist outside the Marxist camp who has formulated a theory of economic evolution. However, the close connection of his theory with Marxian ideas is obvious.

the limits of a purely static theory of equilibrium usually denies the possibility of a theory of economic evolution. He is too much accustomed to see in the evolution of what he regards as the pure data of his science a certain kind of "accident" which may be described by the historian and statistician but which cannot be accounted for causally, at any rate not by economic theory. His argument is in general that the phenomena are too complicated to be capable of theoretical formulation, i.e., to be accounted for by one single principle (or a few principles). He contends that in the study of economic evolution so many factors must be taken into account that economic evolution can virtually only be described historically and cannot be forced into the pattern of an over-simplified (and therefore wrong) theory.* However, this argument is scarcely convincing, it is too much like that put forward by the historical school against the possibility of even static economic theory. The pricing problem, so the historical and purely institutionalist economist argues, is much too complicated to be explained by one single principle (marginal utility), but should rather be described historically and statistically so as to take due account of all the factors influencing the price of a commodity. And such factors are, besides utility, the cost of production, relative scarcity, the cost of transportation, the extent to which the commodity is imported or exported, its quality, the climate if the commodity is an article of clothing, etc., etc.† How crazy, one might conclude on this type of argument, to explain the complicated result of so many causes by one single principle such as marginal utility.

---

* The same type of argument is generally raised against the theory of historical materialism which explains social evolution in terms of a few definite principles.

† I know, for instance, of an institutional economist who actually maintained that the price level depends on exactly twelve factors. From his enumeration of these factors, I happen to remember: the confidence people have in the national currency; whether the national budget is balanced or not; the balance of foreign trade; the size of agricultural crops (and thus indirectly rainfall). The ratio of the volume of monetary and credit circulation to the volume of trade he recognized as *one* of the factors, of course, but how wrong, he argued, to think of it as *the* principle explaining the price level.

Another argument is that even if a theory of economic evolution is in principle possible, it does not belong to the field of economics. If by this it is meant that the theory of economic evolution requires *additional* assumptions beyond those contained in the theory of economic equilibrium this is obvious, for if the theory of economic equilibrium already contained these assumptions it would deduce a process of evolution instead of a state of equilibrium. Whether, however, the deduction of the necessity for a change of certain data from certain principles is called *economic* theory or not is merely a matter of terminology. It should be noted, however, that in Marxian theory this change of data is deduced from the principle of profit maximization which is at the basis of the theory of economic equilibrium and that the phenomena connected with it were regarded by the classical economists as belonging to the traditionally established body of economic theory. Hence a theory of economic evolution explaining certain changes of data as resulting from "within" the economic process in capitalist society may duly be included in the science of economics.

I have pointed out that the real source of the superiority of Marxian economics is in the field of explaining and anticipating a process of economic evolution. It is not the specific economic concepts used by Marx, but the definite specification of the institutional framework in which the economic process goes on in capitalist society that makes it possible to establish a theory of economic evolution different from mere historical description. Most orthodox Marxists, however, believe that their superiority in understanding the evolution of capitalism is due to the economic concepts with which Marx worked, i.e., to his using the labour theory of value. They think that the abandonment of the classical labour theory of value in favour of the theory of marginal utility is responsible for the failure of "bourgeois" economics to explain the fundamental phenomena of capitalist evolution. That they are wrong can be easily shown by considering the economic meaning of the labour theory of value. It is nothing but a static theory of general economic equilibrium. In an individualistic exchange economy, based on division of labour, in which there is no central authority to direct which commodities, and in what quantities, are to be produced, the problem is solved automatically by the fact that competition enforces such a distribution of productive resources between the various industries that prices are proportional to the amount of labour necessary for producing the respective commodities (these being the "natural prices" of classical economics). In essence this is as static as the modern theory of economic equilibrium, for it explains price and production equilibrium only under the assumption of certain data (i.e., a given amount of labour such as is necessary to produce a commodity—an amount determined by the technique of production). Nor is this theory based on more specialized institutional assumptions than the modern theory of economic equilibrium; it holds not only in a capitalist economy, but in any exchange economy in which there is free competition. To be exact, however, it really holds precisely only in a noncapitalistic exchange economy of small producers, each of whom owns his own means of production (an exchange economy composed of small, self-working artisans and peasant farmers, for instance; Marx calls it *einfache Warenproduktion*). In a capitalist economy it requires, as Marx has shown himself in the third volume of *Das Kapital,* certain modifications due to differences in the organic composition of capital (i.e., the ratio of the capital invested in capital *goods* to the capital invested in payment of wages) in different industries. Thus the labour theory of value has no qualities which would make it, from the Marxist point of view, superior to the modern more elaborate theory of economic equilibrium.* It is only a more primitive form of the latter,

* In the Marxian system, the labour theory of value serves also to demonstrate the exploitation of the working class under capitalism, i.e., the difference between the personal distribution of income in a capitalist economy and in an *einfache Warenproduktion.* It is this deduction from the labour theory of value which makes the orthodox Marxist stick to it. But the same fact of exploitation can also be deduced without the help of the labour theory of value. Also without it, it is obvious that the personal distribution of income in a capitalist economy is different from that in an *einfache Warenproduktion* (or in a socialist economy based on equalitarian principles, in which the distribution of income

restricted to the narrow field of pure competition and even not without its limitations in this field.† Further, its most relevant statement (i.e., the equality of price to average cost plus "normal" profit) is included in the modern theory of economic equilibrium. Thus the labour theory of value cannot possibly be the source of the superiority of Marxian over "bourgeois" economics in explaining the phenomena of economic *evolution*. In fact, the adherence to an antiquated form of the theory of economic equilibrium is the cause of the inferiority of Marxian economics in many fields. The superiority of Marxian economics on the problem of the evolution

---

would be substantially the same as in an *einfache Warenproduktion*), for profit, interest, and rent can obviously be the personal income of a separate class of people only in a capitalist economy. If interest is explained by the marginal productivity of capital, it is only because the workers do not own the capital they work with that interest is the personal income of a separate class of people. If interest is regarded as due to a higher valuation of present than future goods, it is only because the workers do not possess the subsistence fund enabling them to wait until the commodities they produce are ready that the capitalist advancing it to the workers gets the interest as his personal income. Just as in Marx's case, it is because the workers do not possess the means of production that the surplus value is pocketed by the capitalist. To make the Marxian concept of exploitation clearer by contrast it may be noticed that Pigou (*The Economics of Welfare*, 3rd ed., published 1929, p. 556), and Mrs. Robinson (*The Economics of Imperfect Competition*, p. 281, *seq.*) define exploitation of the worker as occurring when he gets less than the value of the marginal physical product of his labour. This means that exploitation is defined by contrasting the distribution of income in monopolistic capitalism and in competitive capitalism. The middle-class character of this idea of social justice is obvious. For the socialist, the worker is exploited even if he gets the full value of the marginal product of his labour, for from the fact that interest or rent is determined by the marginal productivity of capital or land it does not follow, from the socialist point of view, that the capital- or land-owner ought to get it as his personal income. The Marxian definition of exploitation is derived from contrasting the personal distribution of income in a capitalist economy (irrespective of whether monopolistic or competitive) with that in an *einfache Warenproduktion* in which the worker owns his means of production.

† It is limited to the assumption that the ratio of capital goods to labour in each industry is determined by technical considerations alone, i.e., is a datum and not a variable depending on wages and the prices of capital goods. The very moment substitution between capital goods and labour is assumed to be possible, the theory of marginal productivity must be introduced to determine the organic composition of capital, the knowledge of which is necessary in the Marxian system to determine the deviation of "production prices" from the respective labour values.

of capitalism is due to the exact specification of the institutional datum which distinguishes capitalism from *einfache Warenproduktion*. It was thus that Marx was able to discover the peculiarities of the capitalist system and to establish a theory of economic evolution.

The shortcomings of Marxian economics due to its antiquated theory of economic equilibrium and its merits due to its possession of a theory of economic evolution both become conspicuous if the contribution of Marxian and of "bourgeois" economics to the theory of the business cycle are considered. Neither of them can give a complete solution to the problem.

That Marxian economics fails is due to the labour theory of value, which can explain prices only as equilibrium prices (i.e., "natural prices" in the terminology of Ricardo). Deviations of actual from "natural prices" are more or less accidental and the labour theory has nothing definite to say about them. But the central problem of business cycle theory is one of deviation from equilibrium —of the causes, the course, and the effect of such deviation. Here the labour theory of value inevitably fails. The inability of Marxian economics to solve the problem of the business cycle is demonstrated by the considerable Marxist literature concerned with the famous reproduction schemes of the second volume of *Das Kapital*. This whole literature tries to solve the fundamental problems of economic equilibrium and disequilibrium without even attempting to make use of the mathematical concept of functional relationship.

But on the other hand, "bourgeois" economics has also failed to establish a consistent theory of business cycles. It has done an exceedingly good job in working out a number of details of the greatest importance for a theory of business cycles, such as studying the effects of the different elasticities of the legamina in our economic system. And it has elucidated in a manner hitherto unprecedented the role of money and credit in the business cycle. But it has not been able to formulate a complete theory of business cycles. This inability is a direct consequence of its being only a static theory of equilibrium and of adjustment processes. Such a theory can analyse why, if a disturbance of equilibrium has occurred, certain adjustment processes necessarily follow. It can also analyse the nature of the adjustment processes following a given change of data. But it cannot explain why such disturbances recur regularly, for this is only possible with a theory of economic evolution. Thus the modern theory of economic equilibrium can show that a boom started by an inflationary credit expansion must lead to a breakdown and a process of liquidation. But the real problem is to explain why such credit inflations occur again and again, being inherent in the very nature of the capitalist system. Similarly with the case of technical innovations as a cause of the business cycle. In a theory of economic evolution the business cycle would prove to be the form in which economic evolution takes place in capitalist society.*

Only by a theory of economic evolution can the "necessary" recurrence of a constellation of data leading to a constantly recurring business cycle be explained. A mere theory of economic equilibrium which considers the problem of change of data to be outside its scope can tackle the problem of the business cycle only in two ways: (1) either by seeking the regularity of the recurrence of business cycles in a regularity of changes of data resulting from forces outside the economic process as, for instance, meteorological cycles or successive waves of optimism or pessimism; or (2) by denying the existence of a regularly recurrent business cycle and regarding business fluctuations as due to changes of data which are, from the economic theorist's point of view, "accidental" and hence the concern rather of the economic historian. In the latter case the scope of economic theory would be limited to explaining each business fluctuation separately, as a unique historical phenomenon, by applying the principles of the theory of economic equilibrium to the factual material collected by the economic historian.

I have stressed the point that the distinguishing feature of Marxian economics is the precise specification of an

---

* This character of the business cycle as the specific form of economic development under Capitalism has been stated very clearly by Schumpeter.

institutional datum by which Marx defines capitalism as opposed to an *einfache Warenproduktion*, i.e., an exchange economy consisting of small independent producers each of whom possesses his own means of production. The institutional datum, which is the corner-stone of the Marxian analysis of capitalism, is the division of the population into two parts, one of which owns the means of production while the other owns only labour power. It is obvious that only through this institutional datum can profit and interest appear as a form of income separate from wages. I believe that nobody denies the important sociological bearing of this institutional datum. However, the question arises whether this institutional datum which is the basis of the Marxian definition of capitalism has any bearing on economic theory. Most of modern economic theory is based on the tacit assumption or even flat denial that any such bearing exists. It is generally assumed that, however important the concept of capitalism (as distinct from a mere exchange economy), may be for sociology and economic history, it is unnecessary for economic theory, because the nature of the economic process in the capitalist system is not substantially different from the nature of the economic process in any type of exchange economy.

This argument is perfectly right in so far as the theory of economic equilibrium is concerned. The formal principles of the theory of economic equilibrium are the same for any type of exchange economy. The system of Walrasian equations is applicable indiscriminately to a capitalist economy or to an *einfache Warenproduktion*. Whether the persons who own the productive services of labour and capital (labour power and the means of production in the Marxian terminology) are the same or not affects, of course, the concrete results of the economic equilibrium process, but not its formal theoretical aspect. But the same is true of the formulation of the theory of economic equilibrium which was used by Marx, i.e., of the labour theory of value. This theory, too, applies indiscriminately to any type of exchange economy, provided only that there is pure competition. It was argued repeatedly by Marx himself that the "law of value" by which equilibrium asserts itself in an exchange economy based on the division of labour holds for any type of exchange economy, whether capitalistic or an *einfache Warenproduktion*. Even more, Marx develops his theory of value first for an *einfache Warenproduktion* later showing the (unessential from his point of view) slight modification it must undergo if applied to a capitalist economy. Thus the institutional basis of capitalist society has no essential significance for the general theory of economic equilibrium. In so far as the prevailing opinion of economists is right. The whole significance of this datum is in terms of a sociological interpretation of the economic equilibrium process.

However, the institutional datum underlying the Marxian analysis of capitalism becomes of fundamental significance where the theory of economic evolution is concerned. A theory of economic evolution can be established only on very definite assumptions concerning the institutional framework in which the economic process goes on. The instability of the technique of production which is the basis of the Marxian* theory of economic evolution can be shown to be inevitable only under very specific institutional data. It is clear that it could not be shown to exist in a feudal society, or even in an *einfache Warenproduktion*. Of course, a certain amount of technical progress exists in any type of human society, but only under capitalism can it be shown to be the necessary condition for the maintenance of the system.

The necessity of technical progress† for the maintenance of the capitalist system is deduced in Marxian economics by showing that only in a progressive economy can capitalist profit and interest exist.

The profit of the capitalist entrepreneur, from which also interest on capital is derived, is explained by Marx to be due to the difference between the value of the work-

---

* And also of Schumpeter's.

† By technical progress I mean here not only technical improvements in the narrow meaning of the word, but also improvements in organization, etc., i.e., any innovation increasing the efficiency of the optimum combination of factors of production.

er's labour power and the value of the product created by the worker. Now, according to the labour theory of value, the value of labour power is determined by its cost of reproduction. As in any civilized society a worker is able to produce more than he needs for his subsistence he creates a surplus which is the basis of his employer's profit. However, the crucial point in the Marxian theory is the application of the labour theory of value to the determination of wages. If the market price of cotton cloth exceeds its "natural price," capital and labour flow into the cotton cloth industry until, through increase of the supply of cotton cloth, its market price conforms to the "natural price." But this equilibrating mechanism, which is the foundation of labour theory of value, cannot be applied to the labour market. If wages rise above the "natural price" of labour power so as to threaten to annihilate the employers' profits, there is no possibility of transferring capital and labour from other industries to the production of a larger supply of labour power. In this respect labour power differs fundamentally from other commodities. Therefore, in order to show that wages cannot exceed a certain maximum and thus annihilate profits, a principle different from the ordinary mechanism making market prices tend towards "natural prices" must be introduced.

The classical economists found such a principle in the theory of population. They taught that the pressure of the reproductive instincts of the population on the means of subsistence reacts on any increase of wages above the "natural price" of labour power to such an extent as to counteract effectively the increase of wages. Ricardo says explicitly:* "However much the market price of labour may deviate from its natural price, it has, like commodities, a tendency to conform to it. . . . When the market

---

* Marx himself did not see clearly that in his theoretical system the virtual existence of a surplus population created by technical progress is necessary for the maintenance of the capitalist system. He applied the labour theory of value to the labour market without being aware that the equilibrating mechanism at the basis of this theory does not work in respect to labour power. But this theory of surplus population which he opposed to the Malthusian theory allows us to complete Marx's argument so as to bridge the gap in his system. It may be mentioned

price of labour exceeds its natural price, . . . by the encouragement which high wages give to the increase of population, the number of labourers is increased, wages again fall to their natural price." Thus the working class is assumed to be in a vicious circle which it cannot transcend. Marx rejected the Malthusian theory of population, contending that even without such reproductive facilities wages could not rise so as to annihilate profits. For capitalism creates, according to Marx, its own surplus population (industrial reserve army) through technical progress, replacing workers by machines. The existence of the surplus population created by technical progress prevents wages from rising so as to swallow profits. Thus technical progress is necessary to maintain the capitalist system† and the dynamic nature of the capitalist system, which explains the constant increase of the organic composition of capital, is established.

That the labour theory of value is not necessary for this argument is easily seen, for its application to the labour market is a purely formal one, since the equilibrating mechanism which is at the basis of this theory does not work on the labour market. It is technical progress (or the "law of population" in the case of the classical economists) which prevents wages from swallowing profits.

We can now see in what sense Marxian economics deduces from theoretical considerations the "necessity" of economic evolution. Of course, the necessity of the fact that labour-saving technical innovations are always available at the right moment cannot be deduced by economic theory and in this sense the "necessity" of economic evolution cannot be proved. But Marxian economics does not attempt to prove this. All it establishes is that the capitalist system cannot maintain itself without such innova-

---

that a proletarian surplus population can also be created through driving out of small independent producers (for instance, artisans and peasants) from the market through the competition of capitalist industry. This source of surplus population was very important in the early history of capitalism. So long as such a source of surplus population exists the capitalist system might exist, in theory, even without technical progress other than the dynamic process inherent in the destruction of precapitalist systems.

† *Principles*, Ch. 5, p. 71 (of Gonner's ed. 1929).

tions. And this proof is given by an economic theory which shows that profit and interest on capital can exist only on account of the instability of a certain datum, i.e., the technique of production, and that it would necessarily disappear the moment further technical progress proved impossible. The economic theory presented here is, of course, but a mere sketch of how Marx explains the evolution of capitalism and a suggestion as to how his theory can be completed so as to bridge over the gaps he left. The modern development of economic theory, however, makes it possible to construct a far more satisfactory theory of economic evolution.

It is obvious that the necessity of economic evolution under capitalism is entirely due to the institutional datum distinguishing capitalism from an *einfache Warenproduktion* and that it would not exist in the latter form of exchange economy. Therefore, "bourgeois" economics, omitting to specify exactly the institutional datum of capitalism, is unable to establish a theory of economic evolution, for such a theory cannot be evolved from the very broad assumptions of exchange economy in general. From our account of the Marxian theory of economic evolution, it becomes evident that the necessity of economic evolution does not result from the exchange and pricing process as such, but from the special institutional set-up under which this process goes on in a capitalist system.* The specification of institutional data by "bourgeois" economic theory is too broad, since it gives no more than the institutional data common to any type of exchange economy. But since this very broad specification gives results which are too general to be applicable to special problems, it usually superimposes a very narrow specification of institutional data concerning the monetary and banking system (e.g., the existence or nonexistence of the gold standard, whether the banking system makes an inflationary credit expansion possible or not, etc.). But between the first specification of institutional

---

* Similarly Schumpeter's theory of economic evolution is based on very definite institutional data and does not hold for any type of exchange economy.

data which is very broad and the second specification which is very narrow there is a gap: the institutional datum distinguishing capitalism from an *einfache Warenproduktion*. And this is precisely the datum which is of fundamental significance for the theory of economic evolution.

Through the exact specification of the institutional framework of capitalist economy, Marxian economics is able to establish a theory of economic evolution in which certain data evolve "from within" the economic system. But not all changes of data are explained in this way by the Marxian theory. The evolution of certain data resulting from the very mechanism of the economic system influences certain extraeconomic factors, such as the policy of the state, political and social ideas, etc., which, reacting back on the economic system, change other of its data. This consideration supplies the explanation of the transition from *laissez-faire* to state interventionism and from free trade to protectionism and economic nationalism, the emergence of imperialist rivalries, etc. The causal chain through which the evolution of certain economic data influences certain extraeconomic factors and the reaction of these factors back on the data of the economic system is, however, not within the subject matter of economics. It belongs to the theory of historical materialism the object of which is to elucidate the causal chains connecting economic evolution with social evolution as a whole. Therefore, the full evolution of capitalism in all its concreteness cannot be explained by a theory of economic evolution alone. It can be explained only by a joint use of both economic theory and the theory of historical materialism. The latter is an inseparable part of the Marxian analysis of capitalism.

Our results may be summarized as follows:

1   The superiority of Marxian economics in analysing capitalism is not due to the economic concepts used by Marx (the labour theory of value), but to the exact specification of the institutional datum distinguishing from the concept of an exchange economy in general.

2   The specification of this institutional datum allows of the establishment of a theory of economic evolution from which a

"necessary" trend of certain data in the capitalist system can be deduced.

3   Jointly with the theory of historical materialism this theory of economic evolution accounts for the actual changes occurring in the capitalist system and forms a basis for anticipating the future.

Paul Ricoeur

Power and the State

Paul Ricoeur (b. 1913) is a French political and cultural analyst, especially known for a critical study of Freudian thought. This essay, first published in English in Dissent, Winter, 1958, argues for "the autonomy of politics," that is, for the idea that in a socialist society, as in any other, there remains an urgent need to defend the political rights of men, to adhere to norms of legality and democratic procedures, and to find a way of transmitting the values of political liberalism into socialist democracy.

Every political theory which does not recognize the autonomy of politics *vis-à-vis* socioeconomic history rejects out of hand the following propositions:

■ that the problem of political power in a socialist economy is not fundamentally different from the same problem in a capitalist economy;

■ that political power in a socialist economy offers comparable or even greater possibilities for tyranny;

■ and therefore that public controls as strict as, if not stricter than, those imposed in capitalist societies are necessary under socialism.

The autonomy of politics—for which I shall argue in this essay—seems to me to consist of two characteristics. On the one hand, politics embodies a human relationship which is not reducible to class conflict or socioeconomic tensions in general. Even the state that is most in subjection to a dominating class is also a state precisely to the extent that it expresses the fundamental will of the nation as a whole. Moreover, the state as such need not be radically affected by major changes in the economic sphere. Through this primary characteristic, man's political existence develops a specific type of rationality which cannot be reduced to economics.

On the other hand, politics develops evils of its own—evils specific to the exercise of power. These evils cannot be reduced to others, particularly not to economic alienation. Consequently, economic exploitation can disappear while political evil persists. The very means developed by the state to end economic exploitation can provide the occasion for abuses of power, abuses which, while new in expression or effect, are nonetheless essentially the same in their irrational force as those perpetrated by previous states.

Specific rationality, specific evil: such is the double and paradoxical character of politics. It is the task of political philosophy to elucidate the paradox. . . .

If the state is simultaneously both more rational and more irrational than the individual, then the great problem of democracy is that of control of the state by the people. Just as the rationality of the state may not simply be derived from socioeconomic history and its evils attributed to class contradictions, so must the problem of the control of the state be viewed as an irreducible one. The problem of controlling the state consists in developing institutional techniques specially designed to make the exercise of power possible and the abuse of power impossible. The concept of "control" proceeds directly from the central paradox of man's political existence, being the *practical* resolution of this paradox. The state should exist, but not in excess; should direct, organize, and decide, so that the political animal himself may exist; but the tyrant must not be allowed to rise to power.

Only a political philosophy which has recognized the specific function and specific evil of politics is in a position to state the problem of political control correctly.

It is for this reason that the reduction of political alienation to economic alienation seems to me the weak point in Marxist political thinking. This reduction of political alienation has, in effect, led Marxism-Leninism to substitute for the problem of controlling the state that of its withering away. Even as it projects the end of the evil of the state into an indeterminate future, it underestimates the practical problem of limiting that evil in the present. In promising too much tomorrow, the thesis of the withering away of the state also tolerates too much today.

This notion can also serve as cover and pretext for the perpetuation of terrorism. By a malevolent paradox the thesis of the provisional character of the state becomes the best justification for the endless prolongation of the "dictatorship of the proletariat," thus paving the way for totalitarianism. But it is essential to notice that the theory of the withering away of the state is a logical consequence of the reduction of political alienation to economic alienation. For if the state is solely an organ of repression which arises from class antagonism and expresses the domination of a class, then the state will disappear when the class division of society is no more. The problem, however, is to know whether the end of private ownership of the means of production will or can entail the end of *all* forms of alienation. Perhaps private ownership is in itself but one form of man's power over man; perhaps money itself is but one among other means of domination; perhaps the same spirit of domination expresses itself in exploitation through money, bureaucratic tyranny, intellectual dictatorship, and clericalism.

It is true that Marx, Engels, and Lenin attempted to relate to experience the theory of the withering away of the state. They interpreted the Paris Commune as showing that the dictatorship of the proletariat can be something quite different from the simple transfer of the state's repressive power into other hands, that it can actually mean the destruction of the state machine as a "special force" of repression. If the armed people takes the place of the permanent army, if the police can be dismissed at any moment, if the bureaucracy is dismantled as an organized body and reduced to the lowest salaried condition, then the general force of the majority of the people replaces the repressive special force of the bourgeois state and the beginning of the withering away of the state coincides with the dictatorship of the proletariat. As Lenin said, "*It is impossible to pass from capi-*

talism to socialism without some return to primitive de-
mocracy." And Marx could even say: *"The commune was*
no longer a state in the proper sense of the word."

In the thinking of Marx and Lenin the withering away
thesis was not hypocritical but sincere. Few men have so
discounted the state as have the great Marxists: "As long
as the proletariat still needs the state," reads the *Letter to
Bebel,* "it needs it not to guarantee freedom, but to suppress its enemies, and the day when it will become possible to speak of freedom, the state as such will have
ceased to exist."

My working hypothesis, by contrast, is that the state
cannot wither away; it must be controlled by special institutional techniques.

One must go still further and assert that the socialist
state requires a more vigilant popular control than the
bourgeois state. And this precisely because the socialist
state is the more rational, extending design and planning
to areas of human existence that had previously been left
to chance or improvisation. Since the rationality of a state
which plans to end class division is greater than that of
its predecessors, its potential power and the opportunities
offered to tyranny are also greater.

The task of a critique of socialist power is to show,
lucidly and honestly, the new possibilities of political alienation which are linked to the very struggle against
economic alienation and to the increase in state power
which that struggle entails.

Here are some directions in which research on the
problem of power under socialism might move:

1   One must examine to what degree "the administration of things" is necessarily "a government of persons"
and to what degree progress in the administration of
things gives rise to an increase in the political power of
man over man.

Planning implies choice of an economic character concerning order of priority in the satisfaction of needs and
in the utilization of the means of production. But immediately this choice becomes more than economic. It is a

function of a general politics, that is, of a long-term project concerning the orientation of the human community. The ratio of part reinvested to part consumed, the proportion of cultural to material goods in the general equilibrium of the plan derives from a total strategic vision in which economics injects itself into politics. A plan is a technique put at the service of a project animated by implicit values, of a project which in the last analysis concerns the very humanity of man. That is why politics is the soul of economics insofar as it expresses both will and power.

Thus, an administration of things cannot be substituted for a government of persons, because the rational technique of ordering man's needs and works on the macroscopic scale of the state cannot wholly free itself from the ethical-cultural context. Moreover, it is political power which in the final instance mediates between the latent aspirations of the human community and the technological means derived from knowledge of economic laws. This linkage of ethics and technique in the planning "task" is the fundamental reason why an administration of things implies a government of persons.

2 It must also be shown how reinforcement of state power, linked to the growth of the socialist state's spheres of action, develops *possibilities of abuses intrinsic to it as a socialist state*. This will be putting to use the idea developed above that the most rational state has the greatest opportunities for being irrational.

Engels has clearly demonstrated in his *Anti-Dühring* that, as long as there persist the old division of labor and the other alienations which make of work a burden rather than a joy, the organization of production will remain authoritarian and repressive even after the expropriation of the expropriators. The allotment and the choice of work, when the latter is not spontaneous, still arises from coercion and that coercion is linked to the transition from chance to rationalization.

The temptation of forced labor thus becomes one of the greatest available to the socialist state. Since planning gives this state the *economic* monopoly over psychological coercion (culture, press, and propaganda are compre-

hended in the plan and thus *economically* determined by
the state), it will have as its disposal a whole arsenal of
means, ranging from stimulation and emulation to depor-
tation.

To opportunities for abuse which thus arise must be
added the temptation to overcome irrational opposition
by means more rapid than those of discussion and education. The rational state, in effect, encounters resistance of
all sorts. There is, for example, the resistance characteristic of the peasantry and the petty bourgeoisie who cannot
adapt to the rhythm of the technocrats but remain adjusted to former conditions. This may be dismissed as
merely an habituation to outmoded economic conditions;
but not all forms of resistance are so readily explained.
The planning state, which thinks in terms of generations,
has a project more vast and more remote than has the
individual, whose interest is more immediate, usually limited to the horizon of his own life span or that of his
children. The state and the individual do not share the
same time scheme and thus the individual develops interests which are not easily reconciled to the needs of the
state. We are aware of at least two manifestations of this
dichotomy between the state's goal and that of the citizen. One concerns the division between investment and
immediate consumption, the other the determination of
norms and tempo in production. The micro-interests of
individuals and the macro-decisions of power are in constant tension, and this tension develops a dialectic of
individual demand and state compulsion which makes
misuse of power possible. . . .

In short, the socialist state is more "ideological" than
the "liberal" state. It can reclaim for itself the old dreams
of unifying the domain of truth in an orthodoxy encom-
passing all the manifestations of knowledge and all
expressions of the human word. Under the pretext of
revolutionary discipline and technocratic efficiency, the
socialist state can justify the complete regimentation of
human minds. It can do this, because it enjoys a monopoly over the means of subsistence.

All these thoughts converge towards the same conclusion: if it is true that the socialist state rather than abol-

ishing the power problem, renews it; if it is true that it advances its rationality and increases opportunities for perversion, then the problem of democratic control of the state is even more urgent in a socialist than in a capitalist regime and the myth of the withering away of the state is an obstacle to a systematic treatment of this problem.

3 The third task of a critique of power in a socialist regime would be to reassess the critique of the liberal state in the light of this idea of democratic control. The aim here would be to distinguish which of the institutional arrangements of the liberal state are independent of the phenomenon of class domination and specifically adapted to limiting abusive power. Almost inevitably the liberal state had to appear as a hypocritical medium for permitting economic exploitation. But today, after the bitter experience of Stalinism, the distinction between an instrument of class domination and democratic control in general thrusts itself upon us. Perhaps the principle of this revaluation is contained within Marxism itself, in that it teaches us that a class in its ascendant phase fulfills a universal function. In discovering the problem of democratic controls, the *philosophes* of the eighteenth-century discovered true liberalism, which doubtless transcends the destiny of the bourgeoisie. Liberal politics carried an element of universality because it was attuned to the universal problem of the state, beyond that of its specifically bourgeois form.

This is why the revival of liberal politics is possible within a socialist context.

I should like to give several examples of this discrimination between the "universal" and "bourgeois" aspects of the liberal state:

1 Is not the independence of the judge the very first means of recourse against the abuse of power? It seems to me that the judge is a personage who, by the consent of all, must be voluntarily placed on the border of fundamental conflicts of society.

Some will say that the independence of the judge is an abstraction. Precisely! Society requires for its human respiration an "ideal" function, a willed abstraction in which it projects the idea of legality which legitimates the reality of power. Without this projection, in which the state represents itself as lawful, the individual is at the mercy of the state and power itself is unprotected against its own arbitrariness. It is clear that, among other reasons, the trials of Moscow, Budapest, and Prague were possible because the independence of the judge was not technically insured nor ideologically established in a theory of the judge as man above class, as abstraction in human guise, as law incarnate. Stalin was possible because there were always judges to judge according to his decree.

2 Is not the second condition for permanent appeal against the misuse of power that citizens should have access to sources of information, of knowledge and science, independent of those of the state? We have seen that the modern state, from the time that it economically orients all man's choices through the large decisions of its planners, determines his way of life. *And if the citizens cannot by themselves form opinions concerning these massive decisions*, this power will be less and less distinguishable from totalitarian power.

The planning state, more than any other, requires the counter force of public opinion in the true sense of the term, that is, a public which has opinions, and opinion which has public expression. This implies a press which belongs to its readers and not to the state, and whose freedom of inquiry and expression are constitutionally and economically guaranteed. Stalin was possible because no public opinion could begin to criticize him. And even now it is the post-Stalinist state alone which has condemned Stalin; the people have not been allowed to speak.

These two concepts are so important that it is upon them that Stalinism floundered. The revolts in eastern Europe crystallized around the "abstract" ideas of *justice* and *truth*. If the intellectuals, writers, and artists played a decisive role in these events it was because the stake—despite poverty and low salaries—was not economic and social; the stake was political: the new "alienation" which infected political power. Now the problem of polit-

ical alienation, as we know it since Plato's *Gorgias*, is the
problem of *nontruth*; we have also learned of it through
the Marxist critique of the bourgeois state founded on
nontruth, on seeming, mystifying, and lying. It is precisely here that the intellectual as such is involved in
politics. He finds himself pressed to the very fore of the
revolution, not merely into the ranks, when its motive
force is more political than economic, when it concerns
the relationship of power to truth and justice.

3 Thus it seems to me that a labor democracy requires a certain dialectic between the state and the independent workers' organizations. We have seen that the
long-range interests of the state, even aside from economic problems, do not coincide immediately with those
of the workers. This is evident in a socialist period in the
precise sense of the term, that is a period of inequality of
salaries and professional specialization which places
workers, managers, intellectuals in opposition to one another. It is also apparent in a period of rapid and even
forced industrialization. Consequently, only a legitimated
structuring of the tensions between the state and the
trade unions representing the diverse interests of the
workers can guarantee the groping search for a viable
equilibrium, one which is both economically profitable
and humanly tolerable. The right to strike in particular
seems to me to be the only recourse of the workers
against the state, even against the workers' state. The
postulate that the will of the socialist state and the interests of all the workers directly coincide is a pernicious
illusion and a dangerous pretext for the abuse of state
power.

4 In short, the key is that of control of the state by
the people, by the democratically organized base. Do a
plurality of parties, the technique of "free elections," and
parliamentary government arise from the "universality" of
the liberal state or do they belong irremediably to the
bourgeois period of that state? One need not have a
preconceived idea. It is certain that planning techniques
demand that the socialist form of production be as irrevocable as the republican form of our [French] government. Carrying out a plan demands plain powers, a stable

government, and a long-term budget. Now our [French] pareimentary technique of alternating majorities in power does not seem very compatible with the tasks of the new state rationality. On the other hand, it is no less certain that free discussion is a vital necessity for the state: discussion gives it impetus and orientation, discussion curbs its abuses. Democracy is discussion. Thus in one way or another discussion must be *organized*, and it is here that the question of parties poses itself. The case for the multiple parties system is advanced by the fact that in the past this system has not only reflected tensions between social groups as determined by class division, but has also furnished an organization for political discussion as such, thus having "universal" and not only "bourgeois" meaning. Analysis of the concept of the party solely in terms of socioeconomic interests seems to me dangerously simplistic. This is why the notions of multiple parties and single party must not be judged solely from the point of view of class dynamics, but also from the point of view of techniques for controlling the state.

I do not know if the term *political liberalism* can be saved from discredit. Perhaps it has been definitively compromised by linkage with economic liberalism. But if the term can be saved, it will express that which must be said: whether the state established liberty through its rationality or whether liberty, through resistance, limits the irrationality of power, the central problem of politics is liberty.

TRANSLATED BY LEONARD PRAGER

George Lichtheim

Collectivism Reconsidered

> *George Lichtheim (b. 1912) author of the notable volume* Marxism, *is one of the most authoritative contemporary political writers speaking from a democratic-socialist point of view. His essay is a study of the trends toward social and economic collectivism in the contemporary world, the problems these raise, and the complex relations between planning and democracy. "Collectivism Reconsidered" first appeared in* The British Journal of Sociology, March, 1955.

To an outsider whose main concern is with what is generally known as political science, the present state of discussion in the field of sociology presents a puzzle. On the one hand there is a visible growth of interest in political processes, in the determinants of revolutionary movements, in the social significance of "intelligentsia politics," and so on. As against this, one encounters a certain indifference to history and to the historical approach, an apparent tendency to rely on methods appropriate to the natural sciences, and a marked disinclination to consider whether the rise of sociology may not in itself signify the beginning of a political change. I should like in particular to stress the last point, because it seems to me that it leads directly to some institutional problems of modern democracy. First, that of pluralism. It would seem obvious that a genuinely critical sociology of institutions—the state, political parties, and so on—presupposes a climate of political freedom. Totalitarian regimes live on the myth of the monolithic community; investigate their actual functioning, and the myth evaporates. But secondly, we have to determine how far pluralism is itself a myth; in what respect, that is to say, the situation now taken for granted in the West inhibits the further development of critical insight into the workings of modern society. We are all, whether we emphasize it or not, in principle committed to a form of society which does not hide its internal conflicts behind a facade of fictitious harmony. But no community allows full scope to realism without at least some internal resistance. If there are no absolute prohibitions, no lies that everyone must mouth on pain of imprisonment, there are nonetheless intellectual taboos of one kind or another. In a pluralist democracy, which maintains itself—and renews its internal balance—through a constant process of social conflict, the chief taboo perhaps is placed upon the recognition of such conflicts as involving more than the push and pull of sectional interests, all legitimate and capable of being harmonized. There is pressure to maintain what Marx called the utopian illusion, the illusion that all interests are ultimately in harmony. Under conditions of this sort one is liable to get either a purely descriptive sociology, or one which lays excessive stress upon the Paretian element of elite formation—a useful, because politically neutral, subject of academic discussion, since there are elites in every conceivable kind of society. Or one may get an outcrop of literature on social psychology, often very illuminating, but carefully shielded from political reality. In writings of this kind, politics are taboo; possibly they are regarded as unimportant or vulgar. The question whether there may not be pressures in the direction of *making* politics vulgar and unimportant, is not asked; it is probably regarded as being in rather bad taste—like the observation that in the U.S.A. one political party rather than another is in control of nine-tenths of all newspapers and radio or television stations. Circumstances of this kind are left to the politician to worry about; perhaps that is why the more realistic studies of present-day society tend to be written by political theorists, or even political journalists, rather than by social scientists.

In a milieu of this kind, sociology in the end is identified with social psychology, or even with individual psychology. As an example one may take the writings of Mr.

David Riesman, which as it happens fill a small oasis in the desert of my own sociological ignorance. I owe a debt to Mr. Riesman, whose recent collection of essays under the title *Individualism Reconsidered* gave me the idea for a heading to put on this paper. One learns a great deal from him—especially if one happens to live in England —on such subjects as American individual psychology, crowd psychology, the impact of modern forms of sport and entertainment, race relations, and so on. One can also, if one feels so inclined, enter into the mysteries of the "inner-directed" and "other-directed" personality, though speaking for myself I prefer not to do so; and one is inevitably treated to a good deal of character analysis of other writers, analysis which apparently is meant to elucidate the significance of the theories associated with these writers. There are disquisitions on education, on neighbourhood communities, on modern films. All this is very interesting; I only wish that somewhere one came across an indication of awareness that these are the problems of a relatively leisured middle-class milieu. Doubtless it must be very pleasant to be living in so highly civilized a milieu, one where the great questions are what to do with one's spare time, whether to go to the movies or look at a football game; a milieu, too, where the establishment of unimportant distinctions between unimportant subjects can become a fulltime occupation. Perhaps we shall all get there in the end, but I fancy that in order to reach this goal we shall have to wade through a good deal of trouble, of the kind that has become familiar in recent years, and to this end *political* sociology may still be of some use.

Collectivists have good reason to occupy themselves with the problem of such a discipline; it is after all their cause which is at stake when the relevance of sociology is under discussion, for unless we get a science of society one does not see how collectivism can be made to work. This fact presumably accounts for the slight but unmistakable odour of subversiveness which still attaches to the concept of a science of society: once people begin to think in terms of social groups there is no saying where they may not end up. This is particularly true of the state of affairs under a totalitarian regime, whether communist or fascist; for here the bare mention of the possibility of social conflict in the happy new monolithic order becomes an expression of disloyalty, almost high treason. It is one of the pleasanter ironies of the contemporary situation that the Communists have been compelled by the logic of their political choice to abandon the Marxist doctrine of politics as an expression of class conflict, at any rate so far as their own orbit is concerned. In Stalinist literature the state has become once more what it was in the ideology of absolutism—the impartial guardian of the public interest. No hint here of conflicting pressures which have to be resolved by force. It seems regrettable that the now fashionable academic pursuit of Marx-baiting should lend indirect support to this Communist attempt to abolish sociology. But perhaps the science of society has something subversive about it even if it is pursued under conditions of political freedom. Is it not collectivistic by nature? It is difficult to envisage an individualist sociology—a fact that may account for the curious unwillingness of individualist writers to tackle sociological problems properly so called. If society were an assemblage of middle-class people with "status" worries to keep them busy when they are not occupied with the more important business of earning money, a liberal sociology would doubtless in due course make its appearance. Indeed, it has done so, in the United States. But precisely for this reason it is not concerned with those social problems that have become our daily preoccupation.

It is difficult to escape the impression that sociology and collectivism are inherently related to each other. The tendencies making for a collectivist order also make for an attempt to elucidate the functioning of such an order, i.e., they encourage the growth of sociology. Indeed one sometimes wonders whether sociology may not be destined to do for the planned society what political economy did for its predecessor. It was, after all, hardly an accident that the classical doctrine emerged just when the market underwent its fullest development. One sees in retrospect how the new liberal society thus found itself presented with a magnificent intellectual toy: a doctrine which had the twofold attraction of being strictly scientific and of confirming all the verities that liberals happened, on other grounds, to regard as certain. It does not seem implausible that sociology may become the "dismal science" of the new planned and collectivist order into which we are sliding. One seems to catch a glimpse of this relationship in the work of a writer like Mannheim, who did so much to popularize the basic concepts worked out by Max Weber, but who also gave Weber's findings an optimistic twist of which their author would scarcely have approved. Weber's pessimism is that of the liberal who sees the new bureaucratic order coming and dislikes it. Mannheim elected to stress the positive side of the new dispensation: the chance of making society more rational, more stable, more harmonious. If he now and then mentions the dangers of bureaucracy, it is rather in the spirit in which the early nineteenth-century *laissez-faire* economists casually referred to unregulated child labour as being a regrettable phenomenon. I think one may say that Mannheim and others provided the *rationale* for the kind of world view which Laski simultaneously converted into the language of political propaganda. Democracy—the word socialism was rarely used —was identified with planning; "planning under freedom" to be sure, although there were those who did not believe this was possible. Most of us remember the dramatic moment in the 1945 election campaign when Mr. Churchill (as he then was), having apparently read Professor Hayek in his bath, sprang to the microphone and warned the electorate that socialism meant serfdom. We may think the Labour Party was entitled to resent this sudden assault, but it did represent a new departure in political thinking, and perhaps an indirect tribute to the importance of sociology. At any rate it established the fact that planning was a political issue of the first order, not just something for professors and civil servants to worry about.

This, of course, was not quite what sociologists with a bias in favour of planning had in mind when they talked of "reconstruction," a term which became very fashionable in the thirties. There is in Mannheim's writings a sense of urgency which plainly comes out of his own experience with the collapse of democracy in Central Europe. The age, we were frequently told, was one of crisis; or to be exact, it was one of transition, since *laissez-faire* was dying while planning had not yet arrived. But when one turns to Mannheim's war-time writings (published in 1943 under the title *Diagnosis of Our Time*) one is left in some doubt what all this planning is to lead to. We are to plan, but what are we to plan for? There is no clear description of the new order. The term *socialism* is carefully avoided; syndicalism of every kind is taboo—apparently the planners are to be left to do pretty well as they like. We are told that democracy must become "militant," and that Youth (with a capital Y) must be given a more important place. All this, and more of the same kind, is to be found in the introductory essay, where there is also a sentence which runs as follows: "The unbridled criticism of the form of freedom and democracy which has existed in the past decades must therefore cease." Dare one suggest that this is reminiscent of Leopold Bloom's election address in *Ulysses*, with its inspired sketch of the "new Bloomusalem"? One recalls the famous passage: "New worlds for old. Union of all, Jew, Moslem, and Gentile. Three acres and a cow for all children of nature. Compulsory manual labour for all. All parks open to the public day and night. Tuberculosis, lunacy, war, and mendicancy must now cease." It seems that you are bound to get this kind of amiable wishful-thinking unless you specify who is to be charged wih the political task of making the new social order work. On the whole it would perhaps have been better if Mannheim had talked of socialism, instead of asking for a "militant democracy." But that might have been regarded as tactless, and perhaps the "free-floating intelligentsia" would have been taken aback. Today the gloves are off. The prevailing pessimistic doctrine holds that all nineteenth-century programs, socialist as well as liberal, have been outmoded by the rise of modern mass society and by the discovery that twentieth-century technology requires large-scale, hierarchial organization: once you have this pattern, it is argued, industrial democracy turns into a dream. The more planned and scientific modern industry becomes, and the more this pattern spreads outward from the hard industrial core, the less scope is there for individual initiative of the classical entrepreneurial kind. But equally the ancient democratic illusions about workers' control in industry evaporate, and with them goes the heart of the socialist appeal. We seem to be in for Schumpeter's and Hayek's post-liberal society in which the planners govern and socialism becomes the opium of the people. Some of this depressing stuff no doubt is true. It is curious, though, how little attention is being given to what might be described a little unscientifically perhaps, as the other side of the picture.

When one glances through the writings of our modern, hard-headed, nonutopian sociologists—students of industrial organization, of "labour relations", of the corporation and its managerial structure—one notices a strain of controlled optimism in their otherwise businesslike and down-to-earth findings. Much as they would disclaim all sympathy with syndicalist notions or other forms of social romanticism, they are far from hopeless about the human pattern disclosed by large-scale organization. If the outlook is none too good for those at the bottom of the ladder, there are compensations in the offing for the higher and middle grades of the hierarchy: not merely Burnham's "managers,"* but the entire group of administrators, consultants, scientists, technologists, engineers, and skilled workers—what might perhaps be termed the technological stratum. It is not simply that this group is growing in numbers, in social importance, and perhaps in the collective influence it exerts on industrial policy, there is also the emergence of a novel form of "industrial democracy" within this particular corporate body, a democracy based on technical competence; and because of it

---

* Prof. G. D. H. Cole, in a suggestive paper published in the December, 1950 issue of the *British Journal of Sociology*, stresses the vagueness and ambiguity of Burnham's terminology, his tendency to shift from political to economic categories and vice versa, his failure to differentiate between those in control of the industrial set-up and the technologists who merely service it, etc. Certainly a writer who in 1941 predicted that the whole world, America included, would rapidly go fascist, encourages a certain wariness on the part of readers. But I think Burham may be credited with having asked the right question, although he gave the wrong answer. At any rate, he helped to bring sociology down into the political arena—where it belongs.

one may witness the growth of an *esprit de corps* which causes people in this group to hold together, as professionals usually do, against those outside their own order. Some of the most enthusiastic descriptions of modern large-scale industry have been done by people who claim for "the corporation" those virtues of intelligent social cooperation, voluntary discipline, intelligent planning, scientific training, etc., that are in fact aspects of any large-scale organization whose work is rationally planned. In so far as such tributes are deserved they reflect the impact of scientific training on the way in which things are managed under conditions where both the administrator at the top, and the foreman near the bottom of the ladder, must know something about the technology of production. Technical education of workers, and scientific training of managers, are aspects of the same process of what the Germans call *Verwissenschaftlichung*; so, too, is the growing importance of teamwork and, at the higher levels, of what is vaguely known as planning. All this, of course, implies an ethos very different from that of the old-fashioned entrepreneur, who was in the habit of extemporizing means and ends simultaneously and who seldom troubled his head about the connection between them. To "proceed according to plan" is to assume the overriding importance of a general idea—in other words, of a collective idea. It is just because of this that individualism of the traditional sort goes by the board. But its place is not, or not necessarily, taken by bureaucratic routine, not even under a totalitarian regime which tries to stifle initiative in every field save the one in which it remains dependent on the maximum energizing of human activity, that of production. Rather it may be, and often is, succeeded by forms of cooperation which leave considerable scope to personal and team initiative. It depends on who is planning and for what. If the ethos developed in this form of process is radically different from that of the old free-wheeling entrepreneur, it is not necessarily inferior to it in point of willingness to assume responsibility. "Serfdom" would seem to be incompatible with anything as dynamic as modern technology; whether the system is run on capitalist, socialist, or "managerial" lines,

the built-in economic pressures must find their equivalent
at some level in a type of organization which gives scope
to the personality of the organizer.

Such changes in the prevailing pattern are not confined
to industry. They can be traced in, for example, the military field, where science has for decades marched hand in
hand with the emergence of the small highly trained
combat team—or guerrilla group! Recent wars and para-
military struggles have been distinguished by revolutionary innovations in this field rather than by stale routine. The trenches of the First World War marked a
pause between two techniques; since then the stalemate
has been broken and the outcome has been to restore the
importance of both the individual and the small group.
One hears a great deal about push-button warfare, but
what seems to be happening in fact is rather that small
teams of specialists, and somewhat larger groups of technicians, are developing forms of activity denied to the old
foot-slogging infantry. In the 1939–1945 war, mass armies
were already at a disadvantage unless broken up into
small units which could develop initiative. The Germans
were first in this field and owed much of their early
success to this fact. The lesson has now been assimilated
by all modern armies, and where they are still reluctant
to learn it, it is being drummed into them by the success
of guerrilla warfare. Oddly enough, it is in the age of the
thermonuclear bomb that the homemade weapon has
come into its own again. Partisans waylay the armoured
column; the hand grenade proves effective in fighting the
tank. At the very moment when its demise was proclaimed by the totalitarians, democracy thrust its shaggy
head through the window and dropped a submachine
gun on the floor.

At the "managerial" level, so to speak, the process takes
a different form, as befits the distinction between those
who plan and those who merely cooperate. But it is not a
form which lends support to the pessimists who see only
the growth of bureaucracy in an increasingly hierarchial
order. The same world conflict which gave rise to the
resistance movement and the partisan swarm also saw the
emergence of the armoured spearhead racing far ahead
of the infantry, the air armada flying in formation over

the battlefield: at both ends of the scale the specialist breaks loose from the inert fabric geared to an outmoded technology. The armoured division resembles the mechanized plant, a complex organization with hundreds of vehicles and a big repair-and-maintenance problem; clearly a job for the expert, who in turn might reasonably think that he should be called in to advise on general strategy. Where this was not done—as in the France of 1940, or the Germany of 1945—disaster resulted. De Gaulle's career epitomizes the possibilities of the new order. Half his appeal lay in his ideas on scientific warfare, rather than in his old-fashioned patriotism or his unbending refusal to concede defeat. The General, who was also a technical expert, turned out to be the central figure of his country's crisis; below him the military and professional hierarchy included hundreds of his type who later rallied to him, and these military reformers were helped and joined by modern-minded technicians and their political friends. Together they explored the possibilities of a new ethos. Means of destruction, like means of production, can become so closely patterned that the same individual intelligence is able to supervise their technical functioning and to direct their operational use: the tank commander, like the factory manager, is both a technical expert and a leader of men. Hence a certain penchant for elite doctrines which in turn serve to frighten the more conventional democratic spokesmen. In the 1930s de Gaulle encountered resistance both from the conservative leaders of the military hierarchy and from the majority of political figures, some of whom scented authoritarian tendencies behind his scheme for the creation of a highly trained *corps d'élite*. Leon Blum (who later changed his mind on this subject) cried out against the establishment of a "praetorian guard." Such fears unfortunately contributed to the destruction of the Third Republic, whose leaders had identified democracy with egalitarianism. The Fourth Republic, no less democratic than its predecessor, has overcome its fear of mechanized divisions and seems none the worse for it.

It may be asked how this pattern fits the accepted image of a social order in which the producers collec-

tively own their tools, or at least exercise some control
over their use. Does it amount to more than an extension
of privilege for the upper layers of the new technological
hierarchy, civilian or military? In the first place, even the
introduction of a limited form of collective responsibility
at some level would be a net gain. Secondly, it has never
been pretended that democratic control can operate at
every level upon the totality of the system. It is enough,
for a start, if those in charge of their particular sector
take an intelligent interest in its operation, and are given
the right to do so. If every one of the "professional hierarchies" were so organized as to encourage autonomy,
self-government, decentralization of authority—this
would seem to be the sane and healthy core of the "cor-
poratist" idea travestied under regimes which never seriously meant to apply it—a great deal of the present out-
cry against centralized planning would come to an end;
so would phenomena such as the commercialization of
the press and the other media of mass communication.
Why indeed should newspapers and radio stations not be
controlled by those who work on them? "Workers' control" might usefully start in places where there exists no
social prejudice against people who are "merely" workers.
In fact, however, there is scarcely a large-scale organization where a start could not be made if those in control
were not in principle opposed to it. Even under the
1945–1951 Labour Government in Britain, resistance to
the idea of "workers' control" in the mines (where it
would according to some experts, have been feasible)
came from those who had in advance made up their
minds against it. They have had their reward in the form
of disappointing coal output. Nationalization having been
planned on purely bureaucratic lines, its relative failure
in terms of output and of social relations was then
blamed on labour or on the socialist concept. But the only
place where socialism and the workers could come together was precisely the place where it was determined
they should not meet: on the factory floor or at the pit-
head. Giving real authority to production committees
would have meant strengthening shop stewards as against
union organizers who had no intention of furthering such

experiments. So the issue was drowned in a flood of talk about "joint consultation." It may well be that the Labour Government missed a major opportunity in this field.*

A future advance will probably have to start from a concept of technical education which envisages it not simply as a means of improving efficiency, but as a link between the worker and the planner. Pushed far enough, such education, if it cannot altogether eliminate the distinction between mental and physical labour, can at least set up its own hierarchy in the workshop, turn the worker into an amateur technologist, the soldier into a potential N.C.O., and thus overcome the modern "alienation" which undermines efficiency no less than welfare. What the totalitarian regimes have attempted along these lines is just successful enough to give our own society the necessary push. If Stakhanovism can score some degree of success under conditions where labour is deprived of its bargaining power, the reason is surely that, for all its systematic distortion in the interest of maximum output and the deliberate creation of new group privileges, it has tapped some hidden source of willingness to participate. For the worker indeed technology holds the most direct access to science and everything that lies beyond it. But technical education without responsible participation soon loses its spur or degenerates into yet another aspect of "public relations in industry." For collectivists, its significance on the contrary lies in the fact that it arises spontaneously out of the modern process of work, while

---

* Cf. Professor Cole's proposals (in *Is This Socialism?*, New Statesman pamphlet, London, 1954) for introducing workers' control at the factory level: "This I believe to be entirely practicable, provided that the policy receives the full backing of a sympathetic Labour Government— but not otherwise. What it involves is that the Trade Unions shall . . . transfer to the workers, under Trade Union supervision, certain of the functions of workshop discipline and organization that are at present in the hands of foremen and supervisors appointed by the employers to order the workers about." In this context it is of course immaterial whether the employers are private owners or bureaucratic state boards. The London dock strike of October 1954, which involved an issue of labour discipline, will perhaps in retrospect appear as the first major conflict that turned on the worker's status rather than his income. From this standpoint the various personal and political factors which served to inflame this particular dispute appear secondary and not particularly interesting.

at the same time it enables the worker to develop his individuality.

Such ideas are, or should be, in accordance with the traditional aims of the labour movement, in so far as that movement is responsive to socialist tendencies; for socialism is the point where the innate collectivism of the workers' movement encounters the drive for more responsible participation in the process of production. The original aim of organization no doubt is simply the need for collective bargaining; at this level the workers experience the claim of solidarity, which becomes *the* distinctive touchstone of labour organization, and the central concept around which the consciousness of the worker takes shape. "Solidarity" is for him what "honour" was for the feudal order, and "honesty" for the bourgeois: a claim which is felt as absolute because the existence of the individual depends on it. The energizing power of such ideals, and their loss of attraction when confronted with alternative ways of life, makes up three-quarters of the real—as distinct from the official—history of social organization. Implicit in each is an exclusiveness which is both the strength and the limitation of the organism they sustain: since the claim is absolute, the practical consequences which flow from it cannot readily be abridged for the sake of convenience. Thus "loyalty," in its blindness, may become an obstacle to the attainment of aims to which the workers themselves are committed, since leaders who rise from the ranks tend to lose the confidence of their erstwhile followers. The labour movement, especially at the trade union level, is desperately egalitarian. Its ethos is so entirely centered upon "all for one, one for all" that it cannot adapt itself to forms of process in which the hierarchy of skills automatically confers social status. Nor should it be expected or urged to do so. Just because we are moving into an increasingly planned and hierarchical society, the primitive democracy of organized labour becomes the chief safeguard against authoritarian and, ultimately, despotic tendencies. Under Stalinist-fascist rule, where this democracy has been smashed, the safeguard is lost and we confront the spectre of "1984." Yet the unions are potentially an obstacle not merely to totalitarianism, but to forms of planning compatible with democratic control. At all times and in all societies, trade unions have stood for less work, more pay, more leisure, the minimum of rationalization compatible with job security, and a rate of advance geared to that of the slowest and weakest member of the team. To reproach them with this would be absurd: the placing of a brake upon mere efficiency is their *raison d'être*. Unions exist to protect the worker not only against market fluctuations and loss of earnings, but equally against the pressure of mechanization. This has not prevented some trade-union movements, e.g., in the United States, from taking part in rationalizing the production process; but it is only where autonomous labour organizations have been replaced by state-controlled ones that organized resistance to the drive for maximum output has disappeared. Here, though the workers may protect themselves by ca'canny, they can no longer utilize the unions to slow down the rate of technical progress, which thus tends to be high. Moreover, they cannot effectively oppose any collective slogan to a regime which is itself collectivist in appearance and to some extent in intention.

It is only under conditions of political freedom that the tension between labour's prime aims and their socialist derivatives has a chance of working itself out. Here its solution—never completely realized—depends on labour's acceptance of the goal of a freely planned society with a high and rising standard of productive performance. The unions, which necessarily stand in the centre of this difficult process of reorientation from one level of awareness to another, cannot help facing both ways. They must continue to protect their members and yet assist the whole community to realize its aims. This is true even of the typical "mixed economy" of our age, let alone of the planned society which remains the only possible goal of democratic socialism. It is clearly not true of the centralized state-controlled economy of totalitarianism: there the conflict has been violently resolved in favour of one of its elements. The ruling political elite, itself amalgamating ever more thoroughly with the socially dominant stratum, sees to it that exploitation reaches the maximum rate compatible with efficiency. In a sense this is the most rational social order conceivable. It is nonetheless unstable, its internal contradictions showing in the constant need to reinforce the apparatus of repression, and in the gradual emergence of a breach between the planners and the planned. Yet it maintains itself, albeit dictatorially, as long as it has the support of the new social key stratum: the technical intelligentsia. One should not conclude that the ruling party functions as an "organ" of the new directing class, except in a vague and metaphorical sense. The point is that the interests of the party and of the privileged stratum coincide, at any rate in the area where emphasis is placed by both on the aim of maximum productivity. If the technical intelligentsia in a sense is hoist with its own petard—since it is tied to the regime by the latter's unshakable allegiance to planning for higher production—the Communists themselves are held to their task by the need to interpenetrate ever more profoundly with the key stratum. Without the latter's active support they cannot govern, far less meet the competition of political rivals whose own economy is still dynamic enough even by totalitarian standards.

Thus the political issue of our day is joined in the one field where technical progress confers ever greater power and responsibility upon the upper layer of the new social hierarchy. No wonder every Communist movement (starting from the Russian party since the period of the great purges in the thirties) has increasingly transformed itself into an organization (not, however, an "organ") of the new elite. The Stalinist drive for maximum industrialization and maximum output has its own logic, even its own dialect: if it subjects the entire society, including its top stratum, to the tyrannical rule of the planners and the secret police, it also compels the Communists to dispense with working-class support and to transform their own ideology into a crude technocratic vision of endless material advance at the expense of all human and social considerations: a veritable caricature of the standard Victorian confession of faith in a mid-nineteenth century milieu such as the Manchester whose inhuman concentration on money-spinning so horrified the youthful Engels. Once this transformation has occurred, it is not open to the Communist Party to revert to its original role as a representative of working-class aims. It cannot do so without sacrificing the goals it sets for the new directing stratum; for although the workers—or some of them— may incidentally benefit from the headlong drive for greater output, the central energizing concept is no longer democratic but frankly authoritarian and hierarchical: Stalinism recognizes the key role of the technical intelligentsia in the planned society it is building, and it assigns to the party the difficult task of mediating between the directing stratum and the masses. To do this the party must satisfy two apparently contradictory requirements: its power must be absolute, but it must also respond to the major needs of the technocratic stratum. This, however, is the problem of every absolutism. Insoluble in theory—hence the theorists of absolutism are either blind to its function or deliberately dishonest—it is by no means so in the day-to-day business of overcoming its own contradictions by storing up fresh, unsolved problems for the future. Under totalitarian rule, this process takes the form of periodic "purges." The purge indeed is the mechanism whereby the political elite from time to time restores the balance between the conflicting pressures laid upon it by its dual role of absolutist ruler of society and technocratic organizer in the interest of the new directing stratum. There is pressure at both ends of the mechanism, for *raison d'état* may require measures unpalatable to all groups, and it takes an absolute ruler to mediate such conflicts, once the democratic mechanism has been abolished. The party leaders must therefore be treated as infallible—though by a familiar paradox it is precisely these infallible leaders who from time to time are "unmasked" as saboteurs.

No examination of this kind can afford to overlook the political developments of recent years which have brought this type of monolithic organization into being. The Communist Party is what it is, and it functions in the way it does, because its leaders have once and for all made up their minds that a total reorganization of society is possible and necessary and that it must be achieved by force, from above. Similar aims were of course inherent in the various fascist movements, and to the extent that the latter have been superseded by the Stalinist drive it can be said that modern communism is postfascist—not in the superficial sense that it has taken the place of a now defunct threat to democracy, but in the more important one that it has inherited and absorbed the ensemble of fascist organization and ideology. The fact itself is familiar to students of European politics, but its sociological significance is veiled by Communist silence on the key issue.

In a sense, the Communist theorists have been keeping silent about it ever since the German debacle of 1933 which disclosed the fundamental miscalculation of utopian Leninist communism. That miscalculation was the belief in the existence, in industrial countries such as Germany, of a "revolutionary proletariat" with a spontaneous capacity for political organization, even under a hostile totalitarian dictatorship. It was the collapse of working-class resistance to Hitler in 1933, and the almost total passivity of labour during the twelve years that followed, which cured the Comintern of its error. Many factors no doubt went into that experience: the destruction of the traditional working-class parties and organizations, with the resulting loss of leadership; the Nazi regime's success in banishing unemployment, though at the price of war preparations, etc. The great fact remains that for twelve years labour did not stir, while the dictatorship maintained itself, thanks to the more or less whole-hearted support of just that key stratum which was simultaneously beginning to emerge in the U.S.S.R.: the technical intelligentsia. It took some time until the lesson had sunk in, but by 1945 it had been learned: communism must cease to be "proletarian." In the language of overt political discussion this discovery was translated into the harmless formula that the party must "learn to address itself to all groups." The real significance of the change was more profound: the Communist leadership had at last understood that to the Stalinist "revolution from above" there corresponds a social stratum which

organizes the planned society from the top downward—
the technological intelligentsia. If Hitler, with his adven-
turist mentality and program, could govern in this fashion, why not the Communist Party. In this sense, 1933
has become the watershed between the old and the new
doctrine of revolution—between "Communism, utopian
and scientific," to paraphrase Engels. "Revolution" no
longer signifies "liberation of the toilers" but "all power to
the planners." In Marxian terms, this signifies a change in
the class structure of the party. Unquestionably the leaders are aware of it. Hence the peculiar moral climate of
modern communism with its double standard of truth for
the elect, its contempt for "the masses," and its elevation
of the individual conscience to the position of public
enemy number one.

Phenomena of this kind are, it seems to me, of equal
concern to the sociologist and to the political scientist.
They indicate the domain where both disciplines may be
expected in future to overlap. In particular it seems important at the present time to stress the role of the technical intelligentsia under totalitarianism, since it has latterly
become the fashion to analyze revolutionary movements, whether in Tsarist Russia or contemporary India,
in terms of intelligentsia. Such attempts to introduce scientific concepts into political discussion represent an important advance—on condition that the social context is
kept in sight. An effort to define *all* revolutionary movements as expressions of hostility to the *status quo* on the
part of intellectuals may give employment to numerous
historians—some have already gone to work, from this
point of view, on the history of the French Revolution—
but it does not significantly advance our understanding of
the current situation. The modern totalitarian regimes
must be viewed in the context of a rapidly changing
industrial society, in which the growing importance of
planning translates itself into the emergence of a hierarchy centered upon certain key groups. It is not the intelligentsia in general that forms the core of the Soviet
regime, but the technical intelligentsia in particular. We
shall never get anywhere in political science if such dis-

tinctions are not given due weight.* We shall equally, it
may be suggested, make little progress if we abstract
from the reality of class conflict. Every totalitarian regime
in one sense represents an attempt to do away with the
class struggle. Though the monolithic community is an
illusion, the monolithic party is real enough, and what
keeps it in being is the attempt to substitute the state for
society: to make the government, that is to say, the final
arbiter of all social conflicts. Historically, the attempt to
impose such a system grows out of the experience of
political breakdown under conditions where the various
pressure groups of a fully developed mass democracy are
deadlocked, and the state consequently ceases to function. That was true of the situation which brought Mussolini and Hitler to power, and in principle this particular
experience could be repeated in any modern democracy
with fully developed sectional and class organizations
which function as pressure groups. It is a truism that
political parties—and, at a higher level, the state—exist
for the purpose of arbitrating such sectional conflicts. The
distinctive feature of modern monolithic "state parties" is
that they amalgamate the functions of the party with
those of the state: the former becomes all-embracing and
compulsory, while the latter is politicalized to the last
degree. Under fascism the official justification for this
state of affairs can occasionally be reduced to variations
on the theme "the King's government must be carried
on," but the underlying reality is that the state has been
captured by one particular political organization with a
program for arbitrating all social differences. Fascist
theory identifies society with the state, and since the latter is *per definitionem* "above" class and sectional strug-

---

* A suggestion which leads to the further remark that, for all the cultural
resemblances to mid-Victorian society which appear so striking to the
student of Soviet affairs, one cannot speak of a "middle class" or "bourgeoisie" in the U.S.S.R., unless such terms are to be completely emptied
of meaning. The strains within the dictatorship (between the party
leaders, the bureaucracy of planners, the technical intelligentsia, and the
masses) constitute a pattern utterly different from that of Western democratic politics. The term bourgeoisie in any case has long been used to
designate the property-owning minority of the old "middle class" and
should not be employed by historians to fill the gaps in their own conceptual apparatus.

gles, these are viewed as hostile to the real interests of society. In modern communist doctrine, on the other hand, the state-party regime may appear variously as an expression of "true" democracy, or as the political form of the "dictatorship of the proletariat"; but at any rate communist theorists are in no doubt that it is incompatible with the sectional push and pull which is the lifeblood of our modern pluralist democracies.

We have here another instance of the peculiar dialectical relationship between fascist and communist movements and of their tendency to copy each other. It would be unrealistic, however, to overlook the common social factor: both movements ultimately compete for the support of the technical intelligentsia, and their real faith is technocratic, i.e., indifferent to property relations in industry. Communists and fascists can both argue that they are concerned with the overriding interests of the community, and they can do so because from the technocratic standpoint it is a matter of indifference whether the means of production are "owned" by private capitalists or by the state, provided they are "run" by the new directing stratum and the workers are kept well in hand and forbidden to strike. In this sense, and in this sense only, fascism and Stalinism are ideologies of the "new class," which, like every new class, identifies itself with "the state," i.e., the public good. It is only a step from here to the apparently paradoxical phenomenon of communist regimes engaging in forcibly suppressing the class struggle and even banishing it from Marxist-Leninist-Stalinist theory. True, the proximate cause of this drive to establish conformity is the need to erect an unchallengeable centre of authority which shall mediate all sectional conflicts and, if necessary, repress them by force. But the ideology which subserves this purpose would be ineffective if it did not echo the demand of the new ruling stratum for a "strong" authority with power to plan, and its indifference to the conflicting claims of the major classes. The new absolutism, like its predecessor, answers a social need other than the traditional urge of the state bureaucracy to establish conformity and suppress opposition. The more "rational" and "scientific" its ideology, the better its chance to absorb the technical intelligentsia, but the latter's rationality comes to a decided halt before the phenomenon of class. Its own position in the new society is not yet sufficiently assured to permit that degree of objectivity towards social processes which the bourgeoisie achieved a long time ago. Hence the significant hostility of radical "New Dealers" and other representatives of the technocratic stratum to Marxian concepts, which at first sight seem quite innocuous from the standpoint, say, of an administrator or technician with strong leanings in the direction of planning.* The notion that society groups itself into classes with significant social aims inevitably entails the thought that the intelligentsia must at some stage define its relationship to the working class which, in a planned economy, it will have to direct. Such thoughts are disturbing—and not only to "sleek-headed men, and such as sleep o'nights." They point to the necessity of a socialist doctrine which will ultimately make sense to planners and planned alike. Far better to concentrate on problems of "social engineering" which by-pass the political issue.

For in the end the sociology of politics comes down to the simple question of who makes the relevant decisions and in what form. Questions of this kind can never be wholly freed from the odium that attaches to politics. They touch too nearly upon the issue of power and upon the function of those whose business it is to instruct the public, but who more frequently are engaged in misleading both themselves and others. There is indeed no single simple conceptual apparatus which will enable us to sort out valid theories from spurious ones; but there are attitudes favourable to realism in sociology, just as there are others which make for aridity or "doublethink." There is today great need for analysis of the technocratic trend and its political implications, and it may be thought that such an analysis might come equally well from those who

---

* Similar tendencies have long been noticeable in the socialist movement, *vide* the long-standing refusal of the Webbs to accept the Marxian analysis of class. Characteristically, this reluctance disappeared when the Webbs had at last discovered a nominally socialist dictatorship with which, on account of its technocratic character and its successful emancipation from "proletarian" tendencies, they could identify themselves.

on the whole welcome this trend as from those who see only its dangers; but it will not come if sociologists shut themselves off from the political scene. What we need are not more learned disquisitions upon this or that aspect of Marx's or Max Weber's theories, but an attempt in the spirit of Marx and Weber to enter the new world of hierarchical organization, centralized planning, and monolithic political structures, of which the communist regimes so far are the most extreme expression. In all probability we shall then find that the problems exhibited by the new absolutism are not totally irrelevant to our own society.

G. D. H. Cole

Socialism and the Welfare State

G. D. H. Cole (1889–1959), one of the most prolific English socialist writers in the twentieth century, is the author of the monumental work, A History of Socialist Thought. *Cole began as a spokesman for Guild Socialism, a school of thought dedicated to the idea of industrial self-government. Toward the end of his life he served as a major spokesman for the left wing of the English socialist movement. The article below, which first appeared in England in somewhat longer form as a pamphlet under the title,* Is This Socialism?, *argues against what Cole regards as the tacit acceptance by social democrats of the welfare state as their final goal.*

A socialist, we used to be told, is "one who has yearnings for the equal division of unequal earnings." This description neatly slurred over the fact that the inequalities the socialists were most intent on getting rid of did not arise out of earnings at all, but out of the possession of claims to income based on ownership and, above all, on inherited wealth. Socialists saw the gross inequalities of income as proceeding much more from the "rights of property" than from differential rewards in return for unequal services. Most of them did, no doubt, hold that the large disparities of *earned* incomes were due to a considerable extent to the existence of large *unearned* incomes, and that, if the latter were eliminated, it would become much easier to narrow differences in earned incomes. They denied the contention of many orthodox economists that differences in earned incomes corresponded to real differences in the value of services rendered, and were dictated by inexorable economic laws. They held, as against this view, that the high salaries and fees paid to professional and managerial workers were in part a reflection of the social inequality inherent in a social system which accepted unearned incomes based on property as legitimate and as carrying high prestige and were in part due to the near-monopoly of higher education by the children of the well-to-do. They wished to diminish the inequalities of earned as well as of unearned income; but their main attack was concentrated on the inequality due to ownership. On that ground, in the main, they demanded the socialization of the means of production, distribution and exchange, and the elimination of the toll levied by individuals on the social product on the score of ownership.

In practice, however, socialists—as exemplified by the Labor government of 1945—have attacked inequalities of *income* much more than inequalities of *property*, and earned incomes almost, though not quite, as much as unearned. True, they have nationalized a number of industries and services; but they have compensated the owners, if not with generosity, at any rate so as to leave them with their claims to income broadly intact. As against this, they have taken over a structure of taxes on incomes erected to meet the emergency of war and have used it to help finance an expansion of social services in time of peace with very little discrimination between incomes derived from property and incomes received as a return for personal services. Admittedly, it is often difficult, or even impossible, to draw a clear line between earned and unearned incomes where a person gives his services to a business in which his property, or some of it, is also invested; for such cases there is no valid way of deciding how much of his "profit" comes from his invested capital and how much from his work. But, in practice, lines are drawn, however arbitrarily, for tax purposes; and it would have been possible to discriminate further against unearned incomes if the Labor government had really wished to do so. It did not, because it did not really want to: in the main, it concerned itself rather with finding the money to pay for the social services and for other public outgoings in the easiest way, rather than with attacking unearned incomes as such.

Why was this? And why was it that the Labor government made no attempt, or almost none, to attack inequalities of ownership and contented itself with lopping off by taxation a large fraction of the really big incomes, while leaving the property that gave rise to most of them practically intact? . . .

Is the answer that the Labor government of 1945 had no mandate to introduce a socialist system, but only to carry through certain social reforms representing an advance towards the welfare state, and to nationalize certain industries and services only on condition of *not* socializing the property rights of their previous owners? This is part of the answer; and it is reasonable to plead that the Labor government could not have gone beyond what it did without seeking a fresh mandate. That, however, only involves recasting the question. Why, we are impelled to ask, did the Labor Party, when it put forward a program for further advances, beyond what it had received a mandate to do in 1945, produce in succession three further programs in which there was still virtually no attempt to attack inequality at its roots or to advance beyond mere piecemeal nationalizations to the socialization without which it was clearly impossible to set about the establishment of a classless society?

It did not, because it did not want to—at any rate for the time being. Why then, did it not want to do what its professed socialist faith surely required of it? Largely, no doubt, because it did not believe that a majority of the electors would be prepared to give it a mandate to do anything of the kind. The electors who returned the Labor government of 1945 voted, for the most part, not for socialism but for a change—and not too great a change. As far as they envisaged anything clearly, they thought of the change they wanted mainly in terms of better social services, including more equal educational opportunities, and of "full employment" as against a return to the depressed conditions of the 1930s. They did not for the most part think of it at all largely in terms of nationalization of industries, much less of socialization of property, though they were quite prepared to see some industries that had got into a mess taken into public ownership. . . .

Most people are neither socialists nor antisocialists in the sense of having a thought-out view of the social and economic system they want. They have certain wants, for particular things, and certain broad preferences for one sort of society over another. But for most of them, the particular wants are much more clearly present, and much more of a driving force, than the vaguer ideals they entertain; and, in a society such as ours, with its long traditions of gradual adaptation as against revolution, most voters vote on the assumption that the government they vote for will do less than it says it intends to do, even if its declared intentions are not very extensive. Under conditions of universal suffrage, electorates do not vote for revolutions—unless the revolutions have already happened. If, in 1950 or in 1954, the Labor Party had put forward a really challenging election program, involving a large advance in the direction of socialism, one thing certain would have been, and would be, the loss of the ensuing general elections by the defection of the "marginal" voters.

In part, then, the absence of a more socialist program is to be attributed to the Labor Party's wish to get back to power, or at least to office. This is a very natural desire, not only because politicians naturally prefer winning to losing, but also because they honestly believe that they have a better case than their opponents. This latter belief is shared by their active supporters and makes them also eager to win. Accordingly, if a moderate program offers the best prospect of electoral victory, the odds are very heavily in favor of the party, as well as the politicians, preferring it to anything more drastic. . . .

But is this the whole explanation? I feel sure that it is not. I feel sure that many politicians who are professed socialists, and not a few of their active supporters, have lost the simple faith in socialism with which most of them began—and which, up to a point, they still hold to with part of their minds—and have come to entertain doubts whether the attempt to establish socialism does not involve too great risks for the game to be worth the candle. Quite serious and even cogent reasons can be advanced in support of this doubt. They are very often not openly admitted, but haunt the backs of people's minds and are half-repressed. Let us try to drag some of them into daylight.

First—to take one which lies quite near the surface—nationalization, in the form of public management of industries and services, does not look quite so enticing as it did, now that we have had some of it and can see how it works out in our society as it is. It is not so easy as it was to contemplate with ecstasy, or even with equanimity, the prospect of all or most of the means of production, etc., being nationalized, if that is to mean their administration by a series of public boards on the model of the Coal Board, the Transport Commission, and the B.E.A. We may, or may not, approve of these bodies; whether or no, it is not very easy to look forward to their extension to cover most branches of production, nor is it easy to see what alternative socialists have to offer. So we fall to disputing about how much of industry we still need to nationalize after all, in order to infuse *enough* socialism —if it is socialism—into the economic system; and, in doing that, we soon find ourselves a long way off the old formula of socialization, or even nationalization, of "the means of production, distribution and exchange."

Secondly, to go a good deal deeper, equality, or even near-equality, does not look quite so simply desirable and objective as it used to do. The Labor government thought it saw good reasons for paying the administrators and managers it needed for the nationalized enterprises as good salaries as they would have got under private ownership or as those holding analogous positions in capitalist industry were continuing to get. It also thought there were good reasons for not paying those of its own supporters whom it appointed to such positions less than it paid to persons taken over from capitalist industry. It therefore, on what appeared to be valid grounds, created a new labor aristocracy of officials in the public service, and in doing so had at any rate some influence in causing such bodies as trade unions to increase the salaries of officials who were *not* so transferred. In effect, it sanctioned degrees of inequality of earned incomes which would have horrified the socialist pioneers. It did this the more easily and with fewer doubts because there was proceeding at the same time so considerable an uplifting of standards at the bottom of the social scale and because so many workers in positions of superior vantage had actually become able to earn good middle-class incomes that it seemed natural for those who were higher in the scale of incomes earned by honest work to move up too. So, no doubt, it was; but that cannot alter the fact that the consequence was to undermine the old belief in a much nearer approach to economic equality and to make it very much more difficult to launch any attack on middle-class, or even upper middle-class, incomes in general.

Thirdly—and here we come nearest of all to the bone —the experience of one kind of totalitarian rule under Hitler and of another kind of totalitarianism under Stalin unavoidably put into the minds of reasonable persons a fear of placing too much power into the state's hands, even if the state professed to be socialist. The workings of universal suffrage under totalitarian conditions did not encourage the continuance of the faith that, where the "people" had the right to vote, all nominally on equal terms and with the secrecy of the ballot guaranteed, democratic government would necessarily follow as a result. Democracy came to be thought of less exclusively in terms of electoral rights and more in terms of personal freedom, of speech and writing and association, and with this went a greater preparedness to take account of the claims of minorities and of groups within the larger society. This reacted on, and interacted with, the new look of nationalized enterprise. It began to be seen that the government of an industry by a national board could not be simply identified with its government by "the people" and that there was a real problem of finding out how to control the controllers.

In Great Britain, this fear of putting too much power into the state's hands has hardly come, as yet, to be more than an uneasiness. We are in no present danger of losing our rights of free speech or association, or of passing under the control of a "one-party" state machine. But we cannot quite avoid asking ourselves whether our present immunity in this respect may not have something to do with the fact that what we have been engaged in setting up has been, not socialism, but only a partial embodiment, within our limited opportunities, of the welfare state.

Of course socialism involves the welfare state: that is implied in the old slogan "from each according to his capacities, to each according to his needs." It has always been one of the essential socialist objectives to put an end to poverty and to ensure that in the distribution of incomes the children, the aged, and the incapacitated are not pushed aside by the predatory or the strong. To the extent of our success in advancing towards this we have been doing what every socialist must wish to do. But the welfare state is, all the same, not socialism: in the form in which we have been attempting to move towards it in recent years it is at most only socialistic—if even that. For what we have been doing is not to put people on an equal footing, but only to lessen the extremes of inequality by redistributing grossly unequal incomes through taxation; and even this redistribution has quite largely taken the form of making the poor pay for one another's basic needs. . . .

The gains achieved through full employment and the welfare state are beyond doubt considerable in terms of the reduction in the amount of sheer suffering and enfeeblement of human quality by privation. So far, they are a great good. They depend, however, at least as much on full employment as on the expansion of the social services and are precarious to the extent to which there is a danger of severe unemployment coming back. Moreover, these gains have been secured at the expense of a narrowing of the differentials awarded for most, though not for all, kinds of superior manual skill, and *may* be reacting on the future supply of skilled workers by making it less worthwhile to learn a skilled trade. The supply of new recruits for the nonmanual occupations which have declined in relative earning capacity is for the most part less likely to be affected because our educational system has a strong bias in favor of such occupations and because some of them are more attractive in themselves and may still carry higher prestige than better-paid manual jobs.

What does all this indicate in respect of the class structure of the society towards which we have been moving? Certainly not that we are advancing towards a "classless society." Except at the very bottom of the scale, the numbers in which have been reduced, there has been a diminution of economic and social inequality between skilled and less skilled manual workers and between manual and white-collar workers. But there is also a tendency for a new grade, or even class, of highly paid, superskilled manual workers to develop and to increase its distance from the main body. These are not Stakhanovites; for many of them are time-workers or setters-up rather than operators of machines, and even where they are piece workers their exploits are not announced in the newspapers or rewarded with public decorations. But they constitute a new and growing labor aristocracy, with "money to burn" because they are only now adjusting their living standards to their increased earnings. They are still, however, in this country only a small group, not at all comparable with the much bigger labor aristocracy that has grown up in the United States. Nor is there at present any sign of a wish on their part to dissociate themselves as a group from the groups lower down in the economic hierarchy.

More widespread for the present is the economic assimilation between the large body of fairly skilled, but not superskilled, manual workers and the main body of white-collar workers: so that these too are being merged economically and to a considerable extent socially as well into a single stratum. A step above them socially, and sometimes but not always economically, the lesser professional groups and the general run of technicians constitute, together with the middling tradesmen, an intermediate stratum—a *petite bourgeoisie* which, far from dying out, is more than holding its own in relative numbers. With it go a large part of the farmers and many small employers, such as garage keepers, jobbing builders, radio dealers, and electrical contractors; so that this stratum includes groups of widely divergent fortunes and interests. It is linked on the one hand to the major professions and on the other to the group of middling profit makers and industrial executives. A part of it has been losing, and a part gaining ground; it has no common social outlook or political allegiance, though the greater proportion tends to be politically Conservative, with some tendency to swing over when things go badly wrong.

Above all these strata the rich remain. But they have considerably changed their composition. Riches and aristocracy still go together in the case of a limited group of old families which have large holdings of urban or industrial land or have used the accumulations of the past from land to become great investors in business. To these must be added the aristocracy of banking and commerce which has bought or married its way into the "upper classes" in the traditional sense of the term. But side by side with these, and as rich or richer, are those who have made great fortunes in business too recently to be counted among the "idle rich"; and this group of new wealth, including now many high-level business administrators who draw large salaries and have risen by personal exertion from the middle or lower grades, forms a larger proportion than ever before of those who can afford to live at a luxury level and to hobnob, without much feeling of inferiority, with their American opposite numbers.

Such a society as this is definitely not socialist; and I cannot feel that it is even on the way to becoming socialist. It is, of course, much less aristocratic than the society it is displacing: in terms of social origins the top classes of today are a very mixed lot. Oxford and Cambridge are no longer gentlemen's preserves to anything like the same extent as they used to be; a much lower proportion of top civil servants and of the successful members of the higher professions come from a small group of gentlemen's schools; and on the boards of directors of the great business concerns there are to be found a large number of "self-made" men who have risen, if not from the ranks, at all events from quite low beginnings. Our society has become a good deal more "open" than it used to be, in the sense that the old distinction between "gentlemen" and "not-gentlemen" has largely broken down. A "player" can not only captain England, or his county, at cricket: he can also captain the Nuffield Organization of Unilever

—or, of course, the B.E.A. But on the whole the new recruits to both grammar schools and universities tend to come much more from the poorer section of the middle classes than from the families of manual workers—and to come hardly at all from the less skilled sections of the manual working class. No doubt, some children of manual workers get their higher education rather through technical schools and colleges than through grammar schools and universities; and account has to be taken of this in estimating the effects of educational development on the class structure. But in this case, too, the children of the unskilled workers are largely left out.

What we are getting in practice appears to be a society in which the field of recruitment for the superior positions is being considerably widened, so as to give those who can get as far as the higher ranges of grammar or technical education an improved chance of rising further even if their parents cannot afford to help them. But at the same time we are putting an increasingly difficult barrier between those who do get so far and those who do not; and this is still in the main a class barrier, though it has been moved further down the social scale. . . .

If this is a correct picture, the question that arises is whether a society of this sort is on the road to socialism. The question is whether it does not, as a hard matter of fact, offer the prospect of even greater resistance to socialism than the society it has displaced. In other words, is the welfare state, in the form in which it has been developed so far, a step on the road to socialism, or a step in quite a different direction—that is, a step, not towards a classless society, but rather towards a new stratification that is likely to persist and to become more marked?

The situation outlined in the preceding paragraph is, of course, only a new version of a very old dilemma. In France the peasants, when they had got the land and destroyed the old feudal privileges, turned promptly into a conservative class and became a bulwark against socialism. They might easily have done the same in Russia had not the Bolsheviks first stamped hard on the kulaks and then collectivized the villages. In our society, the opening of higher education to wider class groups (by no means to all, regardless of class), combined with full employment and greater social security, may well be creating barriers in the way of socialism rather than helping its advance, especially if a child's whole chance of rising to the higher social and economic levels is to depend on the results of a single test, applied at an age when the nature of the home environment is bound to be of great influence in determining these results. This kind of test looks like it's leading to a new class structure which will on the one hand cut the working class in two: those with a chance of rising further and those without; and will, on the other, animate the upper of these two segments with a desire to protect itself against the lower, and also permeate it with a belief in the virtue of personal advancement and in the values of an acquisitive society. In short, is it towards socialism we are tending, or towards an Anglicized version of the American conception of democracy? Is our goal the classless society, or only the so-called "open" society, which is in fact still closed to a majority of the people? . . .

The first question that arises here is that of the extent to which socialism is to be regarded as compatible with economic inequality in its various forms. I think it is clearly incompatible with any social system that allows great fortunes, or even moderate fortunes *that have been inherited once*, to be transmitted at death. I see no reason why it should be regarded as inadmissible for a person to pass on to his wife or children, or perhaps to other near relatives, moderate sums which he has accumulated by saving in his own lifetime, or of course to transmit in moderation personal possessions which are not of a capital kind; and I see every reason why it should remain possible for security of tenure, subject to good use and payment of rent, to be granted to the families of farmers or householders from one generation to the next. But beyond these reasonable limits I think socialists are bound to stand for doing away with inheritance, because *they cannot recognize any able-bodied person's right to live in idleness on the labor of others or to claim on account of inherited wealth a much bigger income than he can earn by his own exertions.* Accordingly, I believe that not merely higher death duties but positive abolition of the right of inheritance beyond fairly modest limits should take a high place among Labor's next steps toward its declared socialist objective. The transition could, if it were thought fit, be eased by allowing limited additional annuities to be paid for a single further life; but beyond the permitted sums generally applicable, the capital should pass to the public, subject to such transitional charges as might be allowed. . . .

Such taxation of inheritance would, of course, mean that the state would have to be prepared to take over the actual property of those dying with considerable fortunes and not money payments supposed to represent their value. For it would create a situation in which there would be far too few buyers for the estates passing at death to be sold to new private owners. It would therefore mean that the government would be continually acquiring ownership both of shares and bonds of all sorts and of other forms of property, such as houses, landed estates and private businesses. Nationalization, or rather socialization, would thus advance by a new route, even if no further industries were taken over by the methods hitherto adopted. The state would become, to an ever-increasing extent, part proprietor of a host of productive businesses and the holder of mortgage charges on many estates and noncompany businesses remaining in private hands. It could use the powers it would thus acquire to appoint its own directors to joint stock enterprises and to foreclose on concerns which failed to meet their obligations. For a time, it would find itself the partner of profitmaking business men, and engaging in profit-making enterprises. But I can see no valid objection to this, if it is merely a stage in the process of acquiring total, or majority, ownership of the businesses in question; and I can see the positive advantage that it would not involve the creation of more top-heavy centralized administrations of the type of the Coal Board and the Transport Commission. Of course it would be necessary for the directors whom the government would appoint to such businesses, not only to play an active part in their operation in the public interest, but also to work together, through some sort of collective body including all the state directors within an industry, and to follow a collective policy laid down by

the government's planning agencies. It would be necessary to train men specially for these tasks in, order to
ensure well-informed intervention in the affairs of the
businesses concerned; and *the long-run effect would be to
establish socialized production over a wide field without
setting up giant organizations in forms of enterprise better suited to relatively small-scale, and within limits competitive, operation.*

The restriction of inheritance would of itself do nothing to lessen inequalities of earned income, though it
would do a good deal towards leveling those who received large incomes partly from work as managers or
members of the higher professions and partly from ownership of property. In the main, excessive disparities of
earned incomes would have to be tackled by other methods. *As the government now meets a large part of the
cost of higher education and professional training, it is no
longer reasonable for the incomes of those who have received this help to be calculated at rates meant to pay
back the expenses of their professional preparation.* Nor
should there be any need in business occupations to pay
the very large salaries which are based largely on a comparison with what is received by capitalist employers in
the form of profit. . . .

As for the middle incomes, no special action seems to
be called for, except a steady policy of reducing trading
margins so as to squeeze out the inefficient as fast as they
can be replaced by more efficient producing or trading
firms, which should become fully practicable if the level
of new investment is made high enough to keep pace
with technical progress.

Wage incomes and the lower ranges of salary incomes
raise more complex problems. It is fully consistent with
socialist principles to allow whatever differentials turn
out to be needed to procure adequate recruitment for the
more skilled kinds of work and also to offer whatever
piece work or similar incentives turn out to be necessary
in order to secure high output. Nobody, however, can
believe that the existing wage structure complies with
these requirements or is anything other than a confusion
due partly to the varying fortunes of the tug-of-war between employers and trade unions and partly to sheer

accident or tradition. In a socialist society, it will clearly not be possible to continue to allow wage rates to be settled by a large number of uncoordinated bargains, influenced largely by the degree of shelter or exposure of particular industries to outside competition or to the expansion or contraction in the demand for their products. There will have to be both some general way of determining how large an aggregate of wage payments the economy is able to afford, and, broadly, how what is deemed to be available shall be divided among the various claimants. It would be premature today, while non-wage incomes remain uncontrolled and while the greater part of industry is still under capitalist operation for profit, to introduce any "national wages policy" under which a body of highly placed officials would have the right to fix wages as they might think fit. But, as we advance further towards a socialist society, the planning of wages will become indispensable, if only because wages and prices are inevitably linked together, and it will be as a rule a matter of choosing between higher wages and higher prices, with the balance of advantage shifting in favor of lower prices as the toll levied by unproductive consumers is reduced by the erosion of incomes derived from ownership.

Some people say that a more equal society is impossible or will lead to disaster because there are too few able persons to run it. They argue, for example, that the increased numbers in higher education have already involved a fall in average quality. I believe this to be nonsense: I do not profess to know whether the supply of real first-raters can be greatly increased by improving our educational system; but I feel no doubt that the supply of good second-raters can be and that more good second raters are what we chiefly need to do the jobs which the advance towards a fair deal for everybody will require us to fill. No doubt, it would be nice to double our supply of first-raters; but a limited number can go a long way if they have good seconds-in-command at call. . . .

I come now to the major problem of industrial democracy. Given full employment, trade unions are in a powerful bargaining position, because employers cannot afford to lose the services of even moderately efficient workers. *Full employment has been chiefly responsible for the great changes that have come about in factory relations and in industrial discipline as a whole.* The foreman can no longer play the tyrant as easily as he could in the past, and the higher management has to mind its P's and Q's when trade union susceptibilities are in question. In some industries, including those which have been nationalized, there have been considerable developments of joint consultation in the work places as well as at higher levels, and trade-union bargaining has spread to many trades in which it was previously almost nonexistent. So far, so good; but *neither trade union bargaining nor joint consultation makes the worker a responsible partner in industry,* nor necessarily gives the individual a sense that it is up to him to render of his best and to think of himself as a member of a team cooperating in the performance of an essentially social task. He cannot, indeed, be expected to have this sense of responsibility where businesses are still being carried on for the profit of absentee shareholders or where the management still behaves as a caste of superiors issuing orders to inferiors to whom it recognizes no democratic responsibility. Exceptionally, a few managers or employers do contrive, by virtue of sheer personality, to establish really friendly and cooperative relationships; but most managements are incapable of achieving this and will continue to be so as long as they represent a business structure in the control of which the workers have no share. This applies even to the nationalized industries, in which the controlling boards are far too remote from the actual workers to give them any sense of participation—and would remain so even if the trade unions were allowed to appoint members to sit on them in a formally representative capacity.

In the past, in a society explicitly based on inequality, it was for the workers to obey orders and for the representatives of their "masters" to give them. Obedience was enforced partly by custom, partly by inducements such as higher earnings for greater efforts, and partly—and to no small extent—by fear of the sack or of being "laid off" for offending the authorities, or in extreme cases of being blacklisted as well as fired. Nowadays, these fears have become much less potent, though they still exist. Piece-work incentives and other monetary inducements still re-tain their power, but have been to some extent weakened by the introduction of guaranteed minimum wages and by the diminished danger of getting fired for not produc-ing enough. The greatest change of all, however, has been in the lessened prestige of those who give the orders and the sense of increased power to question them among those to whom they are given. The consequence is a relaxation of discipline which is bound, for the time being, to react adversely on output. This is partly to the good, where it prevents slave driving or feverish self-driv-ing under the influence of fear; but it is also to the bad, where it conduces to irresponsibility or to a refusal to cooperate in team work. I am not suggesting that, in most industries, average output has fallen; on the contrary, it has been going up despite a small reduction in average hours of work. But the increases have been due mainly, if not entirely, to greater mechanization and improved working arrangements rather than to higher effort or bet-ter cooperation.

It we mean to constitute a really democratic society, permeated by the spirit of social equality, we shall have to find ways of replacing the old incentives of fear and habit with new inducements more consistent with the recognition of equal human rights. In large enterprises I do not think this can be done as long as they continue to be conducted for private profit: in small ones it *some-times* can, where the human relations are good. Social ownership will not of itself put matters right, as the expe-rience both of the nationalized industries and of coopera-tive employment abundantly shows. *Social ownership is only half the battle; the other half is real participation by the workers in control, not only at the top, but at every level from the work group upwards.* By participation I do not mean merely consultation: I mean *real control.* This is necessary, not only for the sake of its effects in making the workers more conscious of their responsibility for high productivity, on which the standard of living must depend, but also because it is impossible to have a really democratic society if most of the members have to spend most of their lives at work under essentially undemocratic conditions. What a man is at his work he will tend to be also in his pleasure and in his activities as a citizen. Industrial democracy is therefore an indispensable part of social democracy, that is, of socialism. . . .

We have seen already how, by means of the abolition of large inheritances, the ownership of existing capital assets could be transferred to the public by stages not too prolonged. Side by side with this gradual transfer, the state could begin at once to assume public ownership of that part of profits, or of a part of the part, that is needed for new investment. This could be done by *a*) *statutory limitation of dividends*, that is, of the part of profits that can be paid out to shareholders as incomes; *b*) *statutory allocation of a share in profits to a capital fund which would become at once public property* and, if invested in the business, would carry share-holding rights to be exercised by public nominees. The public would thus acquire holdings of capital in what are now private enterprises by a double process—through the lapsing of shares to it at the owners' deaths and through the new shares to be created out of profits placed in reserve. By rapid stages private ownership of joint stock enterprises would be extinguished: they would become public property, and the state would be free to make what arrangements it might think best for their future conduct. It could, for example, sell or lease some of them to the Consumers Cooperative Movement, convert others into producers cooperative societies, and arrange for others to continue as publicly owned joint-stock companies. It could amalgamate businesses into larger concerns where this seemed likely to increase efficiency; but it would be under no necessity to set up huge organizations except where the technical conditions required them. *The outcome would be a highly varied and flexible system of socialized ownership and control, which would not preclude leaving as many small enterprises as might be considered desirable to continue under private ownership and control, subject to due provisions to insure good working conditions and compliance with planning requirements.*

Given a clearly defined socialist program of this sort, I do not see why the workers should not be prepared to collaborate with the dying capitalist under the control of a socialist government pledged to carry it through to the end. There remains, however, the obvious difficulty that under our political system no government can be sure of remaining in office for more than five years, and that accordingly the carrying out of the program might be broken off short by the return of the Conservatives to power after an election victory. To be sure, this difficulty applies to every attempt to advance towards socialism by nonrevolutionary means: *it is part of the price we pay for preferring parliamentary government to dictatorship under a one-party system.* There is no doubt that most people in Great Britain do prefer parliamentary government, and the socialist who wishes to see his ideas carried out has to proceed on that assumption. This, I agree, makes it much more difficult than it would be if continued office could be assured to persuade the workers to modify their traditional attitudes: indeed, they cannot fairly be asked to modify them in any way that would reduce their ability to resume their fighting posture in face of any attempt by a Conservative government to undo the achievements of its predecessor. This means that any collaboration that can be advocated under present conditions must be carefully safeguarded so as to preserve, and where possible to increase, trade-union power.

This I believe to be entirely practicable, provided that the policy receives the full backing of a sympathetic Labor government, but not otherwise. What it involves is, first, that the trade unions shall set out deliberately to *extend the area of collective bargaining* to include much that employers still regard as belonging to the sphere of "managerial functions" and therefore outside trade-union competence, and secondly that they shall use this extension to *transfer to the workers, under trade-union supervision, certain of the functions of workshop discipline and organization* that are at present in the hands of foremen and supervisors appointed by the employers to order the workers about. Under this second head I have in mind the replacement of foremen by elected supervisors chosen by the workers themselves from among properly qualified candidates and the substitution, in suitable cases, of collective contracts under which groups of workers will

undertake to carry through a particular job, or series of
jobs, at a collective price, making their own arrangements
for the organization of the work and sharing the proceeds
in accordance with rules drawn up by the trade unions to
which they belong.

The effect of these changes would be to throw upon
the workers responsibilities which they would exercise,
not jointly with nominees of their employers, but by
themselves, under arrangements negotiated by their trade
unions with their employers and their associations. The
transfer of functions to the workers, far from undermining their collective power, would add to it, and would
provide the foundation for extending their authority into
further fields. Such arrangements could, and should, operate both in nationalized industries and in those remaining in private ownership or in transition from private to
public ownership. *They would constitute the reality of
"workers' control" where the putting of a few trade-union
nominees on national boards would give only the appearance of it.* Indeed, I feel sure that trade union representation on national boards can be desirable only after a
measure of real "workers' control" has been established in
this more real form, if even then.

The alternative is to rest content with what has been
achieved and to give up trying to establish a socialist
society. That, I fear, is what many who continue to call
themselves socialists are really minded to do, sheltering
their apostasy behind the assertion that the majority of
the electors would not be induced to vote for it. But what
is the use of winning an election, except as a means to an
end? To win an election without a policy is the surest
way of losing the next and of spreading dismay and disillusionment among one's supporters. If the end is no
longer socialism, but something else—what else? If it is
still socialism, let us tell the electors frankly how we
propose to advance towards it.

Henry M. Pachter

Three Economic Models:
Capitalism, the Welfare State, and Socialism

Henry M. Pachter (b. 1907) is a veteran of the German socialist movement who has lived in the United States during recent decades. Author of many books in German and English, Pachter here presents a lucid analysis of the differences among three major models of society.

In the capitalist economy, business decisions are made by the owners of resources; capital may take the form of money, real estate, machinery and equipment, or of claims and rights to use or to dispose of these resources, or of powerful positions in organizations. Since labor also is a resource and a commodity, the power to supply or to withhold it may fall under this definition of property as well.

In the welfare state, these powers of free disposal have been curbed. They are regulated and controlled by political organs, and, in large areas of economic activity, government has substituted its purposes for those of independent agents. These purposes are determined politically: i.e., they may range from establishing a strong defense posture to a concern for the well-being of the majority.

In both systems, income is related to the use of *property.* Under capitalism the property itself constitutes a claim on income, to be realized in the market; the welfare state, however, supplements the market by other institutions that create or distribute income. Moreover, it creates a demand for goods and services which results not from consumer preferences and producer expectations but from its own political purpose.

Socialism I shall call an economic system which has divorced income from property, and even from the exertion of labor. In contrast to state capitalism, which still recognizes the property of the state as a claim to income, socialism also divorces capital value from production decisions.

Obviously I am dealing here with "pure types," disregarding intermediate systems such as corporate capitalism, syndicalism, corporativism, market socialism, which have in common this basic feature: that the means of production are not owned by individuals but by collective bodies, which, however, deal with the property claims as though they were individuals. An especially interesting case is the cartel general or state capitalism, by which this feature has been carried to the extreme: all facilities are owned by one big corporation, but production relations are still governed by the market mechanism. Clearly the cartel general can also be used for political ends.

My purpose is to show what other assumptions must be made to realize each of these models as a working system —how each affects the allocation of resources, the general efficiency of production and, above all, the welfare of its citizens.

I deliberately refrain, however, from speculating on possible differences of cultural attitudes or changes of human nature in the three systems. I only assume that humans have a natural aversion to involuntary toil and a natural ambition to excel in self-assigned tasks, but that the degree of their acquisitiveness and cooperativeness is related to environmental conditions which may encourage or stifle their development.

Capitalist theory claims that all resources find their most useful employment if each owner tries to maximize his profit in a free market, where labor also finds its price. Fortunately such a pure capitalism has never existed, or else no one would have organized the police, provided courts of justice, built bridges, laid sewers, embellished the public parks, founded hospitals, or established universities. It has always seemed to me that the fire brigade refutes the pure theory of the free enterprise. What more essential service could one imagine? It ought to command a price and attract the venture capital of an enterprising speculator who wishes to make a profit and therefore allocates resources for this purpose. Yet nothing of the kind happened; instead of waiting for the free play of the market to prove the usefulness and determine the price of a fire brigade, a committee of the ruling classes on the municipal level went ahead and organized one.

Likewise, the business community felt that private coining privileges led to public losses, and it gave central banks the power to regulate the flow of money, the rate of interest, the value of currency, and thereby also the direction of foreign trade, income distribution among various countries, and, to some extent at least, the business cycle. Even the most classically free capitalism is not an entirely "free" economy. To function properly, it polices itself. In the public debate, however, the question of controls usually is confused with the question of who should do the controlling. Business prefers the so-called indirect (orthodox or classical) controls: regulation of the rate of interest, reserve requirements, the marketing of treasury bills, not because they are indirect or because they are not controls but because the controllers of these controls are businessmen.

On the other hand, business expects the state to protect it against foreign competition, and, far from leaving the optimum allocation of mineral resources to the competitive spirit of rapacious speculators, it asks the government to enforce conservation practices, to protect patents, and to finance research. Even the most ardent theorists of economic liberalism, Professors Mises, Hayek, Roepke, point out that it can function only if a "strong state" enforces the laws of the free market and provides the services which free enterprise does not find profitable. In short, it simply is not true that the free market, left to itself, results in the optimum allocation of resources. Adam Smith advocated government intervention for specific purposes and opened the way for a general theory of "expenses of the Sovereign and the Commonwealth."

But quite apart from such empirical observations, which undercut the ideal model of pure capitalism (and we have not spoken yet of the tendency toward concentration and monopoly, of the creation of artifical markets through advertising, of manipulation through government orders or policy, etc.), at least two theoretical factors militate against the contention of the market theorists. Both are inherent in the model and both have been freely admitted by the better representatives of liberal economics. One is the inequality of incomes and the other is the time limit within which investment is expected to pay a return but which may (and increasingly does in big projects of national interest) exceed a man's lifetime. It is generally conceded that both features are incompatible with the optimum use of resources. I shall explain the idea in greater detail.

Apologists for capitalism often say that a free market permits the consumers to "vote" for the goods which they desire and that the price mechanism tells producers which goods might give greatest satisfaction to the greatest number. Hence free enterprise equals democracy, Q.E.D. This analogy limps. The consumers must first *buy* their "ballots": unless they are equipped with purchasing power their desires will not become manifest to the producers. Or, differently expressed, this "democracy" is based on unequal suffrage. Are those who have no votes incapable of satisfactions? If all votes were equal, the sum total of satisfactions would be substantially greater and the allocation of resources would be much closer to the optimum. Even from the angle of developing resources, therefore, pure capitalism does not produce the best distribution of effort. Quite apart from the haphazard method by which the market discovers what is in demand, it does not determine the common good but—at best—the maximum profit for all enterprises.

Paradoxically, this also is the aim of certain types of socialist economy, i.e., the syndicalism practiced in Yugoslavia and preached by Oscar Lange and his German disciples. In the way these systems function they scarcely differ from capitalism, except that the dividend is shared between the workers and the government, instead of being paid out to the shareholders to be taxed later. The Yugoslavs claim two virtues for market socialism: it establishes that "consumer democracy" which capitalism cannot realize, and the producers' association tends to acquire the power of true soviets, the best form of political democracy. One day, both claims might be validated, provided the Communist Party dictatorship disappears; but today Tito's work councils are far from being soviets, and the consumers can express their preferences only months or years after the central planning board has expressed its views through investment priorities.

In a capitalist economy, this decision is guided by the profit expectations of investors. But Mises correctly states that profit can be obtained only by meeting "a *comparatively urgent* demand" (italics mine). If there is no such demand equipped with purchasing power, it may be created artificially, through advertising or by inducing the government to finance it; that way, resources are misappropriated to suit a pressure group. Or a need may exist, but demand may not become effective and supply may not come forth because the projects are too large or too speculative: only big corporations, monopolists, have the means or the foresight to allocate resources for long-term research and development on a large scale. It takes guts, plus a reasonable assurance that no competitor has the same plan,* to construct a bridge, a railway, or a power dam at a time when demand is not yet "urgent," though money might be saved by anticipating it well in advance. If not government initiative, then at least government guarantee of capital and interest is required to bring forth investments in the infrastructure—roads, canals, draining of marshes, harbors, and rivers—which rarely yield profits in the foreseeable future. A paper mill may establish a hundred-year cycle of timber exploitation; but this exception proves the rule, for in any event the mill expects to make a profit on the real estate. Similarly, "octopuses" used railroad construction as a pretext to acquire land and to exploit farm communities in the West. Even this incidental profit did not prevent carrier companies from going broke, and the United States would not have its marvelous rail network had not some speculators miscalculated! One too often forgets that our industrial empire arose over the bodies of expropriated capitalists

---

* For that purpose even Adam Smith would grant a monopoly to a corporation!

and failed investors, or that incidental monopoly profits made up for losses sustained in the production phase of the enterprise.°

Because of this time factor, classical capitalism does not achieve optimum use of resources. Normally, wherever expectations of profit must be referred beyond the planners' lifetime, the investment will be undertaken only for a reason of public policy, be it conservation, development, autarchy, or strategy. This history of foreign aid shows that private capital will not take the risk of developing the infrastructure of the laggard countries in a time interval consistent with the rapid population increase and rising expectations. If rapid development is desired, colonialists, monopolies, or state capitalism seem to be the only alternatives.

After a glorious career of continued primitive accumulation, during which capitalism began to develop modern industrial production all over the world, it now has reached limitations which can be overcome only by more effective methods of organization—the big trust, the monopoly, the government enterprise, state capitalism. The enterprise has become too big, the time span for the return of profits too long, and, on the other hand, the need for political investments too pressing for the free market to remain competitive. In distributing the resources, competition no longer responds to consumer needs (if it ever did) and does not most effectively use all factors at the right time. It still is serviceable on the smaller scale of consumer industries; it may still pioneer in some areas of invention. But big research and big industry are now in the era of imperfect competition, and the claims which continue to be made on behalf of "pure"

° It might be claimed that monopoly anticipates social benefits or development profits accruing from its investments. If we take this argument as seriously as it theoretically deserves, it leads us to recognize the advantages of state capitalism over private capitalism. Likewise, it might be claimed that without the land grants there might have been less railroad promotion and no opportunity for big-time speculators to expropriate the public's savings for the higher purpose of a national railroad policy. While this policy was not a deliberate scheme but resulted from the "cunning of history," in the case of our highway network a depression was required to permit (and excuse) its planning on a national scale.

capitalism are based on a theory which no longer fits the facts. Even Mises admits that under monopoly rule "private profit and social productivity are at a variance"; hence, "however great an evil socialism might be, it would be less harmful than private monopoly."*

To make my point clear: what has been said so far does not amount to Hobson's and Lenin's charge that monopolies suppress technological progress. The few instances in which a significant invention was temporarily withheld from exploitation are far outnumbered by the inventions that originated in a monopolistic enterprise and could be exploited only by monopolistic practices. On the other hand, a socialist or state capitalist system might find it equally necessary to delay exploitation of a new invention which makes obsolete a recent huge investment. Imagine a new gimmick which would force each of us to buy a new television set: private industry would ruthlessly force the expense down our throat, while government-operated stations might mercifully continue to use the old system. The government also refuses to build all the bomber types the military-industrial complex is trying to sell.

The point, rather, is that at a certain level of development the equations of exchange become more rigid: more individual transactions become mutually dependent upon each other, yet at the same time the number of independent variables increases, and the number of indeterminate variables decreases. For instance, the population explosion and government-sponsored research cannot be captured in any system of equilibristic calculations; finally, neither the external nor the internal reserves adjust themselves to the requirements of the equilibrium. There are no precapitalistic spaces left for capitalism to feed on, and the labor force does not obligingly contract while

---

* Ludwig von Mises, *Socialism*, revised edition translated by J. Kahane, New Haven: Yale University Press, 1959. Joseph Schumpeter, however, holds that monopoly is more efficient. *See* also Joan Robinson, *The Economics of Imperfect Competition*, London: Macmillan, 1933. Cf. my contribution "Kapitalistische und Wohlfahrtsplanung in Amerika," in *Modelle für eine neue Welt*, ed. Robert Jungk and Hans J. Mundt, Munich: Desch, 1964, where I show that American planning is meant to restore, not to abolish competition.

automation makes it obsolete.* On the other hand, even
the unemployable now refuse to abandon a standard of
living which in the most advanced countries has become
synonymous with existence. As Marx pointed out, the
human factor does not fit into the equations. Hence we
must turn the problem around. State capitalism and socialism provide different answers to the question of how
to fit the equations to the human situation. We therefore
have to say a brief word on the importance of the equations, or what A. C. Pigou and Abba Lerner call "the
Rule."†

We said that technological progress is now speeding
ahead much faster than old equipment can be written off,
while production units are increasing in size, and, in the
more developed countries, demand is becoming inelastic.
Is greater efficiency the answer? In introducing new production methods, capitalism needs to consider only their
cost to the enterprise. It does not consider the social cost
of firing people—neither the "disutility" of their enforced
leisure nor the money it costs, to maintain them in social
insecurity, the social losses in crime, disease, and illiter-
acy. The welfare state makes a conscious effort to assume
these social costs, or it may even waste more money to
fight those undesirable by-products of capitalistic cost
accounting; but it will not effectively force the enterprise
to take them into account (it cannot even control air and
water pollution, protect us from the din of commercials
and jet noises, preserve scenic views and wild life, etc.).

A state capitalistic system has the means to deal with
the problem of social cost. It may maintain a railway stop
which no longer pays, in order to save the gasoline which
the commuters might have to use otherwise. Yet more

---

* Malthus had no answer but war and pestilence when the problem was
much less desperate: Ricardo and Marx assumed that periodic slumps
forcibly restored the equilibrium. Today we have to use "countervailing" techniques permanently *and* maintain a defense economy. (*See below.*)

† The rule of marginal utility says that output should be carried to the
point where the cost of the last (marginal) unit matches the price it
fetches, or where the marginal social benefit matches the marginal social cost. Since the latter is also measured in prices, the two equations
are identical. The assumption here is that "social benefit" and real
social cost can be so measured; this I am going to deny.

often it will leave human beings to fend for themselves. Wherever state capitalism is operating today, it tends to suppress the problem rather than to solve it. Only a socialist system, operating under conditions of abundance, can make its investment decisions in full view of all economic, social, and human factors that might be affected. It may even make uneconomical investments which might not save labor hours and minimize cost but would spare us exertion and misery. But we are anticipating: any economic system that wishes to balance cost and revenue must earn its investments before it introduces new inventions, or the new production methods must produce savings in excess of the capital they make obsolete. That, anyway, is the iron rule for all systems that aim to produce economically, i.e., that fulfill the exchange equations. A free market economy does so by trial and error, through wasteful competition, and at the cost of misallocated resources. It achieves a dynamic equilibrium at the cost of periodic depressions and, even at its best, through violent fluctuations that can be contained only through monopolistic practices, i.e., by destroying the free market.

State capitalism* fulfills the equations by systematizing monopolistic practices. It avoids the waste of the free market, and it does not permit investments to be misplaced in the stage of development or to become obsolete in the stage of saturation. It can direct investments to-

---

* In *Finanzkapital* (1912), Hilferding had toyed with the idea of a "cartel general"; in his last essay (*"Socialističeski Vestnik,"* 1940) he rejected the term "state capitalism," since "an economy without capitalists and without a market cannot be called capitalistic." He coined the term "bureaucratic economy" for both the Nazi war economy and Soviet collectivism. The same idea, of course, underlies B. Riccio's "managerial society"—*"La Bureaucratisation du monde,"* par *"Z"* (Paris, 1939), to which James Burnham failed to acknowledge his indebtedness—and K. A. Wittfogel's "oriental despotism." Important as the nature of the ruling elite may be, we are here concerned with abstract models of pure economic mechanisms; "capitalism" exists wherever capital must earn its keep. It is interesting to note that by now the Soviet Union is forced to abandon the "uneconomic" (i.e, noncapitalistic) methods of price fixing and accounting. Khrushchev admonished the managers to earn an honest profit, and Kosygin allows a wide discussion of Evgin Liberman's neosocialist theories. There is, of course, a semantic and political advantage in setting "statist economy" aside as a special category; but my interest here is theoretical.

ward ventures which create new demands—Keynes's "pyramids," Tugan-Baranovsky's tower of equipment, a huge defense establishment, or a "New Frontier"—and it may even balance inefficient production units against overproductive units. Not for long, though: in the end, state capitalism, too, must balance its budget as well as its other accounts; it must instruct its managers to produce a profit and not to forget that they must earn interest and amortization charges on the equipment which has been placed at the disposal of each. For state capitalism, like private capitalism, is governed by the Rule, and its current production must be burdened by past investments, some of which may no longer have physical counterparts. (The built-in debt charges in most government budgets are constantly increasing, and the French are still paying for conquests which they have since lost.)

In contrast to private capital, state capitalism must be more prudent in using the resources that have been developed and can be more daring in developing resources still unexploited. Since both, however, are laboring under the regime of scarcity,* commodities and services have prices that constitute costs for the producer. The relations between buyer and seller, employer and employee, debtor and creditor are the same under both systems. Whatever their system of equations, it must be capable of simultaneous resolution: service must be paid; capital must be amortized and bear interest; even though production may be nationalized, property relations still govern all economic calculations. It may seem that some nationalized enterprises do not show a profit because the government is their only customer and it subsidizes them. Taxes and subsidies are hidden in the price system, which the government seems to fix arbitrarily for reasons of national policy. In the Soviet Union, e.g., military "hardware" is sold to the defense establishment at prices below cost. That makes the budget look smaller but has resulted in such confusion of bookkeeping that the managers are now pressing for an honest price system. Today, Gosplan must keep two different sets of books—one of

---

* As state capitalism tends to encourage totalitarian government (*see* below), it tends to create artificial shortages, too.

which shows the real cost of the subsidized articles. These subsidies, however, must be covered by taxes taken from the prosperous enterprises, or from the consumers, and if the budget does not balance, inflation threatens to upset all equations. State capitalism, therefore, is striving to increase efficiency and to raise the productivity of labor even more than free capitalism. The whip of hunger has been replaced by the guillotine of control figures: all accounts must resolve themselves, all equations must be fulfilled. While no shareholders expect a dividend, it is as though the managers were merely executing the abstract striving of capital to become remunerative.

Many people confuse socialism with state capitalism and nationalization with socialization. Oskar Lange was clearly thinking of state capitalism rather than socialism when he wrote: "The equations which have to be solved in a socialist economy are exactly the same equations, and they are solved by the same persons, as in a capitalist economy."* He claimed three advantages for his system of socialism:

- a greater equality of incomes, conducive to a greater welfare effect of production and to greater over-all efficiency in the allocation of resources;
- substitution of social gain for private profit;
- planning, i.e., projecting needs, avoiding waste, and setting public goals.

These three improvements are of greatest importance, but they have not liberated the economy from the thralldom of value equations. Moreover, they are ambiguous: the "social gain" which is being substituted for private profit does not become available to the consumers or even to the producers. Some profit may be used to build public parks and art galleries; but its bulk must be invested in improvements of national resources. Lange knew that the

---

* *Ekonomia Polityczenna*, Warsaw, 1959; in English, New York, 1963, and *Essays on Economic Planning*, Calcutta, 1960. Quoted by Landauer, *op. cit.* Jaurès was of the same opinion: "Collectivism can be regarded as a special case of capitalism" (*ibid.*, p. 1606).

It is true that socialism may degenerate into state capitalism. This will happen inevitably under conditions of international tension and competition, which will force state capitalism to observe the rule of maximum efficiency, and this is the reason why socialism is unthinkable while national states continue to exist.

workers cannot get "the full proceeds of their labor," as some primitive socialists have demanded. His "socialism" must follow the market equations, i.e., it must invest its surplus in the same development which would look inviting to capitalists under the profit incentive. These investments are the "social gain" in Poland today.

Recreation facilities and places of learning, however, do not emerge from the equations; their cost must be taken out of "surplus value." Strangely enough, instead of improving the standard of living, the Polish government has used a large part of its profits to rebuild destroyed cities in the quaint auld style of yore. The point is that under state capitalism, which Lange called socialism, the apportionment of surplus value among welfare and other national purposes is a matter of arbitrary decision. The government may allot its profits to industrial developments, to the creation of a national image, to military power, to welfare institutions and consumer satisfactions, or to a trip to the moon. The equations neither prescribe nor prevent any particular use, and state capitalism therefore is neutral with respect to socialism. It is not incompatible with a distributive economy, but it is also compatible with systems of remuneration according to deserts of social rank. Under conditions of great scarcity or extreme stress for the sake of rapid development, state capitalism (national socialism) will reproduce the very worst features of early capitalism (or worse, as it did under Stalin); but under conditions of abundance it may develop features of the welfare state or even of socialism.

Which path it follows, however, will depend upon the development of democratic institutions, and in this respect state capitalism is not so indifferent. It tends to favor bureaucratic dictatorships; or, more correctly, state capitalism and dictatorship enhance each other. Particularly if the dictator communicates to the nation a "sense of urgency" concerning plans for accelerated development, he may destroy the germs of pressure groups and of pluralistic bargaining. State capitalism always creates economic conditions that tempt the policy makers toward national greatness. It is the ideal basis for a military of defense economy. But statism is not socialism.

The arbitrariness of statist production goals has inspired

violent protests from partisans of a free economy, and not without reason have they denounced state capitalism as "the road to serfdom." Unfortunately, though, they gave it the name "socialism," and this has created theoretical confusion. The socialists were actually the first to dissociate themselves from all theories of bureaucratic rule. At all times they have insisted that the state apparatus should be an instrument, not a taskmaster. In its decadent phase, bourgeois theory no longer has the ability to distinguish between the conceptions of "state" and of "politics." Socialists do not say that the state should organize production and command consumption. They say that demand has come to be politicized.

To explain this distinction I have to go back to my introductory remarks. Ultimately the owners of resources make not one decision but two. They seek profit with only those means which previously they have decided to allot to gainful employment; but they have decided simultaneously that part of their resources and time they wish to retain for themselves. As owner of real estate I might decide to set some of it aside for hunting; as owner of money I might decide to buy jewels or paintings rather than machinery; as owner of labor power I might decide to become a monk, thus withdrawing myself from the market and raising the price of labor. According to the strict theory as taught by Mises and Hayek, all resources should compete in the market place for the highest profit, thereby assuring the optimum allotment for the greatest satisfaction of the whole while assuring workers the "marginal" wage which will induce them to serve. But in practice this has never been the case. Each owner is a monopolist who may decide to leave his resources idle, to consume them unproductively, or to use them for gain. Thus workers may decide that idleness gives greater satisfaction than work at low wages or for long hours, and by withdrawing labor power from the market they raise its price. They conspire to do that, just as landowners conspire to control the use of land and bankers conspire to maintain the value of the currency. These are different kinds of conspiracy, recognized as legal at different stages in the development of modern industrialism; together with the first kind of intervention we mentioned—governmental care for health, welfare, security, and communications—they are "countervailing powers" which mitigate the arbitrariness, brutality, uncertainty, and insecurity of the capitalist market.

The welfare state is a capitalist economy that largely depends on the free market, but in which the countervailing powers have been politicized and are consciously employed to balance the economy, to develop the national resources, or to pursue fixed goals of social policy. Foremost among these goals are economic security, the raising of living standards for the poor, conservation and development of resources. The fully developed welfare state has at its disposal a wide range of economic instruments, classical as well as Keynesian and static. They include the government's power to regulate, to control, to intervene, to tax and to redistribute the product, to plan, and to use its position as a buyer of ten to twenty percent of the national product. The welfare state may achieve techniques of maintaining full employment and minimum incomes; it may use industry-wide planning, price fixing, and over-all control of development. But though it will nationalize the coal industry in France and England, erect a TVA in the United States, and build a government steel mill for India, it stops short of expropriation. On the contrary, its proclaimed aim is to preserve the structure of property and to protect the formation of a free market. Whatever expropriating is to be done must come through the free play of the market, as is happening in our farm economy despite price supports. The basic relationships of buyer and seller, employer and employee, owner and nonowner are no different from those prevailing under pure capitalism, but they are supplemented by state interference in two important areas: where classical capitalism is indifferent to the distribution of income, the welfare state at least tries to make income differentials less steep; also, whereas under pure capitalism the development of resources is an accidental byproduct of the profit incentive, the welfare state sets itself definite goals of developing public and private facilities, consumer satisfactions, even tastes and standards.

In contrast to pure, classical capitalism, which is totally

producer oriented, the welfare state may plan the deliberate increase of consumer satisfactions, be it in the form of more equal distribution of income, increased productivity, or enlarged public services. It does not always go that far. Such planning for satisfaction may stop at "full employment," which may be brought about through defense expenditure or pyramid building without any noticeable increase in the general standard of living and without making more people equal. However, the welfare state just gives its citizens more security than pure capitalism, and its planning usually results in higher wage rates, shorter hours, greater opportunities, or, at the very least, in the maintenance of satisfactions that might otherwise be lost. By virtue of both its means and its aims the welfare state therefore is often dubbed "socialism on installments" or "creeping socialism."*

But we should not be misled by its efforts to plan, regulate, and control production, to redistribute income, and to curb the uninhibited use of private property. At the hub of its mechanics, it is different from socialism. Though some prices and wages are determined politically, on the whole they are determined by the market, and that is true even of the public enterprises. The regime of property prevails throughout with the dead weight of past investments burdening the calculation of profit and decisions on future investments, with at least a theoretical obligation to balance all budgets, and with remuneration still tightly ruled by a man's contribution to the value of the product. Public projects still must be justified in terms of national policy rather than human needs, and expenditure for defense and similar purposes still exceeds the welfare expenditure.

---

* In its degenerated forms, it may also be a "limited liability" economy which merely preserves the welfare of politically powerful groups (or elites). It socializes losses and plans the conservation of guild privileges. This problem of the welfare state is well illustrated by the debate in which every year various pressure groups are pitted against each other. On a higher level, we have witnessed the debate between Dr. Leon Keyserling and Professor Galbraith; the latter advocates expansion of the public sector, the former would rather raise the income level of the underprivileged. Dr. Keyserling has argued his own priority preferences persuasively, though on purely pragmatic grounds, and theoretically no general rule can be established for all countries at all stages of development.

An economy totally controlled by the interests of the ultimate consumers is properly called "socialism" or "distributive economy." We usually distinguish two stages. The ultimate, communism, permits every citizen to draw on the public resources according to his needs. This presupposes a degree of productivity and wealth that probably is not available in any country now, in addition to a development of public morality that may not be achieved in the near future. I therefore confine myself to the penultimate stage, socialism, where distributions may still be proportionate to deserts. Even at this stage, however, a *national dividend* may be distributed among all citizens in two forms: increased public services or the conversion of many essential services (such as higher education, health, transportation, housing, recreation, theater) from private to public operation;* secondly, the distribution of a minimum allowance sufficient to cover the expense of feeding, housing, and clothing a family.† The minimum allowance would not be generous enough to cover luxury expenses and hence there remains an incentive to earn additional wages to keep up with the Joneses. Wage levels may be governed by demand and supply, through collective bargaining, and there will be wage differentials according to skill. But there will be a floor, thanks to the national dividend. A free market will provide goods and services, allowing demand and supply to regulate those prices that are not manipulated for purposes of public policy. Both public enterprise and entrepreneurs or cooperatives may compete for the consumers' favour.

Some prices may be administered to implement public

---

* In the Soviet Union, these public consumer services now amount to 15 percent of wage income and are supposed to rise to 50 percent. This is substantially what Messrs. Galbraith and Theobald are suggesting: the constant enlargement of public services.

† Anton Menger formulates as one of three basic rights "that each member of society may claim that the goods and services necessary to the maintenance of his existence shall be assigned to him, in keeping with the measure of existing means, before the less urgent needs of others are satisfied." (*Das Recht auf den vollen Arbeitsertrag*, Stuttgart, 1891; in English: *The Right to the Whole Produce of Labour*, London, 1899.) The other two are Louis Blanc's "right to work" and Ferdinand Lassalle's right to a just (not the full!) share of the product of one's labor. These "rights" fall short of abolishing inequality and exploitation, but their realization is a condition for a classless society.

policy. It is easy to imagine, for example, that each citizen is allotted a room of ten by ten feet; but if a man's need exceeds the standard house in his community, he may have to pay progressively increasing rent per additional square foot, window, or door. For all these transactions, money will be used as a means of circulation and for purposes of accounting. I can see no reason why a socialist economy should deprive itself of this useful invention, provided the money is not used to form capital and to acquire the control of production facilities.

Capital formation may be prevented by a number of devices, such as steep income and inheritance taxes. This may be important for the period of transition if expropriated owners are to be indemnified. One may also think of "funny money," or a tax on all means of circulation and credit accounts such that money would lose a certain percentage of its value every month. That percentage might even be regulated for purposes of public policy in the same way that we now raise and lower reserve requirements or the rate of interest. The device is not primarily intended to reduce big bankbooks, and it does not even serve that purpose very effectively; its main purpose is to help in divorcing present from past production, a necessity which I shall discuss presently. Here I only wish to insert a remark on private property.

It seems to me that socialists have overestimated the importance of expropriating the expropriators; the symbolic value of this measure far exceeds its economic significance. What matters is not ownership but control, and all systems now are moving in the direction of more public control. A man like Mattei had a strangle hold not only on the whole Italian economy but on Italian foreign policy, too, though he did not own a single drop of the oil on which he had built his power. Or closer to home: if one must have a dictator, one might think of better men than Robert Moses, but he has so much power that if any man were to claim as much merely on the ground that he owns a lot of the state's real estate, he might be harassed by D.A.s in every borough and hounded by tax inspectors in every district. The real question is how a democratic society can control the controllers and the managers of

public enterprises.* Owners may be parasites, but economically speaking they are mere *faux frais*, or overhead.
Their unearned income is not a personal tithe which they
exact from the community but a payment for the use of
the capital. In the capitalist lore, it is indeed the tribute
to capital, not to its owner.†

A socialist economy does not earn "wages of capital"; in
fact, it severs the umbilical cord between capital formation and production or, in Marxian language, between
past labor and current employment. This may sound utopian, and some readers who so far may have gone along,
figuring that the national dividend also is nothing but an
extension of welfare state services, may accuse me of
economic dilettantism. Indeed, every major economist
who has given the matter some thought has emphasized
the need for a socialist economy to heed the equations, to
follow the Rule, to amortize capital and, if it wishes to
invite expansion, to pay itself interest and even ground
rent. Schumpeter said that any other notion is "irrational," Abba Lerner worked out schemata showing how
the ultimate costs must equal prices, and Mises thought
that he had refuted the viability of socialism by showing
that under that system "calculation would be impossible."
Only Kautsky had an inkling of the importance of
"freeing prices from values," but he failed to follow up
his idea, and it was an outsider, Peter F. Drucker, who
laid his finger on the crucial point: "The wage rate is the
symbol of conflict rather than the issue itself. The basic
problem is a conflict between the enterpriser's view of
wage as cost, and the employee's view of wage as income.
The real issue is not an economic one but one over the
nature and function of wage."

Since we already have severed income from cost, we
now have a similar conflict between the state enterprise's

---

* England has done better with the so-called "public corporations,"
which Eldon Johnson has called "a cross between a governmental ad-
jective and a capitalist noun."

† The Socialist International proclaimed in its Frankfort Manifesto of
1952 that "planning does not presuppose public ownership of all means
of production." But when the manifesto continues, "it is compatible with
private enterprise in important fields," I would add: "under controlled
conditions."

view of capital as cost and the consumer's view of capital as expenditure. The issue is not how much interest capital might earn to remain fair in a socialist society, but what its function can be in such an economy.

The difference between a socialist and any other economy is in the divorce of production from capital or property claims. *In the socialist economy, capital goods, once created, enter into the consumption funds of the society, to be drawn upon as the need occurs.* There is no need to amortize it in any given time or to realize a profit on it. We are using facilities, such as roads, which our fathers built, and we are building facilities, such as airports, which our children may use. Strangely enough, such facilities are being paid for out of the current municipal, state, and federal budgets but are not carried on the books of these bodies as "assets"; nevertheless, bonds representing the value of these assets are being held and serviced for generations.

Other examples of divorce between real capital value and use challenge the sense of outrage. Daniel M. Friedenberg has shown in *Dissent* how tax advantages make it profitable for owners to tear down houses which still might be of service for years, while at the same time rat-infested slums are maintained because they still yield a profit. All I suggest is that a socialist society might use this same divorce of past investment from present enjoyment, but for a better purpose. We already have seen that state capitalism is capable of taking losses in one industry while earning profits in another. All that was required to satisfy the Rule was that the profit and loss accounts cancel out each other. But we know that in practice the balance is never achieved in any particular year, for indeed, why must the year be the unit? Why not the decade? Why not the century? In practice we draw on present resources to unbalance the budget, or else we could have no development. But then, having established the new facilities, we forbid ourselves their enjoyment and say, in effect, "Now we must tighten our belts and pay for these goodies." Though we may have created the new investment in order to work less, we now must work more to pay for it. If this is not irrational, words have no meaning.

It is, indeed, a fetishistic way of looking at "value" which makes us demand that capital goods must produce "value" in all types of economies. They do not affect the prices of goods unless someone claims that they "belong" to him and he must be rewarded for letting us use them.*
It is the same fetishistic view, that man creates "values," which makes us demand that all equations must be resolved simultaneously. They don't have to be; in a distributive economy, we don't have to wait until we find a buyer to turn over the merchandise. Such an economy may destroy unserviceable assets or abandon created values—don't we do that to our military hardware anyway? —and yet it need not suffer the kind of loss which spells failure for the capitalist to whom it happens, for the loss really has occurred when the goods were first erroneously produced.

I shall admit that this kind of economy encounters certain difficulties. It is rather wasteful; it cannot account for all its transactions in one set of books; its measurements of efficiency are uncertain, and a number of indeterminate variables enter into its cost calculations, not to speak of the numerous political factors that determine its prices. All this is small discomfort, however.† A distributive economy is possible only at a fairly advanced stage of development; one cannot distribute poverty, but only wealth. Once we have conquered scarcity and are systematically opening further possibilities to augment our resources, we can not only tailor production to needs; we can consider capital as a free resource that may enable society freely to decide at every moment whether to use certain facilities without regard to cost, whether to

---

* We are constantly drawing on such assets as air and water, and only occasionally are we reminded that they may have "value"—whenever the water level sinks and someone can sell us some water which he owns. Value is property! And property—c'est le vol!

† In at least two respects, however, a socialist economy is more economical than any preceding society. One is its concern for human beings, the other conservation. As air and water pollution become ever growing problems and we no longer can take nature's immensity for granted, an economy which saves nothing but that which can be owned becomes a threat to the survival of the human race. Once it used to be said that capitalists would charge a price for the air we breathe if only they could make it scarce. Now, precisely because they are making it scarce, socialism becomes a practical necessity.

promote or to retard a certain development without fears about meeting the dividends. Indeed, *what Mises counts for the refutation of socialism, its indifference to proper cost accounting, I would claim as its virtue.*

Nevertheless, no society has unlimited funds, and even the most liberal economist must economize somewhere. Plans must be drawn up with an eye on citizens who might be stingy with their time. Or certain materials may indeed be scarce, and someone must calculate which of two possible substitutes might be more easily developed. In that case, "easily" means fewer hours of labor, less waste of other materials, cheaper transportation, etc. In other words, a socialist economy may keep a second set of books where all transactions are calculated, either in hours of labor or in prices (provided the price system has not become too distorted). But this set of books will have to allow for a kind of wastage unheard of in our present economy: time wasted in experimentation, machines bought not to increase efficiency but to make work easier, committee meetings and grievance procedures, special privileges granted to attract workers. On the other hand, the surplus value also will be enormous, as workers demand parks, playgrounds, nurseries, and other special distributions. In short, the bookkeepers will be aware that capitalistic enterprise could be much more efficient, and that is the reason why socialist economy must not be managed by the bookkeepers. Indeed, it can survive only so long as it is controlled by organs of democracy on all levels, from the planning board down to the works council.

A socialist economy also can afford to experiment with different sorts of enterprise—communal, cooperative, municipal, union-owned, etc.—and to cater to other preferences. It can even allow a free market and marginal forms of private property (as it certainly will in farming). Enterprise cannot be "free," but the enterpriser as promoter and manager may be welcome (he cannot encounter more difficulty in persuading a state office to place resources at his disposal than he has today in persuading a bank that he can make a profit). Thus socialism can be more "liberal" than state capitalism; it is not the regime of technocrats but a form of economic management that leaves ample room for pluralism and democratic processes of decision making.* In fact, the danger may rather be that, under socialism, the economy could become too politicized and that log-rolling would supplant calculating. Anyway, it is obvious that state capitalism is more conducive to dictatorship, whereas socialism is compatible with many forms of government.

---

* This allusion to multiple centers of decision making and competitive—or even antagonistic—organs of shop democracy must suffice here. My essay deals with only one aspect of the socialist economy, its theory of value. It would take another essay to describe its second, no less essential aspect, the democratic organization of work.

Michael Walzer

Politics in the Welfare State

*Michael Walzer (b. 1935), professor of political
science at Harvard and author of* The Revolution of
the Saints, *first printed this essay in* Dissent, *January,
1968. At various points, the reader may be interested
in comparing Walzer's views with those expressed in
the essays by Cole, Pachter, and Ricoeur.*

One day, not soon, the welfare state will extend its benefits to all those men and women who are at present its
occasional victims, its nominal partial members. That day
will not be the end of political history. But it will represent the end of a particular history, and one in which
socialists have been very much involved, if not always on
our own terms.

It is worth reflecting on what that day will be like—
what will we want *then?*—even while we fight to perfect
the system of benefits and argue among ourselves about
the best strategies. For we are not entering, we are not
going to enter, the new world of state-administered prosperity all at once. It is in the nature of the welfare state, I
think, that men break into it in groups, some sooner, some
much later, some with only moderate difficulty, some
after long and bloody struggles. Many of us are inside
already, better served by machines and bureaucrats than
men ever were by servants and slaves. What do we want
now?

Liberal theorists of the welfare state have always
claimed to know what we want. Their work rests on two
assumptions: first, that politics ought to be the instrument
of human desire; second, that the nature of human desire
is obvious. People want pleasure, but such pleasure as

cannot be shared, individual delight, egoistic satisfaction.
The state cannot at the moment provide any sort of direct
delight; perhaps one day it will simply administer the
appropriate chemicals to its members. Today it can provide only the material prerequisites of individual delight,
that is, first security, and then all those services conveniently grouped under the rubric of "welfare"—education,
public health, economic controls, relief for the aged and
the unemployed, and so on. These are vitally important
services, and liberal theory is vindicated, at least in part,
by the fact that they are in great demand. Every attempt
to restrict them to selected groups of people has been,
and will surely continue to be, resisted. The welfare state
has grown through invasion, a clear tribute to its attractiveness.

In the heat of battle, goals have sometimes been suggested which elude or transcend the liberal definition of
human desire. Wild hopes for equality and fraternity
have been proclaimed. But each success has turned out to
be a further triumph for what might best be called political utilitarianism. If we or our ancestors or our comrades
in this or that struggle have sought the actuality of freedom and love, we have settled readily enough for the
pursuit of private happiness, so readily, indeed, that it
would be difficult to deny that private happiness is all we
ever wanted.

The cumulative effects, the likely future effects, of
these successive triumphs are now becoming visible, even
though there are important victories yet to be won (and
the last battles may be the hardest). What I propose in
this essay is a theoretical examination of these effects, of
the welfare state as our collective project, our common
future. I want to argue that the success, or the likely
success, of welfarism makes necessary (as it makes possible) a new and radical challenge to political utilitarianism. Whatever the nature of our past demands, what we
want *next* is not on any of the liberal lists. But first I must
try to suggest the enormous achievements and the special
characteristics of welfare politics. For we cannot say
what it is we want, until we have understood what we
have got and are getting.

First of all, the development of the welfare state has

generated a pervasive enlightenment about the functions of political organization. For the first time in history, masses of men know with absolute clarity that the state ought to be doing something for them. They are rationalists-of-everyday life, each one demanding, "What has it done for me?" Prewelfare theorists have generally denied the validity of this simple question, insisting that the state always *is* more than it *does*. They have described it as a closely knit body, dense and opaque, whose members were involved emotionally as well as materially, mysteriously as well as rationally, in the fate of the whole. The members ought to be involved it was said, not for the sake of concrete benefits of any sort, but, simply, for the sake of communion. Since loyalty was a gift for which there was to be no necessary return, it could not be predicted on anything so clear-cut as interest. It depended instead on all sorts of ideological and ceremonial mystification: anointed kings, oaths, rituals, divine laws; and so on.

The state still does depend on ideology and mystery, but to a far lesser degree than ever before. It has been the great triumph of liberal theorists and politicians to undermine every sort of political divinity, to shatter all the forms of ritual obfuscation, and to turn the mysterious oath into a rational contract. The state itself they have made over from a "body politic" into a machine, the instrument of its citizens (rather than their mythical common life), devoted to what Jeremy Bentham called "welfare production." It is judged as it ought to be, by the amounts of welfare it produces and by the justice and efficiency of its distributive system.

Political unreason survives, of course, and especially in the form of an extraordinary devotion to the modern nation-state and to its leaders, a collective zeal all-too-often unmitigated by individual interest or by any demand for functional transparency. But here too the direction of political utilitarianism is clearly marked out. Thus an eighteenth-century *philosophe*: "What is patriotism? It is an enlightened love of ourselves, which teaches us to love the government which protects us . . . the society which works for our happiness." This definition suggests that many of us are patriotic, if we are, for wrong or inadequate reasons. I will try to describe some of these reasons a little later on.

Second, the expansion of welfare production gives to the state a new and thoroughly rational legitimacy. The state is always immoral when viewed from the standpoint of its invisible and degraded men. Whatever the ideologies of which they are the primary victims, oppressed classes come eventually to regard the claims of their rulers with a deep-rooted skepticism and hostility.

But the claims of the liberals are of a different sort, not mysterious but hypocritical. Therefore the hostility of the oppressed takes a new form: not sullen and inarticulate disbelief, but a positive demand that the claims be realized. Do the middle classes claim to increase the general prosperity? Let them increase *our* prosperity. Do the police claim to defend public security? Let them defend *our* security. Do the rulers of the welfare state claim to maximize the happiness of the greatest number? Let them maximize *our* happiness.

Now insofar as the state becomes a general welfare state, excluding nobody, it meets these demands and so generates a legitimacy such as no previous political system has ever achieved. If no man is invisible, the state is not immoral. The recognition of its members as concrete individuals with needs and desires may seem a minimal requirement of any political system and hardly capable of producing significant moral attachments. In fact, however, such recognition, when it is finally achieved, will be the outcome of centuries of struggle; the right to be visible is always hard won; and the liberal state which finally recognizes all men and grants them their humanity will inherit from those centuries an extraordinary moral power. The state will never again be so easy to challenge as it was in the days of mass invisibility.

Third, the development of the welfare state has gone hand-in-hand with a transformation in the scale of political organization. This is due not only to increase in the rates of infant and adult survival—the first benefit of the welfare state is life—but also to the progressive extension of political membership to previously invisible men. The tiny political public of an earlier period has been broken into by successive waves of lower-class invaders. It has expanded to absorb each wave; it will probably expand to absorb each future wave.

Liberal theorists and politicians have discovered that there are no necessary limits on the size of the public, so long as its members are conceived as individual recipients of benefits, so long as the problems of political communion, the sharing of a common life, are carefully avoided. Now that there really are concrete benefits to be divided, the first political problem is distribution. And the members of the state, precisely because they are recognized as needful persons, seen by the impersonal public eye and assisted by an impersonal administration, need no longer be able to recognize and assist one another. The size of the citizen body of a Greek polis, like that of an early modern aristocracy, was limited by the requirement that its members be known to each other and so distinguishable from the faceless mass. But once invisibility is banished, the need for political "friendship" is also banished. The members of the welfare state need not have even the most remote acquaintance with each other. And so the welfare state is potentially of infinite extent.

The fourth tendency of successful welfare production is to decrease the importance of politics itself and to turn the state from a political order into an administrative agency. This was always the goal of liberalism, and it is the key reason for the liberal insistence upon the transparent material purposes of the state. Beyond welfare the liberal state cannot go; the world of the mind, philosophy, art, literature, and religion; the world of the emotions, friendship, sex, and love—all these have been freed from politics protected against heavy-handed and intolerant magistrates. Simultaneously, liberal politics has been freed from philosophy, art, literature, religion, friendship, sex, and love.

Politics is now concerned only with the provision of a plentiful and enjoyable external world and with the promotion of longevity so that this world can be enjoyed as long as possible. And it has been the assumption of liberal theorists ever since Hobbes and Locke that once security and welfare were assured, once the utilitarian purposes of politics were achieved, men would turn away from public to private life, to business and family, or to religion and self-cultivation. Indeed, it was this turning away—which might be called legitimate apathy since it rests on the satisfaction of all recognized needs and desires—that would assure the stability of the liberal achievement. Conflict would disappear; the state would become a neutral agency for the administration of security and welfare. This was a liberal even before it was a Marxian vision, as Marx himself suggested when he wrote that political emancipation, as practiced by the liberals, "was at the same time the emancipation of civil society from politics."

The state is an instrument and not an end in itself. Politics is an activity with a purpose and not itself an enjoyable activity. These are axioms of liberal enlightenment; the attack upon the opacity of the traditional policy turns out to be an attack upon the value of political life. Why should we be active in politics? asked Thomas Hobbes, and his sarcastic reply suggests the central animus of liberal theory:

to have our wisdom undervalued before our own facts; by an uncertain trial of a little vain-glory to undergo most certain enmities . . . to hate and be hated . . . to lay open our secret councils and advices to all, to no purpose and without any benefit; to neglect the affairs of our own families.

So long as the state establishes peace and, added later liberal writers, promotes welfare, public activity is a waste of time, positively dysfunctional in the economy of private life. Happiness begins and ends at home. One of the ways in which the welfare state promotes happiness is by encouraging men to stay home. Hence the crucial principles of welfare distribution are first, that benefits ought to be distributed to individuals and, second, that they ought to be designed to enhance private worlds. In the perfected welfare state, enjoyment will always be private; only administration will be public; the policeman and the welfare administrator will be the only public men.

Now obviously this is no description of our present experience. Never in human history has politics been so important to so many people, never have so many been active in politics as in the past century and a half. Never before has the state stood at the center of so large a circle of conflict, agitation and maneuver. Politics has been the crucial means of becoming visible, of winning recognition for mass needs and desires. Nor has it been only a means; political activity has also brought the first joyful sense of membership in a community. It has provided the positive pleasures of self-assertion and mutual recognition, of collective effort and achievement.

Unlike the welfare state itself, the struggle groups which have demanded and won the various benefits the state now provides—the unions, parties, and movements —have been shaped to a human scale; their members have also been colleagues; they have called one another brethren, citizens, comrades. For a brief moment in time they created a communion which was not mysterious or opaque precisely because it was a common creation.

As the organizations of the oppressed win their battles, however, they are gradually integrated into the system of welfare administration. Their purposes are not given up, or not wholly given up, but rather give rise, under new circumstances, to new organizational forms: the struggle groups become pressure groups. Public life ceases to engage the minds and emotions of their members; local activity drops off; popular participation declines sharply. The tenacious sense of detail peculiar to highly qualified bureaucrats replaces the enthusiasm of members: it is more useful, even to the members themselves.

The pleasures of political struggle cannot be sustained once victory has been won. And it is in the nature of the infinitely expandable welfare state that victories can, in fact, be won. Thus it happens that communion is replaced by distribution, generalized aspiration by concrete expectation. Erstwhile militants are isolated and immobilized by the sheer size of the state into which they have won admission, mollified by its apparent legitimacy, by the obvious sincerity of its administrators, and the transparency of their purposes. The history of the welfare state begins with the coerced passivity of invisible and degraded men, mystified by ideology. And it ends, or will one day end, with the voluntary passivity of enlightened men, their human desires recognized and (in part) gratified by the public authorities. So, at any rate, we have been led to believe by liberal writers.

What more can we possibly ask?

All these developments—the growing rationality and legitimacy of the state, the vast increase in its size, and the decline of political life—are not only compatible with classical liberal theory, but actually represent its fulfillment. But there is one further corollary of welfare production which raises the most serious problems for liberalism: the growth of state power.

There can be no question that the development of welfare programs has involved (or required) an extraordinary expansion of the machinery of everyday state administration and therefore an increase in the degree, intensity, and detail of social control. In part, this increase stems directly from the progressive enlargement of bureaucratic systems and from improvements in the training and discipline of their personnel. But it is also closely related to the very nature of the utilitarian service state and to the character of the political struggles of the past century and a half.*

For all that time, liberals (and socialists, too) have been like that character of Gogol's who "wanted to bring the government into everything, even into his daily quarrels with his wife," though some of them would have stopped short at the seat of domestic bliss. Everywhere else the agents of government have been invited to roam. This was true even during the brief moment of *laissez-faire*, for the restrictions on commerce which were then overcome were largely local and corporate, and only the central government could overcome them.

Indeed, the state has been an instrument absolutely necessary to reformers of every sort: it shatters the authority of local and traditional elites; it destroys the old corporations und regulates the new ones; it establishes minimal standards for masses of men whose own organizations, however powerful, cannot do so by themselves;

---

* The single greatest factor in the expansion of state power has, of course, been external war, and it is probably true that the greatest dangers posed by the modern liberal state are not those which its own citizens must face. But I have, perhaps arbitrarily, excluded foreign policy and war from this discussion.

it protects racial and religious minorities. It is, so to speak, the crucial licensing agency of modern society, increasingly the only one; it accords recognitions, turning oppressed subjects into full-fledged members, and it absorbs the power of every defunct agency as it wins the support of every newly enfranchised member.

Nor is its usefulness at an end. Given the continued creation of new groups, the continued raising of the level of material desire, the perfection of welfare production may well be an asymptotic goal and the state an eternally progressive force. But this does not mean that the character of political struggle will remain unchanged as new groups and new desires replace the old. For from a certain point in time, the new groups will almost certainly cease to have the same communal structure as the old. The deprivations of their members are more likely to be experienced by each man in his private, state-protected world, experienced simultaneously but not shared.

Thus the Negro is one kind of invisible man, bound to his fellows in a community of suffering and anger and therefore capable of collective action. The man who drives a dangerous car or breathes polluted air is another kind, largely unaware of the risks he shares with others, only marginally aware of the existence of others, and probably incapable of significant efforts on his own behalf. Precisely because of the privatizing results of the benefits he has already won (his automobile, for example), he now stands alone and helpless in the face of one or another sort of corporate power. He is dependent upon the muckraking of free-lance journalists and academic experts and, much more, upon the benevolence of the state.

This benevolence has its price: the increased power of the benevolent administrators, the increasing control over the recipients of benefits. Perhaps the most impressive feature of modern welfare administration is the sheer variety of its coercive and deterrent instruments. Every newly recognized need, every service received, creates a new dependency and so a new social bond.

"A wife and a child are so many pledges a man gives to the world for his good behavior," wrote Jeremy Bentham. This is true only insofar as the world—economy and state

—actually provides or promises a decent living to the wife and child. If it does, the pledge is serious indeed. And the better the living the world promises, the more good behavior it requires. Welfare politics thus has a dialectical pattern: pressure from below for more protection or benefits meets pressure from above for better (more disciplined, or orderly, or sociable) behavior. A balance is struck, breaks down, is struck again. Each new balance is achieved at a higher level of welfare production, includes more people, provides new reasons (and new sanctions) for good behavior.

Eventually, every antisocial act is interpreted as a demand for increased benefits. So it is. And so welfare is the obvious and only antidote to delinquency and riot. For who would be unwilling, if actually given the chance, to pay the price of social discipline, orderly conduct, hard work, and public decency for the sake of the pursuit of happiness? Only much later does it turn out that the price and the purchase are very nearly the same thing. Happiness *is* good behavior, and this equation, fervently endorsed by the authorities, is the ultimate sanction.

Like the public recognition of needs, so the recognition of men, our hard-won visibility, becomes a source of intensified social control. Never have ordinary citizens been so well-known to the public authorities as in the welfare state. We are all counted, numbered, classified, catalogued, polled, interviewed, watched, and filed away. The IBM card is the very means of our visibility, the guarantee that we are not forgotten among so many millions, even as it is simultaneously a symbol of our bondage to the bureaucratic machine.

Invisible men are invisible first of all to the officials of the state (and that is a worse bondage). Precisely because they are not seen as citizens, they are exposed to arbitrary cruelty and neglect. Because they are not numbered, they are always treated *en masse*. Because they are never polled, they are thought to have no opinions. Even their crimes, so long as they injure only one another, are not recorded. When their country goes to war, they are impressed (that is, kidnapped), but not conscripted. Gradually, with the development of the welfare state, all this changes. An extraordinary traffic opens up between the visible and the previously invisible sections of society. Individuals and groups win public recognition, learn good behavior, and march out of the slums and ghettos. At the same time, policemen, census takers, recruiting officers, tax collectors, welfare workers, radical organizers, and sociologists (in roughly that historical order) march in.

In the long run, the two parts of society will merge into one world of absolutely visible men (that does not mean a world of equals), known not to each other but to the specialists in such knowledge, not personally but statistically. The universal character of this new knowledge doubtless will protect individuals from magisterial whim and prejudice. That is one of its purposes. But it will also involve a new kind of exposure: to the developing administrative sciences of anticipation and prevention.

"It's the anarchy of poverty/Delights me . . ." wrote William Carlos Williams. He was too easily delighted, or rather, his delight was that of an onlooker and not a participant in the "anarchic" culture of the poor. Few men who are actually poor would share it. But having said that, it is still worth adding: "It's the regiment of the contented/That haunts me."

Liberals have not been unaware of the dangers of administrative tyranny. Wherever possible they have sought to avoid even benevolent regimentation by giving those whose welfare is at stake "sovereign" power, that is, by establishing governments representative of everyone who receives benefits. In the past that has generally meant of all property owners, for they have been the most important welfare recipients. It obviously means more today, though just how much more is unclear.

The expansion of the range of state benefits and the extension of the ballot to new social groups have been parallel and related processes. Suffrage is the first badge of membership; it is a means of winning benefits and also, presumably, of determining their character and the nature of their administration. In practice, however, it is something less than this. "Welfare without representation," Sargent Shriver has said. "is Tyranny." That is certainly true. But it is not the case that the only alternative to tyranny is a full-scale democracy.

In theory, of course, the purpose of representative government is to make the mass of people all-powerful. Representatives are to be delegates, asserting popular desires, and then legislators, enacting the popular will. Administrators are to be nothing more than servants of the people, bound absolutely by legislative decree. The quality of security and welfare is thus popularly determined, at only one remove. The government of representatives cannot be made responsible to the people on a day-to-day basis, but its general responsibility can be maintained by periodic elections and, more importantly, by continuous political activity between elections. The ultimate defense against bureaucratic omnicompetence is the self-interested assertiveness of ordinary men.

If things have not worked out this way, and do not seem likely to, it is at least partly because liberals never developed a system of democratic activism sufficient to bind administrators to representatives and representatives to constituents. Political parties might have served this purpose, but in the U.S., at least, parties have not developed as membership organizations capable of stimulating commitment and action on the grass-roots level. Local politics has never been competitive with business and family. And it has been discovered that the enhancement of private life through public welfare really does not require any very rigorous and energetic self-government. It may well require a period of sustained struggle, but once that has been won, continued political participation (beyond occasional voting) seems unnecessary and even uneconomical.

Nor is it obvious that the closely articulated representative system that might make such activity worthwhile is really feasible, given the potentially infinite size and the extraordinary administrative complexity of the modern state. Administration has already outdistanced every other branch of government in the sheer accumulation of resources: competent staff, statistical knowledge, patronage, fiscal controls, regulatory powers, secrecy when that is required, publicity when it is not, and so on. Legislative activity has ceased in virtually every respect to be the central feature of the governmental process. It has been replaced in part by administration itself, in part by bargaining between state bureaucrats and the (non-elected) representatives of a great variety of social constituencies.

Thus a modern worker or farmer is far more usefully represented, his interest more successfully defended, by the Washington-based lobbyist of his union than by his locally-based congressman. This is true even though his congressman is elected in a democratic fashion, while the officers of his union are probably coopted and the lobbyist appointed. It is virtually a law of political life that power be imitated, that those who seek benefits copy the organizational style of those who dispense benefits. Today it is palpably the executive rather than the legislative branch of government that is copied. At least, it is copied by those secondary associations already within the welfare system; outside, other models are still possible. In any case, the electoral process has gradually taken on the character of an outer limit, a form of ultimate popular defense rather than of popular self-government, while the day-to-day visibility of workers and farmers and the legitimacy of their government are both maintained by processes largely, though by no means entirely, independent of democratic elections. The modern welfare state is an example of limited government, but not yet of popular sovereignty.

The failure of self-government reveals the fundamental difficulty of liberal utilitarianism. Its standard of utility is the welfare of an individual absolutely free to make his own choices and measure his own happiness. In fact, however, no such individual has ever existed.

Men live in groups and always find that they have limited choices and share, without having chosen, social measurements. If they are ever free to choose new limits and measurements, they must do so in some cooperative fashion, arguing among themselves, reaching a common decision. But to do this, to act collectively like the sovereign individual of the utilitarians, they must share political power. Government must be responsive to their concrete wills and not merely (as at present) to their conventionally defined desires. If they do not share power, they inevitably become the prisoners of the established social systems which they invade or into which they are admitted.

State recognition of new groups obviously affects the structure of social power and value, but there is very little evidence to suggest that it does so in fundamental ways. It clearly does not do so in the ways anticipated during the long struggles for recognition, that is, it does not open the way to social and economic equality. The welfare state has turned out to be perfectly compatible with inequality. Bureaucratic benevolence even bolsters inequality insofar as it neutralizes the struggle groups. decomposing and privatizing popular willfulness. Fundamental social change would require that the state embody this willfulness, inviting its new members to choose their own limits and measurements. This it does not, perhaps cannot, do.

Instead, welfare administrators function, whether consciously or not, as double agents: serving the minimal material interests of the invaders and upholding at the same time the social system that is being invaded. That is why welfare administration, especially in its more direct forms (social work, for example), tends so generally toward paternalism. The administrators are committed in advance to the common limits and measurements, to the established modes of security and welfare. They are knowledgeable about these modes and patronizing toward anyone who is ignorant or uncommitted. But the invaders have burst into a world they never chose. They have to be helped, guided, educated in the acceptable forms of aspiration and action. They are, in a word, newly licensed to have needs, but not yet intentions or plans of their own.

The perfected welfare state will bring with it an end to the terrible oppressiveness of poverty and invisibility. Once all men are recognized as members (even if only by a distant and powerful government), the sheer magnitude of state terrorism and economic exploitation, and so of human misery, will be enormously reduced. At the same time, it needs to be said that security and welfare are not open-ended categories whose final character will be determined by the freedmen of the liberal state. The pursuit of private happiness may be endless, but its direction, for most of us, is given. The newer welfare recipients are not and are not likely to become self-determining men; they remain subject to the determinations of others, not only in the state, but in society and economy as well. Indeed, the established forms of social and economic (that is, corporate) power are likely to be strengthened just as state power has been strengthened: by the general expansion in scale, by the increase in legitimacy that derives from the admission, however reluctant, of all outsiders; by the universal improvement in everyday social behavior; by the new forms of bureaucratic surveillance and record keeping. For these same reasons, the individual member is taken into account in a new way. When his rulers claim to serve him, the claim is not a lie; it is his political destiny to receive services. The reception of services brings freedom of a limited sort, but of a sort rare enough to be valuable. The citizen of the welfare state is free (and, in many cases, newly enabled) to pursue private happiness within the established social and economic system. He is not free to shape or reshape the system, for he has not seized and, except in minimal ways, he does not share political power.

There is no readily accessible meaning in the frequent assertion that socialism lies "beyond the welfare state." No evidence suggests that socialism represents the next stage of history or that the full development of welfare production entails a socialist society. "Beyond," in that hopeful phrase, has neither a historical nor a logical sense.

Although socialist parties and movements have often been in the forefront of the struggle for welfare, and above all for equality in the distribution of benefits, it remains true that socialist theory belongs to a tradition of thought and aspiration not only different from, but also in perennial competition with liberal utilitarianism. Against the utilitarians, socialists have argued that mere private life, however enhanced by state action, cannot sustain a significant human culture; that the family does not provide an adequate arena for the human emotions; that man has both a mind and a passion for society; that he requires an active public life. Against the private man of liberal theory, socialists have defended the free citizen.

This disagreement is in no sense adequately summed up in the words *individualism* and *collectivism*. In both traditions, the individual is recognized as the ultimate value; socialists and liberals unite in opposing any ideology which assigns to the state a moral being independent of the willfulness and rationality of its particular members. But to deny the claims of statist ideologies is not necessarily to assert a purely instrumentalist political theory.

Individual men can still recognize the pleasures of politics, can still choose political life as an end-in-itself. For politics is something more than welfare production. It is a vital and exciting world of work and struggle; of aspiration, initiative, intrigue, and argument; of collective effort, mutual recognition, and *amour social;* of organized hostility; of public venture and social achievement, of personal triumph and failure.

The welfare state offers no satisfactory substitute for any of these. Its theorists claim that all the intellectual and emotional energies of political men can be rechanneled into private life and their creativity coopted by intelligent administrators. Neither of these claims is true. The welfare state requires the virtual withering away of political energy and the disappearance, at least from public life, of any very significant popular creativity. This requirement is first of all an extreme restriction upon the pursuit of happiness, because political activity is or might be one of the forms that pursuit takes for many people. Even more important, it involves a surrender of everyone's say in the determination of further restrictions (or expansions), a surrender of any popular role in determining the shape and substance, the day-to-day quality, of our common life. This is the socialist indictment of liberal utilitarianism.

The terms of the indictment have not often been made clear in the recent past because so many of us who regard ourselves as socialists have found a kind of political fulfillment in the struggles for the welfare state. We have allied ourselves with the crowds of men battering at the gates of American society. Their cause has been our public passion. This will continue to be so for some time to come, probably for the foreseeable future.

Nevertheless as we campaign for this or that welfare measure, we are driven to ask ourselves John Stuart Mill's famous question: "Suppose that . . . all the changes in institutions and opinions which you [are] looking forward to could be completely effected at this very instant: would this be a joy and a happiness to you?" And as with Mill, so with us, "an irrepressible self-consciousness distinctly answers, No!"

The welfare state is not the name of our desire. And what is more, the achievement of the welfare state might well entail the end of that public activity which has until now been a joy and a happiness to us. When contemporary writers talk about the "end of ideology," the disappearance of generalized aspiration, they are describing just this closing down of the possibilities for public intellectual and emotional commitment. Though their announcements are at the very least premature, they linger in our minds as disturbing predictions.

But if we are right in thinking that there are human desires that the welfare state cannot fulfill, then surely these desires will continue to be expressed in the form of collective demands and claims. If men really do seek the common achievements and shared excitements of politics, then they will have them, in one form or another. And they will produce new ideologies to validate their new activities.

In a sense, the welfare state makes these new activities possible, even though it decrees that they must be pursued without the goad of material need and even though its officials hope that they will not in fact be pursued. Political life, if it is to have any significance, must now be chosen for its own sake, and only now can be chosen for its own sake. I am going to assume that liberal ideologists' predictions of the "end of ideology" are wrong and that large numbers of people (not all people) are prone to make this choice. They demand or will demand some form of political participation, some share in political power. How shall their demand be met?

It might be met by the state itself. For there is no obvious reason why the officials of the welfare state, pressed by their constituents or by their own ambitions, should not move beyond the narrow limits of liberal utilitarianism. They will be, they are already, tempted to do so, for two not entirely consistent reasons: first, to avoid the great difficulties that will inevitably be encountered in the expansion of welfare production beyond its present limits; second, to avoid the boredom of success. In the long run, the second is the more important: while the building of the welfare state will have its exciting and morally significant moments, its administration will not. Its administrators will rarely feel themselves buoyed up and sustained by the zeal of their clients. The pride they may well take in the material services they render will never be elevated by the inner conviction of a higher purpose.

But beyond welfare there are many areas in which such purposes might be sought: education, culture, communications, mental health, city planning (and, most tempting and dangerous of all, though not within the range of this discussion, foreign policy). In all these areas the state can be active, in all of them political energies can be expended and emotional commitments made, in all of them common goods can be discovered, goods to be shared and not merely distributed.

Imagine, then, that the state moves into the field of "culture-promotion." Won't the possibilities of cooperative choice and political self-determination be enhanced? Won't the citizens of such a state, the recipients not only of material but also of spiritual benefits, feel themselves to be members of a moral community, a world of rights and obligations?

Perhaps they will; our feelings are not always under our own control. Indeed, we know they will, for the modern state always intrudes, in greater or lesser degree, into areas that lie beyond welfare, most often in the name of political socialization. Obviously, it does so with considerable success. But all this has nothing to do with socialism or with a meaningful common life, for reasons which go to the very heart of the theory of citizenship and participation.

Unlike the defenders of the welfare state, theorists of citizenship have always been concerned with the problem of social scale. If human emotional and intellectual needs are to be partially fulfilled within political society, they have argued, then that society cannot be of any size or shape. It must be built of a human scale, accessible to our minds and feelings, responsive to our decisions.

Exactly what constitutes a human scale is and ought to be a subject of debate, but this is a debate likely to be carried on chiefly among radical democrats and socialists; it is not a debate in which liberal utilitarians take much interest. For it cannot be established that security and welfare are more efficiently administered to 2 million or 50 million or 200 million people. In fact, it is virtually certain that the quality of security and welfare need not change with the size of the population.

But this is probably not the case with regard to the fulfillment of nonmaterial desires. The quality and authenticity of emotional commitment, for example, does appear to vary with population size, though not absolutely or without reference to other factors: human emotions are more easily manipulated the wider their focus and the more they are cut away from immediate personal experience. Participation in cultural life probably varies the same way: the larger the audience, the more passive its members, the more stereotyped the products they consume. Once again, the formula is too pat, but surely contains an element of truth, and its significance may plausibly be extended to politics as well.

The increasing size of the state, the growing power of administration, the decline of political life: all these turn politics from a concrete activity into what Marx once called the fantasy of everyday life. The state becomes an arena in which men do not act but watch the action and, like other audiences, are acted upon. Patriotic communion is always a fraud when it is nothing more than the communion of an audience with its favorite actors, of passive subjects and heroes of the stage. Our emotions are merely tricked by parades and pageants, the rise and fall of political gladiators, the deaths of beloved chiefs, the somber or startling rites of a debased religion. It could be done to anyone, whereas patriotism ought to be the pride of particular man, the enjoyment of particular activities.

When the modern state moves beyond welfare, it does not bring us the satisfactions of citizenship, but only vicarious participation, the illusion of a common life. We find ourselves as if in a dream, living once again in a world which is morally dense and opaque, mystified by ideologies, dominated by leaders whose purposes are not obvious. We are oppressed in the name of a public interest, a national purpose, a solemn commitment, which is neither yours, nor mine, nor ours, in any usual sense of those perfectly simple pronouns. It is difficult not to conclude, as the liberals do, that with the provision of individual material needs, the state reaches or ought to reach its limits. That is the end of its history, the culmination of its legitimacy. There is no state beyond the welfare state.

The struggle to control the modern state is a battle for the perfection of the welfare system. Any political leader who claims that it is more than this, who claims, for example, that citizens should do more for the state than the state does for them, is a dangerous man. He aims to avoid the problems of welfare production, or he seeks some sort of totalitarian "transcendence" (or he is preparing the nation for one or another kind of imperial adventure).

The fight over welfare is important enough. Given the most immediate desires of the poor themselves, given the sheer avariciousness of the rich and the powerful, the fight for some minimal standards of distributive justice takes on all the moral significance that has been attributed to it in the past century and a half. Nevertheless, it is not the only fight; nor ought the state to be the only focus of contemporary political struggle.

Even if the welfare state were to be perfected under the best possible conditions and under socialist auspices, the dangers of bureaucratic omnicompetence and popular passivity would not be avoided. Nor would a socialist government create a socialist society. That requires a different kind of politics, not the kind to which we are all so well accustomed, aimed permanently at the state, but a politics of immediate self-government, a politics of (relatively) small groups.

Socialist writers have never had a great deal that was new or interesting to say about the state. Despite vague phrases about its withering away, they seem to presuppose, as they probably must, an efficient and benevolent bureaucracy, hovering, so to speak, in the background, its central offices as far away as possible. The chief concern of the best left-wing theorists has always been with that day-to-day cooperation in productive activity which occupies the foreground of social life. That means, with those "life-giving nuclei," as Simone Weil called them, within which the local, immediate character of work and culture is determined.

Such secondary associations exist, or can exist, *within* the welfare state, but insofar as they are of some human value, they exist in permanent tension with the centralized administrative system necessary to welfare production. It is not the natural tendency even of liberal bureaucracy to encourage the formation of autonomous groups. This is so both because of the individualist bias of the welfare system and because of the perennial efforts of administrators to escape the system's utilitarian limits and meet the demand for meaningful citizenship in their own (fraudulent) fashion.

What socialism requires, then, is not that the welfare state be surpassed or transcended, whatever that would mean, but that it be held tightly to its own limits, drained of whatever superfluous moral content and unnecessary political power it has usurped, reduced so far as possible to a transparent administrative shell (overarching, protective, enabling) within which smaller groups can grow and prosper. The state is not going to wither away; it must be hollowed out.

What sorts of groups can fill the shell? Two are of especial interest here.

First, the great functional organizations, labor unions, professional associations, and so on: these are the crucial representative bodies of the present day. Their strength and inclusiveness is the best guarantee we can have of the benevolence of the welfare bureaucracy. Unorganized men are unrepresented and unprotected men, their claims unheard or but distantly heard at the centers of power. If they are benefited at all, they are subject to the most extreme paternalism.

The perfection of the welfare state will require the organization of all possible functional groups, even, or rather especially, the group of those who receive direct state assistance. In a society which still exploits masses of men, poverty is itself a function, and no one so desperately requires representation as the man without an adequate income. But all these organizations, as I have argued, tend to become integrated into the welfare system: for them, success *is* integration. They are then trapped in more or less stable bargaining arrangements with governmental or corporate bureaucracies and forced to discipline their own members. They are agents simultaneously of distributive justice and social control. They are not and probably cannot be expected to become arenas of democratic decision making (even though they will be the occasional focus of democratic revolts).

Second, all the local units of social life, work, education, and culture: cities and towns, factories, union locals, universities, churches, political clubs, neighborhood associations, theater groups, editorial boards, and so on. These might be conceived as overlapping circles of engagement and action, closed circles (though not closed in any coercive sense), whose members face inward at least some of the time, and within which resources are contained.

These are the most likely arenas of a genuinely democratic politics. The great danger of the perfected welfare state is that all or most of them would be broken open, so that resources leak away, independence is lost, and the members turn outward to face the powerful state, where all the action is, from which all good things come. To some extent this has already happened. But the process is by no means so far advanced as some of the more extreme versions of the theory of "mass society" suggest. Associations and neighborhoods continue to provide important social space for agitation and activity. Indeed, it needs to be said that the advance of the liberal state often transforms traditional communities (like the old churches) into new political arenas.

At the same time, however, the same process cuts individuals loose, isolates them from communal ties, drives them into a material and then an emotional dependency on the central authorities. It is in response to the expectant faces of these "liberated" individuals that state administrators proclaim the mysteries of national purpose and decide that they must pursue "excellence" or promote culture (or defend freedom), rewarding their eager, needful and bored constituents with inflated rhetoric and byzantine artifacts, and all too often eliciting from them an irrational and unreflective patriotism.

Now all such pursuits and promotions lie outside the competence of the state; they belong to a different sphere of activity; they require a smaller scale of organization. To make these points and to make them stick is the major purpose of socialist politics in the welfare state. It amounts to saying that what we want *next*, and what we want to share, are the pleasures of power. This demand for local self-determination, since it is made in the face of a state whose power is unprecedented in human history, is sometimes called by the melodramatic but useful name "insurgency."

Any member of the welfare state who is willful as well as desirous and who seeks some local space in which to act out his willfulness can be called an insurgent. He insists on his intentions as well as his needs. He seeks to close the circle (not every circle) against bureaucratic intrusions. He reargues the old democratic proposition that decisions should be made by those who are most affected by them. He calls into question the omnicompetence of the service state and of all the organizations created in its image.

In schools, factories, and neighborhoods, where social workers pursue their errands of decency, or union officials defend the interests of their members, or provosts and deans plan the educational experiences of the young, insurgency is likely to be a perennial phenomenon. It takes the form of wildcat strikes, welfare unions, student rebellions. Already a sense of professional *esprit* is growing up among those who know, or think they know, how to "handle" such outbursts. They believe that insurgency is a repudiation of services rendered, stupidly self-destructive since the services are so obviously helpful, even if they are often ineptly or impersonally delivered.

But insurgency, is or ought to be, very different from this. Its participants are not concerned that bureaucrats be sensitive and warm, but that they be reticent and limited, less imposing, less intrusive than they often are.

Insurgency is a demand that bureaucratic services make possible, instead of replacing, local decision making. Or rather, it is the acting out of a new dialectic, which denies conventional definitions of good behavior and seeks to make the "helpfulness" of the welfare bureaucracy into the starting point of a new politics of popular resistance and self-government.

In the long run, the issue for socialists is not state power, but power *right here*, on this shop floor, in this university, in this city. And the central assumption of insurgent politics is that such power must always be won "from below"—which is also to say, against all the odds. For the triumph of benevolent bureaucrats in virtually every local society has been one of the results, not so much inevitable as overdetermined, of the entrance of masses of men into the political world. It is a function of integration.

Most of the previous forms of radical politics have involved demands for wider and wider systems of integration; every successful revolution has produced such a system. But insurgency is different from revolution (more limited, more immediate) precisely in that it seeks no more extensive unity, but calls instead for the multiplication of diverse and independent unities. And it begins this process with a modest but urgent demand for a share *right now* in the management of *this* community.

Whether this can actually be won and the victory sustained is another matter. It is not difficult to imagine a kind of permanent insurgency, generating marginal but never major disturbances in the welfare state, always asserting its claims, never able to enforce them, capable of staging riots, never capable of building a movement or a new community. Newspapers provide us daily with imitations of such a pattern. We don't know if local organizations of rebellious citizens can displace entrenched officials, sanctioned and supported by the central state; nor do we know if they can win any substantial allegiance from their own members, establish some more or less effective control over the local politics of work and culture, and generate significant cooperative activity. Above all, we don't know if they can create new patterns of democratic responsibility, so that the militants of this or that rebellion don't simply become a new elite. That success is possible must be the socialist's faith, or better the wager that sustains his commitment.

The politics of insurgency and the politics of welfare obviously overlap, both in time and technique, and their different purposes are sometimes confused. Insurgency has been a prominent feature of every struggle for recognition: the sit-in strikes of the 1930s are the classic example. Oppressed groups must always win enough power either to threaten those who refuse to grant their demands or to threaten the general peace and so compel state intervention on their behalf. And "enough" power always means power in some particular place and sufficient to inflict some particular injury.

But so long as the goal of the oppressed is (as it ought to be) membership in the greater society rather than autonomy for the smaller one, such power is largely a means to an end, and it disappears when it ceases to be a necessary means. It gradually seeped away from local unions, for example, once bargaining rights were granted at the national or industry-wide level, and while this was certainly a democratic loss, it must be admitted that what the workers wanted could only have been won at the national level.

Something like this will probably happen in the civil rights movement also, since the problems of the Negro community can not be solved until its activists transform such local power as they may win into national recognition and full admission into the welfare state. And this suggests a lesson which is not easy to learn; that political power must always be twice-won. It must be won first with the help of the state or through the creation of parallel bureaucracies against established local or corporate elites. Then it must be won again by new popular forces against the state. In the U.S. today, the Negro is still fighting the first battle; Americans who have already won national recognition are, hopefully, ready for the second.

Socialism, it has often been said, requires decentralization. But that is not quite accurate, for it implies a process that begins at the center and is, just for that reason, inherently unlikely. It suggests that socialism awaits the triumph of a national movement whose leaders are ready to sponsor the fragmentation and dispersion of the power they have so recently won. Once installed, however, won't they be driven to realize how much good might be done with their power if only it is kept intact . . . for a few years more? (And they may well be right.) We ought, of course, to insist that state officials do as much as they can to encourage the growth of secondary associations independent of themselves, not forming wheels within wheels of their welfare-producing machine. But the vitality of such associations depends finally on those who associate.

Socialism then requires insurgency, that is, self-government within the welfare state and against it whenever necessary. And it is the great paradox of socialist politics that the state toward which we must always remain tense, watchful, and resistant is or will almost certainly become the most legitimate, rationally purposive, and powerful state that has ever existed.

Irving Howe and Lewis Coser

Images of Socialism

Irving Howe (b. 1920) and Lewis Coser (b. 1915) are editors of Dissent. *The essay below first appeared in that magazine in 1954; it is an effort to provide a synoptic view of the continuities and changes in the thought of democratic socialism required by contemporary historical experience. Howe, a professor of English at the City University of New York, is the author of numerous works in literary and social criticism, such as* Politics and the Novel. *Coser, a professor of sociology at the State University of New York at Stony Brook, is the author of such works as* The Functions of Social Conflict *and* Men and Ideas.

. . . Utopia without egalitarianism, utopia dominated by an aristocracy of mind, must quickly degenerate into a vision of useful slavery. Hence the importance of Marx's idea that socialism is to be brought about, in the first instance, by the activities of a major segment of the population, the workers. Having placed the drive toward utopia not beyond but squarely—perhaps a little too squarely—within the course of history, and having found in the proletariat that active "realizing" force which the utopians could nowhere discern on the social horizon, Marx was enabled to avoid the two major difficulties of his predecessors: ahistoricism and the elite theory. He had, to be sure, difficulties of his own, but not these.

Marx was the first of the major socialist figures who saw the possibility of linking the utopian desire with the actual development of social life. By studying capitalism both as an "ideal" structure and a "real" dynamic, Marx found the source of revolt within the self-expanding and self-destroying rhythms of the economy itself. The utopians had desired a revolt against history but they could conduct it, so to speak, only from the space platform of the imaginary future; Marx gave new power to the revolt against history by locating it, "scientifically," within history.

The development of technology, he concluded, made possible a society in which men could "realize" their humanity, if only because the brutalizing burden of fatigue, that sheer physical exhaustion from which the great masses of men had never been free, could not for the first time be removed. This was the historic option offered mankind by the Industrial Revolution, as it is now being offered again by the Atomic Revolution. Conceivably, though only conceivably, a society might have been established at any point in historical time which practiced an equalitarian distribution of goods; but there would have been neither goods nor leisure enough to dispense with the need for a struggle over their distribution; which means bureaucracy, police, and oppressive state; and in sum the destruction of equalitarianism. Now, after the Industrial Revolution, the machine might do for all humanity what the slaves had done for the Greek patriciate.

Marx was one of the first political thinkers to see that both industrialism and "the mass society" were here to stay, that all social schemes which ignored or tried to controvert this fact were not merely irrelevant, they weren't even interesting. It is true, of course, that he did not foresee—he could not—a good many consequences of this tremendous historical fact. He did not foresee that "mass culture" together with social atomization (Durkheim's *anomie*) would set off strong tendencies of demoralization acting in opposition to those tendencies that made for disciplined cohesion in the working class. He did not foresee that the rise of totalitarianism might present mankind with choices and problems that went beyond the capitalist/socialist formulation. He did not foresee that the nature of leisure would become, even under capitalism, as great a social and cultural problem as the nature of work. He did not foresee that industrialism would create problems which, while not necessarily insoluble, are likely to survive the span of capitalism. But what he did foresee was crucial: that the great decisions of history would now be made in a mass society, that the "stage" upon which this struggle would take place had suddenly, dramatically been widened far beyond its previous dimensions.

And when Marx declared the proletariat to be the active social force that could lead the transition to socialism, he was neither sentimentalizing the lowly nor smuggling in a theory of the elite, as many of his critics have suggested. Anyone who has read the chapter in *Capital* on the working day or Engels' book on the conditions of the English workers knows that they measured the degradation of the workers to an extent precluding sentimentality. As for the idea of the proletariat as an elite, Marx made no special claim for its virtue or intelligence, which is the traditional mode of justifying an elite; he merely analyzed its peculiar *position* in society, as the class most driven by the workings of capitalism to both discipline and rebellion, the class that come what may, utopia or barbarism, would always remain propertyless.

There is another indication that Marx did not mean to favor an elite theory by his special "placing" of the proletariat. His theory of "increasing misery"—be it right, wrong, or vulgarized—implied that the proletariat would soon include the overwhelming bulk of the population. The transition to socialism, far from being assigned to a "natural" elite or a power group, was seen by Marx as the task of the vast "proletarianized" majority. Correct or not, this was a fundamentally democratic point of view.

Concerned as he was with the mechanics of class power, the "laws of motion" of the existing society, and the strategy of social change, Marx paid very little attention to the description of socialism. The few remarks to be found in his early work and in such a later book as *The Critique of the Gotha Program* are mainly teasers, formulations so brief as to be cryptic, which did not prevent his disciples from making them into dogmas. An interesting division of labor took place. Marx's predecessors, those whom he called the "utopian socialists," had devoted themselves to summoning pictures of the ideal future, perhaps in lieu of activity in the detested present; Marx, partly as a reaction to their brilliant daydreaming, decided to focus on an analysis of those elements in the present that made possible a strategy for reaching the ideal future. And in the meantime, why worry about the face of the future, why create absurd blueprints? As a response to Fourier, Saint-Simon, and Owen there was much good sense in this attitude; given the state of the European labor movements in the mid-nineteenth century, it was indispensable to turn toward practical problems of national life (Germany) and class organization (England). But the Marxist movement, perhaps unavoidably, paid a price for this emphasis.

As the movement grew, the image of socialism kept becoming hazier and hazier, and soon the haziness came to seem a condition of perfection. The "revisionist" social democrat Eduard Bernstein could write that the goal is nothing, the movement everything; as if a means could be intelligently chosen without an end in view! In his *State and Revolution*, Lenin, with far greater fullness than Marx, sketched a vision of socialism profoundly democratic, in which the mass of humanity would break out of its dumbness, so that cooks could become cabinet ministers, and even the "bourgeois principle of equality" would give way to the true freedom of nonmeasurement: "from each according to his ability and to each according to his need." But this democratic vision did not sufficiently affect his immediate views of political activity, so that in his crucial pamphlet, "Will the Bolsheviks Retain State Power?" written in 1917, Lenin, as if to brush aside the traditional Marxist view that the socialist transformation requires a far greater popular base than any previous social change, could say that "after the 1905 Revolution, Russia was ruled by 130,000 landowners. . . . And yet we are told that Russia will not be able to be governed by the 240,000 members of the Bolshevik Party—governing in the interests of the poor and against the rich."

What happened was that the vision of socialism—would it not be better to say the *problem* of socialism?—grew blurred in the minds of many Marxists because they were too ready to entrust it to history. The fetishistic use of the word "scientific," than which nothing could provide a greater sense of assurance, gave the Marxist movement a feeling that it had finally penetrated to the essence of history and found there once and for all its true meaning. The result was often a deification of history: what God had been to Fourier, history became to many Marxists—a certain force leading to a certain goal. And if indeed the goal was certain, or likely enough to be taken as certain, there was no need to draw up fanciful blueprints, the future would take care of itself and require no advice from us. True enough, in a way. But the point that soon came to be forgotten was that it is we, in the present, who need the image of the future, not those who may live in it. And the consequence of failing to imagine creatively the face of socialism, which is not at all the same as an absurd effort to paint it in detail, was that it tended to lapse into a conventional and lifeless "perfection."

Perfection, in that the image of socialism held by many Marxists, the image which emerged at the level of implicit belief, was a society in which tension, conflict, and failure had largely disappeared. It would be easy enough to comb the works of the major Marxists in order to prove this statement, but we prefer to appeal to common experience, to our own knowledge and memories as well as to the knowledge and memories of others. In the socialist movement one did not worry about the society one wanted; innumerable and, indeed, inconceivable subjects were discussed but almost never the idea of socialism itself, for history, strategy, and the party (how easily the three melted into one!) had eliminated that need. Socialism was the future and sometimes a future made curiously respectable, the middle-class values that the radicals had violently rejected now being reinstated, unwittingly, in their vision of the good society. There could hardly be a need to reply to those critics who wondered how some of the perennial human problems could be solved under socialism: one *knew* they would be. In effect, the vision of socialism had a way of declining into a regressive infantile fantasy, a fantasy of protection.

Our criticism is not that the Marxist movement held to a vision of utopia: that it did so was entirely to its credit, a life without some glimmer of a redeeming future being a life cut off from the distinctively human. Our complaint is rather that the vision of utopia grew slack and static.

Sometimes it degenerated into what William Morris called "the cockney dream" by which efficiency becomes a universal solvent for all human problems; sometimes it slipped off, beyond human reach, to the equally repulsive vision of a society in which men become rational titans as well behaved and tedious as Swift's Houyhnhnms. Only occasionally was socialism envisaged as a society with its own rhythm of growth and tension, change and conflict.

Marx's contribution to human thought is immense, but except for some cryptic if pregnant phrases, neither he nor his disciples have told us very much about the society in behalf of which they called men into battle. This is not quite so fatal a criticism as it might seem, since what probably mattered most was that Marxism stirred millions of previously dormant people into historical action, gave expression to their claims and yearnings, and lent a certain form to their desire for a better life. But if we want sustained speculations on the shape of this better life we have to turn to radical mavericks, to the anarchists and libertarians, to the Guild Socialists, and to such a writer as Oscar Wilde, whose *The Soul of Man Under Socialism* is a small masterpiece. In his paradoxical and unsystematic way, Wilde quickly comes to a sense of what the desirable society might be like. The great advantage of socialism, he writes, is that it "would relieve us from that sordid necessity of living for others which, in the present conditions of things, presses so hard upon almost everybody." By focusing upon "the unhealthy and exaggerated altruism" which capitalist society demands from people, and by showing how it saps individuality, Wilde arrives at the distinctive virtue of socialism: that it will make possible what he calls individualism.

We do not wish to succumb to that which we criticize. Blueprints, elaborate schemes do not interest us. But we think it may be useful to suggest some of the qualities that can make the image of socialism a serious and mature goal, as well as some of the difficulties in that goal:

▪ Socialism is not the end of human history, as the deeply held identification of it with perfection must mean. There is no total fulfillment, nor is there an "end to time." History is a process which throws up new problems, new conflicts, new questions; and socialism, being within history, cannot be expected to solve all these problems or, for that matter, to raise humanity at every point above the level of achievement of previous societies. As Engels remarked, there is no final synthesis, only continued clash. What socialists want is simply to do away with those sources of conflict which are the cause of material deprivation and which, in turn, help create psychological and moral suffering. Freedom may then mean that we can devote ourselves to the pursuit of more worthwhile causes of conflict. The hope for a conflictless society is reactionary, as is a reliance upon some abstract "historical force" that will conciliate all human strife.

■ The aim of socialism is to create a society of cooperation, but not necessarily, or at least not universally, of harmony. Cooperation is compatible with conflict, is indeed inconceivable without conflict, while harmony implies a stasis.

■ Even the "total abolition" of social classes, no small or easy matter, would not or need not mean the total abolition of social problems.

■ In a socialist society there would remain a whole variety of human difficulties that could not easily be categorized as social or nonsocial; difficulties that might well result from the sheer friction between the human being and society, *any* society, from say, the process of "socializing" those recalcitrant creatures known as children. The mere existence of man is a difficulty, a problem, with birth, marriage, pain and death being only among the more spectacular of his crises. To be sure, no intelligent radical has ever denied that *such* crises would last into a socialist society, but the point to be stressed is that, with the elimination of our major material troubles, these other problems might rise to a new urgency, so much so as to become *social* problems leading to new conflicts.

But social problems as we conceive of them today would also be present in a socialist society.

Traditionally, Marxists have lumped all the difficulties posed by critics and reality into that "transitional" state that is to guide, or bump, us from capitalism to socialism, while socialism itself they have seen as the society that would transcend these difficulties. This has made it a little too easy to justify some of the doings of the "transitional" society, while making it easier still to avoid considering, not what socialism *will* be like, but what our image of it should be. Without pretending to "solve" these social problems as they might exist under socialism, but intending to suggest a bias or predisposition, we list here a few of them:

1. *Bureaucracy* Marxists have generally related the phenomenon of bureaucratism to social inequality and economic scarcity. Thus they have seen the rise of bureaucracy in Leninist Russia as a consequence of trying to establish a workers' state in an isolated and backward country which lacked the economic prerequisites for building socialism. Given scarcity, there arises a policeman to supervise the distribution of goods; given the policeman, there will be an unjust distribution. Similarly, bureaucratic formations of a more limited kind are seen as parasitic elites which batten upon a social class yet, in some sense, "represent" it in political and economic conflicts. Thus bureaucratism signifies a deformation, though not necessarily a destruction, of democratic processes.

This view of bureaucratism seems to us invaluable. Yet it would be an error to suppose that because a class society is fertile ground for bureaucracy, a classless society would automatically be free of bureaucracy. There are other causes for this social deformation; and while in a socialist society these other causes might not be aggravated by economic inequality and the accumulation as they are under capitalism, they would very likely continue to operate. One need not accept Robert Michels' "Iron Law of Oligarchy" in order to see this. (Michels' theory is powerful but it tends to boomerang: anyone convinced by it that socialism is impossible will have a hard time resisting the idea that democracy is impossible.) Thus the mere presence of equality of wealth in a society does not necessarily mean an equality of power or status: if Citizen A were more interested in the politics of his town or the functioning of his factory than Citizen B, he would probably accumulate more power and status; hence, the *possibility* of misusing them. (Socialists have often replied, But why should Citizen A want to misuse his power and status when there is no pressing economic motive for doing so? No one can answer this question definitively except by positing some theory of "human nature," which we do not propose to do; all we can urge is a certain wariness with regard to any theory which discounts in advance the possibility that noneconomic motives lead to human troubles.) Then again, the problem of sheer size in economic and political units is likely to burden a socialist society as much as it burdens any other society; and large political or economic units, because they require an ever increasing delegation of authority, often to "experts," obviously provide a setting in which bureaucracy can flourish. But most important of all is the sheer problem of representation, the fact that as soon as authority is delegated to a "representative" there must follow a loss of control and autonomy.

Certain institutional checks can, of course, be suggested for containing bureaucracy. The idea of a division of governmental powers, which many Marxists have dismissed as a bourgeois device for thwarting the popular will, would deserve careful attention in planning a socialist society, though one need not suppose that it would have to perpetuate those elements of present-day parliamentary structure which do in fact thwart the popular will. Similarly, the distinction made in English political theory, but neglected by Marxists, between democracy as an expression of popular sovereignty and democracy as a pattern of government in which the rights of minority groups are especially defended, needs to be taken seriously. In general, a society that is pluralist rather than unitary in emphasis, that recognizes the need for diversification of function rather than concentration of authority—this is the desired goal.

And here we have a good deal to learn from a neglected branch of the socialist movement, the Guild Socialists of England, who have given careful thought to these problems. G. D. H. Cole, for example, envisages the socialist society as one in which government policy is a resultant of an interplay among socioeconomic units that simultaneously cooperate and conflict. Cole also puts for-

ward the provocative idea of "functional representation,"
somewhat similar to the original image of the soviets.
Because, he writes, "a human being, as an individual, is
fundamentally incapable of being represented," a man
should have "as many distinct, and separately exercised,
votes, as he has distinct social purposes or interests," voting, that is, in his capacity of worker, consumer, artist,
resident, etc.

But such proposals can hardly be expected to bulk very
large unless they are made in a culture where the
motives for private accumulation and the values sanc-
tioning it have significantly diminished. If, as we believe, the goal of socialism is to create the kind of man
who, to a measurable degree, ceases to be manipulated
object and becomes a motivated subject, then the growth
of socialist consciousness must prove an important bulwark against bureaucracy. A society that stresses cooperation can undercut those prestige factors that make for
bureaucracy; a society that accepts conflict, and provides
a means for modulating it, will encourage those who
combat bureaucracy.

2 *Planning and decentralization*   Unavoidably, a great
deal of traditional socialist thought has stressed economic
centralization as a prerequisite for planning, especially in
the "transitional" state between capitalism and socialism.
Partly, this was an inheritance from the bourgeois revolution, which needed a centralized state; partly, it reflected
the condition of technology in the nineteenth century,
which required centralized units of production; partly, it
is a consequence of the recent power of Leninism, which
stressed centralism as a means of confronting the primitive chaos of the Russian economy but allowed it to become a dogma in countries where it had no necessary
relevance. Whatever the historical validity of these em-
phases on centralism, they must now be abandoned. According to the economist Colin Clark, the new forms of
energy permit an economical employment of small decentralized industrial units. Certainly, every impulse of democratic socialism favors such a tendency. For if mass participation—by the workers, the citizens, the people as a
whole—in the economic life of the society is to be mean-

ingful, it must find its most immediate expression in relatively small economic units. Only in such small units is it possible for the nonexpert to exercise any real control.

From what we can learn about Stalinist "planning," we see that an economic plan does not work, it quickly breaks down, if arbitrarily imposed from above and hedged in with rigid specifications which allow for none of the flexibility, none of the economic *play*, that a democratic society requires. Social planning, if understood in democratic terms—and can there really be social planning, as distinct from economic regulation, without a democratic context?—requires only a loose guiding direction, a general pointer from above. The rest, the actual working out of variables, the arithmetic fulfillment of algebraic possibilities, must come from below from the interaction, cooperation, and conflict of economic units participating in a democratic community.

All of this implies a considerable modification of the familiar socialist emphasis on nationalization of the means of production, increase of productivity, a master economic plan, etc., a modification but not a total rejection. To be sure, socialism still presupposes the abolition of private property in the basic industries, but there is hardly a branch of the socialist movement, except the more petrified forms of Trotskyism, which places any high valuation on nationalization of industry *per se*. Almost all socialists now feel impelled to add that what matters is the use to which nationalization is put and the degree of democratic control present in the nationalized industries. But more important, the idea of nationalization requires still greater modification: there is no reason to envisage, even in a "transitional" society, that all basic industries need be owned by the state. The emphasis of the Guild Socialists upon separate guilds of workers, each owning and managing their own industries, summons no doubt a picture of possible struggles within and between industries; all the better! Guilds, cooperatives, call them what you will, these provide possible bulwarks against the monster Leviathan, the all-consuming state, which it is the sheerest fatuity to suppose would immediately cease being a threat to human liberty simply because "we" took it over. The presence of numerous political and

economic units, living together in a tension of coopera-
tion-and-conflict, seems the best "guarantee" that power
will not accumulate in the hands of a managerial oligarchy—namely, that the process already far advanced in
capitalist society will not continue into socialism. Such
autonomous units, serving as buffers between government
and people, would allow for various, even contradictory,
kinds of expression in social life. The conflicts that might
break out among them would be a healthy social regulator, for while the suppression of conflict makes for an
explosive accumulation of hostility, its normalization
means that a society can be "sewn together" by noncumu-
lative struggles between component groups. And even in
terms of "efficiency," this may prove far more satisfactory
than the bureaucratic state regulation of Communist Russia.

Only if an attempt is made to encompass the total
personality of the individual into one or another group is
conflict likely to lead to social breakdown. Only then
would conflicts over relatively minor issues he elevated
into "affairs of state." So long as the dogma of "total
allegiance," a dogma that has proven harmful in both its
social democratic and Leninist versions is not enforced,
so long as the individual is able to participate in a variety
of groupings without having to commit himself totally to
any of them, society will be able to absorb a constant
series of conflicts.

Nor would the criterion of efficiency be of decisive
importance in such a society. At the beginning of the
construction of socialism, efficiency is urgently required
in order to provide the material possibility for a life of
security and freedom. But efficiency is needed in order,
so to speak, to transcend efficiency.

Between the abstract norms of efficiency and the living
needs of human beings there may always be a clash. To
speak in grandiose terms, as some anarchists do, of
Efficiency vs. Democracy is not very valuable, since living experience always requires compromise and compli-
cation. All one can probably say is that socialists are not
concerned with efficiency as such but with that type of
efficiency which does not go counter to key socialist values. Under socialism there are likely to be many situa-

tions in which efficiency will be consciously sacrificed, and indeed one of the measures of the success of a socialist society would be precisely how far it could afford to discard the criterion of efficiency. This might be one of the more glorious ideas latent in Engels' description of socialism as a "reign of freedom."

These remarks are, of course, scrappy and incomplete, as we intend them to be, for their usefulness has a certain correlation with their incompleteness; but part of what we have been trying to say has been so well put by R. H. S. Crossman that we feel impelled to quote him:

The planned economy and the centralization of power are no longer socialist objectives. They are developing all over the world as the Political Revolution [the concentration of state powers] and the process is accelerated by the prevalence of war economy. The main task of socialism today is to prevent the concentration of power in the hands of *either* industrial management *or* the state bureaucracy—in brief, to distribute responsibility and so to enlarge freedom of choice. This task was not even begun by the Labour government. On the contrary, in the nationalized industries old managements were preserved almost untouched. . . .

In a world organized in ever larger and more inhuman units, the task of socialism is to prevent managerial responsibility degenerating into privilege. This can only be achieved by increasing, even at the cost of "efficiency," the citizen's right to participate in the control not only of government and industry, but of the party for which he voted. . . . After all, it is not the pursuit of happiness but the enlargement of freedom which is socialism's highest aim.

3 *Work and leisure*   No Marxist concept has been more fruitful than that of "alienation." As used by Marx, it suggests the psychic price of living in a society where the worker's "deed becomes an alien power." The division of labor, he writes, makes the worker "a cripple . . . forcing him to develop some highly specialized dexterity at the cost of a world of productive impulses. . . ." The worker becomes estranged from his work, both as process and product; his major energies must be expended upon tasks that have no organic or creative function within his

life; the impersonality of the social relationships enforced by capitalism, together with the sense of incoherence and discontinuity induced by the modern factory, goes far beyond making the worker a dehumanized part of the productive process rather than an autonomous human being. It is not, of course, to be supposed that this is a description of a given factory; it is a "lead" by which to examine a given factory. This theory is the starting point of much speculation on the nature of modern work, as well as upon the social and psychological significance of the industrial city; and almost all the efforts to "engineer" human relations in the factory, implicitly acknowledge the relevance and power of Marx's idea.

But when Marx speaks of alienation and thereby implies the possibility of nonalienation, it is not always clear whether he has in mind some precapitalist society in which men were presumably not alienated or whether he employs it as a useful fiction derived by a process of abstraction from the observable state of society. If he means the former, he may occasionally be guilty of romanticizing, in common with many of his contemporaries, the life of precapitalist society; for most historians of feudalism and of that difficult-to-label era which spans the gap between feudalism and capitalism, strongly imply that the peasant and even the artisan was not quite the unalienated man that some intellectuals like to suppose. Nonetheless, as an analytical tool and a reference to future possibilities, the concept of alienation remains indispensable.

So long as capitalism, in one form or another, continues to exist, it will be difficult to determine to what degree it is the social setting and to what degree the industrial process that makes so much of factory work dehumanizing. That a great deal of this dehumanization is the result of a social structure which deprives many men of an active sense of participation or decision making and tends to reduce them to the level of controlled objects, can hardly be doubted at so late a moment.

We may consequently suppose that in a society where the democratic ethos had been reinforced politically and had made a significant seepage into economic life, the problem of alienation would be alleviated. But not solved.

In his *Critique of the Gotha Program*, Marx speaks of the highest stage of the new society as one in which "the enslaving subordination of individuals in the division of labor has disappeared, and with it also the antagonism between mental and physical labor; labor has become not only a means of living, but itself the first necessity of life. . . ." Remembering that Marx set this as a *limit* toward which to strive and not as a condition likely to be present even during the beginning of socialism let us then suppose that a society resembling this limit has been reached. The crippling effects of the division of labor are now largely eliminated because people are capable of doing a large variety of social tasks; the division between physical and mental labor has been largely eliminated because the level of education has been very much raised; and—we confess here to being uncertain as to Marx's meaning—labor has become "the first necessity of life." But even now the problem of *the nature of work* remains. Given every conceivable improvement in the social context of work; given a free and healthy society; given, in short, all the desiderata Marx lists—even then there remains the uncreativeness, the tedium, what frequently must seem the meaninglessness, of the jobs many people have to perform in the modern factory.

It may be said that in a socialist society people could live creatively in their leisure; no doubt. Or that people would have to do very little work because new forms of energy would be developed; quite likely. But then the problem would be for men to find an outlet for their "productive impulses," not in the way Marx envisaged but in another way, not in work but in leisure. Except for certain obviously satisfying occupations, and by this we do *not* mean only intellectual occupations, work might now become a minor part of human life. The problem is whether in any society it would now be possible to create, given our irrevocable commitment to industrialism, the kind of "whole man" Marx envisaged, the man, that is, who realizes himself through and by his work.

It is not as a speculation about factory life in a socialist society that this problem intrigues us, but rather as an entry into another problem about which Marx wrote very little: what we now call "mass culture." Socialists have traditionally assumed that a solution to economic problems would be followed by a tremendous flowering of culture; and this may happen, we do not know. But another possible outcome might be a population of which large parts were complacent and self-satisfied, so that if hell is now conceived as a drawing room, utopia might soften into a suburb. In any case, we are hardly likely to feel as certain about the cultural consequences of social equality as Trotsky did when he wrote in *Literature and Revolution* that under socialism men might reach the level of Beethoven and Goethe. This seems implausibly romantic, since it is doubtful that the scarcity of Beethovens and Goethes can be related solely to social inequality; and what is more it does not even seem very desirable to have a society of Beethovens and Goethes.

Between the two extreme forecasts there is the more likely possibility that under socialism a great many people would inevitably engage in work which could not release "a world of productive impulses" but which would be brief and light enough to allow them a great deal of leisure. The true problem of socialism might then be to determine the nature, quality, and variety of leisure. Men, that is, would face the full and terrifying burden of human freedom, but they would be more prepared to shoulder it than ever before. . . .